The Collected Works of J. Krishnamurti

Volume VI

1949-1952

The Collected Works of J. Krishnamurti

Volume VI

1949-1952

The Origin of Conflict

MOTILAL BANARSIDASS PUBLISHERS
PRIVATE LIMITED • DELHI

*First Indian Edition : Delhi, **2014***
First Published : USA, 1991

In Association With
KRISHNAMURTI FOUNDATION OF AMERICA
P.O. Box 1560, Ojai, California 93024 U.S.A
E-mail: kfa@kfa.org. Website: www.kfa.org

ISBN: 978-81-208-3359-3 (Vol. VI)
ISBN: 978-81-208-3090-5 (18 Vols. Set)

MOTILAL BANARSIDASS
41 U.A. Bungalow Road, Jawahar Nagar, Delhi 110 007
8 Mahalaxmi Chamber, 22 Bhulabhai Desai Road, Mumbai 400 026
203 Royapettah High Road, Mylapore, Chennai 600 004
236, 9th Main III Block, Jayanagar, Bengaluru 560 011
Sanas Plaza, 1302 Baji Rao Road, Pune 411 002
8 Camac Street, Kolkata 700 017
Ashok Rajpath, Patna 800 004
Chowk, Varanasi 221 001

Photo: J Krishnamurti, ca 1948 by D.R.D. Wadia

Printed in India

at Nice Printing Press,
A 33/3A, Site IV, Industrial Area, Sahibabad, Ghaziabad, U.P.
and published by JP Jain for Motilal Banarsidass Publishers (P) Ltd,
41 U.A. Bungalow Road, Jawahar Nagar, Delhi-110007

Contents

Preface

Jiddu Krishnamurti was born in 1895 of Brahmin parents in south India. At the age of fourteen he was proclaimed the coming World Teacher by Annie Besant, then president of the Theosophical Society, an international organization that emphasized the unity of world religions. Mrs. Besant adopted the boy and took him to England, where he was educated and prepared for his coming role. In 1911 a new worldwide organization was formed with Krishnamurti as its head, solely to prepare its members for his advent as World Teacher. In 1929, after many years of questioning himself and the destiny imposed upon him, Krishnamurti disbanded this organization, saying:

Truth is a pathless land, and you cannot approach it by any path whatsoever, by any religion, by any sect. Truth, being limitless, unconditioned, unapproachable by any path whatsoever, cannot be organized; nor should any organization be formed to lead or to coerce people along any particular path. My only concern is to set men absolutely, unconditionally free.

Until the end of his life at the age of ninety, Krishnamurti traveled the world speaking as a private person. The rejection of all spiritual and psychological authority, including his own, is a fundamental theme. A major concern is the social structure and how it conditions the individual. The emphasis in his talks and writings is on the psychological barriers that prevent clarity of perception. In the mirror of relationship, each of us can come to understand the content of his own consciousness, which is common to all humanity. We can do this, not analytically, but directly in a manner Krishnamurti describes at length. In observing this content we discover within ourselves the division of the observer and what is observed. He points out that this division, which prevents direct perception, is the root of human conflict.

His central vision did not waver after 1929, but Krishnamurti strove for the rest of his life to make his language even more simple and clear. There is a development in his exposition. From year to year he used new terms and new approaches to his subject, with different nuances.

Because his subject is all-embracing, the *Collected Works* are of compelling interest. Within his talks in any one year, Krishnamurti was not able to cover the whole range of his vision, but broad amplifications of particular themes are found throughout these volumes. In them he lays the foundations of many of the concepts he used in later years.

The Collected Works contain Krishnamurti's previously published talks, discussions, answers to specific questions, and writings for the years 1933 through 1967. They are an authentic record of his teachings, taken from transcripts of verbatim shorthand reports and tape recordings.

The Krishnamurti Foundation of America, a California charitable trust, has among its purposes the publication and distribution of Krishnamurti books, videocassettes, films and tape recordings. The production of the *Collected Works* is one of these activities.

Rajahmundry, India, 1949

First Talk in Rajahmundry

There is an art in listening. Listen to find out if what is said is of significance, and after listening, judge, accept, or throw out—but first of all listen. The difficulty with most of us is that we do not listen. We come prepared to be antagonistic or friendly, and not to listen neutrally. If you listen neutrally, surely then only do you begin to discover what lies behind the words. Words are a means of communication. You have to learn my vocabulary, the meaning behind my words, and then you will find the significance of the subject. The thing of first importance is to learn to listen rightly. If you read a poem and are biased, how can you understand it? To appreciate what the poet wants you to understand, you must come with freedom to do so.

The problem that confronts most of us at this juncture is whether the individual is merely the instrument of society or the end of society. Are you and I as individuals to be used, directed, educated, controlled, shaped to a certain pattern by society, government; or does society, the state, exist for the individual? Is the individual the end of society, or is he merely a puppet to be taught, exploited, butchered as an instrument of war? That is the problem that is confronting most of us. That is the problem of the world: whether the individual is a mere instrument of society, a plaything of influences to be molded, or whether society exists for the individual.

How are you going to find this out? It is a serious problem, isn't it? If the individual is merely an instrument of society, then society is much more important than the individual. If that is true, then we must give up individuality and work for society; then our whole educational system must be entirely revolutionized and the individual turned into an instrument to be used and destroyed, liquidated, got rid of. But if society exists for the individual, then the function of society is not to make him conform to any pattern, but to give him the feel, the urge of freedom. So we have to find out which is false.

How would you inquire into this problem? It is a vital problem, isn't it? It is not dependent on any ideology, either of the left or of the right; and if it is dependent on an ideology, then it is merely a matter of opinion. Ideas always breed enmity, confusion, conflict. If you depend on books of the left or of the right, or on sacred books, then you depend on mere opinion, whether of Buddha, of Christ, of capitalism, communism, or what you will. They are ideas, not truth. A fact can never be denied. Opinion about fact can be denied. If we can discover what the truth of the matter is, we shall be able to act independently of opinion.

Is it not, therefore, necessary to discard what others have said? The opinion of the leftist or other leaders is the outcome of their conditioning. So if you depend for your discovery on what is found in books, you are merely bound by opinion. It is not a matter of knowledge.

How is one to discover the truth of this? On that we will act. To find the truth of this, there must be freedom from all propaganda, which means you are capable of looking at the problem independently of opinion. The whole task of education is to awaken the individual. To see the truth of this, you will have to be very clear, which means you cannot depend on a leader. When you choose a leader you do so out of confusion, and so your leaders are also confused, and that is what is happening in the world. Therefore you cannot look to your leader for guidance or help.

The problem, then, is how to find the truth of this matter: whether the individual is the instrument of society or whether society exists for the individual. How are you going to find this out—not intellectually, but factually? What do you mean by the individual? What is the 'you'? What are we, physically and psychologically, outwardly and inwardly? Are we not the result of environmental influences? Are we not the result of our culture, nationality, religion, and so on? So the individual is the result of education, technical or classical. You are the result of environment. There are those who say that you are not only physical but something more—in you is reality, God. This, after all, is but an opinion, the result of the influence of society. It is a conditioned response, nothing more. Here in India, you believe you are more than the outcome of material influences. Others believe they are nothing more than that. Both beliefs are conditioned. Both are the result of social, economic, and other influences—which is fairly obvious. Therefore we have first to recognize that we are the result of the social influences about us. Whether you believe in Hinduism, Christianity, the leftist ideology, or in nothing at all, you are the result of that conditioning.

Now, to find out if you are something more, there must be freedom from conditioning. To be free, you must question the whole social response, and only then can you find out whether the individual is merely the result of society or something more. That is, you can find out the truth of this only through questioning the social, economic, environmental influence, the ideologies, and so on. Only those who question are capable of creating social revolution. Such individuals, being free of patterns, beliefs, ideologies, are able to help to create a new society which is not based on any conditioning.

So, seeing that the world at the present time is in conflict, with imperialism, wars, starvation, increase in population, unemployment, antagonism—seeing all this, the person who is really serious has to find out whether the individual is the end of society, that is, whether society exists for the individual. If it does, then the relationship between the individual and society is entirely different. Then the individual is a free being in relation to society, which is also free. This requires an enormous understanding of oneself. Without self-knowledge, there is no basis for thinking; you are merely shaped by the winds of circumstance. Without knowing the total self, there can be no right thinking. The understanding of oneself is not to be found in withdrawal from life, in running away from society to the woods; on the contrary, it is to be found in relationship with one's wife, with one's son, with society. Relationship is a mirror in which you see yourself, but you cannot see yourself as you are if you condemn what you see. After all, if you want to understand someone, you do not condemn him, but study, observe him under all conditions. You are a silent watcher observing, not condemning—and then only do you understand. Out of that understanding comes clarity, which is the basis of right thinking. But by the mere repetition of ideas, however wonderful they may be, we become gramophones playing according to various influences, but still gramophones. It is only when we cease to be gramophones that the individual acquires significance. We are then true revolutionaries because we discover the real. Freedom from ideas, from conditioning, can alone bring revolution—which must begin with you, not with a blueprint. Any clever person can draw up a blueprint, but it is useless. To discover what one is brings about a radical revolution, and that discovery does not depend on a blueprint. Such a discovery is essential to bring about a new state.

I have been handed several questions. Before I answer them, it is important to find out why you ask questions. Is it to strengthen your opinions or to create a controversy or to deny what is said? Because, if you cling to your views, you will listen with your arguments; you will not listen to find out what is being said. I hope you will listen, not in the spirit of antagonism, but to find out what the truth is. If you meet what is being said with your opinions, of what value is it to listen?

Question: In your talks, you say that man is the measure of the world and that when he transforms himself, the world will be at peace. Has your own transformation shown this to be true?

KRISHNAMURTI: What is implied in this question? That though I say I recognize that I am the world, and the world is not separate from me, though I talk against wars and so on, exploitation still goes on, so what I say is futile. Let us examine this. You and the world are not two different entities. You are the world, not as an ideal, but factually. You are the result of climate, of nationality, of various forms of conditioning, and what you think, what you feel, that you project—and you create a world of division. You want to be Telugus against Tamils, God knows why. What you project is the world; you create the world. If you are greedy, that you project—so the world is yourself. As the world is yourself, to transform the world you must know yourself. In the transformation of yourself, you produce a transformation in society. The questioner implies that since there is no cessation of exploitation, what I am saying is futile. Is that true? I am going around the world trying to point out truth, not doing propaganda. Propaganda is a lie. You can propagate an idea, but you cannot propagate truth. I go around pointing out truth, and it is for you to recognize it or not. One man cannot change the world, but you and I can change the world together. This is not a political lecture. You and I have to find out what is truth, for it is truth that dissolves the sorrows, the miseries of the world. The world is not far away in Russia or America or England. The world is where you are, however small it may seem; it is you, your environment, your family, your neighbor, and if that is transformed, you bring transformation in the world. But most of us are lazy, sluggish. What I say is real in itself, but it is futile if you are unwilling to understand it. Transformation can be brought about only by the individual. Great things are performed by individuals, and you can bring about a phenomenal, radical revolution when you understand yourselves. Have you not noticed in history that it is individuals who transform, not the mass? The mass may be influenced, used, but the radical revolutions in life take place with individuals only. Wherever you live, at whatever level of society you may be placed, if you understand yourselves you will bring about transformation in your relationship with others. What is important is to put an end to sorrow, for the ending of sorrow is the beginning of revolution, and that revolution brings about transformation in the world.

Question: You say that gurus are unnecessary, but how can I find truth without the wise help and guidance which only a guru can give?

KRISHNAMURTI: The question is whether a guru is necessary or not. Can truth be found through another? Some say it can, and some say it cannot. As this is a question of importance, I hope you will pay sufficient attention. We want to know the truth of this, not my opinion as against the opinion of another. I have no opinion in this matter. Either it is so, or it is not. Whether it is essential that you should or should not have a guru is not a question of opinion. The truth of the matter is not dependent on opinion, however profound, erudite, popular, universal. The truth of the matter is to be found out in fact.

First of all, why do we want a guru? We say we need a guru because we are confused and the guru is helpful—he will point out what truth is, he will help us to understand, he knows much more about life than we do, he will act as a father, as a teacher to instruct us in life, he has vast experience and we have but little, he will help us through his greater experience, and so on and on. That is, basically, you go to a teacher because you are confused. If you were clear, you would not go near a guru. Obviously, if you were profoundly happy, if there were no problems, if you understood life completely, you would not go to any guru. I hope you see the significance of this. Because you are confused, you seek out a teacher. You go to him to give you a way of life, to clarify your own confusion, to find truth. You choose your guru because you are confused, and you hope he will give you what you ask. That is, you choose a guru who will satisfy your demand; you choose according to the gratification he will give you, and your choice is dependent on your gratification. You do not choose a guru who says, "Depend on yourself"; you choose him according to your prejudices. So, since you choose your guru according to the gratification he gives you, you are not seeking truth but a way out of confusion, and the way out of confusion is mistakenly called truth.

Let us examine first this idea that a guru can clear up our confusion. Can anyone clear up our confusion?—confusion being the product of our responses. We have created it. Do you think someone else has created it—this misery, this battle at all levels of existence, within and without? It is the result of our own lack of knowledge of ourselves. It is because we do not understand ourselves, our conflicts, our responses, our miseries, that we go to a guru who we think will help us to be free of that confusion. We can understand ourselves only in relationship to the present, and that relationship itself is the guru, not someone outside. If I do not understand that relationship, whatever a guru may say is useless because if I do not understand relationship, my relationship to property, to people, to ideas, who can resolve the conflict within me? To resolve that conflict, I must understand it myself, which means I must be aware of myself in relationship. To be aware, no guru is necessary. If I do not know myself, of what use is a guru? As a political leader is chosen by those who are in confusion and whose choice therefore is also confused, so I choose a guru. I can choose him only according to my confusion; hence he, like the political leader, is confused.

So, what is important is not who is right—whether I am right or whether those are right who say a guru is necessary—but to find out why you need a guru is important. Gurus exist for exploitation of various kinds, but that is irrelevant. It gives you satisfaction if someone tells you how you are progressing. But to find out why you need a guru—there lies the key. Another can point out the way, but you have to do all the work, even if you have a guru. Because you do not want to face that, you shift the responsibility to the guru. The guru becomes useless when there is a particle of self-knowledge. No guru, no book or scripture can give you self-knowledge. It comes when you are aware of yourself in relationship. To be is to be related; not to understand relationship is misery, strife. Not to be aware of your relationship to property is one of the causes of confusion. If you do not know your right relationship to property, there is bound to be conflict, which increases the conflict in society. If you do not understand the relationship between you and your wife, between you and your child, how can another resolve the conflict arising out of that relationship? Similarly with ideas, beliefs, and so on. Being confused in your relationship with people, with property, with ideas, you seek a guru. If he is a real guru, he will tell you to understand yourself. You are the source of all misunderstanding and confusion, and you can resolve that conflict only when you understand yourself in relationship.

You cannot find truth through anybody else. How can you? Surely, truth is not something static; it has no fixed abode; it is not an end, a goal. On the contrary, it is living, dynamic, alert, alive. How can it be an end? If truth is a fixed point, it is no longer truth; it is then a mere opinion. Sir, truth is the unknown, and a mind that is seeking truth will never find it. For mind is made up of the known; it is the result of the past, the outcome of time—which you can observe for yourself. Mind is the instrument of the known; hence it cannot find the unknown; it can only move from the known to the known. When the mind seeks truth, the truth it has read about in books, that "truth" is self-projected, for then the mind is merely in pursuit of the known, a more satisfactory known than the previous one. When the mind seeks truth, it is seeking its own self-projection, not truth. After all, an ideal is self-projected; it is fictitious, unreal. What is real is *what is,* not the opposite. But a mind that is seeking reality, seeking God, is seeking the known. When you think of God, your God is the projection of your own thought, the result of social influences. You can think only of the known; you cannot think of the unknown, you cannot concentrate on truth. The moment you think of the unknown, it is merely the self-projected known. So, God or truth cannot be thought about. If you think about it, it is not truth. Truth cannot be sought—it comes to you. You can go only after what is known. When the mind is not tortured by the known, by the effects of the known, then only can truth reveal itself. Truth is in every leaf, in every tear; it is to be known from moment to moment. No one can lead you to truth, and if anyone leads you, it can only be to the known.

Truth can only come to the mind that is empty of the known. It comes in a state in which the known is absent, not functioning. The mind is the warehouse of the known, the residue of the known; and for the mind to be in that state in which the unknown comes into being, it must be aware of itself, of its previous experiences, the conscious as well as the unconscious, of its responses, reactions, and structure. When there is complete self-knowledge, then there is the ending of the known, then mind is completely empty of the known. It is only then that truth can come to you uninvited. Truth does not belong to you or to me. You cannot worship it. The moment it is known, it is unreal. The symbol is not real, the image is not real, but when there is the understanding of self, the cessation of self, then eternity comes into being.

Question: In order to have peace of mind, must I not learn to control my thoughts?

KRISHNAMURTI: To understand this question properly, we must go into it deeply, and that requires close attention. I hope you are not too tired to follow it.

My mind wanders. Why? I want to think about a picture, a phrase, an idea, an image, and in thinking about it, I see that my mind has gone off to the railway or to something that happened yesterday. The first thought has gone, and another has taken its place. Therefore I examine every thought that arises. That is intelligent, isn't it? But you make an effort to fix your thought on something. Why should you fix it? If you are interested in the thought that comes, then it gives you its significance. The wandering is not distraction—do not give it a name. Follow the wandering, the distraction; find out why the mind has wandered; pursue it, go into it fully. When the distraction is completely understood, then that particular distraction is gone. When another comes, pursue it also. Mind is made up of innumerable demands and longings, and when it understands them, it is capable of an awareness which is not exclusive. Concentration is exclusiveness; it is resistance against something. Such concentration is like putting on blinkers—it is obviously useless, it does not lead to reality. When a child is interested in a toy, there is no distraction.

Comment from the audience: But that is momentary.

KRISHNAMURTI: What do you mean? Do you want a sustained wall to hold you in? Are you a human being or a machine, to be limited, circumscribed? All concentration is exclusive. In that concentrated exclusion, nothing can penetrate your desire to be something. So concentration, which so many practice, is the denial of real meditation. Meditation is the beginning of self-knowledge, and without self-knowledge, you cannot meditate. Without self-knowledge, your meditation is valueless; it is merely a romantic escape. So, concentration, which is a process of exclusion, of resistance, cannot open the door to that state of mind in which there is no resistance. If you resist your child, you do not understand him. You must be open to all his vagaries, every one of his moods. Likewise, to understand yourself, you must be alive to every movement of the mind, every thought that arises. Every thought that comes implies some interest—do not call it distraction and condemn it; pursue it completely, fully. You want to concentrate on what is being said, and your mind wanders off to what a friend said last evening. This conflict you call distraction. So you say, "Help me to learn concentration, to fix my mind on one thing." But if you understand what causes distraction, then there is no necessity to try to concentrate—whatever you do is concentration. So the problem is not the wandering away but why the mind wanders. When the mind is wandering away from what is being said, then you are not interested in what is being said. If you are interested, you are not distracted. You think you ought to be interested in a picture, an idea, a lecture, but your interest is not in it, so the mind goes off all over the place. Why should you not acknowledge that you are not interested and let the mind wander? When you are not interested, it is a waste of effort to fix the mind, which merely creates a conflict between what you think you should be and the actual. It is like a motor car moving with the brakes applied. Such concentration is futile. It is exclusion, a pushing away. Why not acknowledge the distraction first? That is a fact. When the mind becomes quiet, when all the problems are resolved, it is like a pool with still waters in which you can see clearly. It is not quiet when it is caught up in the net of problems, for then you resort to suppression. When the mind follows and understands every thought, there is no distraction, and then it is quiet. Only in freedom can the mind be silent. When the mind is silent, not only the upper part, but fully, when it is free from all values, from the pursuit of its own projections, then there is no distraction—and only then reality comes into being.

November 20, 1949

Second Talk in Rajahmundry

It is very obvious that all problems require, not an answer, a conclusion, but the understanding of the problem itself. For the answer, the solution to the problem, is in the problem, and to understand the problem, whatever it is—personal or social, intimate or general—a certain quietness, a certain quality of unidentification with the problem is essential. That is, we see in the world at the present time great conflicts going on—ideological conflicts, the confusion and struggle of conflicting ideas, ultimately leading to war—and through it all, we want peace. Because, obviously, without peace one cannot create individually, which requires a certain quietness, a sense of undisturbed existence. To live quietly, peacefully, is essential in order to create, to think anew about any problem.

Now, what is the major factor that brings about this lack of peace within and without? That is our problem. We have innumerable problems of various types, and to resolve them, there must be a field of quietness, a sense of patient observation, a silent approach; and that is essential to the resolution of any problem. What is the thing which prevents that peace, that silent observation of *what is?* It seems to me that before we begin to talk of peace, we ought to understand the state of contradiction because that is the disturbing factor which hinders peace. We see contradiction in us and about us, and as I have tried to explain, what we are, the world is. Whatever our ambitions, our pursuits, our aims, it is upon them that we base the structure of society. So, because we are in contradiction, there is lack of peace in us and, therefore, outside of us. There is in us a constant state of denial and assertion—what we want to be and what we are. The state of contradiction creates conflict, and this conflict does not bring about peace—which is a simple, obvious fact. This inward contradiction should not be translated into some kind of philosophical dualism because that is a very easy escape. That is, by saying that contradiction is a state of dualism, we think we have solved it—which is obviously a mere convention, a contributory escape from actuality.

Now, what do we mean by conflict, by contradiction? Why is there a contradiction in us? You understand what I mean by contradiction—this constant struggle to be something apart from what I am. I am this, and I want to be that. This contradiction in us is a fact, not a metaphysical dualism, which we need not discuss. Metaphysics has no significance in understanding *what is.* We may discuss, say, dualism—what it is, if it exists, and so on—but of what value is it if we don't know that there is contradiction in us, opposing desires, opposing interests, opposing pursuits? That is, I want to be good, and I am not able to be. This contradiction, this opposition in us must be understood because it creates conflict, and in conflict, in struggle, we cannot create individually. Let us be clear on the state we are in. There is contradiction, so there must be struggle, and struggle is destruction, waste. In that state, we can produce nothing but antagonism, strife, more bitterness and sorrow. If we can understand this fully and hence be free of contradiction, then there can be inward peace, which will bring understanding of each other.

So, the problem is this. Seeing that conflict is destructive, wasteful, why is it that in each of us there is contradiction? To understand that, we must go a little further. Why is there the sense of opposing desires? I do not know if we are aware of it in ourselves—this contradiction, this sense of wanting and not wanting, remembering something and trying to forget it and face something new. Just watch it. It is very simple and very normal. It is not something extraordinary. The actual fact is: there is contradiction. Then why does this contradiction arise? Is it not important to understand this? Because, if there were no contradiction, there would be no conflict, there would be no struggle; then *what is* could be understood without bringing into it an opposing element which creates conflict. So, our question is, is it not, why is there this contradiction and hence this struggle which is waste and destruction? What do we mean by contradiction? Does it not imply an impermanent state which is being opposed by another impermanent state? That is, I think I have a permanent desire. I posit in myself a permanent desire, and another desire arises which contradicts it, and this contradiction brings about conflict, which is waste. That is, there is a constant denial of one desire by another desire, one pursuit overcoming another pursuit. Now, is there such a thing as a permanent desire? Surely, all desire is impermanent—not metaphysically, but actually. Don't translate this into something metaphysical and think you have understood it. Actually, all desire is impermanent. I want a job. That is, I look to a certain job as a means of happiness, and when I get it, I am dissatisfied. I want to become the manager, then the owner, and so on and on, not only in this world, but in the so-called spiritual world—the teacher becoming the principal, the priest becoming the bishop, the pupil becoming the Master.

So, this constant becoming, arriving at one state after another, brings about contradiction, does it not? Therefore, why not look at life, not as one permanent desire, but as a series of fleeting desires always in opposition to each other? Hence the mind need not be in a state of contradiction. If I regard life, not as a permanent desire, but as a series of temporary desires that are constantly changing, then there is no contradiction. I do not know if I am explaining myself clearly, because it is important to realize that wherever there is contradiction there is conflict, and conflict is unproductive, wasteful, whether it is a quarrel between two people or a struggle within; like war, it is utterly destructive.

So, contradiction arises only when the mind has a fixed point of desire, that is, when the mind does not regard all desire as moving, transient, but seizes upon one desire and makes that into a permanency—only then, when other desires arise, is there contradiction. But all desires are in constant movement; there is no fixation of desire. There is no fixed point in desire, but the mind establishes a fixed point because it treats everything as a means to arrive, to gain; and there must be contradiction, conflict, as long as one is arriving. I do not know if you see that point.

It is important to see, first of all, that conflict is essentially destructive, whether it is the communal conflict, the conflict between nations, between ideas, or the conflict within the individual. It is unproductive, and that struggle is utilized, exploited by the priests, by the politicians. If we realize this, actually see that struggle is destructive, then we have to find out how to bring about the cessation of struggle and must therefore inquire into contradiction; and contradiction always implies the desire to become, to gain, the desire to arrive—which after all is what we mean by the so-called search for truth. That is, you want to arrive, you want to succeed, you want to find an ultimate God or truth which will be your permanent satisfaction. Therefore, you are not seeking truth, you are not seeking God. You are seeking lasting gratification, and that gratification you clothe with an idea, a respectable-sounding words such as *God, truth;* but actually you are each one seeking gratification, and you place that gratification, that satisfaction, at the highest point, calling it God, and the lowest point, drink. As long as the mind is seeking gratification, there is not much difference between God and drink. Socially, drink may be bad, but the inward desire for gratification, for gain, is even more harmful, is it not? If you really want to find truth, you must be extremely honest, not merely at the verbal level, but altogether; you must be extraordinarily clear, and you cannot be clear if you are unwilling to face facts. That is what we are attempting to do at these meetings—to see clearly for ourselves *what is.* If you do not want to see, you can walk away, but if you want to find truth, you must be extraordinarily and scrupulously clear. Therefore, a man who wants to understand reality must obviously understand this whole process of gratification—gratification not only in the literal sense, but in the more psychological sense. As long as the mind is fixed as a "permanent" center, identified with an idea, with a belief, there must be contradiction in life, and that contradiction breeds antagonism, confusion, struggle, which means there can be no peace. So, merely to force the mind to be peaceful is utterly useless because a mind that is disciplined, forced, compelled to be peaceful is not at peace. That which is made peaceful is not peaceful. You can impose your will, your authority on a child to make him peaceful, but that child is not peaceful. To be peaceful is quite a different thing.

So, to understand this whole process of existence in which there is constant struggle, pain, constant disagreement, constant frustration, we must understand the process of the mind, and this understanding of the process of the mind is self-knowledge. After all, if I do not know how to think, what basis have I to think rightly? I must know myself. In knowing myself, there comes quietness, there comes freedom, and in that freedom there is discovery of what is truth—not truth at an abstract level, but in every incident of life, in my words, in my gestures, in the way I talk to my servant. Truth is to be found in the fears, in the sorrows, in the frustrations of daily living because that is the world we live in, the world of turmoil, the world of misery. If we do not understand that, merely to understand some abstract reality is an escape, which leads to further misery. So, what is important is to understand oneself, and understanding oneself is not apart from the world because the world is where you are—it is not miles away; the world is the community in which you live, your environmental influences, the society which you have created—all that is the world; and in that world, unless you understand yourself, there can be no radical transformation, no revolution, and hence no individual creativeness. Don't be frightened of that word *revolution.* It is really a marvelous word with tremendous significance if you know what it means. But most of us do not want change; most of us resist change; we would like a modified continuity of *what is,* which is called revolution—but that is not revolution. Revolution can come into being—and it is essential for such a revolution to take place—only when you as an individual understand yourself in relation to society and therefore transform yourself; and such a revolution is not momentary, but constant.

So, life is a series of contradictions, and without understanding those contradictions, there can be no peace. It is essential to have peace, to have physical security, in order to live, to create. But everything we do contradicts. We want peace, and all our actions produce war. We want no communal strife, and yet that hope is denied. So, until we understand this process of contradiction in ourselves, there can be no peace, and therefore no new culture, no new state; and to understand that contradiction, we must face ourselves, not theoretically, but as we are, not with previous conclusions, with quotations from the Bhagavad-Gita, from Shankara, and so on. We must take ourselves as we really are, the pleasant as well as the unpleasant, which requires the capability of looking at exactly *what is;* and we cannot understand *what is* if we condemn, if we identify, if we justify. We must look at ourselves as we would look at that man walking on the road, and that requires constant awareness—awareness, not at some extraordinary level, but awareness of what we are, of our speech, our responses, our relationship to property, to poor people, to the beggar, to the scholar, and so on. Awareness must begin at that level, because to go far, one must begin near, but most of us are unwilling to begin near. It is much easier—at least we think it is much easier—to begin far away, which is an escape from the near. We all have ideals. We are experts at escape, and that is the curse of these escapist religions. To go far, one must begin near. This does not require some extraordinary renunciation but a state of high sensitivity because that which is highly sensitive is receptive, and only in that state of sensitivity can there be a reception of truth—which is not for the dull, the sluggard, the unaware. He can never find truth. But the man who begins near, who is aware of his gesture, of his talk, the manner of his eating, the manner of his speech, the ways of his behavior—for him there is a possibility of going very extensively, very widely into the causes of conflict. You cannot climb high if you do not begin low, but you do not want to begin low, you do not want to be simple, you do not want to be humble. Humility is humor, and without humor you cannot go far. But humor is not a thing which you can cultivate. So, a man who would really seek, who would know what truth is, or who would be open to truth must begin very near; he must sensitize himself through awareness so that his mind is polished, clear, and simple. Such a mind is not pursuing its own desires; it does not worship a homemade ideal. Only then can there be peace, for such a mind discovers that which is immeasurable.

Question: Why don't you feed the poor instead of talking?

KRISHNAMURTI: It is essential to be critically aware, but not to pass judgment, because the moment you pass judgment, you have already concluded. You are not critically aware. The moment you come to a conclusion, your critical capacity is dead. Now, the questioner implies that he is feeding the poor, and I am not. I wonder if the questioner is feeding the poor! So, put to yourself this question, "Are you feeding the poor?" I am trying to inquire into the mentality of the questioner. Either he is criticizing to find out and therefore is at perfect liberty to criticize, to inquire, or he is criticizing with a conclusion and therefore is no longer critical, is merely imposing his conclusion; or, if the questioner is feeding the poor, then his question is justified. But, are you feeding the poor? Are you at all aware of the poor? On the average, people in India die at 27; in America and New Zealand it is 64 to 67. If you were aware of the poor, this state of things would not go on in India.

Now, the questioner wants to know why I am talking. I will tell you. To feed the poor, you must have complete revolution—not a superficial revolution of the left or of the right, but a radical revolution, and you can have radical revolution only when ideas have ceased. A revolution based on an idea is not a revolution because an idea is merely the reaction to a particular conditioning, and action based on a conditioning is not productive of fundamental change. So, I am talking to produce not mere superficial change but fundamental change. This is not a matter of inventing new ideas. It is only when you and I are free of ideas, whether of the left or of the right, that we can produce a radical revolution, inwardly and so outwardly. Then there is no question of rich and poor. Then there is human dignity, the right to work, opportunity and happiness for each one. Then there is no man with too much who must feed those with too little. There is no class difference. This is not a mere idea; it is not a utopia. It is an actuality when this radical revolution is inwardly taking place, when in each one of us there is fundamental change. Then there will be no class, no nationalities, no wars, no destructive separatism, and that can come about only when there is love in your heart. Real revolution can come only when there is love, not otherwise. Love is the only flame without smoke; but unfortunately we have filled our hearts with the things of the mind, and therefore our hearts are empty and our minds are full. When you fill the heart with thoughts, then love is merely an idea. Love is not an idea, but if you think about love, it is not love—it is merely a projection of thought. To cleanse the mind, there must be fullness of heart, but the heart must be emptied of the mind before it can be full, and that is a tremendous revolution. All other revolutions are merely the continuation of a modified state.

Sir, when you love somebody—not the way we love people, which is only thinking about them—when you love people completely, wholly, then there is neither rich nor poor. Then you are not conscious of yourselves. Then there is that flame in which there is no smoke of jealousy, envy, greed, sensation. It is only such a revolution that can feed the world—and it is up to you, not to me. But most of us have grown accustomed to listening to talks because we live in words. Words have become important because we are newspaper readers; we listen habitually to political talks which are full of words without much meaning. So we are fed on words, we survive on words; and most of you are listening to these talks merely on the verbal level, and therefore there is no real revolution in you. But it is up to you to bring about that revolution, not the revolution of blood, which is a modified continuity which we miscall revolution, but that revolution which comes into being when the mind is no longer filling the heart, when thought is no longer taking the place of affection, compassion. But you cannot have love when the mind is predominant. Most of you are not cultured but merely well-read, and you live by what you have learned. Such knowledge does not bring about revolution, does not bring about transformation. What brings about transformation is understanding everyday conflicts, everyday relationships. When the heart is empty of the things of the mind, then only does that flame of reality come. But one must be capable of receiving it, and to receive it, one cannot have a conclusion based on knowledge and determination. Such a mind, being peaceful, not bound by ideas, is capable of receiving that which is infinite, and therefore it creates revolution—not merely to feed the poor or to give them employment or to give power to those who have no power, but it will be a different world of different value, not based on monetary satisfaction.

So, words don't feed hungry men. Words to me are not important; I am using words merely as a means of communication. We can use any word as long as we understand each other; and I am not giving you ideas, I am not feeding you words. I am talking so that you can see clearly for yourselves that which you are, and from that perception you can act clearly and definitely and purposefully. Only then is there a possibility of cooperative action. Talking merely to amuse ourselves is of no value, but talking to understand ourselves and thus bring about transformation is essential.

Question: In your talks in 1944, the following question was put to you: "You are in a happy position. All your needs are met. We have to earn money for ourselves, our wives and families. We have to attend to the world. How can you understand us and help us?" That is the question.

KRISHNAMURTI: I tried to answer the question; I did not evade it, but perhaps I may have put it in a way that appears to the questioner as evasion. Life is not a thing to be settled with yes or no; life is complicated; it has no such permanent conclusion. It is like your wanting to know if there is or is not reincarnation. We must go into it. In discussing it, you think I am evading because your mind is fixed on one thing, either "there is" or "there is not." So, from your point of view, it is obviously an evasion, but if you look into it a little more clearly, you will see that it is not evasion.

Now, the questioner wants to know—since my needs are provided by others, how can I understand those who are struggling with life to provide for their families and themselves? What is the implication of this question? That you are privileged and we are not, and how can the privileged class understand the unprivileged? So, the question is: Can the privileged person understand the unprivileged?

First of all, am I privileged? I am privileged only when I accept position, authority, power, the prestige of asserting myself to be somebody—which I have never done because to be somebody is highly immoral, unethical, and unspiritual. To be somebody denies reality, and it is only the one who is somebody that is privileged. He exploits and denies, but I am not in that position. I go about speaking, and for that I am paid as you are paid for your job, and I am treated exactly on that level. My needs are not very great because I do not believe in great needs. A man who is burdened with many possessions is thoughtless, but the man who avoids possessions and the man who is identified with a few possessions are equally thoughtless. So, I earn my living as you earn yours. I speak, and I am asked to go to different parts of the world. Those who ask me to go, pay for it. If they do not ask, if I do not talk, it is all right. For me, talking is not a means of self-expression or exploitation. I do not find gratification in it; it is not a means of exploiting you or getting your money because I do not want you to do any charity, to believe this or not to believe that. I am talking merely to help you see that which you are, to be clear in yourself. For in clarity there is happiness; in understanding there is enlightenment. There is happiness in discussing together, for in that discussion we can see ourselves as we are. This relationship may act as a mirror, for all relationship is a mirror in which you and I discover ourselves.

But the questioner wants to know how I can understand and help those who are earning money in order to maintain their families. In other words, the questioner says, "You don't have a family. You don't go through the daily routine of the school, being insulted by the boys. You are not in a position to be heckled by the wife. So, how can you understand me, who have to encounter all this horror every day?"

Perhaps I understand because it is very simple, and it may be that you do not understand. It may be that you are not facing the thing as it is. When you go through the turmoil, the responsibilities, how do you go through them? Why do you go through the routine of going to the office? You call that a responsibility, a duty. Why do you put up with ugly things in life? Why do you put up with your wife and children, or why do you love them—if you do love them? Sir, think it out for yourself. Don't answer me. Don't laugh at it. That is one of the easiest ways of brushing it aside—to make a joke of it. Apparently your wife and children are merely a duty, a responsibility, and so you find life a hollow bore. And I say to you, why do you put up with all that? You say, "I can't help it. To run away from it is impossible. I would like to be free of it, but society would condemn my action. What would happen to my children, to my wife, to my husband?" So, you say it is your karma, it is your duty, it is your responsibility, and you postpone the problem. You do not want to look at the thing as it is. It is only when you think it out without fear, when you directly face it, that you will see that you have a different relationship with your wife, with your child. Sir, it is because you don't love your wife and children that you have this horror of family life. You have made sex into an enormous problem because you have no other relationship mentally, emotionally, morally. You are bound by your religion, by society, and the only other release possible to you is to have success, and as you are caught, bound and held, you rebel against it; you want to be free, and yet you are not. That is the contradiction, and therefore you struggle, which is such a wasteful thing. And, after all, why have we to live in the routine of an office to earn money, to have a job? Sir, have you ever tried not doing anything, really giving up, not calculating? Then you will see that life will feed you. But renunciation with a calculation is not renunciation. Renunciation with an end in view, giving up in order to find God, is merely the search for power. It is not renunciation. To renounce, you cannot look to tomorrow. But you see, we dare not think in these terms. We are respectable people. We have cultivated minds. We play a double game. We are not honest with ourselves and therefore with our families, with our children, with society. Being inwardly uncertain, insecure, we cling to outward things, to the position, to the wife, to the husband, to the children, and they become a means of gratification. I want somebody to be with me, to encourage me, generally the wife or the husband—so we use another for our own gratification. Surely, all this is not very difficult to understand. It is difficult only when you merely examine the superficial side of it. Most of us do not want to go deeply into these questions, so we try to evade them. Sir, a person who evades, who avoids looking at *what is,* will never find reality. The religious person who sees directly *what is* does not seek reality away from that. Reality is in your relationship with your wife and children, in the way you earn money; it is not somewhere else. You cannot earn money through wrong means; you must have a right means of livelihood. Truth is not away from that but is to be discovered in everyday action, and because we avoid all these things, our life is a misery. Our life is empty, has no meaning, except to breed children, earn a living, master a few words of Sanskrit, and do some puja. This we call existence. This we call living—an empty thing without much significance. Surely, to point out all this is not evading the question. To understand it, obviously you and I must go into it. I am not your guru; because, if you choose me as your guru, you will make me into another escape, and what you choose out of your confusion must also be confused. So, truth is a thing to be discovered from moment to moment, in every movement of life, and to understand that, you and I can talk it over, think it out together. I am not imposing something on you which you will never look into. We are talking it over to see our problem clearly, with the dignity of human beings, not with the desire to worship each other.

So, what is important in this question is whether I can really help you to understand yourself. I can help you only if you want to understand yourself; if you don't, the problem is simple—I cannot help you. That is neither wrong nor right. It simply cannot be done. But if we both want to understand, and therefore you and I have a relationship in which there is no fear, no subservience, then you can discover yourself as you are. That is all relationship can do—to offer a mirror in which to discover oneself, and the more you understand, the more there is quietness, tranquillity in the mind; and in that peace, in that silence, reality comes into being.

Question: What is the purpose of prayer?

KRISHNAMURTI: To answer this question, we must go into it fully, because it is a complex problem. Let us see what we mean by prayer, then we will find out its purpose. What do you mean by prayer? When do you pray? Not when you are happy, not when you are delighted, not when there is joy or pleasure in you. You pray only when you are in confusion, when you are in trouble, and then your prayer is a petition. A man in trouble prays, which means he is begging, he wants help. He is petitioning, he is asking to be comforted. (Laughter) There is nothing to laugh at. So, the man who is content, the man who is happy, the man who sees very clearly and understands reality in the action of everyday—such a man is not in need of prayer. You don't pray when you are joyous; you don't pray when there is delight in your heart. You pray only when there is confusion, or your prayer is merely a begging petition, a demand for help, for comfort, for alleviation. Is it not? In other words, you are in confusion, and you want some outside agency to get you out of that confusion. You want somebody to help you, and the more there is of the psychological element in your problem, the more urgent the demand for outside help. So, either you pray to God or, if you are a modern person, you go to a psychologist; or in order to escape from that confusion, you repeat a lot of words. You attend various prayer meetings where you are shepherded together and mesmerized into a certain state, and you think you have the answer. These are all actual facts. I am not inventing; I am just showing the implications of what you mean by prayer. As we go to a doctor when in physical pain, so when we are in psychological confusion, we escape into mass hypnotism or petition some outside agency for help. That is what we do, is it not? I am thinking aloud for you, that is all; I am not imposing anything on you. So, our prayer is addressed not to truth but to an outside agency, which we call a guide, a guru, or God. That is, when in pain, when in psychological conflict, we turn to somebody. It is the natural instinct of a boy turning to his father for help. When I do not understand my relationships with people, when I am in confusion, I call somebody to help me—which is a natural instinct, is it not?

Now, can an outside agency help me? Not that there is no outside agency—we will go into that another time—but can an outside agency help me when I have a problem, when I am in conflict, in confusion, which I have created myself? I have created conflict in my relationship with society. I have done something which brings about conflict. Surely, I am responsible for that confusion, not another; and until I understand it, what is the value of my turning to an outside agency? The outside agency may help me to get out of it, may help me to escape from it, but as long as I do not understand my turmoil, I will create another. That is what we are doing: we create a confusion, find some way to get out of it, and plunge into another confusion. So, until I understand the maker of confusion, which is myself, until I clear that confusion for myself, merely turning to an outside agency is of very little value. I know you won't like this; you will resist it because you do not want to look at things as they are, but surely I have to look at myself clearly in order to understand the cause of confusion. So, that is one fact.

Then we know the simple way of escaping from *what is* by denying it. We either cover it up through a repetition of words or escape from it by going to a mass prayer meeting. We know these various ways. You go to a temple and repeat a lot of words; you keep on repeating, and you think you are transformed. You have an answer, you have found a conclusion. It is merely a way of evading the problem. You have not looked at the problem. What happens when you pray? What do you do when you pray? You repeat certain words, certain phrases. What does it do to the mind when you constantly repeat certain prayers? By the repetition of phrases, the mind is made quiet. It is not quiet, but it is made quiet. There is a difference between a quiet mind and a mind that is made quiet. The mind that is made quiet by repetition is compelled, hypnotized into silence. Now, what happens when the mind is hypnotized into silence? What happens when the mind is made artificially quiet? Have you thought it out? Think it out, and see where it leads. You have to pay a little attention, experiment with yourself and not be distracted by those who come in and go out. Those of you who are interested, sit near.

Now, what happens to a mind that is made quiet? That is, you have a problem, and you want to find an answer. Therefore you pray, which is a repetition of certain phrases, and through that the mind is made quiet. What is the relationship between that hypnotized mind and the problem? Please follow this a little. You desire to find an answer to the problem and therefore use, chant, certain words to make the mind quiet; that is, you want a satisfactory answer to the problem, an answer that will be gratifying, not an answer that may contradict you. So, when you pray and make the mind quiet through words, you are looking for an answer which will be satisfying. You have already conceived the answer which must be satisfactory; therefore, you will find a satisfactory answer. Please see the importance of this, sir. You create what you want through dulling and making the mind quiet; by forcing the mind to pray, you have already established what you want—an answer which will be satisfactory, peaceful, completely satisfying. Therefore, the mind which is seeking an answer to the problem through prayer will find the answer which is satisfactory. Therefore, it is settled, and you say the answer is from God. That is why political leaders shout that they represent God, or that God has spoken to them directly; because they have identified themselves with the country, they get a satisfactory answer.

So, what happens to a mind that is unwilling to understand the problem and thus seeks the answer from an outside agency? Consciously or unconsciously, it gets a satisfactory answer; otherwise, it would reject the answer. That is, those who pray are seeking satisfaction and are therefore incapable of understanding the problem itself. When the mind is made quiet through prayer, the unconscious, which is the residue of your own satisfactory conclusions, projects itself into the conscious mind, and therefore your prayer is answered. So, when you pray, you are seeking an escape, happiness, and the outside agency which answers you is your own gratification, your own conscious or unconscious identification with the particular desire which you want to gratify.

So, I have a problem. I do not want to escape from it, I do not want an answer, I do not want a conclusion. I want to understand because the moment I understand something, I am free of it. So, need I go through the process of hypnotizing myself in order to understand, or of being hypnotized by words, forcing the mind to be quiet? Surely not. When I have a problem, I want to understand it. Understanding can come only when the mind is no longer judging the problem—that is, when the mind can look at it without condemnation or justification. Then the mind is quiet, not made quiet; and when the mind is quiet, then you will see that the problem unfolds itself. If you do not condemn, if you do not try to find an answer, the mind is quiet; in that quietness the problem reveals its own answer, not one satisfying to you. Therefore, the truth of the problem comes from the problem itself, but you cannot see the truth of the problem if you approach it with a conclusion, a prayer, a petition, which intervenes between yourself and the problem.

So, the man who wants to understand any problem can understand it only when the mind is quiet, not taking sides. When you want to understand the problem of unemployment, of human misery, you cannot take sides. But your politicians want you to take sides. If you are to understand the problem, there can be no sides, because the problem is not a matter of opinion, it does not demand an ideology. It demands that you should look at it clearly so as to understand its content, and you cannot understand the content of a problem if you have a screen of ideology between you and the problem. Similarly, prayer without self-knowledge leads to ignorance, to illusion. Self-knowledge is meditation, and without self-knowledge there is no meditation. Meditation is not fixing the mind on some object; meditation is understanding *what is* in relationship. Then the mind need not be forced to be quiet. Then the mind is extremely sensitive and therefore highly receptive. But to discipline the mind to be quiet destroys receptivity.

Perhaps we shall discuss this again next Sunday. To understand a problem, you must understand the creator of the problem, which is yourself. The problem is not apart from you. So, to understand yourself is of the highest importance; and to understand yourself you cannot withdraw from relationship, because relationship is a mirror in which you see yourself. Relationship is action, not abstract action but everyday action: your quarrels, your anger, your grief; and as you understand all that in relation to yourself, there comes quietness of mind, a tranquillity. In that tranquillity there is freedom. Only with that freedom is there the perception of truth.

November 27, 1949

Third Talk in Rajahmundry

There will be a discussion tomorrow morning at 7:45, and also on Tuesday at the same time; but there will be no talk next Sunday. This is the last talk.

I have said that there is an art in listening, and perhaps I can go a little more into it, because I think it is important to listen rightly. We generally hear what we want to hear and exclude everything that is disturbing. To any expression of a disturbing idea we turn a deaf ear, and especially in matters that are profound, religious, that have significance in life, we are apt to listen very superficially. If we hear at all, it is merely the words, not the content of the words, because most of us do not want to be disturbed. Most of us want to carry on in our old ways because to alter, to bring about a change, means disturbance: disturbance in our daily life, disturbance in our family, disturbance between wife and husband, between ourselves and society. As most of us are disinclined to be disturbed, we prefer to follow the easy way of existence; and whether it leads to misery, to turmoil and conflict, is apparently of very little importance. All that we want is an easy life—not too much trouble, not too much disturbance, not too much thinking; and so, when we listen, we are not really hearing anything. Most of us are afraid to hear deeply, but it is only when we hear deeply, when the sounds penetrate deeply, that there is a possibility of a fundamental, radical change. Such change is not possible if you listen superficially, and if I may suggest, at least for this evening, please try to listen without any resistance, without any prejudice—just listen. Do not make tremendous effort to understand, because understanding does not come through effort, understanding does not come through striving. Understanding comes swiftly, unknowingly, when the effort is passive; only when the maker of effort is silent does the wave of understanding come. So, if I may suggest, listen as you would listen to the water that is flowing by. You are not imagining, you are not making an effort to listen, you are just listening. Then the sound conveys its own meaning, and that understanding is far deeper, far greater, and more lasting than the mere understanding of words that comes through intellectual effort. The understanding of words which is called intellectual comprehension is utterly empty. You say, "I understand intellectually, but I cannot put it into practice," which means, really, that you do not understand. When you understand, you understand the content; there is no intellectual understanding. Intellectual understanding is merely a verbal understanding. Hearing the words is not the understanding of their content. The word is not the thing. The word is not understanding. Understanding comes when the mind has ceased to make an effort, which means, when it does not put up a resistance, when it is not prejudiced but listens freely and fully. And, if I may suggest, that is what we should try to do this evening, because then there is in listening a great delight—like listening to a poem, to a song, or seeing the movement of a tree. Then that very observation, listening, gives a tremendous significance to existence.

Religion, surely, is the uncovering of reality. Religion is not belief. Religion is not the search for truth. The search for truth is merely the fulfillment of belief. Religion is the understanding of the thinker; for what the thinker is, that he creates. Without understanding the process of the thinker and the thought, merely to be caught in a dogma is surely not the uncovering of the beauty of life, of existence, of truth. If you seek truth, then you already know truth. If you go out seeking something, the implication is that you have lost it, which means you already know what it is. What you do know is belief, and belief is not truth. No amount of belief, no amount of tradition, none of the religious ceremonies in which there are so many preconceptions of truth, lead to religion. Nor is religion the belief, the God of the irreligious, of the believer who does not believe.

Religion, surely, is allowing truth to come into being, whatever that truth is—not the truth that you want, for then it is merely the gratification of a particular desire which you call belief. So, it is necessary to have a mind that is capable of receiving whatever the truth is, and such a mind is possible only when you listen passively. Passive awareness comes into being when there is no effort, no suppression or sublimation, because after all, to receive, there must be a mind that is not burdened with opinion or busy with its own chatter. Out of an opinion or a belief the mind can project an idea or an image of God; but it is a projection of itself, of its own chatter, of its own fabrication, and therefore it is not real. The real cannot be projected or invited, but can come into being only when the mind, the thinker, understands himself. Without understanding the thought and the thinker, there is no possibility of receiving truth, because the maker of effort is the thought, which is the thinker. Without thought, there is no thinker; and the thinker, seeking further security, takes refuge in an idea which he calls God, religion. But that is not religion, that is merely an extension of his own egotism, a projection of himself. It is a projected righteousness, a projected respectability, and this respectability cannot receive that which is truth. Most of us are very respectable in the political, economic, or religious sense. We want to be something, here or in another world. The desire for existence in another world, in a different form, is still self-projection; it is still the worship of oneself, and such a projection is surely not religion. Religion is something much wider, much deeper than the projections of the self, and after all, your belief is a projection. Your ideals are self-projections, whether national or religious, and the following of such projections is obviously the gratification of the self and therefore the enclosing of the mind within a belief; therefore, it is not real.

Reality comes into being only when the mind is still, not made still. Therefore, there must be no disciplining of the mind to be still. When you discipline yourself, it is merely a projected desire to be in a particular state. Such a state is not the state of passivity. Religion is the understanding of the thinker and the thought, which means the understanding of action in relationship. The understanding of action in conduct is religion, not the worship of some idea, however gratifying, however traditional, whoever has said it. Religion is understanding the beauty, the depth, the extensive significance of action in relationship. Because, after all, life is relationship; to be is to be related—otherwise you have no existence. You cannot live in isolation. You are related to your friends, to your family, to those with whom you work. Even though you withdraw to a mountain, you are related to the man who brings food; you are related to an idea which you have projected. Existence implies being, which is relationship, and if we do not understand that relationship, there is no understanding of reality. But because relationship is painful, disturbing, constantly changing in its demands, we escape from it to what we call God, which we think is the pursuit of reality. The pursuer cannot pursue the real. He can only pursue his own ideal, which is self-projected. So, our relationship and the understanding of it is true religion and nothing else is, because in that relationship is contained the whole significance of existence. In relationship, whether with people, with nature, with the trees, with the stars, with ideas, with the state—in that relationship is the whole uncovering of the thinker and the thought, which is man, which is mind. The self comes into being through the focus of conflict; the focusing of conflict gives self-consciousness to the mind. Otherwise there is no self, and though you may place that self on a high level, it is still the self of gratification.

So, the man who would receive reality—not seek reality—who would hear the voice of the eternal, whatever that eternal is, must understand relationship; because in relationship there is conflict, and it is that conflict which prevents the real. That is, in conflict there is the fixing of selfconsciousness, which seeks to eschew, to escape conflict; but only when the mind understands conflict is it capable of receiving the real. So, without understanding relationship, the pursuit of the real is the pursuit of an escape, is it not? Why not face it? Without understanding the actual, how can you go beyond? You may close your eyes, you may run away to shrines and worship empty images; but the worship, the devotion, the puja, the giving of flowers, the sacrifices, the ideals, beliefs—all that has no meaning without understanding the conflict in relationship. So, the understanding of conflict in relationship is of primary importance and nothing else, for in that conflict you discover the whole process of the mind. Without knowing yourself as you are, not as you are technically supposed to be—God enclosed in matter, or whatever the theory is—but actually, in the conflict of daily existence, economic, social, and ideological—without understanding that conflict, how can you go beyond and find something? The search for the beyond is merely an escape from *what is,* and if you want to escape, then religion or God is as good an escape as drink. Don't object to this putting drink and God on the same level. All escapes are on the same level, whether you escape through drink, through puja, or whatever it be.

So, the understanding of conflict in relationship is of primary importance and nothing else, because out of that conflict we create the world in which we live every day—the misery, the poverty, the ugliness of existence. Relationship is response to the movement of life. That is, life is a constant challenge, and when the response is inadequate, there is conflict; but to respond immediately, truly, adequately to the challenge, brings about a completeness. In that response which is adequate to the challenge there is the cessation of conflict, and therefore it is important to understand oneself, not in abstraction, but in actuality, in everyday existence. What you are in daily life is of the highest importance; not what you think about or what you have ideas about, but how you behave to your wife, to your husband, to your children, to your employees. Because, from what you are, you create the world. Conduct is not an ideal conduct. There is no ideal conduct. Conduct is what you are from moment to moment, how you behave from moment to moment. The ideal is an escape from what you are. How can you go far when you do not know what is near you, when you are not aware of your wife? Surely, you must begin near to go far, but nevertheless, your eyes are fixed on the horizon, which you call religion, and you have all the paraphernalia of belief to help you to escape.

So, what is important is not how to escape because any escape is as good as another—the religious escapes and the worldly escapes are all the same—and escapes do not solve our problem. Our problem is conflict, not only the conflict between individuals, but the world conflict. We see what is happening in the world—the increasing conflict of war, of destruction, of misery. That you cannot stop; all you can do is to alter your relationship with the world, not the world of Europe or America, but the world of your wife, your husband, your work, your home. There you can bring change, and that change moves in wider and wider circles, but without this fundamental change there can be no peace of mind. You may sit in a corner or read something to put yourself to sleep, which most people call meditation, but that is not the uncovering, the receiving of the real. What most of us want is a satisfying escape; we do not want to face our conflicts because they are too painful. They are painful only because we never look to see what they are all about; we seek something which we call God but never look into the cause of conflict. But if we understand the conflict of everyday existence, then we can go further, because therein lies the whole significance of life. A mind that is in conflict is a destructive mind, a wasteful mind, and those in conflict can never understand; but conflict is not stilled by any sanctions, beliefs, or disciplines, because the conflict itself has to be understood. Our problem is in relationship, which is life, and religion is the understanding of that life, which brings about a state in which the mind is quiet. Such a mind is capable of receiving the real. That, after all, is religion—not your sacred threads, your pujas, your repetition of words, phrases, and ceremonies. Surely, all that is not religion. Those are divisions, but a mind that is understanding relationship has no division. The belief that life is one is merely an idea and, therefore, has no value; but for a man who is understanding relationship, there is no "outsider" or "insider," there is neither the foreigner nor the one who is near. Relationship is the process of understanding oneself, and to understand oneself from moment to moment in daily life is self-knowledge. Self-knowledge is not a religion, an ultimate end. There is no such thing as an ultimate end. There is such a thing for the man who wants to escape, but the understanding of relationship, in which there is ever-unfolding self-knowledge, is immeasurable.

So, self-knowledge is not the knowledge of the self placed at some high level; it is from moment to moment in daily conduct, which is action, which is relationship; and without that self-knowledge there is no right thinking. You have no basis for right thinking if you do not know what you are. You cannot know yourself in abstraction, in ideology. You can know yourself only in relationship in your daily life. Don't you know that you are in conflict? And what is the good of going away from it, of avoiding it, like a man who has a poison in his system which he does not reject and who is therefore slowly dying? So, self-knowledge is the beginning of wisdom, and without that self-knowledge you cannot go far; and to seek the absolute, God, truth, or what you will, is merely the search after a self-projected gratification. Therefore, you must begin near and search every word that you speak, search every gesture, the way you talk, the way you act, the way you eat—be aware of everything without condemnation; then in that awareness you will know what actually is and the transformation of *what is*—which is the beginning of liberation. Liberation is not an end. Liberation is from moment to moment in the understanding of *what is*—when the mind is free, not made free. It is only a free mind that can discover, not a mind molded by a belief or shaped according to a hypothesis. Such a mind cannot discover. There can be no freedom if there is conflict, for conflict is the fixing of the self in relationship.

Many questions have been sent in, and naturally it is impossible to answer them all. We have therefore chosen some which seem to be representative, and if your question is not answered, don't feel that it has been overlooked. After all, all problems are related, and if I can understand one problem in its entirety, then I can understand all the related problems. So, listen to these questions as you would listen to the talk, because questions are a challenge, and only in responding to them adequately do we find the problems resolved. They are a challenge to you as well as to me, and therefore, let us think them out together and respond fully.

Question: What is right education? As teachers and as parents, we are confused.

KRISHNAMURTI: Now, how are we going to find the truth of this matter? Merely forcing the mind into a system, a pattern, is obviously not education. So, to discover what is right education, we must find out what we mean by "education." Surely, education is not to learn the purpose of life, but to understand the meaning, the significance, the process of existence; because if you say life has a purpose, then the purpose is self-projected. Surely, to find out what is right education, you have first to inquire into the whole significance of life, of living. What is present education? Learning to earn a few rupees, acquiring a trade, becoming an engineer, a sociologist, learning how to butcher people, or how to read a poem. If you say education is to make a person efficient, which means to give him technical knowledge, then you must understand the whole significance of efficiency. What happens when a person becomes more and more efficient? He becomes more and more ruthless. Don't laugh. What are you doing in your daily life? What is happening now in the world? Education means the development of a particular technique, which is efficiency, which means industrialization, the capacity to work faster and produce more and more, all of which ultimately leads to war. You see this happening every day. Education as it is leads to war, and what is the point of education? To destroy or be destroyed. So, obviously, the present system of education is utterly futile. Therefore, what is important is to educate the educator. These are not clever statements to be listened to and laughed off. Because, without educating the teacher, what can he teach the child except the exploiting principles on which he himself has been brought up? Most of you have read many books. Where are you? You have money or can earn it, you have your pleasures and ceremonies—and you are in conflict; and what is the point of education, of learning to earn a few rupees, when your whole existence leads to misery and war? So, right education, surely, must begin with the educator, the parent, the teacher; and inquiry into right education means inquiry into life, into existence, does it not? What is the point of your being educated as a lawyer if you are only going to increase conflict and maintain litigation? But there is money in that, and you thrive on it. So, if you want to bring about right education, you must obviously understand the meaning, the significance, of existence. It is not only to earn money, to have leisure, but to be able to think directly, truly—not "consistently," because to think consistently is merely to conform to a pattern. A consistent thinker is a thoughtless person; he merely repeats certain phrases and thinks in a groove. To find out what is right education, there must be the understanding of existence, which means the understanding of yourself, because you cannot understand existence abstractly. You cannot understand yourself by theorizing as to what education should be. Surely, right education begins with the right understanding of the educator.

Look at what is happening in the world. Governments are taking control of education—naturally, because all governments are preparing for war. Your pet government, as well as the foreign government, must inevitably prepare for war. A sovereign government must have an army, a navy, an air force; and to make the citizens efficient for war, to prepare them to perform their duties thoroughly, efficiently, ruthlessly, the central government must control them. Therefore, they educate them as they manufacture mechanical instruments, to be ruthlessly efficient. If that is the purpose and end of education—to destroy or be destroyed—then it must be ruthless, and I am not at all sure that that is not what you want. Because, you are still educating your children in the same old fashion. Right education begins with the understanding of the educator, the teacher, which means that he must be free of established patterns of thought. Education is not merely imparting information, knowing how to read, gathering and correlating facts; but it is seeing the whole significance of education, of government, of the world situation, of the totalitarian spirit which is becoming more and more dominant throughout the world. Being confused, you create the educator who is also confused, and through so-called education you give power to destroy the foreign government. Therefore, before you ask what right education is, you must understand yourself, and you will see that it does not take a long time to understand yourself if you are interested to find out. Sir, without understanding yourself as the educator, how can you bring about a new kind of education? Therefore, we come back to the eternal point—which is yourself—and you want to avoid that point; you want to shift the responsibility onto the teacher, onto the government. The government is what you are, the world is what you are; and without understanding yourself, how can there be right education?

Question: What do you mean by living from moment to moment?

KRISHNAMURTI: A thing that continues can never be new. Just think it out and you will see—it is not a complicated problem. Surely, if I can complete each day and not carry over my worries, my tribulations, to the next, then I can meet tomorrow afresh. Meeting the challenge afresh is creation, and there can be no creation without ending. That is, you meet the new with the old; therefore, there must be an ending of the old to meet the new. There must be an ending every minute, so that every minute is a new one. That is not a poetical imagination or indulgence. If you try, you will find out what happens. But, you see, we want to continue. We want to have continuation from moment to moment, from day to day, because we think without continuation we cannot exist.

Now, that which is capable of continuing, can that renew itself? Can that be new? Surely, there can be a new thing only when there is an ending. Your thought is continuous. Thought is the result of the past, thought is founded upon the past; it is a continuance of the past, which in conjunction with the present creates, modifies, the future. But the past, through the present to the future, is still a continuity. There is no break. It is only when there is a break that you can see something new. Merely to continue the past, modified by the present, is not to perceive the new. Therefore, thought cannot perceive the new. Thought must end for the new to be. But, you see what we are doing. We are using the present as a passage from the past to the future. Are we not doing that? To us, the present is not important. Thought, which is the present action, which is the present relationship, we do not think is important. We think what is important is the outcome, the result of thought, which is the future or the past. Have you not noticed how the old look to the past, and also how the young sometimes look to the past or to the future? They are occupied with themselves in the past or in the future but never give their full attention to the present. So, we use the present as a passage way to something else, and therefore there is no consideration, no observation of the present; and to observe the present, the past must end. Surely, to see *what is,* you cannot look through the past to the present. If I want to understand you, I must look at you directly, I must not bring up my past prejudices and through those prejudices look at you. Then I am only looking at my prejudices. I can look at you only when the prejudices are not; therefore, there must be an end to prejudices.

So, to understand *what is,* which is action, which is relationship at every moment, there must be a freshness; therefore, there must be an ending of the past, and this is not a theory. Experiment with it, and you will see that this ending is not as difficult as you think. While you are listening, try it, and you will see how easily and completely you can end thought and so discover. That is, when you are not induced, when you are interested in something vitally, profoundly, you are looking at it anew. The very interest drives away the past. You are only concerned to observe *what is* and to allow *what is* to tell its story. When you see the truth of this, your mind is emptied from moment to moment. Therefore, the mind is discovering everything anew, and that is why knowledge can never be new. It is only wisdom that is new. Knowledge can be taught in a school, but wisdom cannot be taught. A school of wisdom is nonsense. Wisdom is the discovery and the understanding of *what is* from moment to moment, and how can you be taught to observe *what is?* If you are taught, it is knowledge, then knowledge intervenes between you and the fact. Therefore, knowledge is a barrier to the new, and a mind full of knowledge cannot understand *what is.* You are learned, are you not? And is your mind new? Or is it filled up with memorized facts? And a mind which becomes more and more a mere accumulation of facts—how can such a mind see anything new? To see what is new, there must be an emptiness of past knowledge. Only in the discovery of *what is* from moment to moment is there the freedom which wisdom brings. Therefore, wisdom is something new, not repetitive, not something which you learn out of a school book or from Shankara, the Bhagavad-Gita, or Christ.

So, knowledge which is continued is a barrier to understanding the new. If in listening you bring in your previous knowledge, how can you understand? First you must listen. Sir, an engineer has knowledge of stresses and strains, but if he comes to build a bridge, he must first study the location and the soil. He must look at it independently of the structure which he is going to build, which means he must regard it anew, not merely copy from a book. But there is a danger in similes, so use it lightly. What is important is that there be a renewal in which there can be creation, that creative impulse, that sense of constant rebirth, and that can come into being only when there is death every minute. Such a mind can receive that which is truth. Truth is not something absolute, final, far away. It is to be discovered from moment to moment, and you cannot discover it in a state of continuity. There can be no freedom in continuity. After all, continuity is memory, and how can memory be new? How can memory, which is experience, which is the past, understand the present? Only when the past is wholly understood and the mind is empty is it capable of seeing the present in all its significance. But most of our minds are not empty. They are filled with knowledge, and such a mind is not a thinking mind. It is only a repetitive mind, a gramophone changing the records according to circumstances. Such a mind is incapable of discovering the new. There is the new only in ending, but you are afraid of that. You are afraid of ending, and all your talk, your accumulation of facts, is merely a safeguard, an escape from that. Therefore, you are seeking continuity, but continuity is never new; in it there can be no renewal, no emptiness in which you can receive. So, the mind can renew itself only when it is empty, not when it is filled with your worries from day to day, and when the mind has come to an end, there is a creation which is timeless.

Question: The more I listen to you, the more I feel the truth of the ancient teachings of Christ, Shankara, the Bhagavad-Gita, and Theosophy. Have you really not read any of them?

KRISHNAMURTI: I will first answer the second part of the question and then take up the first part. "Have you really not read any of them?" No, sir, I have not read any of them. What is wrong with that? Are you surprised? Are you shocked? And why should you read them? Why do you want to read others' books when there is the book of yourself? Why do you want to read the Bible or Shankara? Surely, because you want confirmation, you want to conform. That is why most people read—to be confirmed in what they believe or what they express, to be sure, to be safe, to be certain. Can you discover anything in certainty? Obviously not. A man who is certain psychologically can never discover. So, why do you read? You may read for mere amusement or to accumulate facts; or you read to acquire what you call wisdom, and you think you have understood everything because you can quote Shankara; you think by quoting Shankara you have got the full significance of life. The man who quotes is a thoughtless man because he is merely repeating what somebody has said. Sirs, if you had no book, no Bhagavad-Gita, no Shankara, what would you do? You would have to take the journey by yourself into the unknown, you would have to venture out alone. When you discover something, what you discover is yours; then you need no book. I have not read the Bhagavad-Gita nor any of the religious, psychological, or philosophical books, but I have discovered something, and that discovery can come only in freedom, not through repetition. That discovery is far greater than the experience of another, because discovery is not repetition, not copy.

Then, the first part of the question. Sir, why do you compare? What is the process of comparison? Why do you say, "What you say is like Shankara"? Whether it is or is not is unimportant. Truth can never be the same; it is ever new. If it is the same, it is not truth because truth is living from moment to moment; it cannot be today what it was yesterday. But why do you want to compare? Don't you compare in order to feel safe, in order to feel that you do not have to think, since what I say is what Shankara said? You have read Shankara, and you think you have understood; so you compare and relax, which is all very quick and effortless. In fact, you have not understood, and that is why you compare. When you compare, there is no understanding. To understand, you must look directly at the thing that is presented to you, and a mind that compares is a sluggish, wasteful mind; it is a mind that lives in security, that is enclosed in gratification. Such a mind cannot possibly understand truth. Truth is a living thing, not static, and a thing that is living is incomparable; it cannot be compared with the past or with the future. Truth is incomparable from moment to moment, and for a mind that tries to compare it, weigh it, judge it, there is no truth. For such a mind there is only propaganda, repetition; and repetition is a lie, it is not truth. You repeat because you are not experiencing, and a man who is experiencing never repeats, because truth is not repeatable. You cannot repeat truth, but your conclusion, your judgment about it can be repeated. Therefore, a mind that compares, that says, "What you are saying is exactly what Shankara said"—such a mind merely wants to continue and so is enervated, dead.

Sir, there is no song in your heart if you merely repeat a song and therefore follow the singer. What is important is not whether I have read sacred books, or whether what I say is comparable to Shankara, the Bhagavad-Gita, or Christ, but what is important is why you repeat, why you compare. Understand why you compare, then you will be understanding yourself. The understanding of yourself is far more important than your understanding of Shankara, because you are far more important than Shankara or any ideology. It is only through you that you discover truth. You are the discoverer of truth, not Shankara, not the Bhagavad-Gita, which has no meaning—it is only a means of hypnotizing yourself, like reading the newspaper. So, a mind that is capable of receiving truth is a mind that does not compare, for truth is incomparable. To receive truth the mind must be alone, and it is not alone when it is influenced by Shankara or Buddha. Therefore all influence, all conditioning must cease. Only in that state when all knowledge has ceased is there an ending and therefore the aloneness of truth.

Question: What exactly do you mean by meditation? Is it a process or a state?

KRISHNAMURTI: Though I talk and you listen, let us experience and discover together what is meditation. I am not going to teach you how to meditate, but together let us find out what is meditation. So, listen and experience as we go along, for words have meaning only when we move, when we journey together.

What is meditation? Meditation is the understanding of the meditator; the meditator is the meditation. Meditation is not exclusion, concentration. What do you mean by concentration? I am going to explain. We are taking a journey together. You are discovering and I am discovering, and the important thing is to discover, not merely to copy, to follow. Most of us consider that concentration is meditation, but it is not, and I will show you why it is not. Concentration means exclusion—focusing on one interest to the exclusion of other interests. You concentrate and resist, so concentration is the focusing of resistance. You try to concentrate on a picture, on an image, on an idea, and your mind wanders to other interests; and the exclusive resistance of the various interests you call meditation. Surely, that concentration is not meditation, because in that effort there is conflict between that which resists and that which encroaches. That is, you spend your time in resisting, in battling, in disciplining against something. You spend days and years in this battle until at last you can focus your mind on the object of your desire. The object of your desire is self-projected, it is part of the thought process, it is of your own creation, and on that you try to focus; so, you are concentrating upon yourself, though you call it the ideal. Therefore it is an enclosing, exclusive process.

Now, meditation is not exclusion. We are discovering what meditation is interrogatively; to say what it is, is merely to copy. Only when you say what it is not, you say what it is. So, concentration is not meditation. When a schoolboy is interested in a toy, he has concentration. Surely, that is not meditation. The toy is not God, and the pursuit of virtue is not meditation. Let us see then what that means. The cultivation of virtue—is that virtue? To cultivate goodness—is that virtue? To say "I am going to be brotherly" and meditate upon brotherliness—is that virtue? Such meditation upon virtue is merely self-calculation. Virtue implies freedom, and you are not free when you are plotting to become virtuous. So, the man who meditates daily to become virtuous is not virtuous. It is a cloak, which is mere respectability. Sir, when you talk of humility, are you really humble, or are you only taking the cloak of humility? Do you know what it is to be humble? You cannot cultivate it. You cannot cultivate nongreediness. Because you are greedy, you want to be nongreedy. How can stupidity become intelligence? Where there is stupidity, there is no intelligence. Stupidity is what it is under all circumstances. Only with the ending of stupidity is there intelligence; only with the ending of greed is there freedom from greed. Therefore, virtue is freedom, not becoming something, which is endless continuity.

So, we see that concentration is not meditation, that pursuit of virtue is not meditation. Devotion obviously is not meditation, for the object of your devotion is self-projected. Your ideal is the outcome of your own thinking. Obviously, sir, your ideal is self-projected, is it not? You are this, and you want to become that. The that of your becoming is out of yourself, out of your own desire. You are violent, and you want to become nonviolent. The ideal is within yourself. Therefore, your ideal is homemade. Therefore, when you give your devotion to the ideal, you are giving devotion to the thing which you have created. So, your devotion is self-gratification. You are not devoted to something which you do not like, which is painful. You are devoted to something which gives you pleasure, which means, obviously, that it is self-created, and therefore that is not meditation. And it is not meditation to search for truth, because you cannot search for something which you do not know. You can only search for that which you know. If you know truth, it is no longer truth. What you know is the outcome of the past, of memory, therefore it is not truth. Therefore, when you say, "Through meditation I am seeking truth," you are merely burdening the mind with your own creation, which is not truth. So, concentration, devotion, the pursuit of virtue, the search for truth, is not meditation.

Then, what is meditation? The things that we have been doing regularly, practicing, disciplining, forcing the mind—obviously all that is not meditation because in it there is no freedom, and only in freedom can truth come into being. Nor is prayer meditation, as we have discussed previously. When all that superstructure is removed from the mind—the pursuit of the ideal, the search for truth, the becoming virtuous, the concentration, the effort, the discipline, the condemning, the judging—when all that is gone, what is the mind? When that is not, the meditator is not; therefore, there is meditation. When the meditator is not, there is meditation, but the meditator can never meditate. He can only meditate upon himself, project himself, think about himself, but he knows no meditation. When the meditator understands himself and comes to an end, only then is there meditation, for the ending of the meditator is meditation. Concentration, seeking truth, becoming virtuous, condemning, judging, disciplining—all that is the process of the meditator, and without understanding the process of the meditator, there is no meditation. Therefore, without self-knowledge there is no meditation. There is no meditation without tranquillity of mind, but tranquillity does not come about through the seeking or the directing of the meditator. When the whole, total process of the meditator is not, then there is a silence that is not brought about by the mind as an idea, as an ideal, which is self-projected gratification. But when the projector, the meditator, the self, is completely absent, wholly ended, then there is silence which is not the product of the mind. Meditation is that silence which comes into being when the meditator and his processes are understood. That silence is inexhaustible; it is not of time, therefore it is immeasurable. Only the meditator compares, judges, measures; but when the measurement is not, the immeasurable is. Therefore, only when the mind is completely silent, completely still, tranquil, not projecting, not thinking—only then does the measureless come into being. But that measureless is not to be thought of. What you think about is the known, and the known cannot understand the unknown. Therefore, only when the known ends does the unknown come into being. Then only is there bliss.

December 4, 1949

Madras, India, 1949–1950

First Talk in Madras

Perhaps if we can understand this whole problem of searching, seeking, we may be able to understand the complex problem of dissatisfaction and discontent. Most of us are seeking something at various levels of existence, physical comfort or psychological well-being, or we say we are seeking truth or seeking wisdom. We are apparently always seeking something. Now, what does this mean, actually? What is it that we are seeking? We can only seek something that we know; we cannot seek something that we do not know. We cannot search for something that we do not know exists; we can only search for something that we have had and have lost. The search is the desire for satisfaction.

Most of us are dissatisfied both outwardly and inwardly, and if we observe ourselves closely, we find that this discontent is merely the search for an enduring satisfaction at different levels of existence, which we call truth, happiness, understanding, or any other term. Basically, this urge is to find lasting gratification; and being discontented with everything we do, finding no gratification in any of the things we have tried, we go from one teacher, one religion, one path, to another, hoping to find ultimate satisfaction. So, essentially our search is not for truth, but for satisfaction. Most of us are discontented, dissatisfied, with things as they are, and our psychological inward struggle is to find a permanent refuge; whether the refuge is one of ideas or of immediate relationship, the basic urge is a desire to achieve complete satisfaction. This drive is what we call seeking.

We try various gratifications, various isms, Communism included, and when these do not satisfy, we turn to religion and pursue one guru after another, or we become cynics. Cynicism also gives great satisfaction. Our search is always for a state of mind in which there will be no disturbance whatever, in which there will no longer be a struggle, but complete satisfaction. Is there the possibility of complete satisfaction in anything which the mind seeks? The mind is searching for its own projections, which are satisfying, gratifying, and the moment it finds one of these projections troublesome, it leaves it and goes to another. That is, we are seeking a psychological state which will be so pacifying, so reconciled, that it eliminates all conflicts. If we look into it deeply, we shall see that no such state is possible unless we are in illusion or attached to some form of psychological assertion.

Can discontent ever find permanent satisfaction? And what is it that we are discontented with? Are we seeking a better job, more money, a better wife, or a better religious formulation? If we examine it closely, we shall find that all our discontent is a search for permanent satisfaction and that there can be no permanent satisfaction. Even physical security is impossible. The more we want to be secure, the more we become enclosed, nationalistic, ultimately leading to war. So, as long as we are seeking satisfaction, there must be ever-increasing conflict.

Is it possible ever to be content? What is contentment, actually? What brings contentment, how does it come about? Surely, contentment comes only when we understand *what is.* What brings discontent is the complex approach to *what is.* Because I want to change *what is* into something else, there is the struggle of becoming. But mere acceptance of *what is* also creates a problem. Surely, to understand *what is,* there must be passive watchfulness without the desire to change it into something else, which means that one must be passively aware of *what is.* Then it is possible to go beyond the mere outward show of *what is. What is* is never static, though our response may be static.

Our problem, therefore, is not the search for an ultimate gratification, which we call truth, God, or a better relationship, but the understanding of *what is.* To understand *what is* requires an extraordinarily swift mind which sees the futility of the desire to change *what is* into something else, of comparing or trying to reconcile *what is* with something else.

This understanding comes, not through discipline, control, or self-immolation, but through the removal of hindrances which prevent us from seeing *what is* directly.

There is no ending to satisfaction—it is continuous, and unless we see that, we are incapable of dealing with *what is* as it is. Direct relationship with *what is* is right action. Action based upon an idea is merely a self-projection. The idea, the ideal, the ideology, is all a part of the thought process, and thought is a response to conditioning at any level. Therefore, the pursuit of an idea, of an ideal or an ideology, is a circle in which the mind is caught. When we see the whole process of the mind and all its crafty maneuvering, only then is there understanding which brings transformation.

Question: We see inequality among men, and some are far above the rest of mankind. Surely, then, there must be higher types of beings like Masters and devas who may be deeply interested in cooperating with mankind. Have you contacted any of them? If so, can you tell us how we can contact them?

KRISHNAMURTI: Most of us are interested in gossip, and gossip is an extraordinarily stimulating thing, whether it is about Masters and devas or about our neighbors. The more dull we are, the more we love gossip. When one is fed up with social gossip, one wants to gossip about something higher. We are interested, not in the problem of inequality, but in gossipy tidbits about strange entities we do not see, thus seeking a means of escaping from our shallowness. After all, the Masters and devas are your own projections; when you follow them, you follow your own projections. If they were to say to you, "Drop your nationalism, your societies, do not be greedy, do not be cruel," you would soon leave them and pursue others who would satisfy you. You want me to help you to contact the Masters. I am really not interested in the Masters. There is a lot of talk about them, and it has become a cunning means of exploiting people. We make a mess in the world, and we want a big brother to come and help us out of it. A great deal of that is cant. This division between Master and pupil, the hierarchical climbing of the ladder of success—is it really spiritual? This whole idea of hierarchical becoming, struggling to become what you call spiritual, to attain liberation—is it spiritual? When our hearts are empty, we fill them with the images of Masters, which means there is no love. When you love someone, you are not conscious of equality or inequality. Why are you so occupied with the question of Masters? The Masters are important to you because you have a sense of authority, and you give authority to something which has no authority. You give authority because it pleases you; it is self-flattery.

The problem of inequality is more fundamental than the desire to contact the Masters. There is inequality in capacity, in thought, in action—between the genius and the dull-witted man, the man who is free and the man who practices a routine. Every kind of revolution has tried to break this down and in the process has created another inequality. The problem is how to go beyond the sense of inequality, of the inferior and the superior. That is true spirituality—not seeking Masters and thereby maintaining the sense of inequality. The problem is not how to bring about equality, because equality is an impossibility. You are entirely different from another. You see more, you are much more alert than the other; you have a song in your heart, the other's is empty and to him a dead leaf is a dead leaf which he burns. Some people have extraordinary capacity, they are swift and capable. Others are slow, dull, unobserving. There is no end to physical and psychological differences, and you cannot break them down—that is an utter impossibility. All that you can do is to give an opportunity to the dull and not kick him, not exploit him. You cannot make him a genius.

So the problem is not how to contact Masters and devas but how to transcend the sense of inequality; seeking to contact Masters is the pursuit of the very, very dull. When you know yourself, you know the Master. A real Master cannot help you because you have to understand yourself. We are all the time pursuing phony Masters; we seek comfort, security, and we project the kind of Master we want, hoping that Master will give us all that we desire. Since there is no such thing as comfort, the problem is much more fundamental—that is, how to go beyond this sense of inequality. Wisdom is not the struggle to become more and more.

Now, is it possible to transcend the sense of inequality? For inequality is there, we cannot deny it. What happens when we do not deny inequality, when we do not come to it with a prejudiced mind, but face it? There is the dirty village, and there is also the nice clean house—both are *what is.* How do you approach ugliness and beauty? In that lies the solution. The beautiful you wish to be identified with, and the ugly you put aside. For the inferior you have no consideration, but for the superior you have the greatest consideration and deference. Your approach is identification with the higher and rejection of the lower; you look upward with cringing and downward with contempt.

Inequality can be transcended only when we understand our approach to it. As long as we resist the ugly and identify ourselves with the beautiful, there is bound to be all this misery. But, if we approach inequality without condemnation, identification, or judgment, then our response is entirely different. Please try it, and you will see what an extraordinary change occurs in your life. The understanding of *what is* brings contentment—which is not the contentment of stagnation, not the contentment caused by the possession of property, of an idea, of a woman. Contentment is the state of approach to *what is* as it is, without any barrier whatsoever. Then only is there love, the love which destroys the sense of inequality, and this is the only thing that is revolutionary, that can transform. Since we have not that flame of revolution, we fill our hearts and minds with ideas of revolution of the left or the right, the modification of what has been. That way there is no hope. The more you reform, the greater the need for further reforms.

It is not important to know how to contact the Masters, for they have no significance in life. What is important is to understand yourself; otherwise, your Master is an illusion. Without understanding yourself, you are creating more and more misery in the world. Look at what is happening in the world and see the narrow spirit displayed by the zealous votaries of peace, of the Masters, of love and brotherhood. You are all out for yourselves, though you wrap it up in beautiful words. You want the Masters to help you to become more glorified and self-enclosed.

I know I have answered this question at different times in different ways. I also know that in spite of all I say, you are going to perform your rituals and rattle your swords for king and country. You do not want to understand and solve this problem of inequality. People have written to me saying, "You are very ungrateful to the Masters who have brought you up." It is so easy to make these statements. It is all cant. One has to discover for oneself that no Master can help one. Is it ungrateful to see that which is false and say it is false? You want me to be grateful to your idea, to your formulation of a Master, and when your ideas are disturbed, you call me ungrateful. The problem is not one of gratitude to the Masters, but of understanding yourself.

There is great joy in understanding and discovering what you are, the whole content of what you are, from moment to moment. Self-knowledge is the beginning of wisdom. Without self-knowledge, you cannot know anything—or if you know something, you will misuse it. To pursue the Master is easy, but to have self-knowledge, to be passively watchful of every thought and feeling, is arduous. You cannot watch if there is judgment or identification, for identification and judgment prevent understanding. If you watch passively, the thing that you watch begins to unfold, and then there is understanding which renews itself from moment to moment.

Question: In one of your talks you have stated that if a person prays, he receives, but he will pay for it in the end. What do you mean by this? What is the entity that grants our prayers, and why do we not succeed in getting all that we pray for?

KRISHNAMURTI: Are you not happy that all you pray for is not granted? Would that not be deadly boring? You should see the whole picture, not only the part you like. Most of you pray to be satisfied. Your prayers are petitions, supplications for help to get away from your own confusion. Obviously, you pray only when you are confused, in trouble, unhappy. You do not pray when you are joyous, but only when there is fear and when there is pain. What happens when you pray? Please experiment with yourself and watch what happens. When you pray, you quiet the mind by the repetition of certain phrases; that is, the mind is made quiet, is drugged, by repeating a word or by looking at a picture or an image. When the superficial mind is quiet, into that upper layer of the mind comes the response which is most satisfactory. Mass prayer also has a similar effect. You supplicate, you put out the begging bowl to receive; you want gratification, you want an escape from your confusion. So, when the mind is drugged into insensitivity or is partly asleep, into it is projected unconsciously the satisfying answer, which is the general influence of the world about you. There is the collective reservoir of greed, of the universal demand away from *what is,* and when you tap it, you obviously get what you want. But that reservoir—is it God, the ultimate truth? Please do look at it, watch it closely, and you will see.

When you pray to God, you pray to something with which you have a relationship, and you can have a relationship only with what you know; therefore, your God is a projection of yourself, either inherited or acquired. When the mind is begging, it will have an answer, but that answer will always be more enclosing and more troublesome, and will create further problems. That is the price you pay. When you sing or chant together, you are only avoiding, seeking an escape from *what is.* The escapes have their satisfaction, but their price is that you have yet to meet the problem which pursues you like a shadow. Your prayers may be gratifying most of the time, but you are in misery all the time, and you want to run away. Your search is the search of avoidance. To understand requires watchfulness, knowing every thought, every gesture. But you are lazy; you have convenient escapes which help you to avoid the understanding of yourself, the creator of pain. Until you understand the problem of yourself, your ambitions, your greed, your exploitation, your desire to maintain inequality; until you face the fact that you are the creator of pain and suffering in the world, of what value are your prayers? You are the problem—you cannot ultimately avoid it—and you can dissolve it only by understanding the whole of it.

So, your prayer is a hindrance to understanding. There is a different kind of prayer—a state of mind where there is no demand, no supplication. In that prayer—perhaps this is a wrong word to use—there is no forward movement, no denial; it is not put together, it cannot be brought about by any kind of trick. That state of mind is not seeking a result—it is still; it cannot be thought of, practiced, or meditated upon. That state of mind alone can discover and allow truth to come into being, and it alone will solve our problem. That quiet state of mind comes when *what is* is observed and understood, and then the mind is capable of receiving the inexhaustible.

Question: There is widespread misery in the world, and all religions have failed, yet you seem to be talking religion more and more. Will any religion help us to be free from misery?

KRISHNAMURTI: We must find out what we mean by religion. Religions have failed throughout the world, perhaps, because we are not religious. You may call yourselves by certain names, but your beliefs, your images, your incense-burning are not religious at all. To you, all these have become important—not religion. Look at what we have done throughout the world. Ideas have set man against man. The extension of dogma is not freedom from dogma. Belief is separating people. Separation is the emphasis of belief, and it is a good means of exploiting the credulous. In belief, you find comfort, security—which is all illusion. Wherever there is a tendency to separativeness, there must be disintegration. Where there is the enclosing force of belief, there must be disintegration. You call yourselves Hindus, Muslims, Christians, Theosophists, and whatnot, and thereby you enclose yourselves. Your ideas create opposition, enmity, and antagonism; so also your philosophies, however clever, idealistic, and amusing. As a man is addicted to drink, you are addicted to your beliefs. That is why organized religions have failed throughout the world.

True religion is experiencing, and it has nothing to do with belief. It is that state of mind which, in the process of self-knowledge, discovers truth from moment to moment. Truth is not continuous, it is never the same, it is incomparable. Truth is the alone; it is not the symbol of anything. The worship of any symbol brings about disaster, and a mind that is addicted to belief in any form can never be a religious mind. It is only the religious mind, not the ideological mind, that is capable of solving the problem. Quoting others is no good. A mind that quotes, whether it be Plato or Buddha, is incapable of experiencing reality. To experience reality, the mind must be completely stripped, and such a mind is not a seeking mind.

Religion, therefore, is not belief; religion is not ceremonies; religion is not an idea or various ideas put together to form an ideology. Religion is experiencing the truth of *what is* from moment to moment. Truth is not an ultimate end—there is no ultimate end to truth. Truth is in *what is;* it is in the present, it is never static. A mind that is clouded with the past cannot possibly understand truth. All religions, as they are, divide man. The beliefs of these religions are not truth. Truth is not to be found in any belief in reincarnation; truth is experienced only when there is an ending, the ending which is implied in death. Your belief in God is not religion, is not truth. There is little difference between the believer and the nonbeliever; they are both conditioned by their respective environments; they bring separation in the world, through ideas, through beliefs. Therefore, neither the believer nor the nonbeliever can experience reality.

When you see things as they are without any prejudice, without praise or condemnation, in direct relationship with *what is,* there is action. When the idea intervenes, there is postponement of action. The mind, which is the structure of ideas, the residue of all memories and thoughts, can never find reality. Your reading and quoting will not help you to experience reality. Reality must come to you. You can search only for something that you know; you cannot search for reality. Please do see the truth of this matter, see the beauty of the mind that is experiencing directly and therefore acting without a reward, without a punishment. But experience is not the criterion of truth. Experience only nurtures memory. Your self is thought, and thought is memory; experience is memory as thought. Therefore, such a mind can organize the word *truth* and exploit people, but it is incapable of experiencing reality. Only the mind that has no idea can experience reality.

A religious man is the truly revolutionary man. The man who acts on ideas may kill others. In direct relationship with *what is* there is experiencing, and such a mind is no longer fabricating ideas. A mind that has no idea is sensitive, is able to see *what is* directly, and is therefore capable of action. Such action alone is revolutionary.

Question: It has been said that the acquirement of wisdom is the ultimate goal of life, and that wisdom has to be sought little by little through a life of purification and dedication, with the mind and the emotions directed to high ideals through prayer and meditation. Do you agree?

KRISHNAMURTI: Let us find out what you mean by wisdom and then see whether we can find that wisdom. What do you mean by wisdom? Is it the goal of life? If it is and if you know the goal, the purpose of life, then wisdom is the known. Can you know or acquire wisdom, or can you only know facts, acquire knowledge? Surely, knowledge and wisdom are two separate things. You may know all about something, but is that wisdom? Is wisdom to be acquired little by little, life after life? Is wisdom the storing up of experience? Acquisition implies accumulation; experience implies residue. Residue, accumulation—is that wisdom? You have already accumulated the racial, the inherited residues in conjunction with the present. Is that process of accumulation wisdom? You accumulate to safeguard yourself, to live securely; you acquire experience gradually.

The accumulation of knowledge, the slow gathering of experience—is that wisdom? Your whole life is accumulation, acquiring more and more. Will that make you wise? You have acquired something; you have had an experience which has left a residue, and that residue conditions your further experience. Your response is this experience, and it is the continuation of the background in a different way. So when you say that wisdom is experience, you mean the collection of many experiences. Why are you not wise? Can the man who is constantly acquiring be wise? Can the man burdened with experience be wise? Can the man who knows be wise? The man who knows is not wise, and the man who does not know is wise. Do not smile and pass it off.

When you know, you have experienced, you have accumulated, and the projection of that accumulation is further knowledge. Therefore, wisdom is not a slow process, it is not to be gathered little by little like a bank account. To believe that gradually, through several lives, you are going to become Buddha is immature thinking and feeling. Such statements appear wonderful, especially when ascribed to a Master. When you inquire to find out the truth, then you will see it is only your own projection that wants to continue to experience the same thing as before.

So, accumulation is never wisdom because there can be accumulation only of what is known, and what is known can never be the unknown. The emptying of the mind is not a slow process, but trying to empty it is a hindrance. If you say, "I will empty the mind," then it is the same old process. Just see the truth that a mind that is acquiring can never be wise—in six lives or in ten. A man who has acquired is already rich, and a rich man is never wise. You want to be rich in knowledge, which is the acquisition of experience in words, but the man who has can never be wise. Also, the man who deliberately has not can never be wise.

Truth cannot be accumulated. It is not experience. It is experiencing in which there is neither the experiencer nor the experience. Knowledge always has the accumulator, the gatherer, but wisdom has no experiencer. Wisdom is as love is and without that love, we attempt to pursue wisdom through continuous acquisition. What continues must decay. Only that which ends can know wisdom. Wisdom is ever fresh, ever new. How can you know the new if there is continuity? There is continuity as long as you are continuing experience. Only when there is ending is there the new, which is creative. But, we want to continue, we want accumulation, which is the continuity of experience, and such a mind can never know wisdom. It can only know its own projection, its own creations, and the reconciliation between its creations. Truth is wisdom. Truth cannot be sought out. Truth comes only when the mind is empty of all knowledge, of all thought, of all experience—and that is wisdom.

December 18, 1949

Second Talk in Madras

Let us see what place the individual has in society—whether the individual can do anything to bring about a radical change in society; whether the transformed entity, the intelligent human being who has fundamentally transformed himself, has any influence, any action, upon the current of events; or whether the individual I am talking of, the transformed entity, cannot do anything himself but can, merely by his very existence, inject some kind of order into society, into the stream of chaos and confusion. We see all over the world that mass action obviously produces results. Seeing that, we feel that individual action has very little importance, that you and I, though we may transform ourselves, can have very little influence; and so we ask what value do we have when we cannot affect the stream.

Now, why do we think in mass terms? Are fundamental revolutions brought about by the mass, or are they started by the few who see and who, by their talk and energy, influence very many people? That is how revolutions are brought about. Is it not a mistake to think that, as individuals, we cannot do anything? Is it not a fallacy to think that all fundamental revolutions are produced by the mass? Why do we think that individuals are not important as individuals? If we have this attitude of mind, we will not think for ourselves but will respond automatically. Is action always of the mass? Does it not spring essentially from the individual and then spread from individual to individual? There is really no such thing as the mass. After all, the mass is an entity formed of people who are caught, hypnotized by words, by certain ideas. The moment we are not hypnotized by words, we are outside that stream—something no politician would like. Should we not remain outside the stream and collect more and more from the stream in order to affect the stream? Is it not important that there should be a fundamental transformation in the individual first, that you and I should radically change first, without waiting for the whole world to change? Is it not an escapist's view, a form of laziness, an avoidance of the issue to think that you and I, in however small a degree, cannot affect society as a whole?

When we see so much misery, not only in our own lives, but also in the society around us, what is it that prevents us from transforming ourselves, from changing ourselves fundamentally? Is it merely habit, lethargy, the quality of the mind that likes the pattern in which it is enclosed and does not want it to break? Surely, it is not only that, because economic circumstances break up that pattern, but the inward psychological pattern persists. Why does it persist? In order to change fundamentally, radically, do we need an outside influence or agency—like sorrow, economic or social revolution, or a guru—all of which are a form of compulsion? An outside agency implies conformity, dependence, compulsion, fear. Do we change fundamentally through dependence? And is it not one of our difficulties that we are dependent for change on outside agencies, economic upheavals, and so on? This dependence upon an outside agency prevents radical revolution, because radical revolution can come about only in understanding the total process of oneself. If you depend on an outside agency of any kind to bring about transformation, you have introduced fear and certain other factors which actually prevent transformation. A man who really wants transformation does not depend upon any outside agency; he has no struggle within himself, he sees the necessity and transforms himself.

Is the transformation of the individual really difficult? Is it difficult to be kind, to be compassionate, to love somebody? After all, that is the very essence of a radical transformation. The difficulty with us is that we have a dualistic nature in which there is hate, dislike, various forms of antagonism, and so on, which takes us away from the central issue. We are so caught up in the impulses that incite hatred, dislike, that the very flame is lost and we are left with the smoke, and then our problem is how to get rid of the smoke. We have not got the flame of creation at all, but we think the smoke is the flame. Is it not necessary to investigate what the flame is—that is, see things anew without being caught in a pattern, look at things as they are without naming them? Is it really difficult? The difficulty with most of us is that we have committed ourselves up to the hilt, we have assumed innumerable responsibilities, duties, and so on, and we say that we cannot get out of them. Surely, that is not a real difficulty. When we feel something deeply we do what we want to do, irrespective of the family, of society, and all that. So, the only difficulty which stands in the way is that we do not sufficiently feel the importance of radical individual transformation. It is imperative to bring about transformation. Transformation will take place when we live without verbalization, when we see things as they are and accept truth as it is. It must begin with us as individuals. It does not begin merely because we do not pay enough attention, we do not give our whole being to the understanding of this one thing; we see so much misery outside of us and confusion within us, and yet we do not want to break through it.

Now, what happens when I have a problem and try to resolve it? In the resolution of that problem, I find several others that have come in—in solving one problem, I have multiplied it. So, I want to find the solution to the problem without increasing the problem; I want to live happily, I want to be free of psychological sorrow without finding a substitute for it. Is it possible to find out if one can really resolve sorrow, to inquire into it without anybody's authority, to go into it in oneself, watching oneself all the time in every kind of relationship? Is not that the only way out of the difficulty?—watching ourselves constantly, what we think, what we feel, what we do, being in that state of watchfulness in which everything is revealed. You must experiment with it and not merely say it cannot be done or accept my authority and merely repeat it. Let us say that you are happy and I am not, and I want to be happy; I do not want to be drugged by belief and all that, but I want to go to the very end of it. So I come to you and inquire, and I go deeper and deeper into it. What is preventing you from doing that now? Why is it you do not have the feeling of happiness, of creation, of seeing things as they are? Why do you not operate in that deep sense? Because you say that sorrow is helpful to happiness, that sorrow is a means to happiness, and you have accepted sorrow, or some kind of substitution. We have made ourselves so dull that we do not see the need for changing; that is the difficulty.

You may say that you want to change but that there is something which prevents the change from taking place. Explanations will not bring about change. To say that the ego is in the way is explanation, mere description. You want me to describe how to overcome the impediments, but we must find a way of jumping the hurdle if we can; we must venture out into the stream and see what happens—not sit on the shore and speculate. What is actually preventing us from taking the jump? Tradition—which is memory, which is experience—prevents us, does it not? We are so satisfied with words, with explanations, that we do not take the jump even when we see the necessity for jumping. It is suggested that there is no venturing out in the stream because of fear of the unknown. But can I ever know what will happen, can I ever know the unknown? If I knew, then I would have no fear, and it would not be the unknown. I can never know the unknown without venturing.

Is it fear that is holding us from venturing forth? What is fear? Fear can exist only in relation to something, it is not in isolation. How can I be afraid of death, how can I be afraid of something I do not know? I can be afraid only of what I know. When I say I am afraid of death, am I really afraid of the unknown, which is death, or am I afraid of losing what I have known? My fear is not of death, but of losing my association with things belonging to me. My fear is always in relation to the known, not to the unknown.

So, my inquiry now is how to be free from the fear of the known, which is the fear of losing my family, my reputation, my character, my bank account, my appetites, and so on. You may say that fear arises from conscience, but your conscience is formed by your conditioning, it may be foolish or wise, so conscience is still the result of the known. What do I know? Knowing is having ideas, having opinions about things, having a sense of continuity as the known, and no more. Ideas are memories, the result of experience, which is response to challenge. I am afraid of the known, which means I am afraid of losing people, things, or ideas; I am afraid of discovering what I am, afraid of being at a loss, afraid of the pain which might come into being when I have lost, or have not gained, or have no more pleasure.

There is fear of pain. Physical pain is the nervous response; psychological pain arises when I hold on to things that give me satisfaction, for then I am afraid of anyone or anything that may take them away from me. The psychological accumulations prevent psychological pain as long as they are undisturbed; that is, I am a bundle of accumulations, experiences, which prevent any serious form of disturbance—and I do not want to be disturbed. Therefore, I am afraid of anyone who disturbs them. Thus, my fear is of the known; I am afraid of the accumulations, physical or psychological, that I have gathered as a means of warding off pain or preventing sorrow. But sorrow is in the very process of accumulating to ward off psychological pain. Knowledge also helps to prevent pain. As medical knowledge helps to prevent physical pain, so beliefs help to prevent psychological pain, and that is why I am afraid of losing my beliefs, though I have no perfect knowledge or concrete proof of the reality of such beliefs. I may reject some of the traditional beliefs that have been foisted on me because my own experience gives me strength, confidence, understanding, but such beliefs and the knowledge which I have acquired are basically the same—a means of warding off pain.

Fear exists as long as there is accumulation of the known, which creates the fear of losing. Therefore, fear of the unknown is really fear of losing the accumulated known. Accumulation invariably means fear, which in turn means pain, and the moment I say, "I must not lose," there is fear. Though my intention in accumulating is to ward off pain, pain is inherent in the process of accumulation. The very things which I have create fear, which is pain.

The seed of defense brings offense. I want physical security; thus I create a sovereign government, which necessitates armed forces, which means war, which destroys security. Wherever there is a desire for self-protection, there is fear. When I see the fallacy of demanding security, I do not accumulate any more. If you say that you see it but you cannot help accumulating, it is because you do not really see that, inherently, in accumulation there is pain.

Fear exists in the process of accumulation, and belief in something is part of the accumulative process. My son dies, and I believe in reincarnation to prevent me psychologically from having more pain, but in the very process of believing, there is doubt. Outwardly I accumulate things, and bring war; inwardly I accumulate beliefs, and bring pain. As long as I want to be secure, to have bank accounts, pleasures, and so on, as long as I want to become something, physiologically or psychologically, there must be pain. The very things I am doing to ward off pain, bring me fear, pain.

Fear comes into being when I desire to be in a particular pattern. To live without fear means to live without a particular pattern. When I demand a particular way of living, that in itself is a source of fear. My difficulty is my desire to live in a certain frame. Can I not break the frame? I can do so only when I see the truth—that the frame is causing fear and that this fear is strengthening the frame. If I say I must break the frame because I want to be free of fear, then I am merely following another pattern which will cause further fear. Any action on my part based on the desire to break the frame will only create another pattern and therefore fear. How am I to break the frame without causing fear, that is, without any conscious or unconscious action on my part with regard to it? This means that I must not act, I must make no movement to break the frame. So, what happens to me when I am simply looking at the frame without doing anything about it? I see that the mind itself is the frame, the pattern; it lives in the habitual pattern which it has created for itself. So, the mind itself is fear. Whatever the mind does goes towards strengthening an old pattern or furthering a new one. This means that whatever the mind does to get rid of fear causes fear. Seeing the truth of all this, seeing the process of it, what happens? The mind becomes sensitive, quiet.

Now, why is not the mind quiet all the time? Each time the pattern crystallizes, why does not the mind see the truth of it? Because, the mind wants permanency, stability, a refuge from which it can act. The mind wants to be secure. There is the breaking up of one particular pattern, and a few minutes later there is again crystallization; and instead of examining this new crystallization and understanding it fully, the mind goes back to the old experience and says, "I have seen the truth, and that must continue." In seeking continuation, the mind creates a new pattern and gets caught in it. Each time the crystallization takes place, it has to be watched and understood, and the repetition occurs because of the incompleteness of understanding.

Truth is noncontinuity. The truth of yesterday is not the truth of today. Truth is not of time and so, not of memory; it is not something to be experienced, to be remembered, gained, lost, or achieved. We pursue truth in order to gain it and give it a continuity, and once we really see this, then the pattern will break up because then the mind is already adrift.

January 29, 1950

Third Talk in Madras

In all our relationships—with people, with nature, with ideas, with things—we seem to create more and more problems. In trying to solve one problem, whether economic, political, social, collective, or individual, we introduce many other problems. We seem somehow to breed more and more conflict and need more and more reform. Obviously, all reform needs further reform, and therefore it is really retrogression. As long as revolution, whether of the left or the right, is merely the continuity of what has been in terms of what shall be, it also is retrogression. There can be fundamental revolution, a constant inward transformation, only when we, as individuals, understand our relationship to the collective. The revolution must begin with each one of us, and not with external environmental influences. After all, we are the collective; both the conscious and the unconscious in us is the residue of all the political, social, cultural influences of man. Therefore, to bring about a fundamental outward revolution, there must be a radical transformation within each one of us, a transformation which does not depend on environmental change. It must begin with you and me. All great things start on a small scale, all great movements begin with you and me as individuals; and if we wait for collective action, such collective action, if it takes place at all, is destructive and conducive to further misery.

So, revolution must begin with you and me. That revolution, that individual transformation, can take place only when we understand relationship, which is the process of self-knowledge. Without knowing the whole process of my relationship at all the different levels, what I think and what I do has no value at all. What basis have I for thinking if I do not know myself? We are so desirous to act, so eager to do something, to bring some kind of revolution, some kind of amelioration, some change in the world; but without knowing the process of ourselves both at the periphery and inwardly, we have no basis for action, and what we do is bound to create more misery, more strife. The understanding of oneself does not come through the process of withdrawal from society or through retirement into an ivory tower. If you and I really go into the matter carefully and intelligently, we will see that we can understand ourselves only in relationship and not in isolation. Nobody can live in isolation. To live is to be related. It is only in the mirror of relationship that I understand myself, which means that I must be extraordinarily alert in all my thoughts, feelings, and actions in relationship. This is not a difficult process or a superhuman endeavor; and as with all rivers, while the source is hardly perceptible, the waters gather momentum as they move, as they deepen. In this mad and chaotic world, if you go into this process advisedly, with care, with patience, without condemning, you will see how it begins to gather momentum and that it is not a matter of time.

Truth is from moment to moment in relationship; it is to see each action, each thought and feeling as it arises in relationship. Truth is not something that can be accumulated, stored up; it has to be found anew in the movement of thought and feeling at every moment—which is not an accumulative process and is not therefore a matter of time. When you say you will eventually understand through experience or knowledge, you are preventing that very understanding because understanding does not come through accumulation. You can accumulate knowledge, but that is not understanding. Understanding comes when the mind is free of knowledge. When the mind does not demand the fulfillment of desires, when it is not seeking out experience, there is stillness, and when the mind is still, then only can there be understanding. It is only when you and I are quite willing to see things clearly as they are that there is a possibility of understanding. Understanding comes, not through discipline, through compulsion, through enforcement, but when the mind is quiet and willing to see things clearly. Quietness of mind is never brought about by any form of compulsion, conscious or unconscious; it must be spontaneous. Freedom is not at the end, but at the beginning; because the end and the beginning are not different, the means and the end are one. The beginning of wisdom is the understanding of the total process of oneself, and that self-knowledge, that understanding, is meditation.

Question: We all experience loneliness; we know its sorrow and see its causes, its roots. But what is aloneness? Is it different from loneliness?

KRISHNAMURTI: Loneliness is the pain, the agony of solitude, the state of isolation when you as an entity do not fit in with anything, neither with the group nor with the country, with your wife, with your children, with your husband; you are cut off from others. You know that state. Now, do you know aloneness? You take it for granted that you are alone, but are you alone?

Aloneness is different from loneliness, but you cannot understand it if you do not understand loneliness. Do you know loneliness? You have surreptitiously watched it, looked at it, not liking it. To know it, you must commune with it with no barrier between it and you, no conclusion, prejudice, or speculation; you must come to it with freedom and not with fear. To understand loneliness, you must approach it without any sense of fear. If you come to loneliness saying that you already know the cause of it, the roots of it, then you cannot understand it. Do you know its roots? You know them by speculating from outside. Do you know the inward content of loneliness? You merely give it a description, and the word is not the thing, the real. To understand it, you must come to it without any sense of getting away from it. The very thought of getting away from loneliness is in itself a form of inward insufficiency. Are not most of our activities an avoidance? When you are alone, you switch on the radio, you do pujas, run after gurus, gossip with others, go to the cinema, attend races, and so on. Your daily life is to get away from yourselves, so the escapes become all-important and you wrangle about the escapes, whether drink or God. The avoidance is the issue, though you may have different means of escape. You may do enormous harm psychologically by your respectable escapes, and I, sociologically, by my worldly escapes, but to understand loneliness, all escapes must come to an end, not through enforcement, compulsion, but by seeing the falseness of escape. Then you are directly confronting *what is,* and the real problem begins.

What is loneliness? To understand it, you must not give it a name. The very naming, the very association of thought with other memories of it, emphasizes loneliness. Experiment with it and see. When you have ceased to escape, you will see that until you realize what loneliness is, anything you do about it is another form of escape. Only by understanding loneliness can you go beyond it.

The problem of aloneness is entirely different. We are never alone; we are always with people except, perhaps, when we go for solitary walks. We are the result of a total process made up of economic, social, climatic, and other environmental influences, and as long as we are influenced, we are not alone. As long as there is the process of accumulation and experience, there can never be aloneness. You can imagine that you are alone by isolating yourself through narrow individual, personal activities, but that is not aloneness. Aloneness can be, only when influence is not. Aloneness is action which is not the result of a reaction, which is not the response to a challenge or a stimulus. Loneliness is a problem of isolation, and we are seeking isolation in all our relationships, which is the very essence of the self, the 'me'—my work, my nature, my duty, my property, my relationship. The very process of thought, which is the result of all the thoughts and influences of man, leads to isolation. To understand loneliness is not a bourgeois act; you cannot understand it as long as there is in you the ache of that undisclosed insufficiency which comes with emptiness, frustration. Aloneness is not an isolation, it is not the opposite of loneliness; it is a state of being when all experience and knowledge are not.

Question: You have been talking for a number of years about transformation. Do you know of anyone who has been transformed in your sense of the word?

KRISHNAMURTI: What is the point of your singing, what is the point of your laughter? Do you laugh, do you smile, in order to convince somebody, to make somebody happy? If you have a song in your heart, you sing. So it is with my talking. It is your responsibility to transform yourself, and not mine. You want to know if anyone has been transformed. I don't know. I have not looked to see who has been transformed and who has not been. It is your life of sorrow, of misery, and I am not the judge. You are yourself the judge. Neither you nor I are propagandists. To do propaganda is to tell a lie; to see truth is quite a different matter. If you who are responsible for this misery, chaos, corruption, these degrading wars, do not see that you are responsible and that you must transform yourselves to bring about a revolution in the world, it is your affair. Unless you want to change, you will not change. You cannot be a singer by listening to songs, but if you have a song in your heart, you will not be repetitive.

The important thing in this is to find out why you listen so much and so often, why you come and listen at all. Why do you waste your time if you are not doing anything about it? Why are you not changed? I am not putting this question to you; you should put it to yourself. When you see so much misery, so much corruption, not only in your individual life, but in your social relationship and in every political endeavor, what do you do about it? Why are you not interested in this? Merely reading the newspaper is obviously no solution. Is it not a vital matter to find out what you are doing and why? Most of us are dull, insensitive to the whole process that is going on around us, though the things in front of us demand action. Why are you dull, insensitive? Is it not because of your worship of authority, political or religious? You have read the Bhagavad-Gita and so many other books, which you can repeat like parrots, but you have not even one thought of your own; and the man who can repeat in a nice voice, who explains texts over and over again, you worship. So, authority dulls the mind, and imitation or repetition makes the mind insensitive, unpliable. That is why gurus multiply and followers destroy. You want direction, and the desire for direction is the building up of authority; and being caught in authority, your minds, seeking comfort, seeking satisfaction, become insensitive, dull. The performance of rituals or the constant reading of a so-called sacred book is the same as having a drink. What would you do if there were no books? You would have to think everything out for yourself; you would have to search, find out, inquire every moment to discover, to understand the new. Are you not in that position now? All the social and political systems have come to nothing though they promise everything, and yet you go on reading religious books and repeating what you have read, which makes your mind dull. Your education is merely the accumulation of book knowledge to pass an examination or to get a job. Thus you yourself have made your mind dull, and your knowledge has corrupted you.

So, your transformation is your own problem. What need have you to find out who has or who has not transformed himself? If you have beauty within you, you do not seek. A happy man does not seek; it is the man who is unhappy that seeks. Unhappiness is not resolved by search, but only by understanding, by watching every gesture, spontaneously seeing every one of your thoughts and feelings so that it reveals its story. Then only is truth discovered.

Question: You have never talked about the future. Why? Are you afraid of it?

KRISHNAMURTI: What is the importance of the future in our life? Why should it have any importance? What do we mean by the future? The tomorrow, the ideal, the everlasting hope of the utopia, of what I should be, the pattern in different forms of an ideal society—is that what you mean by the future? We live by hope, and hope is a means of our death. When you hope, you are dead because hope is an avoidance of the present. You do not hope when you are happy. It is only when you are unhappy, frustrated, restrained, when you are suffering, when you are aching, when you are a prisoner, that you look to the future. When you are really joyous, happy, time is not. We live with hope from birth to death because we are unhappy from the beginning to the very end, and hope is the way of escape; it is not the resolution of our actual state, which is unhappiness. We look to the future as a means of avoiding the present, and the man who avoids the present by going to the past or to the future is not living; he does not know life as it is lived, he only knows life in relation to the past or to the future. Life is painful, tortuous, so we seek an escape from it, and if we are promised heaven, we are perfectly happy. That is why the party, whether of the left or the right, ultimately wins. The parties always promise something tomorrow, five years later, and we fall for it, we gobble it up, and we are ultimately destroyed. Because we want to escape from the present, if we cannot look to the future, we turn to the past—the past teachers, the past books, the knowledge of what has been said by Shankara, Buddha, and others. So we either live in the past or in the future, and a man who lives in the past or in the future has actually the responses of the dead, for all such responses are mere reactions. It is therefore no good talking about the past and the future, about rewards and punishments. What is important is to find out how to live, how to be free from misery in the present. Virtue is not tomorrow. A man who is going to be merciful tomorrow is a foolish man. Virtue is not to be cultivated; it is in the understanding of *what is* in the present.

How are you to live in the present without the ache, the pain, of sorrow? Sorrow is to be resolved, not in terms of time, but by understanding; it can be resolved only in the present, and that is why I don't talk about the future. There comes an extraordinary activity and vitality when there is a direct observation of *what is,* but you want to play with things, and when you play with serious things, you get burned. You are swept away by hopes and rewards, and a man who pursues hope lives in death.

Our problem is whether sorrow can come to an end through the process of time, which is continuity. Sorrow cannot come to an end through time because the process of time is continuance of suffering and, therefore, no resolution of suffering. Sorrow can come to an end instantly; freedom is not at the end, but at the beginning. To understand this, there must be the beginning of freedom, the freedom to see the false as false, the capacity to see things as they are, not in time but now. You do this when you are vitally interested, when you are in a crisis. After all, what is a crisis? It is a situation which demands your full attention without taking refuge in beliefs. When there is no solution, when there is no response of the mind, when the mind has no ready-made answer, no conclusion, and you are unable to resolve the problem—then you are in a crisis. But unfortunately, through your study of books and your following of teachers, your mind has an explanation for every problem; therefore, you are never in a moment of crisis. There is a challenge every minute, and a crisis comes when the mind has no ready-made answer. When you cannot find a way out, consciously or unconsciously, through words or through escapes, then you are in a crisis. Death is a crisis, though you can explain it away. You are in a crisis when you lose your money, when thousands are destroyed in a single second. Ending is the crisis, but you never end; you always want things to continue. It is only when there is a crisis without avoidance or escape and you are therefore confronted with it directly—it is only then that the problem is resolved. The concern with the future is the avoidance of the crisis; hope is avoidance of *what is.* To meet the crisis there must be complete denudation of the future and the past; therefore, it is no good talking about the future.

Question: What should be the relationship, according to you, between the individual and the state?

KRISHNAMURTI: Do you want a blueprint? Now you are back again at what should be. Speculation is the easiest and most wasteful thing that one can indulge in. Beware of the man who offers you hope; do not trust him, he will lead you to death; he is interested in his idea of the future, in his conception of what ought to be, and not in your life.

Are the state and the individual two different processes? Are they not interacting? How can you live without me, without another, and does not our relationship make society? You and I and another are a unitary process, we are not separate processes. The 'you' implies the 'me' and the 'other'. You are the collective, not the single, though you would like to consider yourself single. You are the result of all the collective, and the individual can never be single. You have put a wrong question because you have divided the individual from the state. You are a result of the total process, of all the influences of the collective, and though the result can call itself individual, it is a product of the process which is going on. The understanding of this process is to be found in relationship, whether with the single or with the collective, and that understanding and the action springing from it will create a new society, a new order of things; but to paint a picture of what should be and to leave it to the reformers, the politicians, or the so-called revolutionaries, is merely to seek satisfaction in ideas. There can be fundamental revolution only when you meet the crisis directly without the intervention of the mind.

Question: You have talked about relationship based on usage of another for one's own gratification, and you have often hinted at a state called love. What do you mean by love?

KRISHNAMURTI: We know what our relationship is—a mutual gratification and use, though we clothe it by calling it love. In usage there is tenderness for and the safeguarding of what is used. We safeguard our frontier, our books, our property; similarly, we are careful in safeguarding our wives, our families, our society, because without them we would be lonely, lost. Without the child, the parent feels lonely; what you are not, the child will be, so the child becomes an instrument of your vanity. We know the relationship of need and usage. We need the postman and he needs us, yet we don't say we love the postman. But we do say that we love our wives and children, even though we use them for our personal gratification and are willing to sacrifice them for the vanity of being called patriotic. We know this process very well, and obviously, it cannot be love. Love that uses, exploits, and then feels sorry, cannot be love because love is not a thing of the mind.

Now, let us experiment and discover what love is—discover, not merely verbally, but by actually experiencing that state. When you use me as a guru and I use you as disciples, there is mutual exploitation. Similarly, when you use your wife and children for your furtherance, there is exploitation. Surely, that is not love. When there is use, there must be possession; possession invariably breeds fear, and with fear come jealousy, envy, suspicion. When there is usage, there cannot be love, for love is not something of the mind. To think about a person is not to love that person. You think about a person only when that person is not present, when he is dead, when he has run off, or when he does not give you what you want. Then your inward insufficiency sets the process of the mind going. When that person is close to you, you do not think of him; to think of him when he is close to you is to be disturbed, so you take him for granted—he is there. Habit is a means of forgetting and being at peace so that you won't be disturbed. So, usage must invariably lead to invulnerability, and that is not love.

What is that state when usage—which is thought process as a means to cover the inward insufficiency, positively or negatively—is not? What is that state when there is no sense of gratification? Seeking gratification is the very nature of the mind. Sex is sensation which is created, pictured by the mind, and then the mind acts or does not act. Sensation is a process of thought, which is not love. When the mind is dominant and the thought process is important, there is no love. This process of usage, thinking, imagining, holding, enclosing, rejecting, is all smoke, and when the smoke is not, the flame of love is. Sometimes we do have that flame, rich, full, complete; but the smoke returns because we cannot live long with the flame, which has no sense of nearness, either of the one or the many, either personal or impersonal. Most of us have occasionally known the perfume of love and its vulnerability, but the smoke of usage, habit, jealousy, possession, the contract and the breaking of the contract—all these have become important for us, and therefore the flame of love is not. When the smoke is, the flame is not, but when we understand the truth of usage, the flame is. We use another because we are inwardly poor, insufficient, petty, small, lonely, and we hope that by using another, we can escape. Similarly, we use God as a means of escape. The love of God is not the love of truth. You cannot love truth; loving truth is only a means of using it to gain something else that you know, and therefore there is always the personal fear that you will lose something that you know.

You will know love when the mind is very still and free from its search for gratification and escapes. First, the mind must come entirely to an end. Mind is the result of thought, and thought is merely a passage, a means to an end. When life is merely a passage to something, how can there be love? Love comes into being when the mind is naturally quiet, not made quiet, when it sees the false as false and the true as true. When the mind is quiet, then whatever happens is the action of love, it is not the action of knowledge. Knowledge is mere experience, and experience is not love. Experience cannot know love. Love comes into being when we understand the total process of ourselves, and the understanding of ourselves is the beginning of wisdom.

February 5, 1950

Colombo, Ceylon, 1949–1950

First Talk in Colombo

I think it is important to know how to listen. Most of us do not really listen at all; we are so accustomed to putting away the things we don't want to hear that we have almost become deaf to the problems that concern us. It is important, is it not, how we listen to everything that is going on about us—how we listen not only to the song of the birds, the sounds in nature, but to each other's voices—that is, how extensively we are aware of the problems of the day at different levels. Because, it is only in hearing rightly, and not as we want to hear, that we begin to understand the many problems, whether economic, social, or religious. Life itself is a complex problem which cannot be solved at any one particular level. So we must be able to listen completely and fully, particularly to what is being said. This evening, at least, we might try to listen, so that we understand each other as fully as we can. The difficulty is that most of us listen with prejudice to what is being said; we come to a conclusion about what is being said based on our own ideas, and our minds are already made up. We compare what is being said with the words of some other teacher, and naturally our reaction is conditioned and not a direct response to what is being said. So, if I may suggest it this evening, please listen fully without any prejudice, without any conclusion, without comparing; listen to find out what is actually being said. Because, the world is in a very terrible state; and whether you have riches, own several cars, a comfortable house, a good bank account, or have barely enough to live; whether you belong to a particular religious or political party or to none, these problems have to be understood. I shall be dealing with these problems during the next five weeks, not only here, but also at the discussions to be held on Tuesdays and Thursdays, and we must first learn the art of listening—which is quite a difficult task—so that we get the full significance of what is being said. You cannot get the full significance of what is being said if you listen through the screen of your own prejudice, and the art of listening consists in removing that prejudice, if only for the time being, and trying to understand the problem completely. Thus we shall be able to deal with the problems that arise every day in our lives.

Now, we all have problems, have we not, and we cannot shut our eyes to them or approach them with a pattern of action, either of the left or of the right, with a prejudice which we have formed out of our own knowledge or the knowledge of experts. Surely, the problem is always new; any problem is always new at any level, and if we approach the problem with a pattern of action, whether of the left, the right, or the center, then our response is obviously conditioned, which creates a barrier in understanding the problem itself. That is our difficulty. Life is a process of challenge and response—otherwise, there is no life. Life is a response, a reaction to a demand, to a challenge, to a stimulus, and if our response is conditioned, obviously that creates conflict, which is a problem. Consciously or unconsciously, whether we are aware of it or not, most of us are in conflict, in turmoil; and to understand this inward confusion, which has brought about confusion outwardly—whether political, religious, or economic—we must know how to approach the problem, how to approach this enormous and increasing confusion and misery. There is no decrease, no lessening of sorrow—politically, religiously, socially, or in any other way. Whatever we do, whatever religious or political leaders we follow, creates further disaster, and our problem is how to act so that that very action does not create a new problem, does not produce a further catastrophe, so that reformation does not need further reform. That is the situation each one of us has to face.

Surely, this increasing confusion arises because we approach the problem with a pattern of action, with an ideology, whether political or religious. Organized religion obviously prevents the understanding of the problem because the mind is conditioned by dogma and belief. Our difficulty is how to understand the problem directly, not through any particular religious or political conditioning; how to understand the problem so that the conflict may cease, not temporarily but completely, so that man can live fully, without the misery of tomorrow or the burden of yesterday. Surely, that is what we must find out: how to meet the problem anew, because every problem, whether political, economic, religious, social, or personal, is ever new, and it cannot be met with the old. Perhaps this is putting it in a way different from that to which you are accustomed, but it is actually the issue. After all, life is a constantly changing environment. We would like to sit back and be comfortable; we would like to shelter ourselves in religion and belief, or in knowledge based on particular facts. We would like to be comfortable, we would like to be gratified, we would like not to be disturbed; but life, which is ever changing, ever new, is always disturbing to the old. So, our question is how to meet the challenge afresh. We are the result of the past; our thought is the outcome of yesterday, and with yesterday we obviously cannot meet today because today is new. When we approach the new with yesterday, we are continuing the conditioning of yesterday in understanding today. So our problem in approaching the new is how to understand the old and therefore be free of the old. The old cannot understand the new—you cannot put new wine in old bottles. So, it is important to understand the old, which is the past, which is the mind based on thinking. Thought, idea, is the outcome of the past; whether it is historical or scientific knowledge, or mere prejudice and superstition, idea is obviously the outcome of the past. We would not be able to think if we had no memory; memory is the residue of experience; memory is the response of thought. To understand the challenge, which is new, we have to understand the total process of the self, which is the outcome of our past, the outcome of our conditioning—environmentally, socially, climatically, politically, economically—the whole structure of ourselves. Therefore, to understand the problem is to understand ourselves; the understanding of the world begins with the understanding of ourselves. The problem is not the world but you in relationship with another, which creates a problem, and that problem extended becomes the world problem. So, to understand this enormous, complex machine, this conflict, pain, confusion, misery, we must begin with ourselves—but not individualistically, in opposition to the mass. There is no such thing as that abstraction called the mass, but when you and I do not understand ourselves, when we follow a leader and are hypnotized by words, then we become the mass and are exploited. So, the solution to the problem is not to be found in isolation, in withdrawal to a monastery, to a mountain or a cave, but in understanding the whole problem of ourselves in relationship. You cannot live in isolation; to be is to be related. So, our problem is relationship, which causes conflict, which brings misery, constant trouble. As long as we do not understand that relationship, it will be a source of endless pain and struggle. Understanding ourselves, which is self-knowledge, is the beginning of wisdom, and for self-knowledge you cannot go to a book—there is no book that can teach it to you. Know yourself, and once you understand yourself, you can deal with the problems that confront each one of us every day. Self-knowledge brings tranquillity to the mind, and then only can truth come into being. Truth cannot be sought after. Truth is the unknown, and that which you seek is already known. Truth comes into being unsought when the mind is without prejudice, when there is the understanding of the whole process of ourselves.

Several questions have been sent in, and I am going to answer some of them. It is very easy to ask questions. Anybody can ask a flippant or stupid question, but to ask the right question is much more difficult. Only in asking a right question is there a right answer because only then is the problem of the questioner revealed.

Question: You say that you are not going to act as a guru to anyone. Cannot one who has understood the truth convey his understanding to another to help him also to understand?

KRISHNAMURTI: Surely, whether a guru is necessary or not is not important; the problem is why we want a guru, why we seek a guru. That is the problem, isn't it? If we can understand that, then we will find out whether truth can be conveyed to another. Why do you need a guru, a teacher, a leader, a guide? Obviously, you will say, "I need him because I am confused, I do not know what to do, and I am seeking truth." Let us not deceive ourselves about it. You don't know what truth is; therefore, you go to a teacher, asking him to teach you what truth is. You want someone to help you, to guide you out of your confusion; you are unhappy, and you want to be happy; you are dissatisfied, and you want to be satisfied. So, you choose your guru according to your satisfaction. (Laughter) May I suggest something? When you laugh at something serious, it indicates a very superficial state of mind. By laughing, you pass off the disturbing idea; so, if I may suggest, let us be a little more serious. Because, our problems are very serious, and we cannot approach them like flighty schoolboys—which is the way we are behaving, though we may have gray beards.

So, the question is not whether a guru is necessary but why do we want one? We want someone to give us a comforting hand—that is what we want. We don't want the truth because the truth can be extraordinarily disturbing. We really don't want to understand what truth is, so we go to a guru to give us the satisfaction we want, and as we are confused, obviously we choose a guru or a leader who is also confused. When we choose a guru out of our confusion, that guru must also be confused, otherwise we wouldn't choose him. To understand yourself is essential, and a guru who is worthy of that name must obviously tell you that. But to most of us, this is a tiresome business; we want quick relief, a panacea, so we turn to a guru who will give us a satisfactory pill. We are searching not for truth but for comfort, and the man who gives us comfort enslaves us.

Can truth be conveyed to another? I can give you a description of something which is over, which is past, and therefore not real; I can tell you about the past, and we can communicate with each other on the verbal level about what is known, but we cannot communicate with each other about something which we are not experiencing. Description is always of the past, not the present; therefore, the present cannot be described, and reality is only in the present. So, when you go to another to be told what truth is, he can only tell you of the experience which is over, and the experience which is over is not truth—it is merely knowledge. Knowledge is not wisdom; there can be description on the verbal level of knowledge and facts, but to describe something which is in constant movement is impossible. That which is described is not truth. Truth must be experienced from moment to moment, and if you meet today with the measure of yesterday, you will not understand truth.

So, a guru is not essential. On the contrary, a guru is an impediment. Self-knowledge is the beginning of wisdom. No guru can give you self-knowledge; and without self-knowledge, do what you will, act in any manner you like, follow any leader, any social or religious pattern—you are only creating further misery. But when through self-knowledge the mind is free of impediments and limitations, then truth comes into being.

Question: You are reported as having said that ideas are not going to bring people together. Please explain how, according to you, people can be brought together to create a better world.

KRISHNAMURTI: Let us find out what we mean by ideas, and as I have said, please listen, not with prejudice, not with a conclusion, but listen as you would to someone whom you really like. What do you mean by ideas, what do you mean by belief, what do you mean by ideology? Let us think this out, investigate together. Do ideas bring people together, or separate people? Idea is obviously the verbal version of thought. Thought is response to conditioning, is it not? You are Sinhalese, Buddhists, Christians, or what you will, and your thought is conditioned according to your background. Background is memory, obviously; memory responds to stimulus, to challenge, and the response of memory to challenge is called thinking. Surely, you think according to the pattern in which you have been brought up—as Buddhists, as Christians, according to the left or the right, or God knows what. You are conditioned to believe certain things, and not to believe other things. That conditioning is memory, and the response of memory is thought. Thought examines ideas and, being conditioned, responds according to that conditioning, going either to the left or to the right. So, ideas gather people according to the particular pattern in which they have been brought up, and obviously ideas can oppose ideas.

As it is perhaps a little too abstract, let us put it differently. Suppose you are a real Buddhist, not a verbal Buddhist, but an active one—what does it mean? You believe in certain things and act according to that belief, and a Christian or a communist will act according to a different ideology. How can these two ideas ever meet? Each idea, each thought, is the result of its own conditioning, and how can one idea meet another? All one idea can do is to expand and gather people around itself, as also does any other idea. So, ideas can never bring about unity. On the contrary, they divide people. You are a Christian, I am a Buddhist, another is a Hindu or a Muslim; I believe, you don't believe, so we are at loggerheads. Why? Why are we so divided by ideas? Because that is the only thing we have—the word is the only thing we have; therefore, ideas have become extraordinarily important, and we gather around ideas to act—the Christian in opposition to the communist, labor in opposition to capitalism, capitalism in opposition to socialism. Idea is not action; idea prevents action. We will have to think it out; we will go into it at another discussion. Action based upon idea divides people. That is why there is starvation in the world, there is hunger, there is misery, there is war. We have ideas about it, but idea prevents our understanding of the problem because the problem is not an idea. The problem is pain and conflict. It is very comforting to have an idea about pain, suffering, trouble, exploitation; then you can talk about it and not act. Think it out and you will see, if you are really going into the problem and not merely reacting according to a certain pattern, that ideas are dividing people. Have you not noticed? You Sinhalese are fighting for nationalism, which is just an idea; Hindus are against Europeans, Germans and Americans against Russians. All over the world nationalism, which is an idea, prevents people from coming together, and because nationalism is elementarily gratifying and stupid, you are satisfied with it. Everywhere the word *nationalism* arises like a wall and keeps people apart. So, throughout the world, ideas are separating people, setting man against man. The ideas which we worship are the very denial of love; they have no significance; they cannot bring about a radical transformation. To bring about this fundamental revolution, you must begin to understand yourself; it is only then that you can bring about unity, and not through ideas.

Question: I feel uncertain about everything and consequently find it difficult to act well, as I fear that my action will only lead to further confusion. Is there a way I can act to avoid confusion?

KRISHNAMURTI: Obviously, without knowing yourself, whatever you do is bound to increase confusion; if you don't know the whole structure of your being, your action will inevitably create mischief, though you may have a perfect pattern of conduct. That is why reformation, revolution according to a pattern, is a disintegrating factor in society—it merely carries on the past in a modified way. Self-knowledge, which you cannot buy in a book or get from any teacher, is to be discovered in relationship with people, with ideas. Relationship is a mirror in which you see yourself as you are. Nothing can live in isolation. One must understand relationship and not merely condemn it, justify it, or identify oneself with it. We condemn because that is the easiest way to get rid of something, like putting a child in the corner. If I want to understand my child, my neighbor, my wife, I must study that person, I must be aware in my relationship with that person, mustn't I? So, to act without increasing confusion is possible only through self-knowledge.

Question: You are reported as having said that religion cannot provide a solution to the problems of humanity. Is that correct?

KRISHNAMURTI: Now, what do we mean by religion? As we know it, it is organized belief, dogma, action according to a particular pattern, is it not? Organized belief is the experience of someone else, arranged according to a pattern of yesterday, and you are conditioned by that belief. Is that religion? The pattern may be of the left, of the right, or of the center, or it may be a so-called divine plan—there is not much difference between them—all have their ideals, all have their utopia or heaven, so all may be called religion, each perpetuating exploitation. Now, is that religion? Obviously, belief with its authority and dogmas, with its pageantry and sensation, is not religion. So, what is religion? That is our question. It is simply a word. The word *door* is not a door but only the symbol of something else. Similarly, religion is something behind the conditioned response evoked by that word, which means that we have to discover the thing behind the word. That thing is the unknown, isn't it? What you know has already receded into the past. There must be direct experiencing of *what is,* and for this the first requirement is freedom, which means you must be free of the false, which is belief, not at the end but at the beginning. You must have the freedom to discover what is false—surely that is religion. The whole process of yourself must be understood, for without understanding yourself, there is no wisdom. The beginning of wisdom is the understanding of yourself, and that is meditation.

December 25, 1949

Action

The problems that confront each one of us, and so the world, cannot be solved by politicians or by specialists. These problems are not the result of superficial causes and cannot be so considered. No problem, especially a human problem, can be solved at any one particular level. Our problems are complex; they can be solved only as a total process of man's response to life. The experts may give blueprints for planned action, and it is not the planned actions that are going to save us but the understanding of the total process of man, which is yourself. The experts can only deal with problems on a single level, and so increase our conflicts and confusion.

It is disastrous to consider our complex human problem on a single particular level and allow the specialists to dominate our lives. Our life is a complex process which requires deep understanding of ourselves as thought and feeling. Without understanding ourselves, no problem, however superficial or however complex, can be understood. Without understanding ourselves, our relationship must inevitably lead to conflict and confusion. Without understanding ourselves, there can be no new social order. A revolution without self-knowledge is merely a modified continuation of the present state.

Self-knowledge is not a thing to be bought in books, nor is it the outcome of a long painful practice and discipline, but it is awareness, from moment to moment, of every thought and feeling as it arises in relationship. Relationship is not on an abstract ideological level but an actuality—the relationship with property, with people, and with ideas. Relationship implies existence, and as nothing can live in isolation, to be is to be related. Our conflict is in relationship, at all the levels of our existence, and the understanding of this relationship, completely and extensively, is the only real problem that each one has. This problem cannot be postponed nor be evaded. The avoidance of it only creates further conflict and misery. The escape from it only brings about thoughtlessness which is exploited by the crafty and the ambitious.

Religion then is not belief, nor dogma, but the understanding of truth that is to be discovered in relationship, from moment to moment. Religion that is belief and dogma is only an escape from the reality of relationship. The man who seeks God, or what you will, through belief which he calls religion, only creates opposition, bringing about separation, which is disintegration. Any form of ideology, whether of the right or of the left, of this particular religion or of that, sets man against man—which is what is happening in the world.

The replacement of one ideology by another is not the solution to our problems. The problem is not which is the better ideology but the understanding of ourselves as a total process. You might say that the understanding of ourselves takes infinite time, and in the meanwhile the world is going to pieces. You think that if you have a planned action according to an ideology, then there is a possibility of bringing about, soon, a transformation in the world. If we look a little more closely into this, we will see that ideas do not bring people together at all. An idea may help to form a group, but that group is against another with a different idea, and so on, until ideas become more important than action. Ideologies, beliefs, organized religions separate people.

Humanity cannot be integrated by an idea, however noble and extensive that idea may be. For idea is merely a conditioned response, and a conditioned response, in meeting the challenge of life, must be inadequate, bringing with it conflict and confusion. Religion that is based on idea cannot bring man together. Religion as the experience of some authority may bind a few people together, but it will breed inevitably antagonism; the experience of another is not true, however great the experiencer may be. Truth can never be the product of self-projected authority. The experience of a guru, of a teacher, of a saint, of a savior, is not the truth which you have to discover. The truth of another is not truth. You may repeat the verbal expression of truth to another, but that becomes a lie in the process of repetition.

The experience of another is not valid in understanding reality. But, the organized religions throughout the world are based on the experience of another and, therefore, are not liberating man but only binding him to a particular pattern which sets man against man. Each one of us has to start anew, afresh, for what we are, the world is. The world is not different from you and me. This little world of our problems, extended, becomes the world and the problems of the world.

We despair of our understanding in relation to the vast problems of the world. We do not see that it is not a problem of mass action but of the awakening of the individual to the world in which he lives, and of resolve the problems of his world, however limited. The mass is an abstraction which is exploited by the politician, by one who has an ideology. The mass is actually you and I and another. When you and I and another are hypnotized by a word, then we become the mass, which is still an abstraction, for the word is an abstraction. The mass action is an illusion. This action is really the idea about an action of the few, which we accept in our confusion and despair. Out of our confusion and despair, we choose our guides, whether political or religious; and they must inevitably, because of our choice, be also in confusion and despair. They may put on an air of certainty and all-knowingness, but actually, as they are the guides of the confused, they must be equally confused, or they would not be the guides. In the world, where the leader (guide) and the led (guided) are confused, to follow the pattern or an ideology, knowingly or unknowingly, is to breed further conflict and misery.

The individual then is important, not his idea or whom he follows, his country or his belief. You are important, not to what ideology or nation you belong, to what color and creed; the ideology is only a projection of our own conditioning. These conditionings may, at one level, be useful as knowledge; but at another level, at the deeper levels of existence, they become extremely harmful and destructive. As these are your own projections—the religions and the ideologies, the nationalism and the patterns—any action based on them must be the activity of the dog chasing its tail. For all ideals are homemade. They are the result of your own projection, and they do not reveal truth.

It is only when each one of us realizes the present structure of existence, the structure of self-projected ideals and conclusions, then only is there a possibility of freeing ourselves and looking at the problem anew. The crisis, the impending disasters, cannot be dissolved by another set of self-projected ideologies, but only when you, as an individual, realize the truth of this and so begin to understand the total process of your thought and feeling. The individual is important only in this sense, and not in the isolated, ruthless response to the problem.

After all, the problem throughout the world is the inadequate response to the new, changing challenge of life. This inadequacy creates conflict that brings about the problem. Until the response is adequate, we must have a multiplicity of problems. The adequacy does not demand a new conditioning but the freedom from all conditioning. That is, as long as you are a Buddhist, a Christian, a Muslim, a Hindu, or belonging to the left or to the right, you cannot respond adequately to the problems which are your own creation and so of the world. It is not the strengthening of the conditioning, religious or social, that is going to bring peace to you and to the world.

The world is your problem, and to comprehend it, you must understand yourself. This understanding of yourself is not a matter of time. You exist only in relationship; otherwise, you are not. Your relationship is the problem—your relationship to property, to people, and to ideas or to beliefs. This relationship is now friction, conflict; and so long as you do not understand your relationship, do what you will, hypnotize yourself by any ideology or dogma, there can be no rest for you. This understanding of yourself is action in relationship. You discover yourself as you are directly in relationship. Relationship is the mirror in which you can see yourself as you are. You cannot see yourself as you are in this mirror if you approach it with a conclusion and an explanation, or with condemnation, or with justification.

The very perception of what you are, as you are, in the moment of action of relationship, brings a freedom from *what is.* Only in freedom can there be discovery. A conditioned mind cannot discover truth. Freedom is not an abstraction but it comes into being with virtue. For, the very nature of virtue is to bring liberation from the causes of confusion. After all, nonvirtue is disorder, conflict. But virtue is freedom, the clarity of perception that understanding brings. You cannot become virtuous. The becoming is the illusion of greed or acquisitiveness. Virtue is the immediate perception of *what is.* So, self-knowledge is the beginning of wisdom, and it is wisdom that will resolve your problems and so the problems of the world.

Broadcast by Radio Ceylon
December 28, 1949

Second Talk in Colombo

We were saying how important it is, before we ask what to do or how to act, to discover what is right thinking because without right thinking, obviously there cannot be right action. Action according to a pattern, according to a belief, has set man against man, as we discussed last Sunday. There can be no right thinking as long as there is no self-knowledge because without self-knowledge, how can one know what one is actually thinking? We do a great deal of thinking, and there is a great deal of activity; but such thought and action produce conflict and antagonism, which we see not only in ourselves but also about us in the world. So, our problem is, is it not, how to think rightly, which will produce right action, thereby eliminating the conflict and confusion which we find, not only in ourselves, but in the world about us.

Now, to find out what is right thinking, we must inquire into what is self-knowledge because if we don't know what we think, or if our thought is based on the background which is our conditioning, whatever we think is obviously merely a reaction and therefore leads to further conflict. So, before we can find out what is right thinking, we have to know what is self-knowledge. Self-knowledge, surely, is not mere learning a particular kind of thinking. Self-knowledge is not based on ideas, belief, or conclusion. It must be a living thing; otherwise, it ceases to be self-knowledge and becomes mere information. There is a difference between information—which is knowledge, and wisdom—which is knowing the processes of our thoughts and feelings. But most of us are caught up in information, superficial knowledge, and so we are incapable of going much deeper into the problem. To discover the whole process of self-knowledge, we have to be aware in relationship. Relationship is the only mirror we have, a mirror that will not distort, a mirror in which we can exactly and precisely see our thought unfolding itself. Isolation, which many people seek, is the surreptitious building up of resistance against relationship. Isolation obviously prevents the understanding of relationship—relationship with people, with ideas, with things. As long as we don't know our relationship, actually *what is,* between ourselves and our property, ourselves and people, ourselves and ideas, obviously there must be confusion and conflict.

So, we can find out what is right thinking only in relationship. That is, we can discover in relationship how we think from moment to moment, what are our reactions, and thereby proceed step by step to the unfoldment of right thinking. This is not an abstract or difficult thing to do—to watch exactly what is taking place in our relationship, what are our reactions, and thus discover the truth of each thought, each feeling. But if we bring to it an idea or a preconception of what relationship should be, then obviously that prevents the uncovering, the unfoldment of *what is.* That is our difficulty: we have already made up our minds as to what relationship should be. To most of us, relationship is a term for comfort, for gratification, for security; and in that relationship we use property, ideas, and persons for our gratification. We use belief as a means of security. Relationship is not merely a mechanical adjustment. When we use people, it necessitates possession, physical or psychological; and in possessing someone, we create all the problems of jealousy, envy, loneliness, and conflict. Because, if we examine it a little more closely and deeply, we will see that using a person or property for gratification is a process of isolation. This process of isolation is not actual relationship at all. So our difficulty and our mounting problems come with the lack of understanding of relationship, which is essentially self-knowledge. If we do not know how we are related to people, to property, to ideas, then our relationship will inevitably bring about conflict. That is our whole problem at the present time, is it not?—relationship, not only between people, but between groups of people, between nations, between ideologies, either of the left or of the right, religious or secular. Therefore, it is important to understand fundamentally your relationship with your wife, with your husband, with your neighbor, for relationship is a door through which we can discover ourselves, and through that discovery we understand what is right thinking.

Right thinking, surely, is entirely different from right thought. Right thought is static. You can learn about right thought, but you cannot learn about right thinking because right thinking is movement; it is not static. Right thought you can learn from a book, from a teacher, or gather information about, but you cannot have right thinking by following a pattern or a mold. Right thinking is the understanding of relationship from moment to moment, which uncovers the whole process of the self.

At whatever level you live, there is conflict, not only individual conflict, but also world conflict. The world is you; it is not separate from you. What you are, the world is. There must be a fundamental revolution in your relationship with people, with ideas; there must be a fundamental change, and that change must begin, not outside you, but in your relationships. Therefore, it is essential for a man of peace, for a man of thought, to understand himself, for without self-knowledge his efforts only create further confusion and further misery. Be aware of the total process of yourself. You need no guru, no book, to understand from moment to moment your relationship with all things.

Question: Why do you waste your time preaching instead of helping the world in a practical way?

KRISHNAMURTI: Now, what do you mean by "practical"? You mean bringing about a change in the world, a better economic adjustment, a better distribution of wealth, a better relationship—or, to put it more brutally, helping you to find a better job. You want to see a change in this world—every intelligent man does—and you want a method to bring about that change, and therefore you ask me why I waste my time preaching instead of doing something about it. Now, is what I am actually doing a waste of time? It would be a waste of time, would it not, if I introduced a new set of ideas to replace the old ideology, the old pattern. Perhaps that is what you want me to do. But instead of pointing out a so-called practical way to act, to live, to get a better job, to create a better world, is it not important to find out what are the impediments which actually prevent a real revolution—not a revolution of the left or the right, but a fundamental, radical revolution, not based on ideas? Because, as we have discussed it, ideals, beliefs, ideologies, dogmas, prevent action. There cannot be a world transformation, a revolution, as long as action is based on ideas because action then is merely reaction; therefore, ideas become much more important than action, and that is precisely what is taking place in the world, isn't it? To act, we must discover the impediments that prevent action. But most of us don't want to act—that is our difficulty. We prefer to discuss, we prefer to substitute one ideology for another, and so we escape from action through ideology. Surely, that is very simple, is it not? The world at the present time is facing many problems: overpopulation, starvation, division of people into nationalities and classes, and so on. Why isn't there a group of people sitting together trying to solve the problems of nationalism? But if we try to become international while clinging to our nationality, we create another problem, and that is what most of us do. So, you see that ideals are really preventing action. A statesman, an eminent authority, has said the world can be organized and all the people fed. Then why is it not done? Because of conflicting ideas, beliefs, and nationalisms. Therefore, ideas are actually preventing the feeding of people, and most of us play with ideas and think we are tremendous revolutionaries, hypnotizing ourselves with such words as *practical*. What is important is to free ourselves from ideas, from nationalisms, from all religious beliefs and dogmas, so that we can act, not according to a pattern or an ideology, but as needs demand; and, surely, to point out the hindrances and impediments that prevent such action is not a waste of time, is not a lot of hot air. What you are doing is obviously nonsense. Your ideas and beliefs, your political, economic, and religious panaceas, are actually dividing people and leading to war. It is only when the mind is free of idea and belief that it can act rightly. A man who is patriotic, nationalistic, can never know what it is to be brotherly, though he may talk about it; on the contrary, his actions, economically and in every direction, are conducive to war. So, there can be right action and therefore radical, lasting transformation, only when the mind is free of ideas, not superficially, but fundamentally, and freedom from ideas can take place only through self-awareness and self-knowledge.

Question: I am a teacher, and after studying what you say, I see that most of the present education is harmful or futile. What can I do about it?

KRISHNAMURTI: Surely, the question is what we mean by education and why we are educating people. We see throughout the world that education has failed because it is producing more and more destruction and war. Education so far has furthered industrialism and war; that has been the process for the last century or so. What is actually taking place is war, conflict, unceasing waste of one's own effort, everything leading to more conflict, greater confusion and antagonism—and is that the end of education? So, to find out how to educate, not only must the educator be educated, but there must be an understanding of what it is all about and what we are living for, the end and purpose of life. When we seek the purpose of life, we can find it only as a self-projection. The end and purpose of life, obviously, is living. But living is not a goal; happiness is not a goal. It is only when we are unhappy that we seek the goal of happiness. Similarly, when life is confused, then we want a purpose, an end. So, we have to find out what living means. Is it merely a technique, a capacity to earn money mechanically, or is it a process of understanding the total way of our whole existence? What is happiness? Is it to be educated, to pass the B.A. or M.A., or God knows what? Apart from profession, what are you actually? What is your state of being apart from your social status, so many rupees earned from such and such a job—strip yourselves of these, and what are you? Hardly anything; nothing very great, but something shallow and empty.

Knowledge is what we call education. You can get information from any book as long as you can read; so education so far has actually been an escape from ourselves; and, as with all escapes, it must inevitably create further confusion and further misery. Without understanding the total process of yourself, which is understanding relationship, mere gathering of information and mere memorizing of books in order to pass examinations is utterly futile. Surely I am not exaggerating. Education is understanding, and helping others to understand, the total process of our existence. The teacher must understand the whole significance of his action in relationship with society, with the world; so it is essential that the educator be educated. To bring about revolution in the world, transformation must take place in you, but we avoid radical revolution in ourselves and try to bring about revolution in the state, in the economic world. Therefore, education must begin with you, with the guru. When you give your background to the child, the mind of the child responds to that conditioning, and it is only through freedom from conditioning that there can be the true salvation of the world.

Question: I am a smoker, and I am trying to break myself of the habit of smoking. Can you help me? (Laughter)

KRISHNAMURTI: I do not know why you are laughing. The questioner wants to know how to stop smoking. It is a problem to him, and by merely laughing it away, you have not solved it. Perhaps you also smoke or have some other habit. Let us find out how to understand this whole process of habit forming and habit breaking. We can take the example of smoking, and you can substitute your own habit, your own particular problem, and experiment with your own problem directly as I am experimenting with the problem of smoking. It is a problem, it becomes a problem, when I want to give it up; as long as I am satisfied with it, it is not a problem. The problem arises when I have to do something about a particular habit, when the habit becomes a disturbance. Smoking has created a disturbance, so I want to be free of it. I want to stop smoking; I want to be rid of it, to put it aside, so my approach to smoking is one of resistance or condemnation. That is, I don't want to smoke, so my approach is either to suppress it, condemn it, or to find a substitute for it—instead of smoking, to chew. Now, can I look at the problem free of condemnation, justification, or suppression? Can I look at my smoking without any sense of rejection? Try to experiment with it now as I am talking, and you will see how extraordinarily difficult it is not to reject or accept. Because, our whole tradition, our whole background, is urging us to reject or to justify rather than to be curious about it. Instead of being passively watchful, the mind always operates on the problem. So, the problem is not smoking but our approach to smoking, which creates the problem. Because, if you find smoking rather stupid, a waste of money, and so on—if you really see that, you will drop it, there will be no problem. Smoking, drinking, or any other habit is an escape from something else; it makes you feel socially at ease. It is an escape from your own nervousness or from a disturbed state, and the habit becomes a means of your conditioning. So, smoking is not the problem. When you approach smoking with your memory, your recollection of previous trials and failures, you approach it with a conclusion already made. Therefore, the problem is not in the fact but in your approach to the fact. You have tried by discipline, control, denial, and you have not succeeded. So you say, "I shall go on smoking; I cannot stop"—which is, after all, an attempt to justify yourself, which means your approach is not very intelligent. So, smoking or any other habit is not a problem. The problem is thought, which is your approach to the fact. You are the problem, not the habit which you have created; and thus you will see, if you really try, how difficult it is for the mind to be free from the sense of condemnation and justification. When your mind is free, the problem of smoking—or any other problem—is nonexistent.

Question: Is continence or chastity necessary for the attainment of liberation?

KRISHNAMURTI: The question is wrongly put. For the attainment of liberation, nothing is necessary. You cannot attain it through bargaining, through sacrifice, through elimination; it is not a thing that you can buy. If you do these things, you will get a thing of the marketplace, therefore not real. Truth cannot be bought, there is no means to truth; if there were a means, the end would not be truth, because means and end are one, they are not separate. Chastity as a means to liberation, to truth, is a denial of truth. Chastity is not a coin with which you buy it. You cannot buy truth with any coin, and you cannot buy chastity with any coin. You can buy only those things which you know, but you cannot buy truth because you don't know it. Truth comes into being only when the mind is quiet, still; so the problem is entirely different, is it not?

Why do we think chastity is essential? Why has sex become a problem? That is really the question, isn't it? We shall understand what it is to be chaste when we understand this corroding problem of sex. Let us find out why sex has become such an extremely important factor in our life, more of a problem than property, money, and so on. What do we mean by sex? Not merely the act but thinking about it, feeling about it, anticipating it, escaping from it—that is our problem. Our problem is sensation, wanting more and more. Watch yourself, don't watch your neighbor. Why are your thoughts so occupied with sex? Chastity can exist only when there is love, and without love there is no chastity. Without love, chastity is merely lust in a different form. To become chaste is to become something else; it is like a man becoming powerful, succeeding as a prominent lawyer, politician, or whatever else—the change is on the same level. That is not chastity but merely the end result of a dream, the outcome of the continual resistance to a particular desire. So, our problem is not how to become chaste or to find out what are the things necessary for liberation but to understand this problem which we call sex. Because, it is an enormous problem, and you cannot approach it with condemnation or justification. Of course, you can easily isolate yourself from it, but then you will be creating another problem. This all-important, engrossing, and destructive problem of sex can be understood only when the mind liberates itself from its own anchorage. Please think it out, don't brush it aside. As long as you are bound through fear, through tradition, to any particular job, activity, belief, idea, as long as you are conditioned by and attached to all that, you will have this problem of sex. Only when the mind is free of fear is there the fathomless, the inexhaustible, and only then does this problem take its ordinary place. Then you can deal with it simply and effectively; then it is not a problem. So, chastity ceases to be a problem where there is love. Then life is not a problem; life is to be lived completely in the fullness of love, and that revolution will bring about a new world.

Question: The idea of death terrifies me. Can you help me to overcome the dread of my own death and that of my loved ones?

KRISHNAMURTI: Let us think this problem out together and go to the end of it, because we must find the truth of it, and not merely an opinion. Opinions are not truth. Death is a fact. You may like to dodge it, to escape from it through belief in reincarnation, continuity, growth, but it is a fact. Why are we terrified of it? What do we mean by death? Surely, we mean the end of something—of the body and of our experiences which we have gathered throughout life—the psychological ending of accumulated experiences. Innumerable books are written about death, about the hereafter. But we are afraid of death. So, we try to find immortality, continuity, through property, through title, through name, through achievement, so that desire, memory, can be immortalized. Why do you want to continue? What is there to continue? Your memories? Memories are but accumulated experiences. Only in ending is there creation, not in continuity; therefore, there must be death. In death only is there renewal, not in continuing. Incompleteness of action in the present creates fear of death, and as long as there is the desire for continuity, there must be fear. That which continues must decay; it cannot be renewed, but in dying there is creation of the new.

January 1, 1950

Third Talk in Colombo

One of our major problems is this question of creative living. Obviously, most of us have dull lives; we have only a very superficial reaction. After all, most of our responses are superficial and thereby create innumerable problems. Creative living does not necessarily mean becoming a big architect or a great writer. This is merely capacity, and capacity is entirely different from creative living. No one need know that you are creative, but you yourself can know that state of extraordinary happiness, a quality of indestructibility, but that is not easily realized because most of us have innumerable problems—political, social, economic, religious, family—which we try to solve according to certain explanations, certain rules, traditions, any sociological or religious pattern with which we are familiar. But our solution of one problem seems inevitably to create other problems, and we set up a net of problems ever multiplying and increasing in their destructiveness. When we try to find the answer, a way out of this mess, this confusion, we seek the answer at one particular level. One must have the capacity to go beyond all levels because the creative way of living cannot be found at any particular level. That creative action comes into being only in understanding relationship, and relationship is communion with another. So, it is not really a selfish outlook to be concerned with individual action. We seem to think that we can do very little in this world, that only the big politicians, the famous writers, the great religious leaders are capable of extraordinary action. Actually, you and I are infinitely more capable of bringing about a radical transformation than the professional politicians and economists. If we are concerned with our own lives, if we understand our relationship with others, we will have created a new society; otherwise, we will but perpetuate the present chaotic mess and confusion.

So, it is not out of selfishness, not because of a desire for power, that one is concerned with individual action; and if we can find a way of living which is creative, not merely conforming to religious, social, political, or economic standards as we are doing at the present time, then I think we will be able to solve our many problems. At present we are merely repetitive gramophones, perhaps changing records occasionally under pressure, but most of us always play the same tunes for every occasion. It is this constant repetition, this perpetuation of tradition, that is the source of the problem with all its complexities. We seem to be incapable of breaking away from conformity, though we may substitute a new conformity for the present one or try to modify the present pattern. It is a constant process of repetition, imitation. We are Buddhists, Christians, or Hindus; we belong to the left or to the right. By quoting from the various sacred books, by mere repetition, we think we shall solve our innumerable problems. Surely, repetition is not going to solve human problems. What has the "revolutionary" done for the so-called masses? Actually, the problems are still there. What happens is that this constant repetition of an idea prevents the understanding of the problem itself. Through self-knowledge one has the capacity to free oneself from this repetition. Then it is possible to be in that creative state, which is always new, and therefore one is always ready to meet each problem afresh.

After all, our difficulty is that having these immense problems, we meet them with previous conclusions, with the record of experience, either our own or acquired through others; and so we meet the new with the old, which creates a further problem. Creative living is being without that background; the new is met as the new; therefore, it does not create further problems. Therefore, it is necessary to meet the new with the new until we can understand the total process, the whole problem of mounting disaster, misery, starvation, war, unemployment, inequality, the battle between conflicting ideologies. That struggle and confusion is not to be solved by repetition of old ways. If you will really look a little more closely without prejudice, without religious bias, you will see much bigger problems; and being free from conformity, from belief, you will be able to meet the new. This capacity to meet the new with the new is called the creative state, and that surely is the highest form of religion. Religion is not merely belief; it is not the following of certain rituals, dogmas, the calling yourself this or that. Religion is really experiencing a state in which there is creation. This is not an idea, a process. It can be realized when there is freedom from self. There can be freedom from self only through understanding the self in relationship—but there can be no understanding in isolation.

As I suggested in answering the questions last Sunday, it is important that we experience each question as it arises, and not merely listen to my answers; that we discover together the truth of the matter, which is much more difficult. Most of us would like to be apart from the problem, watching others; but if we can discover together, take the journey together, so that it is your experience and not mine, though you are listening to my words—if we can go together, then it will be of lasting value and importance.

Question: Do you advocate vegetarianism? Would you object to the inclusion of an egg in your diet?

KRISHNAMURTI: Is that really a very great problem, whether we should have an egg or not? Perhaps most of you are concerned with nonkilling. That is really the crux of the matter, is it not? Perhaps most of you eat meat or fish. You avoid killing by going to a butcher, or you put the blame on the killer, the butcher—that is only dodging the problem. If you like to eat eggs, you may get infertile eggs to avoid killing. But this is a very superficial question—the problem is much deeper. You don't want to kill animals for your stomach, but you do not mind supporting governments that are organized to kill. All sovereign governments are based on violence; they must have armies, navies, and air forces. You don't mind supporting them, but you object to the terrible calamity of eating an egg! (Laughter) See how ridiculous the whole thing is; investigate the mentality of the gentleman who is nationalistic, who does not mind the exploitation and the ruthless destruction of people, to whom wholesale massacre is nothing—but who has scruples as to what goes into his mouth. (Laughter) So, there is much more involved in this problem—not only the whole question of killing, but the right employment of the mind. The mind may be used narrowly, or it is capable of extraordinary activity; and most of us are satisfied with superficial activity, with security, sexual satisfaction, amusement, religious belief—with that we are satisfied and discard entirely the deeper response and wider significance of life. Even the religious leaders have become petty in their response to life. After all, the problem is not only killing animals but human beings, which is more important. You may refrain from using animals and degrading them, you may be compassionate about killing them, but what is important in this question is the whole problem of exploitation and killing—not only the slaughter of human beings in wartime, but the way you exploit people, the way you treat your servants and look down on them as inferiors. Probably you are not paying attention to this because it is near home. You would rather discuss God, reincarnation—but nothing requiring immediate action and responsibility.

So, if you are really concerned with not killing, you should not be a nationalist, you should not call yourself Sinhalese, German, or Russian. Also you must have right employment, make right use of machinery. It is very important in modern society to have right employment because today every action leads to war, the whole thing is geared for war; but at least we can find out the wrong professions and avoid them intelligently. Obviously, the army, the navy, are wrong professions; so is the profession of law which encourages litigation; and the police, especially the secret police. So, right employment must be found and exercised by each one, and only then can there be the cessation of killing, which will bring about peace among men. But the economic pressure is so great in the modern world that very few can withstand it. Almost no one is concerned with seeking right profession, and if you are concerned not to kill, then you have to do far more than merely avoid the killing of animals, which means you have to go into this whole problem of right employment. Though the question may appear very petty, if you go into it a little more carefully, you will see that it is a very great question because what you are, you make the world to be. If you are greedy, angry, dominating, possessive, you will inevitably create a social structure that will bring about further conflict, misery, further destruction. But unfortunately, most of us are not concerned with any of these things. Most of us are concerned with immediate pleasures, with everyday living; and if we can get them, we are satisfied. We do not want to look into the deeper and wider problems; though we know they exist, we want to avoid them. By avoiding these problems, they are increased, you have not solved them. To solve them, they cannot be approached through any particular ideology, either of the left or of the right. Look at these problems more closely and effectively, and you will begin to understand the total process of yourself in relation to others, which is society.

But you will tell me that I have not answered the question about the egg, whether to eat an egg or not. Surely, intelligence is the important thing—not what goes into your mouth, but what comes out of it; and most of us have filled our hearts with the things of the mind, and our minds are very small, shallow. Our problem is to find out how to bring about a transformation in that which is shallow and small, and this transformation can come about only through understanding the shallow. Those of you who want to go into the question more deeply will have to find out whether you are contributing to war and how to avoid it, whether indirectly you are the cause of destruction. If you can really solve that question, then you can easily settle the superficial matter of whether you should be a vegetarian or not. Tackle the problem at a much deeper level, and you will find the answer.

Question: You say that reality or understanding exists in the interval between two thoughts. Will you please explain.

KRISHNAMURTI: This is really a different way of asking the question, "What is meditation?" As I answer this question, please experiment with it, discover how your own mind works, which is after all a process of meditation. I am thinking aloud with you, not superficially—I have not studied. I am just thinking aloud with you about the question, so that we can all journey together and find the truth of this question.

The questioner asks about the interval between two thoughts, in which there can be understanding. Before we can inquire into that, we must find out what we mean by thought. What do you mean by thinking? Is this getting a little too serious? You must have patience to listen to it. When you think something—thought being an idea—what do you mean by that? Is not thought a response to influence, the outcome of social, environmental influence? Is not thought the summation of all experience reacting? Say, for example, you have a problem, and you are trying to think about it, to analyze it, to study it. How do you do that? Are you not looking at the present problem with the experience of yesterday—yesterday being the past—with past knowledge, past history, past experience? So, that is the past, which is memory, responding to the present; and this response of memory to the present you call thinking. Thought is merely the response of the past in conjunction with the present, is it not, and for most of us thought is a continuous process. Even when we are asleep, there is constant activity in the form of dreams; there is never a moment when the mind is really still. We project a picture and live either in the past or the future, like many old and some young people do, or like the political leaders who are always promising a marvelous utopia. (Laughter) And we accept it because we all want the future, so we sacrifice the present for the future, but we cannot know what is going to happen tomorrow or in fifty years' time.

So, thought is the response of the past in conjunction with the present; that is, thought is experience responding to challenge, which is reaction. There is no thought if there is no reaction. Response is the past background—you respond as a Buddhist, a Christian, according to the left or to the right. That is the background, and that is the constant response to challenge—and that response of the past to the present is called thinking. There is never a moment when thought is not. Have you not noticed that your mind is incessantly occupied with something or other—personal, religious, or political worries? It is constantly occupied; and what happens to your mind, what happens to any machinery that is in constant use? It wears away. The very nature of the mind is to be occupied with something, to be in constant agitation, and we try to control it, to dominate it, to suppress it; and if we can succeed, we think we have become great saints and religious people, and then we stop thinking.

Now, you will see that in the process of thinking there is always an interval, a gap, between two thoughts. As you are listening to me, what exactly is happening in your mind? You are listening, perhaps experiencing what we are talking about, waiting for information, the experience of the next moment. You are watchful, so there is passive watching, alert awareness. There is no response; there is a state of passiveness in which the mind is strongly aware, yet there is no thought—that is, you are really experiencing what I am talking about. Such passive watchfulness is the interval between two thoughts.

Suppose you have a new problem—and problems are always new—how do you approach it? It is a new problem, not an old one. You may recognize it as old, but as long as it is a problem, it is always new. It is like one of those modern pictures to which you are entirely unaccustomed. What happens if you want to understand it? If you approach it with your classical training, your response to that challenge, which is that picture, is rejection; so if you want to understand the picture, your classical training will have to be put aside—just as, if you want to understand what I am talking about, you have to forget you are a Buddhist, a Christian, or whatnot. You must look at the picture free of your classical training, with passive awareness and watchfulness of mind, and then the picture begins to unfold itself and tell its story. That is possible only when the mind is in a state of watchfulness, without trying to condemn or justify the picture; it comes only when thought is not, when the mind is still. You can experiment with that and see how extraordinarily true is a still mind. Only then is it possible to understand. But the constant activity of the mind prevents the understanding of the problem.

To put it around the other way, what do you do when you have a problem, an acute problem? You think about it, don't you? What do you mean by "think about it"? You mean working for an answer, searching for an answer, according to your previous conclusions. That is, you try to shape the problem to fit certain conclusions which you have, and if you can make it fit, you think you have solved it. But problems are not solved by being put into the pigeonholes of the mind. You think about the problem with the memory of past conclusions and try to find out what Christ, Buddha, X, Y, or Z has said, and then apply those conclusions to the problem. Thereby you do not solve the problem but cover it up with the residue of previous problems. When you have a really big and difficult problem, that process will not work. You say you have tried everything and you cannot solve it. That means you are not waiting for the problem to tell its story. But when the mind is relaxed, no longer making an effort, when it is quiet for just a few seconds, then the problem reveals itself and it is solved. That happens when the mind is still, in the interval between two thoughts, between two responses. In that state of mind understanding comes, but it requires extraordinary watchfulness of every movement of thought. When the mind is aware of its own activity, its own process, then there is quietness. After all, self-knowledge is the beginning of meditation, and if you do not know the whole, total process of yourself, you cannot know the importance of meditation. Merely sitting in front of a picture or repeating phrases is not meditation. Meditation is a part of relationship; it is seeing the process of thought in the mirror of relationship. Meditation is not subjugation but understanding the whole process of thinking. Then thought comes to an end, and only in that ending is there the beginning of understanding.

Question: What happens to an individual at death? Does he continue, or does he go to annihilation?

KRISHNAMURTI: Now, it is very interesting to find out from what point of view we are approaching this question. Please put this question to yourself and find out how you as an individual approach it. Why do you put this question? What is the motive that makes you ask about total annihilation? Either you are approaching the question because you want to know the truth of it, and are therefore not seeking self-gratification, or you want a solution because you are afraid. If you approach it with the idea that you are afraid of death and want to continue, then your question will have a gratifying answer because you are merely seeking consolation. Then you may just as well adopt a new belief that will satisfy you or take a drug that will make you dull. When you suffer, you want to be made dull. Suffering is the response of sensitiveness; that is, sensitiveness makes for pain, and when there is pain you want a drug. So, either you want to find the truth of this question or you are merely seeking a means to lull yourself to sleep—only you don't put it so crudely. You want to be comforted; you ask because you are afraid of death, and you want to be sure of continuity. According to your approach, you will find the answer, obviously. If you are seeking consolation, then you are not seeking truth; if you are afraid, then you are not trying to find out what is real. So, first you have to be very earnest in your thinking. Most of us are afraid of seeking the truth. Most of us are scared of there being no continuity, and we want to be assured that we will continue. Let us find out whether there is continuity—you may want it, but it may not be there.

What do you mean by continuity and coming to an end? What is it that continues? We are trying to find the truth of continuity and the truth of noncontinuity, so we have to examine what it is that continues in your daily life. Have you noticed yourself in continuation—in relation to your property, your family, your ideas? You say a hundred times, "This is my property, my reputation," and it becomes continuity. You say, "This is my name, my wife, my work, my job, these are my ambitions, my characteristics or tendencies; I am a big entity, or a little entity trying to become a big entity"—and that is what you are in daily life, not spiritually, but actually. Obviously, those are all memories, and you want to know if that bundle of memories, identified as yourself, will continue. You are not separate from the bundle. There is no 'you' as an entity different from memory. The 'you' may be placed at a higher level, but even at that level it is within the whole field of memory, of thought; and you want to know whether it will continue. Memory is word, symbol, picture, image; without the word there is no memory. The symbol, the image, the past picture, the memory of certain relationships—all that is 'you', which is the word. You want to know whether that word, which is identified with memory, will continue. In other words, you are seeking immortality through memory identified as 'you'. You are not different from the various qualities which go toward making the 'you'. So, you are the house, the memory, the experience, the family; you are not separate from the idea. And you want to know whether that 'you' continues.

Now, why do you want to know? What is the motive, what is the urge? You say, "I am finished, I must have space in which to grow, to become; life is too short, I must have another chance." Now, have you noticed that idea, thought, can continue? You can experience it for yourself—it is simple. Thought as memory, as idea, continues. So you have the question answered. The 'you' that continues is merely a bundle of memories; that is, when there is identification of thought as 'I am,' this superficial thing in some form or other continues, as thought did before. The 'you' as an idea, as thought, continues, but that is not very satisfactory because you have an idea that you are something more than thought, and you want to know if that something more continues. There is nothing more—'you' are merely the result of social, environmental influences; that is, 'you' are the result of conditioning. You may say, "What nonsense it is to talk of a future life—it is superstitious rot"; others, who are differently conditioned, believe there is something more. Surely, there is not much difference between the two. Both are conditioned, one to believe and the other not to believe. Belief in any form is detrimental to the discovery of truth. Belief in continuity and belief in noncontinuity are both detrimental to the discovery of truth. To find out what truth is, there can be no fear and no belief—which fetter the mind. Only when continuity ends can you know the truth of what is beyond continuity.

To put it differently, death is the unknown, it is ever new, and to understand it, you must go to it with a fresh mind, a mind that is new, not merely a continuation of the past. In that state you are capable of knowing the significance of death. At present we know neither life nor death, and we are anxious to know what death is. Thought must end for life to be. There must be death in order for life to flourish. When life is only the continuation of thought, such continuity can never know reality. If you are seeking continuity, you have it in your house, in your work, in your children, in your name, in your property, in certain qualities—all that is 'you', it is thought continued. Immortality can be known only when thinking ceases, when, through understanding, the process of thought comes to an end. You can only think about something that you know. So when you think of yourself as a spiritual entity, it is your own projection, something born out of the past; therefore, it is not spiritual. It is only when you understand continuity that thought comes to an end—which is an extraordinary process requiring a great deal of alertness, not discipline, vows, dogmas, creeds, beliefs, and all the rest of it. There is immortality only when the mind is completely still, and that stillness comes when thought is wholly understood.

Question: I pray to God, and my prayers are answered. Is this not proof of the existence of God?

KRISHNAMURTI: If you have proof of the existence of God, then it is not God (Laughter) because proof is of the mind. How can the mind prove or disprove God? Therefore, your god is a projection of the mind according to your satisfaction, appetite, happiness, pleasure, or fear. Such a thing is not God but merely a creation of thought, a projection of the known, which is past. What is known is not God, though the mind may look for it, may be active in the search for God.

The questioner says that his prayers are answered and asks if this is not proof of the existence of God. Do you want proof of love? When you love somebody, do you seek proof? If you demand proof of love, is that love? If you love your wife, your child, and you want proof, then love is surely a bargain. So your prayer to God is merely bargaining. (Laughter) Don't laugh it off, look at it seriously, as a fact. The questioner approaches what he calls God through supplication and petition. You cannot find reality through sacrifice, through duty, through responsibility, because these are means to an end, and the end is not different from the means. The means are the end.

The other part of the question is, "I pray to God, and my prayers are answered." Let us examine that. What do you mean by prayer? Do you pray when you are joyous, when you are happy, when there is no confusion, no misery? You pray when there is misery, when there is disturbance, fear, turmoil, and your prayer is supplication, petition. When you are in misery, you want somebody to help you out, a higher entity to give you a helping hand, and that process of supplication in different forms is called prayer. So, what happens? You put out your begging bowl to someone; it does not matter who it is—an angel, or your own projection whom you call God. The moment you beg, you have something—but whether that something is real or not is a different question. You want your confusion, your miseries solved, so you get out your traditional phrases, you turn on your devotion, and the constant repetition obviously makes the mind quiet. But that is not quietness—the mind is merely dulled and put to sleep. In that induced quiet, when there is supplication, there is an answer. But it is not at all an answer from God—it is from your own ornamental projection. Here is the answer to the question. But you do not want to inquire into all this, that is why the question is put. Your prayer is supplication—you are only concerned to get a response to your prayer because you want to be free from trouble. Something is gnawing at your heart, and by praying, you make yourself dull and quiet. In that artificial quietness there is a response—obviously satisfying, otherwise you would reject it. Your prayer is satisfying, and therefore it is what you yourself have created. It is your own projection that helps you out—that is one type of prayer. Then there is the deliberative type of prayer to make the mind quiet, receptive, and open. How can the mind be open when it is conditioned by tradition, the background of the past? Openness implies understanding, the capacity to follow the imponderable. When the mind is held, tethered to a belief, it cannot be open. When it is deliberately opened, obviously any answer it receives is a projection of itself. Only when the mind is unconditioned, when it knows how to deal with each problem as it arises—only then is there no longer a problem. As long as the background continues, it must create a problem; as long as there is continuity, there must be everincreasing turmoil and misery. Receptivity is the capacity to be open, without condemnation or justification, to *what is;* and it is that from which you try to escape through prayer.

January 8, 1950

Fourth Talk in Colombo

Surely, there is great confusion everywhere, not only within ourselves individually, but also in the world and among our so-called leaders. When there is confusion, there is a desire to find someone who will lead us out of our difficulties, and we turn to some kind of authority. We turn the responsibility over to our leaders, or seek a pattern of action, or look to the past or to the future to try to find out what ought to be done. Our morality is based on the pattern of yesterday or the ideal of tomorrow, and when tradition and the ideal of the future both fail, we turn to some authority. Because, most of us want security, we want some kind of refuge from all this turmoil, and we seek it in morality according to a pattern of the past, or in some sort of ideal; we cling to an example, hoping to see our way out of our confusion, out of our uncertainty. Our ideal is a projection of ourselves, created by the interpretation of various books, and our whole intention and purpose is to find something—a person, an idea, or a system—that will lead us out of this confusion. So, being confused, being uncertain, we seek external or inward authority and spend our energies in trying to conform ourselves either to the pattern of tradition or the ideal of what should be. Obviously, conformity at any level denies intelligence, which is the capacity to adjust, the capacity of quick response to challenge; and when that intelligence is not functioning, then we conform to a pattern, to authority. That is what is happening in the world at present, is it not? We are confused individually, and being confused, being insecure in ourselves, we turn to somebody. To find out, is it not necessary to be insecure, to be uncertain? Can you find anything if you are certain? Is it not essential to be uncertain to discover reality, or what you will? There must be this state of uncertainty, this state of constant inquiry—not to find a result, but to inquire into each incident, each thought and feeling as it arises, which is to understand experience from moment to moment.

So, being confused, being uncertain, is not the following of a pattern detrimental to intelligence, to real inward integrity? Because, the pattern, the system, eventually leads to security, and how can a person who is psychologically secure ever find anything? Obviously, you must be physically secure, but physical security is destroyed as long as we are seeking psychological security. Surely, the desire for psychological security prevents creative response to life, which is intelligence. So, our problem is obviously not the substitution of one pattern for another, but how to be free of patterns, so that we can respond to every challenge anew. This is reality, is it not? Reality is to understand every moment of life as it is, without interpreting it according to our past experience. A mind that is bound by authority, whether its own or that of another, a mind that is conforming, imitating, following a particular pattern of action—how can such a mind be capable of understanding the real, of understanding *what is* at every moment of thought and feeling? The mind that is burdened with authority, with confusion, with discipline, obviously cannot find that which is free. Can a mind that is disciplined, controlled, subjugated, ever be free? Can a wrong means lead to a right end? To discover the real, the mind must be free at the beginning, not at some ultimate end. How can there be freedom for the mind that is conforming, that is merely imitating, following a certain course of action? And the mind will follow patterns of action, it will discipline itself, it will conform, as long as there is fear of psychological uncertainty. Physically you must have clothes, food, shelter; but when there is psychological certainty, does it not exclude inquiry and so discovery? Surely, discovery is possible only in freedom, not in a course of action disciplined according to a pattern.

So, our inquiry is about not what is discipline, or what system or course of action to follow, but how to free the mind from the fear of being insecure. Is it not essential for the mind to be insecure? Obviously, only in insecurity can there be understanding of what is false. It requires a certain alertness, the nonacceptance of any authority. So, a mind that desires to understand reality must be free at the very beginning from all compulsion, inward or outward; that is, it must be in a state of uncertainty, not tethered to any particular belief or ideal, which is merely a refuge. Only then, surely, is the mind carefree, aloof, happy, and only such a mind is capable of understanding that which is true. The capacity to understand requires freedom from conformity, which is freedom from fear. After all, we conform because we do not know, and we are afraid, but is it not a fact that not-knowing is essential for the unknown to be? If you observe, you will see how the mind is constantly moving from the known to the known, but only when the mind is free from the known is it possible to receive the unknown, which means it must be entirely free from all sense of conformity, authority, or imitation. The major calamity of modern civilization is that we are like so many gramophone records repeating what is said in the books, whether it is the Koran, the Bible, or what you will. Surely, a mind that repeats is not really in search of understanding, for it is incapable of being uncertain, and uncertainty is essential in order to find.

Question: Why don't you participate in politics or in social reform?

KRISHNAMURTI: Have you noticed how politics and social reform have become extraordinarily predominant in our lives at the present time? All our newspapers and most of the magazines, except the purely escapist ones, are full of politics, economics, and other problems. Have you ever asked yourself why they are that way, why human beings are giving such extraordinary importance to politics, economics, and social reform? Reforms are obviously necessary because of the economic, social, and political confusion and the general deterioration of the state of man following the two wars. So, crowds gather round political leaders; people line the streets, watching them as though they were strange animals trying to solve the problem on the economic, social, or political level, independent of the total process of man. Are these problems to be tackled separately, unrelated to the whole psychological problem of man? You may have a perfect system that you think will solve the economic problems of the world, but another will also have a perfect system, and the two systems, representing two different ideologies, will fight each other. As long as you are fighting over ideas, systems, there cannot be a true, radical revolution, there cannot be fundamental social transformation. Ideas do not transform people. What brings about transformation is freedom from ideas. Revolution based on ideas is no longer revolution but merely a continuation of the past in a modified state. Obviously, that is not revolution.

The questioner wants to know why I don't take part in politics or in social reform. Surely, if you can understand the total process of man, then you are dealing with the fundamental issues, not merely trimming particular branches of the tree. But most of us are not interested in the entire problem. We are concerned merely with reconciliation, superficial adjustment, not with the fundamental understanding of man as a total process. It is very much easier to be an expert on one particular level. The experts on the economic or political level leave the psychological level to other experts, and so we become slaves to experts; we are sacrificed by experts for an idea. So, there can be fundamental revolution only in understanding the total process of yourself, not as an individual opposed to the mass, to society, but as an individual interrelated with society; because without you there is no society, without you there is no relationship with another. There is no revolution, no fundamental transformation, as long as we do not understand ourselves. Reformers and so-called revolutionists are really factors of retrogression in society. A reformer tries to patch up the present society, or create a new one, on the basis of an ideology, and his idea is the conditioned response to a pattern; and such revolution, based on an ideology, can never produce a fundamental, radical transformation in social relationships. What we are concerned with is not reformation or modified continuity, which you call revolution, but the fundamental transformation of man in his relationship with man; and as long as that basic change does not take place in the individual, we cannot produce a new social order. That fundamental transformation does not depend on belief, on religious organizations, or on any political or economic system—it depends on your understanding of yourself in relationship with another. That is the real revolution that must take place, and then you as an individual will have an extraordinary influence in society. But without that transformation, merely to talk about revolution or to sacrifice yourself for a so-called practical idea—which is not really sacrifice at all—is obviously mere repetition, which is retrogression.

Question: Do you believe in reincarnation and karma?

KRISHNAMURTI: Now I suppose you will settle back in your seats and feel comfortable. What do you mean by "believe," and why do you want to believe? Is belief necessary to find out what is true? To find out what is true, you must approach life afresh, you must have the capacity to see things anew, but the mind that is cradled in belief is obviously incapable of discovering what is new. So, before you can discover whether there is reincarnation or not, you must find out if your mind is free from belief. Most of us believe because it is convenient, because it is satisfying; in it there is a great deal of hope. It is like taking some drug or narcotic and feeling pacified. Such a belief is a projection of our own desire. So, to find out the truth of any matter, obviously there must be freedom from hypothesis, from belief, from any form of conclusion—whether of Buddha, Christ, yourself, or your grandmother. You must approach it afresh, and only then are you capable of discovering what is true. Belief is an impediment to reality, and that is a very difficult pill to swallow for most of us. We are not seeking reality; we want gratification, and belief gives us gratification, it pacifies us. So, we are essentially seeking gratification, escaping from the problem, from pain and suffering. Therefore we are not really seeking the truth. To find the truth, there must be the direct experiencing of sorrow, pain, and pleasure, but not through a screen of belief.

So, similarly, let us find out what you mean by reincarnation—the truth of it, not what you like to believe, not what someone has told you, or what your teacher has said. Surely, it is the truth that liberates, not your own conclusion, your own opinion. Now, what do you mean by reincarnation? To reincarnate, to be reborn—what do you mean by that? What is it that actually comes into birth again?—not what you believe or do not believe. Please put all that aside, it is only childish stuff. Let us find out what it is that comes back again or reincarnates. To find that out, you must first know what it is that you are. When you say, "I shall be reborn," you must know what the 'I' is. That is the question, is it not? I am not dodging it. Don't think this is a clever move of mine. You will see the problem clearly as we proceed, as we explore. You say, "I shall be reborn." What is the 'I' that is to be reborn? Is the 'I' a spiritual entity, is the 'I' something continuous, is the 'I' something independent of memory, experience, knowledge? Either the 'I' is a spiritual entity or it is merely a thought process. Either it is something out of time which we call spiritual, not measurable in terms of time, or it is within the field of time, the field of memory, thought. It cannot be something else. Let us find out if it is beyond the measurement of time. I hope you are following all this. Let us find out if the 'I' is in essence something spiritual. Now, by "spiritual" we mean, do we not, something not capable of being conditioned, something that is not the projection of the human mind, something that is not within the field of thought, something that does not die. When we talk of a spiritual entity, we mean by that something which is not within the field of the mind, obviously. Now, is the 'I' such a spiritual entity? If it is a spiritual entity, it must be beyond all time; therefore it cannot be reborn or continued. Thought cannot think about it because thought comes within the measure of time, thought is from yesterday, thought is a continuous movement, the response of the past; so thought is essentially a product of time. If thought can think about the 'I', then it is part of time; therefore that 'I' is not free of time, therefore it is not spiritual—which is obvious. So, the 'I', the 'you' is only a process of thought; and you want to know whether that process of thought, continuing apart from the physical body, is born again, is reincarnated in a physical form. Now go a little further. That which continues—can it ever discover the real, which is beyond time and measurement? We are experimenting to discover truth, not exchanging opinions. That 'I', that entity which is a thought process—can it ever be new? If it cannot, then there must be an ending to thought. Is not anything that continues inherently destructive? That which has continuity can never renew itself. As long as thought continues through memory, through desire, through experience, it can never renew itself; therefore, that which is continued cannot know the real. You may be reborn a thousand times, but you can never know the real, for only that which dies, that which comes to an end, can renew itself.

The other part of the question is whether I believe in karma. What do you mean by the word *karma?* To do, to act, to be. Let us try to find out in spite of old women's tales. Karma implies, does it not, cause and effect—action based on cause, producing a certain effect; action born out of conditioning, producing further results. So karma implies cause and effect. And are cause and effect static, are cause and effect ever fixed? Does not effect become cause also? So there is no fixed cause or fixed effect. Today is a result of yesterday, is it not? Today is the outcome of yesterday, chronologically as well as psychologically; and today is the cause of tomorrow. So cause is effect, and effect becomes cause—it is one continuous movement; there is no fixed cause or fixed effect. If there were a fixed cause and a fixed effect, there would be specialization, and is not specialization death? Any species that specializes obviously comes to an end. The greatness of man is that he cannot specialize. He may specialize technically, but in structure he cannot specialize. An acorn seed is specialized—it cannot be anything but what it is. But the human being does not end completely. There is the possibility of constant renewal; he is not limited by specialization. As long as we regard the cause, the background, the conditioning, as unrelated to the effect, there must be conflict between thought and the background. So the problem is much more complex than whether to believe in reincarnation or not, because the question is how to act, not whether you believe in reincarnation or in karma. That is absolutely irrelevant. Your action is merely the outcome of certain causes, and that action modifies future action—therefore there is no escape from conditioning.

So, to put our problem differently, can action ever bring about freedom from this chain of cause-effect? I have done something in the past; I have had experience, which obviously conditions my response today, and today's response conditions tomorrow. That is the whole process of karma, cause and effect; and obviously, though it may temporarily give pleasure, such a process of cause and effect ultimately leads to pain. That is the real crux of the matter: Can thought be free? Thought, action, that is free does not produce pain, does not bring about conditioning. That is the vital point of this whole question. So, can there be action unrelated to the past? Can there be action not based on idea? Idea is the continuation of yesterday in a modified form, and that continuation will condition tomorrow, which means action based on idea can never be free. As long as action is based on idea, it will inevitably produce further conflict. Can there be action unrelated to the past? Can there be action without the burden of experience, the knowledge of yesterday? As long as action is the outcome of the past, action can never be free, and only in freedom can you discover what is true. What happens is that as the mind is not free, it cannot act; it can only react, and reaction is the basis of our action. Our action is not action but merely the continuation of reaction because it is the outcome of memory, of experience, of yesterday's response.

So, the question is, Can the mind be free from its conditioning? Surely, that is implied in this question of karma and reincarnation. As long as there is continuity of thought, action must be limited; and such action creates opposition, conflict, and karma—the response of the past in conjunction with the present, creating a modified continuity. So, a mind which has continuity, which is based on continuity—can such a mind be free? If it cannot be free, is it possible for continuity to cease? This is a most important question. To discover whether the mind can ever be free from the background implies a tremendous inquiry. Is not the mind based on the background? Is not thought founded upon the past? So, can thought ever free itself from the past? All that thought can do is to come to an end—but obviously not through compulsion, not through effort, not through any form of discipline, control, or subjugation. As an observer, see the truth of what it means for thought to come to an end. See the truth, the significance of it, and the false response is removed. That is what we are trying to do in answering this particular question. When there is action not based on idea or on the past, then the mind is silent, absolutely silent. In that silence, action is free from idea. But you will want an answer to your question: whether I believe or not in reincarnation. Do you know, are you any wiser, if I say I believe in it or do not believe in it? I hope you are confused about it. To be satisfied by words of explanation indicates a petty mind, a stupid mind. Examine the whole process of yourself. That examination can take place only in relationship, and to discover the truth in any relationship, there must be a state of constant watchfulness, constant, passive alertness. That will show you the truth, for which you need no confirmation from anybody. As long as thought continues, there can be no reality; as long as thought continues as the yesterday, there must be confusion and conflict. Only when the mind is still, passively watchful, is it possible for the real to be.

Question: Why are you against nationalism?

KRISHNAMURTI: Aren't you against nationalism? Why are you a nationalist? Is not nationalism, calling yourself English, Tamil, or God knows what else, one of the fundamental reasons for war, for the appalling destruction and misery in the world? What is this process of identifying yourself with a group, with a particular country, whether economically, socially, or politically? What is the reason for calling yourself a man of Ceylon, an Indian, a German, an American, a Russian, or whatever it is? Social conditioning and economic pressure make you identify yourself with a group. That is one factor. But why do you identify yourself with something? That is the problem. You identify yourself with the family, with an idea, or with what you call God. Why do you identify yourself with something that you consider great? I live in a little village; I am nobody, but if I call myself a Hindu, if I identify myself with a certain class or caste, then I am somebody. Psychologically, I am nobody—empty, insufficient, lonely, poor; but if I identify myself with something great, I become great. (Laughter) Don't laugh it off, this is what you are actually doing—you call it nationalism, for which you sacrifice everything. A sovereign government must always be on the defensive against attack by some enemy, but you are willing to destroy yourself for an idea, which is your desire to be something great. Actually, you are not great, you are still what you were, only you call yourself a big man. Nationalism is false; like belief, it divides people, and as long as you are nationalistic, you cannot have physical security.

Question: What do you mean when you say that the thinker and the thought are one?

KRISHNAMURTI: This is a serious question, and you will have to be a little attentive. Now, are we not aware that there is the thinker apart from the thought, that the thinker is an entity separate from the process of thought? Because, the thinker is operating on thought, trying to control, subjugate, modify, or even find a substitute for thought. So, we say there is the thinker separate from thought. Now, is that so? Is the thinker separate from thought? If he is, why is he separate; what has brought about this separation? Is it so in reality, or is it an illusion? Is there actually a thinker separate from thought, or only thought separating itself as the thinker? Surely, thought has created the thinker; the thinker is not beyond thought, the thinker is the product of thought. So, the idea that the thinker is separate from thought is false. It is thought that makes the thinker, and if there were no capacity to think at all, there would be no thinker. The thinker comes into being through thought, and why has this separation taken place? Obviously, for the simple reason that thought is constantly changing; that is, recognizing itself to be in transformation, in change, in constant flux, thought creates an entity, the thinker, to give itself permanency. So desire for permanency creates the thinker. Obviously, thoughts are impermanent, but the entity, the thinker, feels himself to be permanent. Actually, there is no thinker at all; there is only thought creating a permanent entity because there is fear of impermanency. Therefore, it is an illusion. Most of us think this false process is a real process, and because there is the thinker and the thought, because there is the experiencer who is always experiencing, there is no integration. There is integration only when thought does not create the thinker, which means that thought does not identify itself as "my" thought, "my" achievement, "my" experience—for it is this "my" that separates the thought from the thinker. When there is the experience of integration between thought and the thinker, there is a fundamental revolution in thinking. Then there is no entity dominating or controlling thought, there is no longer the idea of a 'me' becoming something, growing more perfect, more virtuous. The complete integration is when there is only the thought to be understood through right meditation. There is no time now to discuss what is right meditation, we will do it next Sunday—it requires a great deal of time; but integration, that complete revolution in thinking, can be understood only in relationship.

Question: Is belief in God necessary or helpful?

KRISHNAMURTI: As I said, belief in any form is a hindrance. A man who believes in God can never find God. If you are open to reality, there can be no belief in reality. If you are open to the unknown, there can be no belief in it. After all, belief is a form of self-protection, and only a petty mind can believe in God. Look at the belief of the aviators during the war who said God was their companion as they were dropping bombs! So you believe in God when you kill, when you are exploiting people. You worship God and go on ruthlessly extorting money, supporting the army—yet you say you believe in mercy, compassion, kindliness. Obviously, such belief is a hindrance to the understanding of reality. All belief in any form is a hindrance, including your belief in God. Your belief is a hindrance to the discovery of the real because it is based on an idea or patterned after a tradition. As long as belief exists, there can never be the unknown; you cannot think about the unknown; thought cannot measure it. The mind is the product of the past; it is the result of yesterday, and can such a mind be open to the unknown? It can only project an image, but that projection is not real; so your god is not God—it is an image of your own making, an image of your own gratification. There can be reality only when the mind understands the total process of itself and comes to an end. When the mind is completely empty—only then is it capable of receiving the unknown. The mind is not purged until it understands the content of relationship—its relationship with property, with people—until it has established the right relationship with everything. Until it understands the whole process of conflict in relationship, the mind cannot be free. Only when the mind is wholly silent, completely inactive, not projecting, when it is not seeking and is utterly still—only then that which is eternal and timeless comes into being. This is not speculation, something which you can learn from another; it is not sentiment or sensation—it is a thing that has to be experienced. You cannot experience it as long as the mind is active. Silence of the mind is not achieved by action; it is not a thing to be gone after; it comes only when conflict ceases. To understand one's conflict in relationship is the beginning of wisdom, and when the mind is tranquil, that which is eternal comes into being.

January 15, 1950

Fifth Talk in Colombo

This is the last talk, and it will be more or less a summary of what we have been discussing here for the last four or five weeks.

It must seem very odd to most of us that life has become such a struggle at all levels of existence—not only physically, but psychologically as well; inwardly as well as outwardly. We seem to be on a battlefield of the world, and we have accepted, we have taken for granted, that conflict is the natural state of man. This conflict, this struggle, is the picture of man which so-called philosophers seem to have created; and we have accepted that as our normal life in relationship, not only with regard to property, but also in our relationship with people. There is this constant battle, individual and collective, between men and women, between man and man, between man and society; and there is also conflict between ideas, between the ideology of the left and of the right, between various beliefs, whether religious or secular, whether economic, social, or political. So, there is constant division going on between man and man, not only outwardly, but inwardly.

Can we understand, can we actually create anything, in a state of conflict? Can you write a book, paint a picture, can you appreciate another human being, feel with him or love him, if there is conflict? Surely, conflict is the antithesis of understanding, and through conflict there can be no understanding at any time, at any level. We have philosophically accepted that conflict is inevitable, and perhaps we are entirely wrong to accept such a thesis, such an idea. Can understanding come from conflict, from warfare, from a proletarian revolution? To understand the structure of society and bring about a radical revolution, must you not understand what is actual, and not create the opposite and thus bring about conflict? Does conflict bring about a synthesis? To understand, surely, we must see, examine, *what is* actually, and not bring in other ideas about it; obviously, only then is it possible to solve the problem. As long as we approach the problem with ideas, with a conclusion, with opinions, with belief, with schemes, with systems of any kind, surely it prevents understanding. There are the problems of starvation, of unemployment, of war, to be solved. What is actually happening? The systems, based on left or right ideologies, are setting man against man; and in the meantime, there is still starvation. So, systems, ideologies, obviously do not solve the problem, yet we are fighting each other over ideas and particular systems. Surely, we must approach the problem without any conclusions of the past, for it is obvious that conclusions prevent understanding of the problem.

So, we can see that conflict at any level indicates deterioration—it is a sign of the disintegration of society as well as of the individual. If we see, not theoretically but actually, that conflict invariably prevents understanding, that through conflict you can never bring about harmony, surely then our approach to the problem is entirely different, is it not? Then our attitude undergoes a fundamental change. Up to now, our approach to the problem has created other problems, mounting sorrow and pain, which are ever the result of conflict and lack of understanding of the problem, and understanding can come only when there is no conflict. If I want to understand you, there must not be any conflict; on the contrary, I must look at you, I must observe you, I must study you, not with previous conclusions, schemes, or systems. Those are all prejudices, and prejudice prevents understanding. I must have a very clear mind, undimmed by any prejudice, any previous knowledge. Only such a mind is capable of understanding the problem, and in that approach lies the solution. The purgation of the mind, surely, is the first requirement in understanding the problem. The mind which is constantly in conflict, grappling, must be free from its own conditioning to meet the problem, whether economic, personal, or social.

So, what is important is how we approach any problem. It is essential that we see very clearly the relationship which creates conflict. It is the lack of right relationship that brings about conflict; and it is therefore essential that we understand conflict in relationship, the whole process of our thought and action. Obviously, if we do not understand ourselves in relationship, whatever society we create, whatever ideas, opinions we may have, will only bring about further mischief and further misery. Therefore, the understanding of the whole process of oneself in relationship with society is the first step in understanding the problem of conflict. Self-knowledge is the beginning of wisdom, because you are the world, you are not separate from the world. Society is your relationship with another; you have created it, and the solution lies through your own understanding of that relationship, the interaction between you and society. Without understanding yourself, to seek for a solution is utterly useless—it is merely an escape. Therefore, what is important is understanding relationship. It is relationship which causes conflict, and that relationship cannot be understood unless we have the capacity to be passively watchful; then, in that passive alertness, in that awareness, there comes understanding.

Question: What is the simple life, and how can I live a simple life in the modern world?

KRISHNAMURTI: The simple life has to be discovered, is it not so? There is no pattern for a simple life. Having few clothes, a loincloth, and a begging bowl does not indicate a simple life. It must be discovered. Surely, to make a pattern for a simple life does not bring about simplicity; on the contrary, it creates complexity. What do we mean by the simple life? Having but few clothes, going about half-naked, possessing little—does that indicate the simple life? Is not life much more complex than that? Obviously, one must have but few things. It is silly, foolish, stupid, to have many things and depend on them. Man has many possessions, and he clings to them—his property, his title, and so on. But is it the simple life for a man to have innumerable beliefs, or even one belief? Dependence on systems, authority, the urge to become, to attain, to acquire, to imitate, to conform, to discipline oneself according to a particular pattern—is that the simple life? Does that indicate simplicity? Surely, simplicity must begin, not merely in the expression of outward things, but much deeper. The man who is simple has no conflict. Conflict indicates an escape towards the more or towards the less. That is, conflict indicates acquisitiveness, the desire to become something more or something less, and a man who wants to become something, is he a simple entity? You despise the man who is trying to acquire wealth, possessions, and you appreciate the man who is supposed not to be interested in worldly things but who is striving to become virtuous, or to become like Buddha, Christ, or to follow a certain pattern—you will say he is a marvelous entity. Surely, the man who is striving to become something in the world is the same as the man who wants to be spiritual. Both are united in one desire—to become someone or something, either respectable or so-called spiritual.

Surely, the simple life is not something theatrical. It can be discovered in daily life; in this rotten world, which after two dreadful wars is perhaps preparing for a third, we can live simply, not only outwardly but inwardly. Why do we give such importance to the outward manifestations of simplicity? Why do we inevitably begin at the wrong end? Why don't we begin at the right end, which is the psychological? Surely, we must begin at the psychological end to find what is the simple life because it is the inner that creates the outer. It is inward insufficiency that makes people cling to property, to beliefs; it is this sense of inward insufficiency that forces us to accumulate goods, clothes, knowledge, virtue. Surely, in that way we can only create much more mischief, much more harm. It is extraordinarily difficult to have a simple mind—not the so-called intellectual mind of the educated, but the simplicity that comes when we understand something, that simplicity that perceives the problem of *what is.* Surely, we cannot understand anything when our mind is complex. I don't know if you have noticed that when you are worried over a problem, when you are concerned about something, you do not see anything very clearly; it is all out of focus. Only when the mind is simple and vulnerable is it possible to see things clearly, in their true proportion. So simplicity of the mind is essential for simplicity of life. The monastery is not the solution. Simplicity comes when the mind is not attached, when the mind is not acquiring, when the mind accepts *what is.* It really means freedom from the background, from the known, from the experience it has acquired. Only then is the mind simple, and then only is it possible to be free. There cannot be simplicity as long as one belongs to any particular religion, to any particular class or society, to any dogma, either of the left or of the right. To be simple inwardly, to be clear, to be vulnerable, is to be like a flame without smoke, and therefore you cannot be simple without love. Love is not an idea; love is not thought. It is only in the cessation of thinking that there is the possibility to know that simplicity which is vulnerable.

Question: I find that loneliness is the underlying cause of many of my problems. How can I deal with it?

KRISHNAMURTI: What do you mean by loneliness? Are you actually aware that you are lonely? Surely, loneliness is not a state of aloneness. Very few of us are alone; we don't want to be alone. It is essential to understand that aloneness is not isolation. Surely, there is a difference between being alone and isolation. Isolation is the sense of being enclosed, the sense of having no relationships, a feeling that you have been cut off from everything. That is entirely different from being alone, which is to be extraordinarily vulnerable. When we are lonely, a feeling of fear, anxiety, the ache of finding oneself in isolation, comes over one. You love somebody, you feel that without that somebody you are lost, so that person becomes essential to you in order for you not to feel the sense of isolation. So, you use the person in order to escape from what you are. That is why we try to establish relationship, a communion with another, or establish a contact with things, property—just so that we feel alive; we acquire furniture, dresses, cars, we seek to accumulate knowledge or become addicted to love. By loneliness we mean that state which comes upon the mind, a state of isolation, a state in which there is no contact, no relationship, no communion with anything. We are afraid of it; we call it painful, and being afraid of what we are, of our actual state, we run away from it, using so many ways of escape—God, drink, the radio, amusements—anything to get away from that sense of isolation. And are not our actions, both in individual relationship and in relationship with society, an isolating process? Is not the relationship of father, mother, wife, husband, an isolating process for us at the present time? Is not that relationship almost always a relationship based on mutual need? So, the process of self-isolation is simple—you are all the time seeking, in your relationships, an advantage for yourself. This isolating process is going on continually, and when awareness of isolation comes upon us through our own activities, we want to run away from it; so we go to the temple, or back to a book, or turn on the radio, or sit in front of a picture and meditate—anything to get away from *what is.*

So, we come to the actual question which is the desire to escape. What do you fear, why are you afraid of the unknown, that insufficiency in yourself, that emptiness? If you are afraid, why do you not look into it? Why should you be afraid of losing what you have, of losing association, contact? What exactly do you know, with your pretensions of knowledge? Your knowledge is but memory; you don't know the living; you know the past—the dead things, the decadent things. So, is it not our trouble that we never find *what is?* We never face the conflict of our insufficiency—we keep smothering it down and suppressing it, running away from it, and we don't know *what is.* Surely, when we approach it without any fear or condemnation, then we come to find the truth of it, and it may be extraordinarily more significant than the significance we give it through fear. Through fear of insufficiency, the mind is operating upon thought—the mind never looks at it, and it is only when we have the capacity to look at thought that there is the possibility of understanding what has made that thought, and thus is revealed to us the whole process of escape from *what is.* Then loneliness is transformed; it becomes aloneness, and that aloneness is a state of vulnerability which is capable of receiving the unknown, the imponderable, the measureless. Therefore, to understand that state of vulnerability, we must understand the whole process of thinking, which means that we must look at it and see its extraordinary qualities. That state cannot be accepted verbally—it must be experienced.

Question: You lay great emphasis on being aware of our conditioning. How can I understand my mind?

KRISHNAMURTI: Is not conditioning inevitable—inevitable in the sense that it is actually taking place all the time? You condition your children as Buddhists, Sinhalese, Tamil, Englishmen, Chinese, communists, and so on. There is a constant impingement of influences—economic, climatic, social, political, religious—acting all the time. Look at yourself: you are either a Buddhist, Sinhalese, Hindu, Christian, or capitalist. That is the whole process—the mind is constantly being conditioned, which means the mind is a result of the past, is founded upon the past. Thought is the response of the past. Mind is the past, mind is part of the past, and the past is tradition, morality. So, action is patterned on the past, or on the future as the ideal. This is the actual state of all who are conditioned. We are the product of the environment—social, economic, or what you will. What you believe is the product of what your father and society have put into you. If they had not put into you the idea of Buddhism, surely you would be something else—Roman Catholic, Protestant, or communist. Your beliefs are the result of your environment, and these beliefs are also created by you because you are the product of the past, and the past in conjunction with the present creates the present social entity. So, your mind is conditioned; that conditioned mind meets the challenge, the stimulus, and invariably responds according to its conditioning, and this is what creates a problem. So, a conditioned mind meeting the challenge creates a problem, which brings on conflict.

Now, if you ask, "Can I be free from conditioning?" your question has validity, not otherwise. As long as the mind is conditioned according to a pattern, it will always respond according to that pattern. There are those who say that the mind cannot be unconditioned, that it is an impossibility; therefore, they substitute a new form of conditioning for the old. Instead of the capitalist, there is the communist; instead of the Roman Catholic, the Protestant or the Buddhist. That is what is actually happening now all over the world. They speak of revolution; it is not revolution, but merely substitution of ideas. Ideas don't produce revolution; they only produce a modified continuity, not revolution. So, there are those who say the mind cannot be unconditioned but can only be reconditioned in a different way. The very assertion implies conditioning. If you say that it can, or that it cannot, you are already conditioned. Therefore, what is important is to find out if the mind can be unconditioned—completely, not superficially or momentarily. How can we do it?

Now, why do you call yourselves Buddhists? You have been told from childhood that you are Buddhists—and why do you accept it and hold on to it? If you can understand that, you will be free of it. What would happen if you didn't hold on to it? If you didn't call yourself a Buddhist, you would feel that you were left out and isolated. So, you do it for economic reasons—that is one factor. Another factor is that you identify yourself with something larger, otherwise you feel lost. You are nobody, but when you say you are a Buddhist, you are somebody; it gives you coloration. So, your desire to be somebody, your desire to be identified with something great, conditions you. The desire to be somebody is the very essence of conditioning. If you had no desire to be somebody, you would not be conditioned in the deeper sense. Surely, being *what is* is the beginning of virtue; contentment is the understanding of *what is.* The desire to be something invariably conditions thought and therefore creates a problem ever deeper and wider, increasing conflict and misery. To be free from conditioning is very simple—experiment with it. When you don't want to be an artist, a Master, a minister, a great, wise, or learned person, then you are nobody. That is the fact, but we don't like to accept it; so we cling to possessions, furniture, books, property. Instead of indulging in pretensions, why not just be small? Then you will see that the mind is extraordinarily pliable, capable of quickly responding to challenge. Such a mind is capable of responding anew to the challenge. Surely, that is clear. Conditioning is not only superficial, in the upper layer of the mind—it is also in the deeper layers; in both the hidden as well as the upper content of the mind there is the desire to be somebody. It is the desire to be somebody, to seek a result, that brings about conditioning, and a conditioned mind can never be revolutionary; it is merely acting according to a pattern—it is somnambulant, not revolutionary. Revolution comes into being when the mind is free, when it does not act according to the past and is aware of its conditioning. Only when the mind is quiet can it be free.

Question: What is right meditation?

KRISHNAMURTI: This is a very complex subject, and it requires a great deal of understanding. Let us go into the question. You and I are going to find out what is right meditation, which means that you and I are going to meditate. How do we understand anything? What is the state of mind for understanding? We are going to find out the many implications of what is meditation. To understand something, you must have communion with it—there must be no barriers. There must be complete integration if you want to understand something new. How would you approach it? You will have to look at it, not condemn or justify it. To understand the problem, the mind must be passively watchful. Meditation is the process of understanding; it is the passive state which brings about discovery of truth. I have discussed meditation before, but now we are discussing it anew. The mind must be extremely quiet to understand deeply. If I want to understand something, my mind must be silent. If I have a problem and want really to understand it, I must not go to it with a worried and agitated mind. I must go with a free mind, for only a passive, alert mind can understand. A mind that is capable of being silent is in a position to receive the truth. Because, you don't know what truth is; if you know the truth, it is not truth. Truth is utterly new, free. It cannot be approached through preconceptions; it is not the experience of another. So, to discover truth, reality, the mind must be absolutely still. That is a requisite for the understanding of any problem, political, economic, or mathematical.

So, it is essential for the mind to be quiet in order to understand. The mind is new only when it is quiet; it is free, tranquil, only when it is not conditioned by the past. It is only then that the unknown is instinctively discovered. So, there must be freedom, and a mind that is disciplined, regimented, is not a free mind—it is not still. Its function is conditioned when it is under discipline. Such a mind is made still by discipline; it is controlled, shaped to be still. For the mind to be really still, there must be freedom, not at the end, but at the beginning. A mind that is overburdened, or a disciplined mind, is incapable of understanding a problem. What brings about freedom?—not a qualified freedom prompted by desire. How does freedom come into being so that the mind may receive the truth? Such freedom can be only when there is virtue. At present, you are striving to become virtuous, and to become something obviously means another form of conditioning. When you strive to become nonviolent, the actual process of striving is violence. That is, in trying to become nonviolent, you are imitating the ideal of nonviolence, which is your own projection. So, the ideal is homemade; it is the outcome of your own violence. Being violent, you create the opposite, but the opposite always contains its own opposite; therefore, the ideal of nonviolence must inevitably contain the element of violence—they are not different. So, the mind that is trying to become merciful, to become humble, is conditioned and therefore can never see the truth. Virtue is the understanding of *what is* without escape. You cannot understand *what is* if you resist it, because understanding requires freedom from conditioned response to *what is;* it not only requires freedom from condemnation and justification, but also from the whole process of terming, or giving a name. Virtue is a state of freedom because virtue brings order and clarity. Virtue is free from becoming; it is the understanding of *what is.* Understanding is not a matter of time, but time is required to escape through the process of acquiring virtue. So, only the mind that is silent can receive the unknown because the unknown is immeasurable. That which is measured is not the unknown; it is known; therefore, it is not true, not real. Freedom comes from virtue, not through discipline. A disciplined mind is an exclusive mind, and there is freedom only when each thought is completely understood without exclusion or distraction. What is called concentration is merely a process of exclusion, and the mind that knows how to exclude, to resist, is not a free mind. You cannot understand thought if you resist it. The mind must be free to meet each thought and understand it fully, and then you will see that thought as an accumulative process comes to an end.

There is also the question of making the mind still through various practices. Is not the thinker, the observer, the same as the thought which he observes? They are not two different processes but one process. As long as there is the thinker as an observer apart from thought, there is no freedom. Meditation is the process of understanding the thinker; meditation is the process of understanding the meditator—that is, understanding oneself at all levels as "my house," "my property," "my wife," "my beliefs," "my knowledge," "my acquisition," "my work." As long as the thinker is separate from thought, there must be conflict, there cannot be freedom. So, understanding the meditator is self-knowledge, which is what we have been doing this evening. The beginning of meditation is the beginning of self-knowledge, because we cannot be free without self-knowledge. Understanding yourself requires passive alertness. There must be freedom at the beginning, not at the end. Truth is not an ultimate end to be personally achieved; it is to be experienced, lived at every minute in relationship. The mind that is silent—not made silent—alone can perceive the immeasurable. The solution to the problem of bringing about quietness without compulsion lies in understanding relationship; therefore, meditation is the beginning of self-knowledge, and self-knowledge is the beginning of wisdom. Wisdom is not the accumulation of knowledge and experience; wisdom is not acquired from books, from ceremonies, or by compulsion. Wisdom comes into being only when there is freedom of the mind, and a still mind will find the timeless, which is the immeasurable come into being. That state is not a state of experience; it is not a state to be remembered. What you remember, you will repeat, and the immeasurable is not repeatable, it cannot be cultivated. The mind must be moved to receive it afresh each time, and a mind that accumulates knowledge, virtue, is incapable of receiving the eternal.

January 22, 1950

Relationship

Relationship is action, is it not? Action has meaning only in relationship; without understanding relationship, action on any level will only breed conflict. The understanding of relationship is infinitely more important than the search for any plan of action. The ideology, the pattern for action, prevents action. Action based on ideology hinders the understanding of relationship between man and man. Ideology may be of the right or of the left, religious or secular, but it is invariably destructive of relationship. The understanding of relationship is true action. Without understanding relationship, strife and antagonism, war and confusion are inevitable.

Relationship means contact, communion. There cannot be communion where people are divided by ideas. A belief may gather a group of people around itself. Such a group will inevitably breed opposition and so form another group with a different belief.

Ideals postpone direct relationship with the problem. It is only when there is direct relationship with the problem, that there is action. But, unfortunately, all of us approach the problem with conclusions, with explanations, which we call ideals. They are the means of postponing action. Idea is thought verbalized. Without the word, the symbol, the image, thought is not. Thought is response of memory, of experience, which are the conditioning influences. These influences are not only of the past but of the past in conjunction with the present. So, the past is always shadowing the present. Idea is the response of the past to the present and so, shadowing the present. Idea is the response of the past to the present and so, idea is always limited, however extensive it may be. So, idea must always separate people.

The world is always close to catastrophe. But it seems to be closer now. Seeing this approaching catastrophe, most of us take shelter in idea. We think that this catastrophe, this crisis, can be solved by an ideology. Ideology is always an impediment to direct relationship, which prevents action. We want peace only as an idea, but not as an actuality. We want peace on the verbal level, which is only on the thinking level, though we proudly call it the intellectual level. But the word *peace* is not peace. Peace can only be when the confusion which you and another make ceases. We are attached to the world of ideas, and not to peace. We search for new social and political patterns, and not for peace; we are concerned with the reconciliation of effects, and not in putting aside the cause of war. This search will bring only answers conditioned by the past. This conditioning is what we call knowledge, experience; and the new changing facts are translated, interpreted, according to this knowledge. So, there is conflict between *what is* and the experience that has been. The past, which is knowledge, must ever be in conflict with the fact, which is ever in the present. So, this will not solve the problem but will perpetuate the conditions which have created the problem.

We come to the problem with ideas about it, with conclusions and answers according to our prejudices. We interpose between ourselves and the problem the screen of ideology. Naturally the answer to the problem is according to the ideology, which only creates another problem without resolving that with which we began.

Relationship is our problem, and not the idea about relationship, not at any one particular level, but at all the levels of our existence. This is the only problem we have. To understand relationship, we must come to it with freedom from all ideology, from all prejudice—not merely from the prejudice of the uneducated, but also from the prejudice of knowledge. There is no such thing as understanding of the problem from past experience. Each problem is new. There is no such thing as an old problem. When we approach a problem, which is always new, with an idea, which is invariably the outcome of the past, our response is also of the past, which prevents understanding the problem.

The search for an answer to the problem only intensifies it. The answer is not away from it but only in the problem itself. We must see the problem afresh, and not through the screen of the past. The inadequacy of response to challenge creates the problem. This inadequacy has to be understood, and not the challenge. We are eager to see the new, and we cannot see it, as the image of the past prevents the clear perception of it. We respond to challenge only as Sinhalese or Tamilians, as Buddhists or as of the left or of the right; this invariably produces further conflict. So, what is important is not seeing the new but the removal of the old. When the response is adequate to the challenge, then only is there no conflict, no problem. This has to be seen in our daily life, and not in the issues of newspapers.

Relationship is the challenge of everyday life. If you and I and another do not know how to meet each other, we are creating conditions that breed war. So, the world problem is your problem. You are not different from the world. The world is you. What you are, the world is. You can save the world, which is yourself, only in understanding the relationship of your daily life, and not through belief, called religion, of the left or of the right, or through any reform, however extensive. The hope is not in the expert, in the ideology, or in the new leader, but it lies in you.

You might ask how you, living an ordinary life in a limited circle, could affect the present world crisis. I do not think you will be able to. The present struggle is the outcome of the past which you and another have created. Until you and another radically alter the present relationship, you will only contribute to further misery. This is not oversimplification. If you go into it fully, you will see how your relationship with another, when extended, brings about world conflict and antagonism.

The world is you. Without the transformation of the individual, which is you, there can be no radical revolution in the world. The revolution in social order without the individual transformation will only lead to further conflict and disaster. For, society is the relationship of you and me and another. Without radical revolution in this relationship, all effort to bring peace is only a reformation, however revolutionary, which is retrogression.

Relationship based on mutual need brings only conflict. However interdependent we are on each other, we are using each other for a purpose, for an end. With an end in view, relationship is not. You may use me and I may use you. In this usage, we lose contact. A society based on mutual usage is the foundation of violence. When we use another, we have only the picture of the end to be gained. The end, the gain, prevents relationship, communion. In the usage of another, however gratifying and comforting it may be, there is always fear. To avoid this fear, we must possess. From this possession there arises envy, suspicion, and constant conflict. Such a relationship can never bring about happiness.

A society whose structure is based on mere need, whether physiological or psychological, must breed conflict, confusion, and misery. Society is the projection of yourself in relation with another, in which the need and the use are predominant. When you use another for your need, physically or psychologically, in actuality there is no relationship at all; you really have no contact with the other, no communion with the other. How can you have communion with the other when the other is used as a piece of furniture for your convenience and comfort? So, it is essential to understand the significance of relationship in daily life.

We do not understand relationship; the total process of our being, our thought, our activity, makes for isolation—which prevents relationship. The ambitious, the crafty, the believer, can have no relationship with another. He can only use another, which makes for confusion and enmity. This confusion and enmity exist in our present social structure; they will exist also in any reformed society as long as there is no fundamental revolution in our attitude towards another human being. As long as we use another as a means towards an end, however noble, there will be inevitably violence and disorder.

Conflict is an indication of not being related; conflict will never bring about the understanding of any problem, whether personal and so of the world. It is imperative that we understand our relationship in our daily life. You might ask, "How will this affect the organization of a new social order?" Society is the relationship of you and me and another.

If you and I bring about fundamental revolution in ourselves, not based on mutual need—either physical or psychological—then has not our relationship to the other undergone a fundamental transformation? Our difficulty is that we have a picture of what the new organized society should be, and we try to fit ourselves into that pattern. The pattern is obviously fictitious. But what is real is that which we are actually. In the understanding of what you are, which is seen clearly in the mirror of daily relationship, to follow the pattern only brings about further conflict and confusion.

The present social disorder and misery must work itself out. But you and I and another can and must see the truth of relationship and so start a new action which is not based on mutual need and gratification. Mere reformation of the present structure of society without altering fundamentally our relationship is retrogression. A revolution which maintains the usage of man towards an end, however promising, is productive of further wars and untold sorrow. The end is always the projection of our own conditioning. However promising and utopian it might be, the end can only be a means of further confusion and pain. What is important in all this is not the new patterns, the new superficial changes, but the understanding of the total process of man, which is yourself.

In the process of understanding yourself, not in isolation but in relationship, you will find that there is a deep, lasting transformation in which the usage of another as a means for your own psychological gratification has come to an end. What is important is not how to act, what pattern to follow, or which ideology is the best, but the understanding of your relationship with another. This understanding is the only revolution, and not the revolution based on idea. Any revolution based on an ideology maintains man as a means only.

As the inner always overcomes the outer, without understanding the total psychological process, which is yourself, there is no basis for thinking at all. Any thought which produces a pattern of action will only lead to further ignorance and confusion.

There is only one fundamental revolution. This revolution is not of idea, it is not based on any pattern of action. This revolution comes into being when the need for using another ceases. This transformation is not an abstraction, a thing to be wished for, but an actuality which can be experienced as we begin to understand the way of our relationship. This fundamental revolution may be called love—it is the only creative factor in bringing about transformation in ourselves and so in society.

Broadcast by Radio Ceylon
January 22, 1950

Bombay, India, 1950

First Talk in Bombay

Is it not important to find out how to listen? It seems to me that most of us do not listen at all. We listen through various screens of prejudice, examining what is being said, either as a Hindu, a Muslim, a Christian, or with a mind already made up. We do not listen freely, easily, and silently. We listen with the intention to agree or to disagree, or we listen in a spirit of argumentation; we do not listen to find out, and it seems to me very important to know how to listen, how to read, to see, to observe. Most of us are incapable of listening truly, and it is only through right listening and hearing that we understand. Understanding comes, not through effort, not through any form of conformity or compulsion, but only when the mind is very quiet. In trying to find out what the other man is saying, there is no strain, no effort, but an easy flow, a swift delight, but we cannot find out what the other man is saying if we listen with any kind of prejudice. Perhaps I may have something new to say, and it will be most difficult for those who are prejudiced, in favor or against, to really understand. Because most of us are conditioned by social, economic, religious influences, and so on, we are copyists, we imitate, and therefore we disregard that which is new; we call it revolutionary or absurd and put it aside. But if we can examine, if we can look at it with freedom from all prejudices, from all limitations, then perhaps it is possible to understand and to commune with each other. There is communion only when there is no barrier, and an idea, a prejudice, is a barrier. When you love somebody, you commune; you have no idea about the person whom you love. Similarly, if we can establish a relationship of real communion between us so that you and I understand the problem together, then there is a possibility of a radical revolution in the world. After all, the world does need, not mere reformation, not a superficial revolution, but a fundamental, radical revolution, a revolution which is not based on an idea. Revolution that is the outcome of an idea is not a fundamental transformation but merely the continuance of a modified idea or pattern. So, let us see if during these talks we can establish between the speaker and the listener a communion that is beyond mere words. Words are necessary for communication, but if we merely remain on that level, surely there is no understanding. Understanding comes when we go beyond the verbal level, but the highly cultivated mind lives on words; it is capable of examining only through the screen of words, and such examination is obviously not understanding; on the contrary, it merely leads to further arguments and disputations.

So, is it not possible for us to establish real communion, not merely on the verbal level, but at a deeper, more worthwhile level? Surely, that is possible, but to do it, you and I have to look at our problems anew—our problems being those of living, of relationship, of the strife between man and man, between groups of people—we have to approach and examine them afresh, for only then is there a possibility of bringing about a fundamental change in our lives and therefore in the life of society. Our first basic problem is one of relationship, is it not, and that relationship is based on the morality of the past or of the future, that is, on traditional precepts, or on an idea of what ought to be. Our morality, upon which our action is based, is the outcome of the past, of the traditional, or of the future, which is the ideal; and when we base our action on the future or on the past, obviously there is no action at all. As long as we live by hope, we cannot act, because hope is obviously the response of a future demand, and as long as we base our action on a hope, on a utopia, on the ideal of perfection or a scheme of what ought to be, we are not living in the present. An idea is always of the future or of the past, and when relationship is considered in terms of the future or the past, naturally no action is possible—action being immediate, always in the present, in the now.

One of our enormous problems is, is it not, to bring about a fundamental revolution in the present existing order. Seeing the disproportion and maldistribution, the whole economic structure of rich and poor, the conflict between those who have and those who have not, and so on, we try to solve the economic and social problems through a scheme, through an idea, through a pattern. There is the pattern, the system of the left and of the right, and these systems are invariably based on an idea. That is, the left starts out to resolve the problem by having a new system which is in conflict with the right, and as long as we are in conflict over ideas, on which all systems are based, obviously there is no solution. To put it differently, there are the problems of starvation, of unemployment, of wars, and we approach them, having already in mind a certain definite system for resolving each one of them. Can any system, whether of the left or of the right, resolve any problem? Both those who are committed to the left and those who are committed to the right consider that they have the perfect, the final, the absolute system, and so both approach the problem of starvation, of unemployment and wars, with an idea, with a prejudice. The result is that the systems, the ideas, the beliefs are in conflict with each other, and the problems remain. If you and I really want to start resolving a problem, surely we must examine the problem directly without the prejudice or screen of a system, for it is only when the mind is free from systems, whether of the left or of the right, that it is possible for us to face the problem itself.

Now, is it possible to have action without idea?—that is really the basic question. The idea is obviously a hope; it is based on the future or on the past, and can we live without hope? Obviously, to live without hope implies understanding the present directly, not in terms of the past or of the future. If we look into our own minds and examine the basis of our thought, we will see that we are thinking in terms of the ideal, of the future, of the hope of becoming something, of attaining a new state. Hope always leads to death, in hope there is no life, for life is in the present, not in the future. Life is neither in the future nor in the past but in the process of living now. So, is it not possible to examine all our problems anew, whatever they be—economic, individual, or collective—to look at them without the pattern, the hope of the future, and without the prejudice, the conditioning of the past? Surely, every challenge is new; otherwise, it is not a challenge, and to meet that challenge, our minds must be fresh, new, not burdened with the past or with the hope of the future. And is it possible for the mind to meet a problem without either the conditioning of the past or the escape, the hope of the future? Surely, it is possible only when you and I as individuals are capable of understanding the problem, whatever it be, personal or collective, and responding to the challenge adequately, fully, and completely; and it is only when the mind is not burdened with knowledge, with experience, that one can respond to the challenge adequately, naturally. That actually means, does it not, that the mind must be capable of being very quiet, because it is only when we are not struggling, when we do not put forward an idea, when the mind is very quiet, that understanding comes. I do not know if you have noticed this in your own daily life. When you are agitated, worrying over a problem, surely you do not understand it, but when the mind is very quiet, free from the past and the future, then it is capable of meeting the challenge adequately. It is the inadequacy of our response to the challenge that creates the problem, and our response to the challenge must be inadequate as long as our actions are based on either the past or the future, on either tradition or hope. Therefore, a man who would really understand the problem of existence and so bring about a radical revolution must be free from the past and the future, from hope and from tradition, from the ideal and from what has been. Such a state of mind is creative, and it is only the creative mind that can understand the present problems, not the mind that is riddled with ideas, inventing schemes, and following ideals, not the mind that is merely copying, imitating, because the challenge is always new, and if we want to understand, we must meet it anew.

So, reality, or whatever name you like to give it, is a state of being in which the mind is no longer swinging between the past and the future, but is perceiving and understanding *what is* from moment to moment. The past and the future are not *what is*. The *what is* is the new; it is unrelated to the past and the future, and to meet it, the mind itself must not be caught in the swing of the past and the future, the mind must not be a passage, a movement of the past to the future. The understanding of *what is* is reality, and reality is not of time, and a mind that is the product of time cannot understand reality. So, the mind must be utterly still, not made still, not compelled, disciplined, or controlled; and it is still only when it understands this whole process of becoming, this movement of time from the past through the present to the future.

Several questions have been sent in, and before I answer them, may I suggest that you and I together try to find the right answers. It is very easy to ask a question and wait for an answer—that is merely a schoolboy trick—but it requires a mature, an intelligent, exploring mind, a mind that is free from prejudices, to take the journey of discovery. So, in considering these questions, we are going to take a journey together and find the truth—not an answer to suit you or me. Truth, surely, is not opinion; truth is not dependent on knowledge, and where there is knowledge, truth is not. Truth is not the result of experience, for experience is memory, and merely to live in memory is to deny truth. To discover truth, the mind must be free, swift, and pliable. Therefore, there must be that art of listening, of hearing, which reveals the truth without effort, because effort is obviously desire, and where there is desire, there is conflict, and conflict is never creative. So, in considering these questions, please do not wait for an answer, because there is no answer. Life has no such answer as a yes or a no; it is much too vast, immeasurable, and to fathom the immeasurable, the mind must be free, silent. Our quest is not to find an opinion, a conclusion with its admissions and denials, but to discover the right answer, the truth of the question. If I may suggest, you and I are going to see if we cannot discover the truth of the problem because it is truth alone that frees you from the problem, not your or my opinion, however wise, however erudite. The man of knowledge, the man of opinion, the man of experience, will never find truth, for the mind must be very simple to find truth, and simplicity is not achieved through learning.

Question: Our lives are empty of any real impulse of kindness, and we seek to fill this void with organized charity and compulsive justice. Sex is our life. Can you throw any light on this weary subject?

KRISHNAMURTI: To translate the question: Our problem is, is it not, that our lives are empty, and we know no love; we know sensations, we know advertising, we know sexual demands, but there is no love. And how is this emptiness to be transformed, how is one to find that flame without smoke? Surely, that is the question, is it not? So, let us find out the truth of the matter together.

Why are our lives empty? Though we are very active, though we write books and go to cinemas, though we play, love, and go to the office, yet our lives are empty, boring, mere routine. Why are our relationships so tawdry, empty, and without much significance? We know our own lives sufficiently well to be aware that our existence has very little meaning; we quote phrases and ideas which we have learned—what so and so has said, what the mahatma, the latest saints, or the ancient saints have said. If it is not a religious, it is a political or intellectual leader that we follow, either Marx or Adler or Christ. We are just gramophone records repeating, and we call this repetition "knowledge." We learn, we repeat, and our lives remain utterly tawdry, boring, and ugly. Why? Why is it like that? If you and I really put that question to ourselves, won't we find the answer? Why is it that we have given so much significance to the things of the mind? Why has the mind become so important in our lives?—mind being ideas, thought, the capacity to rationalize, to weigh, to balance, to calculate. Why have we given such extraordinary significance to the mind?—which does not mean that we must become emotional, sentimental, and gushy. We know this emptiness, we know this extraordinary sense of frustration, and why is there in our lives this vast shallowness, this sense of negation? Surely, we can understand it only when we approach it through awareness in relationship.

What is actually taking place in our relationships? Are not our relationships a self-isolation? Is not every activity of the mind a process of safeguarding, of seeking security, isolation? Is not that very thinking which we say is collective a process of isolation? Is not every action of our life a self-enclosing process? You yourself can see it in your daily life, can't you? The family has become a self-isolating process, and being isolated, it must exist in opposition. So, all our actions are leading to self-isolation, which creates this sense of emptiness; and being empty, we proceed to fill the emptiness with radios, with noise, with chatter, with gossip, with reading, with the acquisition of knowledge, with respectability, money, social position, and so on and on. But these are all part of the isolating process, and therefore they merely give strength to isolation. So, for most of us, life is a process of isolation, of denial, resistance, conformity to a pattern; and naturally in that process there is no life, and therefore there is a sense of emptiness, a sense of frustration. Surely, to love someone is to be in communion with that person, not on one particular level, but completely, integrally, profusely, but we do not know such love. We know love only as sensation—my children, my wife, my property, my knowledge, my achievement; and that again is an isolating process, is it not? Our life in all directions leads to exclusion; it is a self-enclosing momentum of thought and feeling, and occasionally we have communion with another. That is why there is this enormous problem.

Now, that is the actual state of our lives—respectability, possession, and emptiness—and the question is, How are we to go beyond it? How are we to go beyond this loneliness, this emptiness, this insufficiency, this inner poverty? I do not think most of us want to. Most of us are satisfied as we are; it is too tiresome to find out a new thing, so we prefer to remain as we are—and that is the real difficulty. We have so many securities; we have built walls around ourselves with which we are satisfied, and occasionally there is a whisper beyond the wall; occasionally there is an earthquake, a revolution, a disturbance which we soon smother. So, most of us really do not want to go beyond the self-enclosing process; all that we are seeking is a substitution, the same thing in a different form. Our dissatisfaction is so superficial; we want a new thing that will satisfy us, a new safety, a new way of protecting ourselves—which is again the process of isolation. We are actually seeking, not to go beyond isolation, but to strengthen isolation so that it will be permanent and undisturbed. It is only the very few who want to break through and see what is beyond this thing that we call emptiness, loneliness. Those who are seeking a substitution for the old will be satisfied by discovering something that offers a new security, but there are obviously some who will want to go beyond that, so let us proceed with them.

Now, to go beyond loneliness, emptiness, one must understand the whole process of the mind, must one not? What is this thing we call loneliness, emptiness? How do we know it is empty, how do we know it is lonely? By what measure do you say it is "this" and not "that"? Do you understand the problem? When you say it is lonely, it is empty, what is the measure? How do you know it is empty? You can know it only according to the measurement of the old. You say it is empty, you give it a name, and you think you have understood it. Is not the very naming of the thing a hindrance to the understanding of it? Look, sirs, most of us know what this loneliness is, don't we?—this loneliness from which we are trying to escape. Most of us are aware of this inner poverty, this inner insufficiency. It is not an abortive reaction; it is a fact, and by calling it some name, we cannot dissolve it—it is there. Now, how do we know its content, how do we know the nature of it? Do you know something by giving it a name? Do you know me by calling me by a name? You can know me only when you observe me, when you have communion with me, but calling me by a name, saying I am this or that, obviously puts an end to communion with me. Similarly, to know the nature of that thing which we call loneliness, there must be communion with it, and communion is not possible if you name it. To understand something, the naming must cease first. If you want to understand your child at all, which I doubt, what do you do? You look at him, watch him in his play, observe him, study him, don't you? In other words, you love that which you want to understand. When you love something, naturally there is communion with it, but love is not a word, a name, a thought. You cannot love that which you call loneliness because you are not fully aware of it, you approach it with fear—not fear of it but of something else. You have not thought about loneliness because you do not really know what it is. Sirs, don't smile; this is not a clever argument. Experience the thing while we are talking, then you will see the significance of it.

So, that thing which we call the 'empty' is a process of isolation, which is the product of everyday relationship, because in relationship, we are consciously or unconsciously seeking exclusion. You want to be the exclusive owner of your property, of your wife or husband, of your children; you want to name the thing or the person as "mine," which obviously means exclusive acquisition. This process of exclusion must inevitably lead to a sense of isolation, and as nothing can live in isolation, there is conflict, and from that conflict we are trying to escape. All forms of escape of which we can possibly conceive—whether social activities, drink, the pursuit of God, puja, the performance of ceremonials, dancing, and other amusements—are on the same level; and if we see in daily life this total process of escape from conflict and want to go beyond it, we must understand relationship. It is only when the mind is not escaping in any form that it is possible to be in direct communion with that thing which we call loneliness, the alone, and to have communion with that thing, there must be affection, there must be love. In other words, you must love the thing to understand it. Love is the only revolution, and love is not a theory, not an idea; it does not follow any book or any pattern of social behavior. So, the solution of the problem is not to be found in theories, which merely create further isolation; it is to be found only when the mind, which is thought, is not seeking an escape from loneliness. Escape is a process of isolation, and the truth of the matter is that there can be communion only when there is love, and it is only then that the problem of loneliness is resolved.

Question: India has an ancient tradition of simple living and few wants. At present, however, millions are held in the grip of involuntary poverty and privation, while at the other end of the scale this land is dominated by the rich upper classes who are already living a European mode of life. How can one discover the right relationship to possessions and comforts?

KRISHNAMURTI: Sir, what do you mean by simplicity? Is it not important to find out first what is simplicity of life? Having but few clothes, a couple of loincloths—is that a simple life? Is it a simple life to have few needs and be satisfied with one meal a day? The outward show of simplicity—is that simple? Or must simplicity begin at quite a different level, not at the periphery, but at the center? So, let us find out what we mean by simplicity.

A mind that is complex, struggling to develop virtues, seeking power by trying to follow an ideal, to be nonviolent, disciplining itself, conforming to something, aiming at something, forcing itself in order to become something—is such a mind simple? Obviously not. But we want the outward show of simplicity because that is very profitable; that is the traditional, the ideal. A mind that pursues the ideal is not a simple mind—it is an escaping mind. A mind in conflict, a mind that is conforming to a pattern, whatever it be, is not a simple mind, but where there is simplicity at the center, there will be simplicity also at the periphery.

Now, the questioner wants to know how to discover the right relationship to possessions and comforts. If we use possessions for psychological gratification, then obviously possessions lead to complexity. We use things, possessions, not as mere necessities, but to satisfy a psychological need, do we not? That is, property becomes a means of self-aggrandizement. Most of us are seeking titles, position, property, land, virtues, recognition; and all that implies, does it not, a psychological need, an inward demand to be something. When our relationship to property is based on a psychological need, obviously we cannot lead a simple life, and therefore there must be conflict—which is so clear. That is, when I use property, people, or ideas as a means towards my psychological gratification, then I must possess—whatever it is, it is "mine." Therefore, I must protect it, I must fight for it, and hence the conflict begins.

So, it is important, is it not, to understand our relationship to property, but obviously, you cannot understand that relationship if you approach it through any particular pattern. Understanding is not according to any plan, whether communist or socialist, whether of the right or of the left. As long as we use property as a means of self-aggrandizement, there must be conflict, there must be a society which is based on violence. It is not merely an economic problem but much more a psychological problem, and the economists who are trying to solve it on the economic level will always fail because the significance is much deeper. Aren't you using property, comforts, power as a means of self-aggrandizement? To know that you have so much money in the bank, that you have a title, an estate—does it not give you importance, a sense of power? If it is not property you are after, then you want to be an official, a bureaucrat, a commissar, an ambassador, and God knows what else, and from that you get a sense of satisfaction, the feeling that you are somebody.

So, we base our relationship on self-aggrandizement, and as long as we use people, ideas, and things for our self-aggrandizement, there must be violence. The problem cannot be solved through any pattern of economic or social action but requires the understanding of our whole psychological being; therefore there must be an inward revolution, and not merely a revolution on the outside. It is very difficult to be as nothing, not to demand to be something, because most of us want to be successful; we are all after success in some form or other, are we not? In the business or social world, in politics, as a writer, as a poet, we want recognition, we want success in some form, so the problem is really much more inward and psychological than outward and objective. As long as we base our relationship on property, there must be this appalling division of those who have and those who have not, the rich and the poor; and we are trying to abolish that division through revolution based on an idea, which is a pattern of outside action determining how individuals shall behave in society without a fundamental, radical transformation at the center, which is the psyche. That is why a revolution which merely substitutes one pattern for another is no revolution at all. We think that by having an outward revolution we can bring about a new world based on what should be. On the contrary, revolution can only be at the center, in the psyche, and then it will produce real outward revolution; but do what you will, mere outward revolution can never bring about an internal revolution.

So, our problem is not how to bring about a new pattern or a new substitution but how to awaken the radical revolution in ourselves. That is the real problem, because what you are, the world is. Your problem is the world's problem; you are not separate from the world; you and the world are an integrated process; the world is not, without you. So, unless there is a revolution at the center, revolution on the outside has very little meaning. Most of us do not want to change, or we want to change only superficially while maintaining certain things as they are in relation to our psychological demands, but it is only a radical inward revolution that will transform the world. It must begin with you as an individual; you cannot look to the mass, for it is only individuals, not the mass, that can bring about transformation. Therefore, you and I must radically transform ourselves, and in that there is tremendous beauty, in that there is creative thinking. A man who is happy, who loves, does not want possessions; he is not carried away by success, by power, position, or authority. It is the unhappy, the sorrowful, who seek power and success as an escape from their own insufficiency. Superficial discontent only leads to gratification and further discontent, and as most of us are only superficially discontented, we do not want to be free from discontent. To be free from discontent is to bring about a fundamental revolution. Contentment, which is not the opposite of discontent, is that state in which there is the understanding of *what is,* and the understanding of *what is* is not a matter of time; it is not in the movement of the past to the future. The mind can be free only when it is simple, clean, and such a mind alone can be content. Only the mind that is free can establish right relationship to property. You will say, "That will take a very long time because it is only a few who can do it. In the meantime, the world is going to pieces, and therefore we must organize collectively." That is a very facile and specious argument. Actually, even though you organize yourselves to bring about a collective revolution, that also will take time, and how do you know that you have the key to the future? What gives you the authority and the certainty that by your particular revolution you are going to create a marvelous utopia?

Surely, then, it is really important that the problem be viewed, not on a particular level, but profoundly, intimately, and with an integrated approach, for in that alone is there a solution. You cannot be integrated if you approach the problem with any sense of resistance, through any form of compulsion or conformity. Therefore, the thing that brings about integration is love, but to love the problem, you cannot impose on it any particular theory or discipline. If you really want to solve this problem of right relationship to property, you must be able to understand the whole structure of your being. But you see, you want quick answers, you want an immediate response, an easy solution to this problem, and no one on earth can give it to you. There is no immediate solution to a very complex problem. The immediacy is in the response of the individual, not in the solution of the problem. You can change immediately if you so desire—but you don't. It is when you have a crisis that you have to change. A crisis means that you approach the problem with extraordinary completeness, otherwise it is not a crisis. But you do not want crises in your lives; that is why you have lawyers, that is why you have priests, that is why you have official revolutionaries. You avoid crisis, but when you are up against it, then you will find the right answer.

Question: What is self-knowledge? The traditional approach to self-knowledge is the knowledge of atma as distinct from the ego. Is that what you mean by self-knowledge?

KRISHNAMURTI: Look, sirs, you are all well-read, aren't you? You have read all the religious books, and that is how you know about the atma; otherwise, you do not know anything about it. You have read it in the books, and you like the idea, so you accept it, but you don't really know whether it exists or does not exist. You want permanency, and the atma guarantees it. Now, suppose you had not read a single religious book about the atma, the super-atma, and all the rest of it, what would you do? You might invent, but if you had no previous knowledge, what would be your approach? And that is my approach—I have not read a single religious or psychological book because I do not want them. Not that I am conceited, but since the whole business is inside you, you can discover it for yourself—but not by looking outside. Otherwise, how do you know that Shankaracharya, Buddha, or the very latest authority is not wrong?

So, to discover truth, there must be freedom; freedom, not at the end; but at the very beginning. Freedom is not at the end; liberation is not an end product; it must be at the beginning; otherwise, you cannot discover. Therefore, there must be freedom, freedom from the past—and that is what you and I are going to find out. You want to know what is self-knowledge. It is not of the ego, not of the atma—you do not know what that means. All that you know is that you are here—an entity in relationship with another, with your wife and children, with the world—that is all you know. That is the actual fact. Whether the atma exists or not is merely a theory, a speculation, and speculation is a waste of time—it is for the sluggish, the thoughtless.

Now, what am I? That is all that matters—what am I? I am going to find out what I am; I am going to see how far I can go in that direction and find out where it leads. Because, that is the fact—not the atma, not the ego, not the super-super-super. I do not think about those things even though Buddha and Christ and everybody may have talked about them. What I can know is my relationship with property, with people, with ideas. So, the beginning of self-knowledge lies in the understanding of relationship, and that relationship plays on all levels, not on one particular level only. I have to find out what my relationship is with my wife, with my children, with property, with society, with ideas. Relationship is the mirror in which I see myself as I am, and to see myself as I am is the beginning of wisdom. Wisdom is not something that you can buy in books or go to a guru to acquire—that is mere information, and wisdom is not information. Wisdom is the beginning of self-knowledge, and that wisdom comes when you understand relationship.

Now, to understand relationship, to see very clearly in relationship the fact of what you are, there must be no condemnation or justification—you must look at the fact with freedom. How can you understand something if you condemn it or wish it to be something other than it is? Through your understanding of relationship there comes the discovery from minute to minute of the ways of your thinking, the structure of your mind, and as long as the mind does not understand its total process, both the conscious and the unconscious, there can be no freedom. So, through the relationship of everyday contacts, of everyday action, you come to a point when you see that the thinker is not different from thought. When you say the atma is different from the ego, it is still within the field of thought, and without understanding the process, the functioning of thought, it is utterly futile to talk of reality and the atma, because they have no existence, they are merely the prejudices of thought. What we have to do is to understand the thought process, and that can be understood only in relationship. Self-knowledge begins with the understanding of relationship, which we shall discuss later.

Then there is the question of the thinker and the thought, the experiencer and the experienced, with which we are familiar. Is there a thinker as an entity separate from thought? Surely there is no separate entity; there is only thought, and it is thought that has created this separate entity called the thinker. Thought is the response of memory, both the conscious as well as the unconscious, the hidden and the open; memory is experience, and experience is response to a challenge, which becomes the experienced—that is the total process of our consciousness, is it not? There is memory, then experience, which is the response to challenge, then the naming process, which further cultivates memory. Memory responds as thought in relationship, and this whole process of thought, this cycle of memory, challenge, response, experience, and naming, which becomes further memory, is what we call consciousness. That is all I am, that is all I know. So, I see that my mind functions within the field of time, within the field of the known, and can it function beyond that field? I see now the whole process of my thinking, which leads me to the question, Can the mind go beyond thought, which is the result of the known? Obviously not, because when thought seeks to go beyond, it is pursuing its own projection. Thought cannot experience the unknown; it can only experience that which it has projected, which is the known. Thought is the mind, which is the result of time, the result of the past, and I want to know if the mind can go beyond itself. Obviously, it cannot because the "beyond" is the unknown, it is not of time. So, the mind must come to an end, which means the mind must be still, meditative. Meditation is not the becoming of something but the understanding of the total process of relationship, which is self-knowledge. It is only when the mind is still, not compelled to be still, that there is a possibility of experiencing the unknown.

So, then, can the mind, which is the result of experience, which is memory—can such a mind experience the unknown? Do you understand the problem? Can the mind, which is memory, the product of time, experience the timeless? It is the function of the mind to remember, and is truth a matter of experience and remembrance? We will discuss all this further as we go along, but just listen to what is being said, go with it, play with it, do not resist it. The point is: the mind is the result of time, time being memory, and memory says, "I have experienced or have not experienced." Is truth, the unknown, the immeasurable, a matter of experience, which means something to be remembered? If you remember something, it is already the known, is it not? So, is it not possible to experience something which is not in terms of time, which means experiencing in the sense of seeing the truth from moment to moment? If I remember truth, it is no longer truth because memory is a matter of time, of continuity, and truth is not of time, truth is not a continuity. The truth of the Buddha is not the truth which you discover today. Truth is never the same—it has no continuity, it is only from moment to moment, it cannot be remembered. There is truth only when mind is completely silent. Truth is not something to be sought after, experienced, held, and worshipped. There can be the experiencing of the timeless only when the mind is free from all conditioning. So, self-knowledge is the understanding of conditioning.

What is important is to understand the total process of the mind. We will discuss it later, but we will have to see that truth is not something to be remembered. That which is remembered is of time; it is a thing of the past, and the truth can never be of the past or of the future; truth can only be in the present, in that state where there is no time. Time is the process of the mind; the mind is thought, and thought is the response of memory. Memory is the experience of challenge and response, and because the response is inadequate, it creates the problem in relationship. So, the understanding of the total process of the self lies in the understanding of relationship in daily life, and that understanding frees the mind from time, and therefore it is capable of experiencing reality from moment to moment, which is not a process of remembering—it can no longer be termed "experience," it is quite a different state altogether. That state of being is bliss, it is not something that you learn in books and repeat like gramophone records. Such a man is happy, he does not repeat, for him life has no problems. It is only the mind that creates problems.

February 12, 1950

Second Talk in Bombay

When there is so much confusion and contradiction, not only in our own lives, but also among the specialists and the learned, action becomes extremely difficult, and to know what to do, to find a right mode of conduct, a right way of living, is hazardous and uncertain. This confusion is on the increase at the present time, not only in ourselves, but also about us, and we have to find, have we not, a way of action that will not bring more conflict, more misery, more strife, and destruction. We see that whatever the experts, the political leaders and religious authorities assert only leads to further misery, further chaos, further confusion. So, the problem of action—not only individual but also collective action—is very important, and to find out how to live is much more significant than merely to follow a certain pattern of action.

Now, to act, obviously there must be true individuality, but though we have separate bodies, we are actually not individuals at all—psychologically we are not separate. We are not individuals in the true sense of the word but are made up of many layers of memory, of tradition, conflict, and patterns, both conscious and otherwise, and that is the whole structure of our being. So, if we examine the individual closely, we will see that in actuality there is no individuality at all, there is no uniqueness. After all, by individuality we mean the quality of uniqueness, the quality of creativeness, the quality of aloneness that is creative. Sirs, the action which does not contribute to further misery, to further chaos, to further destruction, is possible only when there is true individuality, and individuality is possible only when we understand this whole process of conformity and imitation. For most of us, living is merely the pursuit of a pattern—the pattern that has been, or the pattern that will be. If we examine our daily conduct, our daily way of thinking, we will see that the process of our action is a continual imitation, a mere copying. All that we know and all that we have acquired is based on imitation. It is because we are imitative, copying, that we are not individuals at all. We quote what so and so has said, what Shankaracharya, Buddha, or Christ has said because it has become the pattern of our existence never to discover, never to find out the truth for ourselves, but to repeat what someone else has discovered, what someone else has experienced. When we use the experience of another, however true, as the pattern for our action, our action then is really founded on imitation, and that action is a lie. Please sit down, sir—these meetings are not meant for those who are not serious. This is not a political meeting or a show where you can show off your faces or get your photographs taken. (Laughter) You would not do this in a religious temple, would you? We are dealing with life, not with the mere outward show of things, and to understand life, we have to understand this complete process of living, which is ourselves. To understand ourselves, we must understand the whole content of the conscious and of the unconscious mind, and if you merely pay scant attention to what is being said, I am afraid you will not gather the full significance of it.

So, action which is based on imitation, on copying, on conformity, on the pursuit of a pattern, must inevitably lead to confusion—which is actually what is happening in the world at the present time. Why is it that we conform, why is it that we imitate, copy, quote authorities, cling to the sanction of what has been or what will be? Why is it that we cannot discover how to live, directly, for ourselves, instead of copying somebody? Is it not because most of us are afraid to be without security? Most of us want a certain state which we call "peace," but which is really a state in which one does not want to be disturbed. Most of us are not adventurous, and that is why we merely live by copying and are satisfied with imitation. It is only when we break through, when we understand the process of imitation, that there is a possibility of individual action, which is creation.

Especially in these times, when there is so much confusion in the world, when there are so many authorities, so many gurus, so many leaders—each asserting and denying, each giving a new pattern of action—is it not important to find out what is action independent of the pattern, independent of the copy? And you can find that out only when you understand the process and the significance of imitation—not only the imitation of an external example but the imitation and the conformity brought about by the authority of your own experience. Authority comes into being, does it not, when you want to be secure, and the more you desire security, the less you will have it—which is being shown by these endless wars. Each group consisting of so-called individuals wants to be secure, so each creates a system, a pattern for security based on its own authority in conflict with the authority of others. So, as long as you seek security in any form, psychological or physical, there must be conflict, there must be destruction. The desire for security implies conformity, and it is only when the mind is really insecure, completely uncertain, when it has no authority, either external or inward, when it is not imitating an example, an ideal, or clinging to the authority of what has been—it is only then that the mind is without any conformity and therefore free to discover, and only then is there creation.

So, our problem is not how to act, but how to bring about that state of creation which is true individuality. That state is obviously not based on an idea because creation can never be an ideation. Ideation must cease for the creative to be. There cannot be creative action as long as there is a pattern, an idea, and as our life is based on idea, on conformity to the ideal, we are not creative—and that is the real problem, and not how to act. Anybody will tell how you to act, any politician, any clever system will tell you what to do, but in doing it, you will create more mischief, more misery, more confusion, more strife because your action is not the outcome of creation. That is why it is important to be free from conformity and to be a true individual. To do that, you must know what you are at every moment, and in the understanding of what you are, there is a possibility of bringing about a society which is not based on conflict, destruction, and misery. Such an individual is a happy individual, and happiness does not demand the imitation of virtue; on the contrary, happiness creates virtue. A happy man is a virtuous man—it is the unhappy man who is not virtuous, and however much he may try to become virtuous, as long as he is unhappy, for him there is no virtue. He may become respectable, but respectability only covers up unhappiness. So, what is important is to discover for ourselves the pattern of conformity and to see the truth about that conformity, for only when we see that the pattern is created by fear of insecurity can there be a state of creation.

I have as usual been given many questions, and while considering them together, may I suggest that you do not resist what is being said but rather hear it just as you would listen to music. Just listen to me without disputation. To dispute and deny is the usual and easy way, but the disputatious mind can never be in a state of tranquillity, in which alone understanding comes. Also, if I may suggest, do not merely wait for explanations; do not look to me for a conclusion or an answer—which I shall not give. There is no categorical answer for the real problems of life; there is only understanding, and understanding is catching the full significance of the problem, seeing the whole content of it. So, please be good enough to listen to me with friendliness, and with the intention to find out the significance of the problem itself rather than merely wait for an answer.

Question: You assert that you have not read a single book, but do you really mean it? Don't you know that such loose statements cause resentment? You appear to know the latest jargon of politics, economics, psychology, and the sciences; and are you trying to suggest that you get all this information by some superhuman powers?

KRISHNAMURTI: Sir, whether you like it or not, it is a fact that I have not read a single religious book, nor any books on psychology or science, and it is also a fact that when I was young I was not put through a rigorous course of learning in philosophy or psychology. Somehow or other I have been reluctant to read them—they bore me; that is a fact. Obviously, I meet large numbers of people of every type—scientists, philosophers, analysts, religious people, and so on—who come to discuss, and occasionally I read some weekly magazines on politics and world affairs. That is all I have in the way of general information. Now, why do you resent it? Is it not because you have read so much, and your own ignorance is shown up by someone who has not read? Sir, do you read in order to become wise? Is knowledge wisdom? Is wisdom not something entirely different from knowledge? But there are two problems in this: one is why there is resentment in you, and the other is how I gather all that I am talking about. So, let us first inquire into why you resent.

Is it not important to find out why you feel resentment? You read newspapers, magazines, sacred books, all the commentaries on philosophy, psychology, and science, and you keep on reading. Why do you read, why do you keep your mind so constantly occupied? And why do you resent it when somebody who has not read points out something? Is it because you are frustrated and you dislike, you hate anyone who shows a different attitude towards life? What is the process of your own resentment? Surely, it is important to find out whether wisdom, understanding, comes through books, and why is it that you read; why do you fill your minds with information, with what so and so has said? Does it not indicate a very sluggish mind, an uninquiring mind? Does it not also indicate a mind that is not capable of really investigating, directly experiencing? Such a mind is living on other people's experience, and so it is satisfied, it is put to sleep, it is made dull; and can a mind that is filled with chatter, with information, ever be receptive to wisdom?

The second problem is this: though I may talk, I have not read any book, and you ask, "Are you trying to suggest that you get all this information by some superhuman powers?" Now, if you do not read, you have to know how to listen, you have to see and understand more clearly, observe more delicately and acutely, do you not? You have to be much more subtly aware of everything about you—not only of the people you meet, the people who come to see you, but also of the people in the tramcar, in the taxi, on the road. You have to watch everything, haven't you, more acutely, more clearly; and you are prevented from doing it, if you are cluttered up with information. When you are living fully, with undivided attention, there is direct experience; you do not have authorities and sanctions, and besides, why do you want to look to others when you have the whole treasure in yourself? After all, you are the total result of all humanity, are you not, both the collective and the so-called individual. You are the sum total of all the fathers and all the mothers, and if you know how to look into yourself, you do not have to read a single book on religion, on philosophy or psychology, because the book is yourself. You may have to read for scientific information, to learn mathematics, and so on, but all that can be kept in libraries. Why do you want to fill your mind with facts when you have a treasure in yourself which requires a great deal of attention, a great deal of watchfulness? You see, that is the whole gist of the matter. Though we come across people of every type, of every degree of learning, it is the understanding of oneself that brings infinite knowledge, infinite wisdom.

Sirs, I am sure that in the olden days before books were published, before there were followers, teachers, and gurus, there were original discoverers who had never read any book. Because there was no Bhagavad-Gita, no Bible, no book of any kind, they had to find out for themselves, had they not? How did they go about it? Obviously, they neither had sanctions nor did they stupidly quote the authority of some individual. They searched out the truth for themselves; they found it in the sacred places of their own minds and hearts. Surely, we also can discover the truth for ourselves in the sacred places of our minds and hearts. But to discover, to see *what is* without condemnation or justification is extraordinarily difficult. The mind is merely a process of the past using the present as a passage to the future, and how can such a mind see *what is?* To see *what is,* the mind must be free from all acquisition, from all accumulation—but that is a different problem. We are now trying to understand the problem of why we read, and why we have resentment against those who do not read; and is it possible for one who has read, who has accumulated so much information, to be free to see, to listen, and to hear?

Now, it is no good being resentful; that is stupid, that is only a waste of time, but we are all indulging in action which has no meaning, and surely, sirs and ladies, if you want to find out what wisdom is, you have in yourselves the key and also the door which must be opened. Self-knowledge is the beginning of wisdom, but self-knowledge begins very near; it is not at some supreme atmic level—which is merely another invention of a clever mind seeking security. Self-knowledge is reflected in your relationship with your wife, with your children, with your neighbor, with your boss, with your property, with the trees, and with the world. To go very far, you must begin very near. But most of us dislike to begin near because we are so ugly and so frightened of ourselves, so we imagine something marvelous in the distance and make that our goal, our motto, the pattern which we have to follow. Because we are not willing to see and understand what we are from moment to moment, we make of our life a contradiction, a misery, an utter mess. Sir, truth is here, not far; happiness is in the discovery of *what is,* and that is virtue.

Question: Is beauty to be cultivated or acquired? What does beauty mean to you?

KRISHNAMURTI: Beauty, surely, is something which is not of the mind; therefore, beauty is not sensation. Most of us seek sensation, which we call beauty. The fashion, the style which can be changed, adjusted, or dropped; the expensive furniture which you buy or have copied for your particular home if you have money; the beautiful woman, the beautiful child, the beautiful picture, the beautiful house—surely, all that is really the response of sensation; which is the response of the mind, is it not? And is beauty sensation, is beauty merely of external form and shape? Putting on a sari in the right way, having one's lips carefully curved by lipstick, walking in a particular manner—is that beauty? And is beauty the denial of the ugly? Is virtue the denial of evil? Is there beauty in any denial? Surely, there is denial—the pleasing and the not-pleasing—only when there is sensation. Just listen to it, do not contradict, do not oppose; just listen, and you will discover what we mean by beauty.

While the outward form must obviously be given certain respect and needs certain care, cleanliness, and all the rest of it, both as part of necessity and for aesthetic reasons, surely that is not beauty, is it? Beauty which is a sensation is of the mind, and the mind can make anything beautiful or ugly; therefore, beauty that depends on the mind is not beauty, is it? So, what is beauty? The mind is sensation, and if the mind judges beauty and gives it a name as goodness or truth, is that beauty? If beauty is perceived through the mind, it is sensation, and sensation comes to an end—and can that ever be beautiful? Do you understand what I mean? Is it beauty that comes to an end as sensation? I see a tree in the evening lights, the sun dancing and sparkling on the palm leaves, and it is very beautiful. The mind, becoming attached to it, says, "How beautiful it is," and holds to it, resuscitating and reviving that image. At the moment of perception it has great pleasure, a deep sense of satisfaction, which it calls the beautiful, but a second later it is over, it is only a memory, so the mind gives continuity to the sensation of what it calls beauty.

The mind, then, is continually picturing, imagining the beautiful, which is always of the past. But is beauty of time? If it is not of time, then beauty is something illimitable, is it not?—it is not within the frame of the word *beauty*. The mind can invent the beautiful, but the experience of the illimitable cannot be known by a mind that is pursuing the sensation of beauty. You and I can see beauty externally, but the mere appreciation of that expression is not beauty, is it? So, beauty is something beyond the mind, beyond sensation, beyond time limits, beyond the time-binding quality of thought; and that measureless sense, in which all things are, is beauty—which is to be really infinitely sensitive. The man who denies evil, who denies the ugly, can never know what beauty is because the very denial is the cultivation of the ugly. The illimitable is not to be found in a dictionary, in any religious or philosophical book.

So, beauty is not something of the mind, but unfortunately, modern civilization is making beauty a thing of the mind. All the picture magazines, all the cinemas are doing it; most of our efforts go to making wonderful paintings, marvelous furniture, building beautiful houses, buying the most fashionable dresses, the latest lipstick, or whatever is displayed in the advertisements. We are caught in the things of the mind, and that is why our lives are so ugly, so empty; that is why we decorate ourselves—which does not mean that we should not decorate ourselves. But there is an inner beauty, and when you see it, then it gives significance to the outer, but merely decorating the outer while ignoring the inner is just like beating a drum—it is still empty. Beauty is a thing beyond the mind, and to find that which is beautiful—call it truth, God, or what you will—there must be freedom from the thought process. But that is another problem which we can discuss some other time.

Question: Through such movements as the United Nations Organization and the World Pacifist Conferences recently held in India, men all over the world are making an individual and collective effort to prevent the third world war. How does your attempt differ from theirs, and do you hope to have any appreciable results? Can the impending war be prevented?

KRISHNAMURTI: Let us first dispose of the obvious facts and then go more deeply into the matter. The first fact is the impending war, and can we prevent it? Sir, what do you think? Men are bent on slaughtering each other; you are bent on slaughtering your neighbor—not with swords, perhaps, but you are exploiting them, aren't you, politically, religiously, and economically. There are social, communal, lingual divisions, and are you not making a great ado about all this? You do not want to prevent the impending war because some of you are going to make money. (Laughter) The cunning are going to make money, and the stupid also will want to make more. For God's sake, see the ugliness, the ruthlessness of it. Sir, when you have a set purpose of gain at all costs, the result is inevitable, is it not? The third world war is arising from the second world war, the second world war arose from the first, and the first was the result of previous wars. Until you put an end to the cause, mere tinkering with the symptoms has no significance. One of the causes of war is nationalism, sovereign governments, and all the ugliness that goes with them—power, prestige, position, and authority. Most of us do not want to put an end to war because our lives are incomplete; our whole existence is a battlefield, a ceaseless conflict, not only with one's wife, one's husband, one's neighbor, but with ourselves—the constant struggle to become something. That is our life, of which war and the hydrogen bomb are merely the violent and spectacular projections, and as long as we do not understand the whole significance of our existence and bring about a radical transformation, there can be no peace in the world.

Now, the second problem is much more difficult, much more demanding of your attention—which does not mean that the first one is not important. It is that most of us pay scant attention to the transformation of ourselves because we do not want to be transformed. We are contented and do not want to be disturbed. We are satisfied to go along as we are, and that is why we are sending our children to war, why we must have military training. You all want to save your bank accounts, hold on to your property—all in the name of nonviolence, in the name of God and peace, which is a lot of sanctimonious nonsense. What do we mean by peace? You say the U.N.O. is trying to establish peace by organizing its member nations, which means it is balancing power. Is that a pursuit of peace?

Then there is the gathering of individuals around a certain idea of what they consider to be peace. That is, the individual resists war either according to his moral persuasion or his economic ideas. We place peace either on a rational basis or on a moral basis. We say we must have peace because war is not profitable, which is the economic reason, or we say we must have peace because it is immoral to kill, it is irreligious, man is godly in his nature and must not be destroyed, and so on. So, there are all these various explanations of why we should not have war: the religious, moral, humanitarian, or ethical reasons for peace on the one hand, and the rational, economic, or social reasons on the other.

Now, is peace a thing of the mind? If you have a reason, a motive for peace, will that bring about peace? Do you understand what I mean? If I refrain from killing you because I think it is immoral, is that peaceful? If for economic reasons I do not destroy, if I do not join the army because I think it is unprofitable, is that peaceful? If I base my peace on a motive, on a reason, can that bring about peace? If I love you because you are beautiful, because you please me bodily, is that love? Sirs, please pay a little attention to it because it is very important. Most of us have so cultivated our minds, we are so intellectual, that we want to find reasons for not killing—the reasons being the appalling destructiveness of the atomic bomb, the moral and economic arguments for peace, and so on, and we think that the more reasons we have for not killing, the more there will be peace. But can you have peace through a reason, can peace be made into a cause? Is not the very cause part of the conflict? Is nonviolence, is peace an ideal to be pursued and attained eventually through a gradual process of evolution? These are all reasons, rationalizations, are they not? So, if we are at all thoughtful, our question really is, is it not, whether peace is a result, the outcome of a cause, or whether peace is a state of being, not in the future or in the past, but now. If peace, if nonviolence is an ideal, surely it indicates that actually you are violent, you are not peaceful. You wish to be peaceful, and you give reasons why you should be peaceful, and being satisfied with the reasons, you remain violent. Actually, a man who wants peace, who sees the necessity of being peaceful, has no ideal about peace. He does not make an effort to become peaceful but sees the necessity, the truth of being peaceful. It is only the man who does not see the importance, the necessity, the truth of being peaceful who makes nonviolence an ideal—which is really only a postponement of peace. And that is what you are doing: you are all worshipping the ideal of peace and in the meantime enjoying violence. (Laughter) Sirs, you laugh; you are easily amused, aren't you? It is another entertainment, and when you leave this meeting, you will go on exactly as before. Do you expect to have peace by your facile arguments, your casual talk? You will not have peace because you do not want peace—you are not interested in it, you do not see the importance, the necessity of having peace now, not tomorrow. It is only when you have no reason for being peaceful that you will have peace.

Sirs, as long as you have a reason to live, you are not living, are you? You live only when there is no reason, no cause—you just live. Similarly, as long as you have a reason for peace, you will have no peace. A mind that invents a reason for being peaceful is in conflict, and such a mind will produce chaos and conflict in the world. Just think it out and you will see. How can the mind that invents reasons for peace be peaceful? You can have very clever arguments and counter-arguments, but is not the very structure of the mind based on violence? The mind is the outcome of time, of yesterday, and it is always in conflict with the present, but the man who really wants to be peaceful now has no reason for it. For the peaceful man, there is no motive for peace. Sir, has generosity a motive? When you are generous with a motive, is that generosity? When a man renounces the world in order to achieve God, in order to find something greater, is that renunciation? If I give up this in order to find that, have I really given up anything? If I am peaceful for various reasons, have I found peace?

So, then, is not peace a thing far beyond the mind and the inventions of the mind? Most of us, most religious people with their organizations, come to peace through reason, through discipline, through conformity because there is no direct perception of the necessity, the truth of being peaceful. Peacefulness, that state of peace, is not stagnation;

on the contrary, it is a most active state. But the mind can only know the activity of its own creation, which is thought, and thought can never be peaceful; thought is sorrow, thought is conflict. As we know only sorrow and misery, we try to find ways and means to go beyond it, and whatever the mind invents only further increases its own misery, its own conflict, its own strife. You will say that very few will understand this, that very few will ever be peaceful in the right sense of the word. Why do you say that? Is it not because it is a convenient escape for you? You say that peace can never be achieved in the way I am talking about; it is impossible; therefore, you must have reasons for peace, you must have organizations for peace, you must have clever propaganda for peace. But all those methods are obviously mere postponement of peace. Only when you are directly in touch with the problem, when you see that without peace today you cannot have peace tomorrow, when you have no reason for peace but actually see the truth that without peace life is not possible, creation is not possible, that without peace there can be no sense of happiness—only when you see the truth of that will you have peace. Then you will have peace without any organizations for peace. Sir, for that you must be so vulnerable, you must demand peace with all your heart, you must find the truth of it for yourself, not through organizations, through propaganda, through clever arguments for peace and against war. Peace is not the denial of war. Peace is a state of being in which all conflicts and all problems have ceased; it is not a theory, not an ideal to be achieved after ten incarnations, ten years, or ten days. As long as the mind has not understood its own activity, it will create more misery and the understanding of the mind is the beginning of peace.

Question: You repeat again and again that the mind must cease for reality to come into existence. Why then do you attack prayer, worship, and ceremonials, which are really meant to still the mind?

KRISHNAMURTI: By a trick the mind can be made quiet; you can take a drug or a drink; you can do ceremonials, worship, pray. There are many means by which you can make the mind still. But is the mind still when it is made still? Some of you pray, don't you? You repeat the *Gayatri,* you chant to still the mind, or you clasp your hands and mesmerize yourself into a state which you call peace. Self-hypnosis by the repetition of words is very simple. When you keep on repeating certain words, your mind becomes very still, quiet; by taking certain postures, breathing a certain way, forcing the mind, you can obviously reduce the activity of the mind. That is, through various tricks of discipline, compulsion, conformity, the mind is made still, but when the mind is made still, is it really still? It is dead, is it not? It is in a state of hypnosis. When you pray, you repeat certain phrases, and that quietens the mind, and in that quietness there are certain responses; you hear voices which you, of course, attribute to the highest. That highest always replies to your most urgent demand, and the reply gives you gratification. This is all a well-known psychological process. But when the mind is made still through prayer, through ceremonials, through repetition, through chanting, through songs, is the mind really still, or merely dull? The mind has hypnotized itself into quietness, has it not? And most of you enjoy that hypnotized state because in that state you have no problems; you are completely enclosed, isolated, and insensitive. In that state you are obviously unconscious, the response of the conscious being blocked. When the mind is artificially made quiet, the upper layer of the mind is able to receive intimations, not only from its own unconscious, but from the collective unconscious, and the intimations are translated according to the conditioned mind. Therefore, a Hitler can say he is guided by God in what he does, and somebody else in India that God is all for something quite different. It is a very simple psychological process, which you can discover for yourself if you watch your own mind in action and see how it can hypnotize itself into tranquillity. Therefore, when the mind is forced into stillness through concentration, through conformity, through any kind of discipline or self-hypnosis, it is obviously incapable of discovering reality. It can project itself and hear its own ugly voice, which we call the voice of God, but surely that is entirely different from the state of a mind that is really still.

Now, the mind is active, it is constantly thinking of the things that have been and the things that will be, and how can such a mind be still—not be made still, which any fool can do? How is the mind to be really still? Surely, the mind is still only when it understands its own activity. As the waters of a pond become very quiet, very peaceful, when the breezes stop, so the mind is still when it is no longer creating problems. So, our question is not how to make the mind still but how to understand the creator of problems, because the moment you understand the creator of problems, the mind is still. Do not close your eyes and go off because that word *still* is mentioned. The understanding of the creator of problems brings tranquillity to the mind. So, you have to understand thought because thought is the maker of problems. Thought creates the thinker; thought is always seeking a permanent state; seeing its own state of transition, of flux, of impermanence, thought creates an entity which it calls the thinker, the atma, the paramatma, the soul—a higher and higher security. That is, thought creates an entity which it calls the observer, the experiencer, the permanent thinker as distinct from the impermanent thought, and the wide distance between the two creates the conflict of time.

Now, the understanding of this whole process of thought creating the thinker, and the incarnation of thought as the thinker, brings about tranquillity of mind. This means that one has to understand what is thought. What is this thing which you call thinking? Until we understand that, whatever thought does only creates more confusion; until we know the whole significance and depth of thought, the conscious as well as the unconscious, the individual as well as the collective, merely to indulge in further thinking, further speculation, only creates more misery. So, a mind which is ceaselessly active, chattering, always using the present as a passage from the past to the future, how can such a mind be still? Such a mind can never be still. A stupid mind is always stupid; it can never become intelligent; you may become what you call clever, but that is only further stupidity. A mind that is wandering cannot be still, cannot be tranquil. It is only when the mind understands its own process, when it begins to be aware of itself, that you will see the end of thought. After all, what is our thinking, of which we are so proud? Our thinking, surely, is merely the response of memory, the response of experience, which we call knowledge; our thinking is merely the response of yesterday, is it not? And how can such thinking, which is of time, understand something which is beyond time?

Sir, is it not important for the mind to be aware of its own action—not as an entity apart from action, but aware of itself as action? And it can be aware only in relation to property, to people, to ideas. It is in understanding relationship that we understand thought, for there is no thinker apart from thought, no thinker who thinks thoughts—there is only thought. When we see the truth of that, then the thinker is not, and when there is no thinker, the mind becomes very quiet. When there is no entity attempting to make the mind still, then the mind, which is only the result of time, of the past, becomes still of itself; and then only is it possible to understand truth, or for truth to come into being. Truth is not a thing of memory; truth is not of knowledge, of information. Truth is neither of the mind nor of emotion; it has nothing to do with sensations; it is not the projection of the self as the image, the voice of the Almighty. Truth is not of memory; therefore, truth is not of time. As truth is not of the mind, it can come into being only when the mind is still, when thought is silent. Truth must be seen from moment to moment, and it is only truth that can resolve our problems, not the mind or the inventions of the mind.

February 19, 1950

Third Talk in Bombay

I would again like to lay emphasis on the importance of listening rightly. Most of us listen without understanding; we listen merely to words, but the word is not the thing—the word can never be the real. The word becomes real only when it has deep significance, but to catch the deep significance of the word, one must know how to listen. This evening I want to talk about the question of virtue, and perhaps it may be something which is not along the old traditional lines; it may be something new, so I hope you will kindly listen to it without any resistance, without denial. Listen to it with the intention of really grasping its significance, and then, perhaps, we shall be able to understand the extraordinary importance of virtue. The difficulty in grasping the significance of whatever is said will be, I am quite sure, to cross the barriers of our own prejudices and personal experiences.

Now, virtue is essential, and to understand it, we have to go beyond the struggle to be virtuous, beyond the conventional meaning or definition of that word. Because we have made virtue into something very tiresome and tedious, something very ugly, there is no joy in being virtuous. It is a constant effort; it is a strain, a travail. Virtue is a fact, and to understand the fact, one must be free to look at it as a fact. It is only the unhappy man who struggles to be virtuous, and the very struggle to be virtuous is the denial of virtue, but the man who is free from unhappiness, from strife, from struggle, such a person is virtuous without effort. The understanding of a fact is extraordinarily difficult because the fact is one thing, and the desire to change the fact is another. To understand the fact is to be virtuous. Anger is a fact, and to understand it without condemning it, without trying to defend it or find excuses for it, liberates one from the fact, and liberation from the fact is virtue. So, virtue is in the understanding of the fact, whatever it be, not in becoming something away from the fact.

With most of us, virtue is the ideal, which is a means of escape from the fact, and therefore we are never virtuous at any time. We are always becoming virtuous, and therefore we are not virtuous. Surely, one must see the fact of what one is, whatever it be, without denial, acceptance, or identification, because when one identifies oneself with a fact, accepts or denies it, one does not understand the fact. Mere denial or acceptance is obviously not understanding. So, virtue is not an end to be pursued. The understanding of the fact is virtue, and without virtue there can be no freedom. It is the unvirtuous who are not free, and it is only in freedom that truth can be discovered. Freedom is virtue, and virtue is understanding the fact of what you are, which is not an ultimate process.

You can see the fact immediately, so virtue is immediate, not in the future. If you will think about this, you will see the significance of it. Naturally, we have not the time to go into all the details, but if you can see the fact of what you are as you would see any other fact, then you will discover there is a freedom from that fact, and it is only in that freedom that truth can be realized.

So, virtue is not a process, not an ultimate thing to be gained or to be practiced. What is practiced merely becomes habit, and habit can never be virtue. Habit is merely an automatic response. A fact is something that is constantly fresh, free; but a virtue that is practiced only leads to respectability, and a respectable man can never be happy. Happiness is not something that is gained by position, prestige; it is not arrived at through any means. We say we are happy because we have money, a position, or some means of sensation, but surely, that is not happiness. Happiness is a state of being in which there is no dependence, for where there is dependence, there is fear, and a man who is fearful can never be happy, however much he may cover up his fear. There is happiness only in freedom, and there must be virtue for freedom. An unvirtuous man can never be free because his mind is confused. So, the understanding of the fact is freedom from that fact, and freedom from the fact is virtue. It is only when there is freedom that there is discovery, and freedom is not at the end, but at the beginning. Truth is not something distant: it must be discovered in the immediate, in the very first step. To discover the truth in the immediate, there must be freedom, which means the understanding of the fact, which is virtue.

Now I shall answer some questions. It is always difficult to answer questions, and to be precise, because life is not a matter of yes and no. It is much too vast to be encompassed by a few words; it is too vital to be put in a frame. But if we can see the significance of the problem, then the answer is in the problem itself. It is open to anyone to discover the significance, the beauty, the truth of the problem, and that is possible only when you can see the fact and do not wander away from the fact.

Question: One watches the people near you for any visible sign of transformation. How do you explain that, while you walk in light, your nearest followers remain dull and ugly in their life and their behavior?

KRISHNAMURTI: First of all, the follower destroys the leader. To follow anyone is not to find truth. If one would understand what truth is, there can be neither the follower nor the teacher. There is no guru who will lead you to truth, and to follow anyone is to deny that freedom which virtue brings. This is not a mere rhetorical response. Just see the truth of it—that to follow authority of any kind is to deny intelligence. We follow because we ourselves are in confusion, and out of that confusion we choose the leader; therefore, the leader also can only be confused. (Laughter) Sir, please do not laugh it off. You choose the guru to have your appetite for security satisfied, and what you follow is your own projection, your own gratification, not the truth. When you follow somebody, you are destroying that somebody, which is to destroy yourself. I have no followers, nor am I a teacher to anybody; if I were, you would destroy me, and I would destroy you. Then there would be no love between us; there would be mere following, for those who follow and those who lead have no love in their hearts.

Now, the questioner is very concerned with those who are about me. Why? Why is he concerned with whether others are beautiful or ugly? Surely, what is important is one's own condition, not that of another. If my mind is petty, narrow, limited, then I will see the same in others. This desire to criticize others is really quite extraordinary. How can I know what another is when I do not know what I myself am? How can I judge another, when my own measurement is at fault? What is the instrument, the balance by which I weigh another, when I do not know the whole process of 'myself'? And when I do away with the 'myself' in its totality, there is no time to judge another, nor do I feel the inclination to judge another. It is the sluggish, agitated, worrying mind that judges; it is the restless mind that is forever criticizing others, and how can a restless mind that does not know itself ever look clearly at anything? It is only when you are capable of looking at things directly and clearly that you are free of those things.

The third point in this question is, is it not, How do you know that I "walk in light"? You assume that I do, but how can you know anything about it? This extraordinary desire to accept and to take things for granted is one of the indications of a dull mind. On the contrary, you should be skeptical. Skepticism is not cynicism or denial; it is the state of a mind that does not agree quickly, that does not accept or take things for granted. A mind that accepts is seeking, not enlightenment or wisdom, but refuge. The important thing is, surely, not whether I walk in light but whether you do. It is your life, not mine; it is your happiness, your strife, your misery. What is the good of thinking someone else walks in light? He may or may not, and of what value is it to you when you are yourself in misery? If you merely believe in the light of another, you become a follower, a copyist, an imitator, which means you are a gramophone record playing some tune over and over again without a song in your own heart.

In this question there is also another point: instead of criticizing, tackling me, you go for the so-called followers. It is like whipping a boy instead of the king; the king can do no wrong, so you go for the boy. Similarly, you go for those whom you regard as my followers. Fortunately, there are no followers as far as I am concerned. As I said, to follow anyone is destruction, and that is what is the matter with the world at the present time. We are mere copyists, imitators; we follow eagerly, both politically and religiously, and so we are led to destruction. This does not mean that we must become rampant individualists, which is the other extreme, but to be able to live happily, to see the truth for oneself, does not demand following another. A happy man does not follow. It is the miserable, the confused man who eagerly pursues another, hoping for refuge; and he will find a refuge, but that refuge is his darkness, it is his undoing. It is only the man who tries to find out the fact of what he is in himself that will know freedom and therefore happiness.

Question: The more one listens to you, the more one feels that you are preaching withdrawal from life. I am a clerk in the Secretariat; I have four children, and I get only Rs. 125/a month. Will you please explain how I can fight the gloomy struggle for existence in the new way you are proposing? Do you really think that your message can mean anything significant to the starving and to the stunted wage earner? Have you lived among such people?

KRISHNAMURTI: First of all, let us dispose of the question as to whether I have lived among such people. It implies, does it not, that in order to understand life, you must go through every phase of life, every experience; you must live among the poor and the rich; you must starve and pass through every condition of existence. Now, to put the problem very briefly: must you go through drunkenness to know sobriety? Does not one experience—fully, completely understood—reveal the whole process of life? Must you go through all the phases of life to understand life? Please see that this is not an avoidance of the question—on the contrary. We think that to know wisdom, we must go through every phase of life and experience, from the rich man to the poor man, from the beggar to the king. Now, is that so? Is wisdom the accumulation of many experiences? Or is wisdom to be found in the complete understanding of one experience? Because we never completely and fully understand one experience, we wander from experience to experience, hoping for some salvation, for some refuge, for some happiness. So, we have made our life a process of continuous accumulation of experiences, and therefore it is an endless struggle, a ceaseless battle to attain, to acquire. Surely, that is a tedious, an utterly stupid approach to life, is it not?

Is it not possible to gather the full significance of an experience and so understand the whole width and depth of life? I say it is possible and that it is the only way to understand life. Whatever the experience, whatever the challenge and response to life, if one can understand it fully, then the pursuit of every experience has no meaning; it becomes merely a waste of time. Because we are incapable of doing that, we have invented the illusory idea that by accumulating experiences, we shall ultimately arrive, God knows where.

Now, the questioner wants to know if I am preaching withdrawal from life. What do we mean by life? I am thinking out this problem aloud, so let us follow it together. What do we mean by life? Living is possible only in relationship, is it not? If there is no relationship, there is no life. To be is to be related; life is a process of relationship, of being in communion with another, with two or ten, with society. Life is not a process of isolation, of withdrawal. But for most of us, living is a process of isolation, is it not? We are struggling to isolate ourselves in action, in relationship. All our activities are self-enclosing, narrowing down, isolating, and in that very process there is friction, sorrow, pain. Living is relationship, and nothing can exist in isolation; therefore, there can be no withdrawal from life. On the contrary, there must be the understanding of relationship—your relationship with your wife, your children, with society, with nature, with the beauty of this day, the sunlight on the waters, the flight of a bird, with the things that you possess and the ideals that control you. To understand all that, you do not withdraw from it. Truth is not found in withdrawal and isolation; on the contrary, in isolation, whether it is conscious or unconscious, there is only darkness and death.

So, I am not proposing a withdrawal from life, a suppression of life; on the contrary, we can understand life only in relationship. It is because we do not understand life that we are all the time making an effort to withdraw, to isolate, and having created a society based on violence, on corruption, God becomes the ultimate isolation.

Then the questioner wants to know how, earning so little, he is to live what we are talking about. Now, first of all, the earning of a livelihood is not only the problem of the man who earns little, but it is also yours and mine, is it not? You may have a little more money, you may be well off, have a better job, a better position, a bigger bank account, but it is also your problem and mine because this society is what all of us have created. Until we three—you, I, and another—really understand relationship, we cannot bring about revolution in society. The man who has no food in his stomach obviously cannot find reality; he must first be fed, but the man whose stomach is full, surely it is his immediate responsibility to see that there is a fundamental revolution in society, that things do not go on as they are. To think, to feel out all these problems is much more the responsibility of those who have time, who have leisure, than it is of the man who earns little and has such a struggle to make both ends meet, who has no time and is worn out by this rotten, exploiting society. So, it is you and I, those of us who have a little more time and leisure, who must go into these problems completely—which does not mean that we have to become professional talkers, offering one system as a substitute for another. It is for you and me, who have time, who have leisure for thought, to seek out the way of a new society, a new culture.

Now, what happens to the poor man who is earning Rs. 125/-, or whatever it is? He has to carry the family with him; he has to accept the superstitions of his grandmother, his aunts, nephews, and so on; he has to marry according to a certain pattern; he has to do puja, ceremonies, and fit in with all that superstitious nonsense. He is caught in it, and if he rebels, you, the respectable people, throttle him.

So, the question of right livelihood is your problem and mine, is it not? But most of us are not concerned with right livelihood at all; we are glad and thankful simply to have a job, and so we maintain a society, a culture, that renders right livelihood impossible. Sirs, do not treat it theoretically. If you find yourself in a wrong vocation and actually do something about it, do you not see what a revolution it will bring in your life and in the life of those around you? But if you listen casually and carry on as before because you have a good job and for you there is no problem, obviously you will continue to cause misery in the world. For the man with too little money there is a problem; but he, like the rest of us, is only concerned with having more, and when he gets more, the problem continues because he wants still more.

Now, what is a right means of livelihood? Obviously, there are certain occupations that are detrimental to society. The army is detrimental to society because it plans and encourages murder in the name of the country. Because you are a nationalist, holding to sovereign governments, you must have armed forces to protect your property, and property is much more important to you than life, the life of your son. That is why you have conscription, that is why your schools are being encouraged to have military training. So, in the name of your country, you are destroying your children. Your country is yourself identified, your own projection, and when you worship your country, you are sacrificing your children to the worship of yourself. That is why the army, which is the instrument of a separate and sovereign government, is a wrong means of livelihood. But it is made easy to enter the army, and it becomes a sure means of earning a little money. Just see this extraordinary fact in modern civilization. Surely, the army is a wrong way to earn one's livelihood because it is based on planned and calculated destruction, and until you and I see the truth of this, we are not going to bring about any different kind of society.

Similarly, you can see that a job in a police force is a wrong means of livelihood. Do not smile and pass it off. The police become a means of investigating private lives. We are not talking of the police as a means of helping, guiding, but as an instrument of the state, the secret police, and all the rest of it. Then the individual becomes merely an instrument of society; the individual has no privacy, no freedom, no rights of his own; he is investigated, controlled, shaped by the government, which is society. Obviously, that is a wrong means of livelihood.

Then there is the profession of law. Is that not a wrong means of livelihood? I see some of you are smiling. Probably you are lawyers, and you know better than I do what that system is based on. Fundamentally, not superficially, it is based on maintaining things as they are, on disagreements, disputation, confusion, quarrels, encouraging disruption and disorder in the name of order.

There is also the wrong profession of the man who wants to become rich, the big business man, the man who is gathering, accumulating, storing up money through exploitation, through ruthlessness—though he may do it in the name of philanthropy or in the name of education.

Obviously, then, these are all wrong means of livelihood, and a complete change in the social structure, a revolution of the right kind, is possible only when it begins with you. Revolution cannot be based on an ideal or a system, but when you see all this as a fact, you are liberated from it, and therefore you are free to act. But, sirs, you do not want to act; you are afraid of being disturbed, and you say, "There is already sufficient confusion; please do not make any more." If you do not make more confusion, others are there making it for you and utilizing that confusion as a means of gaining political power. Surely, it is your responsibility as an individual to see the confusion within and without and to do something about it—not merely accept it and wait for a miracle, a marvelous utopia created by others into which you can step without effort.

Sirs, this problem is your problem as well as the poor man's problem. The poor man depends on you, and you depend on him; he is your clerk while you ride in a big car and get a fat salary, accumulating money at his expense. So, it is your problem as well as his, and until you and he alter radically in your relationship, there will be no real revolution; though there may be violence and bloodshed, you will maintain things essentially as they are. Therefore, our problem is the transformation of relationship, and that transformation is not on the intellectual or verbal level but it can take place only when you understand the fact of what you are. You cannot understand it if you theorize, verbalize, deny, or justify, and that is why it is important to understand the whole process of the mind. A revolution which is merely the outcome of the mind is no revolution at all, but revolution which is not of the mind, which is not of the word, of the system—that is the only revolution, the only solution to the problem. But unfortunately, we have cultivated our brains, our so-called intellects, to such an extent that we have lost all capacities except the merely intellectual and verbal capacity. It is only when we see life as a whole, in its entirety, in its totality, that there is a possibility of a revolution which will give both the poor man and the rich man his due.

Question: The conscious mind is ignorant and afraid of the unconscious mind. You are addressing mainly the conscious mind, and is that enough? Will your method bring about release of the unconscious? Please explain in detail how one can tackle the unconscious mind fully.

KRISHNAMURTI: This is quite a complex and difficult problem; it requires a great deal of penetration, and I hope you will pay attention, not merely verbally, but by really listening and by seeing the truth of it.

Now, we are aware that there is the conscious and the unconscious mind, but most of us function only on the conscious level, in the upper layer of the mind, and our whole life is practically limited to that. We live in the so-called conscious mind, and we never pay attention to the deeper unconscious mind, from which there is occasionally an intimation, a hint; but that hint is disregarded, perverted, or translated according to our particular conscious demands at the moment. Now, the questioner asks, "You are addressing mainly the conscious mind, and is that enough?'' Let us see what we mean by the conscious mind. Is the conscious mind different from the unconscious mind? We have divided the conscious from the unconscious, and is this justified? Is this true? Is there such a division between the conscious and the unconscious? Is there a definite barrier, a line where the conscious ends and the unconscious begins? We are aware that the upper layer, the conscious mind, is active, but is that the only instrument that is active throughout the day? So, if I were addressing merely the upper layer of the mind, then surely what I am saying would be valueless; it would have no meaning. And yet, most of us cling to what the conscious mind has accepted because the conscious mind finds it convenient to adjust to certain obvious facts, but the unconscious may rebel, and often does, and so there is conflict between the so-called conscious and the unconscious.

So, our problem is this, is it not?—there is in fact only one state, not two states such as the conscious and the unconscious; there is only a state of being, which is consciousness, though you may divide it as the conscious and the unconscious. But that consciousness is always of the past, never of the present; you are conscious only of things that are over. You are conscious of hearing me the second it is over, are you not?—you understand it a moment later. You are never conscious or aware of the now. Watch your own hearts and minds, and you will see that consciousness is functioning between the past—and the future, and that the present is merely a passage of the past to the future. So, consciousness is a movement of the past to the future. Please follow this. It is a little too abstract to give examples, similes; and to think in similes is not to think at all, because similes are limited. You must think abstractly or negatively, which is the highest form of thinking.

If you watch your own mind at work, you will see that the movement to the past and to the future is a process in which the present is not. Either the past is a means of escape from the present, which may be unpleasant, or the future is a hope away from the present. So, the mind is occupied with the past or with the future and sloughs off the present. That is, the mind is conditioned by the past—conditioned as an Indian, a Brahmin or a non-Brahmin, a Christian, a Buddhist, and so on—and that conditioned mind projects itself into the future; therefore, it is never capable of looking directly and impartially at any fact. It either condemns and rejects the fact or accepts and identifies itself with the fact. Such a mind is obviously not capable of seeing any fact as a fact. That is our state of consciousness, which is conditioned by the past, and our thought is the conditioned response to the challenge of a fact; and the more you respond according to the conditioning of belief, of the past, the more there is the strengthening of the past. That strengthening of the past is obviously the continuity of itself, which it calls the future. So, that is the state of our mind, of our consciousness—a pendulum swinging backwards and forwards between the past and the future. That is our consciousness, which is made up not only of the upper layers of the mind but of the deeper layers as well. Such consciousness obviously cannot function at a different level because it only knows those two movements of backwards and forwards.

Now, if you watch very carefully, you will see that it is not a constant movement, but that there is an interval between two thoughts; though it may be but an infinitesimal fraction of a second, there is an interval that has significance in the swinging backwards and forwards of the pendulum. So, we see the fact that our thinking is conditioned by the past, which is projected into the future, and the moment you admit the past, you must also admit the future because there are not two states as the past and the future but one state which includes both the conscious and the unconscious, both the collective past and the individual past. The collective and the individual past, in response to the present, give out certain responses which create the individual consciousness; therefore, consciousness is of the past, and that is the whole background of our existence. And the moment you have the past, you inevitably have the future because the future is merely the continuity of the modified past, but it is still the past. So, our problem is how to bring about a transformation in this process of the past without creating another conditioning, another past. I hope you are following all this. If it is not clear, perhaps we will discuss it on Tuesday or Thursday.

To put it differently, the problem is this: most of us reject one particular form of conditioning and find another form—a wider, more significant or more pleasant conditioning. You give up one religion and take on another, reject one form of belief and accept another. Such substitution is obviously not understanding life—life being relationship. So, our problem is how to be free from all conditioning. Either you say it is impossible, that no human mind can ever be free from conditioning, or you begin to experiment, to inquire, to discover. If you assert that it is impossible, obviously you are out of the running. Your assertion may be based on limited or wide experience, or on the mere acceptance of a belief, but such assertion is the denial of search, of research, of inquiry, of discovery. To find out if it is possible for the mind to be completely free from all conditioning, you must be free to inquire and to discover.

Now, I say it is definitely possible for the mind to be free from all conditioning—not that you should accept my authority. If you accept it on authority, you will never discover; it will be another substitution, and that will have no significance. When I say it is possible, I say it because for me it is a fact, and I will show it to you verbally, but if you are to find the truth of it for yourself, you must experiment with it and follow it swiftly.

The understanding of the whole process of conditioning does not come to you through analysis or introspection, because the moment you have the analyzer, that very analyzer himself is part of the background, and therefore his analysis is of no significance. That is a fact, and you must put it aside. The analyzer who examines, who analyzes the thing which he is looking at, is himself part of the conditioned state, and therefore whatever his interpretation, his understanding, his analysis may be, it is still part of the background. So that way there is no escape, and to break the background is essential because to meet the challenge of the new, the mind must be new; to discover God, truth, or what you will, the mind must be fresh, uncontaminated by the past. To analyze the past, to arrive at conclusions through a series of experimentations, to make assertions and denials, and all the rest of it, implies, in its very essence, the continuance of the background in different forms; and when you see the truth of that fact, then you will discover that the analyzer has come to an end. The background is still there, but the analyzer has come to an end. Then there is no entity apart from the background; there is only thought as the background—thought being the response of memory, both conscious and unconscious, individual and collective.

So, the mind is the result of the past, which is the process of conditioning, and how is it possible for the mind to be free? To be free, the mind must not only see and understand its pendulum-like swing between the past and the future but also be aware of the interval between thoughts. That interval is spontaneous; it is not brought about through any causation, through any wish, through any compulsion. Just experiment with me this evening and see your own mind in operation as I go slowly into the matter. Don't worry, I am not mesmerizing you. (Laughter) I am not interested in mesmerizing or influencing you, because to be mesmerized, to be influenced, consciously or unconsciously, is to become a follower; and to become a follower is to destroy yourself and him whom you follow, and therefore there is no love between us. When there is love, there is no mesmerism; there is neither the follower nor the teacher, neither the man nor the woman; there is only that flame of love, and it is that love which brings communion between us.

Now, although it is difficult with a large audience, this evening I am going to try to show how the mind actually works, and you can experiment and see it for yourself. We know thinking is a response of the background. You think as a Hindu, as a Parsee, as a Buddhist, or as God knows what else, not only in your conscious thinking, but also in your unconscious thinking. You are the background, you are not separate, there is no thinker apart from the background, and the response of that background is what you call thinking. That background, whether it is cultured or uncultured, learned or ignorant, is constantly responding to any challenge, to any stimulant, and that response creates not only the so-called present, but also the future—and that is our process of thinking.

Now, if you watch very carefully, you will see that though the response, the movement of thought, seems so swift, there are gaps, there are intervals between thoughts. Between two thoughts there is a period of silence which is not related to the thought process. If you observe you will see that that period of silence, that interval, is not of time; and the discovery of that interval, the full experiencing of that interval, liberates you from conditioning—or rather, it does not liberate 'you', but there is liberation from conditioning. So, the understanding of the process of thinking is meditation—which we will discuss another time. We are now not only discussing the structure and the process of thought, which is the background of memory, of experience, of knowledge, but we are also trying to find out if the mind can liberate itself from the background. It is only when the mind is not giving continuity to thought, when it is still with a stillness that is not induced, that is without any causation—it is only then that there can be freedom from the background. I hope I have explained this question sufficiently.

Question: Why does the human mind cling so persistently to the idea of God in many different ways? Can you deny that belief in God has brought consolation and meaning to lonely and desolate people all over the world? Why are you depriving man of this consolation by preaching a new type of nihilism?

KRISHNAMURTI: Sirs, this is as important a question as the previous one because all vital human questions are important. So, please, do not resist but try to understand what I am talking about, and you will see.

Now, belief is a denial of truth; belief hinders truth—to believe in God is not to find God. Neither the believer nor the nonbeliever will find God because reality is the unknown, and your belief or nonbelief in the unknown is merely a self-projection and therefore not real. So, if I may suggest, do not resist but let us go into it together. I know you believe, and I know it has very little meaning in your life. There are many people who believe; millions believe in God and take consolation. First of all, why do you believe? You believe because it gives you satisfaction, consolation, hope, and you say it gives significance to life. But actually, your belief has very little significance because you believe and exploit, you believe and kill, you believe in a universal God and murder each other. The rich man also believes in God; he exploits ruthlessly, accumulates money, and then builds a temple or becomes a philanthropist. Is that belief in God? And the man who drops an atomic bomb says that God is his copilot on the airplane. (Laughter) Do not laugh, sirs. Your turn is coming also. The man who plans murder on a vast scale calls on the Almighty; the man who is cruel to his wife, to his children, to his neighbor, he also sings, sits down, kneels, clasps his hands, and calls on the name of God.

So, you all believe in different ways, but your belief has no reality whatsoever. Reality is what you are, what you do, what you think; and your belief in God is merely an escape from your monotonous, stupid, and cruel life. Furthermore, belief invariably divides people: there is the Parsee, the Hindu, the Buddhist, the Christian, the communist, the socialist, the capitalist, and so on. Belief, idea, divides; it never brings people together. You may bring a few people together in a group, but that group is opposed to another group. So, ideas and beliefs are never unifying; on the contrary, they are separative, disintegrating, and destructive. Therefore, your belief in God is really spreading misery in the world; though it may have brought you momentary consolation, in actuality it has brought you more misery and destruction in the form of wars, famines, class divisions, and the ruthless action of separate individuals. So, your belief has no validity at all. If you really believed in God, if it were a real experience to you, then your face would have a smile, then you would not be destroying human beings. I am not being rhetorical, but please look at the facts first.

You do not really believe in God, because if you did you would not be rich, you would have no temples, you would have no poor people, you would not be a philanthropist with a big title after exploiting people. So, your belief in God is worthless; and though it may give you temporary consolation, compensate for and hide you from your own misery, give you a respectable escape which mankind recognizes as making you a religious person, it is all without validity, it has no significance whatsoever. What is significant is your life, the way you live, the way you treat your servant, the way you look at another human being.

So, what I am preaching is not negation. I am saying that you spread misery by clinging to illusions, which help you to avoid looking at things as they are. To face a fact is freedom from the fact, and belief is a hindrance to the perception of *what is.* After all, your belief is the result of your conditioning. You can be conditioned to believe in God, and another can be conditioned not to believe, to deny that there is God. Obviously, then, belief impedes the realization of *what is,* and to see the truth of this fact is to be free from belief. Then only can the mind inquire and find out if there is that thing which is called God.

Now, what is reality, what is God? God is not the word, the word is not the thing. To know that which is immeasurable, which is not of time, the mind must be free of time, which means the mind must be free from all thought, from all ideas about God. Because, what do you know about God or truth? You do not really know anything about that reality. All that you know is words, the experiences of others, or some moments of rather vague experience of your own. Surely, that is not God, that is not reality, that is not beyond the field of time. So, to know that which is beyond time, the process of time must be understood—time being thought, the process of becoming, the accumulation of knowledge. That is the whole background of the mind; the mind itself is the background, both the conscious and the unconscious, the collective and the individual. So, the mind must be free of the known, which means the mind must be completely silent, not made silent. The mind that achieves silence as a result, as the outcome of determined action, of practice, of discipline, is not a silent mind. The mind that is forced, controlled, shaped, put into a frame and kept quiet, is not a still mind. You may succeed for a period of time in forcing the mind to be superficially silent, but such a mind is not a still mind. Stillness comes only when you understand the whole process of thought, because to understand the process is to end the process, and the ending of the process of thought is the beginning of silence. Only when the mind is completely silent, not only on the upper level, but fundamentally, right through, on both the superficial and the deeper levels of consciousness—only then can the unknown come into being. The unknown is not something to be experienced by the mind; silence alone can be experienced, nothing but silence. If the mind experiences anything but silence, it is merely projecting its own desires, and such a mind is not silent; and as long as the mind is not silent, as long as thought in any form, conscious or unconscious, is in movement, there can be no silence. Silence is freedom from the past, from knowledge, from both conscious and unconscious memory; and when the mind is completely silent, not in use, when there is the silence which is not a product of effort, then only does the timeless, the eternal come into being. That state is not a state of remembering—there is no entity that remembers, that experiences. So, God or truth, or what you will, is a thing that comes into being from moment to moment, and it happens only in a state of freedom and spontaneity, not when the mind is disciplined according to a pattern. God is not a thing of the mind, it does not come through self-projection, it comes only when there is virtue, which is freedom. Virtue is facing the fact of *what is,* and the facing of the fact is a state of bliss. Only when the mind is blissful, quiet, without any movement of its own, without the projection of thought, conscious or unconscious—only then does the eternal come into being.

February 26, 1950

Fourth Talk in Bombay

Unless we understand the whole problem of effort, the question of action will not be completely understood. Most of us live by a series of efforts, striving to achieve a result, striving either for the general welfare, for general upliftment, or to achieve personal advancement. Effort is ultimately, is it not, a process of ambition, whether collective or individual, and it is ambition that seems to drive most of us into political activity or into work for social and religious advancement. For most of us, ambition seems to be the goal, the way of living; and when the pursuits of that ambition are thwarted, there is frustration, there is sorrow, leading to a series of escapes. Surely, effort ultimately implies not only the ambition for personal advancement but also the ambition for social and political advancement, and if we do not succeed in worldly matters, we turn our ambition to so-called spiritual matters. If I do not become somebody in this world, I want to become somebody in the next world, and that is considered to be spiritual, more worthy, more significant; but ambition in any direction, by whatever name we may call it, is still ambition. The acquiring of capacity, of technique and efficiency, the desire for the power to do good, for the power to speak, to write, to think clearly, the desire for power in any form, implies ambition, does it not? And does the search for power bring about creation or creativeness? Does creativeness come into being through effort, through advancement, personal or collective? Does creativeness come into being through the cultivation of capacity and efficiency, which is ultimately power? Until we understand the state of being which is creation, until there is that ingrained sense of creativeness, conflict is inevitable. If we can understand that question of creation, then perhaps we shall be able to act without multiplying the problems through action, and to understand the state of creativeness, surely we must understand the process of effort.

Now, where there is effort to achieve something, obviously there cannot be understanding. Understanding comes only when there is the cessation of the whole process, the whole mechanism of striving to be or not to be, to advance or not to advance. It is really only the imitator who makes an effort to become something, and the man who has disciplined his mind according to a certain pattern is obviously an imitator, a copyist. He must make an effort to conform to the pattern, and conformity to the pattern he calls living. However subtle, however hidden and widely extended, any effort in which there is imitation, copy, is obviously not creation. Because most of us are caught in imitation, we have lost the feeling for creation, and having lost it, we get entangled in technique, in making effort more and more perfect, more and more efficient; that is, we develop more and more technical capacity without having the flame, and the search for efficiency in action without the flame is the curse of the present age. Most of us who are concerned with action which we hope will bring about a revolution are caught in action based on an idea, which is merely copy, and therefore, it is invalid. Surely, our problem—sociological, religious, individual, collective, or what you will—can be solved only when we understand the whole process, the mechanism of effort, and the understanding of effort is meditation.

So, until we understand and are utterly free from the whole process of ambition, which is the search for power, for efficiency, for domination, there cannot be creative action; and it is only the creative man who can solve these problems, not the man who is merely copying a pattern, however efficient, however worthy. The search for a pattern is not the search for creation; the search for a pattern is not the search for true revolution. As long as we do not understand the process of effort, in which is implied power, imitation, ambition, there cannot be creation. It is only the creative man who is happy, and only the happy man is virtuous, and the happy, virtuous man is a really creative social entity who will bring about revolution.

There are several questions. To most of us, the problems of life are not very serious, and we want ready-made answers. We do not want to delve into the problem, we do not want to think it out completely, fully, and understand the whole significance of it; we want to be told the answer, and the more gratifying the answer, the quicker we accept it. When we are made to think about a problem, when we have to go into it, our minds rebel because we are not used to inquiring into problems. In considering these questions, if you merely wait for a ready-made answer from me, I am afraid you will be disappointed; but if we can go into the question together, think it out anew, not according to old patterns, then perhaps we shall be able to solve the many problems which confront us, and which we are usually so unwilling to look at. We have to look at them; that is, there must be the capacity to face the fact, and we cannot face the fact, whatever it be, as long as we have explanations, as long as words fill our minds. It is words, explanations, memories that cloud the understanding of the fact. The fact is always new because the fact is a challenge, but the fact ceases to be a challenge, it is not new, when we consider it merely as the old and discard it. So, in considering these questions, I hope you and I will think out the problem together. I am not laying down the answer, but we are going to think out each problem together and discover the truth of it.

Question: You seem to be preaching something very akin to the teachings of the Upanishads; why then are you upset if someone quotes from sacred books? Do you mean to suggest that you are expounding something no one has ever said before? Does quotation from another person interfere with the peculiar technique of hypnotism which you are employing?

KRISHNAMURTI: Why do you quote, and why do you compare? Either you quote because you say, "By quoting I can compare and understand," or you quote because in your mind you are nothing else but quotation. (Laughter) Do not laugh, sirs, just see the truth of the matter. A gramophone record repeats what someone else has said. Has that any validity in the search of truth? Do you understand by quoting the Upanishads or any other book? No book is sacred, I assure you; like the newspaper, it is only words printed on paper, and there is nothing sacred in either. Now, you quote because you think that by quoting and comparing you will understand what I am talking about. Do we understand anything through comparison, or does understanding come only when you deal directly with whatever is said. When you say that the Upanishads have said it, or someone else has said it, what is actually taking place in your psychological process? By saying that someone else has said it, you do not have to think any more about it, do you? You think you have understood the Upanishads, and when you compare what the Upanishads say with what I am saying, you say it is alike, and you give no further thought to the problem. That is, by comparing you are really seeking a state in which you will not be disturbed. After all, when you have read the Upanishads or the Bhagavad-Gita and think you have understood it, you can sit back and keep on repeating it, and it will have no effect on your daily life; you can keep on reading and quoting and be undisturbed, perfectly safe. Then you are very respectable, and you can carry on with your daily life, which is monstrously ugly and stupid; and when someone else comes along and points out something, you immediately compare it with what you have read, and you think you have understood. Actually, you are avoiding disturbance—that is why you compare, and that is what I object to.

I do not know whether what I am saying is new or old, I am not interested in whether someone else has said it or not, but what I am really interested in is to find out the truth of every problem—not according to the Upanishads, the Bhagavad-Gita, the Bible, or Shankara. When you are seeking the truth of a problem, it is stupid to quote what others have said. Sir, this is not a political meeting, and the question fundamentally is, Do you understand anything by comparison? Do you understand life by having your mind full of the sayings of others, by following the experience, the knowledge of others? Or does understanding come only when the mind is still—not made still, which is dullness? Through inquiry, through search, through exploration, inevitably the mind becomes quiet, and then the problem gives its full significance; and it is only when the mind is quiet that there is understanding of the significance of the problem, not when you are constantly comparing, quoting, judging, weighing. Surely, sir, the man of knowledge, the scholar, can never know truth; on the contrary, knowledge and erudition must come to an end. The mind must be simple to understand truth, not filled with the knowledge of others or with its own restlessness. Look, if you had no books of any kind, no so-called religious or sacred books, what would you do to find truth? If you were interested in it at all, you would have to search your own heart, you would have to seek out the sacred places of your mind, would you not? You would have to look to yourself; you would have to understand the way your mind is working, because the mind is the only instrument you have, and if you do not understand that instrument, how can you go beyond the mind? Surely, sir, those who first wrote the sacred books could not have been copyists, could they? They didn't quote somebody else. But we are quoting because our hearts are empty, we are dry, we have nothing in us. We make a lot of noise, and that we call wisdom; and with that knowledge we want to transform the world, and thereby we make more noise. That is why it is important for the mind which really wants to bring about a fundamental revolution to be free from copy, from imitation, from patterns.

Now, the questioner asks, "Does quotation from another person interfere with the peculiar technique of hypnotism which you are employing?" Am I hypnotizing you? Don't answer me—because the hypnotized man does not know he is being hypnotized. The problem is not whether I am hypnotizing you, but why you are listening to me. If you are listening merely to find a substitute, another leader, another picture to worship and put flowers before, then what I am saying will be utterly useless. Your walls are already filled with pictures, you have innumerable images, and if you are listening to find further gratification, you will be hypnotized no matter what is said. As long as you are seeking gratification, you will find the means that will gratify you, and therefore you will be hypnotized—as most of you are. Those who believe in nationalism are hypnotized; those who believe in certain dogmas about God, about reincarnation, or what you will, are hypnotized by words, by ideas. And you like to be hypnotized, mesmerized, either by another or by yourselves, because in that state you can remain undisturbed; and as long as you are seeking a state in which you will have no disturbance, which you call peace of mind, you will always find the means, the guru—anyone or anything that will give you what you want. That state is hypnosis. Surely, that is not what is taking place here, is it? Actually, I am not giving you anything. On the contrary, I say: Wake up from your hypnosis; whether you are hypnotized by your Upanishads, or by the latest guru—be free of them. Look at your own problems; see the truth of the nearest problems, not the farthest, and understand your relationship with society. Surely, that is not to hypnotize you; on the contrary, it is to bring you down to facts, to make you see the facts. The avoidance of the fact, the escape from the fact, is the process of hypnosis, and that is helped along by the newspapers, the cinema, the sacred books, the gurus, the temples, the repetition of words and chants. The fact is not something very extraordinary; the fact is that you are exploiting, that you are responsible for the mess in the world; it is you who are responsible, not some economic maladjustment. That is the fact, which you are unwilling to look at; and as long as you do not want to look at the fact, you will be hypnotized, not by me, but by your own desire, which seeks a way of not being disturbed, of walking along the usual path and becoming respectable. Sir, the respectable man, the so-called religious man, is the hypnotized man, because his ultimate escape is his belief; and that belief is invariably gratifying, it is never disturbing; otherwise, he would not believe in it.

So, either the desire for comfort, for security, for gratification, for a state of nondisturbance creates the outside entity who hypnotizes you, or you are inwardly hypnotized by your own desire for security; but to understand truth, the mind must be free. Freedom is not something to be achieved ultimately; it must be at the beginning, but we do not want to be free at the beginning because to be free at the beginning means inward revolution, a drastic perception of the facts all the time, which demands constant awareness, alertness of mind. Because we do not want to be awake to the facts, we find the usual ways of escape, either in social activities or personal ambition, and the mind which is caught in social activity and ambition is much more hypnotized than the mind which is merely self-enclosed in its personal misery; but both are hypnotized by their own want, by their own desires. You can be free from your own self-hypnosis only when you understand the whole, total process of yourself; therefore, self-knowledge is the beginning of freedom, and without self-knowledge you are perpetually in a state of hypnosis.

Question: You are preaching a kind of philosophical anarchism, which is the favorite escape of the highbrow intellectuals. Will not a community always need some form of regulation and authority? What social order could express the values you are upholding?

KRISHNAMURTI: Sir, when life is very difficult, when problems are increasing, we escape either through the intellect or through mysticism. We know the escape through the intellect: rationalization, more and more cunning devices, more and more technique, more and more economic responses to life, all very subtle and intellectual. And there is the escape through mysticism, through the sacred books, through worshipping an established idea—idea being an image, a symbol, a superior entity, or what you will—thinking that it is not of the mind, but both the intellectual and the mystic are products of the mind. One we call the intellectual highbrow, and the other we despise, because it is the fashion now to despise the mystic, to kick him out, but both function through the mind. The intellectual may be able to talk, to express himself more clearly, but he too withdraws himself into his own ideas and lives there quietly, disregarding society and pursuing his illusions, which are born of the mind; so I do not think there is any difference between the two. They are both pursuing illusions of the mind, and neither the highbrow nor the lowbrow, neither the mystic, the yogi who escapes, withdraws from the world, nor the commissar has the answer. It is you and I, ordinary common people, who have to solve this problem without being highbrow or mystical, without escaping either through rationalization or through vague terms and getting hypnotized by words, by methods of our own self-projection. What you are the world is, and unless you understand yourself, what you create will always increase confusion and misery, but the understanding of yourself is not a process through which you have to go in order to act. It is not that you must first understand yourself and then act; on the contrary, the understanding of yourself is in the very action of relationship. Action is relationship in which you understand yourself, in which you see yourself clearly, but if you wait to become perfect or to understand yourself, that waiting is dying. Most of us have been active, and that activity has left us empty, dry; and once we have been bitten, we wait and do not act further, because we say, "I won't act until I understand." Waiting to understand is a process of death, but if you understand the whole problem of action, of living from moment to moment, which does not demand waiting, then understanding is in what you are doing; it is in action itself, it is not separate from living. Living is action; living is relationship, and because we do not understand relationship, because we avoid relationship, we are caught in words; and words have mesmerized us into action that leads to further chaos and misery.

"Will not a community always need some form of regulation and authority?" Obviously, there must be authority as long as a community is based on violence. Is not our present social structure based on violence, on intolerance? The community is you and another in relationship, and is not your relationship based on violence? Are you not ultimately out for yourself, either as a commissar or as a yogi? The yogi wants his salvation first and so does the commissar, only you call it by different names. Is not our present relationship based on violence—violence being the process of self-enclosure, isolation? Is not our daily action a process of isolation? And since each one is isolating himself, there must be authority to bring about cohesion—either the authority of the state or the authority of organized religion. To the extent that we have been held together at all, we have been held so far through fear of religion or through fear of government, but a man who understands relationship, whose life is not based on violence, has no need for authority. The man who needs authority is the stupid man, the violent man, the unhappy man—which is yourself. You seek authority because you think that without it you are lost; that is why you have all these religions, illusions, and beliefs; that is why you have innumerable leaders, political as well as religious. In moments of confusion you produce the leader, and that leader you follow; and since he is the outcome of your own confusion, obviously, the leader himself must be confused. So, authority is necessary as long as you are producing conflict, misery, and violence in your relationships.

"What social order could express the values you are upholding?" Sir, do you understand what values I am upholding? Am I upholding anything—at least for those few who have listened with serious intention? I am not giving you a new set of values for an old set of values; I am not giving you a substitution, but I say: Look at the very things that you hold, examine them, search out their truth, and the values that you then establish will create the new society. It is not for somebody else to draw up a blueprint which you can follow blindly without knowing what it is all about, but it is for you to find out for yourself the value, the truth of each problem. What I am saying is very clear and simple if you will follow it. Society is your own product, it is your projection. The world's problem is your problem, and to understand that problem, you have to understand yourself, and you can understand yourself only in relationship, not in escapes. Because you escape through them, your religion, your knowledge, have no validity, no significance. You are unwilling to alter, fundamentally, your relationship with another because that means trouble, that means disturbance, revolution; so you talk about the highbrow intellectual, the mystic, and all the rest of that nonsense. Sir, a new society, a new order, cannot be established by another; it must be established by you. A revolution based on an idea is not a revolution at all. Real revolution comes from within, and that revolution is not brought about through escape but comes only when you understand your relationships, your daily activities, the way you are acting, the way you are thinking, the way you are talking, your attitude to your neighbor, to your wife, to your husband, to your children. Without understanding yourself, whatever you do, however far you may escape, will only produce more misery, more wars, more destruction.

Question: Prayer is the only expression of every human heart; it is the cry of the heart for unity. All schools of Bhaktimarga *are based on the instinctive bent for devotion. Why do you brush it aside as a thing of the mind?*

KRISHNAMURTI: Most people pray—you all do—either in a temple, in your private room, or quietly in your own heart. When do you pray? Surely, you pray when you are in trouble, do you not? When you are faced with a serious problem, when you are in sorrow, when there is no one to help you in your difficulty, when you are unhappy, confused, disturbed, and you want someone to help you out—then you pray. That is, prayer is the cry of every human being who seeks someone to help him out of his misery; so prayer is generally a petition, is it not? It is a supplication to someone outside of yourself, to a separate entity, to help you, and you want to be united with that entity.

Now, sirs, most of you pray in one way or another, so try to understand what I am talking about; do not resist it, but first find out. I am not mesmerizing you; I am trying to tell you that to resist something new is not to understand it. Do not say that I am condemning prayer, that I think it is futile, because there may be a different approach to the whole problem. Unless you follow this rather closely, I am afraid you won't understand what is going to come out of it. Prayer is a supplication, a petition, an appeal to something outside of ourselves. Is there anything beyond ourselves? Do not quote the Upanishads or Marx, because quotation has no meaning. The Upanishads may say that there is something beyond yourself, and the Marxist may say there is nothing beyond yourself, but both of them may be wrong. You have to find out the truth of it, and to find out the truth of it, you have to examine the process of yourself in prayer, you have to understand why you pray. For the moment we are not considering whether there is an answer to prayer or how the answer comes; we will go into that presently. When you pray, it is taken for granted that you pray to another, to an entity who is superior, who is beyond yourself, but before we go into that, surely, we must find out why you pray.

What is the process of prayer? First, obviously, we pray because we are confused. A happy man does not pray, does he? A man with joy, with delight, does not pray. It is the man who is in sorrow, the man who is faced with a difficulty, who is in confusion, in pain—it is he who prays, and his prayer is either for the clarification of his confusion or it is a supplication for some other need in which there is urgency. So, the man who prays is confused, in misery, in travail; and what happens when he prays? Have you ever observed yourself praying? You either kneel or sit quietly, you take a certain physical posture, don't you? Or, while you are walking, your mind is praying. Now, what happens in that process? Please follow it and you will see. When you pray, your mind is repeating certain words, certain Christian or Sanskrit phrases, and the repetition of these phrases makes the mind quiet, does it not? Try it and you will see that if you keep on repeating certain words, certain phrases, the superficial, upper layers of the mind are made quiet—which is not real stillness but a form of hypnosis. Now, when the upper, the superficial mind is made quiet, what happens? Obviously, the deeper layers of the mind give their intimation, do they not? All the deeper levels of consciousness, the racial accumulations, the individual experiences, the past memories and knowledge—it is all there; but our daily life, our daily activities are merely on the surface of the mind, and most of us are not concerned at all about the deeper levels. We are concerned with them only when we are disturbed, or occasionally when there is a remembrance, a dream. But obviously, the deeper layers of consciousness are always there, and they are ceaselessly acting, waiting, watching; and when the superficial mind, which is ordinarily so completely occupied with its own troubles, necessities, and worries, becomes somewhat quiet or is made quiet, naturally the inward memories give their intimations, and these intimations we call the voice of God. But is it the voice of God? Is it something beyond yourself? When these intimations come, obviously, they must be the result of collective and individual experience, of racial memory, which is a little more alert, a little wiser than the superficial mind; but the response is still from yourself, it is not from outside. The collective memories, the collective instincts, the collective idiosyncrasies and responses—all these project the hint into the quiet mind, but it is still from the limited entity, from the conditioned consciousness; it is not from beyond that consciousness. That is how your prayers are answered. You are part of the collective, and your prayers are answered from the collective in yourself, and the response to prayer must be satisfactory to the conscious mind; otherwise, you will never accept it. You believe and you pray because you want a way out of your difficulty, and the way out of your difficulty is always satisfying—somehow your prayers are always answered according to your gratifications. So, our prayers, which are supplications, have an answer from our deeper selves, not from beyond ourselves.

The next question is, Is there something beyond ourselves? To find that out requires quite a different way of thinking, not through prayer, not through meditation, not through quotation, but through understanding the whole process of consciousness. The mind can project ideas about God or reality, but what the mind projects is not beyond the field of thought, and as long as the mind is active in the projection of its own conceptions, it obviously cannot find out if there is something beyond itself. To find out if there is something beyond itself, the mind must cease to project, because whatever it can think of is still within the field of thought, whether conscious or unconscious. What the mind can project is not outside the field of itself, and to find out if there is something beyond the mind, the mind as thought must come to an end. Any activity, any movement on the part of the mind, is still its own projection, and as long as thought continues, it can never find what is beyond itself. That which is beyond the mind can be discovered only when the mind is still, and the stilling of the mind is not a process of will, of determined action. The mind that is made still through the action of will is obviously not a still mind, so the problem is how thought can come to an end without willing it to come to an end, because if I discipline the mind to be still, then it is a dead mind, it is an enclosed mind, it is not a free mind. It is only the free mind that can discover what is beyond itself, and that freedom cannot be imposed on the mind. Imposition is not freedom, discipline is not freedom, conformity is not freedom; but when the mind sees that conformity is not freedom, then it is free. Seeing the fact is the beginning of freedom, which is seeing the false as the false and the true as the true, not at a distant future, but from moment to moment; then only is there that freedom in which the mind can be simple and still, and such a still mind can know what is beyond itself.

Question: Do you accept the law of reincarnation and karma as valid, or do you envisage a state of complete annihilation?

KRISHNAMURTI: Now, most of you probably believe in reincarnation and karma, so please do not resist what I am going to say. Through resistance we do not understand, through exclusion there is no communion; to understand something, we must love it, which means we must be in communion with it and not be afraid of it.

First of all, belief in any form is the denial of truth; a believing mind is not an exploring mind; a believing mind can never be in a state of experiencing. Belief is merely a tether created by a particular desire. A man who believes in reincarnation cannot know the truth of it, because his belief is merely a comfort, an escape from death, from fear of noncontinuity; such a man cannot find the truth of reincarnation because what he wants is comfort, not truth. Truth may give him comfort or it may be a disturbing factor, but if he starts with the desire to find comfort, he cannot see the truth. Now, if you are serious, you and I are going to find out the truth of the matter, and what is important is how we approach the problem. How do you and I approach the problem of reincarnation? Are you approaching it through fear, through curiosity, through the desire for continuity? Or do you want to know *what is?* I am not avoiding the question. A mind that wants to know the truth, whatever it is, is surely in a different state from the mind which is afraid of death and is seeking comfort, continuity, and therefore clings to reincarnation. Such a mind is obviously not in a state of discovery. So, the approach to the problem matters, and I am taking it for granted that you are approaching the problem rightly, not through any desire for comfort, but to find out the truth of the matter.

Now, what do you mean by reincarnation? What is it that reincarnates? You know there is death, and do what you will, you cannot avoid it. You may postpone death, but this is a fact, which we will go into presently. What is it that reincarnates? It is either one of two things, is it not? Either it is a spiritual entity or it is a thing which is merely an accumulation of experience, of knowledge, of memory, not only individual but collective, which takes form again in another life. So, let us examine those two things. What do we mean by a "spiritual entity"? Is there a spiritual entity in you—something which is not of the mind, which is beyond sensation, something which is not of time, something immortal? You will say, "Yes"—all religious people do. You say that there is a spiritual entity, which is beyond time, beyond the mind, beyond death. Please do not resist, let us think it out. If you say there is a spiritual entity in you, it is obviously the product of thought, is it not? You have been told about it; it is not your experience. As a man is conditioned by being brought up with the idea that there is no spiritual entity, but only the coming together of various social, economic, and environmental influences, so you are conditioned to the idea of a spiritual entity, are you not? Even if it is your own discovery that there is a spiritual entity, surely it is still within the field of thought, and thought is the result of time, thought is the product of the past, thought is accumulation, memory. That is, if you can think about the spiritual entity, surely that entity is still within the field of thought; therefore, it is the product of thought, the projection of thought, and therefore it is not a spiritual entity. What you can think about is still within the field of thought, so it cannot be something beyond thought.

Now, if there is no spiritual entity, what is it that reincarnates? And if there is a spiritual entity, can it reincarnate? Is it a thing of time; is it a thing of memory that comes and goes at your convenience, at your desire? If it is born, if it is a process in time, if it has progress, surely it is not a spiritual entity; and if it is not of time, then there can be no question of reincarnating, taking on a new life. So, if the spiritual entity is not, then the 'you' is merely a bundle of accumulated memories; the 'you' is your property, your wife, your husband, your children, your name, your qualities. The accumulation of the experiences of the past in conjunction with the present is the 'you', both the conscious and the unconscious, the collective as well as the individual—that whole bundle is the 'you', and that bundle asks, "Shall I reincarnate, shall I have continuity, what happens after death?" If there is a spiritual entity, it is beyond thought; it cannot be caught in the net of the mind; and to discover that entity, that spiritual state, the mind must be quiet; it cannot be agitated with the functioning of thought. Now you are asking whether the 'you' has continuity—the 'you' being the name, the property, the furniture, the memories, the idiosyncrasies, the experiences, the accumulated knowledge. Has that continuity? That is, has conditioned thought a continuity? Obviously, thought has continuity; for that you do not have to inquire far. You have continuity in your children, in your property, in your name; obviously, that continues in one form or another. But you are not satisfied with that continuity, are you? You want to continue as a spiritual entity, not merely as thought, a bundle of reactions—there is no fun in that. But are you anything more than that? Are you anything more than your religion, your beliefs, your caste divisions, your superstitions, traditions, and future hopes? Are you anything more than that? You would like to think you are more than that, but the fact is you are that and nothing else. There may be something beyond, but to discover something beyond, all this has to come to an end. So, when you inquire into the problem of reincarnation, you are concerned, not with what is beyond, but with the continuity of thought identified as the 'you', and obviously there is continuity.

Now, another question involved in this is the problem of death. What is death? Is death merely the ending of the body? And why is it that we are so afraid of death? Because we cling to continuity, and we see that there is an ending of continuity when we die, we want assurance of continuity on the other side, and that is why we believe in life after death; but any amount of guarantees of continuity, all the research societies, all the books and information, will never satisfy you. Death is always the unknown; you may have all the information about it, but the known is afraid of the unknown and will always be. So, one of the problems in this question is this: is continuity creative? Can that which is continuous discover anything beyond itself? Sir, can that which has continuity know something beyond its own field? That is the problem, and it is a problem which you are unwilling to face—and that is why you are afraid of death. That which continues can never be creative; it is only in ending that there is the new. Only when the known comes to an end is there creation, the new, the unknown; but as long as we cling to the desire for continuity, which is thought identified as the 'me', that thought will continue, and that which continues has in it the seed of death and decay; it is not creative. It is only that which ends that can see the new, the fresh, the whole, the unknown. Sir, this is simple and very clear. As long as you are continuing in the habit of a particular thought, surely you cannot know the new, can you? As long as you cling to your traditions, to your name, to your properties, you cannot know anything new, can you? It is only when you let all that go completely that the new comes. But you dare not let go of the old because you are afraid of the new; that is why you are afraid of death, and that is why you have all the innumerable escapes. More books are written on death than on life because life you want to avoid. Living is to you a continuity, and that which continues withers, has no life; it is always afraid of coming to an end—and that is why you want immortality. You have your immortality in your name, in your property, in your furniture, in your son, your clothes, your house; all that is your immortality—you have it, but you want something more. You want immortality on the other side, and you have that too, which is your thought, identified as yourself, continuing—'yourself' being your furniture, your hats, your substitutions, your beliefs. But should you not find out whether that which continues can ever know the timeless? That which continues implies a process of time: the past, the present, and the future. That is, continuance is the past in conjunction with the present breeding the tomorrow, the future, which again breeds another future—and so there is continuity. But does that continuity bring about, can that continuity discover the unknown, the unknowable, the eternal? And if it cannot, what is the point of having that thought, identified as the 'me', continue? The 'me', which is identified thought, must be in a state of ceaseless conflict, constant suffering, perpetual worry over problems, and so on—and that is the lot of continuity. It is only when the mind comes to an end, when it is not identified as the 'me', that you will know that which is beyond time, but merely to speculate what is beyond is a waste of energy, it is the action of a sluggard. So, that which has continuance can never know the real, but that which has an ending shall know the real. Death alone can show the way to reality—not the death of old age or of disease, but the death of every day, dying every minute, so that you see the new.

In this question is also involved the problem of karma. I wonder if you would rather I discussed this another time? It is already half past seven. Do you want me to go into it?

Comment from the audience: Yes, sir.

KRISHNAMURTI: Have you understood what I have said about reincarnation? Have you, sirs? Why this strange silence? (Interruption) This is not a discussion, sir. We will discuss next Tuesday the question of time, and on Thursday evening we will discuss meditation; but if you really think about what has just been said, you will see the extraordinary depth of ending, of dying. The mind that can die every minute shall know the eternal, but the mind that has continuance can never know that which is beyond the mind. Sir, that is not a thing to be quoted, discussed; you must live it, and then only you will know the beauty of it; you will know the depth and the significance of dying each minute. Dying is merely the ending of the past, which is memory—not the memory, the recognition of facts, but the ending of the psychological accumulation as the 'me' and the 'mine'; and in that ending of identified thought, there is the new.

Now you want me to answer the question on karma. Please approach it with freedom, not with resistance, not with superstition, not with your beliefs. Obviously, there is cause and effect. The mind is the result of a cause; you are the result, the product of yesterday, and of many, many thousands of yesterdays; cause and effect are an obvious fact. The seedling has in it both cause and effect. It is specialized; a particular seed cannot become something different. The seed of wheat is specialized, but we human beings are different, are we not? That which specializes can be destroyed; anything that specializes comes to an end, biologically as well as psychologically, but with us it is different, is it not? We see that cause becomes effect, and what was effect becomes a further cause—it is very simple. Today is the result of yesterday, and tomorrow is the result of today; yesterday was the cause of today, and today is the cause of tomorrow. What was effect becomes cause, so it is a process without an end. There is no cause apart from effect; there is no division between cause and effect because cause and effect flow into each other, and if one can see the process of cause and effect as it actually operates, one can be free of it. As long as we are concerned with the mere reconciliation of effects, cause takes patterns, and the patterns then become the issue, the motive of action; but is there at any time a line of demarcation where cause ends and effect begins? Surely not, because cause and effect are in constant movement. In fact, there is no cause and no effect but only a movement of the "what has been" through the present to the future; and for a mind that is caught in this process of the "what has been" using the present as a passage to the "what will be," there is only a result. That is, such a mind is only concerned with results, with the reconciliation of effects, and hence for such a mind there is no escape beyond its own projections. So, as long as thought is caught in the process of cause and effect, the mind can proceed only in its own enclosure, and therefore there is no freedom. There is freedom only when we see that the process of cause and effect is not stationary, static, but in movement; when understood, that movement comes to an end—and then one can go beyond.

So, as long as the mind is merely responding to stimuli from the past, whatever it does is merely furthering its own misery; but when it sees and understands the fact of this whole process of cause and effect, of this whole process of time, that very understanding of the fact is freedom from the fact. Then only can the mind know that which is not a result or a cause. Truth is not a result, truth is not a cause; it is something which has no cause at all. That which has a cause is of the mind; that which has an effect is of the mind; and to know the causeless, the eternal—that which is beyond time—the mind, which is the effect of time, must come to an end. Thought, which is the effect as well as the cause, must come to an end, and only then can that which is beyond time be known.

March 5, 1950

Fifth Talk in Bombay

This is the last talk that will be held here. I believe there is a talk on Tuesday, the 14th at Dadar at 9 o'clock; probably you are already informed about it.

I think it is important, is it not, to understand the meaning of words, not only superficially, according to the dictionary, but also to see their significance beyond the mere superficial level, because we are mesmerized by words, and we think that by understanding a word we understand the whole content of that word. The word becomes significant only when we go beyond the superficial level, the ordinary or common usage, and see the deeper meaning of it. We have been mesmerized by certain words like *God, love, the simple life;* and especially in these times when there is so much confusion, when there are so many leaders, books, theories, and opinions, we tend to be easily mesmerized by the word *activity* or *action.* So, I think it would be worthwhile to go into the problem of what we mean by action and not merely be hypnotized by that word. We think we are very much alive and active when we keep going, when we are constantly in movement, when we are doing something, either at the club, in politics, in the family, or what you will. We think activity is life—and is it life? Living in the mechanical responses of everyday existence—is that life? Since mere activity takes most of our energy, is it not important to understand and not be mesmerized by the words *action* and *activity?* Action is obviously necessary; action is life, but at what level? We act according to opinion, according to memory; we are a whole series of conditioned responses, memories, and traditions. Our action and our morality are based on what has been or what will be, and our thinking, which is obviously the basis of our action, is almost mechanical; most of us are like machines in what we do. You give a machine certain information, and it gives you certain responses; similarly, we receive certain information through our senses and then respond. So, our thinking and our activities are almost mechanical, and this mechanical thinking with its responses and activity we call "living." We are satisfied to live on that level, and we are mesmerized by our leaders, by ourselves, by our environmental influences, to continue living in that state.

Now, can we go beyond and find out what is action? To most of us, action is mere mechanical response to a challenge. I ask you something, and you reply. There is constant impingement of stimuli, and there is a constant response, conscious or unconscious; and this process of the background, the tradition of what has been, mechanically responding to challenge, to stimuli, is our whole existence; it is our thinking and our activity. Religiously as well as politically, we are always responding to a challenge, and that response we call activity. But is that response action? Can it ever be action? Surely, it is not action; it is only reaction, and is it possible to go beyond reaction, to go beyond the mechanical process of the mind? We know the structure of the mind, which is merely accumulated information, accumulated experience, the conditioning of the past; and this conditioned mind is always responding, reacting; and this reaction we call action. But action based on reaction must obviously lead to confusion, because there is no newness, there is no freshness, no vitality, no clarity; it is a mechanical response. It is like a motor-car—you put in oil and fuel, start it, keep it going, and occasionally overhaul it. That is exactly what our life is—a series of mechanical responses to stimuli, to challenge, and this we call living. Obviously, such an approach to any problem can solve it only according to reaction, and a problem that is solved according to reaction is not solved at all.

So, is it possible to go beyond the mechanical responses and find out what is action? Action is obviously not a response, not a reaction, and it is only when we see that action itself is challenge that there is a quality of newness. To come to that, one must understand the whole process of thinking, the whole process of responding, reacting, and that is why it is so important to understand oneself. The self is obviously reaction, and to go beyond reaction, there must be complete understanding of the self, of the 'me', on all levels—not only on the physical but also on the psychological. As long as there is reaction, there must be the self, and the understanding of the self is the ending of reaction. Thinking in terms of reaction with regard to any problem will only multiply the problems, the complexities, the miseries of life; and the ending of reaction, of response, is the understanding of the self, the 'me'. The 'me' is at all levels; it is still the 'me', whether you place it at the highest level, calling it the atma, the paramatma or soul, or whether it is the 'me' that owns property, that is seeking power, virtue. The 'me' is merely reaction, and therefore the ending of reaction is the ending of the self. That is why it is important to understand the whole process of the self, which means, obviously, the process of thinking. Because our thinking is based on reaction, it is mechanical. The self is mechanical, and therefore it can respond mechanically; and to go beyond, there must be complete self-knowledge. The self is reaction, and when there is the understanding of the self, then we will find out what is action, because then action is challenge, then action is not a response, a reaction; it is from the center which is without a point. Now we always act from a center with a point, which is the 'me'—my fears, my hopes, my frustrations, my ambitions, my sociological, environmental, or religious conditioning; that is the center from which we react, and as long as that center is not completely understood, however much we may try to solve our problems, they will only multiply, and the misery, the struggle, the catastrophe will only increase. To understand that center with a point is to put an end to reaction and to bring about a center without a point, and when there is that center without a point, then there is action, and action is itself challenge.

The understanding of the mind is possible only in relationship—in your relationship to property, to people, and to ideas. At present that relationship is reaction, and a problem that is created by reaction cannot be solved by another reaction; it can be solved only when the whole process of reaction is understood—which is the self, the 'me'. Then you will find there is an action which is not reaction, which is the challenge itself, which is creative; but that state is not realized by closing your eyes and going into deep, peculiar meditation, fancies, and whatnot. Therefore, religion is self-knowledge, the beginning of the understanding of reaction; and without self-knowledge, there is no basis for thinking, there is only a basis for reaction. Thinking is action without a center—but then it is no longer thinking, because then there is no verbalization, there is no accumulation of memory, of experience. We can solve our problems only when we approach them anew, when there is creativeness, and there can be no creativeness if there is mechanical response. A machine is not creative, however marvelously put together, and we have a mind which is marvelously put together, which is mechanical, and which creates problems. To resolve those problems, occasionally we give it a shock, and then more and more shocks, but the shock method is not the solution of a problem. The solution of problems comes only when there is action which is not a reaction, and that is possible only when we understand the whole process of the mind in its relationships in daily life.

So, religion is the understanding of daily life, not a theory or a process of isolation. A religious man who repeats certain words while ruthlessly exploiting others is obviously an escapist; his morality, his respectability, is without any meaning. The understanding of the self is the beginning of wisdom, and wisdom is not reaction. It is only when the whole process of reaction, which is conditioning, is understood that there is a center without a point, which is wisdom.

Apparently it is easy to ask questions, for many have been sent in. Out of all those questions, résumés have been made of the more representative ones, and here they are; so if your particular question is not answered exactly as you put it, it is only being answered differently, but the problems are the same. As I answer these questions, please do not merely follow on the verbal level what is being said, but experience it as we go along. Let us take the journey together and observe, as it were, every shadow, every flower, every stone, every dead animal on the road, all the dirt and beauty that lie along the wayside. That is the only way we can solve any of our problems—by clearly, definitely, and closely observing everything that we see and feel.

Question: Will you please explain the process of your mind when you are actually speaking here. If you have not gathered knowledge, and if you have no store of experience and memory, from where do you get your wisdom? How do you manage to cultivate it? (Pause)

KRISHNAMURTI: I am hesitating because I have not seen the questions before. I shall answer spontaneously, so you also will have to follow spontaneously and not think along traditional lines. The question, then, is how my mind works, and how I have gathered wisdom. "If you have no store of experience and memory, from where do you get your wisdom? How do you manage to cultivate it?" First of all, how do you know that what I am saying is wisdom? (Laughter) Sirs, do not laugh. It is easy to laugh and pass it by. How do you know that what I am saying is true? By what measurement, by what yardstick do you measure? Is there a measurement for wisdom? Can you say this is wisdom and that is not? Is sensation wisdom, or is the response to sensation wisdom? Sir, you do not know what wisdom is; therefore, you cannot say I am speaking wisdom. Wisdom is not that which you experience, nor is it to be found in a book. Wisdom is not something that you can experience at all, that you can gather, accumulate. On the contrary, wisdom is a state of being in which there is no accumulation of any kind; you cannot gather wisdom.

The questioner wants to know how my mind works. If I may go into it a little, I will show you. There is no center from which it is acting, there is no memory from which it is responding. There is memory of the road which I took just now, of the road where I live, there is the recognition of people, of incidents, but there is no accumulating process, no mechanical process of gradual gathering, from which comes response. If I did not know the usage of English or some other language, I would not be able to speak. Communication on the verbal level is necessary in order to understand each other, but it is what is said, how it is said, from where it is said, that is important. Now, when a question is put, if the answer is the response of a mind which has accumulated experiences and memories, then it is merely reaction, and therefore it is not reasoning; but when there is no accumulation, which means no response, then there is no frustration, no effort, no struggle. The accumulating process, the accumulating center, is like a deep-rooted tree in a stream which gathers debris around itself, and thought, sitting on the top of that tree, imagines it is thinking, living. Such a mind is only accumulating, and the mind which accumulates—whether knowledge, money, or experience—is obviously not living. It is only when the mind moves, flows, that there is living.

The questioner wants to know how wisdom is come by, and how to cultivate it. You cannot cultivate wisdom; you can cultivate knowledge, information, but you cannot cultivate wisdom because wisdom is not a thing that can be accumulated. The moment you begin to accumulate, it becomes mere information, knowledge, which is not wisdom. The entity that cultivates wisdom is still part of thought, and thought is merely a response, a reaction to challenge. Therefore, thought is merely the accumulation of memory, of experience, of knowledge, and so thought can never find wisdom. Only when there is a cessation of thinking is there wisdom, and there can be cessation of thinking only when there is an end to the process of accumulation—which is the recognition of the 'me' and the 'mine'. While the mind functions within the field of 'me' and the 'mine', which is merely reaction, there cannot be wisdom. Wisdom is a state of spontaneity which has no center, which has no accumulating entity. As I am talking, I am aware of the words I am using, but I am not reacting from a center to the question. To find out the truth of a question, of a problem, the process of thinking—which is mechanical and which we know—must come to an end. Therefore, it means there must be complete inward silence, and then only will you know that creativeness which is not mechanical, which is not merely reaction. So, silence is the beginning of wisdom.

Look, sirs, it is fairly simple. When you have a problem, your first response is to think about it, to resist it, to deny it, to accept it, or to explain it away, is it not? Watch yourself and you will see. Take any problem that arises, and you will see that the immediate response is to resist or to accept it; or, if you do not do either of those things, you justify it, or you explain it away. So, when a question is asked, your mind is immediately set into motion; like a machine, it immediately responds. But if you will solve the problem, the immediate response is silence, not thinking. When this question was asked, my response was silence, complete silence, and being silent, I saw immediately that where there is accumulation, there cannot be wisdom. Wisdom is spontaneity, and there can be no spontaneity or freedom as long as there is accumulation as knowledge, memory. So, a man of experience can never be a wise man nor a simple man, but the man who is free from the process of accumulation is wise; he knows what silence is, and whatever comes from that silence is true. That silence is not a thing to be cultivated; it has no means, there is no path to it, there is no "how." To ask "how" means cultivating; it is merely a reaction, a response of the desire to accumulate silence. But when you understand the whole process of accumulating, which is the process of thinking, then you will know that silence from which springs action which is not reaction, and one can live in that silence all the time; it is not a gift, a capacity—it has nothing to do with capacity. It comes into being only when you closely observe every reaction, every thought, every feeling; when you are aware of the fact without explanation, without resistance, without acceptance or justification; and when you see the fact very clearly without intervening blocks and screens, then the very perception of the fact dissolves the fact, and the mind is quiet. It is only when the mind is very quiet, not making an effort to be quiet, that it is free. Sir, it is only the free mind that is wise, and to be free the mind must be silent.

Question: How can I as an individual meet, overcome, and resolve the growing tension and war fever between India and Pakistan? This situation creates a mentality of revenge and mass retaliation. Appeals and arguments are completely inadequate. Inaction is a crime. How does one meet a problem like this?

KRISHNAMURTI: Sir, why do you call inaction a crime? There are only two ways of dealing with this according to you—which is either to become a pacifist or to take a gun. That is the only way you respond, is it not? That is the only way most people know in which to answer a problem of this kind. To you, the gun and pacifism are the only means of action, are they not? You think you are answering the challenge when you take revenge with a gun, or whatever it is you do, and if you think that violence is no solution, you become a pacifist. In other words, you want recognition for your action, and the recognition satisfies you; you say, "I am a pacifist," or "I have a gun," and this labeling of yourself satisfies you, and you think you have answered the problem. Surely, that is the general response, is it not? So, that is why you say inaction is a crime. Of course it is a crime from those two points of view. A man who does not carry a gun or call himself a pacifist is to you a criminal because you think according to the recognized labels, according to those two ways. Now, seeing that, let us find out if inaction is a crime—inaction being not to act along either of those two lines or their equivalents. Is that a crime? Is it a crime to say, "I am neither a pacifist nor do I carry a gun"? When would you say that? When you see that both are merely reactions to the challenge, and that through reaction you cannot solve the problem. Surely, the man who carries a gun is doing so because of his reaction, which is the outcome of his conditioning as a nationalist, as an Indian, as a Pakistani, or whatever he is called. The carrying of the gun is merely a reaction according to his conditioning. And the man who does not carry a gun, who calls himself a pacifist, is also reacting according to his particular view, is he not? Those are the two reactions which we know, with which we are all acquainted. During wartime you make the pacifist a martyr, and so on, but both are recognized means of activity, and when you act along either of those two lines, with all their implications, you are satisfied, you feel that at least you are doing something about the war, and people recognize that you are doing it. You feel satisfied, and they feel satisfied, and the more carrying of guns, the better.

Now, the man who in wartime neither carries a gun nor calls himself a pacifist, who is inactive in the deep sense of the word, who does not respond to the challenge as a reaction—such a man you call inactive and therefore criminal. Now, is he the criminal? Is he inactive? Are you not the criminals, both the pacifist and the man who carries a gun? Surely, the criminal is not the man who says, "I will not react to war in any way," because such a man has no country; he belongs to no religion, no dogma; he has no leader—political, religious, or economic; he does not belong to any party, because these are all reactions, and therefore he is neither a pacifist nor does he carry a gun. And a man who does not react to the challenge but who is the challenge, such a man you call inactive, a useless entity, because he does not fit into either of these two categories. Surely, the whole thing is wrong, pacifism as well as carrying a gun, because they are mere reactions, and through reaction you will never solve any problem. You will solve the problem of war only when you yourself are the challenge and not merely a reaction.

So, the man who carries a gun does not solve the problem; he only increases the problem, for each war produces another war—it is a historical fact. The first world war produced the second world war, the second will produce the third, and so the chain keeps going. Now, when you see that, you react against it and say, "I am a pacifist, I won't carry a gun, and I will go to prison, I will suffer for it; I have a cause for which I am acting." The suffering, the martyrdom, is still a reaction, and so it cannot solve the problem either. But the man who is not reacting to war in any way is the challenge itself; he is in himself the breaker of old traditions, and such a man is the only entity that can resolve this problem. That is why it is important to understand yourself—your conditioning, your upbringing, the way you are educated—because the government, the whole system, is your own projection. The world is you, the world is not separate from you; the world with its problems is projected out of your responses, out of your reactions, so the solution does not lie in creating further reactions. There can be a solution only when there is action which is not reaction, and that can come into being only when you understand the whole process of response to stimuli, both from outside and inside, which means that you understand the structure of your own being from which society is created.

Question: We know sex as an inescapable physical and psychological necessity, and it seems to be a root cause of chaos in the per-

sonal life of our generation. It is a horror to young women who are victims of man's lust. Suppression and indulgence are equally ineffective. How can we deal with this problem?

KRISHNAMURTI: Why is it that whatever we touch we turn into a problem? We have made God a problem, we have made love a problem, we have made relationship, living, a problem, and we have made sex a problem. Why? Why is everything we do a problem, a horror? Why are we suffering? Why has sex become a problem? Why do we submit to living with problems; why do we not put an end to them? Why do we not die to our problems instead of carrying them day after day, year after year? Surely, sex is a relevant question, which I shall answer presently, but there is the primary question, Why do we make life into a problem? Working, sex, earning money, thinking, feeling, experiencing; you know—the whole business of living—why is it a problem? Is it not essentially because we always think from a particular point of view, from a fixed point of view? We are always thinking from a center towards the periphery, but the periphery is the center for most of us, and so anything we touch is superficial. But life is not superficial; it demands living completely, and because we are living only superficially, we know only superficial reaction. Whatever we do on the periphery must inevitably create a problem, and that is our life—we live in the superficial, and we are content to live there with all the problems of the superficial. So, problems exist as long as we live in the superficial, on the periphery—the periphery being the 'me' and its sensations, which can be externalized or made subjective, which can be identified with the universe, with the country, or with some other thing made up by the mind. So, as long as we live within the field of the mind, there must be complications, there must be problems, and that is all we know. Mind is sensation; mind is the result of accumulated sensations and reactions, and anything it touches is bound to create misery, confusion, an endless problem. The mind is the real cause of our problems—the mind that is working mechanically night and day, consciously and unconsciously. The mind is a most superficial thing, and we have spent generations, we spend our whole lives cultivating the mind, making it more and more clever, more and more subtle, more and more cunning, more and more dishonest and crooked—all of which is apparent in every activity of our life. The very nature of our mind is to be dishonest, crooked, incapable of facing facts, and that is the thing which creates problems, that is the thing which is the problem itself.

Now, what do we mean by the problem of sex? Is it the act, or is it a thought about the act? Surely, it is not the act. The sexual act is no problem to you any more than eating is a problem to you, but if you think about eating or anything else all day long because you have nothing else to think about, it becomes a problem to you. (Laughter) Do not laugh and look at somebody else—it is your life. So, is the sexual act the problem, or is it the thought about the act? And why do you think about it? Why do you build it up, which you are obviously doing? The cinemas, the magazines, the stories, the way women dress, everything is building up your thought of sex. And why does the mind build it up, why does the mind think about sex at all? Why, sirs and ladies? It is your problem. Why? Why has it become a central issue in your life? When there are so many things calling, demanding your attention, you give complete attention to the thought of sex. What happens, why are your minds so occupied with it? Because that is a way of ultimate escape, is it not? It is a way of complete self-forgetfulness. For the time being, at least for the moment, you can forget yourself—and there is no other way of forgetting yourself. Everything else you do in life gives emphasis to the 'me', to the self. Your business, your religion, your gods, your leaders, your political and economic actions, your escapes, your social activities, your joining one party and rejecting another—all that is emphasizing and giving strength to the 'me'. That is, sirs, there is only one act in which there is no emphasis on the 'me', so it becomes a problem, does it not? When there is only one thing in your life which is an avenue to ultimate escape, to complete forgetfulness of yourself if only for a few seconds, you cling to it because that is the only moment you are happy. Every other issue you touch becomes a nightmare, a source of suffering and pain, so you cling to the one thing that gives complete self-forgetfulness, which you call happiness. But when you cling to it, it too becomes a nightmare because then you want to be free from it; you do not want to be a slave to it. So you invent, again from the mind, the idea of chastity, of celibacy, and you try to be celibate, to be chaste, through suppression, denial, meditation, through all kinds of religious practices, all of which are operations of the mind to cut itself off from the fact. This again gives particular emphasis to the 'me', who is trying to become something; so again you are caught in travail, in trouble, in effort, in pain.

So, sex becomes an extraordinarily difficult and complex problem as long as you do not understand the mind which thinks about the problem. The act itself can never be a problem, but the thought about the act creates the problem. The act you safeguard; you live loosely or indulge yourself in marriage, thereby making your wife into a prostitute, which is all apparently very respectable, and you are satisfied to leave it at that. Surely, the problem can be solved only when you understand the whole process and structure of the 'me' and the 'mine': my wife, my child, my property, my car, my achievement, my success; and until you understand and resolve all that, sex as a problem will remain. As long as you are ambitious—politically, religiously, or in any way—as long as you are emphasizing the self, the thinker, the experiencer, by feeding him on ambition, whether in the name of yourself as an individual or in the name of the country, of the party, or of an idea which you call religion—as long as there is this activity of self-expansion, you will have a sexual problem. Surely, you are creating, feeding, expanding yourself on the one hand, and on the other you are trying to forget yourself, to lose yourself if only for a moment. How can the two exist together? So, your life is a contradiction: emphasis on the 'me', and forgetting the 'me'. Sex is not a problem; the problem is this contradiction in your life, and the contradiction cannot be bridged over by the mind because the mind itself is a contradiction. The contradiction can be understood only when you understand fully the whole process of your daily existence. Going to the cinemas and watching women on the screen, reading books which stimulate the thought, the magazines with their half-naked pictures, your way of looking at women, the surreptitious eyes that catch you—all these things are encouraging the mind through devious ways to emphasize the self, and at the same time you try to be kind, loving, tender. The two cannot go together. The man who is ambitious, spiritually or otherwise, can never be without a problem because problems cease only when the self is forgotten, when the 'me' is nonexistent; and that state of the nonexistence of the self is not an act of will, it is not a mere reaction. Sex becomes a reaction, and when the mind tries to solve the problem, it only makes the problem more confused, more troublesome, more painful. So, the act is not the problem, but the mind is the problem—the mind which says it must be chaste. Chastity is not of the mind. The mind can only suppress its own activities, and suppression is not chastity. Chastity is not a virtue; chastity cannot be cultivated. The man who is cultivating humility is surely not a humble man; he may call his pride humility, but he is a proud man, and that is why he seeks to become humble. Pride can never become humble, and chastity is not a thing of the mind—you cannot become chaste. You will know chastity only when there is love, and love is not of the mind nor a thing of the mind.

So, the problem of sex, which tortures so many people all over the world, cannot be resolved until the mind is understood. We cannot put an end to thinking, but thought comes to an end when the thinker ceases, and the thinker ceases only when there is an understanding of the whole process. Fear comes into being when there is division between the thinker and his thought; when there is no thinker, then only is there no conflict in thought. What is implicit needs no effort to understand. The thinker comes into being through thought; then the thinker exerts himself to shape, to control his thoughts, or to put an end to them. The thinker is a fictitious entity, an illusion of the mind. When there is a realization of thought as a fact, then there is no need to think about the fact. If there is simple, choiceless awareness, then that which is implicit in the fact begins to reveal itself. Therefore, thought as fact ends. Then you will see that the problems which are eating at our hearts and minds, the problems of our social structure, can be resolved. Then sex is no longer a problem, it has its proper place, it is neither an impure thing nor a pure thing. Sex has its place, but when the mind gives it the predominant place, then it becomes a problem. The mind gives sex a predominant place because it cannot live without some happiness, and so sex becomes a problem; but when the mind understands its whole process and so comes to an end, that is, when thinking ceases, then there is creation, and it is that creation which makes us happy. To be in that state of creation is bliss, because it is self-forgetfulness, in which there is no reaction as from the self. This is not an abstract answer to the daily problem of sex—it is the only answer. The mind denies love, and without love there is no chastity, and it is because there is no love that you make sex into a problem.

Question: Love, as we know and experience it, is a fusion between two people, or between the members of a group; it is exclusive, and in it there is both pain and joy. When you say love is the only solvent of life's problems, you are giving a connotation to the word which we have hardly experienced. Can a common man like me ever know love in your sense?

KRISHNAMURTI: Sir, everybody can know love, but you can know it only when you are capable of looking at facts very clearly, without resistance, without justification, without explaining them away—just look at things closely, observe them very clearly and minutely. Now, what is the thing that we call love? The questioner says that it is exclusive, and that in it we know pain and joy. Is love exclusive? We shall find out when we examine what we call love, what the so-called common man calls love. There is no common man. There is only man, which is you and I. The common man is a fictitious entity invented by the politicians. There is only man, which is you and I, who are in sorrow, in pain, in anxiety, and fear. Now, what is our life? To find out what love is, let us begin with what we know. What is our love? In the midst of pain and pleasure we know it is exclusive, personal: my wife, my children, my country, my God. We know it as a flame in the midst of smoke, we know it through jealousy, we know it through domination, we know it through possession, we know it through loss when the other is gone. So, we know love as sensation, do we not? When we say we love, we know jealousy, we know fear, we know anxiety. When you say you love someone, all that is implied: envy, the desire to possess, the desire to own, to dominate, the fear of loss, and so on. All this we call love, and we do not know love without fear, without envy, without possession; we merely verbalize that state of love which is without fear; we call it impersonal, pure, divine, or God knows what else, but the fact is that we are jealous, we are dominating, possessive. We shall know that state of love only when jealousy, envy, possessiveness, domination, come to an end, and as long as we possess, we shall never love. Envy, possession, hatred, the desire to dominate the person or the thing called 'mine', the desire to possess and to be possessed—all that is a process of thought, is it not? And is love a process of thought? Is love a thing of the mind? Actually, for most of us, it is. Do not say it is not—it is nonsense to say that. Do not deny the fact that your love is a thing of the mind. Surely it is, is it not? Otherwise, you would not possess, you would not dominate, you would not say, "It is mine." And as you do say it, your love is a thing of the mind; so love, for you, is a process of thought. You can think about the person whom you love, but thinking about the person whom you love—is that love? When do you think about the person whom you love? You think about her when she is gone, when she is away, when she has left you. But when she no longer disturbs you, when you can say, "She is mine," then you do not have to think about her. You do not have to think about your furniture; it is part of you—which is a process of identification so as not to be disturbed, to avoid trouble, anxiety, sorrow. So, you miss the person whom you say you love only when you are disturbed, when you are in suffering; and as long as you possess that person, you do not have to think about that person, because in possession there is no disturbance. But when possession is disturbed, you begin to think, and then you say, "I love that person." So your love is merely a reaction of the mind, is it not?—which means your love is merely a sensation, and sensation is surely not love. Do you think about the person when you are close to him, sirs and ladies? When you possess, hold, dominate, control, when you can say, "She is mine" or "He is mine," there is no problem. As long as you are certain in your possession, there is no problem, is there? And society, everything you have built around you, helps you to possess so as not to be disturbed, so as not to think about it. Thinking comes when you are disturbed—and you are bound to be disturbed as long as your thinking is what you call "love." Surely, love is not a thing of the mind, and because the things of the mind have filled our hearts, we have no love. The things of the mind are jealousy, envy, ambition, the desire to be somebody, to achieve success. These things of the mind fill your hearts, and then you say you love, but how can you love when you have all these confusing elements in you? When there is smoke, how can there be a pure flame? Love is not a thing of the mind, and love is the only solution to our problems. Love is not of the mind, and the man who has accumulated money or knowledge can never know love because he lives with the things of the mind; his activities are of the mind, and whatever he touches he makes into a problem, a confusion, a misery.

So, what we call our love is a thing of the mind. Look at yourselves, sirs and ladies, and you will see that what I am saying is obviously true; otherwise, our lives, our marriage, our relationships would be entirely different; we would have a new society. We bind ourselves to another, not through fusion, but through contract, which is called love, marriage. Love does not fuse, adjust—it is neither personal nor impersonal; it is a state of being. The man who desires to fuse with something greater, to unite himself with another, is avoiding misery, confusion; but the mind is still in separation, which is disintegration. Love knows neither fusion nor diffusion; it is neither personal nor impersonal; it is a state of being which the mind cannot find—it can describe it, give it a term, a name, but the word, the description, is not love. It is only when the mind is quiet that it shall know love, and that state of quietness is not a thing to be cultivated. Cultivation is still the action of the mind; discipline is still a product of the mind, and a mind that is disciplined, controlled, subjugated, a mind that is resisting, explaining, cannot know love. You may read, you may listen to what is being said about love, but that is not love. Only when you put away the things of the mind, only when your hearts are empty of the things of the mind, is there love. Then you will know what it is to love without separation, without distance, without time, without fear—and that is not reserved to the few. Love knows no hierarchy; there is only love. There are the many and the one, an exclusiveness, only when you do not love. When you love, sir, there is neither the 'you' nor the 'me'; in that state there is only a flame without smoke.

It is already half past seven, and there is one more question. Do you want me to answer it? You are not tired?

Question: The question of what is truth is an ancient one, and no one has answered it finally. You speak of truth, but we do not see your experiments or efforts to achieve it, as we saw in the lives of people like Mahatma Gandhi and Dr. Besant. Your pleasant personality, your disarming smile and soft love, is all that we see. Will you explain why there is such a difference between your life and the lives of other seekers of truth. Are there two truths?

KRISHNAMURTI: Do you want proof? And by what standard shall truth be judged? There are those who say that effort and experiment are necessary for truth, but is truth to be gotten through effort, through experiment, through trial and error? There are those who struggle and make valiant efforts, who strive spectacularly, either publicly or quietly in caves—and shall they find truth? Is truth a thing to be discovered through effort? Is there a path to truth, your path and my path, the path of the one who makes an effort, and the path of the one who does not? Are there two truths, or has truth many aspects?

Now, this is your problem, it is not my problem; and your problem is this, is it not?—you say, "Certain people—two, or several, or hundreds—have made efforts, have struggled, have sought truth whereas you do not make an effort, you lead a pleasant, unassuming life." So, you want to compare, that is, you have a standard, you have the picture of your leaders who have struggled to achieve truth; and when someone else comes along who does not fit into your frame, you are baffled, and so you ask, "Which is truth?" You are baffled—that is the important thing, sir, not whether I have truth or someone else has truth. What is important is to find out if you can discover reality through effort, will, struggle, striving. Does that bring understanding? Surely, truth is not something distant; truth is in the little things of everyday life—in every word, in every smile, in every relationship—only we do not know how to see it; and the man who tries, who struggles valiantly, who disciplines himself, controls himself—will he see truth?

The mind that is disciplined, controlled, narrowed down through effort—shall it see truth? Obviously not. It is only the silent mind that shall see the truth, not the mind that makes an effort to see. Sir, if you are making an effort to hear what I am saying, will you hear? It is only when you are quiet, when you are really silent, that you understand. If you observe closely, listen quietly, then you will hear; but if you strain, struggle, to catch everything that is being said, your energy will be dissipated in the strain, in the effort. So, you will not find truth through effort; it does not matter who says it, whether the ancient books, the ancient saints, or the modern ones. Effort is the very denial of understanding, and it is only the quiet mind, the simple mind, the mind that is still, that is not overtaxed by its own efforts—only such a mind shall understand, shall see truth. Truth is not something in the distance; there is no path to it; there is neither your path nor my path; there is no devotional path; there is no path of knowledge or path of action, because truth has no path to it. The moment you have a path to truth, you divide it, because the path is exclusive, and what is exclusive at the very beginning will end in exclusiveness. The man who is following a path can never know truth because he is living in exclusiveness; his means are exclusive, and the means are the end, the means are not separate from the end. If the means are exclusive, the end is also exclusive.

So, there is no path to truth, and there are not two truths. Truth is not of the past or of the present, it is timeless; and the man who quotes the truth of the Buddha, of Shankara, of the Christ, or who merely repeats what I am saying, will not find truth, because repetition is not truth. Repetition is a lie. Truth is a state of being which arises when the mind—which seeks to divide, to be exclusive, which can think only in terms of results, of achievement—has come to an end. Only then will there be truth. The mind that is making effort, disciplining itself in order to achieve an end, cannot know truth, because the end is its own projection, and the pursuit of that projection, however noble, is a form of self-worship. Such a being is worshipping himself, and therefore he cannot know truth. Truth is to be known only when we understand the whole process of the mind, that is, when there is no strife. Truth is a fact, and the fact can be understood only when the various things that have been placed between the mind and the fact are removed. The fact is your relationship to property, to your wife, to human beings, to nature, to ideas; and as long as you do not understand the fact of relationship, your seeking God merely increases the confusion because it is a substitution, an escape, and therefore it has no meaning. As long as you dominate your wife or she dominates you, as long as you possess and are possessed, you cannot know love; as long as you are suppressing, substituting, as long as you are ambitious, you cannot know truth. It is not the denial of ambition that makes the mind calm, and virtue is not the denial of evil. Virtue is a state of freedom, of order, which evil cannot give, and the understanding of evil is the establishment of virtue. The man who builds churches or temples in the name of God with the money which he has gathered through exploitation, through deceit, through cunning and foul play, shall not know truth; he may be mild of tongue, but his tongue is bitter with the taste of exploitation, the taste of sorrow. He alone shall know truth who is not seeking, who is not striving, who is not trying to achieve a result. The mind itself is a result, and whatever it produces is still a result, but the man who is content with *what is* shall know truth. Contentment does not mean being satisfied with the status quo, maintaining things as they are—that is not contentment. It is in seeing a fact truly and being free of it that there is contentment, which is virtue. Truth is not continuous; it has no abiding place; it can be seen only from moment to moment. Truth is always new, therefore timeless. What was truth yesterday is not truth today; what is truth today is not truth tomorrow. Truth has no continuity. It is the mind which wants to make the experience which it calls truth continuous, and such a mind shall not know truth. Truth is always new; it is to see the same smile and see that smile newly, to see the same person and see that person anew, to see the waving palms anew, to meet life anew. Truth is not to be had through books, through devotion, or through self-immolation, but it is known when the mind is free, quiet; and that freedom, that quietness of the mind comes only when the facts of its relationships are understood. Without understanding its relationships, whatever it does only creates further problems. But when the mind is free from all its projections, there is a state of quietness in which problems cease, and then only the timeless, the eternal comes into being. Then truth is not a matter of knowledge, it is not a thing to be remembered, it is not something to be repeated, to be printed and spread abroad. Truth is that *which is;* it is nameless, and so the mind cannot approach it.

March 12, 1950

Sixth Talk in Bombay

This is going to be rather difficult, and I hope those who understand English will have the patience to listen to Marathi.

It must be fairly obvious to most of us that a different kind of thinking and action must be brought about in the world, and that requires very careful observation of ourselves, not mere analysis, but deep penetration into the activities of each one of us. The problems of our daily existence are numerous, and we have not the means or the capacity to deal with them; and as our lives are so drab, dull, and stupid, we try to escape from them, either intellectually or mystically. Intellectually we become cynical, clever, and very learned, or mystically we try to develop some powers or follow some guru, hoping to make our hearts more lovely and give our life more zest. Or, seeing the drabness of our life and the implication of our problems, and seeing that the problems are always on the increase, always multiplying, we think that to bring about a fundamental change, we cannot act as individuals, but must act in a mass, collectively. I think it is a great mistake to say that our problems are to be solved through collective or mass action. We believe that individual action is of very little importance and has no place when the problems are so vast, so complex, so demanding; therefore, we turn to collective or mass action. We think that if you and I acted individually, it would have very little result, so we join mass movements and take part in collective action. But if we examine collective action very closely, we will see that it is really based on you and me. We seem to regard mass action as the only effective action because it can produce a result, but we forget that individual action is much more effective, because the mass is composed of many individuals, the mass is not an independent entity, it is not different or separate from you and me.

So, what is important is to understand that any creative, any definitely effective action can be brought about only by individuals, that is, by you and me. Mass action is really an invention of the politician, is it not? It is a fictitious action in which there is no independent thought and action on the part of the individual. If you look at history, all great movements which resulted in collective action began with individuals like you and me, individuals who are capable of thinking very clearly and seeing things as they are; those individuals, through their understanding, invite others, and then there is collective action. After all, the collective is composed of individuals, and it is only the response of the individual, of you and me, that can bring about a fundamental alteration in the world; but when the individual does not see his responsibility, he throws the responsibility onto the collective, and the collective is then used by the clever politician, or by the clever religious leader. Whereas, if you see that you and I are responsible for the alteration of the conditions in the world, then the individual becomes extraordinarily important and not merely an instrument, a tool, in the hands of another.

So, you, the individual, are part of society; you are not separate from society; what you are, society is. Though society may be an entity apart from you, you have created it, and therefore you alone can change it. But instead of realizing our responsibility as individuals in the collective, we as individuals become cynical, intellectual, or mystical; we avoid our responsibility towards definite action, which must be revolutionary in the fundamental sense; and as long as the individual, which is you and I, does not take responsibility for the complete transformation of society, society will remain as it is.

We seem to forget that the world problem is the individual problem, that the problems of the world are created by you and me as individuals. The problems of war, starvation, exploitation, and all the other innumerable problems that confront each one of us are created by you and me, and as long as we do not understand ourselves at every level, we will maintain the rottenness of the present society. So, before you can alter society, you have to understand what your whole structure is: the manner of your thinking, the manner of your action, the ways of your relationship with people, ideas, and things. Revolution in society must begin with revolution in your own thinking and acting. The understanding of yourself is of primary importance if you would bring about a radical transformation in society, and the understanding of yourself is self-knowledge. Now, we have made self-knowledge into something extraordinarily difficult and remote. Religions have made self-knowledge very mystical, abstract, and far away, but if you look at it more closely, you will see that self-knowledge is very simple and demands simple attention in relationship—and it is essential if there is to be a fundamental revolution in the structure of society. If you, the individual, do not understand the ways of your own thought and activities, merely to bring about a superficial revolution in the outer structure of society is to create further confusion and misery. If you do not know yourself, if you follow another without knowing the whole process of your own thinking and feeling, you will obviously be led to further confusion, to further disaster.

After all, life is relationship, and without relationship there is no possibility of life. There is no living in isolation, because living is a process of relationship, and relationship is not with abstractions; it is your relationship to property, to people, and to ideas. In relationship you see yourself as you are, whatever you are, ugly or beautiful, subtle or gross; in the mirror of relationship you see precisely every new problem, the whole structure of yourself as you are. Because you think that you cannot alter your relationship fundamentally, you try to escape intellectually or mystically, and this escape only creates more problems, more confusion, and more disaster. But if, instead of escaping, you look at your life in relationship and understand the whole structure of that relationship, then there is a possibility of going beyond that which is very close. Surely, to go very far, you must begin very near, but to begin near is very difficult for most of us because we want to escape from *what is,* from the fact of what we are. Without understanding ourselves, we cannot go far, and we are in constant relationship; there is no existence at all without relationship. So, relationship is the immediate, and to go beyond the immediate, there must be the understanding of relationship. But we would much rather examine that which is very far away, that which we call God or truth, than bring about a fundamental revolution in our relationship, and this escape to God or to truth is utterly fictitious, unreal. Relationship is the only thing that we have, and without understanding that relationship, we can never find out what reality is or God is. So, to bring about a complete change in the social structure, in society, the individual must cleanse his relationship, and the cleansing of relationship is the beginning of his own transformation.

I am going to answer some questions which have been handed to me. Now, in considering these questions, I shall not give any definite conclusion or final answer because what is important is to find out the truth of the problem, and the truth is not in the answer but in the problem itself. Most of us are accustomed to repeat what we have been told, to recite something that we have learned from a book, and so, in putting questions, we expect answers which will fit into our particular ways of thinking. We think we understand the problems of life by quoting some sacred book, which merely makes us into gramophone records, and if the song is not the same, we get lost. The so-called religious person and the so-called nonbeliever are both repeating machines. They are neither religious nor revolutionary; they merely repeat a formula, and repetition does not make one a religious or a revolutionary person. So, in considering these questions, let us travel together and go into the problem fully and extensively, not merely look at it from outside.

Question: Political freedom has not yet brought a new faith and joy. We find everywhere cynicism, communal and linguistic antagonism, and class hatred. What is your diagnosis and remedy for this tragic situation?

KRISHNAMURTI: Sir, this is not a problem only in India but a problem all over the world. It is a world problem, not merely an Indian problem. Now, one of the factors of disintegration is when people divide themselves into communal, linguistic, or sectional groups. We seem to think that through nationalism we shall be able to solve our problems, but nationalism, however widely extended, is an exclusion; it is still separatism, and where there is separatism, there is disintegration. Though full of promise at the beginning, full of hope, joy, and expectation, nationalism becomes a poison as you can see in this country—and that is exactly what is happening in every country. How can there be unity when there is exclusion? Unity implies no separation into Hindu and Muslim. Unity is destroyed when it becomes exclusive, when it is limited to a particular group. Unity is not the opposite of exclusion; it is the inner integration of the whole being of the individual in himself, not mere identification with a particular group or society. Why are you a nationalist; why do you belong to a particular class? Why this emphasis on a name? Let us examine this process of identification with a country, with a people, with a linguistic group, and so on. Why is it that you call yourself a Hindu? Why is it that you call yourself an Indian, a Gujarathi, or by some other name? Is it not because through identification with something greater, you feel yourself to be greater? In yourself you are nobody—you are dry, empty, hollow—

and by identifying yourself with something greater called India, England, or some other country, you think you become important. So, your calling yourself a nationalist, your identifying yourself with a particular country, obviously indicates that in yourself you are empty, dull, dry, ugly; and in identifying yourself with something greater, you are merely escaping from what you are. Now, such identification must lead to disintegration because you as an individual are the basis of all society, and if you are dishonest in your own thinking, the society you produce or project outside of yourself will be founded on dishonesty, without any fundamental reality. And the clever politicians or religious leaders use nationalism as a means of producing a result which is merely artificial, because it is without the understanding of the whole structure of human thought and feeling. We seem to think that by gaining independence we have achieved freedom. Freedom is not achieved; it does not come through mere political independence. Freedom comes when there is happiness. By merely exchanging a white bureaucracy for a brown bureaucracy, you are not free, are you? You are still the exploiter and the exploited; you are still saddled with the clever politicians and the innumerable leaders who are trying to lead you to God knows what. Nationalism is like a poison that is working subtly—and before you know what is happening, you are in the middle of a war. Sovereign governments with their nationalism and armed forces must lead to war, and to avoid war is not to become a mere pacifist or to join an antiwar movement but to understand the whole structure of ourselves as human entities, as individuals in relationship with each other, which is society.

So, to understand yourself is much more important than to call yourself by a name. A name is readily exploited, but if you understand yourself, no one can exploit you. Nationalism always produces war, and the problem is not to be solved by bringing about further nationalism, which is only an avoidance of the fact and an extension of the same poison, but by being free of nationalism, of the sense of belonging to a particular group, to a particular class or society.

Question: Can the starving and ignorant people of this land understand your message? How can it have any meaning or significance for them?

KRISHNAMURTI: The problem of starvation and unemployment is not only in this country, though it is much more aggravated here, but it exists all over the world. It has definite causes, and until we understand those causes, merely to scratch on the surface will have no result. Nationalism is one of the causes, separate sovereign governments is another. There is enough scientific knowledge to bring about conditions so that people all over the world can have food, clothing, and shelter. Why is it not done? Is it not because we are quarreling over systems? Realizing that there is starvation and unemployment in the world, we turn to systems and formulas which promise a better future, and have you ever noticed that those who have a system for the solution of unemployment and starvation are always fighting another system? So, systems become much more important than the solution of the problem of starvation itself. The fact of starvation can never be solved by an idea because ideas will only produce more conflict, more opposition, but facts can never produce opposition. There is starvation and unemployment in this country and throughout the world, and seeing the problem, we approach it with an idea about the problem. So idea, theory, system, becomes much more important than the fact. That is, we turn from the fact to a theory, an idea, a belief about the fact, and around the belief, groups are being formed, and these groups battle and liquidate each other, and the fact remains. (Laughter) What is important is the understanding of the fact, not an idea about the fact, and that understanding does not depend on idea. Idea is merely a fabrication of the mind, but understanding is not a result of the mind. We have enough intelligence and capacity and knowledge to solve the fact of starvation and unemployment, but what prevents us from solving it is our idea about the solution. The fact is there, and we have created several approaches to the fact: there is the approach of the yogi, of the commissar, of the capitalist, of the socialist, and so on. Now, can the fact be grasped through a particular approach? A particular approach must obviously prevent the understanding of the fact. So, the fact of starvation and unemployment can be solved only when idea, belief, does not interfere with the understanding of the fact. That means, does it not, that you, who are part of society, must be free of nationalism, free of belief in a particular religion, free of identification with a particular idea or group. So, the solution of this problem is not in the hands of the commissar or the yogi but in your hands, because it is what you are that prevents the solution of all these problems. If you are a nationalist, if you belong to a particular class or caste, if you have narrow religious traditions, obviously you are hindering the welfare of man.

Question: Are you not against institutional marriage?

KRISHNAMURTI: Please listen carefully and hear intelligently; do not merely oppose or resist. It is so easy to be against something; it is so stupid to resist without understanding. Now, the family is exclusive, is it not? The family is a process of identification with the particular, and when society is based on this idea of family as an exclusive unit in opposition to other exclusive units, such a society must inevitably produce violence. We use family as a means of security for ourselves, for the individual, and where there is search for individual security, for individual happiness, there must be exclusion. This exclusion is called "love," and in that so-called family or married state, is there really love? Now, let us examine what the family actually is and not cling to a theory about it. We are not considering the ideal of what it should be, but let us examine exactly what the family is as you know it. You mean by family your wife and children, do you not? It is a unit in opposition to other units, and in that unit it is you who are important—not your wife, not your children or society, but you who are seeking security, name, position, power, both in the family and outside the family. You dominate your wife; she is subservient to you; you are the maker and the dispenser of money, and she is your cook and the bearer of your children. (Laughter) So, you create the family which is an exclusive unit in opposition to other units; you multiply by millions and produce a society in which the family is an exclusive, self-isolating, separative entity, antagonistic and opposed to another. All revolutions try to do away with the family, but invariably they fail because the individual is constantly seeking his own security through isolation, exclusion, ambition, and domination. So, the family, which you have created as a separative unit, becomes a danger to the collective, which is also the result of the individual; therefore, there can be no reform in the collective as long as you, the individual, are exclusive and self-isolating in every action, narrowing down your interest to yourself.

Now, this process of exclusion is surely not love. Love is not a creation of the mind. Love is not personal, impersonal, or universal—those words are merely of the mind. Love is something that cannot be understood as long as thought, which is exclusive, remains. Thought, which is the reaction of the mind, can never understand what love is; thought is invariably exclusive, separative, and when thought tries to describe love, it must of necessity enclose it in words, which are also exclusive. The family as we know it is the invention of the mind, and therefore it is exclusive; it is a process of the enlargement of the self, of the 'me', which is the result of thought; and in the family, to which we cling so constantly, so desperately, surely there is no love, is there? We use that word *love;* we think we love, but actually we do not, do we? We say that we love truth, that we love the wife, the husband, the children; but that word is surrounded by the smoke of jealousy, envy, oppression, domination, and constant battle. So, family becomes a nightmare; it becomes a battlefield between the two sexes, and therefore family invariably becomes opposed to society. The solution lies not in legislation to destroy the family but in your own understanding of the problem, and the problem is understood and therefore comes to an end only when there is real love. When the things of the mind do not fill the heart, when individual ambition, personal success and achievement do not predominate, when they have no place in your heart, then you will know love.

Question: Why are you trying to shake our belief in God and religion? Is not some faith necessary for spiritual endeavor, both individual and collective?

KRISHNAMURTI: Why do we need faith, why do we need belief? If you observe, is not belief one of the factors that separate man from man? You believe in God, and another does not believe in God, so your beliefs separate you from each other. Belief throughout the world is organized as Hinduism, Buddhism, or Christianity, and so it divides man from man. We are confused, and we think that through belief we shall clear the confusion; that is, belief is superimposed on the confusion, and we hope that confusion will thereby be cleared away. But belief is merely an escape from the fact of confusion; it does not help us to face and to understand the fact but to run away from the confusion in which we are. To understand the confusion, belief is not necessary, and belief only acts as a screen between ourselves and our problems. So, religion, which is organized belief, becomes a means of escape from *what is,* from the fact of confusion. The man who believes in God, the man who believes in the hereafter, or who has any other form of belief, is escaping from the fact of what he is. Do you not know those who believe in God, who do puja, who repeat certain chants and words, and who in their daily life are dominating, cruel, ambitious, cheating, dishonest? Shall they find God? Are they really seeking God? Is God to be found through repetition of words, through belief? But such people believe in God, they worship God, they go to the temple every day, they do everything to avoid the fact of what they are—and such people you consider respectable because they are yourself.

So, your religion, your belief in God, is an escape from actuality, and therefore it is no religion at all. The rich man who accumulates money through cruelty, through dishonesty, through cunning exploitation, believes in God; and you also believe in God, you also are cunning, cruel, suspicious, envious. Is God to be found through dishonesty, through deceit, through cunning tricks of the mind? Because you collect all the sacred books and the various symbols of God, does that indicate that you are a religious person? So, religion is not escape from the fact; religion is the understanding of the fact of what you are in your everyday relationships; religion is the manner of your speech, the way you talk, the way you address your servants, the way you treat your wife, your children, and neighbors. As long as you do not understand your relationship with your neighbor, with society, with your wife and children, there must be confusion; and whatever it does, the mind that is confused will only create more confusion, more problems and conflict. A mind that escapes from the actual, from the facts of relationship, shall never find God; a mind that is agitated by belief shall not know truth. But the mind that understands its relationship with property, with people, with ideas, the mind which no longer struggles with the problems which relationship creates, and for which the solution is not withdrawal but the understanding of love—such a mind alone can understand reality. Truth cannot be known by a mind that is confused in relationship, or that escapes from relationship into isolation, but by the mind that understands itself in action, and only such a mind shall know the truth. A quiet mind, a silent mind, cannot come into being through any form of compulsion, through any form of discipline, because the mind is quiet only when it understands its relationship to property, to people, and to ideas, and, do what it will, the mind is not quiet when it is disturbed by the fact of its relationship to these. The mind that is made quiet without understanding its relationships is a dead mind, but the mind that has no belief, that is quiet because it understands relationship—such a mind is silent, creative, and it shall know reality.

March 14, 1950

Paris, France, 1950

First Talk in Paris

Most of us are confronted with many problems, not only individual but collective; there are problems that not only touch our personal lives, but also affect us as citizens of a particular country, as part of a collective group, and so on. We have problems that are not only sociological and economic, but also, if I may use the word, spiritual. We are confronted with problems of every kind, and the more we deal with these problems, the more they seem to increase and multiply and become confused.

This translation business is going to be rather difficult, but perhaps it will go fairly smoothly as we get used to it. I have not done this kind of thing for many years, so I hope you will have a little patience if there is hesitation on my part.

As I was saying, the more we deal with these problems, the more they seem to increase, and with the increase of problems, there arises greater suffering, greater misery, and greater confusion. Surely, what is important is not how to solve any one particular problem but to find out how to deal with the problems as they arise, so as not to increase or multiply them. That is, we must obviously deal with the problems of existence, not on any one particular level, but at all levels, because if we deal with a problem merely on its own level, surely such a problem cannot be solved. If we deal with the economic problem, whether individual or collective, apart from the spiritual or psychological problem, the economic problem can never be solved. In order to solve a particular problem, we have to understand the creator of the problem, and to understand the creator is surely much more important than to understand the problem itself because when once we understand the creator or maker of the problem, then we can resolve the problem. So, our difficulty is to understand, not only superficially but also fundamentally, the creator of problems—which is oneself. Therefore the study of oneself is not an avoidance of the problem, whether superficial or profound; on the contrary, to understand oneself is of far greater importance than to bring about a result by dealing with the problem, by transforming or being active about the problem.

Now, as I said, the important thing is not to seek a mere solution to the problem, whether economic or any other, whether individual or collective, but to understand the maker of the problem; and to understand the maker is much more difficult, it requires much greater awareness, greater attention, than merely to study the problem. The creator of the problem is oneself, and the understanding of oneself does not imply a process of isolation, a process of withdrawal. We seem to think that we must be agitated, active about the problem, for then we can at least feel that we are doing something about it; but any concern with the study, with the understanding of the maker of the problem, we regard as a process of isolation, of enclosure, and therefore a denial of action. So, it is important to see that the study of oneself is not a withdrawal, is not a process of isolation or inactivity; on the contrary, it is a process of extraordinary attention, of alert awareness, which demands not only superficial but also inward clarity.

After all, when we talk of action, we really mean reaction, do we not? Most of us react to any outside influence, and in this process of reaction we are caught, and this reaction we call dealing with the problem. So, the understanding of reaction is the beginning of the understanding of oneself. As I pointed out, what is important is not so much the understanding of the problem itself, but the understanding of the reactions that each one has in response to any particular stimulus, to any particular influence or condition. The study of oneself is far more significant than the study of the problem—to which most of us have devoted our lives. We have studied the problems from every angle, but we have never studied profoundly or deeply the maker of the problems; and to understand the maker of the problems, we have to understand our relationships because the maker of the problems exists only in relationship. Therefore, the study of relationships in order to understand the maker of the problems is our main question, and the understanding of relationships is the beginning of self-knowledge. I do not see how we can understand life, or any of our problems, without understanding ourselves because without knowing oneself, there is no basis for thinking, there is no basis for action, there is no basis for any kind of transformation or revolution.

So, the beginning of the understanding of relationships, by which one discovers the maker of the problems, is of the highest importance, and the maker of the problems is the mind. To understand the maker of the problems, which is the mind, is not merely to be very clever, but to study the whole process of psychological reaction in oneself; and without understanding the total process of the mind, do what we will with regard to the many problems, whether individual or collective, the economic problem, the problems of war, of nationalism, and so on—without understanding the mind, we have no way out of all these problems. Our question, then, is really not war, not the economic problem, but the study, the understanding of the mind, because it is the mind that creates the problems in relationship, whether that relationship be with people, with ideas, or with things. And the mind cannot be understood as something apart, to be studied in a laboratory, but only in the action of relationship.

The mind is, after all, the result of the past. What you and I are is the outcome of many yesterdays, we are the total summation of the past, and without understanding that past we cannot proceed. Now, to understand that past, must we study the whole content, the background of the past? That is, to study the past, we can either dig into it, delve deeply into all the memories of the race, of the group, of the individual, which implies studying the analyzer, or we can go into the problem of whether the analyzer is different from the analyzed, whether the observer is different from the observed. Because, as long as there is an analyzer examining the past, surely that analyzer is also a result of the past; therefore, whatever he analyzes, examines, must be conditioned and hence inadequate. The analyzer is part of the analyzed, the two are not separate—which is an obvious fact when we look at it. There is no thinker apart from the thought, and as long as there is a thinker apart from the thought, a thinker examining the thought, then whatever the outcome of that examination may be, it is inevitably conditioned and therefore inadequate. That is why, before we try to understand the problem of war, the economic or any other problem, we must first understand the thinker who is analyzing the problem. Because, the problem is not different from the thinker, the thinker is not separate from the thought—it is the thought that creates the thinker. If we can see that, then we will discover that there is only thinking and not a thinker, an observer, an experiencer. There is only thinking and not a thinker. The moment we see that, our approach to the problem, whatever it be, is entirely different because then there is no thinker trying to dissect, to analyze or shape a particular thought—there is only thinking. Therefore, it is possible for thought to come to an end without the process of struggle, without the process of analyzing. As long as there is a thinker as the 'me' and the 'mine', there is a center from which action is always taking place. That center is obviously the result of our thinking, and our thinking is the outcome of conditioning; and when the thinker merely detaches himself from the conditioning and tries to bring about action, change, or revolution, there is always the center which remains as permanent. So, the real question is to understand and dissolve that center which is the thinker.

The difficulty with most of us is, is it not, that our thinking is so conditioned. We are either French or English or German or Russian or Hindu, with particular religious, political, and economic backgrounds, and through this screen of conditioning we try to meet the problems of life, and thereby increase the problems. We do not meet life without conditioning; we meet it as an entity with a particular background and training, with particular experience. Being conditioned, we meet life according to our particular patterns, and this reaction according to pattern only creates more problems. Obviously, then, we have to understand and remove these conditionings which increase our problems; but most of us are unaware that we are conditioned and that our conditioning is the result of our own desire, of our own longing for security. After all, the society about us is the outcome of our desire to be secure, to be safe, to be permanent in our own particular form of conditioning; and being unaware of our conditioning, we continue to create more problems. We have such an accumulation of knowledge, so many prejudices, so many ideologies, so many beliefs to which we cling, and these backgrounds, these conditionings, prevent us from actually meeting life as it is. We are always meeting life, which is a challenge, with our inadequate responses, and so we never understand life except through our particular conditioning. The challenge is life, which is in constant transformation, in constant flux; and we have to understand, not the challenge, but our reaction to the challenge.

Now, our conditioning is the mind; the mind is the seat of all our conditioning—conditioning being knowledge, experience, belief, tradition, identification with a particular party, with a particular group or nation. The mind is the result of conditioning, the mind is the conditioned state; therefore, any problems that the mind tackles must further increase those problems. As long as the mind deals with any problem, at any level, it can only create more trouble, more misery, and more confusion. Is it possible, then, to meet the challenge of life without the process of thinking, without this accumulated experience which is the mind? That is, is it possible to meet the challenge of life without the reaction of the mind, which is the conditioning of the past? When there is a challenge, we have a reaction; the mind immediately responds, and as one watches, one sees that the response of the mind is always conditioned. Therefore, when there is a challenge, the mind which responds can only create more problems, more confusion, and always does.

So, though we have innumerable problems at all levels of our existence, as long as the mind meets them, as long as thought reacts to them, there must be further confusion; and is it possible to meet life without the reaction of the conditioned mind? We can meet the challenge without thought responding to it only when there is a crisis. When there is an acute crisis, we will see that thought has no response; the background does not react. It is only in that state, when the mind does not react to the problem as a process of thought—only then can we resolve the problems that confront each one of us.

I have been given some questions, and I shall answer them.

Question: The only weapon you give to the victims of social injustice is self-knowledge. This, to me, is derision. History teaches us that people have never freed themselves except through violence. The state of society conditions me; therefore, I have to smash it.

KRISHNAMURTI: Before we begin to break up society, we must understand what society is and how one is to act, to respond, to that society in which one is caught. So, what is important is not how to break society to be free from it but to understand the structure of society, because the moment I understand the structure of society in relation to myself, I shall be able to act in the right way with regard to it.

What is society? Is it not the product of our relationship, the relationship between you and me and another? Our relationship is society, and society is not something apart from us. Therefore, to alter the structure of the present society without understanding relationship is merely to continue the present society in a modified form. The present society is pretty rotten, it is a process of corruption, of violence, in which there is always intolerance, conflict, and pain; and to bring about a fundamental alteration in this society of which we are a part, there must be the understanding of ourselves. Surely, this understanding of ourselves is not a derision, nor is it in opposition to the present order. There is opposition only as a reaction. A fundamental alteration in society can come about, not through ideas, not through a revolution based on ideas, but through the transformation of myself in my relationship with another. Society obviously needs transformation—all societies always need transformation. Should that transformation be based on an idea, that is, on thought, on calculation, on clever dialectic assertions and denials, and all the rest of it? Or, since patterns only create opposition, should such a revolution take place not according to any particular pattern? A revolution can come into being only when the idea of 'me', as an entity apart from society, ceases; and that 'me' exists only as long as thought, which is the conditioned desire to be secure in different forms, continues.

We all know and admit that there must be some kind of radical change in the structure of society. There are those who say such a transformation, such a change, must be based on an idea, on an ideology; but an idea invariably creates opposition, and therefore you have a revolution according to the left or to the right. Now, is revolution possible, is it a true revolution when it is based on an idea, on a belief? That is, when revolution is the outcome of a process of thought, which is merely a reaction of the background giving a modified continuity to the past, is that a revolution at all? Surely, a revolution based on an idea is not a revolution, it is merely a modified continuity of the past, however intelligent, however cunning. Therefore, revolution in the right sense of the word is possible only when the mind is not the center of action, when belief, idea, is not the dominant influence. That is why, to bring about a radical transformation in society, one must understand oneself—the 'oneself' being the conditioned background of idea, experience, knowledge, memory.

Question: My husband was killed during one war, my children died during another, and my house has been destroyed. You say that life is an eternal state of creation, but every spring is broken in me, and I do not find it possible to partake of that renewal.

KRISHNAMURTI: What is it that prevents this constant renewal in our life, that prevents the new from coming into being? Is it not that we do not know how to die each day? Because we live in a state of continuity, a constant process of carrying over from day to day our memories, our knowledge, our experiences, our worries, our pain and suffering, we never come to a new day without yesterday's memory. To us, continuity is life. To know that 'I' continue as memory identified with a particular group, with particular knowledge, with particular experience—to us that is life; and that which has continuity, which is carried on through memory—how can that ever renew? Surely, renewal is possible only when we understand the whole process of the desire to continue; and only when that continuity as an entity, as the 'I' in thought, comes to an end, is there a renewal.

After all, we are a collection of memories—the memories of experience, the memories which we have gathered through life, through education—and the 'I' is the result of identification with all that. We are the result of identifying ourselves with a particular group, whether French, Dutch, German, or Hindu. Without identification with a group, with a house, with a piano, with an idea, or with a person, we feel lost; so, we cling to memory, to identification, and this identification gives us continuity, and continuity prevents renewal. Surely, it is possible to renew ourselves only when we know how to die and to be reborn each day, that is, to be free from all identification, which gives continuity.

Creation is not a state of memory, is it? It is not a state in which the mind is active. Creation is a state of mind in which thought is absent, and as long as thought is functioning, there can be no creation. Thought is continuous; it is the result of continuity, and for that which has continuity, there cannot be creation, renewal; it can only proceed from the known to the known, and therefore it can never be the unknown. Therefore, the understanding of thought, and how to bring thought to an end, is important. This ending of thought is not a process of living in an ivory tower of abstraction; on the contrary, the ending of thought is the highest form of understanding. The ending of thought brings about creation, and in that there is renewal; but as long as thought continues, there can be no renewal. That is why, to understand how we are thinking is much more important than to consider how to renew ourselves. Only when I understand the ways of my own thinking, see all its reactions, not only on the superficial level, but on the deeper unconscious levels—only then, in the understanding of myself, does thought come to an end.

The ending of thought is the beginning of creation, the ending of thought is the beginning of silence; but the ending of thought cannot come through compulsion, through any form of discipline, through any enforcement. After all, we must have had moments when the mind was very quiet—spontaneously quiet, without any sense of compulsion, without any motive, without any desire to make it silent. We must have experienced moments when the mind was utterly still. Now, that stillness is not the result of a continuity, that stillness can never be the outcome of a particular form of identification. The mind in that state comes to an end; that is, thinking, as the reaction of particular conditioning, comes to an end. That ending of thought is renewal, it is the freshness in which the mind can begin anew.

So, the understanding of the mind, not as the thinker, but only as thought, the direct awareness of the mind as thought without any sense of condemnation or justification, without any choice, brings about the ending of thought. Then you will see, if you will experiment with it, that with the ending of thought, there is no thinker, and when there is no thinker, the mind is quiet. The thinker is the entity that has continuity. Thought, seeing itself to be transient, creates the thinker as a permanent entity and gives to the thinker continuity; and then the thinker becomes the agitator, maintaining the mind in a state of constant agitation, constant search, inquiry, longing. Only when the mind understands the total process of itself, without any form of compulsion, is there tranquillity, and therefore a possibility of renewal.

Surely, then, in all these matters the important thing is to understand the process of the mind, and to understand the process of the mind is not a self-isolating or introspective action—it is not a denial of life, a withdrawal into a hermitage or monastery, or an enclosing of oneself in a particular religious belief. On the contrary, any belief conditions the mind. Belief creates antagonism, and a mind that believes can never be quiet, a mind that is caught in dogma can never know what it is to be creative. So, our problems can be resolved only when we understand the process of the mind, which is the creator of the problems, and the creator can come to an end only when we understand relationship. Relationship is society, and to bring about a revolution in society we have to understand our reactions in relationship. Renewal, that creative state, comes into being only when the mind is utterly tranquil, not enclosed in any particular activity or belief. When the mind is quiet, utterly still, because thinking has come to an end—only then is there creation.

April 9, 1950

Second Talk in Paris

Surely, one of our great difficulties is that in trying to find security, not only in the economic world, but also in the psychological or so-called spiritual world, we destroy physical security. In the search for economic and psychological security, we create certain ideas, we cling to certain beliefs, we have certain anxieties, certain acquisitive instincts, and that very search ultimately destroys physical security for most of us. So, is it not important to find out why it is that the mind attaches itself so strongly to ideas, to beliefs, to conclusions, to systems and formulas? Because, obviously, this attachment to ideas and beliefs with the hope of inward security in view ultimately destroys outward or physical security. Physical security is made impossible by the desire, by the anxiety, by the psychological necessity of seeking inward security; therefore, it is surely important to find out why the mind, why each one of us, so ardently pursues inward security.

Now, it is obvious that we must have physical security, food, clothing, and shelter, and it is important to find out, is it not, how the mind, in seeking inward security, destroys security outwardly. In order to bring about physical security, we have to investigate this desire for inward security, this inward attachment to ideas, to beliefs, to conclusions. Why does the mind seek inward security? Why do we attach such enormous importance to ideas, to property, to certain people? Why do we take refuge in belief, in seclusion, which ultimately destroys outward security? Why does the mind hold so strongly, so determinedly, to ideas? Nationalism, belief in God, belief in a formula of one sort or another are merely attachment to an idea, and we see that ideas, beliefs, divide people. Why are we attached so strongly to ideas? If we can be free from the desire to be secure inwardly, then perhaps it will be possible to organize outward security because it is the desire for inward security that divides us, not the desire for outward security. We must have outward security—that is obvious, but outward security is prevented by the desire to be inwardly secure. Until this problem is solved, not superficially but radically, fundamentally, and seriously, there can be no outward security.

So, our problem is not to seek a formula or system which will bring about outward security, but to find out why the mind is constantly seeking inward isolation, inward gratification, psychological security. It is easy to put the question, but to discover the right answer, which must be true, is very arduous. Because most of us want to be certain, we avoid uncertainty; we want to be certain in our affections, we want to be certain in our knowledge, we want to be certain in our experiences, because that certainty gives us a sense of assurance, a sense of well-being, in which there is no disturbance, no shock of experience, the shock of a new quality coming into being. It is this very desire for certainty which prevents us from inquiring into the need for freedom from all inward security. We obviously find great satisfaction in our capacity to do things with our hands or with our mind, which is accumulated knowledge, experience; and in that capacity we seek certainty because in that state, the mind need never be disturbed—there is no anxiety, no fear, no new experience.

So the mind, seeking inward certainty through property, through people, through ideas, does not desire to be disturbed and made uncertain. Have you not often noticed how the mind rebels against anything new—a new idea, a new experience, a new state? When it does experience a new state, the mind immediately brings it into the field of itself, into the field of the known. The mind is always functioning, is it not, within the field of certainty, within the field of the known, within the field of security, which is its own projection, and therefore it can never experience something beyond itself. The state of creation, surely, is the experiencing of something beyond the mind, and that state of creation cannot come into being as long as the mind is attached to any particular form of security, inward or outward. Obviously then, what is important is for each one to find out where one is attached, where one is seeking security, and if one is really interested, one can easily find this out for oneself—one can discover in what manner, through what experience, through what belief, the mind is seeking security, certainty. When one discovers that, not theoretically but actually, when one directly experiences attachment to belief, to a particular form of affection, to a particular idea or formula, then one will see that there comes a freedom from that particular form of security. And in that state of uncertainty, which is not isolation, which is not fear, there is creative being. Uncertainty is essential for creative being.

We see in the world that beliefs, ideas, and ideologies are dividing people, are bringing about catastrophes, miseries, and confusion. Holding on to our beliefs, being divided by our personal opinions and experiences which we cling to as being the ultimate truth, we then try to bring about collective action, which is obviously impossible. There can be collective action only when there is freedom from all desire to take refuge in any ideology, in any belief, in any system, in any group, in any one person, in any particular teacher or teaching. It is only when there is freedom from all desire to be inwardly secure that there is a possibility of being outwardly secure, having the physical things that are necessary for human survival.

I am going to answer some of these questions, but please bear in mind that there is no categorical yes and no to any human problem. One must think out each problem, go into it, see the truth of it, and only then does the problem reveal its own answer.

Question: What is thought? From whence does it come? And what is the relation of the thinker to thought?

KRISHNAMURTI: Now, who puts this question? Does the thinker put the question? Or, is the question the outcome of thought? If the thinker puts the question, then the thinker is an entity separate from thought, he is merely the observer of thought, he is the experiencer outside the experience. So, when you put this question, you have to find out whether the thinker is separate from the thought. Are you putting the question as though you were outside of, apart from the process of thinking? If you are, then you have to find out if the thinker is really separate from thought. Thought is a process of reaction, is it not? That is, there is a challenge and a response, and the response is the process of thinking. If there is no challenge of any kind, conscious or unconscious, violent or very subtle, there is no response, there is no thinking. So, thinking is a process of response to challenge. Thinking, thought, is a process of reaction. There is first perception, then contact, sensation, desire, and identification—and thought has begun. Thought is a process of response to challenge, conscious or unconscious—that is fairly obvious. There is no response if there is no challenge. So, thinking is a process of response, reaction, to any form of stimulus or challenge.

Now, is that all? Is the thinker the outcome of thought, or is he an entity in his own right, not created by thought, but outside all thought and apart from time? Because, thought is a process of time; thought is the response of the background, and the response of the background is the process of time. So, is the thinker apart from time? Or, is the thinker part of the process of time, which is thought?

This is a difficult problem to deal with in two languages, and it would be much simpler if I could speak in French. As I cannot—although I talk and understand it a little—let us proceed, and we will see.

The question is, What is thought and what is the thinker? Is the thinker separate from thought, or is he the outcome of thinking? If he is separate from thought, then he can operate on thought, he can control, change, modify thought; but if he is part of thinking, then he cannot operate on it. Though he may think he can control thought, change or modify it, he is not capable of doing that because he is himself the product of thinking. So, we have to find out whether thought produces the thinker or whether the thinker, being separate, apart, is independent of thought and therefore can control it.

Now, we can see very well that the thinker is the result of thought because there is no thinker if there is no thought, there is no experiencer if there is no experiencing. The experiencing, the observing, the thinking, produces the experiencer, the observer, the thinker. The experiencer is not separate from the experience, the thinker is not separate from the thought. Why then, has thought made the thinker into a separate entity? When we know that our daily thinking, which is a response to challenge, produces the thinker, why do we believe that there is an entity separate from our daily thinking? Thought has created the thinker as a separate entity because thought is always changing, modifying, and it sees its own impermanence. Being transient, thought desires permanency, and so creates the thinker as an entity who is permanent, who is not caught in the net of time. So, we create the thinker—which is merely a belief. That is, the mind, seeking security, holds to the belief that there is a thinker separate from thought, a 'me' that is apart from my daily activities, from my daily thoughts, from my daily functions. So, the thinker becomes an entity apart from thought, and then the thinker proceeds to control, modify, dominate thought, which creates conflict between the thinker and the thought, between the actor and the action.

Now, if we see the truth of that—that the thinker is thought, that there is no thinker separate from thought, but only the process of thinking—then what happens? If we see that there is only thinking and not a thinker trying to modify thought, what is the result? I hope I am making myself clear. So far, we know that the thinker is operating upon thought, and this creates conflict between the thinker and the thought; but if we see the truth that there is only thought and not a thinker, that the thinker is arbitrary, artificial, and entirely fictitious—then what happens? Is not the process of conflict removed? At present our life is a conflict, a series of battles between the thinker and the thought—what to do and what not to do, what should be and what should not be. The thinker is always separating himself as the 'me' remaining outside of action. But when we see that there is only thought, have we not then removed the cause of conflict? Then we are able to be choicelessly aware of thought and not as the thinker observing thought from outside. When we remove the entity that creates conflict, surely then there is a possibility of understanding thought. When there is no thinker observing, judging, molding thought, but only choiceless awareness of the whole process of thinking, without any resistance, without battle, without conflict, then the thought process comes to an end.

So, the mind, in understanding that there is no thinker but only thought, eliminates conflict, and therefore there is merely the process of thinking; and when there is an awareness of thinking without any choice because the chooser has been eliminated, then you will see that thought comes to an end. Then the mind is very quiet, it is not agitated, and in that quietness, in that stillness, the problem is understood.

Question: Considering the world's present condition, there must be immediate action on the part of some who are not caught in any system either of the left or of the right. How is this group to be created, and how will it act with regard to the present crisis?

KRISHNAMURTI: How is this group to be created, the group that does not belong to the left or to the right, or to any particular belief? How is such a group to be formed? How do you think it is to be formed? What is a group? Surely, it is you and I, isn't it? To form such a group, you and I must free ourselves from the desire to be secure, to be identified with any particular idea, belief, conclusion, system, or country. That is, you and I must begin to free ourselves from seeking shelter in an idea, in a belief, in knowledge; then, obviously, you and I are the group who are free from the exclusiveness of belonging to something. But are we such a group? Are you and I such entities? If we are not free from belief, from conclusion, from system, from idea, we may form a group, but we will create again the same confusion, the same misery, the same leadership, the same liquidation of those who disagree, and so on and on. So, before we form a group at all, we must first be free of the desire to be secure, to take shelter in any belief, in any idea, in any system. Are you and I free of that desire? If we are not, then let us not think in terms of groups and future action; but what is important, surely, is to find out, not merely verbally, but inwardly and deeply, both in the conscious as well as in the hidden parts of our own minds and hearts, whether we are really free from any sense of identification with a particular group, with a particular nation, with a particular belief or dogma. If we are not, then in starting a group we are bound to create the same mess, the same misery.

Now, you will probably say, "It will take a long time for me to be free from my own beliefs, from the dogmas which I have projected and which are the result of my own thinking; therefore I cannot operate, I cannot do anything, I will have to wait." That is your reaction, is it not? You say, "As I am not free, what am I to do? I can't act." Isn't that your question? And while you wait, the world is going on creating more confusion, more misery, more horrors and destruction. Or, being anxious to help, you plunge in with your own beliefs, with your own dogmas, and so create greater confusion. Surely, what is important is to see that there can be no right action as long as the mind is holding on to a particular conclusion or belief, either of the left or of the right, because if you really see the truth of that, then obviously you will be in a position to act. And that does not take time, it is not a matter of progress, gradual evolution. Seeing a fact is not a process of evolution, is it? But you are not interested, you do not want to see the truth of it. You just say, "Well, it is a matter of time for me to be free"—and there you drop it.

The question, then, is this: Is it possible for an ordinary person like you and me, a person who is not very intellectual and all the rest of it, to be free immediately of the desire to hold on to a particular belief or a particular dogma? Is it possible to be free immediately from belief? When you put that question seriously to yourself, is there any doubt left? Is it a matter of time for you to think about it? When you see that belief divides people, when you actually see and inwardly understand it, doesn't belief fall away from you? That does not require an effort, a struggle, a process of time. But we are not willing to see that fact—and that is our trouble. We want to act, so we join groups which are perhaps a little more cultured, a little more kindly, a little more pleasant. Such a group may act, but it can only produce the same chaos in another direction. But if you and I see the truth that each one of us can be free from dogma, from belief, then surely, whether we form a group or not, we will act, and it is this action that is needed, not action based on an idea.

So, the important point in this question is, is it not, whether there can be action without idea, without belief. We see throughout the world that action based on a belief, on a dogma, on a conclusion, on a system, on a formula, has led to division, to conflict, and to disintegration. Is it possible, then, to act without idea, without belief? You have to find that out, have you not?—not accept or reject it. You have to discover for yourself whether such action is possible, and you will discover it only in experiencing, not in believing or rejecting it. When you see that all action based on belief, on dogma, on conclusion, on calculation, must inevitably create separation, and therefore disintegration—when you see that, then you will experience action without the imposition of an idea.

Question: What is the relationship of the individual to society? Has he any respon-

sibility towards it? If he has, should he modify it, or disown it?

KRISHNAMURTI: Now, what is the individual, and what is society? What are you and I? Are we not the product of our background, of our education, of our social, environmental influences, of our religious training? We are the result of everything about us, and the things about us are in turn created by us, are they not? The society that exists at the present time is the product of our desires, of our responses, of our actions. We project the society and then become the instruments of that society. So, are you not the product of the society which you yourself have created? Surely, there is no extraordinary division or line of demarcation between the individual and society. Individuality comes into being later, much later, when we begin to free ourselves from the social influences.

So, are you an individual? Though you may have a particular name, own a piece of land, a private house, have a personal relationship, a separate bank account, are you really an individual or merely a product of the environment? Though all this makes you think that you are separate, are you not part of the whole? And how can you have a relationship to it unless you are separate from it? After all, our mind is the result of the past, is it not? All our thoughts are founded upon the past, and the past, both the conscious and the unconscious, is the result of the thoughts, efforts, struggles, intentions, and desires of all human beings. So, we are the sum total, are we not, of the entire human struggle, and since we are the result of the mass, of society, we cannot say that we are separate, that we are definitely apart from it. We are society; we are part of the whole, we are not separate. The separation takes place only when the mind begins to see where the false is, and therefore rejects it. Then only is there an individuality which is not resisting, which is not in opposition to society, an individuality not based on opposition, on resistance, on acquisition, but which has understood the false and has therefore separated itself from it. Only such an entity can operate on society, and therefore its responsibility to society is entirely different. Then it will act, not in terms of disowning or modifying society, but out of its own understanding, its own vitality, which comes through the discovery of that which is false.

So, as long as you and I are without self-knowledge, as long as we do not understand the whole process of ourselves, merely to modify or to disown society has no meaning. In order to bring about a fundamental revolution in society, self-knowledge is essential, and self-knowledge is to become aware of the false. Out of that awareness there comes the understanding of aloneness—that aloneness which is not a withdrawal, not an isolation, but which is essential if we are to act truly—because only that which is alone is creative. Creation does not come when all the influences of the past are impinging upon the present; creation comes only when there is an aloneness which is not loneliness, which is not a state of apartness, division. It is an aloneness which comes through understanding both the hidden as well as the conscious; and in that state of aloneness there can be action which will be effective in the transformation of society.

Question: What relation has death to life?

KRISHNAMURTI: Is there a division between life and death? Why do we regard death as something apart from life? Why are we afraid of death? And why have so many books been written about death? Why is there this line of demarcation between life and death? And is that separation real or merely arbitrary, a thing of the mind?

Now, when we talk about life, we mean living as a process of continuity in which there is identification. Me and my house, me and my wife, me and my bank account, me and my past experiences—that is what we mean by life, is it not? Living is a process of continuity in memory, conscious as well as unconscious, with its various struggles, quarrels, incidents, experiences, and so on. All that is what we call life, and in opposition to that, there is death, which is putting an end to all that. So, having created the opposite, which is death, and being afraid of it, we proceed to look for the relationship between life and death; and if we can bridge the gap with some explanation, with belief in continuity, in the hereafter, we are satisfied. We believe in reincarnation or in some other form of continuity of thought, and then we try to establish a relationship between the known and the unknown. We try to bridge the known and the unknown, and thereby try to find the relationship between the past and the future. That is what we are doing, is it not, when we inquire if there is any relationship between life and death. We want to know how to bridge the living and the ending—surely, that is our fundamental thinking.

Now, can the end, which is death, be known while living? That is, if we can know what death is while we are living, then we shall have no problem. It is because we cannot experience the unknown while we are living that we are afraid of it. So, our struggle is to establish a relationship between ourselves, which is the result of the known, and the unknown, which we call death. And can there be a relationship between the past and something which the mind cannot conceive, which we call death? And why do we separate the two? Is it not because our mind can function only within the field of the known, within the field of the continuous? One only knows oneself as a thinker, as an actor with certain memories of misery, of pleasure, of love, affection, of various kinds of experience; one only knows oneself as being continuous; otherwise, one would have no recollection of oneself as being something. Now, when that something comes to the end, which we call death, there is fear of the unknown; so, we want to draw the unknown into the known, and our whole effort is to give continuity to the unknown. That is, we do not want to know life which includes death, but we want to know how to continue and not come to an end. We do not want to know life and death, we only want to know how to continue without ending.

Now, that which continues has no renewal. There can be nothing new, there can be nothing creative, in that which has continuance—this is fairly obvious. It is only when continuity ends that there is a possibility of that which is ever new. But it is this ending that we dread, and we don't see that only in ending can there be renewal, the creative, the unknown—and not in carrying over from day to day our experiences, our memories and misfortunes. It is only when we die each day to all that is old that there can be the new. The new cannot be where there is continuity—the new being the creative, the unknown, the eternal, God, or what you will. The person, the continuous entity who seeks the unknown, the real, the eternal, will never find it because he can find only that which he projects out of himself, and that which he projects is not the real. So, only in ending, in dying, can the new be known; and the man who seeks to find a relationship between life and death, to bridge the continuous with that which he thinks is beyond, is living in a fictitious, unreal world—which is a projection of himself.

Now, is it possible, while living, to die—which means coming to an end, being as nothing? Is it possible, while living in this world where everything is becoming more and more or becoming less and less, where everything is a process of climbing, achieving, succeeding—is it possible, in such a world, to know death? That is, is it possible to end all memories—not the memory of facts, the way to your house, and so on, but the inward attachment through memory to psychological security, the memories that one has accumulated, stored up, and in which one seeks security, happiness? Is it possible to put an end to all that—which means dying every day so that there may be a renewal tomorrow? It is only then that one knows death while living. Only in that dying, in that coming to an end, putting an end to continuity, is there renewal, that creation which is eternal.

April 16, 1950

Third Talk in Paris

Is it not very important that those who would know what truth is should discover it through their own experience, and not merely accept or believe according to any particular pattern? Surely, it is essential to discover for oneself what reality is, what God is—the name you give to it is not of great importance—because that is the only thing that is really creative, that is the only door through which one can find that happiness which is not merely transient, which is not dependent. Most of us are seeking happiness in one form or another, and we try to find it through knowledge, through experience, through constant struggle. But surely, happiness that depends on something is not happiness. The moment we depend for happiness on possessions, on people, or on ideas, those things become very important, and happiness passes us by. The very things on which we depend for our happiness become more important than happiness itself. If you and I depend on certain people for happiness, then those people become important, and if we depend on ideas for our happiness, then ideas become important. The same thing happens with regard to property, name, position, power—the moment we depend for our happiness on any of these things, they become all-consumingly essential in our lives.

So, dependence is the denial of happiness, and the moment one depends on ideas, on people, or on things, obviously that relationship must isolate one. The very dependence implies isolation, and where there is isolation, there cannot be true relationship. Only in understanding true relationship is it possible to liberate oneself from the dependence which brings out isolation, and that is why I think it is important to go very deeply and fully into the question of relationship. If relationship is merely a dependence, then obviously it leads to isolation, and such a relationship must inevitably create various forms of fear, of self-enclosure, possessiveness, jealousy, and so on. When we seek happiness through relationship, whether it be with property, with people, or with ideas, invariably we possess those things; we must possess them because through them, we derive our happiness—at least, we think so. But from the very possession of the things on which we depend, there arises the process of self-enclosure; and so relationship, which should lead to the destruction of the self, of the 'me', of the narrowing influences of life, becomes more and more stringent, more and more restricted, limited, and destroys the very happiness we seek.

So, as long as we merely depend for our happiness on things, on people, or on ideas, relationship is a process of self-enclosure, of isolation, and I think it is very important to realize this. At present, all relationship tends to limit our action, our thought, our feelings, and until we realize that dependence is hampering our action and destroying our happiness, until we really see the truth of that, there is no possibility of wider, freer movement of thought and feeling. After all, we go to books, to Masters, to teachers; we turn to disciplines or to experience and knowledge in order to find a lasting happiness; a safe refuge, a protection—and so we multiply Masters, books, ideas, knowledge. But surely, no one can give us that happiness; no one can free us from our own desires, from our own narrowing influences, and therefore it is important, is it not, to know oneself completely, not only the conscious, but also the inward part of oneself. That self-knowledge comes only through relationship because the understanding of relationship discloses the process of the self, of the 'me'. It is only when we understand the full extent of the 'me' and its activities, not only at the superficial level but on all the deeper levels, that there is freedom from dependence, and therefore a possibility of realizing what happiness is. Happiness is not an end in itself any more than virtue is, and if we make happiness or virtue an end, then we must depend upon things, upon people or ideas, upon Masters or knowledge. But none except ourselves, through understanding relationship in our daily life, can give us freedom from our own narrowing confusion, conflicts, and limitations.

We seem to think that the understanding of the self is extremely difficult. We have the impression that to discover the process of the self, the ways of one's thought in the secret places of one's own mind and heart, we must go to somebody else and be told or given a method. Surely, we have made the study of the self extremely complicated, have we not? But is the study of the self so very difficult? Does it need the aid of another, however advanced, at whatever level the Master may be? Surely, no one can teach us the understanding of the self. We have to discover the whole, total process of the self, but to discover it, there must be spontaneity. One cannot impose upon oneself a discipline, a mode of operation; one can only be aware from moment to moment of every movement of thought, of every feeling, in relationship. And for most of us, it is that which is difficult—to be choicelessly aware of every word, of every thought, of every feeling. But to be aware does not require that you should follow anyone; you do not require a Master, you do not require a sage, you do not require a belief. To know the whole process of the mind, what you need is only the intention to watch, to be aware, without condemnation or justification. You can know yourself only when you are aware in relationship, in your relationship with your wife, with your children, with your neighbor, with society, with the knowledge which you have acquired, the experiences you have gathered. It is because we are lazy, slothful, that we turn to someone, to a leader, to a Master, who will instruct us or give us a mode of conduct. But surely, this desire to look to another for help only makes us dependent, and the more we are dependent, the further we are away from self-knowledge. It is only through self-knowledge, through understanding the complete process of oneself, that there is liberation, and in liberating oneself from one's own enclosing, narrowing, isolating process, there is happiness.

So, it is important, is it not, that one should understand oneself thoroughly, deeply, and comprehensively. If I do not know myself, if you do not know yourself, what basis have we for thought, for action? If I do not know myself, not only superficially, but also at the profound levels from which spring all the motives, the responses, the accumulated desires and impulses, how can I think, act, live, be? So, is it not important to know oneself as completely as possible? If I do not know myself, how can I go to another and search out the truth? I can go to another, I can choose a leader out of my confusion, but because I have chosen him out of my confusion, the leader, the teacher, the Master, must also be confused. So, as long as there is choice, there can be no understanding. Understanding does not come through choice; understanding does not come through comparison, nor through criticism, nor through justification. Understanding comes only when the mind has become completely aware of the whole process of itself and so has become quiet. When the mind is completely silent, without any demand—only in that stillness is there understanding, is there a possibility of experiencing that which is beyond time.

Before I answer some of these questions, may I point out, if you don't mind, that it is important to discover the answer for oneself. That is, you and I are going to investigate the truth of each problem and discover it for ourselves, experience it for ourselves; otherwise, it will be merely on the verbal level, and therefore utterly valueless. If we can experience the truth of every question, every problem, then perhaps that problem will be resolved completely; but merely to remain on the verbal level, merely to discuss, to argue with each other through words, will not bring about the solution of the problem. So, in considering these questions, I am not merely giving an expression to words, but you and I are trying to find out the truth of the matter; and to find the truth, we must be free from our anchors, from our commitments, from the influence of ideas, and proceed step by step to inquire into the truth of the matter.

Question: As creative individuals may disrupt society according to their own particular idiosyncrasies and capacities, should not creativeness be at the command of society?

KRISHNAMURTI: Now, what do we mean by creativeness? Is it creative to invent the atomic bomb or to discover how to kill another? Is it creative to have a capacity, a gift? Is it creative to be able to speak very cleverly, to write very intelligent books, to solve problems? Is it creative to discover the process of nature, the hidden processes of life? Is any of that a state of creativeness? Or, is creativeness something entirely different from creative expression? I may have the capacity to translate into marble a certain vision, a certain feeling, or being a scientist, I may be able to discover something, according to my tendencies and capacities. But is that creativeness? Is the expression of a feeling, the making of a discovery, the writing of a book or a poem, the painting of a picture—is any of that necessarily creative? Or, is creativeness something utterly different which is not dependent on expression? To us, expression seems to matter so enormously, does it not? To be able to say something in words, in a picture, in a poem, to be able to concentrate on the discovery of a particular scientific fact—is that a process of creation? Or, is creation something which is not of the mind at all? After all, when the mind demands, it will find an answer, but is its answer the creative answer? Or, is there creativeness only when the mind is completely silent—not asking, not demanding, not searching out?

Now, we are the result of society, we are the depositories of society, and we either conform to society or break away from society. The breaking away from society depends upon our background, our conditioning; therefore, our breaking away from society does not indicate that we are free—it may be merely the reaction of the background to certain incidents. So, a man who is creative merely in the accepted sense of the word may be dangerous, disruptive, without transforming in any fundamental way the respectable, exploiting society which is ours; and the questioner wants to know whether society should not command his creativeness. But who is going to represent society? The leaders, the people in power, the people who are respectable and who have the means of controlling others? Or, must the problem be approached quite differently? That is, society is the outcome of our own projections, of our own intentions, and therefore we are not separate from society, and since the man who goes against society is not necessarily a revolutionary, is it not important to understand what we mean by revolution? Surely, as long as we base revolution on an idea, it is not a revolution, is it? A revolution based on a belief, on a dogma, on knowledge, is obviously no revolution at all—it is merely a modified continuation of the old. That is, a reaction of the background against the conditioning influence of society is an escape, it is obviously not a revolution.

There is real revolution, which is not dependent on idea, only when one understands the whole total process of oneself. As long as we accept the pattern of society, as long as we produce the influences which create a society based on violence, intolerance, and static progress—as long as that process exists, society will try to control the individual. And as long as the individual is attempting to be creative within the field of his conditioning, obviously he cannot be creative. There is creativeness only when the mind is completely understood, and then the mind does not depend on mere expression—the expression is of secondary importance.

Surely, then, the important thing is to discover what it is to be creative, and creativity can be discovered and understood, the truth of it seen, only when I understand the whole total process of myself. As long as there is a projection of the mind, whether at the verbal or any other level, there cannot be a creative state. Only when every movement of thought is understood and therefore comes to an end—only then is there creativeness.

Question: I have prayed for my friend's health, and it has produced certain results. If I now pray to have peace in my heart, can I come in direct contact with God?

KRISHNAMURTI: Obviously a demand, a supplication, a petition, brings results. You ask, and you receive—that is an obvious psychological fact which you can test out for yourselves. Psychologically you pray, you demand, you petition, and you will have a reply, but is it the reply of reality? To find reality there must be no demand, no petition, no supplication. After all, you pray only when you are confused, when you are in trouble and misery, do you not? Otherwise you do not pray. It is only when you are confused, when you are miserable, that you want somebody's help; and prayer, which is a process of demand, must necessarily have an answer. The answer may be the outcome of the deep unconscious layers of oneself, or it may be the result of the collective, but it is obviously not the reply, the response, of reality. And one can see that through prayer, through posture, through the constant repetition of certain words and phrases, the mind is made quiet. When the mind is quiet, after struggling with a problem, obviously there is an answer, but the answer is surely not from that which is beyond time. Your demand is within the field of time, and therefore the reply must also be within the field of time. So, that is one part of the question—as long as we pray, which is a petition, a demand, there must be an answer, but the answer is not the response of reality.

Now, the questioner wants to know whether through prayer it is possible to come directly into contact with reality, with God. Through making the mind still, through forcing the mind, through discipline, through the repetition of words, through taking certain postures, through constant control and subjugation—is it possible in that way to come into contact with reality? Obviously not. A mind that is shaped by circumstances, by environment, by desire, by discipline, can never be free. It is only the free mind that can discover, it is only the free mind that can come into contact with reality. But a mind that is seeking, that is demanding, a mind that is trying to be happy, to become virtuous—such a mind can never be quiet, and therefore it can never come into contact with that which is beyond all experience. After all, experience is within the field of the transient, is it not? To say, "I have experienced," is to put that experience within the net of time. And is truth something to be experienced? Is truth something to be repeated? Is truth a thing of memory, of the mind? Or, is truth something which is beyond the mind, and therefore beyond the state of experiencing? When one experiences, there is memory of that experience, and that memory, which is repetition, is obviously not true. Truth is something which is from moment to moment, not to be experienced as a thing of the experiencer.

So, the mind must be free to come into contact with reality, but that freedom does not come through discipline, through demand, through prayer. The mind can be made quiet through desire, through various forms of compulsion, effort, but the mind that is made quiet is not a still mind—it is only a disciplined mind, a mind that is in prison, shaped, under control. He who would come into contact with reality need not pray. On the contrary, he must understand life—life being relationship. To be is to be related, and without understanding its relationship with things, with people, and with ideas, the mind will inevitably be in conflict, in a state of agitation. You may for the time being suppress that agitation, but such suppression is not freedom. Freedom comes in understanding yourself, and only then is it possible to come into contact with that which is not the projection of the mind.

Question: Is the individual the result of society or the instrument of society?

KRISHNAMURTI: This is an important question, is it not? On this question the world is being divided by two opposing ideologies—whether the individual is the instrument of society or the result of society. The experts, the authorities on one side, say that the individual is the result of society, and those on the other maintain that he is the instrument of society. Now, is it not important for you and me to find out for ourselves what is the truth of this matter, and not depend on specialists, on authorities, whether of the left or of the right? It is the truth, and not opinion, not knowledge, that will liberate us from the false, and it is important, is it not, for each one of us to discover the truth, and not merely depend on words or on the opinion of another.

So, how are you to find the truth of it? To find the truth of it, it is obvious that there must be no dependence on the expert, on the specialist, on the leader. And to know the truth of it for yourself, you cannot depend on previous knowledge. When you depend on previous knowledge, you are lost because each authority contradicts the other, each translates history according to his particular prejudice or idiosyncrasy. So, the first obvious thing is to be free from the external influences of knowledge, of the specialist, of the power politicians, and so on.

Now, to discover the truth of this matter, you may reject outer authorities and rely on your own experience, on your own knowledge, on your own study, but will your own experience give you the truth of it? You may say that you have nothing else to go on, that to judge whether the individual is the instrument of society or the result, the product of society—to find the truth of that, you will have to rely on your own experience. Now, is the discovery of truth dependent on experience? After all, what is your experience? It is the result of accumulated beliefs, influences, memories, conditions, and so on. It is the past—experience is the accumulated knowledge of the past, and through the past you are trying to find the truth of this matter. So, can you rely on your experience? And if you cannot, then by what will you judge?

I hope I am making the problem clear. To see, to find the truth of this matter, you must know what your experience is. What is your experience? Your experience is the response of your conditioning, obviously, and your conditioning is the result of the society about you. So, you are looking for the truth of this matter according to your conditioning, are you not? You would like to think that you are only the result of society—it's easier and therefore more pleasant, but you actually think you are spiritual, that you are God incarnate, the manifestation of something ultimate, and so on, which is all a result of the conditioning influences of your society, of your religion. So, according to that, you will judge. But is that the true measure of truth? Is the measure of truth ever dependent on experience? Is not experience itself a barrier to the understanding of truth? At the present time you are both the product and the instrument of society, are you not? All education is conditioning the child to this end. If you look at it very factually, you are the product of society—you are a Frenchman, an Englishman, a Hindu, believing this or that. And also, you are the instrument of society. When society says, "Go to war," you all troop to war; when society says, "You belong to this particular religion," you repeat the formula, the phrases, the dogma. So, you are both the instrument of society and the product of society—which is an obvious fact. Whether you like it or not, that is so.

Now, to find out what is beyond, to find out if there is something more to life than merely to be shaped by society for society—to find the truth of that, all influences must come to an end, all experience, which is the measure, must cease. To discover truth, there must be no measurement because the measurement is the result of your conditioning, and that which is conditioned can see only its own projection, and therefore it can never perceive that which is real. It is important to find out for yourself the truth of this matter because only the truth can deliver you, and then you will be a real revolutionary, not a mere repeater of words.

Question: Why do you speak of the stillness of the mind, and what is this stillness?

KRISHNAMURTI: Is it not necessary, if we would understand anything, that the mind should be still? If we have a problem, we worry over it, don't we? We go into it, we analyze it, we tear it to pieces in the hope of understanding it. Now, do we understand through effort, through analysis, through comparison, through any form of mental struggle? Surely, understanding comes only when the mind is very quiet. I do not know if you have experimented with it, but if you will, you can easily find out for yourself. We say that the more we struggle with the question of starvation, of war, or any other human problem, the more we come into conflict with it, the better we shall understand it. Now, is that true? Wars have been going on for centuries, the conflict between individuals, between societies; war, inward and outward, is constantly there. Do we resolve that war, that conflict, by further conflict, by further struggle, by cunning endeavor? Or, do we understand the problem only when we are directly in front of it, when we are faced with the fact? And we can face the fact only when there is no interfering agitation between the mind and the fact. So, is it not important, if we are to understand, that the mind be quiet?

But you will invariably ask, "How can the mind be made still?" That is the immediate response, is it not? You say, "My mind is agitated, and how can I keep it quiet?" Now, can any system make the mind quiet? Can a formula, a discipline, make the mind still? It can, but when the mind is made still, is that quietness, is that stillness? Or, is the mind only enclosed within an idea, within a formula, within a phrase? And such a mind is dead, is it not? That is why most people who try to be spiritual, so-called spiritual, are dead—because they have trained their minds to be quiet, they have enclosed themselves within a formula for being quiet. Obviously, such a mind is never quiet; it is only suppressed, held down.

Now, the mind is quiet when it sees the truth that understanding comes only when it is quiet; that if I would understand you, I must be quiet, I cannot have reactions against you, I must not be prejudiced, I must put away all my conclusions, my experiences, and meet you face to face. Only then, when the mind is free from my conditioning, do I understand. When I see the truth of that, the mind is quiet—and then there is no question of how to make the mind quiet. Only the truth can liberate the mind from its own ideation, and to see the truth, the mind must realize the fact that as long as it is agitated, it can have no understanding. So, quietness of mind, tranquillity of mind, is not a thing to be produced by willpower, by any action of desire; if it is, then such a mind is enclosed, isolated, it is a dead mind, and therefore it is incapable of adaptability, of pliability, of swiftness. Such a mind is not creative.

Our question, then, is not how to make the mind still, but to see the truth of every problem as it presents itself to us. It is like the pool that becomes quiet when the wind stops. Our mind is agitated because we have problems, and to avoid the problems, we make the mind still. Now, the mind has projected these problems, and there are no problems apart from the mind, and as long as the mind projects any conception of sensitivity, practices any form of stillness, it can never be still. But when the mind realizes that only by being still is there understanding, then it becomes very quiet. That quietness is not imposed, not disciplined; it is a quietness that cannot be understood by an agitated mind.

Many who seek quietness of mind withdraw from active life to a village, to a monastery, to the mountains. Or, they withdraw into ideas, enclose themselves in a belief, or avoid people who give them trouble. But such isolation is not stillness of mind. The enclosure of the mind in an idea or the avoidance of people who make life complicated does not bring about stillness of mind. Stillness of mind comes only when there is no process of isolation through accumulation, but complete understanding of the whole process of relationship. Accumulation makes the mind old, and only when the mind is new, when the mind is fresh, without the process of accumulation—only then is there a possibility of having tranquillity of mind. Such a mind is not dead, it is most active. The still mind is the most active mind, but if you will experiment with it, go into it deeply, you will see that in that stillness there is no projection of thought. Thought, at all levels, is obviously the reaction of memory, and thought can never be in a state of creation. It may express creativeness, but thought in itself can never be creative. But when there is silence—that tranquillity of mind which is not a result—then we shall see that in that quietness there is extraordinary activity, an extraordinary action which a mind agitated by thought can never know. In that stillness, there is no formulation, there is no idea, there is no memory, and that stillness is a state of creation that can be experienced only when there is complete understanding of the whole process of the 'me'. Otherwise, stillness has no meaning. Only in that stillness which is not a result is the eternal discovered which is beyond time.

April 23, 1950

Fourth Talk in Paris

The problem of effort, struggle, of striving after something, should be thoroughly understood, because it seems to me that the more we strive, the more we struggle to become something, the greater becomes the complexity of the problem. We have never really gone into this question of striving after something. We make great efforts, spiritually, physically, and in every department of life; our whole existence, positively or negatively, is a process of constant effort—effort, either to become something or to avoid something. Our whole social structure, as well as our religious and philosophical existence, is based, is it not, on striving to achieve a result or to avoid an outcome.

Now, do we understand anything through struggle, through strife, through conflict? Is there a possibility of adjustment, of pliability, through conflict, through struggle? And, is the effort that we are making practically the whole of the time, consciously and unconsciously—is that effort really essential? I know, obviously, that the present structure of society is based on struggle, on effort, on becoming successful or avoiding a result which one does not desire. It is a constant psychological battle. Through psychological effort, in trying to become something, do we understand? I think that is a problem we should really face and go into rather deeply. Perhaps it may not be possible this morning to go into details, but one can see quite clearly that there is effort of every kind, and that the effort of adjustment in relationship is the most prominent effort that we make. Struggle, conflict, exists in relationship—we always trying to adjust ourselves to a different category of society or to an idea; and will this constant striving really lead anywhere?

Now, striving creates a center in one's consciousness around which we build the whole structure of the 'me' and the 'mine'—my position, my achievement, my will, my success; and as long as the 'me' exists, surely there is no possibility of really understanding the total process of oneself. And is it not possible to live a life without struggle, without conflict, without the center of the 'me'? Surely, such a manner of living is not mere oriental escapism—to call it that would be really absurd, that would be merely brushing it aside. On the contrary, let us consider whether it is possible to live in the world and build a new society, whether this whole process of becoming successful, becoming virtuous, achieving or avoiding something, can be completely set aside. And is it not important that we should set aside this constant striving after something, if we would really understand what living is? After all, can we grasp the significance of anything through effort, through struggle, through conflict with it? Or, do we understand it only when we have the capacity to look at it directly, without this battle, this conflict between the observer and the observed?

We can see in everyday experience that if we would really understand something, there must be a certain sense of quietness, a certain tranquillity—not enforced, not disciplined or controlled, but a spontaneous tranquillity in which one sees the significance of any problem. After all, when we have a problem, we struggle with it, we analyze it, we dissect it, we tear it to pieces, trying to find out how to resolve it. Now, what happens when we give up struggling with it? In that quiet state of relaxed tranquillity, the problem has a different aspect—one understands it more clearly. Similarly, is it not possible to live in that state of alertness, in that state of choiceless observation, which brings about tranquillity and in which alone there can be understanding?

After all, our conditioning—social, economic, religious, and so on—is all based on the worship of success. We all want to be successful; we all want to achieve a result. If we fail in this world, we hope to make a success of it in the next. If we are not very successful politically, economically, we want to be successful spiritually. We worship success. And in becoming successful, there must be effort—which means constant conflict, within and without. Surely, one can never understand anything through conflict, can one? Is not the very nature of the self, the 'me', a process of conflict, a process of becoming something? And is it not necessary to understand this 'me', which is the field of conflict, in order to think, to feel directly? And can one understand this whole structure of oneself without the conflict of trying to alter *what is?* In other words, can one look at, consider, what one is essentially, factually, and not try to alter it? Surely, it is only when we are capable of looking at the fact as it is that we can deal with it, but as long as we are struggling with the fact, trying to alter it, make it into something else, we are incapable of understanding *what is.* Only when we understand *what is,* can we go beyond it.

So, in order to understand the structure of myself, which is the central problem of all existence, it is essential, is it not, to be aware of the whole process of the 'me'—the 'me' that seeks success, the 'me' that is cruel, the 'me' that is acquisitive, the 'me' that separates all action, all thought, as 'mine'. In order to understand that 'me', must you not look at it as it is factually, without struggling with it, trying to alter it? Surely, only then is it possible to go beyond. Therefore, self-knowledge is the beginning of wisdom. Wisdom is not bought in books; wisdom is not experience; wisdom is not the accumulation of any kind of virtue or the avoidance of evil. Wisdom comes only through self-knowledge, through the understanding of the whole structure, the whole process, of the 'me'.

For the 'me' to be understood clearly, it must be seen, experienced, in relationship. It is only in the mirror of relationship that I discover the whole process of myself, conscious as well as unconscious; and obviously, all effort to transform it is a process of avoidance, a process of resistance, which prevents understanding. So, if one is really serious, and not merely living on the verbal level, one must understand this process of the 'me'—not theoretically, not according to any philosophy or doctrine, but actually, in relationship; and that process can be discovered and understood completely only when there is no effort to change or alter it. That is, understanding can come only when there is observation without choice.

I do not think most of us realize that the problems of the world are not something apart from us. The problems of the world exist because of you and me; the world's problems are our problems because the world is not different from you and me. And if one would really, seriously and earnestly, understand the whole problem of existence, surely one must begin with oneself—but not in isolation, not as an individuality opposing the mass or withdrawing from society. The problem of the mass is the problem of the 'me', and it is essential, if we would understand the world and bring about a new structure of society, that we should understand ourselves. I don't think we seriously realize the capacity that each one has to transform himself. We look to leaders, to teachers, to saviors, but I am afraid they will not transform the world, they will not bring about a new world order. No teacher can ever do it, but only you and I in understanding ourselves, and I don't think we see the immensity of that. We think that as individuals we are so small, so unimportant, so ordinary, that we cannot do anything in this world. Surely, great things are started in little ways. Fundamental revolution takes place, not outwardly, but inwardly, psychologically, and that fundamental, lasting revolution can come about only when you and I understand ourselves.

So, this understanding of oneself is not a withdrawal from life into a monastery or into some religious meditation. On the contrary, to understand oneself is to understand one's relationship with things, with people, and with ideas. Without relationship, we are not; we exist only in relationship; to be is to be related. Relationship is with property, with people, with ideas, and as long as we do not understand the total process of the 'me' in relationship, we are bound to create conflict within—which projects outwardly and makes misery in the world. So, it is essential to understand oneself, and the understanding of oneself does not lie through any book, through any philosophy. It can be understood only from moment to moment, in all the daily relationships. Relationship is life, and without understanding relationship, our life is a conflict, a constant struggle to transform *what is* into what we desire. Without understanding the 'me', merely to transform or reform the world outside only leads to further misery, further conflict, and further destruction.

I have been given some questions, and I shall answer them. But before I answer them, may I say that while it is easy to ask questions, to follow the question and discover the answer for oneself is extremely difficult. Most of us, when we ask a question, hope for an answer, but life is not made up of questions and answers. It is what is true, and when one puts a question, one must follow it through, go to the very end of it, and find the true answer. So, in considering these questions, I hope that you and I will try to find the truth of the matter, and not merely live on the verbal level.

Question: Why are we afraid of death? And how are we to overcome this fear?

KRISHNAMURTI: Fear is not an abstraction; it obviously exists only in relationship to something. Now, what is it in death that we are afraid of? Of not being, of not continuing—surely, that is the primary thing. We are afraid of not having continuity, are we not—which means, basically, we are afraid of not knowing the future, the unknown. If there is an assurance of continuity, that is, if we can know the future, if we can know the unknown, then there is no fear.

Now, can we know the unknown—that which is beyond all the fabrications, all the projections of the mind? We can know the projections of the mind, but that is not the unknown. We can withhold the projections and try to feel out the unknown, but that is still a form of projection. So, as long as we are trying to find out intellectually, verbally, through desire, how to conquer the unknown, surely there must be fear. We are afraid essentially because of the future, of the unknown, and if another can guarantee, assure us, that there is continuity, then we are no longer afraid. But does continuity in any form bring about understanding of the unknown? Can continuity bring creativeness or creative feeling? Surely, the moment there is continuity, there is no ending, and only in ending, in dying, is there creativeness, is there the new. We do not want to die, and so we make life a process of continuity, but only in death can we know living.

So, our problem is, is it not: can the mind ever conceive, ever formulate, the unknown? And is not the mind the result of the past, of time? Is it not a mere accumulation of experiences, knowledge, and so a storehouse of time, of the past? So, can the mind, which is the result of time, know the timeless, that which is beyond time? Obviously not. Whatever the mind projects is still within the field of time, and there will be fear as long as the mind is projecting itself or trying to understand the future, the unknown. There will be the cessation of fear only when I see the truth of this—that continuity means the projection of myself, the 'myself' being conflict, the constant swing between pleasure and pain. As long as there is a continuity of the 'me', there must be pain, there must be fear; and the mind, which is the center of the 'me', can never find that which is beyond the field of time.

Our difficulty is, is it not, that we really don't know how to live. Because we have not understood life, we think we want to understand death, but if we can understand the process of living, then there will be no fear of death. It is because we do not know how to live that we are afraid of death. Look at the books that have been written on death, look at all the effort made to understand what is beyond! Surely, fear of what is beyond comes only when I do not know how to live in the present, when I do not know the whole significance of life.

Our life is a process of struggle, of pain and pleasure, a constant movement from one thing to another, from the known to the known; it is a battle of adjustment, a battle of achievement, a battle of change. That is our whole life—with occasional rays of clarity. And since we do not understand life, we are afraid of death. Now, need life be a battle, a struggle, a constant becoming? Or, can there be freedom from this becoming so that one can live without conflict?—which means dying each day, dying to all the things that one has accumulated, all the things that one has gathered as experience, as knowledge. Then there is a quality of newness because life is no longer a movement from the known to the known, but a freedom from the known to meet the unknown. Then only is there a possibility of being free from the fear of death.

Question: What is the process of experience? Is it different from self-consciousness?

KRISHNAMURTI: First, let us see what is experience. Surely, experience is the response to challenge and the recognition of the response, is it not? Stimulus, response, and recognition of the response—that is experience, is it not? If you do not respond to a challenge, to a stimulus, or if you do not recognize that response, is there experience? So, experience, surely, is the recognition of the response to a challenge—the recognition being the naming, the terming, giving it the appropriate value. That is, experience is the response to a challenge and the recognition of that response, giving it a term, either verbally or symbolically, consciously or unconsciously. Without the process of recognition, there is no experience.

So, this process of response to a challenge and recognition of the response is surely experience. And is that different from self-consciousness? As long as the response to the challenge is adequate, complete, obviously there can be no friction, there can be no conflict, between the response and the challenge. So, self-consciousness comes into being, does it not, only when there is conflict between challenge and response. You can work this out for yourself; it is very simple, and you will see that it is not a question of believing or discarding, but only of experimenting and being aware, seeing actually what happens.

As long as you have no conflict, no battle, no struggle, is there self-consciousness? Are you aware that you are happy? The moment you are aware that you are happy, happiness ceases, does it not? And the desire for something, the desire for happiness, is the conflict which makes for self-consciousness. When there is conflict, when there is disturbance, there is recognition, and the very recognition is the process of self-consciousness.

So, experience, which is the recognition of the response to challenge, is the beginning of self-consciousness. There is no difference, then, between experiencing, which is recognizing, and self-consciousness. To understand this, it is not necessary, surely, to read books about consciousness, or to study very deeply, or listen to others. One can discover it by actually observing the whole total process of one's own experiencing, one's own consciousness. That is exactly what we are trying to do. I am not propounding a new philosophy—I hope not—nor am I putting something over on you. All that we are trying to do is to see what is consciousness. Surely, consciousness is experience, then the naming of that experience as good or bad, pleasant or unpleasant, and the desire for more of it or less of it; and the very naming, the very terming, gives it strength, gives it permanence. So, consciousness is a process of experiencing, naming or terming, and storing as memory, recollection. This total process is either conscious or unconscious, and as long as we give a name, a term, to the experience, it must be made permanent, it must be fixed in the mind, held in the net of time. This whole, total process is self-consciousness—whether it is on the verbal level or very deep, covered up.

Now, as long as we give a name, a term, a symbol, to an experience, that experience can never be new because the moment we recognize an experience, it is already old. When there is an experience and the naming of it, it is merely the process of recording, remembering. That is, every reaction, every experience, is translated by the mind and put away in the mind as memory, and with that memory we meet the new, which is the challenge. In meeting the new with the old, we transform the new into the old—and so there is no understanding of the new at all.

The understanding of the new is possible only when the mind is capable of not giving it a name, and it is only then that experience can be fully, completely understood and gone beyond so that every meeting of the challenge has a new quality and is not merely recognized and put into the record. There is freedom from self-consciousness, from the 'me', only when we understand this whole, total process of experiencing, naming, and recording. Only when that process ceases, which is the process of the 'me' and the 'mine', is there a possibility of going beyond and discovering things which are not of the mind.

Question: I cannot conceive of a love which is neither felt nor thought of. You are probably using the word love *to indicate something else. Is it not so?*

KRISHNAMURTI: When we say "love," what do we mean by it? Actually, not theoretically, what do we mean? It is a process of sensation and thought, is it not? That is what we mean by love—a process of thought, a process of sensation.

Now, is thought love? When I think of you, is that love? Or, when I say that love must be impersonal, universal—is that love? Surely, thought is the result of a feeling, of sensation, and as long as love is held within the field of sensation and thought, obviously there must be conflict in that process. And must we not find out if there is something beyond the field of thought? That is what we are trying to do. We know what love is in the ordinary sense—a process of thought and sensation. If we do not think of a person, we think we do not love him; if we do not feel, we think there is no love. But is that all? Or, is love something beyond? And to find out, must not thought, as sensation, come to an end? After all, when we love somebody, we think about them, we have a picture of them. That is, what we call love is a thinking process, a sensation, which is memory—the memory of what we did or did not do with him or her. So, memory, which is the result of sensation, which becomes verbalized thought, is what we call love. And even when we say that love is impersonal, cosmic, or what you will, it is still a process of thought.

Now, is love a process of thought? Can we think about love? We can think about the person or think of memories with regard to that person, but is that love? Surely, love is a flame without smoke. The smoke is that with which we are familiar—the smoke of jealousy, of anger, of dependence, of calling it personal or impersonal, the smoke of attachment. We have not the flame, but we are fully acquainted with the smoke, and it is possible to have that flame only when the smoke is not. Therefore, our concern is not with love, whether it is something beyond the mind or beyond sensation, but to be free of the smoke—the smoke of jealousy, of envy, the smoke of separation, of sorrow and pain. Only when the smoke is not shall we know, experience, that which is the flame. And the flame is neither personal nor impersonal, neither universal nor particular—it is just a flame, and there is the reality of that flame only when the mind, the whole process of thought, has been understood. So, there can be love only when the smoke of conflict, of competition, struggle, envy, comes to an end because that process breeds opposition, in which there is fear. As long as there is fear, there is no communion, for one cannot commune through the screen of smoke.

So, it is clear that love is possible only without the smoke, and as we are acquainted with the smoke, let us go into it completely, understand it fully, so as to be free of it. Then only shall we know that flame which is neither personal nor impersonal, which has no name. That which is new cannot be given a name. Our question is not what love is, but what are the things that are preventing the fullness of that flame. We don't know how to love—we only know how to think about love. In the very process of thinking we create the smoke of the 'me' and the 'mine'—and in that we are caught. Only when we are capable of freeing ourselves from the process of thinking about love, and all the complications that arise out of it—only then is there a possibility of having that flame.

Question: What is good and what is evil?

KRISHNAMURTI: As I said, it is easy to ask a question, but it is much more difficult to go into it fully. But let us try.

Why do we always think in terms of duality, in terms of the opposite? Why is it that we are so conditioned by the thought that there is good and that there is evil? Why this division, why this dual process always at work within us? Surely, if we can understand the process of desire, we shall understand this problem, shall we not? The division of good and evil is a contradiction in us. We are attached to the good because it is more pleasurable, and we are conditioned to avoid the evil, which is painful. Now, if we can understand the process of desire, which makes life a contradiction, then perhaps we shall be able to be free from the conflict of the opposites.

So, the problem is not what is good and what is evil, but why this contradiction exists in our daily life. I want something, and in that very wanting there is the opposite. Now, is good the avoidance of evil? Is beauty the avoidance of the ugly? As long as I avoid something, do I not of necessity bring about resistance against it and therefore create its opposite? So, is there a clear line of demarcation between good and evil? Or, is it that when I understand the process of desire, then perhaps I shall know what virtue is? Because, the man who is trying to become virtuous can obviously never be virtuous. The man who is trying to become kindly, loving, tolerant, can never be virtuous; he is merely trying to achieve something, and virtue is not a process of achievement. The avoidance of evil is a process of achievement, but if I can understand the desire which creates duality, the conflict of the opposites, then I shall know what virtue is.

Virtue is not putting an end to desire, but understanding desire. Putting an end to desire is merely another form of desire. In the very desire to end desire, I create the opposite, and therefore I perpetuate the conflict, the battle, between the ideal and what I am. So, the man who pursues the ideal only creates conflict, and the man who is becoming virtuous can never know virtue—he is merely entangled in the battle of opposites. This conflict between himself and what he thinks he should be gives him a sense of living, but the man of ideals is really a man of escape.

Now, if one can understand what virtue is, which means if one can understand desire, then there is freedom from the opposites; and one can understand desire only when one looks at it factually, sees it as it is, without any sense of comparison, without condemnation, without resistance. Then only is there freedom from desire. As long as one is condemning desire, there must be the conflict of the opposites as good and evil, as important and unimportant; as long as one is resisting desire, there must be the conflict of duality. But when one looks at desire as it is, without any sense of comparison, condemnation, or justification, then one will see that desire comes to an end.

So, the beginning of virtue is the understanding of desire. To be caught in the conflict of the opposites is merely to strengthen desire, and most of us do not want to understand desire fully—we enjoy the conflict of the opposites. The conflict of the opposites we call virtue, becoming spiritual, but it is only another form of strengthening the continuity of 'myself', and in the continuity of 'myself' there can be no virtue. It is only when there is no fear that there is freedom, and fear ceases with the understanding of desire.

There is one more question. Shall I answer it, or not?

Audience: Yes, yes.

Question: You say that if I am creative, all the problems will be solved. How am I to change myself so as to be creative?

KRISHNAMURTI: This question is as important as the first question, and I hope you are not too tired to go into it as fully as we can within a few minutes.

We see that in trying to resolve one problem, we create many other problems—which is an obvious fact. In trying to resolve the economic problem, we come upon a multitude of other problems, not only outward, external, but also inward problems. When I have a problem, I try to solve it, and in the very solution of it, I find other problems on my hands. So, that is what we know of the problem—that it is never finally resolved but is constantly increasing.

Now, that being the case, how is it possible to approach the problem of living, or any other problem, without multiplying it? That means, is it possible to approach the problem anew? Surely, that is the question, is it not? If I can approach any problem anew, which is to approach it creatively, then perhaps I shall not only resolve that particular problem but also not introduce many other problems. So, how is it possible to be creative? What are the things that are hindering this sense of creativity, the sense of newness? And I think that is the best question: How is it possible to approach everything anew, with a fresh mind, a mind that is not loaded with experience, with knowledge, with imitation?

What is it that is preventing us from being creative? Obviously, technique. We always know what to do; we have the means. All our education is a process of learning a technique—which means a process of imitation, a process of copy. After all, knowledge is imitation, copy, and isn't that one of the major burdens that prevent us from meeting things anew? Is not authority in any form, spiritual or mundane, external or inward, an impediment to creative understanding? And why do we have authorities? Because, without authority we think we are lost. We must have some anchor. So, in the desire to be secure, inwardly and outwardly, we create authority, and that very authority, which obviously means imitation, destroys creativeness, newness.

Is truth, God, that state of creativeness, something that can come through imitation, through copy, through authority, through compulsion? Must one not be free from authority, from all sense of imitation and copy? You will say, "No, we must begin with authority in order to be free; we must begin through imitation, through compulsion, in order ultimately to arrive at freedom." If you take the wrong means, can you come to the right end? If the end is freedom, must not the beginning also be free? Because, if you use a wrong means, obviously the end must be equally wrong, and if you have no freedom at the beginning, you will have no freedom at the end. If at the beginning your mind is controlled, shaped, disciplined, molded according to authority, obviously it will still be encompassed, held in a frame, at the end, and such a mind, surely, can never be in a state of creativeness. So, the beginning is the end; the end and the means are one.

Surely, if we are to understand creativeness, the beginning matters enormously—which means understanding all those things that impede the mind and prevent its freedom. Freedom comes only when we understand the desire to be secure. It is the desire to be secure that creates authority, that creates discipline, the pattern of imitation, the pursuit of the ideal, the whole process of conformity. The loftier the ideal, the nobler, the holier, the more spiritual we think it is, but it is still merely a pattern, and a mind caught in a pattern is obviously not capable of being creative. But seeing that the mind is caught in a pattern, merely to reject it, as a reaction, is obviously not freedom. In understanding why the mind creates a pattern and holds to it, why the mind is caught in technique, in the addiction to knowledge, why the mind always moves from the known to the known, from security to security, from imitation to imitation—in the direct understanding of all that, and not merely reacting against it, there is freedom from the desire for security and hence from the sense of fear. As long as there is a center of the 'me' from which there is action and reaction, denial and acceptance, obviously there must be a process of imitation and copy. As long as we are mere repeaters, reading books, quoting authorities, pursuing ideals, conforming to a formula or to a dogma, holding on to a particular religion or joining new cults, seeking new teachers, in the hope of being happy—as long as that process exists, obviously there can be no freedom.

So, creativeness comes only when the mind is free from all imitation, from all experience, which is merely the continuity of the 'me'. The mind is free when there is no center which is experiencing, and that center in the mind disappears only when the whole process of desire is understood. Then only is there quietness of mind—not an imposed quietness, a disciplined stillness, or the tranquillity of conformity, but that spontaneous quietness which comes through understanding. And when the mind is still, there is creativeness, there is the creative state of being. Stillness is not a process of imitation, of conformity; you cannot think about stillness. Tranquillity does not come through any projection of the mind. Only when thought is silent, not merely on the upper level, but right through the consciousness as well as the unconscious, only when the thought process comes to an end is there a sense of tranquillity, a stillness. In that silence there is a creation which is not mere technique, but which has its own vitality, its own way of expression. As long as you are concerned with expression, with technique, with knowledge, with any form of addiction, there can be no creativeness because that creativeness comes only when the mind is utterly still. That stillness is not a process of avoidance, it does not come through learning a technique of meditation. Those who learn a technique of how to meditate will never know what silence is, will never be creative—their state will be a state of death and denial. There can be creation only when thought has come to an end, not only at the conscious upper level, but at those levels that are deep down, concealed, hidden. When the mind is utterly still, then there is creation.

April 30, 1950

Fifth Talk in Paris

We seem to think that by pursuing a particular course of philosophy, or a belief, or a system of thought, we shall be able to clear up the confusion, not only in ourselves, but also about us. We have innumerable beliefs, doctrines, and hopes, and in trying to follow them, in trying to be sincere in regard to our ideals, we hope to clear the path to happiness or the path to knowledge and comprehension. Surely, there is a difference between sincerity and earnestness. One can be faithful to an idea, to a hope, to a doctrine, to a particular system; but merely copying, pursuing an idea, or conforming oneself to a particular doctrine—all of which may be called sincerity—will surely not help us to clear up the confusion in ourselves and so the confusion about us.

So, it seems to me that what is necessary is earnestness—not the earnestness that comes from merely following a particular tendency, a particular path, but that earnestness which is essential in the understanding of ourselves. To understand ourselves, there need be no particular system, no particular idea. One is sincere only in regard to a thing, to a particular attitude, to a particular belief, but such sincerity cannot help us because we can be sincere and yet be confused, foolish, and ignorant. Sincerity is a hindrance when it is mere copying, trying to follow a particular ideal, but earnestness is quite a different thing. To be earnest is essential—not in the pursuit of anything, but in the understanding of the process of ourselves. In the understanding of the process of ourselves, there need be no belief, no doctrine, no particular philosophy. On the contrary, if we have a philosophy, a doctrine, it will become an impediment to the understanding of ourselves.

The understanding of ourselves has nothing to do with following a doctrine, a philosophy, a formula, or trying to imitate a particular ideal. Surely, all that is the process of the 'me', the 'I'. And in the understanding of our various conditionings, sincerity is not necessary—but it is essential to be earnest, which is quite different. Earnestness does not depend on a mood; it is the beginning of the understanding of ourselves. Because, without being earnest, without being really serious, one cannot go very far. But our seriousness, our earnestness, is generally applied to the following of a particular idea, a particular belief or hope, and what is important is to understand ourselves. The understanding of ourselves does not demand imitation, copy, the approximation to an ideal. On the contrary, we have to understand ourselves as we are from moment to moment, whatever it be, and for that there must be earnestness which does not depend on any particular mood or tendency.

Now, it is clear that we cannot resolve any human problem, either external or inward, without understanding ourselves, and the understanding of ourselves is possible only when we do not condemn or justify that of which we are aware. To be aware, without condemnation, justification, or comparison, of every thought, of every mood, of every reaction, does not demand the approximation to an idea. What it does require is earnestness—a sense of going into it fully, completely. But most of us do not want to understand any problem deeply, fully; we would rather escape from it through an idea, through approximation, through comparison or condemnation, and thereby we never solve the particular issue in front of us.

So, it is important, is it not, in order to understand ourselves, that we be aware of every reaction, every feeling as it arises, and awareness does not depend on any formula, on any doctrine or belief—which are merely self-projected escapes. To understand every mood, every sense of reaction, surely one must be aware without choice because the moment we choose, we set into motion a process of conflict. That is, when we choose, there is resistance, and in resistance there is no understanding. Choice is merely fixing the mind on a particular interest and resisting other interests, other demands, other pursuits, and obviously, such choice will not help us to resolve or understand the whole process of ourselves. Each one of us is made up of many entities, conscious as well as unconscious, and to choose one particular entity, one particular desire, and pursue that is surely an impediment to the understanding of ourselves.

So, seeing the whole process of ourselves is the beginning of wisdom. Wisdom is not something that can be bought in books, that can be learned through another, that can be gathered even through experience. Experience is merely memory, and the accumulation of memory or knowledge is not wisdom. Wisdom is surely the experiencing of each moment without condemnation or justification; it is understanding each particular experience or reaction fully, completely, so that the mind comes to every problem anew. After all, the 'me' is the center of recognition, and if we do not understand that center but merely recognize every experience or reaction and give it a name, a term, it does not mean that we have understood that particular reaction or experience; on the contrary, when we name, or recognize, a particular experience, we only strengthen the 'me'—that isolated consciousness which is the center of recognition. So, merely recognizing every experience, every reaction, is not the understanding of oneself. The understanding of oneself comes only when we are aware of the process of recognition and allow a gap between experience and recognition—which means a state of mind in which there is stillness.

Surely, if we would understand anything, any problem, there must be quietness of mind, must there not? But the mind cannot be forced to be quiet, and silence that is cultivated is mere resistance, isolation. The mind is spontaneously quiet only when it sees the necessity, the truth of being quiet, and therefore begins to understand the process of recognition, which is the whole consciousness of the 'me'. Without understanding oneself, obviously there is no basis for thought, and without knowing oneself, merely to know the outward problems, to acquire external knowledge, will only lead us to further confusion and misery. But the more we know ourselves, both the conscious and the unconscious, the more we see the whole process of the 'me', the more we are able to understand and resolve our problems and therefore bring about a better society, a different world. So, we must begin with ourselves. You may say that to begin with oneself is a very small affair, but if we would tackle great things, we must begin very near. The world's problem is our problem, and without understanding ourselves, any problem with which we come face to face in the world will never be resolved. So, the beginning of wisdom is self-knowledge, and without self-knowledge we cannot resolve any human problem.

Before I answer some of these questions, may I suggest that when listening to the answers, you and I should both experience what is being said. That is, let us take a journey together in understanding these problems which I am going to try to explain verbally. So, please do not remain on the verbal level or merely try to understand intellectually—whatever that word may mean. Because, the intellect cannot understand; it can only project its own particular accumulations. It can accept, deny, or resist, which is the process of recognition and verbalization, but the intellect cannot understand any human problem—it can only make it more confusing, more conflicting, more sorrowful. If, instead of trying to understand merely on the verbal level, we go beyond the intellect, then perhaps we shall be able to see the truth of these questions. To go beyond the intellect is not to become sentimental, emotional, which would be the opposite, and in the conflict of the opposites there is no comprehension, obviously. But if we can see that the process of the intellect, of the mind, can only bring about further argumentations, further conflict—if we can see the truth of that, then perhaps we shall discover the truth of every question, of every human problem, that confronts us.

Question: Beyond all superficial fears there is a deep anguish which eludes me. It seems to be the very fear of life—or perhaps of death. Or is it the vast emptiness of life?

KRISHNAMURTI: I think most of us feel this; most of us feel a great sense of emptiness, a great sense of loneliness. We try to avoid it, we try to run away from it, we try to find security, permanency, away from this anguish. Or, we try to be free of it by analyzing the various dreams, the various reactions. But it is always there, eluding us, and not to be resolved so easily and so superficially. Most of us are aware of this emptiness, of this loneliness, of this anguish. And, being afraid of it, we seek security, a sense of permanency, in things or property, in people or relationship, or in ideas, beliefs, dogmas, in name, position, and power. But can this emptiness be banished by merely running away from ourselves? And is not this running away from ourselves one of the causes of confusion, pain, misery, in our relationships and therefore in the world?

So, this is a question not to be brushed aside as being bourgeois, or stupid, or merely for those who are not active socially, religiously. We must examine it very carefully and go into it fully. As I said, most of us are aware of this emptiness, and we try to run away from it. In running away from it, we establish certain securities, and then those securities become all-important to us because they are the means of escape from our particular loneliness, emptiness, or anguish. Your escape may be a Master, it may be thinking yourself very important, it may be giving all your love, your wealth, jewels, everything, to your wife, to your family; or it may be social or philanthropic activity. Any form of escape from this inward emptiness becomes all-important, and therefore we cling to it desperately. Those who are religiously-minded cling to their belief in God, which covers up their emptiness, their anguish; and so their belief, their dogma, becomes essential—and for these they are willing to fight, to destroy each other.

Obviously, then, any escape from this anguish, from this loneliness, will not solve the problem. On the contrary, it merely increases the problem and brings about further confusion. So, one must first realize the escapes. All escapes are on the same level; there are no superior or inferior escapes, there are no spiritual escapes apart from the mundane. All escapes are essentially similar, and if we recognize that the mind is constantly escaping from the central problem of anguish, of emptiness, then we are capable of looking at emptiness without condemning it or being afraid of it. As long as I am escaping from a fact, I am afraid of that fact, and when there is fear, I can have no communication with it. So, to understand the fact of emptiness, there must be no fear. Fear comes only when I am trying to escape from it, because in escaping, I can never look at it directly. But the moment I cease to escape, I am left with the fact. I can look at it without fear, and then I am able to deal with the fact.

So, that is the first step—to face the fact, which means not to escape through money, through amusement, through the radio, through beliefs, through assertions, or through any other means, because that emptiness cannot be filled by words, by activities, by beliefs. Do what we will, that anguish cannot be wiped away by any tricks of the mind, and whatever the mind does with regard to it will only be an avoidance. But when there is no avoidance of any kind, then the fact is there, and the understanding of the fact does not depend on the inventions, on the projections or calculations of the mind. When one is confronted with the fact of loneliness, with that immense anguish, the vast emptiness of existence, then one will see whether that emptiness is a reality—or merely the result of naming, of terming, of self-projection. Because, by giving it a name, by giving it a term, we have condemned it, have we not? We say it is emptiness, it is loneliness, it is death, and these words—*death, loneliness, emptiness*—imply a condemnation, a resistance, and through resistance, through condemnation, we do not understand the fact.

To understand the fact which we call emptiness, there must be no condemnation, no naming, of the fact. After all, the recognition of the fact creates the center of the 'me', and the 'me' is empty, the 'me' is only words. When I do not name the fact, give it a term, when I do not recognize it as this or that, is there loneliness? After all, loneliness is a process of isolation, is it not? Surely, in all our relationships, in all our efforts in life, we are always isolating ourselves. That process of isolation must obviously lead to emptiness, and without understanding the whole process of isolation, we shall not be able to resolve this emptiness, this loneliness. But when we understand the process of isolation, we shall see that emptiness is merely a thing of words, mere recognition; and the moment there is no recognition, no naming of it, and hence no fear, emptiness becomes something else, it goes beyond itself. Then it is not emptiness, it is aloneness—something much vaster than the process of isolation.

Now, must we not be alone? At present we are not alone—we are merely a bundle of influences. We are the result of all kinds of influences—social, religious, economic, hereditary, climatic. Through all those influences, we try to find something beyond, and if we cannot find it, we invent it and cling to our inventions. But when we understand the whole process of influence at all the different levels of our consciousness, then, by becoming free of it, there is an aloneness which is uninfluenced; that is, the mind and heart are no longer shaped by outward events or inward experiences. It is only when there is this aloneness that there is a possibility of finding the real. But a mind that is merely isolating itself through fear can have only anguish, and such a mind can never go beyond itself.

With most of us, the difficulty is that we are unaware of our escapes. We are so conditioned, so accustomed to our escapes, that we take them as realities. But if we will look more deeply into ourselves, we will see how extraordinarily lonely, how extraordinarily empty we are under the superficial covering of our escapes. Being aware of that emptiness, we are constantly covering it up with various activities, whether artistic, social, religious, or political. But emptiness can never finally be covered—it must be understood. To understand it, we must be aware of these escapes, and when we understand the escapes, then we shall be able to face our emptiness. Then we shall see that the emptiness is not different from ourselves, that the observer is the observed. In that experience, in that integration of the thinker and the thought, this loneliness, this anguish, disappears.

Question: Is it possible for Westerners to meditate?

KRISHNAMURTI: I think this is one of the romantic ideas of Westerners—that only Easterners can meditate. So, let us find out, not how to meditate, but what we mean by meditation. Let us experiment together to find out what meditation means, what are the implications of meditation. Merely to learn how to meditate, to acquire a technique, is obviously not meditation. Going to a yogi, a swami, reading about meditation in books and trying to imitate, sitting in certain postures with your eyes closed, breathing in a certain way, repeating words—surely, all that is not meditation; it is merely pursuing a pattern of conformity, making the mind repetitive, habitual. The mere cultivation of a habit, whether noble or trivial, is not meditation. This practice of cultivating a particular habit is known both in the East and in the West, and we think that it is a process of meditation.

Now, let us find out what is meditation. Is concentration meditation? Concentration on a particular interest chosen from among many other interests, focusing the mind on an object or an entity—is that meditation? In the process of concentration, obviously there is resistance to other forms of interest; therefore, concentration is a process of exclusion, is it not? I do not know if you have tried to meditate, tried to fix your mind on a particular thought. When you do that, other thoughts come pouring in because you are also interested in those other thoughts, not only in the particular thought you have chosen. You have chosen one particular thought, thinking it is noble, spiritual, and that you should concentrate on it and resist other thoughts. But the very resistance creates conflict between the thought that you have chosen to think about and other interests; so you spend your time concentrating on one thought and keeping off the others, and this battle between thoughts is considered meditation. If you can succeed in completely identifying yourself with one thought and resisting all others, you think you have learned how to meditate. Now, such concentration is a process of exclusion and therefore a process of gratification, is it not? You have chosen a particular interest that you think will ultimately give you satisfaction, and you go after it by repeating a phrase, by concentrating upon an image, by breathing, and so on. That whole process implies advancement, becoming something, achieving a result. That is what we are all interested in—we want to be successful in meditation. And the more successful we are, the more we think we have advanced. So obviously, such forms of concentration, which we call meditation, are mere gratification; they are not meditation at all. So, mere concentration on an idea is not meditation.

What, then, is meditation? Is prayer meditation? Is devotion meditation? Is the cultivation of a virtue meditation? The cultivation of a virtue only strengthens the 'me', does it not? It is I who am becoming virtuous. Can the 'I', the 'me', ever become virtuous? That is, can the center of resistance, of recognition, which is a process of isolation—can that ever be virtuous? Surely, there is virtue only when there is freedom from the 'I', from the 'me', so the cultivation of virtue through meditation is obviously a false process. But it is a very convenient process because it strengthens the 'me', and as long as I am strengthening the 'me', I think I am advancing, becoming successful spiritually. But obviously, that is not meditation, is it? Nor is prayer—prayer being mere supplication, petition, which is again a demand of the self, a projection of the self towards greater and wider satisfaction. Nor is meditation the immolation of oneself to an image, to an idea, which we call devotion, because we always choose the image, the formula, the ideal, according to our own satisfaction. What we choose may be beautiful, but we are still seeking gratification.

So, none of these processes—concentration, repeating certain phrases, breathing in a special manner, and all the rest of it—can really help us to understand what meditation is. They are very popular because they always produce results, but they are all obviously foolish ways of trying to meditate.

Now, what is meditation? The understanding of the ways of the mind is meditation, is it not? Meditation is the understanding of myself, it is being aware of every reaction, conscious as well as unconscious—which is self-knowledge. Without self-knowledge, how can there be meditation? Surely, meditation is the beginning of self-knowledge, because if I do not know myself, whatever I do must be merely an escape from myself. If I do not know the structure, the ways of my own thinking, feeling, reacting, of what value is it to imitate, to try to concentrate, to learn how to breathe in a particular way, or to lose myself in devotion? Surely, in that way I will never understand myself; on the contrary, I am merely escaping from myself.

Meditation, then, is the beginning of self-knowledge. In that there is no success, there are no spectacular processes. It is most arduous. As we do not want to know ourselves but only to find an escape, we turn to Masters, religious books, prayers, yogis, and all the rest of it, and then we think we have learned how to meditate. Only in understanding ourselves does the mind become quiet, and without understanding ourselves, the tranquillity of the mind is not possible. When the mind is quiet, not made quiet through discipline—when the mind is not controlled, not encased in condemnation and resistance, but is spontaneously still—only then is it possible to find out what is true and what is beyond the projections of the mind.

Surely, if I want to know if there is reality, God, or what you will, the mind must be absolutely quiet, must it not? Because, whatever the mind seeks out will not be real—it will merely be the projection of its own memories, of the things it has accumulated; and the projection of memory is obviously not reality or God. So, the mind must be still, but not made still; it must be naturally, easily, spontaneously still. Only then is it possible for the mind to discover something beyond itself.

Question: Is truth absolute?

KRISHNAMURTI: Is truth something final, absolute, fixed? We would like it to be absolute because then we could take shelter in it. We would like it to be permanent because then we could hold on to it, find happiness in it. But is truth absolute, continuous, to be experienced over and over again? The repetition of experience is the mere cultivation of memory, is it not? In moments of quietness, I may experience a certain truth, but if I cling to that experience through memory and make it absolute, fixed—is that truth? Is truth the continuation, the cultivation of memory? Or, is truth to be found only when the mind is utterly still? When the mind is not caught in memories, not cultivating memory as the center of recognition, but is aware of everything I am saying, everything I am doing in my relationships, in my activities, seeing the truth of everything as it is from moment to moment—surely, that is the way of meditation, is it not? There is comprehension only when the mind is still, and the mind cannot be still as long as it is ignorant of itself. That ignorance is not dispelled through any form of discipline, through pursuing any authority, ancient or modern. Belief only creates resistance, isolation, and where there is isolation, there is no possibility of tranquillity. Tranquillity comes only when I understand the whole process of myself—the various entities in conflict with each other which compose the 'me'. As that is an arduous task, we turn to others to learn various tricks which we call meditation. The tricks of the mind are not meditation. Meditation is the beginning of self-knowledge, and without meditation, there is no self-knowledge. Meditation is watching, observing, being aware of oneself, not only at one particular hour of the day, but all the time—when we are walking, eating, talking, reading, in relationship—all that is the process in which we discover the ways of the 'me'.

When I understand myself, then there is quietness, then there is stillness of the mind. In that stillness, reality can come to me. That stillness is not stagnation, it is not a denial of action. On the contrary, it is the highest form of action. In that stillness there is creation—not the mere expression of a particular creative activity, but the feeling of creation itself.

So, meditation is the beginning of self-knowledge, and merely to cling to formulas, to repetitions, to words, does not reveal the process of the self. It is only when the mind is not agitated, not compelled, not forced, that there is a spontaneous stillness in which truth can come into being.

May 7, 1950

New York City, New York, 1950

First Talk in New York

I think it is important to bear in mind that there is a difficulty in understanding each other. Most of us listen casually, and we hear only what we want to hear; we disregard that which is penetrating or disturbing and listen only to the things that are pleasurable, satisfying. Surely, there can be no real understanding of anything if we listen only to those things which gratify and soothe us. It is quite an art to listen to everything without prejudice, without building up defenses; and may I suggest that we try to set aside our acquired knowledge, our particular idiosyncrasies and points of view, and listen to find out the truth of the matter. It is only the truth that really and fundamentally frees us—not speculations, not conclusions, but only the perception of what is true. The true is the factual, and we are incapable of looking at the factual when we approach it with our private conclusions, prejudices, and experiences. So, if I may suggest it, during these talks we should try to hear not only what is being said verbally but the inward content of it; we should try to discover the truth of the matter for ourselves.

Now, truth can be discovered only when we are not pursuing any form of distraction, and most of us want to be distracted. Life, with all its struggles, problems, wars, business crises, and family quarrels, is a bit too much for us, so we want to be distracted, and we have probably come to this meeting in search of distraction. But distraction, whether outward or inward, will not help us to understand ourselves. Distraction—whether the distraction of politics, of religion, of knowledge, of amusement, or the distraction of pursuing so-called truth—however stimulating for the time being, ultimately dulls the mind, encloses, circumscribes, and limits it. Distractions are both outward and inward. The outward ones we know fairly well; as we grow older we begin to recognize them if we are at all thoughtful. But though we may discard the obvious distractions, it is much more difficult to understand the inward ones; and if we merely make these meetings into a new form of distraction, a new stimulation, I am afraid they will have very little value in the understanding of oneself—which is of primary importance.

Therefore, one has to understand the whole process of distraction, because as long as the mind is distracted, seeking a result, trying to escape through stimulation or so-called inspiration, it is incapable of understanding its own process. And, if we are to think out any of the innumerable problems that confront each one of us, it is essential to know the whole process of our own thinking, is it not? Self-knowledge is ultimately the only way of resolving our innumerable problems, and self-knowledge cannot possibly be a result, an outcome, of stimulation or distraction. On the contrary, distraction, stimulation, and so-called inspiration merely take one away from the central issue. Surely, without knowing oneself fundamentally, radically, and deeply, without knowing all the layers of consciousness, both the superficial as well as the profound, there is no basis for thinking, is there? If I do not know myself in both the upper and the deeper layers of the mind, what basis have I for any thinking? And in order to know oneself, no form of distraction is helpful. Yet most of us are concerned with distractions. Our religious, political, social, and economic activities, our pursuit of various teachers with their particular idiosyncrasies, our clamoring after what we call knowledge—these are all escapes, they are obviously distractions away from the central issue of knowing oneself. Though it has often been said that it is essential to know oneself, we actually give very little time or thought to the matter; and without knowing oneself, whatever we think or do must inevitably lead to further confusion and misery.

So, it is essential in all things to understand the process of oneself because without knowing oneself, no human problem can be resolved. Any resolution of a problem without self-knowledge is merely distraction, leading to further misery, confusion, and struggle—this, when one thinks about it, is fairly obvious. Seeing the truth of that, how is it possible to know the whole content, the whole structure of oneself? I think this is a fundamental question which each one of us has to face, and in considering it together, you are not merely listening to me giving you a series of ideas, nor am I expounding a particular system or method. On the contrary, you and I are trying to find out together how it is possible to know oneself—the ''oneself'' who is the actor, the observer, the thinker, the watcher. If I do not know the whole process of myself, mere conclusions, theories, speculations, are obviously of very little significance.

Now, to know myself, I must know my actions, my thoughts, my feelings because I can only know myself in action, not apart from action. I cannot know myself apart from my activities in relationship. My activities, my qualities, are myself. I can know the whole process of my thinking, the conscious as well as the unconscious, only in relationship—my relationship to ideas, to people, and to things, property, and money; and to study myself apart from relationship has very little meaning. It is only in my relationship to these things that I can know myself. To divide myself into the 'higher' and the 'lower' is absurd. To think that I am the higher self directing or controlling my lower self is a theory of the mind, and without understanding the structure of the mind, merely to invent convenient theories is a process of escape from myself.

So, the important thing is to find out what my relationship is to people, to property, and to ideas, because life is a process of relationship. Nothing can live in isolation, except theoretically, and to understand myself, I must understand the whole process of relationship. But the understanding of relationship becomes extremely difficult and almost impossible when I look into the mirror of relationship with a sense of condemnation, justification, or comparison. How can I understand relationship if I condemn, justify, or compare it with something? I can understand it only when I come to it anew, with a fresh mind, a mind which is not caught in the traditional background of condemnation and acceptance.

To understand myself is essential because whatever the problems, they are projected by me. I am the world, I am not independent of the world, and the world's problems are my own. To understand the problems around me, which are the projection of myself, I have to understand myself in relationship to everything, but there cannot be understanding if I begin by comparing, condemning, or justifying. Now, it is the nature of the mind to condemn, to justify, to compare, and when we see in the mirror of relationship our own reactions and idiosyncrasies, our instinctive response is to condemn or justify them. The understanding of this process of condemnation and justification is the beginning of self-knowledge—and without self-knowledge, we cannot go very far. We can invent a lot of theories and speculations, join various groups, follow teachers and Masters, perform rituals, gather into little cliques and feel superior to others—but all this leads nowhere, it is merely the immature action of thoughtless people. To find out what is real, to discover whether or not there is reality, God, one must first understand oneself because whatever the conception one may have of reality or of God, it is merely a projection of oneself, which can obviously never be real. It is only when the mind is utterly tranquil—not forced to be tranquil, not compelled nor disciplined—that it is possible to find out what is real, and the mind can be still only in the understanding of its own structure. Only the real, that which is not a projection of the mind, can free the mind from all the tribulations, from all the problems that confront each one of us.

So, we must first see the importance, the necessity of understanding oneself, for without understanding oneself, no problem can be resolved, and the wars, the antagonisms, the envy and strife will continue. A man who would really understand truth must have a mind that is quiet, and that quietness can come only through the understanding of himself. Tranquillity of the mind does not come through discipline, through control, through subjugation, but only when the problems, which are the projections of oneself, are completely understood. Only when the mind is quiet, when it is not projecting itself, is it possible for the real to be. That is, for reality to come into being, the mind must be quiet—not made quiet, not controlled, subjugated, or suppressed, but silent spontaneously because of its understanding of the whole structure of the 'me', with all its memories, limitations, and conflicts. When all this is completely and truly understood, the mind is quiet, and then only is it possible to know that which is real.

Some questions have been given to me, and I shall answer a few of them this morning, but before doing so, let me say that it is very easy to ask a question, hoping for an answer. I am afraid, however, that life has no answer like yes or no. We have to discover the true answer for ourselves, and to discover the true answer, we must examine the problem. To examine the problem, especially a problem that concerns us intimately, is very difficult, for most of us approach it with a prejudice, with a desire to find a result, a satisfactory answer. So, in considering these questions, let us investigate the problem together, and not wait for me to tell you the answer, because truth must be discovered each minute, not merely explained. Truth is not knowledge—knowledge is merely the cultivation of memory, and memory is a continuity of experiences—and that which is continuous can never be the truth. So, let us investigate these questions together. I am not saying this merely to be rhetorical—I actually mean it. You and I are going to find out the truth of the matter. If you discover it for yourself, it is yours, but if you wait for me to give the answer, it will have very little value, for then you will merely remain on the verbal level and hear only words, and the words will not carry you very far.

Question: What system would assure us of economic security?

KRISHNAMURTI: Now, what do we mean by a system? The world is torn at the present time between two systems, the left and the right. The world is broken up by beliefs, by ideas, by formulas, and we seek economic or physical security along certain lines. Now, can there be security according to any particular system? Can you base existence on any particular belief, conclusion, or theory? There is the system of the left and the system of the right. Both of them promise economic security, and they are at war with each other—which means that you are not secure. You are not secure because you are quarreling over systems and cultivating war in the process. So, as long as you depend on a system for security, there must be insecurity. Surely, that is fairly clear, is it not? Those who hold to beliefs, to utopian promises, are not concerned with people—they are concerned with ideas; and action based on ideas must inevitably breed separatism and disintegration—which is actually what is taking place. So, as long as we look for security through a system, through an idea, obviously there must be separatism, contention, and disintegration, which invariably brings about insecurity.

The next problem is this: Is economic security a matter of legislation, of compulsion, of totalitarianism? We all want to be secure. It is essential to be physically secure, to have food, clothing, and shelter, otherwise we cannot exist. But is that security brought about by legislation, by economic regulation—or is it a psychological problem? So far, we have considered it merely as an economic problem, a matter of economic adjustment, but surely it is a psychological problem, is it not? And can such a problem be solved by economic experts? Since the economic problem is obviously the result of our own inclinations, desires, and pursuits, it is really a psychological problem; and in order to bring about economic security, we must understand the psychological demand to be secure. I do not know if I am making myself clear.

The world is now torn up into different nationalities, different beliefs, different political ideologies, each promising security, a future utopia; and obviously, such a process of separatism is a process of disintegration.

Now, can there ever be unity through ideas? Can ideas, beliefs, ever bring people together? Obviously, they cannot—it is being proved throughout the world. So, to bring about security, not for a small group of people, but for the whole of mankind, there must be freedom from this process of division created by ideas—the idea of being a Christian, a Buddhist, a Hindu, a nationalist, a communist, a socialist, a capitalist, an American, a Russian, or God knows what else. It is these things that are separating us, and they are nothing but beliefs, ideas; and as long as we cling to beliefs as a means of security, there must be separation, there must be disintegration and chaos.

So, this is fundamentally a psychological, not an economic problem; it is a problem of the individual psyche, and therefore we have to understand the process of individuality, of the 'you'. Is the 'you' in America different from the 'me' that lives in India or in Europe? Though we may separate ourselves by customs, by formulas, by certain beliefs, fundamentally we are the same, are we not? Now, when the 'me' seeks security in a belief, that very belief gives strength to the 'me'. I am a Hindu, a socialist, I belong to a particular religion, a particular sect, and I cling to that and defend it. So, the very attachment to belief creates separatism, which is obviously a cause of contention between you and me. The economic problem can never be solved as long as we separate ourselves into nationalities, into religious groups, or belong to particular ideologies. So, it is essentially a psychological problem, that is, a problem of the individual in relationship to society; and society is the projection of oneself. That is why there can be no solution to any human problem without understanding oneself completely—which means living in a state of complete inward insecurity. We want to be outwardly secure, and so we pursue inward security; but as long as we are seeking inward security through beliefs, through attachments, through ideologies, obviously we will create islands of isolation in the form of national, ideological, and religious groups, and therefore be at war with each other.

So, it is important to understand the process of oneself. But self-knowledge is not a means of ultimate security—on the contrary, reality is something which has to be discovered from moment to moment. A mind that is secure can never be in a state of discovery, and a mind that is insecure has no belief, it is not caught in any particular ideology. Such a mind is not seeking inward security, therefore it will create outward security. As long as you are seeking security inwardly, you will never have security outwardly. Therefore, the problem is not to bring about outward security but to understand the desire to be inwardly, psychologically secure, and as long as we do not understand that, we shall never have peace, we shall never have security in the outer world.

Now, one is horrified, very often, to discover in oneself appalling distortions. How is one to be free from them? There are different ways of attempting to be free, are there not? There is the psychoanalytical process, and there is the process of control, of discipline, and the process of escape. Can one be free fundamentally through the psychoanalytical process? I am not condemning psychoanalysis—but let us examine it. First of all, the 'me', the whole structure of the 'me', is the result of the past. You and I are the result of the past, of time, of many incidents, experiences; we are made up of various qualities, memories, idiosyncrasies. The whole structure of the 'me' is the past. Now, in the past there are certain qualities which I dislike and want to get rid of, so I go into the past and look at them; I bring them out and analyze them, hoping to dissolve them; or, using the actions of the present as a mirror to reflect the past, I try to dissolve the past. Either I go to the past and try to dissolve it through analysis, or I use the present as a means through which the past is discovered; that is, in present action I seek to discover and understand the past. So, that is one way.

Then there is the way of discipline. I say to myself, "These particular distortions are not worthwhile, I am going to suppress, subjugate, control them." This implies, does it not, that there is an entity separate from the thought process—call it the higher self or what you will—that is controlling, dominating, choosing. Surely that is implied, is it not? When I say, "I am going to dissolve the distortions," I am separate from those distortions. That is, I don't like the distortions—they hinder me, they bring about fear, conflict—and I want to dissolve them, so there arises the idea that the 'me' is separate from the distortions and is capable of dissolving them.

Before we discuss this further, we will have to find out if the 'me', the examiner, the observer, the analyzer, is different from the qualities. Am I making it clear? Is the thinker, the experiencer, the observer, different from the thought, from the experience, from the thing which is observed? Is the 'me', whether you place it at the highest or at the lowest level—is that 'me' different from the qualities which compose it? Is the thinker, the analyzer, different from his thoughts? You think that he is—that the thinker is separate from thought; therefore, you control thought, you shape thought, you subjugate, push it aside. The thinker, you say, is different from thought. But is that so? Is there a thinker without thought? If you have no thought, where is the thinker? So, thought creates the thinker; the thinker doesn't create thought. The moment we separate the thinker from the thought, we have the whole problem of trying to control, dissipate, suppress thought, or of trying to be free from a particular thought. This is the conflict between the thinker and the thought in which most of us are caught—it is our whole problem.

One sees certain distortions in oneself which one doesn't like, and one wants to be free of them; so one tries to analyze or to discipline them, that is, to do something about the thoughts. But before we do that, should we not find out if the thinker is actually separate from thought? Obviously he is not—the thinker is the thought, the experiencer is the experienced—they are not two different processes, but a single, unitary process. Thought divides itself and creates the thinker for its own convenience. That is, thought is invariably transient; it has no resting place, and seeing itself as transient, thought creates the thinker as the permanent entity. The permanent entity then acts upon thought, choosing this particular thought and rejecting that. Now, when you really see the falseness of that process, you will discover that there is no thinker, but only thoughts—which is quite a revolution. This is the fundamental revolution which is essential in order to understand the whole process of thinking. As long as you establish a thinker independent of his thoughts, you are bound to have conflict between the thinker and the thought, and where there is conflict, there can be no understanding. Without understanding this division in yourself, do what you will—suppress, analyze, discover the cause of struggle, go to a psychoanalyst, and all the rest of it—you will inevitably remain in the process of conflict. But if you can see and understand the truth that the thinker is the thought, the analyzer is the analyzed—if you can understand that, not merely verbally, but in actual experience, then you will discover that an extraordinary revolution is taking place. Then there is no permanent entity as the 'me' choosing and discarding, seeking a result, or trying to achieve an end. Where there is choice there must be conflict, and choice will never lead to understanding because choice implies a thinker who chooses. So, to be free of a particular distortion, a particular perversion, we must first discover for ourselves the truth that the thinker is not separate from thought; then we will see that what we call distortion is a process of thinking, and that there is no thinker apart from that process.

Now, what do we mean by thinking? When we say, "This is ugly," "That is fear," "This must be discarded," we know what that process is. There is the 'me' who is choosing, condemning, discarding. But if there is not the 'me' but only that process of fear, then what happens? Am I explaining the problem? If there is not the one who condemns, who chooses, who thinks that he is separate from that which he dislikes, then what happens? Please experience this as we go along, and you will see. Don't merely listen to my words, but actually experience that there is only thought, and not the thinker. Then you will see what thinking is. What is thought? Thought is a process of verbalization, is it not? Without words, you cannot think. So, thought is a process of memory, because words, symbols, names, are the product, the result of memory. So, thinking is a process of memory, and memory gives a name to a particular feeling and either condemns or accepts it. By giving a name to something, you condemn or accept it, don't you? When you say someone is an American, a Russian, a Hindu, a negro, you have finished with him, haven't you? By labeling a thing, you think you have understood it. So, when there is a particular reaction which you term *fear,* in giving it a name you have condemned it. That is the actual process you will see going on when you begin to be aware of your thinking.

Is it possible not to name a feeling? Because, by calling a particular feeling "anger," "fear," "jealousy," we have given it strength, have we not? We have fixed it. The very naming is a process of confirming that feeling, giving it strength, and therefore enclosing it in memory. Observe it and you will see. It is possible to be free fundamentally only when the process of naming is understood—naming being terming, symbolizing, which is the action of memory—because memory is the 'you'. Without your memory, without your experiences, the 'you' is not, and the mind clings to those experiences as essential in order to be secure. So, we cultivate memory, which is experience, knowledge, and through that process we hope to control the reactions and feelings which we call distortions. If we would be free of any particular quality, we must understand the whole process of the thinker and the thought; we must see the truth that the thinker is not separate from thought, but that they are a single, unitary process. If you actually realize that, you will see what an extraordinary revolution takes place in your life. By revolution I do not mean economic revolution, which is no revolution at all, but merely a modified continuity of *what is.* But when the thinker realizes that he is not different from thought, then you will see that radically, deeply, there is an extraordinary transformation, because then there is only the fact of thought, and not the translation of that fact to suit the thinker.

Now, what is there to understand about a fact? There is nothing, is there? A fact is a fact, it is self-evident. The struggle to understand comes only when the thinker is trying to do something about the fact. The action of the thinker upon the fact is shaped by his memory, by his past experience; therefore, the fact is always shaped by the thinker, and therefore he never understands the fact. But if there is no thinker, but only the fact, then the fact has not to be understood—it is a fact; and when you are face to face with a fact, what happens? When there is no escape, when there is no thinker trying to give the fact a meaning to suit himself or shape it according to his particular pattern, what happens? When you are face to face with a fact, surely then you have understood it, have you not? Therefore, there is freedom from it. And such freedom is a radical freedom, it is not just a superficial reaction, a result of the mind's trying to identify itself with a particular opposite. As long as we are seeking a result, there must be the thinker, there must be the process of isolation; and a person who, in his thoughts, is isolated as the thinker, can never find what is true. The so-called religious person who is seeking God is merely establishing himself as a permanent entity apart from his thoughts, and such a person can never find reality.

So, then, our problem is this: Being aware of a particular reaction, of a response of fear, of guilt, of anger, of envy, or what you will, how is one to be radically free of it? One can see that it is impossible to be free of it through discipline because a product of conflict is never the truth—it is only a result, the effect of a cause. Whereas, if one sees as true that the thinker can never be separate from his thought, that the qualities and memories of the 'me' are not separate from the 'me'—when one realizes that and has direct experience of it, then one will see that thought becomes a fact and that there is no translating of the fact. The fact is the truth, and when you are confronted with truth and there is no other action but seeing it directly as it is, without condemnation or justification, that very recognition of the fact frees the mind from the fact.

So, only when the mind is capable of seeing itself in its relationship to all things is it possible for the mind to be quiet, to be tranquil. The mind that is tranquil through a process of isolation, of subjugation, of control, is not tranquil, but dead; it is merely conforming to a pattern, seeking a particular result. Only a free mind can be tranquil, and that freedom does not come through any form of identification; on the contrary, it comes only when we realize that the thinker is the thought, and not separate from thought. The tranquillity of freedom, of understanding, is not a matter of knowledge. Knowledge can never bring understanding. Knowledge is merely the cultivation of memory, in which the mind seeks security, and such a mind can never understand reality. Reality can be found only in freedom, which means to face the fact as it is, without distorting it. There must be distortion as long as the 'I' is separate from the thing it observes. Surely, the tranquil mind is a free mind, and it is only in freedom that truth can be discovered.

June 4, 1950

Second Talk in New York

I think it is important to see the necessity of self-knowledge because what we are, that we project. If we are confused, uncertain, worried, ambitious, cruel, or fearful, it is just that which we produce in the world. We do not seem to realize how essential it is for thought and action that there should be a fundamental understanding of oneself—not only of the superficial layers of one's consciousness, but also of the deeper layers of the unconscious, of the totality of one's whole process of thinking and feeling. We seem to regard this understanding of oneself as such a difficult task that we prefer to run away from it into all kinds of infantile, immature activities, such as ceremonies, so-called spiritual organizations, political groups, and so on—anything rather than study and comprehend oneself integrally and completely.

The fundamental understanding of oneself does not come through knowledge or through the accumulation of experiences, which is merely the cultivation of memory. The understanding of oneself is from moment to moment; and if we merely accumulate knowledge of the self, that very knowledge prevents further understanding, because accumulated knowledge and experience become the center through which thought focuses and has its being. The world is not different from us and our activities, because it is what we are which creates the problems of the world; and the difficulty with the majority of us is that we do not know ourselves directly, but seek a system, a method, a means of operation by which to solve the many human problems.

Now, is there a means, a system, of knowing oneself? Any clever person, any philosopher, can invent a system, a method, but surely, the following of a system will merely produce a result created by that system, will it not? If I follow a particular method of knowing myself, then I shall have the result which that system necessitates, but that result will obviously not be the understanding of myself. That is, by following a method, a system, a means through which to know myself, I shape my thinking, my activities, according to a pattern, but the following of a pattern is not the understanding of oneself.

So, there is no method for self-knowledge. Seeking a method invariably implies the desire to attain some result—and that is what we all want. We follow authority—if not that of a person, then of a system, of an ideology—because we want a result which will be satisfactory, which will give us security. We really do not want to understand ourselves, our impulses and reactions, the whole process of our thinking, the conscious as well as the unconscious; we would rather pursue a system which assures us of a result. But the pursuit of a system is invariably the outcome of our desire for security, for certainty, and the result is obviously not the understanding of oneself. When we follow a method, we must have authorities—the teacher, the guru, the savior, the Master—who will guarantee us what we desire, and surely, that is not the way to self-knowledge.

Authority prevents the understanding of oneself, does it not? Under the shelter of an authority, a guide, you may have temporarily a sense of security, a sense of well-being, but that is not the understanding of the total process of oneself. Authority in its very nature prevents the full awareness of oneself, and therefore ultimately destroys freedom, and in freedom alone can there be creativeness. There can be creativeness only through self-knowledge. Most of us are not creative, we are repetitive machines, mere gramophone records playing over and over again certain songs of experience, certain conclusions and memories, either our own or those of another. Such repetition is not creative being—but it is what we want. Because we want to be inwardly secure, we are constantly seeking methods and means for this security, and thereby we create authority, the worship of another, which destroys comprehension, that spontaneous tranquillity of mind in which alone there can be a state of creativeness.

Surely, our difficulty is that most of us have lost this sense of creativeness. To be creative does not mean that we must paint pictures or write poems and become famous. That is not creativeness—it is merely the capacity to express an idea, which the public applauds or disregards. Capacity and creativeness should not be confused. Capacity is not creativeness. Creativeness is quite a different state of being, is it not? It is a state in which the self is absent, in which the mind is no longer a focus of our experiences, our ambitions, our pursuits, and our desires. Creativeness is not a continuous state, it is new from moment to moment, it is a movement in which there is not the 'me', the 'mine', in which the thought is not focused around any particular experience, ambition, achievement, purpose, or motive. It is only when the self is not, that there is creativeness—that state of being in which alone there can be reality, the creator of all things. But that state cannot be conceived or imagined, it cannot be formulated or copied, it cannot be attained through any system, through any method, through any philosophy, through any discipline; on the contrary, it comes into being only through understanding the total process of oneself.

The understanding of oneself is not a result, a culmination; it is seeing oneself from moment to moment in the mirror of relationship—one's relationship to property, to things, to people, and to ideas. But we find it difficult to be alert, to be aware, and we prefer to dull our minds by following a method, by accepting authorities, superstitions, and gratifying theories; so, our minds become weary, exhausted, and insensitive. Such a mind cannot be in a state of creativeness. That state of creativeness comes only when the self, which is the process of recognition and accumulation, ceases to be, because, after all, consciousness as the 'me' is the center of recognition, and recognition is merely the process of the accumulation of experience. But we are all afraid to be nothing because we all want to be something. The little man wants to be a big man, the unvirtuous wants to be virtuous, the weak and obscure crave power, position, and authority. This is the incessant activity of the mind. Such a mind cannot be quiet and therefore can never understand the state of creativeness.

So, to transform the world about us, with its misery, wars, unemployment, starvation, class divisions, and utter confusion, there must be a transformation in ourselves. The revolution must begin within oneself—but not according to any belief or ideology because revolution based on an idea, or in conformity to a particular pattern, is obviously no revolution at all. To bring about a fundamental revolution in oneself, one must understand the whole process of one's thought and feeling in relationship. That is the only solution to all our problems—and not to have more disciplines, more beliefs, more ideologies, and more teachers. If we can understand ourselves as we are from moment to moment without the process of accumulation, then we will see how there comes a tranquillity that is not a product of the mind, a tranquillity that is neither imagined nor cultivated; and only in that state of tranquillity can there be creativeness.

There are several questions, and in considering them together, let us as individuals experiment together to find out the truth of each question. It is not my explanation that is going to dissolve the problem nor your eager search for a solution, but what dissolves any problem is to unravel it step by step and thereby see the truth of it. It is seeing the truth of our difficulties which dissolves them, but to see things as they are is not easy. Listening is an art, and if in listening we can follow what is said experimentally, operationally, then there is a possibility of seeing the truth and thereby dissolving the particular problem which may confront each one of us.

Question: What mental attitude would you consider best suited for the achievement of contentment in today's troubled world, and how would you suggest we attain it?

KRISHNAMURTI: When you want to attain contentment, you have an idea about it, haven't you? You have a preconception of what it is to be contented, and you want to be in that state, so you seek a method, you want to know how to attain it. Is contentment a result, a thing to be achieved? Is not the very search for a result itself the cause of discontent? Surely, the moment I want to be something, I have already sown the seed of discontent; because I want to attain contentment, I have already brought discontent into being.

Please let us see the significance of this desire to achieve an end. The end is always gratifying, it is something that we think will give us permanent security, happiness. That is, the end is always self-projected, and having projected it, or imagined it, or formulated it in words, we want to attain it, and then we seek a method for its attainment. We want to know how to be contented. Does not that very desire to be contented, or the search for a method to that end, show the stupidity of our own minds? A man who says, "I want to attain contentment," is surely already in a state of stagnation. He is only concerned with being enclosed in a state wherein nothing will disturb him, so his contentment is really the ultimate security, which is undisturbed isolation. Contentment which is achieved, and which we call the highest spiritual attainment, is really a condition of decay. But if we can understand the process of discontent, see what it is that brings it about, if without coming to any conclusion, we can be aware of the ways of discontent, choicelessly watching its every movement—then, in that very understanding, there comes a state of contentment which is not a product of the mind, the thought process, or of desire.

Whatever the mind produces is obviously based on thought, and thought is merely the response of memory, of sensation. When we seek contentment, we are pursuing a sensation that will be completely satisfying, and sensation can never be contentment. If I am aware that I am contented, if I am conscious of it, is that contentment? Is virtue self-conscious? Is happiness a state in which I am conscious that I am happy? Surely, the moment I am aware that I am contented, I am discontented—I want more. (Laughter) Please do not laugh at these things, because by laughing you are putting it away, you are not taking it in. It is a superficial reaction to something serious which you do not want to face and look at.

Contentment is a thing that cannot be achieved—though all the religious books, all the saints and the Masters, promise it to you. Their promise is no promise at all; it is just a vanity which gratifies you. But there is a possibility of understanding the whole process of discontent, is there not? What is it that makes me discontented? Surely, it is the desire for a result, a reward, an achievement, the desire to become something. In the very process of achieving a reward, there is punishment, and the man who seeks a reward is already punishing himself. Gaining implies discontent. The longing to achieve creates the fear of loss, and the very desire to attain contentment brings discontent. It is important, is it not, to see this, not as a theory, not as something to be thought about, discussed, and meditated upon, but as a simple fact. The moment you want something, you have already created discontent, and all the advertisements, everything in our society, is instigating this desire to possess, to grow, to achieve, to become. And can this struggle to become something be called evolution, growth, progress?

Surely, there is a process of understanding discontent, and in the process of understanding it, you will see that discontent is the very nature of the self, the 'me'. The 'me' is the center of discontent because the 'me' is the accumulation of memories, and memories cannot thrive unless there are more memories, more sensations. Until you and I understand the 'me', which is the center of discontent, until we go into it and understand this whole process of becoming, achieving, there must always be discontent. How can a mind that is agitated by the desire for a result ever understand anything? It may be quiet for a time in the isolation of its own achievement, but such a mind is obviously self-enclosed, and it can never know the tranquillity of that contentment which is not a result. The mind that is caught up in a result can never be free, and it is only in freedom that there can be contentment.

Question: You say we use physiological needs for our psychological expansion and security. You further show us that security is nonexistent. This gives us a feeling of complete hopelessness and fear. Is this all?

KRISHNAMURTI: This is a complex problem, and let us work it out together. First of all, there must be a physiological security, must there not? You must have food, clothing, and shelter. There must be security in the sense that our physical needs must be satisfied, otherwise we cannot exist at all. But the physical needs are used as a means for our psychological self-expansion, are they not? That is, one uses property, clothes, all the physical necessities, as a means of one's own position, progress, and authority.

To put it in a different way, nationalism, calling oneself an American, a Russian, a Hindu, or what you will, is obviously one of the causes of war. Nationalism is separatism, and that which separates obviously disintegrates. Nationalism destroys physical security, but one is nationalistic because there is a psychological security in being identified with the larger, with a particular country, group, or race. It gives me a sense of psychological security to call myself a Hindu, or by some other name; I feel flattered, it gives me a sense of well-being.

Similarly, we use property, things, as a means of psychological enlargement, expansion of the 'me', and that is why we have all this confusion, conflict, and separation which is taking place in the world. So, the economic problem is not wholly on its own level, but is fundamentally a psychological problem. That is one of the things involved in this question.

Now, as long as we are seeking psychological or inward security, obviously we must deny outward security. That is, as long as we are nationalistic, we must create war, thereby destroying the outward security which is so essential. It is the individual's seeking of inward security that brings about wars, class struggles, the innumerable divisions of religion, and all the rest of the business, ultimately destroying outward security for all. So, as long as I am seeking inward security in any form, I must bring about outward chaos and misery. The mere rearrangement of outward security, individual or collective, without understanding the inward processes of desire, is utterly futile because the psychological necessity for inward expansion will inevitably destroy whatever outward structure has been created. This is a fact which we can discuss and which I will go into later.

Now, inward security is a non-existent state, and when we seek it, what we are doing is merely isolating ourselves, enclosing ourselves in an idea, in a hope, in a particular pattern which gratifies us. That is, we enclose ourselves either in the collective experience and knowledge or in our own particular experience and knowledge and in that state we like to remain because we feel secure. Having a particular name, possessing certain qualities and things, gives you a sense of well-being. Calling yourself a doctor, a mayor, a swami, or God knows what else, gives you a sense of inward security, and that inward security is obviously a process of separation, and therefore of disintegration.

Now, when you actually see that there is no inward security, you say you have a feeling of complete hopelessness and fear. Why is there this sense of hopelessness? Why is there this sense of despair? What do you mean by hope? A man who clings to hope is obviously dead; a man who is hoping is dying, because to him what is important is the future—not *what is,* but what will be. A man who lives in hope is not living at all; he is living somewhere else, in the future, and living in the future is obviously not living. Now, you say that when you are without hope, you become hopeless. Is that so? When you see the truth about hope, how destructive it is, do you become hopeless? Do you? If you see the truth that there is no inward security of any kind—really see the truth of it, not merely speculate about the psychological state of insecurity—are you hopeless, are you in despair? Because we always think in terms of opposites—when we are in despair we want hope, and when there is no hope we become hopeless. Does this not indicate that we are seeking a state in which there will be no disturbance of any kind? And why should we not be disturbed? Must not the mind be completely uncertain in order to find out? But the moment you are uncertain, you fall into a state of hopelessness, despair, and fear, and then you develop a philosophy of despair and pursue that. Surely, if you really see the truth as regards hope, there comes a freedom from both hopelessness and hope, but one must see it, one must realize and experience that state.

What do we mean by fear? Fear of what? Fear of not being? Fear of what you are? Fear of losing, of being at a loss? Fear, whether conscious or unconscious, is not abstract—it exists only in relation to something. What we are afraid of is being insecure, is it not? We are afraid of being insecure—not only economically, but much more so inwardly. That is, we are afraid of loneliness, afraid of being nothing, afraid of a sense of complete denudation, a total purgation of all the beliefs, experiences, and memories of the mind. Of that state, whatever it is, we are afraid; the state of not being loved, of losing, or not achieving. But when once we see what loneliness is, when we know what it is to be lonely without escape, then there is a possibility of going beyond, because aloneness is entirely different from loneliness. There must be aloneness, but at present we are made up of many things, of many influences, and we are never alone. We are not individuals, we are merely a bundle of collective responses, with a particular name and a particular group of memories, both inherited and acquired. Surely, that is not individuality.

Now, to understand what it is to be alone, you must understand the whole process of fear. The understanding of fear ultimately brings you to that state in which you are completely empty, completely alone; that is, you are face to face with a loneliness which cannot be satisfied, which cannot be filled in, and from which there is no escape. Then you will see that one can go beyond loneliness—and then there is neither hope nor hopelessness, but a state of aloneness in which there is no fear.

As I said, a man who hopes is obviously not living because to him the future is extraordinarily important; therefore, he is willing to sacrifice the present for the future. That is what all the ideologists, all the people who build utopias, are doing—they are sacrificing the present, that is, they are willing to liquidate you and me for the future, as though they knew the future. All political parties, all ideologists, dangle a hope in front of us, and those who pursue hope are ultimately destroyed. But if we can understand the desire for inward security, see its whole process, and not merely deny it or live in some fanciful state; if through alert watchfulness we are aware of every response of the self, of the 'me', and see that there is no inward security of any kind, whether through property, through a person, or through an ideology—then, in that state of complete insecurity of the mind, there comes a freedom in which alone there is a possibility of discovering *what is*. But such a state is not for those who hope, or fear, or who want to achieve a result.

Question: How can I experience God in myself?

KRISHNAMURTI: What do we mean by experience? What is the process of experiencing? When do we say, "I have had an experience"? We say that only when we recognize the experience, that is, only when there is an experiencer apart from the experience. This means that our experiencing is a process of recognition and accumulation. Am I explaining myself?

I can experience only when there is a recognition of the experience, and the recognition is recollection, memory; and memory is obviously the center of the 'me'. That is, the whole process of recognition and accumulation of experience is the 'me', and the 'me' then says, "I have had an experience." What is recognized and accumulated as experience is the response to stimuli, the response to challenge. If I do not recognize the response to a challenge, I have no experience. Surely, if you challenge me, and I do not recognize the meaning, the significance of your challenge, nor my response to it, how can I have an experience? There is experiencing only when I respond to a challenge and recognize the response.

Now, the questioner asks, "How can I experience God in myself?" Is God, reality, or what you will, a thing to be experienced, a thing to be recognized, so that you can say, "I have had an experience of God"? Obviously, God is the unknown; it cannot be the known. The moment you know it, it is not God—it is something self-projected, recognized, which is memory. That is why the believer can never know God, and since most of you believe in God, you can never know God because your very belief prevents you. But nonbelief in God, which is another form of belief, also hinders the discovery of the unknown, because all belief is obviously a process of the mind. Belief is the result of the known. You may believe in the unknown, but that belief is born of the known, it is part of the known, which is memory. Memory says, "I do not know God, it is something unknown." So, memory creates the unknown and then believes in it as a means of experiencing the unknown.

Is God to be believed in? The priests, the preachers, the organizers of religions, the bishops, the cardinals, the butcher, the man who flies an airplane and drops a bomb—they all say, "God is with me." The man who makes money, exploits others, the man who accumulates wealth and builds temples or churches, says that God is his companion. All such people believe in God, and surely, their belief is merely a form of self-expansion, it is their own conceit. Such people, those who believe in organized dogmas, who have conditioned their minds according to a particular pattern called religion, obviously can never know the ultimate reality.

For the unknown to be, the mind must be completely empty; there can be no experiencing of reality, because the experiencer is the 'me', with all his accumulated memories, conscious as well as unconscious. The 'me', which is the residue of all that, says, "I am experiencing," but what he can experience is only his own projection. The 'me' cannot experience the unknown; he can only experience the known, the self-projected, the thing believed in or hoped for, which is the creation of thought as a reaction from the past. Such a mind is obviously incapable of being completely empty, completely alone, and therefore it can never be free. It is only a free mind that can know *what is*—that thing which is indescribable, which cannot be put into words for you or me to recognize. The description of it is merely the cultivation of memory; to verbalize it, is to put it in time, and that which is of time can never be the timeless.

So, the important thing is not what you believe or disbelieve, or what your activities are, but to understand the whole process, the whole content, of yourself, and that means being aware from moment to moment without any sense of accumulation. When the mind is utterly tranquil, quiet, without any sense of acceptance or rejection, without any sense of acquisitiveness or accumulation, when there is that state of tranquillity in which the experiencer is not—only then is there that which may be called God. The word is not important. And then there is a state of creation which is not the expression of the self.

June 11, 1950

Third Talk in New York

It is most important, is it not, that the various disintegrating factors in our lives should be understood. These disruptive elements exist, not only at the superficial or economic level, but also at the deeper levels of one's consciousness. We can see throughout the world that there is division, not only between various groups of people, but within the individual himself there is conflict, contradiction. Until we understand this contradiction in ourselves, we shall not be able to deal with the contradictions about us. This contradiction which exists in each one, and of which most of us are aware if we are at all thoughtful, cannot be resolved by the desire to be integrated—which merely becomes another problem to contend with; but if we can be aware of and understand the factors that bring about contradiction, then perhaps there will be a possibility of being integrated.

Now, what brings about contradiction in each one of us? Surely, it is the desire to become something, is it not? We all want to become something—to become successful in the world, and inwardly to achieve a result. So, as long as we think in terms of time, in terms of achievement, in terms of position, there must be contradiction. After all, the mind is the product of time. Thought is based on yesterday, on the past; and as long as thought is functioning within the field of time, thinking in terms of the future, of becoming, gaining, achieving, there must be contradiction because then we are incapable of facing exactly *what is*. Only in realizing, in understanding, in being choicelessly aware of *what is*, is there a possibility of freedom from that disintegrating factor which is contradiction.

So, it is essential, is it not, to understand the whole process of our thinking, for it is there that we find contradiction. Thought itself has become a contradiction because we have not understood the total process of ourselves; and that understanding is possible only when we are fully aware of our thought, not as an observer operating upon his thought, but integrally and without choice—which is extremely arduous. Then only is there the dissolution of that contradiction which is so detrimental, so painful.

As long as we are trying to achieve a psychological result, as long as we want inward security, there must be a contradiction in our life. I do not think that most of us are aware of this contradiction, or if we are, we do not see its real significance. On the contrary, contradiction gives us an impetus to live; the very element of friction makes us feel that we are alive. The effort, the struggle of contradiction, gives us a sense of vitality. That is why we love wars, that is why we enjoy the battle of frustrations. As long as there is the desire to achieve a result, which is the desire to be psychologically secure, there must be a contradiction, and where there is contradiction, there cannot be a quiet mind. Quietness of mind is essential to understand the whole significance of life. Thought can never be tranquil; thought, which is the product of time, can never find that which is timeless, can never know that which is beyond time. The very nature of our thinking is a contradiction because we are always thinking in terms of the past or of the future, and therefore we are never fully cognizant, fully aware of the present.

To be fully aware of the present is an extraordinarily difficult task because the mind is incapable of facing a fact directly without deception. As I explained, thought is the product of the past, and therefore it can only think in terms of the past or of the future, it cannot be completely aware of a fact in the present. So, as long as thought—which is the product of the past—tries to eliminate contradiction and all the problems that it creates, it is merely pursuing a result, trying to achieve an end, and such thinking only creates more contradiction, and hence conflict, misery, and confusion in us, and therefore about us.

To be free of contradiction, one must be aware of the present without choice. How can there be choice when you are confronted with a fact? Surely, the understanding of the fact is made impossible as long as thought is trying to operate upon the fact in terms of becoming, changing, altering. So, self-knowledge is the beginning of understanding, and without self-knowledge, contradiction and conflict will continue. To know the whole process, the totality of oneself, does not require any expert, any authority. The pursuit of authority only breeds fear. No expert, no specialist, can show us how to understand the process of the self. One has to study it for oneself. You and I can help each other by talking about it, but none can unfold it for us—no specialist, no teacher, can explore it for us. We can be aware of it only in our relationship—in our relationship to things, to property, to people, and to ideas. In relationship we will discover that contradiction arises when action is approximating itself to an idea. The idea is merely the crystallization of thought as a symbol, and the effort to live up to the symbol brings about a contradiction.

So, as long as there is a pattern of thought, contradiction will continue, and to put an end to the pattern, and so to contradiction, there must be self-knowledge. This understanding of the self is not a process reserved for the few. The self is to be understood in our everyday speech, in the way we think and feel, in the way we look at another. If we can be aware of every thought, of every feeling, from moment to moment, then we shall see that in relationship the ways of the self are understood. Then only is there a possibility of that tranquillity of mind in which alone the ultimate reality can come into being.

I am going to answer some questions, and when I do so, let us together explore each problem. I am not the authority, the specialist, the teacher, who is telling you what to do; that would be too absurd for grown-up people—if we are grown-up at all. So, in considering these questions, let us try to explore and discover the truth for our-selves. It is the discovery of truth that is going to free us from our problems, but that truth cannot be discovered, it cannot come to us, if the mind is merely agitated in the current of these problems. In order to discover the ways of the problem, the problem must be unfolded and the mind allowed to be quiet; then we see the truth, and it is the truth that frees us.

Question: How am I to get rid of fear, which influences all my activities?

KRISHNAMURTI: This is a very complex problem requiring close attention, and if we do not follow and explore it fully in the sense of experiencing each step as we go along, we will not be able at the end of it to be free of fear.

What do we mean by fear? Fear of what? There are various types of fear, and we need not analyze every type. But we can see that fear comes into being when our comprehension of relationship is not complete. Relationship is not only between people, but between ourselves and nature, between ourselves and property, between ourselves and ideas; and as long as that relationship is not fully understood, there must be fear. Life is relationship. To be, is to be related, and without relationship there is no life. Nothing can exist in isolation, and as long as the mind is seeking isolation, there must be fear. So, fear is not an abstraction; it exists only in relation to something.

Now, the question is how to be rid of fear. First of all, anything that is overcome has to be conquered again and again. No problem can be finally overcome, conquered; it can be understood, but not conquered. They are two completely different processes, and the conquering process leads to further confusion, further fear. To resist, to dominate, to do battle with a problem, or to build a defense against it, is only to create further conflict. Whereas, if we can understand fear, go into it fully step by step, explore the whole content of it, then fear will never return in any form—and that is what I hope we can do this morning.

As I said, fear is not an abstraction; it exists only in relationship. Now, what do we mean by fear? Ultimately, we are afraid, are we not, of not being, of not becoming. Now, when there is fear of not being, of not advancing, or fear of the unknown, of death, can that fear be overcome by determination, by a conclusion, by any choice? Obviously not. Mere suppression, sublimation, or substitution creates further resistance, does it not? So, fear can never be overcome through any form of discipline, through any form of resistance. That fact must be clearly seen, felt, and experienced—that fear cannot be overcome through any form of defense or resistance. Nor can there be freedom from fear through the search for an answer, or through mere intellectual or verbal explanation.

Now, what are we afraid of? Are we afraid of a fact, or of an idea about the fact? Please see this point. Are we afraid of the thing as it is, or are we afraid of what we think it is? Take death, for example. Are we afraid of the fact of death, or of the idea of death? The fact is one thing, and the idea about the fact is another. Am I afraid of the word *death*, or of the fact itself? Because I am afraid of the word, of the idea, I never understand the fact, I never look at the fact, I am never in direct relation with the fact. It is only when I am in complete communion with the fact that there is no fear. But if I am not in communion with the fact, then there is fear, and there is no communion with the fact as long as I have an idea, an opinion, a theory, about the fact. So, I have to be very clear whether I am afraid of the word, the idea, or of the fact. If I am face to face with the fact, there is nothing to understand about it—the fact is there, and I can deal with it. But if I am afraid of the word, then I must understand the word, go into the whole process of what the word, the term, implies.

For example, one is afraid of loneliness, afraid of the ache, the pain of loneliness. Surely, that fear exists because one has never really looked at loneliness, one has never been in complete communion with it. The moment one is completely open to the fact of loneliness, one can understand what it is; but one has an idea, an opinion about it, based on previous knowledge; and it is this idea, opinion, this previous knowledge about the fact, that creates fear. So, fear is obviously the outcome of naming, of terming, of projecting a symbol to represent the fact; that is, fear is not independent of the word, of the term. I hope I am making myself clear.

I have a reaction, say, to loneliness; that is, I say I am afraid of being nothing. Am I afraid of the fact itself, or is that fear awakened because I have previous knowledge of the fact, knowledge being the word, the symbol, the image? How can there be fear of a fact? When I am face to face with a fact, in direct communion with it, I can look at it, observe it; therefore, there is no fear of the fact. What causes fear is my apprehension about the fact, what the fact might be or do.

So, it is my opinion, my idea, my experience, my knowledge about the fact, that creates fear. As long as there is verbalization of the fact, giving the fact a name and therefore identifying or condemning it, as long as thought is judging the fact as an observer, there must be fear. Thought is the product of the past; it can only exist through verbalization, through symbols, through images, and as long as thought is regarding or translating the fact, there must be fear.

So, it is the mind that creates fear, the mind being the process of thinking. Thinking is verbalization. You cannot think without words, without symbols, images; these images, which are the prejudices, the previous knowledge, the apprehensions of the mind, are projected upon the fact, and out of that there arises fear. There is freedom from fear only when the mind is capable of looking at the fact without translating it, without giving it a name, a label. This is quite difficult because the feelings, the reactions, the anxieties that we have are promptly identified by the mind and given a word. The feeling of jealousy is identified by that word. Now, is it possible not to identify a feeling, to look at that feeling without naming it? It is the naming of the feeling that gives it continuity, that gives it strength. The moment you give a name to that which you call fear, you strengthen it, but if you can look at that feeling without terming it, you will see that it withers away. Therefore, if one would be completely free of fear, it is essential to understand this whole process of terming, of projecting symbols, images, giving names to facts. That is, there can be freedom from fear only when there is self-knowledge. Self-knowledge is the beginning of wisdom, which is the ending of fear.

Question: How can I permanently get rid of sexual desire?

KRISHNAMURTI: Why do we want to get permanently rid of a desire? You call it sexual, somebody else calls it attachment, fear, and so on. Why do we want to get rid of any desire permanently? Because that particular desire is disturbing to us, and we don't want to be disturbed. That is our whole process of thinking, is it not? We want to be self-enclosed, without any disturbance, that is, we want to be isolated; but nothing can live in isolation. In his search for God, the so-called religious person is really seeking complete isolation in which he will never be disturbed, but such a person is not really religious, is he? The truly religious are those who understand relationship completely, fully, and therefore have no problems, no conflict. Not that they are not disturbed, but because they are not seeking certainty, they understand disturbance, and therefore there is no self-enclosing process created by the desire for security.

Now, this question requires a great deal of understanding because we are dealing with sensation, which is thought. To most people, sex has become an extraordinarily important problem. Being uncreative, afraid, enclosed, cut off in all other directions, sex is the only thing through which most people can find a release, the one act in which the self is momentarily absent. In that brief state of abnegation when the self, the 'me', with all its troubles, confusions, and worries, is absent, there is great happiness. Through self-forgetfulness there is a sense of quietness, a release, and because we are uncreative religiously, economically, and in every other direction, sex becomes an overwhelmingly important problem. In daily life we are mere gramophone records, repeating phrases that we have learned; religiously we are automatons, mechanically following the priest; economically and socially we are bound, strangled, by environmental influences. Is there a release for us in any of that? Obviously not; and where there is no release, there must be frustration. That is why the sexual act, in which there is a release, has become such a vital problem for most of us. And society encourages and stimulates it through advertisements, magazines, the cinema, and all the rest of it.

Now, as long as the mind, which is the result, the focal point of sensation, regards sex as a means of its release, sex must be a problem, and that problem will continue as long as we are incapable of being creative comprehensively, totally, and not merely in one particular direction. Creativeness has nothing to do with sensation. Sex is of the mind, and creation is not of the mind. Creation is never a product of the mind, a product of thought, and in that sense, sex, which is sensation, can never be creative. It may produce babies, but that is obviously not creativeness. As long as we depend for release on sensation, on stimulation in any form, there must be frustration, because the mind becomes incapable of realizing what creativeness is.

This problem cannot be resolved by any discipline, by any taboos, by any social edicts or sanctions. It can be resolved only when we understand the whole process of the mind because it is the mind that is sexual. It is the mind's images, fancies, and pictures that stimulate it to be sexual, and as the mind is the result of sensation, it can only become more and more sensuous. Such a mind can never be creative because creation is not sensation. It is only when the mind does not seek stimuli in any form, whether outward or inward, that it can be completely quiet, free, and only in that freedom is there creation. We have made sex into something ugly because it is the only private sensation that we have; all other sensations are public, open. But as long as we use sensation in any form as a means of release, it will only increase the problems, the confusion and trouble, because release can never come into being through seeking a result.

The questioner wants to end sexual desire permanently because he has an idea that then he will be in a state in which all disturbances have disappeared; that is why he is seeking it, striving towards it. The very striving towards that state is preventing him from being free to understand the process of the mind. As long as the mind is merely seeking a permanent state in which it will have no disturbance of any kind, it is closed, and therefore it can never be creative. It is only when the mind is free of the desire to become something, to achieve a result, and hence free of fear, that it can be utterly quiet; and only then is there a possibility of that creativeness which is reality.

Question: Should I be a pacifist?

KRISHNAMURTI: I am afraid I cannot tell you what you should or should not be. We are supposed to be mature, and seeking advice from another in a matter of this kind indicates immaturity. The search for authority only creates corruption; it does not bring freedom. It is only in freedom that truth can be discovered. By following another you will never find what it is to be free of violence.

Let us find out what we mean by pacifism. Is pacifism opposed to violence? Is peace the denial of conflict? Is good the opposite of evil? When you deny vice and go to the opposite, is that virtue? If you deny, resist, put away the ugly, are you beautiful? Is the pursuit of an opposite ever peaceful, ever virtuous or beautiful? The opposite implies conflict, does it not? If you deny violence and pursue peace, what happens? The very pursuit of peace creates conflict because you are denying violence. The very denial creates conflict, and is virtue ever the result of conflict? Is peace the denial of war? War is obviously the extension, the projection of ourselves, is it not? War is the spectacular and bloody projection of our own daily existence. We call ourselves Americans or Russians or Hindus or God knows what else out of our desire to be safe, and this identification with a particular country, race, or group of people gives us a sense of security. But identification with a group or nation means separation, leading to disintegration and war. Surely, as long as I am seeking identification in any form—with my family, with my group, with my property, with my particular ideology or belief—there must be separation, disintegration, and war. Although it is the dream of all ideologists, whether of the left or of the right, to have everybody believing in one particular theory or system, such a thing is an impossibility. Belief always separates, and therefore it is a disintegrating factor.

So, as long as you and I are in conflict inwardly, psychologically, there must be the projection of that conflict in the world as war. Without understanding your own inward conflict, merely to become a pacifist or join an organization for peace has no meaning. A man who merely resists war while remaining in psychological conflict only creates further confusion. But if you really understand this total process of inward conflict, which projects itself in the world as war, then obviously you are neither a warmonger nor a mere pacifist—you are something entirely different because you are at peace with yourself, you are at peace with the world. Being at peace inwardly and therefore outwardly, you will obviously not belong to any nationality, to any religion, to any particular group or class, and if you are brought before the tribunal to be conscripted, or whatever it is called, you will probably be shot. But that is not your responsibility—it is the responsibility of society because society rejects you. After all, society is not very intelligent anyhow. What is society? It is your own projection, is it not? What you and I are, society is. So, don't call society stupid and laugh at it. Society is the structure of ourselves in projection, and if we want to bring about a fundamental revolution in society, there must be a fundamental revolution in ourselves—which is an enormously difficult task. Any revolution based on an idea is never a revolution—it is merely a modified continuity. Ideas can never be revolutionary because ideas are merely the reactions of memory. Thought is mere reaction, and an action based on reaction can never be fundamental, can never be true.

Surely, then, whether or not you should be a pacifist is not the problem. We see that everything in the world is contributing to war. War is obviously no means of settling anything, but apparently we are incapable of learning that. We change enemies from time to time, and we seem to be quite satisfied with this process, which is kept going by propaganda, by our own desire to be revengeful, by our own inward, psychological conflict. So, we are encouraging war through nationalism, through greed, through the desire to be successful, to become somebody. That is, we encourage war inwardly, and then outwardly want to be pacifists, and such pacifism obviously has no meaning. It is only a contradiction. We all want to become something: a pacifist, a war hero, a millionaire, a virtuous man, or what you will. The very desire to become involves conflict, and that conflict produces war. There is peace only when there is no desire to become something, and that is the only true state because in that state alone there is creation, there is reality. But that is completely foreign to the whole structure of society—which is the projection of yourself. You worship success. Your god is success, the giver of titles, degrees, position, and authority. There is a constant battle within yourself—the struggle to achieve what you want. You never have a peaceful moment, there is never peace in your heart, because you are always striving to become something, to progress. Do not be misled by the word *progress.* Mechanical things progress, but thought can never progress except in terms of its own becoming. Thought moves from the known to the known, but that is not growth, that is not evolution, that is not freedom.

So, if you want to be a pacifist in the true sense of the word, which is to be free of conflict, you have to understand yourself; and when the mind and heart are peaceful, quiet, then you will know what it is to be without conflict, which will express itself in action, whatever that action may be. But to make up your mind to become something is merely a process of striving, which inevitably creates further conflict and strife. As every war produces another war, so each conflict produces more conflict. There can be real peace only when conflict ends, and to end conflict is to understand the whole process of oneself.

Question: I am not loved and I want to be, for without it life has no meaning. How can I fulfill this longing?

KRISHNAMURTI: I hope you are not merely listening to words because then these meetings will be another distraction, a waste of time. But if you are really experiencing the things that we are discussing, then they will have an extraordinary significance, because though you may follow words with the conscious mind, if you are experiencing what is being said, the unconscious also takes part in it. If given an opportunity, the unconscious will reveal its whole content and so bring about a complete understanding of ourselves. So, I hope you are not merely listening to another talk but are actually experiencing the things as we go along.

The questioner wants to know how to love and to be loved. Is not that the state of most of us? We all want to be loved and also to give love. We talk a great deal about it. All religions, all preachers, talk about it. So, let us find out what we mean by love. Is love sensation? Is love a thing of the mind? Can you think about love? You can think about the object of love, but you cannot think about love, can you? I can think about the person I love; I can have a picture, an image of that person and recall the sensations, the memories, of our relationship. But is love sensation, memory? When I say, "I want to love and be loved," is that not merely thought, a reflection of the mind? Is thought love? We think it is, do we not? To us, love is sensation. That is why we have pictures of the people whom we love, that is why we think about them and are attached to them. That is all a process of thought, is it not?

Now, thought is frustrated in different directions, and therefore it says, "I find happiness in love, so I must have love." That is why we cling to the person we love, that is why we possess the person, psychologically as well as physiologically. We create laws to protect the possession of what we love, whether it be a person, a piano, a piece of property, or an idea, a belief, because in possession, with all its complications of jealousy, fear, suspicion, anxiety, we feel secure. So, we have made love into a thing of the mind, and with the things of the mind we fill the heart. Because the heart is empty, the mind says, "I must have that love," and we try to fulfill ourselves through the wife, through the husband. Through love, we try to become something. That is, love becomes a useful thing, we use love as a means to an end.

So, we have made of love a thing of the mind. The mind becomes the instrument of love, and the mind is only sensation. Thought is the reaction of memory to sensation. Without the symbol, the word, the image, there is no memory, there is no thought. We know the sensation of so-called love, and we cling to that, and when it fails, we want some other expression of that same sensation. So, the more we cultivate sensation, the more we cultivate so-called knowledge—which is merely memory—the less there is of love.

As long as we are seeking love, there must be a self-enclosing process. Love implies vulnerability, love implies communion, and there can be no communion, no vulnerability, as long as there is the self-enclosing process of thought. The very process of thought is fear, and how can there be communion with another when there is fear, when we use thought as a means for further stimulation?

There can be love only when you understand the whole process of the mind. Love is not of the mind, and you cannot think about love. When you say, "I want love," you are thinking about it, you are longing for it, which is a sensation, a means to an end. Therefore, it is not love that you want, but stimulation; you want a means through which you can fulfill yourself, whether it be a person, a job, a particular excitement, and so on. Surely, that is not love. Love can be only when the thought of the self is absent, and freedom from the self lies through self-knowledge. With self-knowledge there comes understanding, and when the total process of the mind is completely and fully revealed and understood, then you will know what it is to love. Then you will see that love has nothing to do with sensation, that it is not a means of fulfillment. Then love is by itself, without any result. Love is a state of being, and in that state, the 'me', with its identifications, anxieties, and possessions, is absent. Love cannot be, as long as the activities of the self, of the 'me', whether conscious or unconscious, continue to exist. That is why it is important to understand the process of the self, the center of recognition which is the 'me'.

June 18, 1950

Fourth Talk in New York

If we could find a way out of our conflict, we would not take recourse to authority, but as we do not find a means of resolving our innumerable and multiplying conflicts, we turn either to inward or outward authority for guidance and comfort. So, authority becomes very important in our lives. Because we are unable to understand and resolve conflict, we use authority as a means of avoiding conflict, and the means then become all-important, and not the fathoming, the exploring of the process of conflict.

So, we have authority of innumerable kinds, inward as well as outward. Outward authority takes the form of knowledge, examples, teachers, and so on, and inwardly it is our own experiences and memories, to which we turn for guidance in moments of conflict and anxiety. So, authority, both outward and inward, offers us a hope of being free of our various troubles.

But can authority of any kind, inward or outward, resolve our problems? The more we seek authorities, ideals, conclusions, hopes, the more we depend on them; and dependence on authority becomes much more significant than the understanding of the conflict itself. The more we depend on authority, the more dependent we become, because dependence ultimately destroys confidence in our own understanding of problems. Most of us have no confidence in our own capacity to find out, to explore the many problems, and when we depend on authority, obviously that confidence is denied.

Confidence is not arrogance. The more one has experienced, the more one is inwardly certain, the more arrogant and obstinate one becomes. Such self-confidence is only self-enclosure, a process of resistance. But there is, I think, a different kind of confidence which is not cumulative. To explore into the nature of conflict, one cannot bring to it that which one has accumulated, and if one explores with previous knowledge, it ceases to be exploration. Then you are merely moving from the known to the known, from certainty to certainty, from what you have experienced to what you hope to experience, and that is not exploration or experimentation. That is merely the cumulative process of knowledge, of experience, and the confidence it brings is assertive arrogance.

Now, I think there is a confidence which is much more subtle, much more worthwhile, and which comes when there is no sense of accumulation of any kind, but a constant exploration and discovery. It is this state of constant discovery, the capacity for constant exploration, that brings about an enduring confidence which is not arrogance. And that confidence, which is so essential, is denied when there is authority of any kind, when we depend on or look up to another for guidance in conduct. When we are dependent, it does give a certain self-assurance even though it entails fear, but that assurance of following someone, belonging to a group, believing in an idea or in certain dogmas, is surely a self-enclosing process, is it not? The mind that is constantly isolating itself is bound to awaken fear, and so there is a wandering from one authority to another, from one emotional exhaustion to another, and in this process our problems are never resolved—they only multiply.

Now, is it possible to look at our conflicts without bringing in any authority, external or inward? Surely, one can be passively aware of conflict without choice or condemnation; that is, one can be aware, not as an observer observing his experience or analyzing the thing in himself which he wishes to destroy, but aware with that passivity in which the observer is the observed. In that state of mind we will see that the problems are understood and resolved; whereas, if we choose the way of action with regard to a problem, or compare or condemn it, we only increase resistance and therefore multiply the problems. This process of choice is going on at all levels of our being, and that is why, instead of decreasing problems, we are multiplying them. The multiplication of problems comes into being only when we seek an answer, a conclusion, and so depend on an authority, outward or inward. Dependence on authority actually prevents our understanding of any problem, which is always new. No problem is old; as long as it remains a problem, it is a challenge, and therefore it is always new. Problems are invariably self-projected, and therefore it is important to understand the whole process of oneself without authority, without following a pattern or looking up to an example, an ideal, or a leader.

Self-knowledge is the beginning of the end of all conflict, and it is only when conflict ceases that there can be creation. Creation cannot be verbalized—it is a state which comes into being when the process of thought is at an end, and only then will the unknowable come to you.

In considering these questions, let us take the journey of exploration together; let each one of us find the truth of every problem for himself. It is no use waiting for the particular answer which you or I might like, or adhering to any particular opinion. To find out what is true, there must obviously be that passive alertness of mind which gives the capacity to explore each problem deeply.

Question: I have many friends, but I am in constant fear of being rejected by them. What should I do?

KRISHNAMURTI: What is the problem? Is the problem one of rejection and fear, or is it a question of dependence? Why do we want to have friends? Not that we should not have friends, but when we feel the necessity of having friends, when there is this dependence on others, what does it indicate? Does it not indicate insufficiency in oneself? Does not loneliness indicate an inward poverty? And being lonely, inwardly poor, insufficient, we turn to friends, to love, to activity, to ideas, to possessions, to knowledge and technique.

That is, being inwardly poor, we depend on outward things, so the outward things become very important to us. When we use something as a means of escape from ourselves, obviously it becomes very important. We cling to things, to ideas, and to people because psychologically we depend on them, and when they are taken away, as when our friends reject us, we are lost, we are afraid. So, dependence indicates inward uncertainty, inward poverty, and as long as we use or depend on others, there must be fear of loss.

Now, can this loneliness, this inward poverty or emptiness, be filled through any action of the mind? If I may suggest, please listen and follow it out by watching your own mind, and you will find the answer for yourself. I am only describing the experience as we go along, but to experience it for yourself, you must be passively alert, and not merely follow words.

So, being inwardly poor, we try to escape from this poverty through work, through knowledge, through love, through many forms of activity. We listen to the radio, read the latest book, pursue an idea or a virtue, accept a belief—anything to escape from ourselves. Our thinking is a process of escape from *what is,* and can that inward emptiness ever be covered up or filled? One can know the truth of that only when one does not escape—which is extremely arduous. One must be aware that one is escaping and see that all escapes are similar, that there is no "noble" escape. All escapes, from drunkenness to God, are the same because one is escaping from *what is,* which is oneself, one's own inward poverty. It is only when one really ceases to escape that one is face to face with the problem of loneliness, of inward insufficiency, which no knowledge, no experience, can cover up; and only then is there a possibility of understanding and so dissolving it. This loneliness, this inward insufficiency, is not merely the problem of people who have leisure, who have nothing else to do in life except study themselves; it is the problem of everyone in the world, the rich and the poor, the man who is brilliant and the man who is dull.

So, can inward emptiness ever be covered up? If you have tried and failed to cover it up by means of one escape, surely you know that all escapes are futile, do you not? You don't have to go from one escape to another to see that psychological insufficiency can never be filled, covered up, or enriched. By thoroughly understanding one escape, the whole process of escape is understood, is it not? Then what happens? One is left with emptiness, with loneliness, and then the problem arises—is that loneliness different from the entity that feels lonely? Obviously not. It is not that the entity feels empty but that he himself is emptiness, and the separation between the entity that feels empty and the state which he calls emptiness arises only in giving that state a name, a term, a label. When you do not name that state, then you will see there is no separation between the observer and the observed: the observer *is* the observed—which is insufficiency. In other words, when there is no naming or terming, an integration takes place between the experiencer and the experienced; and then you can proceed further to find out if that state which you have been avoiding as lonely, insufficient, is really so or is merely a reaction to the word *lonely,* which awakens fear.

Is it the word or the fact that awakens fear? Is any fact ever fearful, or is it an idea about the fact that makes for fear? If you have followed this whole process, you will see that when there is no desire to escape from *what is,* there is no fear; and then there is a transformation of *what is,* because then the mind is no longer afraid to be what it is. In that state there is no sense of being lonely, insufficient—it is what it is. If you proceed deeper, you will see that the mind no longer rejects or accepts that state and is therefore quiet, and only then is it possible to be free from that which is qualified as being lonely or insufficient. But to come to that, you must understand this whole process of inward insufficiency, escape, and dependence; you must see how escape and the means of escape become much more important than the thing from which you are escaping; you must discover this division between the thinker and the condition which he calls lonely, and find out for yourself whether it is merely verbal, or an actual state. If it is verbal, then that separation goes on, but if you do not give it a name, then there is only that state which you no longer term *lonely*—and only then is it possible for the mind to go beyond and discover further.

Question: What is the place of the individual in society?

KRISHNAMURTI: Is the individual different from society? Are you different from your environment? The environment has conditioned us to be Christians, capitalists, communists, socialists, or what you will, and the environment is in turn the projection of ourselves, is it not? Society is the projection of the individual, who is then further conditioned by that society. So, the individual and society are interrelated; they are not two separate states, or two separate entities. As long as you are conditioned by environment, is there a separate individuality? I am not saying that life is one—that is merely a theory. But it is important to discover whether the individual is separate from the environment, is it not? Though we may call ourselves individuals, are we not conditioned by society? Obviously we are. We are an integral part of society; therefore, although we appear to be separate entities, we are not really individuals. Physically, you and I are separate, dissimilar, but there is an extraordinary inward similarity. Whatever may be the superficial differences of race and custom, we are all more or less shaped along the same lines; we are all conditioned by fear, by dependence, by belief, by the desire to be secure, and so on. Surely, as long as we are conditioned by environment, which is our own projection, we are not really individuals, though we may bear different names. There is individuality only when we can go beyond this conditioning. Individuality is a state of creativeness, a state of aloneness, in which there is freedom from the conditioning influences of desire.

So, as long as we are bound by desire, as long as thought is merely the reaction of desire, which it is, there must be the conditioning influence of society, of the environment, and of our own experiences in reaction to society. We are an integral part of society; and if we try to establish a relationship between ourselves and society as though we and society were two separate entities, then surely we shall misunderstand the whole process; then we shall merely resist or fight society. Until we understand how society influences, shapes, controls us through our own instinctual responses of desire, we are obviously not unique individuals though we may say, "I am a separate soul," and all the rest of it. That is merely the assertion of a dogma, a belief—which will inevitably be denied by those who belong to another kind of society; so, we shall be conditioned in one way, and they will be conditioned in another. As long as we consider ourselves as entities separate from society, we shall never understand either society or ourselves, and we shall always be in conflict with society. But if we can understand the process of desire which creates the environmental influences which condition us, then we can go beyond and discover that aloneness which is true individuality, that uniqueness which is a state of creation.

The important thing, then, is not to inquire what is the individual's place in society, but to be aware of how we are conditioned by our beliefs, our desires, our motives. To be aware of the conscious as well as of the unconscious or collective response of the past to the present, to know both the superficial and the deeper layers of one's own thinking—surely, that is of far greater importance than to inquire what is the relationship between the individual and society. If we really see that, then the reformation of society becomes a minor thing. To reform society without understanding ourselves merely creates the need of further reform—and so there is no end to reformation. Whereas, if we can go beyond the limitations of desire, then there is the revolution of individuality, and it is that inward revolution that is so essential to bring about a new world. Merely reforming the world according to a particular ideology has no significance, because revolution based on an idea is no revolution at all. An idea is merely a reaction of the past to the present. There is inward revolution or transformation only when there is the understanding of desire, and it is this inward revolution which is so essential because it alone can bring about a different world.

Question: I love my children, and how am I to educate them to become integrated human beings?

KRISHNAMURTI: I wonder if we do love our children? We say so, and we take it for granted that we love them. But do we? If we loved our children, would there be wars? If we loved them, would we be nationalistic, divided into separate groups, constantly destroying each other? Would we belong to any particular race or religion in opposition to another? This whole process of separation in life ultimately brings about disintegration, does it not? Surely, war, the ceaseless conflict in society between different groups and different classes, is an indication that we do not love our children. If we really loved them, we would want to save them, would we not? We would want to protect them, we would want them to live as happy, integrated human beings, we would not want them to live in outward insecurity or be destroyed. But since we have created a world of conflict and misery, in which outward security is nonexistent, it indicates, does it not, that we do not really love our children at all. If we loved them, we would obviously have a different world. Don't let us become sentimental. But we would have a different world if we really loved our children because then we would quickly see how to prevent wars; then we would not leave it to the clever politicians, who will never prevent wars, but we would assume direct responsibility for it because we would really have the intention of saving the children.

Surely, then, our whole outlook in education, our entire social structure, must be utterly revolutionized, must it not? That means we can no longer use the children for our personal or psychological gratification as we are doing at present—and that is why we are so easily satisfied, so superficial in what we call "love." But if we do not use the children as a means of self-perpetuation, to carry on our name, if we do not use them in any way for our personal gratification, then we will obviously regard them quite differently. Then our concern will be not to educate the children but to educate the educator. At present, education is merely to make the children efficient, to teach them a technique, the manner of earning a livelihood, and efficiency obviously brings about ruthlessness. Not that one must be inefficient, but this drive to be efficient, this constant attention to success, must entail struggle, strife, contention.

Now, we cannot have integrated human beings unless we understand the process of disintegration. Integration is not the pursuit of a pattern, the adjustment to an idea, or the following of a particular example. Integration can come about only when one understands the total process of oneself, and there cannot be the understanding of oneself as long as we are living superficially. Our whole process of thought is superficial, the process of the so-called intellect, and to the cultivation of this intellect we give great emphasis. So, intellectually, which is verbally, we are very far advanced, but inwardly we are insufficient, poor, uncertain, groping, clinging to any form of security. This whole process of thought is a process of disintegration because thought invariably separates; ideas, like beliefs, never bring people together except in conflicting groups. So, as long as we depend on thought as a means of integration, there must be disintegration. To understand the process of thought is to understand the ways of the self, and then only is there a possibility of integration, which is not imitation.

So, there must not only be the educating of the educator, but we, as mature human beings, must understand our relationship with the children, must we not? And if we really love them, obviously we will see to it that there will be no war, that there will be no struggle in society between the rich and the poor, nor the depredations of the ambitious and the acquisitive who seek power, position, and prestige. But if we want our children to be powerful, to have bigger and better positions, to become more and more successful, surely it indicates that we do not love them—we merely love the acclaim, the glamour, the position, the reflected glory which we hope they will afford us. Therefore, we are encouraging confusion, destruction, and utter misery. I know you are listening to all this, but you will probably return home and continue with those very ways which engender war. Most of us are really not interested in these things. We are interested in immediate answers. We do not want to explore and discover the truth. It is not an economic revolution but only the discovery of truth that will free us, that will bring about a new world.

So, the whole question resolves itself into this—not how to educate the children, but how to educate ourselves and thereby bring about a different society. To do that, one must understand oneself, the ways of one's desire, the ways of one's thought. We must be aware of everything: of the things about us and in us, of colors, of people, of ideas, of the words we use, of our memories, both personal and collective. It is only when one is fully aware of this whole process that one is alone, a unique individual, and only such people can bring about a new civilization, a new culture.

Question: Can prayer form the link between life and religion?

KRISHNAMURTI: What do we mean by prayer, and what do we mean by life and religion? Is life different from religion? Apparently with most of us it is, so we use prayer as a means of linking life and religion. Why is life separate from religion? What is religion, and what is life? Is religion the pursuit of an idea? When you say religion is the pursuit of God, surely your God is an idea, is it not? Therefore your God is self-projected. Or, if you deny God and accept another ideology, whether of the left or of the right, it is still a form of religion. So, is religion merely the following of a certain pattern of ideas which promises a reward in the present or in the future? And is religion different from life, from action, from relationship?

What do we mean by life? Life is relationship, is it not? Can there be life without relationship—relationship to people, to ideas, to things, to property, to nature? Can there be life in isolation? And yet, that is what each one of us is pursuing, is it not? In our ideas, in our relationship to everything about us, we are enclosing, isolating ourselves; and being isolated, we want to find a relationship or link with what we call religion—which is merely another form of isolation. That is, because in our relationships we are seeking inward security, we make outward security impossible, and in religion we are also seeking security. Our God is the ultimate happiness, absolute peace. Surely, such a God is an invention of our minds so as to assure ourselves of permanency in the form of ultimate security; and then we ask, "Can prayer form the link between life and religion?" Obviously it can, can it not? Like everything else in our lives, prayer will help us to be more and more isolated because that is what we want. In our relationships, in our possessions, we are seeking isolation, which is a form of security, and in religion also we seek security, permanency. Our God, our virtue, our morality, like our daily activities, are all self-enclosing, self-isolating, so we use prayer as a means of uniting the various isolations.

What do we mean by prayer? And when do we pray? Surely, we pray only when we are suffering, when we are in misfortune, when there is conflict, confusion, when we are in pain. Do we ever pray when we are happy, when there is rejoicing, when our hearts are full? Obviously not. We pray only when we are in confusion, when we are uncertain, when we don't know what to do—and then we turn to somebody for help.

Prayer, then, is generally supplication, is it not? It is a petition, a demand, a psychological extending of the hand for it to be held, to be filled. And when you ask, you receive, do you not? But what you get is what you want—it is never what you don't want—so what you get is your own projection. That which you receive in response to prayer is shaped by your own fancy, your own limitation, your own conditioning. The more you ask, the more you receive of your own projection, and with that you are satisfied.

But is prayer a process of self-gratification? What happens when you pray? You repeat certain words, certain phrases, you take a certain posture, and when there is a constant repetition of words and phrases, obviously the mind becomes quiet, does it not? Try it and you will see. The repetition of words makes the mind still. But that is only a trick, is it not? The mind is not really still—it is acquisitive—but you have made it still in order to receive what you want. You want to be helped because you are confused, you are uncertain, and you will receive what you want. But that response to supplication is not the voice of reality—it is the response of your own projection and also of the collective projection. Because, we all want an answer, do we not? We all want somebody to tell us what wonderful people we are; we all want someone to guide us, to help us in our confusion, in our misery. So, we receive what we want, but what we want is petty, trivial.

So, prayer, which is a supplication, a petition, can never find that reality which is not the outcome of a demand. We demand, supplicate, pray, only when we are in confusion, in sorrow, and not understanding that confusion and sorrow, we turn to somebody else. The answer to prayer is our own projection; in one way or another it is always satisfactory, gratifying, otherwise we would reject it. So, when one has learned the trick of quieting the mind through repetition, one keeps on with that habit, but the answer to supplication must obviously be shaped according to the desire of the person who supplicates.

Now, prayer, supplication, petition, can never uncover that which is not the projection of the mind. To find that which is not the fabrication of the mind, the mind must be quiet—not made quiet by the repetition of words, which is self-hypnosis, nor by any other means of inducing the mind to be still.

Stillness that is induced, enforced, is not stillness at all. It is like putting a child in the corner—superficially he may be quiet, but inwardly he is boiling. So, a mind that is made quiet by discipline is never really quiet, and stillness that is induced can never uncover that creative state in which reality comes into being.

So, when we use prayer as a means of linking life and religion, we are only discovering more ways of self-isolation, more ways of disintegration. To put yourself in a state of receptivity through prayer is a process of disintegration because you want to receive. You may say, "I do not ask anything; I only put myself in a state of receptivity through prayer," but that is merely a subtle form of forcing the mind. Enforcement of any kind can never bring about tranquillity. Tranquillity of mind comes into being only with the cessation of thought, and thought ceases when one understands the thinker, the person who asks, demands. Therefore, self-knowledge is the beginning of wisdom, and without self-knowledge, merely to pray has very little significance. Prayer cannot open the door to self-knowledge. What opens the door to self-knowledge is constant awareness—not practicing awareness, but being aware from moment to moment and discovering. Discovery can never be cumulative. If it is cumulative, it is not discovery. Discovery is new from moment to moment; it is not a continuous state. A man cannot discover if he is accumulating, for accumulation is continuity. Discovery from moment to moment is freedom from the desire which is understood from moment to moment. There is spontaneity of the mind only when you understand the desire that seeks security, permanency, and that desire is the self, the 'me', at all levels. As long as you do not understand yourself wholly, there must be every form of escape, every form of confusion and destruction, and prayers do not help; they merely offer another means of escape. But if you begin to understand the desire that creates confusion, pain, conflict, then you will see that in understanding there comes spontaneity of the mind; then the mind is really tranquil, without wanting to be or not to be, and only such a mind can understand that which is real.

June 25, 1950

Fifth Talk in New York

I think it is quite apparent that there must be a fundamental transformation in society, and it can only begin with a radical revolution within each one of us, for society is not very different from ourselves. What we are, society is. The problems of the world are not separate from our problems. We ourselves have projected them, and therefore we are responsible for them; and the fundamental revolution in outward circumstances, however essential and necessary, can be brought about only when there is a radical revolution in ourselves. A radical revolution, a transformation, a psychological upheaval in ourselves, cannot be brought about through any idea or according to any pattern. Revolution based on an ideology is no longer a revolution—it is merely the modified continuity of an old pattern. Thought can never be revolutionary because thought is the response of memory. Ideas can never bring about a transformation in ourselves because ideas are merely the continuation of that response, either verbalized or in the form of symbols, images, and so on. When we desire to bring about a transformation in ourselves according to a pattern pre-established by thought, such a transformation is only the modified continuation of memory; being a projection of ourselves in a different form, it is a continuation of the conditioned state, and therefore it is no transformation at all. Revolution based on an ideology, however inclusive, is not a revolution because an idea is the projection of thought, which is memory. The response of memory can never bring about transformation. What can bring about transformation in ourselves, and therefore in society, is to understand the whole process of thinking, which is not different from feeling. Feeling is thinking; though we like to keep them separate and rely either on the one or the other, they are interrelated; they are not dualistic but a unitary process.

So, as long as we do not understand the whole process of thinking and feeling, obviously there can be no radical revolution within and so without. The understanding of thought, which is feeling, is self-knowledge, and self-knowledge cannot be bought. No study of books, no going to lectures, will give self-knowledge. Self-knowledge comes only when we are aware of ourselves from moment to moment, naturally, spontaneously, easily, without any sense of enforcement—aware, not only of our conscious thinking, but also of the unconscious, with all its content. It is like looking at a map and allowing it to unfold, and the moment we block it by discipline, by any form of practice, the unfolding of self-knowledge comes to an end.

What is important, surely, is to be aware without choice because choice brings about conflict. The chooser is in confusion; therefore, he chooses; if he is not in confusion, there is no choice. Only the person who is confused chooses what he shall do or shall not do. The man who is clear and simple does not choose—what is, is. Action based on an idea is obviously the action of choice, and such action is not liberating; on the contrary, it only creates further resistance, further conflict, according to that conditioned thinking.

So, then, the important thing is to be aware from moment to moment without accumulating the experience which awareness brings because the moment you accumulate, you are aware only according to that accumulation, according to that pattern, according to that experience. That is, your awareness is conditioned by your accumulation, and therefore there is no longer observation, but merely translation. Where there is translation, there is choice, and choice creates conflict, and in conflict there can be no understanding.

As we have been discussing for the last four weeks, the difficulty in understanding ourselves exists because we have never given thought to it. We do not see the importance, the significance, of exploring ourselves directly, not according to any idea, pattern, or teacher. The necessity of understanding ourselves is perceived only when we see that without self-knowledge there can be no basis for thought, for action, for feeling; but self-knowledge is not the outcome of the desire to achieve an end. If we begin to inquire into the process of self-knowledge through fear, through resistance, through authority, or with the desire to gain a result, we shall have what we desire, but it will not be the understanding of the self and the ways of the self. You may place the self at any level, calling it the higher self or the lower self, but it is still the process of thinking, and if the thinker is not understood, obviously his thinking is a process of escape.

Thought and the thinker are one, but it is thought that creates the thinker, and without thought there is no thinker. So, one has to be aware of the process of conditioning, which is thought; and when there is awareness of that process without choice, when there is no sense of resistance, when there is neither condemnation nor justification of what is observed, then we see that the mind is the center of conflict. In understanding the mind and the ways of the mind, the conscious as well as the unconscious, through dreams, through every word, through every process of thought and action, the mind becomes extraordinarily quiet; and that tranquillity of the mind is the beginning of wisdom. Wisdom cannot be bought, it cannot be learned; it comes into being only when the mind is quiet, utterly still—not made still by compulsion, coercion, or discipline. Only when the mind is spontaneously silent is it possible to understand that which is beyond time.

In considering these questions, as I have often reminded you, there is neither denial nor acceptance. We are going to explore each question, and the answer is not apart from the question. In going into the question as fully and deeply as we can, we shall see the truth of it, and it is that truth that will free us from the problem.

Question: You have shown me the superficiality and the futility of the life I am leading. I should like to change, but I am trapped by habit and environment. Should I leave everything and everyone and follow you?

KRISHNAMURTI: Do you think our problems are solved when we follow another? To follow another, no matter who it is, is to deny the understanding of yourself. And it is very easy to follow somebody. The greater the personality, the greater the power, the easier it is to follow; and in the very following you are destroying that understanding because the follower destroys—he is never the creator, he never brings about understanding. To follow is to deny all understanding and therefore to deny truth.

Now, if you do not follow, what are you to do? Since, as the questioner says, one is trapped by habit and environment, what is one to do? Surely, all that you can do is to understand the trap of habit and environment, the superficiality and the futility of your life. We are always in relationship, are we not? To be is to be related, and if you regard relationship as a trap from which you want to escape, then you will only fall into another trap—the trap of the teacher whom you follow. It may be a little more arduous, a little more inconvenient, a little less comfortable, but it will still be a trap; because, that also is relationship, and there too there are jealousies, envy, the desire to be the nearest disciple, and all the rest of the nonsense.

So, we are trapped because we do not understand relationship; and it is difficult to understand relationship if we are condemning, identifying ourselves with something, or if we are using relationship as a means of escape from ourselves, from that which we are. After all, relationship is a mirror, is it not? Relationship is a mirror in which I can see myself as I am. But to see ourselves directly as we are is very unpleasant, and so we avoid it by condemning it, justifying it, or merely identifying ourselves with it. Without relationship there is no life, is there? Nothing can exist in isolation. And yet all our efforts are towards being isolated; relationship for most of us is a process of self-isolation, self-enclosure, and therefore there is friction. When there is friction, misery, pain, suffering, unhappiness, we want to run away, we want to follow someone else, to live in the shadow of another, and so we turn to the church, to a monastery, or to the latest teacher. They are all the same because they are all escapes, and our turning to them is obviously prompted by the desire to avoid that which is; and in the very running away we create further misery, further confusion.

So, most of us are trapped, whether we like it or not, because that is our world, that is our society; and awareness in relationship is the mirror in which we can see ourselves very clearly. To see clearly, there must obviously be no condemnation, acceptance, justification, or identification. If we are simply aware without choice, then we can observe, not only the superficial reactions of the mind, but also the deep and hidden reactions, which come out in the shape of dreams, or in moments when the superficial mind is quiet and there is spontaneity of response. But if the mind is conditioned, shaped, and bound by a particular belief, surely there can be no spontaneity, and therefore no direct perception of the responses of relationship.

It is important to see, is it not, that no one can give us freedom from the conflict of relationship. We can hide behind the screen of words, or follow a teacher, or run to a church, or lose ourselves in a cinema or a book, or keep on attending talks; but it is only when the fundamental process of thinking is uncovered through awareness in relationship that it is possible to understand and be free of that friction which we instinctively seek to avoid. Most of us use relationship as a means of escape from ourselves, from our own loneliness, from our own inward uncertainty and poverty, and so we cling to the outer things of relationship, which become very important to us. But if, instead of escaping through relationship, we can look into relationship as a mirror and see very clearly, without any prejudice, exactly *what is,* then that very perception brings about a transformation of *what is,* without any effort to transform it. There is nothing to transform about a fact; it is what it is. But we approach the fact with hesitation, with fear, with a sense of prejudice, and so we are always acting upon the fact and therefore never perceiving the fact as it is. When we see the fact as it is, then that very fact is the truth which resolves the problem.

So, in all this the important thing is not what another says, however great or stupid he may be, but to be aware of oneself, to see the fact of *what is,* from moment to moment, without accumulating. When you accumulate, you cannot see the fact; then you see the accumulation, and not the fact. But when you can see the fact independently of the accumulation, independently of the thought process, which is the response of accumulated experience, then it is possible to go beyond the fact. It is the avoidance of the fact that brings about conflict, but when you recognize the truth of the fact, then there is a quietness of mind in which conflict ceases.

So, do what you will, you cannot escape through relationship; and if you do escape, you will only create further isolation, further misery and confusion, because to use relationship as a means of self-fulfillment is to deny relationship. If we look at this problem very clearly, we can see that life is a process of relationship; and if, instead of understanding relationship, we seek to withdraw from it, enclosing ourselves in ideas, in superstitions, in various forms of addiction, these self-enclosures only create more of the very conflict we are trying to avoid.

Question: What is wisdom? Is it dissimilar from knowledge?

KRISHNAMURTI: What is knowledge? Surely, knowledge is the accumulating principle in all of us, which is memory. The acquisitive process is knowledge, is it not? Knowledge is experience and memory. The more we accumulate experience, the more we know. Knowing is a process of verbalizing, and that which has been accumulated, which is experience, memory, or knowledge, can never bring wisdom. Knowledge is the result of experience, and there is experience only when there is an experiencer who is accumulating. The experiencer is the result of his own accumulations, experiences, and knowledge; and what he experiences is according to his conditioning. Therefore, the more he experiences, the more he is conditioned, weighed down. When he experiences, he can only experience according to his background, so the background dictates the knowledge, the translation of experience. Experience, the translation of a fact, cannot bring understanding. Understanding comes only with the suppression of knowledge.

After all, we experience according to our belief. If I believe that there is no God, obviously I experience according to my belief because the background, the conditioning, the training, dictates and translates my experiences; and if I believe in God, then my experience is according to my conditioning as a believer. So, experiencing is a process of the response of the conditioned mind; and where there is knowledge, or the accumulation of experience, of memory, of words, symbols, images, there can be no understanding. Understanding can come only when there is freedom from knowledge. After all, when you have a problem, the more you think about it, worry over it, the less you understand it; but if you can look at it freely, without translating it, without bringing in all the background of your tradition, of your experiences, then you will see that understanding comes out of it.

So, understanding is not the result of accumulation, and wisdom is not knowledge. Wisdom is independent, it is dissimilar from knowledge. Wisdom is from moment to moment, whereas knowledge can never be free from the past, from time. Wisdom is free from time, and knowledge is the very process of time, and the two cannot possibly be joined together. The man who knows can never be wise because the very knowledge of what he has denies wisdom. Knowledge is the process of time, which is the accumulation of experience; and wisdom is freedom from time, which is experience from moment to moment without the process of accumulation.

Question: Though I am young, I am haunted by the fear of death. How am I to overcome this fear?

KRISHNAMURTI: Surely, anything that is overcome has to be overcome again, does it not? When you conquer your enemy, you have to reconquer him again and again. That is why wars continue. The moment you vanquish one desire, there is another desire to be vanquished. So, that which is overcome can never be understood. Overcoming is merely a form of suppression, and you can never be free of that which is suppressed. So, the overcoming of fear is merely the postponement of fear.

Our problem, then, is not how to overcome fear of death but to understand the whole process of death, and understanding it is not a matter of being young or old. There are various forms of death, for the old as well as for the young. All of us are conditioned by our past, by conformity, by the desire for our own advancement, by the subtle accumulation of power, and though we are outwardly active, we may be inwardly dead. So, to understand this process of death needs a great deal of exploration, and not merely adhering to a particular form of belief—that there is, or is not, a continuity after death. Belief in life after death may give you an ideological consolation, and there may be, and probably is, a form of continuity. But then what? What continues? Can that which continues ever be creative? And where there is continuity, is there not always the fear of ending? So, death is a process of time, is it not?

What do we mean by time? There is chronological time, but there is also another kind of time, is there not? It is the psychological process of continuity. That is, we want to continue, and the very desire to continue creates the process of time and the fear of not continuing. It is this fear of not continuing that we are concerned with; it is ending of which we are afraid. We are afraid of death because we think that through continuity we shall achieve something, we shall be happy.

After all, what is it that continues? If we can really understand that, if we can actually experience it as we are sitting here, and not merely listen to words, then perhaps we shall know what it is to die from moment to moment; and knowing death, we shall know life because the two are not very different. If we do not know how to live, we are afraid of death, but if we know how to live, then there is no death. Most of us do not know what living is, and so we regard death as a negation of life, and therefore we are afraid of death. But if we can understand what living is, then we shall know of death in the very process of living. To find that out, we must understand what we mean by continuity.

What is this extraordinary craving to continue that each one of us has? And what is it that continues? Surely, that which continues is name, form, experience, knowledge, and various memories. That is what we are, is it not? To divide yourself into the higher and the lower self is irrelevant—you are still merely the sum total of all that. Though you may say, "No, I am more than that, I am a spiritual entity," that very assertion is part of the process of thinking, which is the conditioned and conditioning response of memory. There are others who are conditioned to say, "We are not spiritual, we are just the product of environment." So, you are your memories, your experiences, your thoughts. At whatever level you place the thought process, you are still that, and you are afraid that when death comes, that process, which is the 'you', will come to an end. Or, you rationalize it and say, "I will continue in some form after death and come back in the next life."

Now, a spiritual entity obviously cannot continue because it is beyond time. Continuity implies time—yesterday, today, and tomorrow; therefore, that which is timeless can have no continuity. To say "I am a spiritual entity" is a comforting thought, but the very process of thinking about it catches it in the net of time; therefore, it cannot be timeless, and therefore it is not spiritual.

So, what we have is only our thinking, which is also feeling. We have nothing but our name, our form, our family, our clothes and furniture, our memories and experiences, our responses, traditions, vanities, and prejudices. That is all we have, and *that* we want to continue. We are afraid it will all come to an end, that we shall be unable to say, "This for which I have struggled is all mine." Now, can that which continues ever renew itself? Obviously not. That which continues cannot be reborn, renewed; it can merely have a continuity. Only that which comes to an end can renew itself. There is creation only when there is an ending. But we are afraid to end, we are afraid to die. We want to carry on from yesterday through today to tomorrow. We are building utopias and sacrificing the present to the future, liquidating people because of the desire for continuity. If we examine very closely what it is that continues, we will see that it is only memory in various forms, and because the mind clings to memory, it is afraid of death. But surely, only in dying, in not accumulating, is there that which is beyond time. The mind cannot possibly conceive, formulate, or experience that which is not of time. It can experience only that which is of time because the mind is the result of time, of the past.

So, as long as the mind is afraid of coming to an end, it clings to its own continuity, and that which continues must obviously decay. Our difficulty is to die to all the things that we have accumulated, to all the experiences of yesterday. After all, that is death, is it not?—to be uncertain, to be in a state of vulnerability. The man who is certain can never know that which is immortal, that which is beyond time. The man of knowledge can never know death, which is beyond time, the unknown. It is only when we die from moment to moment to the things of yesterday and understand the whole significance of continuity that there is the unknown, a new thing. That which continues can never know the truth, the unknown, the new; it can only know its own projection. Most of us live through accumulation; therefore, yesterday and tomorrow become far more important than the present.

There must obviously be chronological time; otherwise, you will miss your train; but as long as we are caught in the projection of the mind, which is psychological time, there is no ending, and that which has continuity is not immortal. Only that which comes to an end is timeless, and that alone can know the immortal.

Question: There are several systems of meditation, both Occidental and Oriental. Which do you recommend?

KRISHNAMURTI: To understand what is right meditation is really a very complex problem, and to know how to meditate, how to be in the state of meditation, is important; but to follow any system, whether Occidental or Oriental, is not to meditate. When you follow a system, all that you learn is to conform, to shape the mind to a particular pattern or drive it along a particular groove. If you pursue it ardently enough, you will produce the result that the system guarantees, but surely, that is not meditation. There is a lot of nonsense taught about meditation, especially by those people who come from the Orient. (Laughter) Please don't laugh or clap—this is not that kind of meeting. We are trying to find out what meditation is.

You can see that those who pursue a system, who drive the mind into certain practices, obviously condition the mind according to that formula. Therefore, the mind is not free. It is only the free mind that can discover, not a mind conditioned according to any system, whether Oriental or Occidental. Conditioning is the same, by whatever name you may call it. To see the truth there must be freedom, and a mind that is conditioned according to a system can never see the truth.

Now, to see the truth that there can be no freedom through the discipline of any system requires the understanding of the process of the mind, because the mind clings to systems, to beliefs, to particular formulas. To discover the truth of that, surely you have to see that you are caught in a system, and to be aware of the process by which the mind gets caught in a system is meditation. To be aware of the whole process of thinking is self-knowledge, is it not? So, meditation is the beginning of self-knowledge. Without knowing the process of your own thinking, merely to sit in a corner and go off into silence, or whatever you do, is not meditation—it is just a wish to become, to acquire, to gain something. And obviously, concentration is not meditation. Merely focusing the mind on an idea, an image, or a phrase and excluding all other thoughts is not meditation, is it? You may learn concentration in that way, but concentration is exclusion, and when the mind excludes, it is not free.

Why do we want to focus the mind on an image or an idea, or practice a system of so-called meditation—the more mysterious the better? Because we think that by concentration, or through prayer, the constant repetition of certain words, the mind will be made quiet. As I said, concentration is a process of exclusion. We choose a particular idea or thought and dwell on it, and while we are forcing the mind to concentrate on it, other thoughts come in; so, there is a conflict going on, and we spend our energy in this wasteful battle. But if we can be open to each thought as it arises and understand it, then we shall see that the mind does not revert to any particular thought. The mind reverts to a thought because it has not understood it; that is, what is not understood is repeated over and over again, and mere exclusion will not prevent it. So, concentration, which is exclusion, is not meditation. Most of us want to live exclusively, with our private memories, private experiences, private knowledge; and concentration, which we call meditation, is merely a further process of self-enclosure, self-isolation. But the mind can never be free through isolation, however wide your projected idea may be.

Now, you can force the mind to be quiet through what is called prayer, the constant repetition of words, but when the mind is hypnotized into quietness, is that a state of meditation? Surely, that only dulls the mind, does it not? Though the mind may be pacified through discipline, which is based on the desire for particular results, such a mind is obviously not a free mind. Freedom can never come through discipline. Though we think we must discipline ourselves in order to be free, the beginning determines the end, and if the mind is disciplined at the beginning, it will be disciplined at the end; therefore, it can never be free. But if we can understand the whole process of discipline, control, suppression, sublimation, substitution, then there will be freedom from the very beginning, for the means and the end are one—they are not two separate processes, either politically or religiously.

So, discipline through concentration is not meditation, nor are the various forms of prayer. Those are all tricks by which the mind is forced to be still, and a mind that is made still through will, through desire, can never be free. If we really look at all these things—concentration, prayer, systems of meditation, and all the various tricks that we learn to quiet, to hypnotize the mind—we shall discover that they are the ways of thought, the ways of the self; and this discovery is the beginning of meditation, which is the beginning of self-knowledge. Without knowing yourself, merely to concentrate, to conform to a pattern, to follow a system, to quiet the mind through a discipline, only leads to further misery, further confusion. But if you begin to know the ways of your own thought by being choicelessly aware of yourself in relationship, in your talking, in your walking, when you are observing a bird or looking at somebody else, then, in that awareness, the responses of your conditioned state come into being—and in that spontaneity there is the discovery of yourself as yourself. And the more you are aware of yourself without choice, without justification or condemnation, the more there is freedom. It is this freedom that is the process of meditation. But you cannot cultivate freedom any more than you can cultivate love. Freedom comes into being, not through the search for it, but when you understand the whole process and structure of yourself.

Meditation, then, is the beginning of self-knowledge. When you begin very near, you can go very far, and then you will see that thought, which is the projection of the mind, comes to an end of itself without being compelled, forced. Then there is silence—not the silence that is willed, created by the mind, but a silence that is not of time; and in that silence there is the state of creation, the timelessness which is reality.

So, without understanding the ways of thought, merely to force the mind to meditate is an utter waste of time and energy and only creates more confusion, more misery. But to understand the process of the self as the thinker, to know the ways of the self as thought, is the beginning of wisdom. For wisdom to be, there must be the understanding of the accumulating process—which is the thinker. Without understanding the thinker, meditation has no meaning because whatever he projects is according to his own conditioning, and that is obviously not reality. Only when the mind understands the whole process of itself as thought, is it capable of being free, and only then does the timeless come into being.

July 2, 1950

Seattle, Washington, 1950

First Talk in Seattle

I think it is important to learn the art of hearing. Most of us listen only to that which is convenient, pleasurable; we do not hear those things that might affect us deeply, that are disturbing, that contradict our particular beliefs and opinions. And surely, it is important that we should know how to listen without making a tremendous effort to understand. When we make an effort to understand, our energy goes into the effort rather than into the process of understanding. Very few can listen without resistance, without creating barriers between themselves and the speaker; but if we can put aside our particular opinions, our accumulated knowledge and experience, and listen easily, without effort, then perhaps we shall be able to understand the nature of the fundamental and radical transformation that is so essential in a crisis of the present kind.

Now, it is obvious that there must be some kind of change. We are at the edge of a precipice, and the crisis is not limited to a particular group, religion, or people, but it is a crisis that involves us all. Whether you are an American or a Korean, a Japanese or a German, a Russian or a Hindu, you are affected by this crisis. It is a world crisis, and to understand it fully, if one is at all serious about it, one has obviously to begin with a fundamental understanding of oneself. The world is not different from each one of us. The world's problems are your problems and mine. This is not a histrionic assertion but an actual fact. If you examine the matter closely, go into it fully, you will see that the collective problems are the problems that confront each one of us individually. I do not think there is a division between the collective problems and those of the individual. The world is what we are; what we are, we project, and that to us becomes the world problem.

So, to understand this extraordinarily complex and ever-increasing problem that we see in the world, we have to understand ourselves—which does not mean that we must become so subjective, so inward-turned, that we lose contact with external affairs. Such an action, such a process, is meaningless, it has no validity at all. But if we can see that the world crisis—the confusion, the tragedy, the appalling murders and disasters that are taking place and are going to take place, this whole beastly mess—if we can see that all this is the result of our own daily life and action, of our particular beliefs, both religious and national, if we can see that this world cataclysm is a projection of ourselves and is not independent of us, then our examination of the problem will be neither subjective nor objective, but will come about through quite a different approach.

Now, we generally approach a problem of this kind either objectively or subjectively, do we not? We try to understand it either on the objective or on the subjective level, and the difficulty is that the problem is neither purely subjective nor purely objective, but is a combination of the two. It is both a social and a psychological process, and that is why no specialist, no economist, no psychologist, no follower of a system, whether of the right or of the left, can ever solve this problem. The specialists and experts can attack the problem only in their own particular fields—they never treat it as a total process—and to understand it, one must approach it in its totality. So, our approach to the problem can obviously be neither subjective nor objective, but we must be capable of seeing it as a total process.

To understand the world crisis as a total process, one has to begin with oneself. Outwardly there is constant war, conflict, confusion, misery, and strife; and through it all there is the search for security, for happiness. Surely, these outward problems are the result, the projection, of our own inward confusion, conflict, and misery. Therefore, in order to solve the external problems, which are not independent of our inward struggles and pains, we must obviously begin to understand the process of our own thinking; that is, there must be self-knowledge. Without knowing ourselves fundamentally, both the conscious and the unconscious, there is no basis for thinking, is there? If I do not know myself deeply, at all the different levels, what basis is there for my thinking, for my action? Though this has been said over and over again by every preacher since the beginning of time, we go on disregarding it because we think that by environmental change, by altering outward circumstances, by bringing about an economic revolution, we can transform fundamentally the process of our thinking. But surely, if we can look at the problem a little more closely and ardently, we will see that mere external alterations can never bring about a fundamental revolution. Without understanding the whole process of the self, of the 'me', the process of our own thinking, the inward confusion in which we live will always overcome the cunning reconstruction of outer circumstances.

So, it is important, is it not, for those who are really serious, who are in earnest, who are not just flippant or pursuing some sectarian belief—surely, it is important for such people to begin to understand the process of their own thinking. Because, after all, our thought is the response of our particular conditioning, and there would be no thought if there were no conditioning. That is, whether you are a socialist, a communist, a capitalist, a Catholic, a Protestant, a Hindu, or what you will, your thinking is the response of that conditioning; and without understanding that conditioning or background, which is the 'you', whatever you do, whatever you think, must obviously be the response of that conditioning. So, to bring about a fundamental revolution, a transformation in oneself, there must be the understanding of the background, of the conditioning influences which create the process of thinking; and this self-knowledge is the beginning of wisdom.

Most of us, unfortunately, seek wisdom through books, through listening to somebody; we think we will understand life by following experts or by joining philosophical societies or religious organizations. Surely, they are all escapes, are they not? Because, after all, we have to understand ourselves, and the understanding of oneself is a very complex process. We do not exist at only one level; our structure of being is at several levels, with different entities all in conflict with each other. Without understanding that whole process of the self, we cannot finally solve any problem, whether political, economic, or social. The basic problem is one of human relationship, and to solve that, we must begin to understand the total process of ourselves. To bring about a change in the world, which is obviously essential, we must be aware of all our psychological responses, must we not? To be aware of our responses is to observe them without choice, without condemnation or justification—just to see the whole process of our own thinking in the midst of relationship, in the midst of action. Then we begin to examine the problem in its totality, that is, we are aware of its full scope; and then we shall see how our responses are conditioned by our particular background, and how those conditioned responses are contributing to the chaos in the world. So, self-knowledge is the beginning of freedom.

Now, to discover anything, to understand what is truth, reality, or God, there must be freedom. Freedom can never come through a belief; on the contrary, there is freedom only when the conditioning influences of belief, and of the process of memory, are understood. When there is that understanding of its own process, then the mind is really still, spontaneously silent; and in that silence, which cannot come through any enforcement, there is freedom. Then only is there a possibility of discovering what is real. So, there can be freedom only with the understanding of the self, of the 'me', of the whole process of our thinking.

There are some questions, and in considering them, may I suggest that you and I should both try to discover the truth of the matter, and not merely wait for an answer. Life has no categorical answer of yes or no. We must go into each problem very deeply, and to go into it deeply, we must begin very near and follow it closely without missing a step. And if we can take the journey together and discover the truth of these problems, then no expert, no pressure of public opinion, no immature thinking, can ever obscure that which has been discovered.

Question: What is my responsibility towards the present world crisis?

KRISHNAMURTI: First of all, is the world crisis something apart from you? Is the present world catastrophe different from the conflict of our daily existence? After all, this disastrous world situation is the collective result of our separative beliefs, of our narrow patriotisms, of our religious bigotries, petty antagonisms, and economic frontiers. It is the result of our daily competition, of our ruthless efficiency, is it not?

So, the world crisis is a projection of ourselves; it is not separate from us. And to bring about a fundamental change in the world, surely we must individually break down and be free from those limitations, barriers, and conditioning influences which create this universal horror and confusion. But our difficulty is that we do not see that we are responsible. We do not really see that nationalism divides people, that so-called religions, with their dogmas, beliefs, and rituals, are separating influences. Though they preach the unity of man, they themselves are a means of setting man against man. We do not see the truth of that, nor of the fact that our own limited thoughts, experiences, and knowledge are again a separative process; and where there is separation, obviously there is disintegration and ultimately war.

Our life, then, is actually a process of disintegration; in it there is nothing creative. We are like gramophone records, repeating certain experiences, certain slogans, and reproducing the knowledge which we have acquired. In repeating, we make a lot of noise, and we think we are living; but this mechanical repetition is obviously a process of disintegration which, when projected, becomes a world crisis of ultimate destruction. So, the world crisis is a projection of our daily existence. What we are makes the world around us. Therefore, for those who are really serious, it is of the highest importance to bring about a fundamental change in what we are, because only in the transformation of ourselves can there be the cessation of this horror that is going on. But unfortunately, most of us are lazy. We want others to do the work for us, to tell us what to do. We are satisfied with our little knowledge, with our little experience, with trite newspaper slogans, and gradually we become set in our narrow ways—we lose the vitality of change, the quickness, the alertness of mind.

So, the problem is not to find out your responsibility towards the world crisis, but to see that what you are, the world is. Without a fundamental transformation in yourself, world crises will go on multiplying, becoming more and more disastrous. The problem, then, is how to bring about a fundamental transformation in oneself, and we shall discuss this during the next four weeks as we go along. It is not an easy problem. Transformation is not mere change, a mere modification in one's attitude. Such change is superficial—it can never be fundamental. So, we must think about the whole problem quite differently, which we will do in the course of the coming weeks.

Question: Is the individual the instrument of society, or does society exist for the individual?

KRISHNAMURTI: This is an important question, is it not? Let us think it out together and find the truth of the matter without depending on the opinion of any authority or any expert. Authorities and experts change their views according to their convenience, according to their latest discoveries, and so on; but if we can discover the truth of the matter for ourselves, then we shall not be dependent on others.

Now, this question implies that the world is divided, does it not? There are those who assert, with enormous knowledge in addition to their personal inclination and idiosyncrasy, that the individual is the instrument of society—which means that the individual is not important at all. There is a tremendous group of people who maintain this and who therefore give all their energies to the reconstruction of society. And there are those who believe with equal emphasis that the individual is above society, that society exists for the individual.

So, you and I have to find out what the truth of this matter is. How are we going to find out? Surely, not by being persuaded to accept this or that opinion, but by going into the whole problem very deeply. That is, our problem is not whether society exists for the individual, or the individual for society, but to find out what is the individual. I hope I am making myself clear. There are those who assert that the individual is not important, and that only society is important, and there are others who maintain that the individual is beyond society. But to find out the truth of the matter, surely we must inquire into the problem of what is individuality.

Are you an individual? You may think you are an individual because you have your own house, your own name, your own family, your own bank account; you have the particular experiences, the memories, both private and collective, of a separate person. But does that constitute individuality? Because, after all, you are conditioned by your environment, are you not? You are an American or a Russian or a Hindu, with all its implications; you have a certain ideology imposed upon you by your society, either of the left or of the right. You are educated in certain ways by your society. Your religious beliefs are a result of your education, of your environmental influence. You believe in God or disbelieve in God, according to your conditioning. So, you, as an entity, are the result of social or environmental conditioning, are you not? That is, you are a conditioned entity, and is a conditioned entity a true individual? Individuality is unique, is it not? Otherwise it is not individuality. And that which is unique is creative—it is beyond all conditioning, it is not limited, controlled by thought. So, there can be individuality only when there is freedom from conditioning, and as long as you are conditioned as a Hindu, a Buddhist, a communist, a capitalist, a Russian, or what you will, there can be no individuality.

Now, society is only concerned with creating an entity which is efficient for its own purposes, including war; it is obviously not concerned with bringing about an individual who is unique, creative. So, the problem is not whether the individual is or is not the instrument of society, but whether we ourselves are individuals; and to find out if we are individuals, surely we must be aware of our conditioning. As long as we are not free from our particular conditioning, there cannot be the creative uniqueness of individuality. There can be individuality only when there is freedom from all conditioning, whether of the left or of the right, and that freedom alone brings about the creative uniqueness of the individual.

You may say that I am giving quite a different significance to that word *individual*. But I don't think we are individuals, are we? And by recognizing that we are not individuals, that we merely respond according to our conditioning—by recognizing that fact, we can go beyond it; but if we deny the fact, then it is obviously impossible to go beyond. And most of us will deny the fact because we like what we are. We like to be comfortable in our own little backyard of thinking—and for that we will fight. But if we can understand our conditioning and the responses of that conditioning, which we so proudly call individuality, if we can be aware of all that, then there is a possibility of going beyond and discovering what is true creation.

Question: There are many concepts of God in the world today. What is your thought concerning God?

KRISHNAMURTI: First of all, we must find out what we mean by a concept. What do we mean by the process of thinking? Because, after all, when we formulate a concept, let us say, of God, our formula or concept must be the result of our conditioning, must it not? If we believe in God, surely our belief is the result of our environment. There are those who are trained from childhood to deny God and those who are trained to believe in God—as most of you have been. So, we formulate a concept of God according to our training, according to our background, according to our idiosyncrasies, likes and dislikes, hopes and fears. Obviously, then, as long as we do not understand the process of our own thinking, mere concepts of God have no value at all, have they? Because, thought can project anything it likes. It can create God and deny God. Each person can invent or destroy God according to his inclinations, pleasures, and pains. Therefore, as long as thought is active, formulating, inventing, that which is beyond time can never be discovered. God, or reality, is to be discovered only when thought comes to an end.

Now, when you ask, "What is your thought concerning God?" you have already formulated your own thought, have you not? Thought can create God and experience that which it has created, but surely, that is not true experience. It is only its own projection that thought experiences, and therefore it is not real. But if you and I can see the truth of this, then perhaps we shall experience something much greater than a mere projection of thought.

At the present time, when there is greater and greater insecurity outwardly, there is obviously a yearning for inward security. Since we cannot find security outside, we seek it in an idea, in thought; and so we create that which we call God, and that concept becomes our security. Now, a mind that seeks security surely cannot find the real, the true. To understand that which is beyond time, the fabrications of thought must come to an end. Thought cannot exist without words, symbols, images, and only when the mind is quiet, free of its own creations, is there a possibility of finding out what is real. So, merely to ask if there is or is not God, is an immature response to the problem, is it not? And to formulate opinions about God is really childish.

To experience, to realize, that which is beyond time, we must obviously understand the process of time. The mind is the result of time; it is based on the memories of yesterday, and is it possible to be free from the multiplication of yesterdays, which is the process of time? Surely, this is a very serious problem; it is not a matter of belief or disbelief. Believing and disbelieving is a process of ignorance whereas understanding the time-binding quality of thought brings freedom, in which alone there can be discovery. But most of us want to believe because it is much more convenient; it gives us a sense of security, a sense of belonging to the group. Surely, this very belief separates us because you believe in one thing, and I believe in another. So, belief acts as a barrier; it is a process of disintegration.

What is important, then, is not the cultivation of belief or disbelief, but to understand the process of the mind. It is the mind, it is thought, that creates time. Thought is time, and whatever thought projects must be of time; therefore, thought cannot possibly go beyond itself. To discover what is beyond time, thought must come to an end—and that is a most difficult thing because the ending of thought does not come about through discipline, through control, through denial or suppression. Thought ends only when we understand the whole process of thinking, and to understand thinking, there must be self-knowledge. Thought is the self, thought is the word which identifies itself as the 'me'; and at whatever level, high or low, the self is placed, it is still within the field of thought. To find God, that which is beyond time, we must understand the process of thought, that is, the process of oneself. And the self is very complex; it is not at any one level but is made up of many thoughts, many entities, each in contradiction with the other. There must be a constant awareness of them all—an awareness in which there is no choice, no condemnation or comparison; that is, there must be the capacity to see things as they are without distorting or translating them. The moment we judge or translate what is seen, we distort it according to our background. To discover reality or God, there can be no belief because acceptance or denial is a barrier to discovery. We all want to be secure, both outwardly and inwardly, and the mind must understand that the search for security is an illusion. It is only the mind which is insecure, completely free from any form of possession, that can discover—and this is an arduous task. It does not mean retiring into the woods or to a monastery, or isolating oneself in some peculiar belief; on the contrary, nothing can exist in isolation. To be is to be related, and it is only in the midst of relationship that we can spontaneously discover ourselves as we are. It is this very discovery of ourselves as we are, without any sense of condemnation or justification, that brings about a fundamental transformation in what we are—and that is the beginning of wisdom.

July 16, 1950

Second Talk in Seattle

With most of us, life is a constant struggle, a constant battle, within ourselves, and therefore outwardly. This battle, this conflict, seems never to end, and the difficulty with most of us is that we are always trying to conform our lives to certain standards, principles, or ideals. Now, the cessation of conflict does not come about through a process of conformity, either to the past or to the future, but through understanding the events, the happenings, of our daily life as they arise from moment to moment; and we are incapable of that full comprehension of events as long as we hold to a particular outlook, opinion, experience, or idea.

Life is relationship, and in relationship, most of us seek isolation. If we observe closely, we will see that our very thinking and action are self-enclosing, and this process of self-enclosing we call experience. Relationship is not only with people, but with ideas and things; and as long as we do not understand this self-enclosing process in relationship, we are bound to have conflict because there must be conflict as long as there is isolation.

Isolation takes many and extraordinary forms. There is the isolation of memory, both personal and collective; there is isolation in the form of belief; and there is the isolation of the experiences that one has accumulated and to which the mind clings. This whole process of isolation, of separation, is obviously a disintegrating factor in our lives—and that is exactly what is happening at the present time in the world. Inwardly, as individuals, and outwardly, as nationalistic and religious groups, we are seeking isolation in self-enclosing ideals, beliefs, dogmas, and opinions; and as long as this process of isolation continues, there must be conflict. Conflict can never be overcome because a thing that is overcome has to be conquered again and again. Conflict ceases only in understanding the process of relationship. We cannot live in isolation because life is relationship. To be is to be related, and without understanding relationship, obviously there must be conflict. So, our problem is to understand relationship—our relationship with people, with property, and with ideas.

Does understanding depend on experience? What do we mean by experience? Experience is a reaction, the response to a challenge, is it not? If the response is not adequate, there is conflict; and the response can never be adequate as long as we do not understand relationship. To understand relationship, we must understand the whole background and process of our thinking. Thought, the whole structure of our thinking, is based on the past, and as long as we do not understand this background, relationship remains inevitably a process of conflict.

To understand thought, which is the process of the self at whatever level it may be placed, is arduous because thought has no break in continuity. That is why, to follow the movement, the reactions of thought, which is the self, the mind must be extraordinarily subtle, quick, and adaptable. The self, the 'me', is obviously made up of the qualities, the tendencies, the prejudices and idiosyncrasies of the mind; and without understanding that whole structure of thinking, merely to solve the outer problems of relationship is obviously futile.

So, understanding does not depend on the process of thought. Thought is never new, but relationship is always new, and thought approaches this thing that is vital, real, new, with the background of the old. That is, thought tries to understand relationship according to the memories, patterns, and conditioning of the old—and hence there is conflict. Before we can understand relationship, we must understand the background of the thinker, which is to be aware of the whole process of thought without choice; that is, we must be capable of seeing things as they are without translating them according to our memories, our preconceived ideas, which are the outcome of past conditioning.

To understand conflict, we must understand relationship, and the understanding of relationship does not depend on memory, on habit, on what has been or what should be. It depends on choiceless awareness from moment to moment, and if we go into it deeply, we shall see that in that awareness there is no accumulative process at all. The moment there is accumulation, there is a point from which to examine, and that point is conditioned; and hence, when we regard relationship from a fixed point, there must be pain, there must be conflict.

Life, then, is a process of constant relationship with ideas, with people, and with things; and as long as we have a fixed point or center of recognition, which is the consciousness of the 'me', there must be conflict. From the center of recognition, that accumulative principle of the 'me', we examine all our relationships, and therefore there must be a constant isolation; and it is this isolation, this desire to be separate, that creates conflict and struggle.

So, our problem in life, in living, is to understand the desire to be separate. Nothing can live in isolation, but all our efforts based on desire must eventually be exclusive, separative. Therefore, desire is the process of disintegration, and desire expresses itself in many ways, subtle and gross, conscious and unconscious. But if we can be aware of desire—not as a discipline, but by being choicelessly aware of it from moment to moment—then we shall see that there comes a swift spontaneity of discovery of that which is true; and it is truth that gives freedom, not all our efforts to be free.

Truth is not cumulative; it is to be seen and understood from moment to moment. The person who accumulates, whether knowledge, property, or ideas, who is caught up in the self-enclosing process of relationship, is incapable of seeing truth. The man of knowledge can never know truth because the process of knowledge is cumulative, and the mind which accumulates is caught in time and therefore cannot know the timeless.

Now, how are we to understand the process of the self, the 'me'? Without understanding this process, there is no basis for action, for thought. To understand the self, we must understand relationship because it is in the mirror of relationship that the self is seen. But the self can be seen clearly as it is only when there is no condemnation, no comparison—that is, when we are capable of observation, alert passiveness, in which all choice has come to an end. As long as the mind is accumulating, it is not free, but when it is capable of perceiving without choice that which is, then that very perception is its own freedom. It is only when the mind is free that it is capable of discovery, and in that freedom there is the cessation of conflict and pain.

I have several questions, and in considering them, let us examine the problem and discover the truth of it together. To do that, the mind must be quick, pliable, actively aware. No problem has an answer, and if we seek an answer, it will lead us away from the problem, but if we understand that problem, the problem comes to an end. As long as we seek an answer to any problem, that problem will continue because the desire to find an answer prevents the understanding of the problem itself. So, our approach to the problem is extraordinarily important, is it not? The man who is looking for the solution to a problem has his whole concentration placed on the discovery of the answer, and so he is really incapable of looking directly at the problem. But if we can look at the problem without the desire to find an answer, we shall see that the problem is quickly resolved because then the problem reveals its whole content. So, if I may suggest, let us in that manner examine these questions together.

Question: What system would give man the greatest physical security?

KRISHNAMURTI: There are several things involved in this question, are there not? What do we mean by a system? And what do we mean by physical security? By a system we mean an ideology, either of the left or of the right, do we not? And can any ideology guarantee physical security? Can a system, an idea, a doctrine, however promising, however cunningly and subtly thought out, however erudite, give security? A political structure built around ideas, knowledge, and experience—that is what we mean by a system, is it not? It is an ideology in opposition to other ideologies, and can that ever bring physical security?

What do we mean by idea? Idea is a process of thinking, is it not? One thinks, and idea is merely the result of accumulated knowledge and experience, and we look to idea as a means of physical security. That is, to put it differently, there are many problems: starvation, war, unemployment, overpopulation, erosion of the soil, and so on. Take starvation—though it is perhaps not the problem in this country that it is in the East. Two opposing systems, the left and the right, try to solve it. That is, we approach the problem of starvation with an idea, with a formula—and then fight over the formula. So, the formula, the system, becomes more important than the problem of starvation. The problem is starvation, not what idea, what formula to use. But we are more interested in the idea than in the problem of starvation, and so we group ourselves against each other, according to our ideas, and fight it out, liquidate each other—and starvation continues.

So, the important thing is to have the capacity to face the problem, to tackle it directly, and not look to a system; and by understanding the problem, we will naturally resolve it. That is entirely different from coming to it with a formula, is it not? After all, there is enough scientific knowledge to solve the problem of starvation. Why is it not done? Because of our nationalism, our power politics, and the innumerable other absurdities of which we are so proud. It is therefore a psychological problem, and not merely an economic problem. No expert can solve it because the expert looks at it from his particular point of view, according to his formula. That is why it is important to understand the whole process of one's own thinking.

Now, can we have physical security as long as we are seeking psychological security? This is another problem which is also involved in this question. We have seen what is implied when we look to a system in order to have physical security; and now we are trying to find out what we mean by physical security and if physical security is independent of psychological security. Is physical security assured if we are seeking psychological security? That is, if we use property as a means of psychological security, are we not creating physical insecurity? Property becomes extraordinarily important to us because psychologically we are weak; it gives us power, position, prestige, and so we put a fence around it and call it "mine." To protect it, we create a police force, an army, and from that arise nationalism and war. So, in the very desire for psychological security, we bring about physical insecurity. Therefore, physical security is entirely dependent on whether or not we are seeking psychological security. If we do not seek psychological security in any form, then obviously there is a possibility of achieving physical security.

Physical security, then, depends upon the understanding of our own psychological process, the whole structure of our inner being, and as long as we do not understand ourselves, no system can give us physical security. A revolution based on an idea can never be a revolution and can therefore never bring about physical security because it is merely a modified continuation of *what is.* Revolution, transformation, is not the outcome of thinking; it comes into being only when thought ceases. Our difficulty is that we are so caught up with utopian promises that we are willing to sacrifice the present for the future, and in the very sacrificing of the present is the destruction of the future. Only when we understand the fact of *what is,* without translating it according to any ideology, is there a possibility of having the physical security which is so essential.

Question: I seek God, truth, understanding. How am I to proceed in finding them?

KRISHNAMURTI: Do not seek, for what you seek is obviously your own projection, is it not? When you say, "I seek God, truth, understanding," you have an idea of what truth or God is, and you are after that; and you will find what you seek—but it will not be God. It will merely be the image of your idea. Only the man who does not seek will find reality—which does not mean that we must become apathetic, lazy, sluggish. On the contrary, not to seek is extremely difficult; it requires great understanding, deep comprehension. When the mind is seeking, it is projecting, manufacturing, fabricating; and it is only when the mind is still—not disciplined to be still, but spontaneously quiet—that there is a possibility of truth coming into being. The man who struggles and tries to seek is caught in the process of conflict, is he not? Because he is continuously seeking, searching out, his mind is agitated, it is never still, and how can such a mind ever be quiet? Such a mind wants a result, it is seeking an end, a goal, which means it wants to be successful, only it does not call it that; it calls it the search for God, for truth, for understanding. But the intention, the background of that search, is the desire to be successful, the desire to be certain, the desire to be secure, to avoid all conflict, to reach a place where all disturbance will cease. When such a mind says, "I am seeking," what it wants is to be enclosed permanently in the security of an ideal, which is its own projection.

So, the man who seeks will never find; but if we can understand the process of our own search, the whole psychological structure of our desire to find, to arrive, to succeed, which is quite complex, then we shall see that when seeking comes to an end there is the beginning of truth, the beginning of understanding. But there can be no understanding as long as the mind is in the process of grasping.

It is the very nature of the mind, is it not, to acquire, to gain, to become; and in acquisition, in becoming, there is always agitation, conflict. Being in conflict, the mind seeks truth or God, and that search is merely avoidance, an escape from conflict. Escape is always the same, whether it is drink or God. So, a mind that is seeking can never find, but when the mind begins to understand its own process, then it is quiet, it is content. That contentment is not the outcome of acquiring or becoming something, it is not the contentment of satisfaction, of arriving at a position. Contentment which is free of all grasping comes only with the understanding of *what is,* but to understand *what is* requires diligence, an awareness without rejection or acceptance. Only when the mind is not struggling, acquiring, grasping, can it be still, and only then is there understanding.

Question: To me, discipline is necessary to the good life, but you say that discipline is a hindrance to the good life. Please explain.

KRISHNAMURTI: We take for granted that discipline is essential to the good life. But is it? What do we mean by discipline? By discipline we mean conformity to a system, to an ideal, do we not? We are afraid to be what we are, so we discipline ourselves to be something else—which is a process of resistance, suppression, sublimation, substitution. Now, does conformity, resistance, suppression, lead to the good life? Are you good when you resist? Are you noble when you are afraid to see what you are and avoid it? Are you virtuous when you are conforming? The man who has enclosed himself in discipline—is he leading a noble life? Surely, he is merely resisting something of which he is afraid, conforming to a pattern that will assure him of security. Is that goodness? Or is goodness something beyond fear, beyond conformity and resistance?

It is easy merely to resist something, is it not? It is easy to comply, to conform, to imitate, but can such a mind ever be noble? After all, virtue is freedom, is it not? Discipline is a process of becoming virtuous, and surely, a mind that is becoming virtuous is never virtuous. Virtue is freedom, and freedom comes through exploring and understanding the whole process of resistance, of conformity to social standards—that process by which the mind moves from the known to the known and so is never in a state of insecurity. So, if we can understand the psychology of resistance, of conformity, of suppression, this whole process of becoming something which we call virtuous—if we can understand all that, only then is there a good life. A good life is a free life, a comprehending life, not a life of resisting, fighting, conforming. To be free, we have to understand the process of our own conditioning which has trained us either to resist or to conform.

So, a mind that is disciplined can never be free. A mind that is disciplined at the beginning will not be free at the end because the beginning is the end. The end and the beginning are not two separate states, they are one continuous process; and if you say, "I will be free through discipline," you are denying freedom at the very beginning. But if at the very beginning you go deeply into and understand the process of discipline, control, shaping, conforming, resisting, then you will see that freedom is now, not in the future.

Now, society makes use of discipline for its own purposes. A political party wants to have disciplined members for concerted action, but that action is never free, and therefore it creates resistance, the opposite, the other party; and so the two parties are in conflict with each other. But if we can understand the process which creates a party, whether of the left or of the right, the process of discipline arising from our conditioning—if we can understand this in its entirety, then we shall see that the good life does not come about through discipline, but comes only through understanding one's desire to conform, to resist, to suppress, to imitate—and that understanding is virtue.

Question: You have said in one of your talks that the thought process must cease for reality to be. How can we know anything if thought ceases?

KRISHNAMURTI: First, let us examine what we mean by thinking and what we mean by experiencing, which is recognizing. As the questioner says, if thought ceases, how can it recognize anything? Now, what do we mean by thinking? Please do not wait for my answer—we are exploring it together. When we say, "I am thinking," what do we mean? If I ask you that, you respond, do you not?—

whether correctly or incorrectly is irrelevant for the time being. So, thinking is a process of response to challenge. The challenge is always new, but the response is always the old; so, thinking is the response of memory, is it not? I ask you if you believe in God, and your immediate response is according to your memory or conditioning. Either you do or you do not believe. So, thinking is the process, the response of memory, which is habit. That is, memory is the result of experience, and experience is knowledge; and according to your memory, experience, knowledge, you respond to any challenge. The challenge is new, and your response is modified according to the newness, the vitality of the challenge; but it is always the response of the background, is it not?

So, thinking is the response of the background, of the past, of accumulated experience; it is the response of memory at different levels, both individual and collective, particular and racial, conscious and unconscious. All that is our process of thinking. Therefore, our thinking can never be new. There can be no "new" idea because thinking can never renew itself; thinking can never be fresh because it is always the response of the background—the background being our conditioning, our traditions, our experiences, our accumulations, collective and personal. So, when we look to thought as a means of discovering the new, we see the utter futility of it. Thought can only discover its own projection, it cannot discover anything new; thought can only recognize that which it has experienced, it cannot recognize that which it has not experienced.

Thought, then, is the process of recognition. Thought exists through verbalization, through symbols, through images, through words; otherwise, there is no thought; therefore, thought can never be new, it can never be creative. When you say you are experiencing something, your experiencing is recognizing, is it not? If you did not recognize, you would not know you were experiencing. Now, can thought experience the new? Obviously not because thought can only recognize the old, that which it has known, that which it has experienced before. The new can never be experienced by thought because thought is the reaction of the old.

This is not something metaphysical, complicated, or abstract. If you will look at it a little more closely, you will see that as long as the 'I'—the entity who is made up of all these memories—is experiencing, there can never be the discovery of the new. Thought, which is the 'I', can never experience God because God or reality is the unknown, the unimaginable, the unformulated; it has no label, no word. The word *God* is not God. So, thought can never experience the new, the unknowable; it can only experience the known, for the mind can function only within the field of the known—it cannot function beyond it. The moment there is thought about the unknown, the mind is agitated; it is always seeking to bring the unknown into the known. But the unknown can never be brought into the known, and hence the conflict between the known and the unknown.

So, only when thought comes to an end is it possible for the unknown to be, and then there is no question of an 'I' experiencing the unknown. The 'I' can never experience the unknown, reality, God, or what you will. The 'I', the mind, the self, is the bundle of the known, which is memory; and memory can only recognize its own projections, it cannot recognize the unknown. That is why thought must come to an end.

Thought as the 'I' must cease to experience; there must be no feeling, no certainty, that "I have experienced." When thought, which is the response of memory, comes to an end, and the mind is no longer functioning in the field of the known, only then is it possible for the unknown to be.

The experiencing of the unknown is not possible because when you "experience" the unknown, you are only experiencing the known as a new sensation. The unknown can never be recognized. The unknown is. But in that state the mind rebels because it can only function within the field of the known.

That is why, for reality to be, you must understand the whole process of thinking, the process of the self. Thought can never discover or come to the unknown, the real; but when the mind is still, utterly silent—not made silent by any practice, by any discipline, by any system of control or meditation—then, in that tranquillity, there is the reality which can never be experienced by the mind; for reality is beyond all projections of the self.

July 23, 1950

Third Talk in Seattle

We ought to be able, I think, to discern the difference between necessity and desire. Desire can never be integrated because desire always creates contradiction, its own opposite; whereas, if we can understand necessity, then we shall see that in it there is no contradiction. And surely, it is important to be aware of this problem of desire, which creates contradiction in each one of us, because desire can never at any time bring about integration, and it is only in the state of integration, in the state of wholeness, that there is a possibility of going beyond the contradictions created in the mind by desire. After all, desire is sensation, and sensation is the basis of thought, of the mind. Sensation is the foundation of all our thinking, and as long as we do not understand the process of desire, we are bound to create in our life the conflict of contradiction.

So, the understanding of desire is essential, and that understanding does not come through merely transferring desire from one level to another. Desire at any level, however high we may place it, is inevitably contradictory and therefore destructive. But if we can understand necessity, then we shall see that desire is binding, that it does not bring about freedom; and to discern what is needful is quite an arduous task because desire constantly interferes with our needs. When we understand need, there is no contradiction, but to understand need, we must understand desire. And our problem is, is it not, that there is a constant battle going on between need and desire. Our whole social structure is based on this contradiction of desire. We think we are making progress when we move from one desire to what we call a higher desire, but desire, whether high or low, is always a contradiction, a source of conflict and great suffering.

So, if we can see how the whole process of desire works out in our daily life, then we shall understand the extraordinary importance of need, of necessity. Necessity is not a matter of choice, is it? When we can understand what is necessary, there is no contradiction, no battle either within or without; but to understand necessity, must we not examine the process of the mind that chooses what is necessary? The moment we bring in choice, does that not block the understanding of necessity? When we choose, do we ever discover what is necessary? Choice is always based, is it not, on our conditioning, and that conditioning is the outcome of our contradictory desires. So, if we choose what is necessary, we are bound to create conflict, we are bound to bring about confusion. There is no thought without sensation; thought is the outcome of sensation—it is founded upon sensation—and if we can understand the ways of sensation, the ways of thought, and not choose what is necessary, then we shall see that necessity is a simple matter; and in that understanding there is no conflict, no contradiction.

Where there is desire, there is conflict and contradiction, and whether we are aware of it or not, contradiction invariably brings pain. So, desire is sorrow, whether we desire trivial things or great things. Desire inevitably brings its own opposite in its wake, and therefore it is important, is it not, to understand the whole process of thought, which is the 'me' and the 'mine'. The understanding of desire is the way of self-knowledge. Without understanding the self, there is no possibility of understanding what is essential, necessary in life. Self-knowledge comes only through the understanding of relationship, which is the beginning of wisdom. Wisdom cannot be bought, it cannot be gathered; it arises from moment to moment in relationship when the mind is aware, clear, and observing, without choice.

So, if we would understand the contradiction in which most of us live, there must be self-knowledge, which is the understanding of desire; and without understanding the whole process of desire, merely to follow one particular desire does not solve our problem. What solves our problem is to understand the nature of contradiction, which is desire. Desire can never be overcome, but when we see the truth that desire always creates its own opposite and therefore is a contradiction, then desire comes to an end; and only then is there a possibility of being content with necessity.

In considering these questions, it is important to find out in what way we are approaching them. If we come to a problem with a preconception, with a conclusion, with an opinion, obviously we cannot understand that problem. As I said, any problem is always new, fresh, and a mind that comes to a problem with a conclusion, with accumulated knowledge, cannot understand it. The mind can understand only when it comes to the problem afresh; and if we can this morning, let us examine each question directly and see the truth of it, for it is the discovery of the truth of the problem that liberates us from the problem itself.

Question: How many centuries will it take for the few who understand to bring about a fundamental transformation in the world?

KRISHNAMURTI: It is important to find out, is it not, from what point of view this question is put. If we say it will take many centuries to bring about a fundamental transformation because there are very few individuals who really desire to transform themselves, we are obviously concerned with the problem of time. That is, we want immediate transformation because we see in the world such confusion, misery, conflict, starvation, economic problems, and wars; we see this unceasing sorrow, and so we are impatient, we desire transformation within a certain period of time. We say, "The transformation of a few individuals will not bring about a fundamental and rapid change in the structure of society. Therefore, the transformation of the few is not very important. Though it is necessary, there must be a quicker way to bring about a fundamental revolution."

Now, is there a rapid, an immediate way to transform man? And if we bring about a rapid change, will that be enduring? The world cannot be changed immediately. Even revolution cannot bring about an immediate and universal change; the millions cannot be fed overnight. But it is important, is it not, to find out whether you and I can change, can bring about a fundamental transformation in ourselves, irrespective of its utilitarian aspect. And is the discovery and understanding of truth, useful? Has truth any use? Is it utilitarian? That is really what is implied in this question—whether truth is useful. Truth has no use whatever, has it? It cannot be used. It is. And the moment we approach truth with the desire to use it in the world of action, we destroy it. But if we can see the truth and allow it to operate without wanting to use it, then it brings about a fundamental transformation in our thinking, in our relationship. So, as long as we regard truth as a thing to be used, as a means of transforming society or ourselves, it becomes merely an instrument—it is not an end in itself, without causation. But if it is an end in itself, without any utilitarian purpose, that is, if we allow it to operate within us, and without any interference from the mind, then unknowingly, unconsciously, it has a far-reaching effect.

So, what is important is not whether the few can bring about a fundamental change—even though fundamental changes generally are brought about by the few—but to find out whether one is, oneself, really in earnest to discover this extraordinary liberating factor, this thing that we call truth or God, irrespective of any social or other value it may have. Because, the mind is always seeking values, is it not? And if it seeks truth as a "value," then that value is recognizable; but truth is not recognizable, it has no "value" for the mind. The mind cannot use it. But if the mind is quiet, then truth will operate, and this operation is extensive, unlimited—and therein lies freedom and happiness.

Question: Religions advocate prayer, and for centuries man has found in it his consolation. This concerted effort through the centuries is surely a significant and vital force. Do you deny its importance?

KRISHNAMURTI: What is the function of prayer? Has prayer any significance? And what do we mean by prayer? Let us go into the whole question without any bias or prejudice. Obviously, man through the centuries has prayed, and it must bring results, it must in some way give him consolation, satisfaction, an answer in accordance with his demand; otherwise, he would not continue to pray. Now, when do we pray? Surely, we pray when we are in trouble, do we not? We pray when we are in a state of uncertainty, of contradiction, that is, when we are unhappy. We do not pray when we are happy, when we see things very clearly, simply, and directly, but only when we are confused. So, prayer is a form of petition, of supplication, is it not? And when we ask, we receive, and we receive according to our demand. When we pray, surely we are always asking for satisfaction in one form or another. One may pray for light or guidance, another for the removal of pain and so on, but the desire, the intention, is always to find peace, gratification. A mind that is seeking gratification at whatever level, high or low, is bound to be gratified, is it not? That is why, when we are confused, when we are in pain, when we are in uncertainty, we turn to prayer. Through prayer we hope to receive certainty, reassurance, the right answer to our problem. Please, I am not for or against prayer. We are examining the problem. I think there is a much greater thing than prayer, and we can discover that only when we understand the ways of prayer, this whole problem of supplication.

So, what happens when we pray? I am sure many of us have prayed. What is the way of prayer? We take a certain posture, repeat certain words or phrases, and gradually, through this repetition, the mind becomes quiet. The mind is made quiet by repetition of certain phrases, and in that quietness you receive an answer to your problem. But the answer is invariably gratifying; otherwise, you would not accept it; though the answer may be painful, yet in the very acceptance of that painful answer there is gratification. That is, through the constant repetition of certain phrases or the prolonged dwelling on certain ideas, the mind is made quiet, and when the mind is quiet, it is capable of receiving an answer. But the answer depends on the petitioner; and the answer he receives is from the concentrated accumulation of innumerable desires, conscious and unconscious longings, and collective effort of many people through many centuries. You can test this out for yourself. When you consciously ask for something in prayer, there is an unconscious response, and that response is from the accumulated and concentrated effort of centuries, modified according to the particular conditioning of the petitioner. But prayer does not ultimately help the individual to understand himself; and it is only in understanding oneself fundamentally, as a total process, that there is a possibility of going beyond the state of demanding, seeking, of striving to achieve a result. As I said, there is something far more important than prayer—which is meditation; and we shall discuss that at another time.

Now, it is important, is it not, to understand this problem of prayer in relation to conflict, pain, and suffering. Because, we never pray when we are happy, when we are joyous, when we have no problems; we pray only when we are in conflict, when we have a difficulty which we cannot solve. There are two different kinds of prayer, which are essentially the same. There is the prayer of active supplication, petition, and there is the prayer in which we simply remain open but are unconsciously waiting to receive something. When we pray, we always have an outstretched hand—we are waiting, hoping, longing for an answer, for some consolation; and in that petitioning, we will find an answer according to our struggles, according to our conditioning. But prayer will never release the mind from creating the very problems that cause us to pray. What will free the mind from manufacturing its own problems is the understanding of itself, and the understanding of itself is self-knowledge. But the whole process of knowing oneself is so complex that few of us are desirous of going into the problem; we would rather find a superficial answer, and so we turn to prayer. For centuries man has built up a concentrated reservoir, a storehouse of thought and desire, from which prayer may evoke an answer, a consolation; but that response is not the solution of the problem. The solution of the problem is to understand the total process of the mind itself.

Questions: At various times in our lives, we have some kind of mystical experience. How do we know that these are not illusions? How can we recognize reality?

KRISHNAMURTI: What do we mean by illusion? What creates illusion? Surely, illusion is created, is it not, when the mind is caught up in desire. As long as the mind interprets what is perceived according to its longings, wishes, and desires, according to its likes and dislikes, there must be illusion. As long as the mind does not understand desire, it translates experience and inevitably creates illusion. That is, if I have an experience which is called "mystical" and do not understand the process of my own mind, that experience is bound to create illusion. And if I am attached to any particular form of experience, if I wish to gather more of it and continue in it, there must also be illusion because I am concerned, not with perceiving *what is,* but with gaining, guarding, accumulating.

Most of us have had some kind of mystical experience which has brought a certain clarity, a certain release, a certain happiness, and when it has passed, the memory of it becomes very important to us. We cling to the memory of that experience, and the very fact that we cling to it indicates that we are caught in illusion. Memory is within the field of time, and what is true is beyond time; and when the mind holds to any particular experience, that experience becomes mere sensation, and sensation makes for illusions. So, when we cling to the memory of any so-called "mystical experience" which we may have had, it indicates that we are concerned with the sensation that the experience has left behind, and therefore there is illusion. We cannot ever cling to the experience itself; we can never hold on to the state of experiencing. We can only accumulate memory, with its sensations, and when we do, we create a hindrance to further experiencing. Clinging to the past prevents the new, and so this attachment to the memory of a particular experience creates illusion.

The next part of this question is, "How can we recognize reality?" To go into that, we must understand the process of experiencing. We experience only when we recognize, do we not? If I meet you and recognize you, I have an experience, but if I do not recognize you, there is no experience. So, where there is recognition, there is the process of experiencing. Now, how do I recognize? Recognition is based on memory, is it not? And can memory, which is the residue of the past, ever recognize the new? Please, as this is an important question, let us go into it a little carefully.

Most of us move from the known to the known; our mind functions within the field of the known, and it cannot function outside. Now, can such a mind recognize what is true? Can it recognize the unknown? Can it recognize God? If God is the unknown, how can we recognize it? We can only recognize something which we have experienced, which we have known before, and when we recognize something, is it the truth, is it the new? As long as there is the old, the new cannot be; only when the old ceases is there a possibility of the new. And when we ask, "How can we recognize reality?" we want to know whether the 'I', the accumulated past, the known, can give a name to the new. When we give a name to the new, has not the new ceased to be? So, God is not a thing to be recognized; truth is not something to be known through memory. It is only when the mind is entirely and absolutely still that the new can be—which is not a process of recognition. On the contrary, when the mind is translating the new in terms of the old, it is not still, and so truth cannot be. The mind cannot translate the new in terms of the old—it can only translate what is supposed to be the new in terms of what it has known.

So, the important thing is not whether you and I can recognize truth, but how to free the mind from desire so that it can be completely still. Stillness of the mind does not come about through any discipline. The mind cannot be made still by any compulsion, with any motive, or for any purpose; but it is spontaneously still when it understands its own conflicting desires, which create problems. The mind is still only when it knows itself as a totality, but as long as it does not know itself completely, it goes on creating problems and can never be still. So, the mind must understand the ways of itself, and for that it must be alertly passive, aware without choice; and only then is there a possibility that the mind can be completely and totally still. We can make the mind superficially still through prayer, through various psychological tricks, but such a mind is not fundamentally still. Stillness comes only when there is complete understanding of the whole process of recognition, demanding, and responding, which is the process of the self—and that is an arduous task.

Question: Will you please explain what you mean by creativeness.

KRISHNAMURTI: Is creativeness a matter of capacity? Is creativeness mastery of a technique? Is creativeness a gift?

One can master a technique through constant practice, through the accumulation of knowledge and experience, both one's own and that of another. But does the perfection of a technique make for creativeness? You may practice the piano for hours and be able to play expertly, your technique may be perfect, but will that make you a creative musician? If you know how to write poetry, if you can make a perfect garland of words, are you thereby a poet? Will technique bring about that freedom in which the 'me', the self, is absent? It is only when the self, the 'me', is absent that there is creativeness; otherwise, technique merely emphasizes or distracts the self, modifying or enlarging it—and surely, that does not bring about creativeness.

As long as the mind is in conflict with what it has produced, is producing, or will produce, there cannot be a creative state, can there? Can there ever be creativeness as long as we are in conflict? Surely, conflict excludes every form of creative action, and creativity comes into being only when the mind is still, not in a state of conflict. As long as the mind is caught between thesis and antithesis, between the opposites, how can there be that state of alert passivity which alone is creative? We think that through conflict, through battle, through probing, analyzing, we shall have a peaceful state, but is there ever a peaceful state through conflict? Is not that peaceful state independent of conflict? As long as there is the desire to achieve a result, the desire to be creative, obviously we must be in a state of conflict, and such a state denies creativeness.

So, how is one to have that creative state? How is it possible to achieve creativeness? It is not possible to achieve creativeness. All that we can do is to understand conflict, which denies creativeness, and the understanding of conflict is the understanding of oneself. You see, we think that to have a technique, to be able to draw, to write a poem or an article, to fulfill oneself in one form or another, is to be creative. But surely, that is not creativeness; that is merely self-expression, satisfying a certain appetite through technique. But if we can understand this whole process of conflict, this striving after attainment which brings in our lives such contradiction, such sorrow and pain, then we shall see that the mind becomes very quiet, without any striving; and when the mind is silent, free of the anxieties and demands of the self, only then is there a possibility for creative being. That creativeness may or may not express itself in words, in marble, in thought—or it may be utterly silent. But we want expression. To most of us, creativeness is a process of expression; it is the power to do something, and we consider that power of expression as far more important than to be free. We crave for expression because it gives us a sense of fulfillment, a sense of importance; it gives us the feeling of being somebody, of being socially useful. All this feeds our vanity in many ways and so destroys the state of creativeness.

Actually, creativeness may not express itself at all because the state of creativeness is silent. To seek expression is to deny creativeness because that which is creative can never be cumulative. Creativeness is only from moment to moment—it is not a state of continuity. The moment it is a continuous state, it is within the field of time, and that which is within the field of time is not creative. Creativeness is timeless, but we would like to hold it within the field of time in order to be able to express it. As long as the mind is seeking to be creative, creativeness can never be, because all the efforts of the mind are within the field of time. Only when the mind is utterly still, silent with a silence that is not induced, is there a possibility of the timeless, the creative. So, what is important is not to verbalize about this creative state but to understand the whole process of conflict in the mind. And as the pool is quiet when the winds stop, so there is creativeness when the problems which the mind creates come to an end.

July 30, 1950

Fourth Talk in Seattle

Most of us seek some kind of result, and we never think of action without result. We do not have the sense of moving, acting, unless there is an end in view. As long as we seek a result, the result is psychologically much more important to us than the means, and the corruption of the means is inevitable when we give a greater significance to the result. Action then is guided by the desire for a result rather than by consideration of the means—and action is thereby stultified. That is, as long as there is the psychological seeking of a result from action, we stultify that action because we are chiefly concerned with the result, and only incidentally with the action. Therefore, as we see throughout the world at the present time, action breeds further confusion, further misery. This outward conflict and suffering can be brought to an end only when we see how the mind is constantly seeking a result in action, that is, security for itself, and is therefore not concerned with the means of action. The means and the end are not two different states—they are a unitary process. The means is the end, and if we understand the means, the right end is inevitable. But as I said, most of us are not concerned with the means. We are mostly concerned with the end, and hoping for a right end, we use wrong methods. But the method produces the result, and if we want peace, we must use peaceful means. Therefore, the means is much more important than the end.

Now, the understanding of the means without searching for an end is a fundamental and necessary revolution in our whole approach to life. Because thought invariably seeks a reward, in each one of us there is a psychological demand for gratification, and the result is that all action, whether political, economic, or social, leads to endless controversy and ultimately to violence. There is no clarity of perception because fundamentally we are not concerned with the means but only with the result, with the goal, with the end; and we do not see that the end and the means are not separate, that they are one. The end is in the means, and if psychologically we seek a result independent of the means, physical action must inevitably produce confusion. That is, when we use the result as a means of inward or psychological security, our working for that result has a conditioning effect on the mind, and this process can be understood fully only when we see the significance of action.

At present, we know action only in terms of achieving a result, a goal. We work towards a goal, in the psychological as well as the physical sense. To us, action is a process of achieving something, not of understanding action itself—which alone will produce the right means, and hence the right end, without the search for a result; and the understanding of action is surely the understanding of the whole process of our thinking. That is why it is so essential to have complete understanding of the total process of one's consciousness—the ways of one's own thought, feeling, and action. Without understanding oneself, merely to achieve a result will only lead to further confusion, misery, and frustration.

To understand the whole process of oneself requires constant alertness, awareness, in the action of relationship. There must be a constant watching of every incident, without choice, without condemnation or acceptance, with a certain sense of dispassion, so that the truth of every incident is revealed. But this self-knowledge is not a result, an end. There is no end to self-knowledge; it is a constant process of understanding which comes about only when one begins objectively and goes deeper and deeper into the whole problem of daily living—which is the 'you' and the 'me' in relationship.

I have several questions, and in considering them, do not let us seek an answer because merely to find an answer is to put an end to further discovery and understanding. But if we can follow the problem as it is revealed step by step, then perhaps we shall be able to see the truth of it; and it is the truth of the problem that will free us from the problem itself.

Question: Though you tell us it is necessary for the mind to become still if we are to experience reality, yet you do everything in your power to stimulate us to think.

KRISHNAMURTI: Am I stimulating you to think? If it is mere stimulation, then weariness will come out of it because every form of stimulation soon comes to an end, leaving the mind dull, unelastic, and weary. If these talks and discussions have become merely a means of stimulation, then I am afraid you will find, when they are over, that you will fall back into your dreary ruts, your old beliefs, your insensitive attitudes and ways of thinking. But if, instead of being a stimulation, they are a process in which you and I examine facts and see them exactly as they are—which is the beginning of the perception of what is true—then these talks and discussions will obviously have been worthwhile. Surely, it is edifying to see things as they are, for then it will bring about a fundamental transformation. Therefore, we are not seeking stimulation but are exploring together all our human problems. Stimulation makes you think along a particular line, it is a process of substitution, which conditions you in a new direction; whereas only when we are trying to see things as they are, very clearly, without bias, without distortion, is it possible for the mind to be quiet. The mind cannot be quiet, cannot be calm or still, when there is any distortion, when it is capable of creating illusion. And as the mind is infinitely capable of creating illusion, to be aware of the power to create illusion, which is to be aware of desire, is surely not stimulation. On the contrary, there is freedom from stimulation only when there is awareness of how the mind works, how it manipulates, connives, distorts; and that freedom alone can bring about tranquillity of mind.

Now, the mind can enclose itself in a particular belief or illusion and thereby think it is tranquil, but such a mind is obviously not tranquil—it is dead, unpliable, insensitive. The mind is tranquil only when it is infinitely pliable, capable of adjusting, of seeing things as they are; and it is only when the mind is capable of seeing things as they are that there is a freedom from that which it has seen. Surely, we must go through all this process of uncovering, exploring, before the mind can be still. Without tranquillity of the mind, obviously there can be no true perception; and to discover what are the distorting factors, the distractions which the mind has cultivated, is not a stimulation. If it is a stimulation, the mind will never be tranquil because it will go from one stimulation to another, and a mind that seeks stimulation is a dull and insufficient mind, incapable of perceiving anything but its own sensations.

So, what is important is not to depend on any stimulation, either of a ritual, of an idea, or of drink. All stimulations are on the same level, for stimulation of any kind makes the mind dull and weary; but to see the fact that the mind depends upon stimulation, is to be free of that fact. Perceiving things without distortion brings about the tranquillity of mind which is so essential for reality to be.

Question: I worry a great deal. Can you tell me how I can be free from worry?

KRISHNAMURTI: Why do you want to be free from worry? You mean you want to be free from a particular worry, from a certain kind of disturbance, but you do not want to be free from all worry, do you? Most of us want to be occupied, and we only know we exist because we are occupied. We say that occupation is necessary for the mind—whether it is occupation with God, with self-fulfillment, with a car, with a family, with success, with virtue, or what you will. Surely, the mind demands to be occupied; otherwise, we would be lost, and this very occupation is worry, is it not? What would happen if you did not worry, if the mind were not occupied with something? Would you not feel utterly lost? If you have no occupation, you will find one. If you do not worry about society, you will worry about God and be occupied with that; or you will worry about the war, about the newspapers, the radio, about what people say or do not say. The mind is constantly occupied—its very existence depends on its occupation. So, for most of us, occupation, which is a form of worry, is essential. If we did not worry, if we were not occupied, we would feel utterly at a loss, we would say there is nothing to do, that life is vain, empty; so, the mind occupies itself and keeps worrying.

For most of us, occupation is an escape from our own essential insufficiency. Being insufficient, we worry over something as a means of escape from that which is. So, the question is not how to be free from a particular worry but to understand the whole problem of occupation—which involves right means of livelihood in one direction, and the psychological occupation of the mind in another. Most of us find that the mind cannot be without thought, without occupation, without worry. Most of us are afraid to be what we are—beautiful or ugly, intelligent or stupid, or whatever it may be—and proceed from there. The mind is afraid to be what it is, and so it seeks an escape, the higher-sounding, the better. This escape from *what is* may be called reality or God, but it is merely a self-enclosing isolation; and the more isolated one is, the more one worries, the more one must be occupied.

Surely, then, freedom from worry is not the problem. The problem is to find out why the mind demands occupation, and if we go into it rather carefully, we will discover that the mind is afraid of being as nothing. Surely, a cup is useful only when it is empty, and the mind is creative only when it is capable of emptying itself, being purged of its whole content. It is only when the mind is empty, silent, that it is creative. But to come to that point, one must understand the total process of the mind, how it is constantly occupied, worrying about a virtue, about death, about success. At however high a level, worry is still worry, and a worrying, agitated mind can never understand any problem. It can only go around in circles, hoping to find a way out—and that is what it does. A mind that is constantly occupied is seeking a result, an end, a goal, and to such a mind, the means is not important at all.

So, the important thing is not how to free oneself from worry but to find out why the mind is so occupied, so desirous of holding on to and identifying itself with a particular idea, belief, or concept. Surely, it does this because of its own insufficiency. Without understanding its own insufficiency, without going into it deeply, the mind tries to run away from it through occupation; and the more you run, the more you worry. The only way out of this process is to come back and look at insufficiency.

Question: I love my son. He may be killed in the war. What am I to do?

KRISHNAMURTI: I wonder if you do love your son? If you really loved your son, would there be war? Would you not prevent war in any form if you really loved your son? Would you not bring about right education—an education which would not be identified with either the Orient or the Occident? If you really loved your son, would you not see to it that no belief divided human beings, that no national frontier stood between man and man?

I am afraid we do not love our children. "I love my son" is merely the accepted phrase. If we loved our sons, there would be a fundamental revolution in education, would there not? Because, at the present time, we are merely cultivating technique, efficiency, and the higher the efficiency, the greater the ruthlessness. The more nationalistic and separative we are, the faster society disintegrates. We are torn apart by our beliefs, by our ideologies, by our religions and dogmas; and inevitably there is conflict, not only between different societies, but between groups in the same society.

So, although we may say that we love our children, we are obviously not deeply concerned about them as long as we are nationalistic, as long as we cling to our property, as long as we are bound, conditioned by our religious beliefs. These are the disintegrating factors in society, leading inevitably to war and utter misery, and if we are really desirous of saving the children, it is for us as individuals to bring about a fundamental transformation in ourselves. This means, does it not, that we have to revalue the whole structure of society. That is a very complex and arduous business, and so we leave it to the experts—religious, economic, and political. But the expert cannot understand that which is beyond his particular specialization. The specialist is never an integrated person, and integration is the only solution to our problem. There must be a total integration of ourselves as individuals, and only then can we educate the child to be an integrated human being; and there obviously cannot be integration as long as there are racial, national, political, and religious prejudices. Until we alter all that in ourselves fundamentally, we are bound to have war—and whatever you may say about loving your son is not going to stop it. What will stop war is the profound realization that one must oneself be free of those disintegrating factors which create war. It is only then that we will put an end to war. But unfortunately, most of us are not interested in all this. We want an immediate result, an immediate answer.

War, after all, is the spectacular and bloody projection of our daily lives, and without altering the fundamental structure of our own existence, we hope that by some miracle, wars will come to an end. Or, we blame some other society, we say some other national group is responsible for wars. It is our responsibility, not that of someone else; and those who are really serious about this thing, who are not seeking an easy explanation, will know how to act, taking into consideration this whole structure of the causation of war.

So, if we do love our children, then the structure of society will be fundamentally altered, and the more we love, the deeper will be our influence on society. Therefore, it is important to understand the whole process of oneself, and no expert, no general, no teacher can give us the key to that understanding. Self-knowledge is the outcome of our own intensity, our own clarity, our own awareness in relationship; and relationship is not only with people but also with property and with ideas.

Question: How am I to overcome loneliness?

KRISHNAMURTI: Can you overcome loneliness? Whatever you conquer has to be conquered again and again, does it not? What you understand comes to an end, but that which you conquer can never come to an end. The battling process only feeds and strengthens that with which you fight.

Now, what is this loneliness of which most of us are aware? We know it, and we run away from it, do we not? We take flight from it into every form of activity. We are empty, lonely, and we are afraid of it, so we try to cover it up by some means or other—meditation, the search for God, social activity, the radio, drink, or what you will—we would do anything else rather than face it, be with it, understand it. Running away is the same, whether we do it through the idea of God or through drink. As long as one is escaping from loneliness, there is no essential difference between the worship of God and addiction to alcohol. Socially there may be a difference, but psychologically, the man who runs away from himself, from his own emptiness, whose escape is his search for God, is on the same level with the drunkard.

What is important, then, is not to overcome loneliness but to understand it, and we cannot understand it if we do not face it, if we do not look at it directly, if we are continually running away from it. And our whole life is a process of running away from loneliness, is it not? In relationship, we use others to cover up loneliness; our pursuit of knowledge, our gathering of experience, everything we do, is a distraction, an escape from that emptiness. So, these distractions and escapes must obviously come to an end. If we are to understand something, we must give our full attention to it, must we not? And how can we give full attention to loneliness if we are afraid of it, if we are running away from it through some distraction? So, when we really want to understand loneliness, when our intention is to go fully, completely into it, because we see that there can be no creativeness as long as we do not understand that inward insufficiency which is the fundamental cause of fear—when we come to that point, then every form of distraction ends, does it not? Many people laugh at loneliness and say, "Oh, that is only for the bourgeois; for God's sake, be occupied with something and forget it." But emptiness cannot be forgotten, it cannot be put aside.

So, if one would really understand this fundamental thing which we call loneliness, all escape must cease; but escape does not cease through worry, through seeking a result, or through any action of desire. One must see that without understanding loneliness, every form of action is a distraction, an escape, a process of self-isolation, which only creates more conflict, more misery. To see that fact is essential, for only then can one face loneliness.

Then, if we go still more deeply into it, the problem arises of whether that which we call loneliness is an actuality or merely a word. Is loneliness an actuality or merely a word which covers something that may not be what we think it is? Is not loneliness a thought, the result of thinking? That is, thinking is verbalization based on memory, and do we not, with that verbalization, with that thought, with that memory, look at the state which we call "lonely"? So, the very giving of a name to that state may be the cause of the fear which prevents us from looking at it more closely; and if we do not give it a name, which is fabricated by the mind, then is that state lonely?

Surely, there is a difference between loneliness and being alone. Loneliness is the ultimate in the process of self-isolation. The more you are conscious of yourself, the more isolated you are, and self-consciousness is the process of isolation. But aloneness is not isolation. There is aloneness only when loneliness has come to an end. Aloneness is a state in which all influence has completely ceased, both the influence from outside and the inner influence of memory; and only when the mind is in that state of aloneness can it know the incorruptible. But to come to that, we must understand loneliness, this process of isolation, which is the self and its activity. So, the understanding of the self is the beginning of the cessation of isolation, and therefore of loneliness.

Question: Is there continuity after death?

KRISHNAMURTI: In this question several things are implied. There is the idea of immortality, which we think is continuity, the question of what we mean by death, and whether there is a spiritual essence in each one of us that will continue in spite of death. So, let us examine this question, however briefly.

You ask if there is continuity after death. Now, what do we mean by "continuity"? Continuity obviously implies cause and effect—a series of incidents or causes which are remembered and which continue. Please, if I may suggest, let us listen very carefully and think it out together, and perhaps we shall see something much greater than the mere desire to continue after death.

Most of us want to continue. To us, life is a series of incidents tied together by memory. We have experiences which are continually accumulated, as the memories of childhood, of pleasant things, and the unpleasant memories are also there, although hidden. This whole process of cause and effect gives a sense of continuity which is the 'me.' The 'me', the self, is a chain of remembered incidents—whether they are pleasant or unpleasant is not important. My house, my family, my experience, my cultivation of virtue, and so on—all that is the 'me'; and you want to know if that 'me' continues after death.

Now, it is obvious that some kind of thought continuity must exist, but we are not satisfied with that, are we? We want immortality, and we say that this process of continuity will eventually lead us to immortality. But will continuity ever lead us to immortality? What is it that continues? It is memory, is it not? It is a bundle of memories moving from the past through the present to the future. And can that which continues ever be free from the net of time?

Surely, only that which comes to an end can renew—not that which has continuity. That which has continuity can only continue in its own state; it can be modified, altered, but it is essentially the same all along. Only for that which comes to an end is there a possibility of fundamental transformation. So, immortality is not continuity. Immortality is that state in which time, as continuity of the 'me', has ceased.

Is there a spiritual essence in each one of us that will continue? What is spiritual essence? If there is a spiritual essence, it must obviously be beyond the field of time, beyond causation; and if the mind can think about it, or if it has already conceived it, it is obviously the product of thought, and so within the field of time, and therefore it is not a spiritual essence. We like to think that there is a spiritual essence, but it is merely an idea, the product of thought, of our conditioning. When the mind clings to the idea of a spiritual essence, it indicates, does it not, that we are seeking security, certainty; and it is the perpetuation of comfort, of security, that we call immortality. As long as the mind continues in the sense of moving from the known to the known, there is always the fear of death.

Now, surely, there is another way of living, which is to die each day to the things of yesterday and not to carry over to tomorrow the things of today. If in living we can die to the things the mind clings to, then in that very dying we shall find that there is a life which is not of memory, which is not of time. To die in that sense is to understand this whole process of accumulation, which creates the fear of losing, which is the cause of the desire to immortalize the 'me' through family, through property, or through continuity in the hereafter. If we can be aware of how the mind is constantly seeking certainty, a state in which there can never be freedom, if we can cease to accumulate inwardly and not be psychologically concerned about the morrow, which means coming to an end each day—if we can do this, then there is immortality, that state in which time is not.

August 6, 1950

Fifth Talk in Seattle

Most of us are very easily satisfied with explanations, theories, and words, and our superficial interest will obviously never bring about a fundamental revolution. What is necessary, surely, at the present time and at all times, is to have a radical transformation in oneself, and this transformation affects not only our personal relationships, but also our relationship to society. Without this deep inner revolution, there can be no lasting happiness, no final solution to any of our problems. It is almost impossible for those who are only superficially interested to go into these matters deeply and understand the whole process of themselves, and only those who are really in earnest can bring about this revolution. This inner revolution is not the search for new explanations, new words, new slogans; it comes only with the freedom from all sense of acquisitiveness.

Now, we are not only acquisitive on the physical plane, where we have built our whole social structure on acquisitiveness, but also in our relationships. That is, in our relationship with one another there is a sense of possessiveness, which is merely an outward indication of deep frustration, loneliness, and so on. We are acquisitive also in the matter of knowledge. We think that acquiring more and more knowledge, more and more explanations, wider and wider information, will in some miraculous way solve our problems. Acquisitiveness at any level only binds the mind, shapes it according to a particular pattern, and a pattern can obviously never produce revolution. Any form of acquisitiveness—whether in the pursuit of worldly things, in relationship, in learning, in experience, or in the desire to find reality—will always create conflict, will always bring about misunderstanding, a series of battles, inward as well as outward. And where there is conflict, there can obviously be no understanding.

It is acquisitiveness that prevents us from living clearly, simply, and directly; and until there is a fundamental revolution in each one, obviously no real social improvement is possible. That is why it is so important to understand the whole process of oneself. The ways of the self can be discovered only in relationship to things, to people, and to ideas; and in the mirror of that relationship we begin to see ourselves as we are. But to understand the process of oneself, there can be no condemnation or justification of one's own reactions. Our difficulty is, is it not, that most of us are continually seeking subtle forms of isolation. Because we have conflict in our relationships, we gradually withdraw, inwardly as well as outwardly, into isolation; and without understanding relationships at all levels, not only with people, but also with ideas and things, it is impossible to go deeply into the problem of reality.

Reality is not something abstract or theoretical—it has nothing to do with philosophy; reality is in the understanding of relationship, in being aware at every moment of our speech, of our conduct, of the way we treat people, the way we consider others; for behavior is righteousness, and in that there is reality. Without understanding relationship, it is impossible to go beyond conflict. To go beyond conflict without that understanding is merely a means of escape, and where there is escape, there is the power to create illusion. Most of us have that power to create illusion extraordinarily developed because we have not understood relationship. It is only in the understanding of relationship, which is to comprehend the total process of oneself fundamentally and deeply, that there is freedom; and only in freedom can there be the discovery of what is real.

The mind can never find reality by searching for it. All that the mind can do is to be quiet, to be tranquil, and then reality comes into being. Reality must come to us; we cannot go after reality. If you seek God, you will never find God because your search is merely a desire to escape from the realities of life. Without understanding the realities of life, every conflict, every movement of thought, the inward workings of the mind, both subtle and obvious, the hidden as well as the open—without understanding all that, merely to seek reality is only an evasion; and the mind is infinitely capable of producing illusory concepts of reality. So, as long as the mind is not understood, as long as the whole process of the self, of the 'me', which is the center of acquisitiveness, is not fully comprehended, there can be no cessation of conflict, and therefore no happiness, no virtue.

Virtue is not an end. Virtue brings freedom; therefore, virtue is essential. Virtue, which is freedom, lies in the understanding of conduct, of our relationship to things, to nature, to people, and to ideas. Surely, then, it is important to know our own thinking and feeling, to be aware of all our actions without any sense of condemnation or justification. To see in the mirror of our relationship exactly what is taking place, there must be choiceless awareness; and in the very perception of *what is,* there is freedom from *what is.* But to perceive clearly exactly what is taking place is most difficult and arduous because we have so many prejudices, so many subtle forms of condemnation and justification, and these prevent fundamental understanding. It is these subtle conditionings of the mind that hinder the further understanding of relationship, of the complex problem of life; and without that understanding, however earnest one may be in search of what is called reality, such a search inevitably becomes an evasion, an escape. In escape there are all kinds of illusions, all kinds of myths, and the more we acquire and cling to these myths, the greater will be the difficulty of liberation.

So, what is important is to understand the whole process of the self, of the 'me', for without that understanding, there is no possibility of a new and fundamental action. If one would understand society and bring about a fundamental revolution in the social structure, one must obviously begin with oneself because we are not different from society. What we are, society is. We have made society from ourselves, from our reactions, from our responses, and without understanding our responses, there is no possibility of a radical change in society.

I have several questions, and I shall try to answer them as briefly as possible, but the solution to any problem does not lie in the answer. The answer is never important; what is important is the understanding of the problem. If we approach the problem merely with a desire to find an answer, we shall not be in a position to understand the problem itself. Most of us are eager to find an answer, a solution, eager to solve the problem, and this very eagerness prevents the full observation and clear understanding of the problem. Whatever the problem may be, as long as we seek an answer away from the problem, the problem cannot give its whole significance. Most of us have problems in our life, and to carry a problem on from day to day exhausts the mind. Conflict can never solve any problem. What brings about the solution of a problem is to study it, to observe it, for only then can it reveal its full significance. But that is arduous, and we are always so anxious to go beyond the problem that we are incapable of living with it, of allowing it to unfold, to give its perfume. Surely, the problem comes to an end only when it is understood completely.

Question: I want to help people. What is the best way?

KRISHNAMURTI: I wonder why you want to help people? Is it because you love people? And if you love, will you ask what is the best way to help? There are different ways of "helping" people, are there not? The market helps people; the doctor, the lawyer, the scientist, the laborer, the priest—they are all "helping" people, are they not? The desire to serve people has become a profession, and this desire always has a reward attached to it. Service organizes itself into efficient groups, and each group is in contention with the other. All desire to serve, to help, and all are in competition with each other, becoming more and more efficient, therefore, more and more ruthless.

So, when you say you want to "help" people, what do you mean by that word? How can you help people? At what level do you want to help people? Is it at the economic level, or at the so-called spiritual or psychological level? Some are content to help people merely at the economic level, at the immediate social level. Their concern, therefore, is to bring about social reformation. But mere reform creates the need for further reform, and there is no end to reformation. And there are those who want to help people psychologically or spiritually. But to help another in the psychological or spiritual sense, must you not understand yourself first? It is so easy to say, "I can help another," to have the desire, the wish, the longing to help; but in the very process of helping, you may bring about confusion.

So, if you would help others at any level, is it not important to see that there must be, not mere patchwork reform, but a fundamental revolution? And can fundamental revolution be based on an idea? Is revolution ever a revolution when it is born of thought? Because, ideas are always limited, they are conditioned responses, are they not? Thought is always the response of memory; therefore, it is always conditioned, and any revolution based on an idea can never be a fundamental transformation. The more there are revolutions based on ideas, the more separation and disintegration there will be because ideas, beliefs, and dogmas always separate people; they can never bring people together, except in mutually exclusive and conflicting groups. They are a most disastrous foundation on which to build a society because they inevitably create enmity.

Now, seeing all that, if you really want to bring about a fundamental revolution in the structure of society, surely you must begin on the psychological level, that is, with yourself. And if you really bring about in yourself a fundamental transformation, then you will be able to help others not to create illusions, not to create more dogmas, more beliefs, more cages for people to be caught in. Then your desire to help another will not be born of any conviction, of any calculation, of any belief. You will help people because you love them, because your heart is full. But your heart can never be full if it is the mind that fills the heart, and most of us have our hearts filled with the things of the mind. It is only when our hearts are filled with the things of the mind that we want to know how to help, but when the heart is empty of the things of the mind and is therefore full, then there is a possibility of helping. When one really loves, one helps. But love is not a thing of the mind. Love is not sensation. You cannot think about love. If you think about love, you are only thinking about sensation, which is not love. When you say, "I love somebody," you are not thinking about love but about the sensation, the image, the picture of that person.

So, thought is not love. Love is something that cannot be captured by the mind. The mind can only capture sensation, and then it is sensation that fills our hearts; and from that sensation there comes the desire to help people through making them better, through reforming them, and so on and on. As long as our hearts are filled with the things of the mind, there is no love; and when there is love, there is no question of how to help people. The very action of love, without the interference of the mind, helps people; but as long as the mind interferes, there can be no love.

Question: My life seems to be aimless, and as a result my behavior is unintelligent. Should I not have an overall purpose?

KRISHNAMURTI: How will you discover an overall purpose? And why do you want a purpose? Can you discover a purpose that will cover the whole significance of existence? And what is the instrument that discovers? Most of us want a purpose, for then we can use it as a guide, and according to our purpose we can build; in its shadow we can live securely, purposefully, with a sense of direction. Without an end, a goal, a purpose, most of us are lost, and our action becomes unintelligent, as the questioner says.

Now, can you find an overall purpose? How will you set about to find it? Who is the entity that will find it? Surely, it is your own mind, your own desire and longing; so, your own desire will shape the end, will it not? That is, your own desire creates the end or the purpose. To put it differently, you are confused, and your actions are therefore unintelligent. Out of this confusion, you want to choose an end, an overall purpose. But can you choose anything when you are confused? And will whatever you choose not also be confused? Surely, it is important to clarify the confusion, and not choose a purpose out of that confusion. There is the purgation of confusion only when you begin to understand every act of that confusion; and in that very process you will discover a clarity which is its own end.

Most of us are confused, struggling, uncertain, we do not know what to do. We have created society and are subject to all of its influences, its demands, its wars, its utter confusion, misery, and destruction. We are part of all that; and if, in that state, we make a choice, whatever we choose will obviously still be confused. And that is what is happening in the world, is it not? Being confused, we choose a leader, and therefore the leader is also confused. But if we can patiently understand our own confusion, going deeper and deeper, ever more widely and extensively, into all the layers of consciousness, then we will see that out of that understanding there comes a clarity; and that clarity brings about a spontaneous behavior which is not chosen by will or guided by any particular pattern.

So, what is essential is not to have a purpose, but to understand oneself. That is, one must begin to see the deep inward source of conflict, misery, pain, uncertainty; and in the very process of that understanding, there comes a direct action which is not in the shadow of a determined end.

Question: What objective proof is there of the experiencing of reality? In the search for reality, is not self-confidence necessary?

KRISHNAMURTI: Surely, there are two kinds of self-confidence, are there not? There is the self-confidence which comes through having a particular faculty, through experience, through repetition or practice, through gain. That is, the more you acquire at any level, the greater the self-confidence. Such confidence only breeds arrogance, defensive attitudes, and enmity, within and without, because it is essentially based on the expansion of the self. The more you possess, the more you acquire, the more you experience, the greater the strength of the self, of the 'me'; and that obviously breeds a certain kind of self-assurance. But surely, such self-confidence is a form of resistance, is it not? It only strengthens the process of isolation, ultimately leading to illusions, to misery.

Now, I think there is a different kind of confidence, which is not based on accumulation. It is the confidence that comes through experimentation, through being sensitive, alert, through continual discovery and understanding of every response, every idea, every movement of thought. That is quite a different kind of confidence, is it not? Because, in that confidence, there is no question of an accumulating center. The moment you have an accumulating center, there can be no rapid adjustment, swift sensitivity, nor the immediate perception that understands fully and extensively every movement of thought and feeling. It is the confidence born of understanding that is essential—not the self-assurance which breeds arrogance; and that confidence comes only when there is constant watchfulness without accumulation. How can you be sensitive when you are accumulating? The person who is accumulating is shrewd and watchful to save himself and his accumulation, but surely that is not sensitivity. The confidence of sensitivity, which is essential, comes into being only when there is no sense of accumulation, when there is no center which is always gathering, which is always craving for more.

The other part of this question is, "What objective proof is there of the experiencing of reality?" What do you mean by objective proof? A demonstration? An argument capable of convincing another? A system of philosophy, carefully devised and sharply defined, so that others can see it? Do you want the authority of another to support your own experience? Is truth, reality, something to be proved, either to another or to yourself? As long as we want proof, which means that we want to be made certain in our own experience, whatever we experience is not truth. Most of us want assurance, we want to be assured that we are experiencing what we call truth. We want to be sure that we are not caught in the net of illusion, of myths, and so on, and that what we experience is real. We want not only objective proof but also subjective proof.

Now, as long as the mind clings to any form of experience, it is bound to be caught in illusion because then it is the residue or memory of the experience that becomes all-significant to the mind. What is remembered is the sensation of the experience. If the sensation is painful, it is avoided; if pleasurable, it is retained. So, as long as the mind clings to any so-called spiritual experience, living around the sensation of it and building that into its own existence, it is bound to be caught in the net of illusion.

Reality is not cumulative, it is not to be gathered, it does not give you any assurance, any gratification. It comes when the mind is quiet, tranquil, not demanding, and it is to be understood from moment to moment. And there is no accumulation, no urge for more, as a result of that experience. The moment you want an assurance of the truth of your experience, you may be sure that the experience is an illusion. A mind that craves to be certain, that seeks certainty as an end, is conditioning itself, and therefore, whatever experience it has will only further condition it, bringing about more struggle and misery.

You may have an experience, and because it is pleasurable, you cling to it; the mind goes back to that pleasure over and over again. So, the past becomes extraordinarily significant, and your memories of it then prevent the experiencing of the new. There is a possibility of experiencing the new only when the mind is not anchored to any particular pleasure or experience.

So, there is no proof of reality, objective or subjective; but what is important is the conduct of life, for behavior is not different from righteousness. Merely to seek proof of subjective experience in no way transforms the conduct of life. On the contrary, it prevents righteous behavior because the past experience then becomes all-important and the mind is made incapable of understanding its own responses in the present. Do not let us be caught in proof and disproof, in assertions and denials, but let us understand confusion, struggle, misery, illwill, enmity, greed, and ambition. When the mind is free from all that, from all the worldly things which it creates and clings to, then there is a real possibility of stillness; and in that stillness, in that tranquillity, reality comes into being. But to ask for proof of reality is to ask the impossible; because, if you want assurance, you do not want truth. For truth or reality to be, the state of uncertainty is essential because only then is there no accumulation, no center around which the mind can dwell.

What is important, then, is not to seek proof of reality, but to look to one's conduct in everyday life, to be choicelessly aware of what we do, what we think, what we say. In the freedom of that understanding, the mind is quiet, not demanding, not projecting—and in that stillness, there is the real.

Question: My thoughts wander to such an extent that I find meditation extremely difficult. Is not concentration necessary for meditation?

KRISHNAMURTI: This is a very complex question, and to understand it fully, I am afraid we will have to go rather deeply into the problem. Meditation of the right kind is essential, but very few people know the full significance of meditation. They may learn a few tricks from some oriental teacher or from their own priest, but that is not meditation. Meditation is something which has no result, nor is meditation the search for a result. We will find out what is right meditation only if we can understand the process of thinking. The questioner wants to know how to concentrate because his thoughts wander.

Now, why do our thoughts wander? Have you ever watched your mind in action? It is always going off, it is always being distracted—at least, that is what we call it. Distracted from what? Distracted from a central thought, a thought which you have chosen and upon which you want to dwell. Please follow this, if you will, and you will see what is right meditation. Without right meditation, self-knowledge is not possible, and without self-knowledge, do what you will, there can be no right thinking. So, meditation is fundamentally necessary. But we must understand what meditation is, so I hope you will follow it patiently.

When we want to focus our attention on a particular thought, the mind wanders off repeatedly, and there is a constant struggle to keep it focused; and the wandering off we call distraction. Now, there are several things involved in this process. First, you choose a central thought upon which you wish to dwell, and as that choice is made out of confusion, there is resistance against other thoughts. That is, as long as you have a chosen central thought upon which you wish to dwell, every other thought is a distraction, and it is important to discover why you choose that central thought. Surely, you have chosen it from among many thoughts because it gives you pleasure or it promises you a reward, a comfort. That is why you wish to dwell on it. But the very desire to dwell on it creates resistance against the other thoughts which come pouring in, and so you keep up the battle, the constant fight between the central thought and the other thoughts. And if ultimately you can conquer all other thoughts and make them one, you think you know how to meditate. Surely, that is really quite immature.

So, it is futile to say, "This is the right thought, and all the rest are distractions." What is important is to find out why the mind wanders. Why does it wander? It wanders because it is interested in all the things that are going on. It has some vested interest in every thought that comes back; otherwise, it would not come back. Every thought has some significance, some value, some hidden meaning, and so, like weeds, they keep coming.

Now, if you can understand each thought and not resist it, not push it away, if you can look at each thought as it arises and uncover its meaning, then you will see that those thoughts never come back—they are finished. Only thoughts that are not fully understood are repetitive. So, the important thing is not the controlling of thought but the understanding of thought. Anybody can learn to control thought, but that is not understanding. In merely controlling thought there is no flexibility; it is only a form of resistance. All disciplining of thought to a particular pattern creates resistance, and how can you understand through resistance?

The questioner asks, "Is not concentration necessary for meditation?" What do we mean by concentration? By concentration we mean exclusion, do we not? To concentrate is to exclude every thought but one. Therefore, with most of us, concentration is a narrowing-down process; and a mind that is narrowed down, limited, disciplined, controlled, shaped, according to its own desires and the influences of its environment, can obviously never be free. So, concentration, as most people practice it in what they call meditation, is a form of exclusion, and therefore a process of self-isolation. This isolation is self-protection, and a mind that is protecting itself must inevitably be in a state of fear. And how can a mind which is fearful ever be open to that which is real?

If you examine and understand the significance of every thought, you will inevitably and naturally come to the question of whether the thinker is separate from thought. If the thinker is separate from thought, then the thinker can operate upon thought, can control and shape thought. But is the thinker separate from thought? Does not the thinker come into being because of his thought? Surely, the two are not separate; the thinker, the experiencer, is not separate from what is experienced.

Now, the moment you see that there is no thinker separate from thought, that there is only thought, then all choice is removed, is it not? That is, if there is only thought and not the translation of thought, then there is no entity that says, "I will choose this thought and reject the others"; there is no translator, no interpreter, no judge, no bearer of the club. Then you will see that there is no conflict between the thinker and the thought, and therefore the mind is no longer chattering, no longer caught in the word *distraction.* Then every movement of thought becomes a significant one. And if you go still deeper, you will find that the mind becomes very quiet. It is no longer made quiet, it is no longer disciplined to be quiet.

A mind which is made quiet by discipline is a dull mind; it lives in its formula of discipline, and such a mind is not sensitive, free. It lives only in the known—it is not an open mind; therefore, it is incapable of receiving the unknown, the imponderable. A mind that is disciplined can never be extensive; it is a limited mind, and whatever it does, is bound to be always petty. God is made petty by a petty mind. So, when the mind sees that whatever it does to control its own thought only makes it more narrow, limited, conditioned, then the thought process as we know it comes to an end because the thinker is no longer fighting with his thoughts. Then the mind becomes quiet, still, without any contradiction, and in that stillness, there are wider and deeper states. But if you merely pursue the deeper, it becomes imagination, speculation. Imagination and speculation must cease for reality to be.

So, this whole process of understanding oneself is the beginning of meditation. There is no technique, no special posture, no acquired method of breathing, nor any of the tricks that one learns from books or from others. Self-knowledge is the beginning of meditation. Without knowing yourself, whatever you think has no reality, no basis. But to know yourself, there must be constant watchfulness—not with a stick, not with condemnation or justification, but just awareness, a passive alertness, in which you see things as they are. In seeing things as they are, you understand yourself, which leads to perfect tranquillity of mind; and only in that tranquillity, that stillness of the heart and mind, can reality be.

August 13, 1950

Madras, India, 1952

First Talk in Madras

I have to make one or two announcements. These meetings on every Saturday and Sunday will go on until the 10th of February, and there will be discussions every Wednesday at 5:30 P.M., the same time as usual.

I think most of us are aware of the extraordinarily complex and vast problems that surround each one of us. There is so much contradiction among the experts—political, social, and religious. There are those who assert constantly that only a certain system must be valid. Religiously, there is a contradiction of belief. It seems to me that if you want to solve any of these problems, you must all think anew and not rely on any one source, on any authority; and that seems most extraordinarily difficult for most of us. Either we turn to the past as a source of information or for purpose of imitation, or rely on some future promise—economic, political, or religious. Either we turn back to the past as a means of solace by asserting that religious conformity is essential, or we rely on the economic authority of revolution and future promise of the ideal state. Until we very carefully and intelligently think out the problems for ourselves, I do not think there is any way of dissolving any of these confusing and contradictory problems.

What I propose to do during these discussions is to think out with each one of you this extraordinarily complex problem of living. You know this problem is not confined to a narrow area. All over the world it is the same. We are confused; we do not know what to do, and we do not know how to set about it or to discover why each group is fighting the other. Ambition, corruption, in the name of peace and other ideals, are rampant throughout the world, not only parochially but all-extensively. Now if we want to really solve this problem, we have to think it out ourselves. We have to find the right answer. I believe there is an answer, and I am completely convinced there is an answer. But the mere discovery of the answer is not a solution. So what you and I have to do is to find out, which means you and I have to listen to each other to find out the right answer. Listening is an extraordinarily difficult art. That is because most of us are incapable of listening because we have so much knowledge, so much information; we have read so much; our prejudices are so strong; our experiences are like the walls that surround us—and through these prejudices, looking over these walls, we try to listen. Can we listen to anything if our mind, at least temporarily, is not free of the prejudices and is not always referring to some knowledge which we have all translated and interpreted? That is one of the greatest difficulties, is it not?

Though we appear to be incapable of listening, it seems to me that it is one of the most necessary and essential things that we have to do, you and I have to do. You should not translate what I am saying, or interpret what I am saying, or understand it according to your background; because when you do that, you stop all thinking, don't you? If you say, "That conforms to my understanding," you have stopped thinking, you have stopped listening; you do not open the door to see greater visions, greater depths of those words. To listen without interpretation requires extraordinary alertness of mind. Please try during these discussions and at home to really listen to each other without interpretation, just to listen without translating according to your prejudices. After all, translations mean that you have previous knowledge which confines thought, prevents it from penetrating further and deeper. So it is essential that you and I should establish the right kind of relationship. I do not believe in authority of any kind, and if you treat what I am saying as authoritarian, then you stop listening. You will have to investigate and try to find out what is the answer, the right answer, what is the way out of this appalling mess of war and peace, of this contradiction between the rich and the poor, between those who are seeking authority in the name of every form of violence and peace. If we do not seek and understand the right answer, I think we have no business or responsibility of sitting and listening to each other and wasting our time. I feel very ardently that if we, even two or three of us, could sit down and go into this thoroughly, setting aside everything to find out, then there is a possibility of starting on a little scale until it becomes a roaring storm; but that requires earnestness, that requires real exchange of thought, and not mere assertion of prejudice and constancy of a particular experience.

So, how is it possible to find out the right answer? I am sure that is what most of us are trying to find out, are we not? Any thoughtful person must be seeking the right solution, the lasting and permanent solution to all this appalling suffering, misery, this contradiction between the rich and the poor, between those who are seeking authority in the name of peace, between the powerful and the downtrodden, between those who have nothing and those who have everything, between those who are seeking power. Surely, there must be an answer to all this, must there not be? How are we going to find it out? Surely, the first essential requirement to understand or to search out the answer must be the understanding that all search is conditioned by desire. Let us think about it for a while. If I seek an economic or other answer to this problem, without understanding the instrument that seeks, that very instrument is limited, confined, conditioned by the desire that is out seeking. If I am seeking the right answer, the right solution to any problem, is not the search conditioned by my desire? So before I can seek an answer, I must understand desire. Is that not so? If I want to know if there is God, if there is such a thing as absolute happiness, surely, before I can seek it, I must understand the mind that seeks it. Otherwise, the mind will condition the object of my search. That is fairly obvious, is it not? Those who seek anything will find what they seek, but what they find will depend on their desire. If you seek comfort and security, you will find them, but that will not be real; on the contrary, that will produce more and more confusion, contradiction, and misery. So, before we begin to seek, we must understand the whole process of desire. In the very search of understanding desire, you will find the answer. But to seek the answer without understanding desire, the center of recognition, is futile. Those who are really earnest, those who really want to see a peaceful world, to have peaceful relationship with each other, to be friendly and compassionate, must surely solve this problem first.

If you really consider what is happening in the world, you will see how man is dividing himself, bringing wars, confusion, and utter misery. To all this confusion, to all this increasing and expanding misery, there must be an answer; that is possible only if we understand the process of desire. Whenever we seek anything without understanding our desire, we are seeking an idea as a means of action; all our search ends in an idea—as a formulation, as a concept, or as an experience; we are seeking a conclusion, an idea, a concept. But an idea, a concept, a formulation can never produce action. I do not know if that is clear or rather abstract and confusing. To us, idea is very important—idea in the shape of experience or in the shape of a conclusion. So, when we are seeking, we are seeking an idea which we will translate afterwards into action. First, I have an idea of what I should do, and then I act. We have the pattern of what a society should be, and then we conform to that pattern. So, there is always a contradiction, a competition, a struggle between action and idea.

Is this search for an idea truly an answer, or is the search to be independent of idea and be only action? This is not very complex if you really think about it. It is really very important to understand this before you proceed further. Because our search is intellectual, there is a contradiction between idea and action, a gap, an interval; and our constant endeavor is to bridge the two together, which is surely a waste of time, stupidity, call it what you will, because we do not understand that the search depends on desire and that desire essentially breeds idea. Surely therefore, those of us who are really earnest, who are not carried away by emotional nonsense or by their own prejudices, by their own vanities, if they really want to find out a peaceful and lasting answer to this problem, have to search out and understand desire, which means action. The very understanding of desire is action, and not idea.

The moment you have an idea, what happens? Watch your own mind and see, discover what happens when you have an idea. You want to translate that idea into action, don't you? You want to put it into a picture or to do something with it, convey, translate, communicate it with somebody. Idea is never action, is it? If peace is based on an idea, then you are bound to have contradictions of how to carry it out, how to implement, and how to bring it about. But if you begin to understand the whole process of desire, then you will see that action is independent of thought, of idea. The mistake we make is that we first have the idea and then act. But if we begin to understand desire, which is a very complex and intricate problem, then you will see that action follows the understanding of each desire.

What do I mean by understanding desire? Desire is not static, is it? You cannot impose certain rules and regulations on desire if you would understand it. Would you? You have to follow it, you have to observe, you have to follow every movement of its intricate, conscious, and unconscious whims and fancies, have you not? You cannot say, "That is right desire. That is wrong desire. This is all right. This, I want to do," and so on. When you say so, you put an end to the understanding and subsequent following of that desire. This is not easy because we have been trained from childhood to repress, to control, to dominate and say, "This is right, that is wrong"; and therefore, we put an end to investigation, to search, and to all understanding. Do not begin to say immediately, "This is right desire or wrong desire." Let us find out. It is like following a path on the map. That is, if you are earnest; but if you want to be flippant about it and want to play about it in the name of peace, obviously that has no meaning. Such people have no experience. If you would really follow it out, then you see that you have a center which is always the process of recognition. There is no experience if there is no recognition. If I do not recognize, I have no experience, have I? You only say, "I have an experience" when there is a process of recognition taking place. Our difficulty is to understand desire without this process of recognition.

Do you understand what I mean by recognition? By recognition, I mean something that happens when you meet or see somebody. You then have a subjective reaction, emotion, and you recognize; you give it a name—and that recognition only strengthens each experience, and each experience limits, conditions, and narrows down the self. So, if you would understand what is reality, what is God, that center of recognition must completely end. Otherwise, what have you? The projection of your mind and memory, what you have learned from the past, with which you recognize what is happening. And what is happening is your own experience projected. If I want to know what truth is, my mind must be in a state in which no recognition can ever take place. Is that possible? Do not, please, accept any of these things if you are not convinced. Have a balanced and sane skepticism about it all. You are not my pupils or my followers. You are dignified human beings trying to find out the right answer to all this appalling misery. To find out the right answer you must be extremely sharp, doubting, questioning, being balanced with skepticism. Is it possible? Do you have an experience which is not recognized? Do you understand what it means? Because that is after all God, that is the truth, that is the eternal or what you will. The moment you have a measure with which to measure, that is not truth. Our Gods are measurable; we know them previously. Our scriptures, our friends, and our religious teachers have so conditioned us that we know what everything is. All that we are doing is merely this process of recognition.

Is it possible to dissolve the center of recognition? After all, it is the desire that gives strength to one's recognition. To say, "I know, I have had experience, it is so," indicates the strengthening of self. There is no higher self, no lower self; self is self. Now, to find out if there is God, if there is truth, if there is such a thing as a state in which recognition is not possible, in which all measurement has ceased, surely we must begin to understand desire. It is so absurd for the so-called religious people to say, "There is God," and for others to say, "There is no God." That is not solving the problem, nor is the repeating of the Bible, or the Bhagavad-Gita, or God knows what else. Surely that is not solving the problem. That is what everybody has been doing through centuries. Yet, we have not solved it. We are increasing our problems more and more, bringing greater and greater miseries upon us. So, to understand this problem of existence with all its confusion, its extraordinary trials, troubles, tribulations, and misery, surely we have to understand desire, to follow it. You can only follow it when the mind is aware of itself, when you are not looking at desire as something outside of you, when you are following it. Look here, sirs. I have a desire. What do I do? My instinctive reaction is to condemn it, to say how idiotic, how stupid it is, or to say how good, how noble it is. Then what happens? I have not really followed the desire—I have not gone into it, I have not understood it; I have put an end to it. Please think it out, and you will see the extraordinary importance of it. Then I assure you, you will have revolution, revolution of the greatest kind—because inward revolution is the only revolution, not economic revolution, because inward revolution will always conquer outward revolution, but outer revolution can never conquer inner. What is important is inward psychological revolution, regeneration; and that can only take place when we follow, understand the whole process, the complex process of psychological desire, motives, urges, conscious as well as unconscious. That is not easy. It is no use saying, "I have got it now, everything is all right, I am transformed," because to say so is only to find yourself back into the whirl of action. If we can understand how to pursue desire, how to be acquainted with it, how not to translate it, then we shall solve all these problems.

How is it possible for an ordinary person like you and me, who has got so many problems—economic, family, religious, the mess we are all in—to pursue desire to the end, to go with it, to understand it? Is that not the question? How am I, who am not intelligent, who have got so many formulations, prejudices, memories, how am I to follow desire? It would be easy if you had a companion who would stop you each time and say, "Look, what are you doing? You are interpreting, translating, condemning desire. You are not really following it. You are really putting a cap on it." If somebody could force you every instant and make you observe what you are doing, then perhaps it would be helpful. But you have no such companion; you too do not want such a companion because it is too difficult, too irritating, too disturbing. But, you will have such a companion in your own mind if you are earnest and say, "I want to understand it." Don't create any intellectual difficulty by asking, "When I say I want it, is that not a desire?" That is only a quibbling of words, that is clever argumentation and has no validity. Then you and I will not understand it because we must use words in order to convey, but if you merely put a stop at a certain point and refuse to go beyond and understand the words in their connotation, then all action ceases. Take any desire—desire to be powerful, which most of us have, desire to dominate, which most of us have; clerk or president or anybody rich or poor has the desire to be powerful. Do not condemn it; do not say, "It is right; it is wrong," but go into it; you will then see where it will lead you. You do not have to read any book. All the subconscious accumulations of desire for power through various means will be open to the conscious. There you have the book of knowledge, and if you do not know how to read it, you will never understand anything. You are following all the rubbish that has no meaning because, in your heart, in your mind, truth lies, and it is no good seeking it outside though it may be pleasing to you to do so. So we lead very complex and contradictory lives, not only individually but collectively, Brahmin against non-Brahmin and so on. They are not only parochial problems but vast problems, world problems, and you cannot solve them through merely being confined to a narrow area. We must think of this thing as a tremendous whole, not as a little person investigating a little problem.

So, that is what we are going to discuss and talk about for the next six weeks, that is, how to understand desire and how, if possible, to go beyond recognition, that center which recognizes, which cripples all creative action. Please do not come if you really are not earnest. It is very much better to have two or three who are really earnest. It is sheer waste of time on your part because I feel I have talked for so many years and with what result? Do not have any sympathy for me, please. I feel there is something in that center that can be grasped and understood; because, as you know, it is something much greater than physical or superficial existence. I would like to convey this to the two or three who are really serious and can go into it. But it is very difficult to find those two or three because we have got all kinds of people with their self-importance, their ambitions, and their refusal to see beyond themselves. So, I beg of you most earnestly not to come if you are not serious, if you are not earnest; because if you are earnest, we can go very far and understand, not eventually but immediately. And that is where there is real transformation—to see a thing very clearly and to act upon it; and that requires enormous patience, observation, and inward integrity.

Question: You have been in retreat for the past sixteen months and that, for the first time in your life. May we know if there is any significance in this?

KRISHNAMURTI: Don't you also want to go away sometimes to be quiet and take stock of things and not merely become a repetitive machine, a talker, explainer, and expounder? Don't you want to do that some time, don't you want to be quiet, don't you want to know more of yourself? Some of you wish to do it, but economically you cannot. Some of you might want to; but family responsibility and so on crowds in your way. All the same, it is good to retreat to quiet and to take stock of everything that you have done. When you do that, you acquire experiences that are not recognized, not translated. Therefore, my retreat has no significance to you. I am sorry. But your retreat, if you follow it rightly, will have significance to you. And I think it is essential sometimes to go to retreat, to stop everything that you have been doing, to stop your beliefs and experiences completely and look at them anew, not keep on repeating like machines whether you believe or do not believe. You would then let in fresh air into your minds. Wouldn't you? That means you must be insecure, must you not? If you can do so, you would be open to the mysteries of nature and to things that are whispering about us, which you would not otherwise reach; you would reach the God that is waiting to come, the truth that cannot be invited but comes itself. But we are not open to love and other finer processes that are taking place within us because we are all too enclosed by our own ambitions, by our own achievements, by our own desires. Surely it is good to retreat from all that, is it not? Stop being a member of some society. Stop being a Brahmin, a Hindu, a Christian, a Muslim. Stop your worship, rituals; take a complete retreat from all those and see what happens. In a retreat, do not plunge into something else, do not take some book and be absorbed in new knowledge and new acquisition. Have a complete break with the past and see what happens. Sirs, do it, and you will see delight. You will see vast expanses of love, understanding, and freedom. When your heart is open, then reality can come. Then the whisperings of your own prejudices, your own noises, are not heard. That is why it is good to take a retreat, to go away, and to stop the routine—not only the routine of outward existence but the routine which the mind establishes for its own safety and convenience.

Try it sirs, those who have the opportunity. Then perhaps you will know what is beyond recognition, what truth is which is not measured. Then you will find that God is not a thing to be experienced, to be recognized, but that God is something which comes to you without your invitation. But, that is only when your mind and your heart are absolutely still, not seeking, not probing, and when you have no ambitions to acquire. God can be found only when the mind is no longer seeking advancement. If we take a retreat from all that, then perhaps the whisperings of desire will cease to be heard, and the thing that is waiting will come directly and surely.

January 5, 1952

Second Talk in Madras

We were talking yesterday about the problem of desire and how to understand it. As it is a very important question, it should not be casually considered and discarded. One can put innumerable questions to find the right answer, but one must have the capacity to listen. Most of us are so eager to get an answer, to have a right response, to find the right solution, that in our eagerness we miss them all. So, as I suggested yesterday, we should have a great deal of patience, not lethargy, but alertness with patience, alert passivity. What I would like to do this evening is to talk over the problems of belief and knowledge. Belief and knowledge are very intimately related to desire, and perhaps, if we can understand these two issues, then we can see how desire works and understand its complexity.

May I suggest that you should listen and not take notes because it is very difficult to take notes and to listen. What I would like to experiment with each one of you here in all my discussions and talks is that we should see the issue directly, understand it directly, and not grope about after you have gone from here. Then you will see that these meetings are worthwhile. I feel most ardently that I am not talking to a large audience or to a small audience, but that I am talking to each individual, and I mean it. It is only the individual that can see, understand, and create a new world, that can bring about an inward revolution and therefore an external revolution also. So, you as an individual and I are discussing the problem together and are going into it as deeply as possible. To do that, you have to listen; you have to be a little receptive, be capable of exposing yourself to what is being said, and find out our own reactions as we go along. So, may I suggest that, as you listen, you should see the thing without interpretation and understand it directly.

As I said, it is really a very interesting problem, this question of belief and knowledge. What an extraordinary part it plays in our life! How many beliefs we have! Surely the more intelligent, the more cultured, the more spiritual, if I can use that word, a person is, the less is his capacity to understand. The savages have innumerable superstitions, even in the modern world. The more thoughtful, the more awake, the more alert are perhaps the less believing. That is because belief binds, belief isolates, and we see that throughout the world, the economic and the political world, and also in the so-called spiritual world. You believe there is God, and perhaps I believe that there is no God; or, you believe in the complete state control of everything and of every individual, and I believe in private enterprise and all the rest of it; you believe that there is only one savior and through him you can get your end, and I don't believe so. So, you with your belief and I with mine are asserting ourselves. Yet we both talk of love, of peace, of unity of mankind, of one life—which means absolutely nothing because actually the very belief is a process of isolation. You are a Brahmin, I a non-Brahmin; you are a Christian, I a Muslim, and so on. But you talk of brotherhood and I also talk of the same brotherhood, love, and peace. In actuality, we are separated, we are dividing ourselves. A man who would want peace and would want to create a new world, a happy world, surely cannot isolate himself through any form of belief. Is that clear? It may be verbal, but if you see the significance and validity and the truth of it, it will begin to act.

So, we see that where there is a process of desire at work, there must be the process of isolation through belief, because obviously, you believe in order to be secure economically, spiritually, and also inwardly. I am not talking of those people who believe for economic reasons because they are brought up to depend on the jobs and therefore they will be Catholics, Hindus—it does not matter what—as long as there is a job for them. We are not also discussing those people who cling to a belief for the sake of convenience. Perhaps with most of you it is equally so. For convenience, we believe in certain things. Brushing aside these economic reasons, you must go more deeply into it. Take the people who believe strongly in anything, economic, social, or spiritual; the process behind it is the psychological desire to be secure. Is it not? And then there is the desire to continue. We are not discussing here whether there is or there is not continuity; we are only discussing the urge, the constant impulse to believe. A man of peace, a man who would really understand the whole process of human existence, cannot be bound by a belief. Can he? It means he sees his desire at work as a means to become secure. Please do not go to the other side and say, "I am preaching non-religion." That is not my point at all. My point is that as long as we do not understand the process of desire in the form of belief, there must be contention, there must be conflict, there must be sorrow, and man will be against man, which is seen every day. So, if I perceive, if I am aware that this process takes the form of belief which is an expression of the craving for inward security, then my problem is not that I should believe this or that but that I should free myself from the desire to be secure. Can the mind be free from it? That is the problem, not what to believe and how much to believe. These are merely expressions of inward craving to be secure psychologically, to be certain about something when everything is so uncertain in the world.

Can a mind, can a conscious mind, can a personality be free from this desire to be secure? We want to be secure and therefore need the aid of our estates, our property, and our family. We want to be secure inwardly and also spiritually by erecting walls of belief, which are an indication of this craving to be certain. Can you as an individual be free from this urge, this craving to be secure, which expresses itself in the desire to believe in something? If we are not free of all that, we are a source of contention; we are not peacemaking; we have no love in our hearts. Belief destroys all that, and this is seen in our everyday life. So, can I see myself when I am caught in this process of desire, which expresses itself in clinging to a belief? Can the mind free itself from it? It should not find a substitute for belief but be entirely free from it. You cannot answer yes or no to this, but you can definitely give an answer if your intention is to become free from belief. You then inevitably come to the point when you are seeking the means to free yourself from the urge to be secure. Obviously, there is no security inwardly which, as you like to believe, would continue. You like to believe there is God who is carefully looking after your petty, little things—whom you should see, what you should do, and how you should do. Obviously, this is childish and immature thinking. You think the Great Father is watching every one of us. That is a mere projection of your own personal liking. It is not obviously true. Truth must be something entirely different. To find out that truth which is not a projection of our liking is our purpose in all these discussions and talks. So, if you are really earnest in your endeavor to find out what truth is, it would be obvious that a mind that is crippled, that is bound, that is trammelled by belief, cannot proceed any distance.

Our next problem is that of knowledge. Is knowledge necessary to the understanding of truth? When I say, "I know," the implication is that there is knowledge. Can such a mind be capable of investigation and search of what is reality? And besides, what is it we know, of which we are so proud? Actually what is it we know? We know information; we are full of information and experience based on our condition, our memory, and our capacities. When you say, "I know," what do you mean? Do please think it out, go along with me, don't merely listen to me. Either the acknowledgment that you know is the recognition of a fact or a certain information, or it is an experience that you have had. The constant accumulation of information, the acquisition of various forms of knowledge, information, all that, constitutes the assertion "I know"; and you start translating what you have read according to your background, your desire, your experience. Your knowledge is a thing in which a process similar to the process of desire is at work. Instead of belief we substitute knowledge. "I know, I have had experience, it cannot be refuted; my experience is that, on that I completely rely"; these are indications of that knowledge. But when you go behind it, analyze it, look at it more intelligently and carefully, you will find that the very assertion "I know" is another wall separating you and me. Behind that wall you take refuge, seeking comfort, security. Therefore, the more knowledge a mind is burdened with, the less capable it is of understanding. Obviously! Surely, sirs, the man who would seek peace, who would seek truth, must be free from all knowledge, because he that has knowledge would interpret in his own way all that he observes and experiences. Therefore, the suppression of all knowledge is essential to experience reality: suppression in the sense—not of subjugation, not enforcing it down.

It is a very interesting thing to watch how in our life these two, knowledge and belief, play an extraordinarily powerful part. Look how we worship those who have immense knowledge and erudition! Can you understand the meaning of it? Sirs, if you would find something new, experience something which is not a projection of your imagination, your mind must be free, must it not be? It must be capable of seeing something new. But unfortunately, every time you see something new, you bring all the information known to you already, all your knowledge, all your past memories; obviously you become incapable of looking, incapable of receiving anything that is new and that is not of the old. Please don't immediately translate this into detail. If I do not know how to get back to Mylapore, I would be lost. If I do not know how to run a machine, I shall be of little use. That is quite a different thing. We are not discussing that here. We are discussing about knowledge that is used as a means of security, psychological and inward security, to be something. What do you get through knowledge? The authority of knowledge, the weight of knowledge, the sense of importance, dignity, the sense of vitality and what not? A man who says, "I know," "There is," or "There is not," surely has stopped thinking, stopped pursuing this whole process of desire.

Our problem then, as I see it, is: "I am bound, weighed down by belief, with knowledge; and is it possible for a mind to be free from yesterday and the beliefs that have been acquired through the process of yesterday?" Do you understand the question? Is it possible for me as an individual and you as an individual to live in this society and yet be free from the beliefs in which the mind has been brought up? Is it possible for the mind to be free of all that knowledge, all that authority? Please, sirs, do pay a little attention to this because I think it is very important if you are at all earnest to really go into this problem of belief and knowledge. We read the various scriptures, religious books. There, they have very carefully described what to do, what not to do, how to attain the goal, what the goal is, and what God is. You all know that by heart, and you have pursued that. That is your knowledge, that is what you have acquired, that is what you have learned; along that path you pursue. Obviously what you pursue and see, you will find. But is it reality? Is it not the projection of your own knowledge? It is not reality. Is it possible to realize that now—not tomorrow, but now—and say, "I see the truth of it," and let it go, so that your mind is not crippled by this process of imagination, of projection, of seeing what it must be?

Similarly, is the mind capable of becoming free from belief? You can only be free from it when you understand the inward nature of the causes that make you hold on to it, not only the conscious but the unconscious motives as well, that make you believe. After all, we are not merely a superficial entity functioning on the conscious level. We can find out the deeper conscious and unconscious activities if you give the unconscious mind a chance, because it is much quicker in response than the conscious mind. If you listen, as I hope you are listening, to what I am saying, your unconscious mind must be responding. While your conscious mind is quietly thinking, listening, and watching, the unconscious mind is much more active, much more alert, and much more receptive; it must, therefore, have an answer. Can the mind which has been subjugated, intimidated, forced, compelled to believe, can such a mind be free to think? Can it look anew and remove the process of isolation between you and me? Please do not say belief brings people together. It does not. That is obvious. Is that not? No organized religion has. Look at ourselves in this country. You are all believers, but are you all together? Are you all united? You yourselves know you are not. You are divided into so many petty, little parties, castes; you know the innumerable divisions, similarly in the West. The process is the same right through the world—Christians destroying Christians, murdering each other for petty, little things, driving people into camps, and so on—the whole horror of the war. So, belief does not bind people. That is so clear. If that is clear and that is true, and if you see it, then it must be followed. But the difficulty is that most of us do not see because we are not capable of facing that inward insecurity, that inward sense of being alone. We want something to lean on, whether it is the state, whether it is the caste, whether it is nationalism, whether it is a Master or a savior or anything we want to hold on to. And when we see the falseness of it, the mind is capable—it may be temporarily for a second—of seeing the truth of it, and when it is too much, it goes back. But to see temporarily is sufficient; if you can see it for a fleeting second, it is enough because you will then see an extraordinary thing taking place. The unconscious is at work though the conscious may reject. And it is not a progressive second, but that second is the only thing, and it will have its own results even in spite of the conscious mind struggling against it.

So, our question is, "Is it possible for the mind to be free from knowledge and belief?" Is not the mind made up of knowledge and belief? Are you following all this? Is not the structure of the mind belief and knowledge? Belief and knowledge are the processes of recognition, the center of the mind. The process is enclosing, the process is conscious. So can the mind be free of its own structure? You understand what I mean? The mind is not as we know the mind to be. It is so easy to ask questions without understanding. Probably, I shall receive many questions tomorrow such as, "How can the mind be like this or that?" Do not, please, ask such questions. Think it out, feel it out, go into it;

do not accept what I am saying, but see the problem with which you are confronted everyday in your life.

Can the mind cease to be? That is the problem. Mind, as we know it, has belief behind it, has desire, the urge to be secure, knowledge, and accumulation of strength. And if, with all its power and superiority, one cannot think for oneself, there can be no peace in the world. You may talk about it, you may organize political parties, you may shout from the housetops, but you cannot have peace because in the mind is the very basis which creates contradiction, which isolates and separates. We will discuss this as we go along. Just leave it alone. You have heard it, let it simmer. If you have already discarded desire, finished with it, so much the better; if you have not, let it operate. And it will operate if you listen rightly because it is something vital, it is something that you have to solve. A man of peace, a man of earnestness, cannot isolate himself and yet talk of brotherhood and peace. It is just a game, political or religious, a sense of achievement and ambition. We shall discuss that later. A man who is really earnest about this, who wants to discover, has to face the problem of knowledge and belief; he has to go behind it to discover the whole process of desire at work, desire to be secure, desire to be certain.

Question: You have condemned discipline as a means of spiritual or other attainment. How can anything be accomplished in life without discipline or at least self-discipline?

KRISHNAMURTI: Again, please let us listen. Let us listen to find the truth of the matter. It does not matter what I say or somebody else says, but we have to find the truth of the matter. First of all, there are many who say that discipline is necessary, or the whole social, economic, and political system would cease, that in order to do this or that, in order to realize God, you must have discipline. You must follow a certain discipline because without discipline, you cannot control the mind; without discipline, you will spill over.

But I want to know the truth of the matter, not what Shankara, Buddha, or Patanjali, or anybody else has said. I want to know what is the truth of it. I do not want to rely on authority to find it out. Would I discipline a child? I discipline a child when I have no time, when I am impatient, when I am angry, when I want to make him do something. But if I help the child to understand why he is mischievous, why he is doing a certain thing, then discipline is not necessary. Is it? If I go and explain, take the trouble, have the patience to understand the whole problem of why the child is acting in such and such a way, surely, discipline is not necessary. What is necessary is to awaken intelligence, is it not? If intelligence be awakened in me, then obviously I shall not do certain things. Since we do not know how to awaken that intelligence, we build walls of control and resistance and call that discipline. So discipline has nothing to do with intelligence; on the contrary, it destroys intelligence. So how am I to awaken intelligence? If I understand that to think in a certain manner—for instance, to think in terms of nationalism—is a wrong process, if I see the whole implication of it, the isolation, the sense of identification with something larger, and so on, if I see the whole implication of desire, of the activity of the mind, if I really understand and see the whole content of it, if my intelligence awakens to it, the desire drops away; I do not have to say, "It is a very bad desire." This requires watchfulness, attention, alertness, and examination, does it not? And because we are not capable of it, we say we must discipline; it is a very immature way of thinking about a very complex problem.

Even modern systems of education are discarding the whole idea of discipline. They are trying to find out the psychology of the child and why he is going in such and such a way; they are watching him, helping him.

Now, look at the process of discipline. What happens? Discipline is, surely, a process of compulsion, of repression, is it not? I want to do something, and I say, "I must, because I want to get there," or "That is bad." Do I understand anything by condemning it? And when I condemn a thing, do I look at it, do I go into it? I have not seen it. So, it is the sluggish mind that begins to discipline without understanding what it is all about, and I am sure all religious rules have been laid down for the lazy. It is so much easier to follow than to investigate, than to inquire, than to understand. The more you are disciplined, the less your heart is open. Do you know all these things, sirs? How can an empty heart understand something which is beyond the influence of the mind?

The problem of discipline is really very complex. The political parties use discipline in order to achieve a particular result, in order to make the individual conform to the ideal pattern of a future society, for which we are only too willing to become slaves because that promises something marvelous. So a mind that is seeking a reward, an end, forces itself to conform to that end, which is always a projection of a clever mind, of a superior mind, a more cunning mind. A disciplined mind can never understand what it is to be peaceful. How can a mind which is enclosed by regulations and restrictions see anything beyond?

If you look at this process of discipline, you will observe that desire is at the back of it—the desire to be strong, the desire to achieve a result, the desire to become something, the desire to be powerful, to become more and not less. This constant urge of desire is at work, this urge to conform, to discipline, to suppress, to isolate. You may suppress, you may discipline. But the conscious cannot control and shape the unconscious mind. If you try to shape your unconscious mind, it is what you call discipline, is it not? The more you suppress, the more you put the lid on your mind, the more the unconscious revolts until ultimately the mind either ends up neurotic or does a crazy thing.

So what is important in this question is not whether I condemn discipline or you approve of it, but to see how to awaken the integrated intelligence, not departmentalized intelligence, but integrated intelligence, which brings its own understanding and therefore avoids certain things naturally, automatically, and freely. It is the intelligence that will guide, not discipline. Sir, this is really a very important and complex question. If we would really go into it, if we watch ourselves and understand the whole process of discipline, we will find that we are not really disciplined at all. Are you disciplined in your lives? Or are you merely suppressing the various cravings, resisting various forms of temptations? If you should resist through discipline, those temptations and those demands are still there. Are they not hidden deep down but still there, waiting for an opening to burst out? Have you not noticed as you grow older that those feelings that are suppressed are coming out again? So you cannot play tricks with your unconscious; it will pay you back thousand-fold.

You have to understand this whole process, not that you are all for discipline, and I am against it. I assert that discipline will lead you nowhere; on the contrary, it is a blind process, unintelligent and thoughtless. But to awaken intelligence is quite a different problem. You cannot cultivate intelligence. Intelligence, when awakened, brings its own mode of operation; it regulates its own life, observes various forms of temptations, inclinations, reactions, and goes into it; it understands, not superficially, but in an integrated, comprehensive manner. To do that, the mind must be constantly alert, watchful, must it not? Surely, for a mind that would understand, the restrictions imposed upon it by itself are of very little significance. To understand, there must be freedom; that freedom does not come through compulsion in any form, and freedom lies not at the end but at the beginning. Our difficulty is to awaken integrated intelligence, and that can only come about when we are capable of understanding the whole.

This complex problem of desire expresses itself through discipline, through conformity, through repression, through belief, through knowledge. When we see the vast structure of desire, then we will begin to understand. Then the mind will begin to see itself and be capable of receiving something which is not the projection of its own.

January 6, 1952

Third Talk in Madras

I have been trying to find out, the last two times that we have met, the action that is not isolated, that is not fragmented, action that is not bound by idea; and I think it is important to go into that matter rather carefully because I feel that without understanding the whole process of ideation, mere action will have very little significance. The conflict between idea and action will always be ever increasing, and it can never be bridged. So, to find out action which is not fragmented, that is not broken up, not isolated, but comprehensive, we have to investigate the whole process of desire. Desire is not a thing that can be annihilated, that can be subjugated or twisted. That is because, as I explained, however much we may wish to abandon desire, it can never be done; for desire is a constant process of the conscious as well as the unconscious, and we may temporarily control the conscious desire, but it is very difficult to subjugate or control the unconscious. I feel that utter confusion and chaos would result from any action which is isolated, and it also seems to me that most of us are occupied with such actions. Experts and specialists have separated action and idea; they have done this at different levels and in different patterns and have told you how to act. There are, as you know, the economists, the politicians, the religious persons, and so on; they have given us fragmentary views of the whole comprehension of life. It seems to me that those who are really very earnest to understand this process of action which is not isolated and not fragmented or broken up, must be on their guard. It can only be done when we understand the whole process of desire. That is more or less what we discussed last Saturday and Sunday.

To understand desire is not to condemn it. As most of us are conditioned, as most of us have fixed ideas and opinions with regard to desire, it is almost impossible for us to follow the movement of desire without condemning it, without having opinions. If I would understand something, I must observe it without any process of condemnatory attitude, must I not? If I would understand you and if you would understand me, we must not judge each other, we must not condemn each other; we must be open and receptive to all the implications of each other's word, to the expression of our face; we must be completely receptive and open-minded. That is not possible when there is condemnation. Is it possible to have action without idea? For most of us, ideas come first and action follows after. Ideas are always fragmentary, they are always isolated, and any action based on idea must be fragmentary, isolated. Is it possible to have an action that is not broken up, that is comprehensive, that is integrated? It seems to me that such an action is the only redemption for us. All other actions are bound to leave further confusion and further conflict. So, how is one to find action which is not based on idea?

What do we mean by idea? Surely idea is the process of thought, is it not? Idea is a process of mentation, of thinking, and thinking is always a reaction either of the conscious or of the unconscious. Thinking is a process of verbalization which is the result of memory; thinking is a process of time. So, when action is based on the process of thinking, such action must inevitably be conditioned, isolated. Idea must oppose idea, idea must be dominated by idea. There is a gap then between action and idea. What we are trying to find out is whether it is possible for action to be without idea. We see how idea separates people. As I have already explained, knowledge and belief are essentially separating qualities. Beliefs never bind people; they always separate people; when action is based on belief or an idea or an ideal, such an action must inevitably be isolated, fragmented. Is it possible to act without the process of thought, thought being a process of time, a process of calculation, a process of self-protection, a process of belief, denial, condemnation, justification? Surely, it must have occurred to you as it has to me, whether action is at all possible without idea. I see as well as you see that when I have an idea and I base my action on that idea, it must create opposition; idea must meet idea and must inevitably create suppression, opposition. I do not know if I am making myself clear. To me this is really a very important point. If you can understand that, not by the mind or sentimentally, but intimately, I feel we shall have transcended all our difficulties. Our difficulties are of ideas, not of action. It is not what we should do, which is merely an idea; what is important is acting. Is action possible without the process of calculation, which is the result of self-protection, of memory, of relationship, personal, individual, collective, and so on? I say it is possible. You can experiment with it when you are here. If we can follow without any condemnation the whole process of desire, then you will see that action is inevitable without idea. That no doubt requires an extraordinary alertness of mind because our whole conditioning is to condemn, justify, to put into various categories—which are all a process of calculation, mentation. For most of us, idea and action are two different things. There is idea first and action follows after. Our difficulty is to bridge action and idea. Let us look at it differently.

We know every form of greed is destructive. Envy leads to ambition—political, religious, collective or individual. Every form of ambition, if we are aware of it, is limited and destructive. We all know that; we do not have to be told; we have not got to think a great deal about it. Ambition produces envy. Ambition is the result of the desire for power and position, for personal advancement, political and religious—politically in the name of an idea of the future or of the present, and spiritually in the name of something equally good or equally bad. We have known such ambitions—to be somebody, to be dominating people in the name of peace, in the name of Master, in the name of God, and heaven knows what else. Where there is ambition, there must be exploitation, man against man, nation against nation, and the very people who are shouting peace are the very ones who are doing things which are highly destructive, perhaps for themselves and for their country or for their idea. Such people do not bring peace. They only verbalize peace, but they have not got peace in their hearts. Such people obviously cannot bring to the world peace or happiness; they must only bring contention, war.

Ambition is the result of greed, envy, desire for power. It is all based on an idea, is it not? Idea is nothing but reaction. It is so, neurologically, psychologically, or physically. Ambition is an idea to be something politically, religiously; "I want to become a great person and work for the future." What does it reflect? We also know political ambition in the name of the country and so on. All this is based on an idea. It is an idea, a concept, a formulation of what I shall be or my party shall be. Having established the idea, then I pursue that idea in action. First of all, morally, an ambitious person is immoral. He is a source of contention, and yet we all encourage ambition. Otherwise, what can we do? There may be no achievement. So, when you look at it, you will see ambition is an idea, the pursuit of an idea in action—"I am going to be something"—in which is involved exploitation, ruthlessness, appalling brutality, etc. After all, the 'me' is an idea which has no actuality. It is a process of time. It is a process of memory, recognition, which are all essentially ideas.

Can ambition be completely put aside when I perceive that action, if based on an idea, must ultimately breed hatred, envy? Can I abandon completely ambition and therefore act without the process of idea? I shall put it more simply. If we are ambitious, is it possible to abandon completely ambition—politically, religiously? Only then, am I a center of peace. But to abandon completely ambition with all its meaning, significance, inward confusion, brutality, with the whole significance of the desire for power and condemnation, is not so easy. I can only drop it integrally, wholly, and completely when I no longer pursue the idea, the idea being the 'me'; then there is no problem of how I am not to be ambitious, or being ambitious, how I am to get rid of it. Is that not our problem? We are all greedy, we are envious; you have more and I have less; you have more power and I want that power, spiritually, secularly. Being caught in it, my problem then is how to get rid of it. How am I to abandon it? We then introduce the problem "how?" That is merely a postponement of action. If I see that action based on an idea must introduce postponement, then I realize the necessity for action without ideation. I wonder if I am making myself clear. Is not ambition destructive? Ambitious nations, individuals after power, or persons immensely bloated with their self-importance are all dangers; you know what misery they cause to themselves and to those around them. How are they to be got rid of—not superficially but profoundly, both in the conscious as well as in the unconscious?

Idea introduced into action creates nonaction. Action not based on idea will be immediate, not tomorrow. If I am able to see without ideation the brutality, the implications of ambition, then there is immediate action. There is no question of how I am not to be ambitious. If we want action which is not separated, which is not fragmented, which is not isolated, we must think it over. Have you not seen man against man, nation against nation, one sect against another, one group against another communally, one dogma against another, one Master against another? You know the whole game of division and brutality. Knowing it, seeing the fact of it clearly, can ambition be abandoned? We are aware of domination—spiritual, economic, and political, and we have noticed the results—which are constant wars, starvation, fragmentation of man, and so on. We know that any action without understanding the whole process of ideation and the course of ideas, will only further breed antagonism.

So, a man who is earnest, who is really peaceful, not just politically peaceful, cannot prejudice this problem through idea because idea is postponement, idea is fragmentary, and it is not integrated intelligence. Thought must always be limited by the thinker who is conditioned; the thinker is always conditioned and is never free; if thought occurs, immediately idea follows. Idea in order to act is bound to create more confusion. Knowing all this, is it possible to act without idea? Yes, it is the way of love. Love is not an idea; it is not a sensation; it is not a memory; it is not a feeling of postponement, a self-protective device. We can only be aware of the way of love when we understand the whole process of idea. Now, is it possible to abandon the other ways and know the way of love which is the only redemption? No other way, political or religious, will solve the problem. This is not a theory which you will have to think over and adopt in your life; it must be actual, and it can only be actual when you see and realize that ambition is destructive and therefore should be pushed away from you.

We have never tried that way of love. We have tried every other way. Please do not shut your eyes and go to sleep over the word *love.* It is not a process of thinking. Your immediate reaction is: "What is love? Can I know it? How am I to live according to that?" What is the way of love which is apart from the process of thinking and idea? When you love, is there idea? Do not accept it; just look at it, examine it, go into it profoundly, because every other way we have tried, and found there is no answer to misery. Politicians may promise it; the so-called religious organizations may promise future happiness; but we have not got it now, and the future is relatively unimportant when we are hungry. We have tried every other way, and we can only know the way of love if we know the way of idea and abandon idea, which is to act. It may sound absurd or foolish to the majority of you when you hear that action can be without idea, but if you go into it a little more deeply, without pushing it aside as silly, if you go into it deeply with earnestness, you will see idea can never take the place of action. Action is always immediate. You see something like ambition or greed; there is no "How to get rid of that? Can you do it?" Please think it out. We can discuss it. You will see that love is the only remedy; that is our only redemption in which man can live with man peacefully, happily, without exploiting, without dominating, without one person becoming greater and superior through ambition, through cunning. We do not know that way. Let us become aware of all this. When we have fully recognized the whole significance of action based on idea, the very recognition of it is to act away from it—which is the way of love.

Question: We are told that India is rapidly disintegrating. Is this your feeling too?

KRISHNAMURTI: What do you think? What do you mean by disintegration? Surely, a nation, a group, an individual is disintegrating when it or he is corrupt, is bound to tradition, when he is imitating, when he is following, when he is not independent in his thinking, when he is not free from the environment so that he, as an individual, cannot look, think, and see clearly. Obviously, when one individual exploits another by his cunning, by his superior knowledge, by his capacities, surely such an individual is a factor of disintegration, is he not? And are not we all in that same position? Are not we all imitating, following, exploiting, afraid, bound to the tradition of others' thoughts? Are we capable of thinking for ourselves without the imposition of others' ideas? Does not all this indicate the process of disintegration? When you worship somebody, however great, is that not a process of disintegration? When you are pursuing an ambition, climbing its ladder, reaching the dung heap, is that not disintegration? The dung heap may be politically satisfying, economically gratifying; is that not also disintegration? Is not that disintegration when you are spiritually influenced by somebody, a special messenger? When you are building for the future, for tomorrow, or for the future of your own existence, next life, and so on, is not that disintegration? You are always living in the future, sacrificing many for an idea. Surely, all this is an indication of disintegration, is it not? This is not only here in India; this is taking place all over the world. Why are we doing this all the time? Is it very difficult to find out the "why"?

We all want to be secure, economically and psychologically. Our petty selves are so narrow and limited that we want to be secure. Therefore we worship authority. So long as we seek security inwardly, there must be disintegration. Outward security we must have. I must be sure of my next meal, shelter, and clothing but that is made impossible if each one of us seeks inward security either through property or nation, or desires to achieve the topmost rung of the ladder. That is, so long as I am seeking personal advancement in any form, which is an indication of the desire for inward security, there must be disintegration because I am fighting my fellow man.

You listen to all this, and what is your action? Not what is your idea, or your opinion, because anybody can have an opinion, but what is your action? If you say, "How am I not to be ambitious, how am I not to be self-protective?" then my question to you is merely an idea, is merely an exchange of thought, opinion. But if it is genuine in the sense that it is a challenge for you to respond through action, then what will you do? That is, you are truly a factor of disintegration. It does not matter what society you belong to—Indian, Russian, American, or English—you are sure to be a factor of destruction and disintegration as long as you consciously pursue security, inwardly or outwardly. What is your action? Surely, that is the only response you can have, not "I shall think over it; how am I to do it?" which is rather a response to an idea. But a man who sees it, acts immediately, and that man will know the way of love; to me, he is the regenerating factor in the world of corruption. That does not require great courage, great intelligence, which are merely factors of the cunning mind; it requires perspective, direct perspective of *what is*. The man who sees clearly, inevitably must act. We do not want to see, and that is where our misery lies. We know all this. We are familiar with all this corruption, disintegration, and we cannot act because we are caught in ideation, in ideas, thought of how and what. So a man who sees corruption and is aware of it without the screen of idea, will act, and such a man knows the way of love.

Question: When the mind ceases to recognize, does it not come to a state of inactivity? What functions then?

KRISHNAMURTI: To answer that question fully, you must understand what has been said previously. I said the process of mind is recognition. Thought, experience, the center of me, is recognition. Without recognition, without knowing, there is no thought process. If I have an experience, I must be able to recognize it either verbally or without verbalization. I must know I have had experience; that is, I must recognize experience as pleasurable, painful, and so on. I must give it a name. There is the center of recognition, which is the 'me', the self—not higher self or lower self—self is one—not superior or inferior; that is the invention of the clever mind. So, this center of recognition is the self, and without recognition, can the mind exist, can the center, the 'me', exist? Obviously not.

The questioner asks if that recognition is not, if the center is not, what is the state of activity of the mind. What is the activity there? What happens then? Have I explained the question? Now, why do you want to know? There is no pushing you back into yourselves. You want to know in order to be able to recognize, do you not? To be able to recognize from my experience when I verbalize it to you, so that you can say I have had it, so that you can recognize your experience as corresponding to mine. Your asking the question is a continuation of the process of the self. Is my experience the same as yours? You are asking the question in order to feel secure in your recognition. Please see how your own mind works. So, what you are interested in is not what happens when the process of recognition is not, but you want an assurance from me that your experience is the same as mine, which is, you want to recognize your experience in relation with mine. So your question has no answer. It is a wrong question.

Let us put it differently. We only know experience through recognition. And each recognition strengthens the mind, the self, gives emphasis, strengthens the security of the self. Each experience is recognized, and you cannot have experience without saying "Yes, I know what it is." So your experience is only a projection of your own thought. Listen without being clever and cunning; just watch it. Psychologically it is a fact. I want to see the Master and I see him and I experience, but it has nothing to do with reality. It is my desire projected and recognized, which only strengthens my experience, my recognition, and so I say, "I believe, I know." So, if I rely on my experience to see what truth is, then it is my projection of what truth should be. And is it possible for the center, for the 'me', to have no recognition, not to aid experience through recognition? You try it. You try to see if your mind can be completely still without recognition, without recognizing things; when this happens, the mind is in a state of stillness. Soon afterwards, it wants to prolong that state thereby reducing that experience to the realm of memory and strengthening the process of thought, of recognition, which is the center of the self; therefore, there is no possibility of experiencing anything anew; recognition persists; there is the desire to hold on to the experience done years ago, to continue it. Can the mind be still, without any of all this? Which means, can the mind be still without verbalization, which is thought process? If the mind is still in that manner, activities that follow cannot be measured, cannot be verbalized, cannot be recognized.

God, truth, is not recognizable. Therefore, to know truth, there must be the understanding and putting away of all knowledge, of all beliefs, because when the mind is not in a state of knowledge, when recognition has ceased, truth can come into it and be there.

Question: If I am myself unable to find truth, how can I prevent my child from being the victim of my conditioning?

KRISHNAMURTI: How would you set about it? Knowing that a parent is conditioned, that he has prejudices, has ambitions, has absurdities, has pronouncements, has secularism, has beliefs, has traditions, has grandmother's opinions, what society will say and will not say—knowing all that, how will you help the child to grow to be a free and integrated human being? That is the problem, is it not? How will you set about it? It requires a whole hour to answer it because the question is how to educate the child. What are we doing for our children? Merely trying to fit them into the present state of society, to help them pass examinations! We have really no idea of what he should be; we want to try to help the child to understand what we have not understood. If I am blind, can I lead you across the road? But being blind, I do not say

I am blind. I am not aware that I am blind. I say, "Yes, I am conditioned, it is so. But I want to help my child." But if I am aware that I am deeply and fundamentally conditioned, I have problems, prejudices, ambitions, superstitions, beliefs, if I am aware of it, am cognizant of it, am in the know of it, then what happens? My action towards my child will be different. If I know I am poisoned, religiously poisoned, will I allow my child to come near me? I will reason with him, show him why he should not come to me, which means, I must love my child. But we do not love our children. We have no love in our hearts for the children; otherwise, if there were, we would prevent wars; we would prevent all this fragmentation of human beings into classes, nationalities, British, Indian, Brahmin and non-Brahmin, white and black, purple and blue. So being conditioned, I cannot help another if I am unaware of my conditioning. But to acknowledge that I am conditioned is to break from it, and not "I am conditioned, how am I to be free from the conditioning?" which is merely an idea which helps me to postpone action. If I am aware of it, if I know I am conditioned, then I cannot but act and help the child. It is really very important to understand this question, not the question of conducting the child, how to help him.

We have to understand the whole problem of idea and action. We have always placed idea first and action afterwards. All our literature—religious, political, economic—is based on idea. Our knowledge is nothing more. A mind that is full of knowledge and ideas can never act. Therefore, belief and knowledge are an impediment to action. They may sound contradictory and absurd, but if you will kindly go into it, you will see the reasonableness behind that statement. So what is important in these questions and talks is not to find the cultivation of ideas, or to exchange opinions, dogmas, and beliefs, or to substitute them for another, but to be free to act, without action being isolating. Action will always be isolating so long as it is based on knowledge and belief, which is idea, which is the process of thinking. When you have a problem as of ambition, you cannot have an idea about it; you can only act about it. Similarly, when I know I am conditioned, a mere thought process regarding it is postponement of the mind from the conditioning. I assure you, it ceases to be a problem only to a man who is earnest, whose function is peace, who is intent on finding love, the way of love, because he is not concerned with idea, because he is concerned with action which is not isolated.

January 12, 1952

Fourth Talk in Madras

I have been trying to find out the solution of the problem of consciousness. It is very important to talk over what individuality or the problem of consciousness is. Being individuals, we strive to fit into the pattern of the community, the collective, the totalitarian. Before we can adequately and truly cover the subject, it is necessary, is it not, to understand the whole question of individuality.

What is the individual? This problem is a question which must be talked over very constantly and wisely without any barriers and without any conclusions and comparisons. If you can listen to what I am going to talk about, not throw up barriers of your own conclusions which may be true or may not be true, barriers of what you have learned from your environmental influence or what you have read from the books, then perhaps you will be able actually to cooperate with me and with each other without dominating, without completely annihilating the individual through legislation, through compulsion, through concentration camps, and so on. I do not know if you feel the importance of this question. If not, I suggest that you should try to because it is really a vital problem. As it is a difficult question, we should be able to talk it over like two friends, not like two antagonists in two opposite camps, you with your opinions and I perhaps with mine. I am not offering an opinion; I am not putting forward a belief, formulation, conception, because I do not indulge in that form of stupidity; because to me it is stupid, when I am incapable of understanding *what is,* that I should want to know *what is.*

We should not speculate about *what is.* I hope to see that difference between speculation of *what is* and understanding *what is.* Surely the two are entirely different. Most of us only speculate, have beliefs, have conclusions about *what is,* and with these conclusions, speculations, formulations, etc., we approach the question of the individual. Truly we must fail if we so approach it, whereas if we can look at it without formulation but merely look at it, then perhaps we will be able to understand the significance of the problems involved in individuality, and perhaps we will be able to go beyond that which we call the individual. That is to understand the whole question of the conscious and the unconscious, not only the barren uppermost consciousness of the mind, of the active mind, but also of the unconscious, the hidden.

So, what is the individual? What is the 'me'? You must examine what we think it is and what we hope it is, that is, look at ourselves without speculation if that is possible. If you say such things as, "I am the highest representative of God," that is mere speculation. We have to put aside such speculations. Obviously! Must we not? They are all words which you have learned, which society has imposed upon you, one way or the other. Politically, you might say that if you belong to the extreme left, you have nothing to bother about but only to let the environmental influence operate; if you are religiously inclined, you have your own phraseology that you are this, you are that, and that something is manifest in you. You know the whole thing about the higher self and the lower self. With that background, obviously you cannot look or examine the problem, can you? You can only look at *what is* by observing very carefully the whole process of the individual, what the individual is, etc. Can you tell me what you are? Please bear in mind what we are discussing, for what purpose. To understand the problem of the conscious and to look into it, if it is possible, not speculatively, not theoretically, but to go beyond the confines of the narrow area called the individual—that is what we are trying to do.

What is the individual? What are you, actually? Obviously, certain physiological responses, bodily responses, and psychological responses of memory, of time, constitute the individual. We are all composed of frustrated hopes, depressions, with an occasional joy, in which the self is, the 'me' with all its fears, hopes, degradations, memories. We are a repository of tradition, of knowledge, of belief, of what we would like to be, and of the desire for certainty, of continuity with a name and a form. That is what actually we are. We are the result of our father and mother, of environmental influences, climatically and psychologically. That is *what is.* Beyond that we do not know. We can only speculate; we can only assert; we can only say that we are the soul, immortal, imperishable; but, actually, that has no existence. That is merely a process of *what is* translated into terms of security.

So, consciousness, as we know it, is a process of time. When are you conscious? When there is response, pleasant or unpleasant. Otherwise you are not conscious, are you? When there is fear, you are conscious. When there is frustration, you are aware of yourself being frustrated. When there is joy, you are aware of it. When consciousness comes into action, when desire is thwarted, frustrated, or when desire finds fulfillment, you are equally aware. So, what we know is that consciousness is a process of time, confined, limited, narrowed down to the thought process. Surely, that is what is actually taking place in each one of us, is it not? That process may be elevated to a high degree or taken down to a low degree, but that is what is actually taking place, what is actually going on.

Consciousness is a process of time in action. I want to do something and when I can do that without any hindrance, without any struggle, without any sense of fear or frustration, there is no effort involved. The moment effort is involved, consciousness as the 'me' comes into being. I hope you are following.

The individual is the product of time, and it is memory, consciousness, the 'me' narrowed down to a particular form and name. 'I' refers to both the conscious mind functioning as well as the unconscious. We all have fear of death, we have fear of innumerable things. You have various levels of frustrations and hopes, according to education, according to environmental influence, and of depression dependent on physiological condition, as well as psychological condition. So, we are all that; we are a bundle of all that. We are conscious only when the movement of consciousness is blocked. You are aware of yourself only when you are hindered. Are you aware of yourself in any other way? You are aware of yourself in fulfilling, in achieving, in arriving, in becoming. Otherwise, you are not conscious, are you? And as long as there is this process of time, there must be fear, must there not be?

What is fear? Fear is in relation to something, is it not? Fear does not exist by itself. Fear of death, of not being, not arriving, not being elected, not achieving, not becoming successful, and so on. There is fear at different levels. There is the fear to be secure economically, mentally. As long as there is fear, there must be struggle, there must be battle, there must be constant friction between being and not being, not only on the conscious level but also on the hidden level. So, being afraid, which is the state of most of us, we are trying to escape from it, and the escapes are many.

Please follow carefully and watch yourself as you follow. Then you and I can proceed further and discover much more than at the mere verbal level. You must watch yourself as I am talking, in the mirror of my words. If you merely stop at the verbal level, you will not be able to proceed further, and you can only proceed further if you are relating what I am saying to yourself. I am not saying something which you have to examine and analyze. I am saying what is actually taking place.

We are all afraid. We have a desire to be secure. You like to be with your husband, I with my wife, with my neighbor, with my society, with God, and so on. There are innumerable forms of desire. We have not solved the problem of fear. What we do is to escape from it through various forms. If we are so-called educated, so-called civilized, our escapes are refined. Sometimes these escapes take the form of superstition.

Now, is it possible to go beyond fear? I know I am afraid; you know you too are afraid, you may not be outwardly, but you are afraid inwardly. What is this fear? Obviously it can be only in relation to something. I am afraid of death; I am afraid because I do not know what is going to happen. I am afraid of losing my job; I am afraid of my neighbor; I am afraid of my wife; I am afraid of having a desire; I am afraid of not arriving at the spiritual height that is expected of me and so on. What is this 'me'? It is fear, consciousness in action, desire to be something or not to be something. Fear finds various escapes. The common variety is identification, is it not? Identification with the country, with the society, with an idea. Haven't you noticed how you respond when you see a procession, a military procession or a religious procession, or when the country is in danger of being invaded? You then identify yourself with the country, with a belief, with an ideology. There are other times when you identify with your child, with your wife, with a particular form of action or inaction. So, identification is a process of self-forgetfulness. As long as I am conscious of the 'me', I know there is pain, there is struggle, there is constant fear. But if I can identify myself with something greater, with something worthwhile, with beauty, with life, with truth, with belief, with knowledge, at least temporarily, there is an escape from the 'me', is there not? If I talk about my country, I forget myself temporarily. Do I not? If I can say something about God, I forget myself. If I can identify my family with a group, with a particular party, with a certain ideology, then there is a temporary escape.

Therefore, identification is a form of escape from the self in as much as virtue is a form of escape from the self. The man who pursues virtue is escaping from the self, and he has a narrow mind. That is not a virtuous mind, for virtue is something which should not be pursued. You are not going to be virtuous because the more you try to become virtuous, the more the strength, the security you give to the self, to the 'me'. So, fear which is common to most of us in different forms, must always find a substitution and must therefore increase our struggle. The more you are identifying with a substitution, the greater the strength to hold on to that for which you are prepared to die, to struggle—because fear is at the back.

Do we now know what fear is? Is it not the nonacceptance of *what is?* We must understand the word *acceptance.* I am not using that word as meaning the effort made to accept. There is no question of accepting when I am able to see *what is* and when I perceive *what is.* When I don't see clearly *what is,* then I bring in the process of acceptance. So, fear is the nonacceptance of *what is.* How can I, who am a bundle of all these reactions, responses, memories, hopes, depressions, frustrations, who am the result of the movement of consciousness blocked, go beyond? That is, can the mind without this blocking and hindrance, be conscious? We know, when there is no hindrance, what extraordinary joy there is. Don't you know when the body is perfectly healthy, there is a certain joy, well-being; and don't you know when the mind is completely free without any block, when the center of recognition as the 'me' is not there, you experience a certain joy? Haven't you experienced this state when the self is absent? Surely we all have. Having experienced, we want to go back and recapture it. This is again the time process. Having experienced something, we want it; therefore, we give consciousness a block. Surely to find out action which is not the result of isolation, there must be action without the self. That is what you are all seeking in one form or other in society, through religious speculation, through meditation, through identification, through belief, through knowledge, through activities of innumerable kinds. That is what each one of us is seeking—to escape from the narrow area called 'self', to get away from it. Can you get away from it without understanding the whole process of *what is?* If I do not know the whole content of *what is* in front of me as the 'me', can I avoid it and run away?

There is understanding and freedom from the self only when I can look at it completely and integrally as a whole, and I can do that only when I understand the whole process of all activity, of desire which is the very expression of thought—for thought is not different from desire—without justifying it, without condemning it, without suppressing it; if I can understand that, then I will know there is the possibility of going beyond the restrictions of the self. And then there can be action which is not isolated, action which is not based on idea. But so long as the mind is confined to the area called the 'self', there must be conflict between man and man; and a man who seeks truth or peace must understand desire. Understanding comes when desire is not blocked intellectually, through fear, through condemnation—which does not mean you must give full vent to desire; you must follow it; there must be movement without contradiction, without condemnation. Then you will see that the conscious, however active it may be, becomes the field in which the unconscious can flower.

Freedom, which is really virtue, is necessary to discover what is truth, and a man who is bound to belief, knowledge, and self, can never find what truth is. That discovery of truth is not the process of time. The process of time is the mind, and the mind can never discover what is truth. Therefore it is necessary to understand the process of consciousness as limited to the 'me'.

Question: What do you feel to be the cause of the great prevalence of mental derangement in the world today? Is it insecurity? If so, what can we do to keep the millions who feel insecure from becoming unbalanced, neurotic, and psychotic?

KRISHNAMURTI: First of all, is there such a thing as inward security? Can there ever be security inwardly, psychologically? If you can find an answer to that, then physical security is possible, because that is what millions want—physical security, the next meal, shelter, and clothing. Millions go to bed half-starved. To solve the problem of food, clothing, and shelter for the many, not for the few, we must inquire why man seeks security, psychological security, because the answer is not in the rearrangement of things; the answer is not economic but psychological. Because each one of us is seeking inward security which prevents outward security for man, because each one of us wants to be something, we use physical substance as a means of psychological security. Are you not doing that? If you and I, if the world were concerned in feeding man, clothing him, and sheltering him, surely we would have to find ways. Is it not so? Nobody is doing that. This is one cause of mental derangement, is it not? If I feel outwardly insecure, I feel all kinds of things which bring about a mentally neurotic state.

So our problem is not wholly economic, as economists would like to think, but rather psychological; which is, that each one of us wants to be secure through belief, through superstition. We know the various forms of belief to which we cling in the hope of feeling secure. Don't you know that the man who believes can never commit suicide? But the man who does not believe is ready to commit suicide, either to kill himself or kill somebody else. So belief is the means of security. And the more I believe in the future life, in God, the more I think of it because it gives comfort and security, and I am fairly balanced, but if I am inquiring, searching, doubting, skeptic, then I begin to lose my mooring and I lose my security, and mentally I cannot stand this. So there is the psychotic state of mind. Have you not noticed it in yourselves? The moment you have something to which you can cling, you feel peaceful, be it a person, or idea or party—it does not matter what it is. As long as you can cling to something, you feel safe and feel more or less balanced. But question that belief and inquire into it, you invite insecurity. That is why all clever and intellectual people end up in some form of belief—because they push their intellects as far as they go, and they see nothing, and then they say, "Let us believe." Surely our question is, is there security, psychological and inward security? Obviously there is not. I can find security in belief, but that is merely a projection of my uncertainty in the form of belief, which becomes certain.

Can I find the truth of security and insecurity? Then only am I a sane being, not if I cling to some belief or some knowledge or some idea. If I can find out the truth of security, then I am an integrated, intelligent being. Is that your question? Obviously not, because you do not want to know if there is security. The moment you doubt it, where are you? The house of cards which you have so cleverly built up comes crumbling down. If you cannot achieve security, you become psychotic. So until you find the truth of security, if there is such a thing as security, obviously you are an unbalanced being.

Is there security, psychological security, inward security? Obviously, there is not. We only like it to be, but there is not. Can you depend on anything? When you do, what happens? The very dependence is an invitation to fear which breeds independence away from it, which is another form of fear. So until you find the truth of insecurity which means continuity, you are bound to have some blockages in the mind which in action creates a neurotic state. There is no permanency, there is no certainty, but there is truth which can only take place if you understand the whole process of desire and insecurity.

Question: Is true regeneration of India possible solely through renaissance of arts and the dance?

KRISHNAMURTI: The word *solely* is important. Is it not? Because what each one of us is occupied with becomes the means of renaissance. If I am an artist, that is the only way through which I can produce a creative world. If I am a religious person, that is the only way. To the economist, economics is the only way of regeneration. So what each one of us is occupied with, that particular gift, that particular tendency, becomes the means of producing a regenerated India.

Does regeneration come through outward organizations, through capacities, through rearrangement of facts, dance, or of arts? What do you mean by regeneration? Rebirth, something new, not continuity of the past in a new form. Surely we mean that, don't we? A new state, a new world in which there is peace, happiness. You know the whole thing for which we are struggling. Is renaissance possible without inward revolution, inward freedom? You may be an expert in dancing; that may be your particular gift. Will that really regenerate India or the world—because you are a marvelous dancer or you are a marvelous chemist or politician? What will produce a fundamental and radical revolution, so necessary, a complete revolution, not fragmentary revolution but integrated revolution, not a superficial rearrangement of the pattern? Surely that revolution must take place in each one of us. Must it not?

Don't be afraid of the word revolution. Either it is or it is not. We would rather like inward evolution, the whole process of becoming more and more worldly, more and more virtuous, which is only the strengthening of the 'me' through time. As long as the 'me' exists, there is no inward revolution. And the 'me' cannot be dissolved through time or through identification with that which we want.

Inward revolution takes place only when you see *what is* and when there is action which is not the basis of idea. Because when you are confronted with *what is,* ideas have no value. Regeneration and renaissance can only take place, not through a particular gift or capacity, but only through inward understanding and revolution.

Question: Have I understood you aright when I say that the solution for all our ills is to put a stop to all recognition and to the vagaries of desire and go beyond it? I have experienced moments of ecstasy, but they drop away soon afterwards, and desires rush in, breaking from the past into the future. Is it possible to annihilate desire once and for all?

KRISHNAMURTI: See, you want a result. You worship success, and you want to get rid of desire altogether in order to achieve that ecstatic state. That is, I would like to be happy and ecstatic, and I want to get rid of desire. So I am inquiring not how to understand desire but how to get rid of desire in order to achieve that state. Please see the impossibility of this. I want a certain result which I have experienced, and that experience I want to continue; and I cannot continue that experience as long as desire exists; therefore, I must get rid of desire. You are not interested in understanding desire but in modifying it at a particular stage; that is what is implied in this question. You want ecstasy, and you know you have experienced it; and you know desire prevents it, and so you have this problem of how to get rid of that. You desire that state of ecstasy, that is all. Only you have transformed your desire from secular, parochial, narrow walls to something which you have experienced. So what are you concerned with? With an experience which is past. Please follow this if you would understand the whole process you are confronted with, the problem of recapturing a past experience like a boy who has had a moment of ecstasy, and who, when he has grown old, would want to return to that. You know it is fragmentary because he is incapable of experiencing anything new.

What do you mean by experience? You can only experience anything which we recognize. So what is happening—the 'me' recognizes something as ecstasy and wants to capture it. The very wanting is a process of desire. It is given a name. At the moment of experiencing, there is no naming. Please follow this. Watch yourself in operation; then what I say will have meaning. When something happens to you unexpectedly, a state of ecstasy develops; in that second, there is no recognition. You then say, "I have had an experience"; you give it a name. This is all the process of mind trying to give it a name so that it can remember, so that through that remembrance it can continue that experience. For most of us, that is our companion.

But to understand desire needs an alert mind and constant watching without condemnation, without justification, constant observation, constant following, because it is never still. It is a movement, and no opposition will be of any use, for it will only create greater resistance in it. When you have an experience which is never recognized, you will see that the so-called experience which you name is not an experience at all but only a continuance of your own desire in a different form. When you understand desire, when you have really followed it, you have a state of being in which recognition is not present, in which there is no naming. That comes only when the mind is not inviting, when the mind is really silent, not made silent. The mind is silent because it understands, it pursues and becomes aware of the whole process of desire. When the mind is silent, it is no longer imaginative, no longer verbalizing; that very silence of the mind leads to the state of being which cannot be measured by the mind.

January 13, 1952

Fifth Talk in Madras

We have been discussing the last few times that we have met, the importance of understanding the ways of the self because, after all, the most thoughtful people must be aware that the self, the 'me', the 'I', is really the cause of all our mischief and all our misery. I think the most thoughtful people are aware of it. One can see that most religious organizations theorize and vaguely insist upon how essential it is that the 'me', the self, should be completely abandoned. We have read in the books about the abandonment of the self. If we are at all religiously inclined, we have various phrases about it all; we may repeat mantras and all the rest of it, but in spite of all this, our own perception and vague comprehensions about the self still continue in a very subtle way or in the grossest manner. I think, if it were at all easy, we must be sure and must understand the various expressions of the self and see if we cannot completely eradicate it, because I feel that without understanding the whole complexity of the self, we can't proceed further—whether the self is or is not divided into the high and the low, which is irrelevant and which is only a matter of the mind which eventually divides it as a means of its own security. Unless we understand this whole complex process, there is no possibility of peace in the world. We know this; we are aware of this fact consciously or unconsciously, but yet in our everyday life, it does not play any part; we do not bring it into reality.

What we have been discussing is this—how are we to recognize the various activities of the self and its subtle forms behind which the mind takes shelter? We see the self, its activity, and its action based on an idea. Action based on an idea is a form of the self because it gives continuity to that action, a purpose to that action. So, idea in action becomes the means of continuing the self. If the idea is not there, action has a different meaning altogether, which is not born of the self. The search for power, position, authority, ambition, and all the rest are the forms of the self in all its different ways. But what is important is to understand the self, and I am sure you and I are convinced of it. If I may add here, let us be earnest about this matter because I feel that if you and I as individuals, not as a group of people belonging to certain classes, certain societies, certain climatic divisions, can understand this and act upon this, then I think there will be real revolution. The moment it becomes universal and better organized, the self takes shelter in that, whereas if you and I as individuals can love, can carry this out actually in everyday life, then the revolution that is so essential will come into being, not because you organized it through the coming together of various groups, but because, individually, there is revolution taking place all the time.

I would like to discuss this evening how experience strengthens the self.

You know what I mean by the self? By that, I mean the idea, the memory, the conclusion, the experience, the various forms of nameable and unnameable intentions, the conscious endeavor to be or not to be, the accumulated memory of the unconscious, the racial, the group, the individual, the clan, and the whole of it all, whether it is projected outwardly in action or projected spiritually as virtue—the striving after all this is the self. In it is included the competition, the desire to be. The whole process of that is the self, and we know actually when we are faced with it that it is an evil thing. I am using the word *evil* intentionally because the self is dividing; the self is self-enclosing; its activities, however noble, are separated and isolated. We know all this. We also know that extraordinary are the moments when the self is not there, in which there is no sense of endeavor, of effort, and which happens when there is love.

It seems to me that it is important to understand how experience strengthens the self. If we are earnest, we should understand this problem of experience. Now, what do we mean by experience? We have experiences all the time—impressions—and we translate those impressions, and we are reacting to them, or we are acting according to those impressions; we are calculated, cunning, and so on. There is the constant interplay between what is seen objectively and our reacting to it, and the interplay between the unconscious and the memories of the unconscious.

Do not, please, memorize all this. Watch, if I may suggest, watch your own minds and activities taking place as I am talking, and you will see. I have not memorized all this; I am just talking as it is happening.

According to my memories, I react to whatever I see, to whatever I feel. In this process of reacting to what I see, what I feel, what I know, what I believe, experience is taking place, is it not? Reaction to the response of something seen is experience. When I see you, I react; the reaction is experience. The naming of that reaction is experience. If I do not name that reaction, it is not an experience. Please do watch it. Watch your own responses and what is taking place about you. There is no experience unless there is a naming process going on at the same time. If I do not recognize you, how can I have experience? It sounds simple and right. Is it not a fact? That is, if I do not react to you according to my memories, according to my condition, according to my prejudices, how can I know that I have had an experience? That is one type of it.

Then there is the projection of various desires. I desire to be protected, to have security inwardly, or I desire to have a Master, a guru, a teacher, a God, and I experience that which I have projected. That is, I have projected a desire which has taken a form, to which I have given a name; to that, I react. It is my projection. It is my naming. That desire which gives me an experience makes me say, "I have got," "I have experienced," "I have met the Master," or "I have not met the Master." You know the whole process of naming an experience. Desire is what you call experience. Is it not?

When I desire silence of the mind, what is taking place? What happens? I see the importance of having a silent mind, a quiet mind, for various reasons—because Upanishads have said so, religious scriptures have said so, saints have said it, and also occasionally, I myself feel how good it is to be quiet because my mind is so very chatty all the day. At times, I feel how nice, how pleasurable it is to have a peaceful mind, a silent mind. The desire to have a silent mind is to experience silence. I want to have a silent mind, and so I ask you how to get it. I know what this book or that book says about meditation and the various forms of discipline. I want a silent mind through discipline, and I experience silence. The self, the 'me', has established itself in the experience of silence. Am I making myself clear?

I want to understand what is truth; that is my desire, my longing; then there is my projection of what I consider to be the truth because I have read lots about it; I have heard many people talk about it; religious scriptures have described it. I want all that. What happens? The very want, the very desire is projected, and I experience because I recognize that state. If I do not recognize that state, that act, that truth, I would not call it truth. I recognize it and I experience it. That experience gives strength to the self, to the 'me', does it not? So, the self becomes entrenched in experience. Then you say, "I know," "the Master exists," "there is God," or "there is no God"; you say that you want a particular political system to come because that is right and all others are not.

So experience is always strengthening the 'me'. The more you are strengthened, the more entrenched you are in your experience and the more does the self get strengthened. As a result of this, you have a certain strength of character, strength of knowledge, of belief, which you put over across to other people because you know they are not so clever as you are and because you have the gift of the pen and you are cunning. Because the self is still acting, your beliefs, your Masters, your castes, your economic system are all a process of isolation, and they therefore bring contention. You must, if you are at all serious or earnest in this, dissolve this completely and not justify it. That is why we must understand the process of experience.

Is it possible for the mind, for the self not to project, not to desire, not to experience? We see all experiences of the self are a negation, a destruction, and yet we call the same a positive action, don't we? That is what we call the positive way of life. To undo this whole process is what you call negation. Are you right in that? There is nothing positive. Can we, you and I as individuals, go to the root of it and understand the process of the self? Now what is the element that dissolves it? What brings about dissolution of the self? Religious and other groups have explained it by identification, have they not? Identify yourself with a larger, and the self disappears; that is what they say. We say here that identification is still the process of the self; the larger is simply the projection of the 'me', which I experience and which therefore strengthens the 'me'. I wonder if you are following this. All the various forms of discipline, beliefs, and knowledge only strengthen the self.

Can we find an element which would dissolve the self? Or, is that a wrong question? That is what we want basically. We want to find something which will dissolve the 'me'. Is it not so? We think there are various forms of finding that, namely, identification, belief, etc., but all of them are at the same level; one is not superior to the other because all of them are equally powerful in strengthening the self, the 'me'. Now, I see the 'me' wherever it functions, and I see its destructive forces and energy. Whatever name you may give to it, it is an isolating force, it is a destructive force, and I want to find a way of dissolving it. You must have asked this yourself—"I see the 'I' functioning all the time and always bringing anxiety, fear, frustration, despair, misery, not only to myself but to all around me. Is it possible for that self to be dissolved, not partially but completely?" Can we go to the root of it and destroy it? That is the only way of functioning, is it not? I do not want to be partially intelligent, but intelligent in an integrated manner. Most of us are intelligent in layers, you probably in one way and I in some other way. Some of you are intelligent in your business work, some others in your office work, and so on; people are intelligent in different ways, but we are not integrally intelligent. To be integrally intelligent means to be without the self. Is it possible? If I pursue that action, what is your response? This is not a discussion, and therefore please do not answer but be aware of that action. The implications which I have tried to point out must produce a reaction in you. What is your response?

Is it possible for the self now to be completely absent? You know it is possible. Now, how is it possible? What are the necessary ingredients, requirements? What is the element that brings it about? Can I find it? Are you following this, sirs? When I put that question, "Can I find it?" surely I am convinced that it is possible. I have already created an experience in which the self is going to be strengthened, is it not? Understanding of the self requires a great deal of intelligence, a great deal of watchfulness, alertness, watching ceaselessly, so that it does not slip away. I, who am very earnest, want to dissolve the self. When I say that, I know it is possible to dissolve the self. Please be patient. The moment I say, "I want to dissolve this," and in the process I follow for the dissolution of that, there is the experiencing of the self, and so, the self is strengthened. So, how is it possible for the self not to experience? One can see that creation is not at all the experience of the self. Creation is when the self is not there, because creation is not intellectual, is not of the mind, is not self-projected, is something beyond all experiencing, as we know. Is it possible for the mind to be quite still, in a state of nonrecognition, which is, nonexperiencing, to be in a state in which creation can take place—which means, when the self is not there, when the self is absent? Am I making myself clear or not? Look, sirs, the problem is this, is it not? Any movement of the mind, positive or negative, is an experience which actually strengthens the 'me'. Is it possible for the mind not to recognize? That can only take place when there is complete silence, but not the silence which is an experience of the self and which therefore strengthens the self.

Is there an entity apart from the self which looks at the self and dissolves the self? Are you following all this? Is there a spiritual entity which supersedes the self and destroys it, which puts it aside? We think there is, don't we? Most religious people think there is such an element. The materialist says, "It is impossible for the self to be destroyed; it can only be conditioned and restrained—politically, economically, and socially; we can hold it firmly within a certain pattern, and we can break it, and therefore it can be made to lead a high life, a moral life, and not to interfere with anything but to follow the social pattern and to function merely as a machine." That, we know. There are other people, the so-called religious ones—they are not really religious, though we call them so—who say, "Fundamentally, there is such an element. If we can get into touch with it, it will dissolve the self."

Is there such an element to dissolve the self? Please see what we are doing. We are merely forcing the self into a corner. If you allow yourself to be forced into the corner, you will see what is going to happen. We would like that there should be an element which is timeless, which is not of the self, which, we hope, will come and intercede and destroy, which we call God. Now is there such a thing which the mind can conceive? There may be or there may not be; that is not the point. When the mind seeks a timeless spiritual state which will go into action in order to destroy the self, is that not another form of experience which is strengthening the 'me'? When you believe, is that not what is actually taking place? When you believe that there is truth, God, timeless state, immortality, is that not the process of strengthening the self? The self has projected that thing which, you feel and believe, will come and destroy the self. So, having projected this idea of continuance in a timeless state as spiritual entity, you are going to experience, and all such experience will only strengthen the self, and therefore what have you done? You have not really destroyed the self but only given it a different name, a different quality; the self is still there because you have experienced it. So, our action from the beginning to the end is the same action; only we think it is evolving, growing, becoming more and more beautiful, but if you observe inwardly, it is the same action going on, the same 'me' functioning at different levels with different labels, with different names.

When you see the whole process, the cunning, extraordinary inventions, the intelligence of the self, how it covers itself up through identification, through virtue, through experience, through belief, through knowledge; when you see that you are moving in a circle, in a cage of its own making, what happens? When you are aware of it, fully cognizant of it, then is not your mind extraordinarily quiet—not through compulsion, not through any reward, not through any fear? When you recognize that every movement of the mind is merely a form of strengthening the self, when you observe it, see it, when you are completely aware of it in action, when you come to that point—not ideologically, verbally, not through experiencing, but when you are actually in that state—then you will see that the mind being utterly still, has no power of creating. Whatever the mind creates is in a circle, within the field of the self. When the mind is noncreating, there is creation, which is not a recognizable process.

Reality, truth, is not to be recognized. For truth to come, belief, knowledge, experiencing, virtue, pursuit of virtue—which is different from being virtuous—all this must go. The virtuous person who is conscious of pursuing virtue can never find reality. He may be a very decent person; that is entirely different from the man of truth, from the man who understands. To the man of truth, truth has come into being. A virtuous man is a righteous man, and a righteous man can never understand what is truth, because virtue to him is the covering of the self, the strengthening of the self, because he is pursuing virtue. When he says, "I must be without greed," the state in which he is nongreedy and which he experiences strengthens the self. That is why it is so important to be poor, not only in the things of the world, but also in belief and in knowledge. A rich man with worldly riches or a man rich in knowledge and belief will never know anything but darkness and will be the center of all mischief and misery. But if you and I, as individuals, can see this whole working of the self, then we shall know what love is. I assure you, that is the only reformation which can possibly change the world. Love is not the self. Self cannot recognize love. You say, "I love," but then, in the very saying of it, in the very experiencing of it, love is not. But, when you know love, self is not. When there is love, self is not.

Question: What is simplicity? Does it imply seeing very clearly the essentials and discarding everything else?

KRISHNAMURTI: Let us see what simplicity is not. Don't say, "That is negation." You do not say anything positive; that is immature, thoughtless expression. Those people who say it are exploiters because they have something to give you which you want and through which to exploit you. We are doing nothing of that kind. We are trying to find out the truth of simplicity. Therefore you must discard, put things aside, and observe. The man who has much is afraid of revolution, inwardly and outwardly. So let us find out what is not simplicity. A complicated mind is not simple, is it? A clever mind is not simple; a mind that has an end in view for which it is working as reward, as punishment, is not a simple mind, is it? Sirs, don't agree with me. It is not a question of agreement. It is your life. A mind that is burdened with knowledge is not a simple mind; a mind that is crippled with beliefs is not a simple mind, is it? A mind that has identified itself with something greater and is striving to keep that identity is not a simple mind, is it? But we think it is a simple life to have a loincloth, one or two; we want outward show of simplicity, and we are easily deceived by that. That is why a man who is very rich worships the man who has renounced.

What is simplicity? Can simplicity be the discarding of nonessentials and pursuing of essentials—which means choice? Please follow this. Does it not mean choice, choosing? I choose essentials and discard nonessentials. What is this process of choosing? Think deeply. What is the entity that chooses? Mind, is it not? It does not matter what you call it. You say, "I will choose this essential." How do you know what is the essential? Either you have a pattern of what other people have said or your own experience says that is the essential. Can you rely on your experience? Because, when you choose, your choice is based on desire; what you call essential is that which gives you satisfaction. So you are back again in the same process, are you not? Can a confused mind choose? If it does, the choice must also be confused.

Therefore, the choice between the essential and the nonessential is not simplicity. It is a conflict. A mind in conflict, in confusion, can never be simple. So when you discard, when you see all the false things and the tricks of the mind, when you observe it, look at it, are aware of it, then you will know what simplicity is. A mind which is bound by belief is never a simple mind. A mind that is crippled with knowledge is not simple. A mind that is distracted by God, by women, by music, is not a simple mind. A mind caught in the routine of the office, of the rituals, of the mantras, such a mind is not simple. Simplicity is action without idea. But, that is a very rare thing; that means creation. As long as there is not creation, we are centers of mischief and misery and destruction. Simplicity is not a thing which you pursue and experience. Simplicity comes, as a flower opens, at the right moment when each one understands the whole process of existence and relationship. Because we have not thought about it or have not observed it, we are not aware of it; we value in a certain way all of the outer forms of simplicity—such as shaving our heads, having clothing or unclothing in a certain way. Those are not simplicity. Simplicity is not to be found. Simplicity does not lie between essential and nonessential. It comes into being when the self is not, when the self is not caught in speculations, in conclusions, in beliefs, in ideations. Such a mind only can find truth. Such a mind alone can receive that which is immeasurable, which is unnameable—and that is simplicity.

Question: Can I, who am religiously inclined and desirous of acting wholly and integrally, express myself through politics? For, to me, it appears that a radical change is necessary in the political field.

KRISHNAMURTI: What the questioner means is this: seeking wholly, seeking religiously the whole, entire, complete, can I politically function, that is, act partially? He says politics is obviously the path for him; when he seeks and follows that path which is not the whole, complete, he merely functions in fields which are partial, fragmentary. Is that not so? What is your answer, not your cunning answer or immediate response? Can I see the whole thing of life, which means, can I love? Let us take love. I have compassion; I feel tremendously and for the whole; can I then act only politically? Can I, seeking the whole, be a Hindu or a Brahmin? Can I, having love in my heart, identify myself with a path, with a particular country, with a particular system—economic or religious? Suppose I want to improve the particular, I want to bring about a radical change in the particular, in the country in which I live; the moment I identify myself with that particular, have I not shut out the whole? This is your problem just as mine. We are thinking about it together. You are not listening to me. When we are trying to find an answer, your opinions and ideas are not the solution. What we are trying to find is, can a truly religious man—not a phoney one that consults others—a really sacred person seeking the whole, can he identify himself with a radical movement for a particular country? And will it do to have revolution—don't be afraid of that word—of one country, of one people, of one state, if I am seeking the whole, if I am trying to understand that which is not within the scope of the mind? Can I, using my mind, act politically? I see there must be political action; I see there must be real change, radical change in our relationship, in our economic system, in the distribution of land, and so on. I see there must be revolution, and yet at the same time, I am pursuing a path, the political path; I am also trying to understand the whole. What is my action there? Is not that your problem, sirs? Can you act politically—that is, partially—and understand the whole? Politics and economics are partial; they are not the whole, integrated life; they are partial, necessary, essential. Can I abandon the whole or leave the whole society and tinker with the particular? Obviously, I cannot. But I can act upon it, not through it.

We want to bring about a certain change; we have certain ideas about it; we pursue so many groups and so on. We use means to achieve the result. And is the understanding of the whole contrary to that? Am I confusing you? I am only telling you what I think; do not accept it, but think it out for yourself and see. For me, political action, economic action are of secondary importance though they are essential. There must be radical change in the political field, but such a change will have no depth if I do not pursue the other. If the other is not primary, if the other is only secondary, then my action towards the secondary will have tremendous significance. But, if I see a certain path and act politically, political action becomes important to me, and not acting integrally. But, if acting integrally is really important to me and if I pursue it, political action, religious action, economic action, will come rightly, deeply, fundamentally. If I do not pursue the other but merely confine myself to the political, the economic, or the social change, then I create more misery.

So it all depends on what you lay emphasis on. Laying emphasis on the right thing—which is the whole—will produce its own action with regard to politics and so on. It all depends on you. In pursuing that whole thing without saying, "I am going to act politically or socially," you will bring about fundamental alterations politically, religiously, and economically.

What is important in this question is: what is it that you are seeking? What is the primary issue in your life? There is really no division between primary and secondary, but yet, in seeking, you will find that when you begin to understand the whole, there is no secondary or primary; then the whole is the path. But, if you say that you must alter a particular part, then you will not understand the whole. Any change in the particular, like the political field, cannot alter the whole thing; this has been shown historically. But if you know, if you are aware of the whole process of the self, dissolve it, and if there is love, this will bring about a fundamental revolution in India.

January 19, 1952

Sixth Talk in Madras

I think it is important to understand the relationship between the speaker and yourself, for one is apt to listen to these talks and discussions with either complete indifference, curiosity, a certain attitude of skepticism, or with a natural inclination to take up a pro or anti attitude, an attitude of addiction. To me, both these approaches seem utterly wrong. What is important is to understand that you and I are two individuals, not a collective group belonging to two sects or religions, that we are, as two individuals, trying to solve the problem. That is always my approach, and not the one where I sit on a platform advising what you should do or laying down the law—which would be stupid. But if you and I as two individuals can look at the problem, understand it, go into the root of it, then perhaps we shall be able to help each other to dissolve the many problems that confront each one of us. That is the only approach, I think, any intelligent person caught in the present confusion must adopt. We are so apt to believe, to accept, and that is because in belief, in acceptance, there is a certain security, a certain escape, self-aggrandizement. If we can look at the problems with clarity and honesty of purpose, then we can solve the problems easily. But that is very difficult because most of us are so corrupt in our thinking, because we have so many vested interests—economic, religious, and psychological. It is difficult for most of us to think apart from these backgrounds. If I may suggest, that is the only approach for solving any of the innumerable problems awaiting solution; you as an individual and I as an individual are resolving our problems in our little world of relationship.

What we have been discussing for the last few weeks has been the question of the self and its ways. Can we see that the self is the root cause of all evils? The 'me', or the self, with all its extraordinary deviations and subtle actions, is responsible for all our ills. Every intelligent man must resolve this problem of 'self', not hedge it about, cover it about; he must understand how, in daily living, he gives sustenance, vitality, and continuity to the self. If we would solve any of the world's problems, we would surely understand the whole process of the self with all its complexities, both the conscious and the unconscious. That is what we have been discussing, taking different aspects of it.

Organized religion, organized belief, and totalitarian states are very similar because they all want to destroy the individual through compulsion, through propaganda, though various forms of coercion. The organized religion does the same thing, only in a different way. There, you must accept, you must believe, you are conditioned. The whole tendency both of the left and of the so-called spiritual organizations is to mold the mind to a particular pattern of conduct because the individual left to himself becomes a rebel. So, the individual is destroyed through compulsion, though propaganda, and is controlled, dominated for the sake of the society, for the sake of the state and so on. The so-called religious organizations do the same, only a little more suspiciously, a little more subtly, because there too, people must believe, must repress, must control, and all the rest of it. The whole process is to dominate the self in one form or another. Through compulsion, collective action is sought. That is what most organizations want, whether they be economic organizations or religious. They want collective action, which means that the individual should be destroyed. Ultimately, it can only mean that. You accept the left, the Marxist theory or the Hindu, Buddhist or the Christian doctrines, and thereby you hope to bring about collective action. Surely cooperation is different from coercion.

How is collective action brought about, or how is it to be brought about? Up to now, it has been through belief, economic promise of a welfare state, promise of a bright future, or it has been through the so-called spiritual method, through fear, compulsion, and various forms of reward. Does not cooperation come when there is intelligence which is not collective, which is neither collective nor individual? That is what I would like to discuss, talk over together, this evening.

To discuss that problem profitably, you must find out what is the function of the mind. What do we mean by the mind? As I have been pointing out, you are not merely listening to me, but you and I are together investigating this question, the function of the mind. By sheer accident, I happen for the moment to be sitting on a platform, talking it over with you, but really you and I are together tackling the problem, together investigating the whole question.

When you observe your own mind, you are observing not only the so-called upper levels of the mind but also watching the unconscious; you are seeing what the mind actually does, are you not? That is the only way you can investigate. You should not superimpose what it should do, how it should think, or how it should act and so on; that would amount to making mere statements. That is, if you say the mind should be this or should not be that, then you stop all investigation and all thinking; or, if you quote some high authority, then you equally stop thinking, don't you? If you quote Shankara, Buddha, Christ, or XYZ, there is an end to all pursuit, to all thinking and all investigation. So, one has to guard against that. You must put aside all these subtleties of the mind, and you must know you are investigating this problem of the 'me' together with me.

What is the function of the mind? To find that out, you must know what the mind is actually doing. What does your mind do? It is all a process of thinking, is it not? Otherwise, the mind is not there. As long as the mind is not thinking consciously or unconsciously, without verbalizing, there is no consciousness. We have to find out what the mind that we use in our everyday life, and also the mind of which most of us are unconscious, does in relation to our problems. We must look at the mind as it is, and not as it should be.

Now what is mind as it is functioning? It is actually a process of isolation, is it not? Fundamentally it is that. That is what the process of thought is. It is thinking in an isolated form, yet remaining collective. When you observe your own thinking, you will see it is an isolated, fragmentary process. You are thinking according to your reactions, the reactions of your memory, of your experience, of your knowledge, of your belief. You are reacting to all that, aren't you? If I say that there must be a fundamental revolution, you immediately react. You will object to that word *revolution*, if you have got good investments, spiritual or otherwise. So, your reaction is dependent on your knowledge, on your belief, on your experience. That is an obvious fact. There are various forms of reaction. You say, "I must be brotherly," "I must cooperate," "I must be friendly," "I must be kind," and so on. What are these? These are all reactions, but the fundamental reaction of thinking is a process of isolation. Please do not readily accept it, for we are together investigating it. You are watching the process of your own mind, each one of you, which means you are watching your own action, belief, knowledge, experience. All these give security, do they not? They give security, give strength to the process of thinking. As we discussed yesterday, that process only strengthens the 'me', the mind, the self whether that self is high or low. All our religions, all our social sanctions, all our laws are for the support of the individual, the individual self, the separative action, and in opposition to that, there is the totalitarian state. If you go deeper into the unconscious, there too it is the same process that is at work. There, we are the collective influenced by the environment, by the climate, by the society, by the father, the mother, the grandfather; you know all that. There again is the desire to assert, to dominate as an individual, as the 'me'.

So, is not the function of the mind, as we know it and as we function daily, a process of isolation? Aren't you seeking individual salvation? You are going to be somebody in the future; in this very life, you are going to be a great man, a great writer. Our whole tendency is to be separated. Can the mind do anything else but that? Is it possible for the mind not to think separatively, in a self-enclosed manner, fragmentarily? That is impossible. Because of this, we worship the mind; the mind is extraordinarily important. Don't you know, the moment you are a little bit cunning, a little bit alert, and have a little accumulated information and knowledge, how important you become in society? You have seen how you worship those who are intellectually superior, the lawyers, the professors, the orators, the great writers, the explainers and the expounders! Haven't you? You have cultivated the intellect and the mind.

The function of the mind is to be separated; otherwise, your mind is not there. Having cultivated this process for centuries, we find we cannot cooperate; only we are urged, compelled, driven by authority, fear, either economic or religious. If that is the actual state, not only consciously but also at the deeper levels, in our motives, our intentions, our pursuits, how can there be cooperation? How can there be intelligent coming together to do something? As that is almost impossible, religions and organized social parties force the individual to certain forms of discipline. Discipline then becomes imperative in order to come together, to do things together.

So, until we understand how to transcend this separative thinking, this process of giving emphasis to the 'me' and the mind whether in the collective form or in individual form, we shall not have peace; we shall have constant conflict and wars. Now, our problem is how to dissolve this, how to bring about an end to the separative process of thought. Can thought ever destroy the self, thought being the process of verbalization and of certain reactions? Thought is nothing else than reactions; thought is not creative, but it is only the expression of the creativeness in words, which we call thought. Can such thought put an end to itself? That is what we are trying to find out, aren't we? I think along these lines: "I must discipline," "I must identify," "I must think more properly," "I must be this or that." Thought is compelling itself, urging itself, disciplining itself, to be something or not to be something. Is that not a process of isolation? Therefore, it is not the integrated intelligence which can function as a whole, from which alone there can be cooperation. Do you see the problem now? I am not proposing a problem myself. You must know that this is your problem, if you are not already aware of it. You may put it in different ways, but fundamentally, this is the problem.

How are you to come to the end of thought, or rather, how is thought to come to an end? I mean the thought which is isolated, fragmentary, and partial. How do you set about it? Will discipline destroy it? Will your so-called discipline destroy it? Obviously, you have not succeeded all these long years; otherwise, you would not be here. You must examine the disciplining process, which is solely a thought process, in which there is subjection, repression, control, domination—all affecting the unconscious. It asserts itself later as you grow older. Having tried discipline for such a long time to no purpose, you must have found that obviously discipline is not the process to destroy the self. Self cannot be destroyed through discipline because discipline is a process of strengthening the self. Yet, all your religions support it; all your meditations, your assertions are based on this. Will knowledge destroy it? Will belief destroy it? In other words, will everything that we are at present doing, all the activities in which we are at present engaged in order to get at the root of the self, will all that succeed? Is not all this a fundamental waste in a thought process which is a process of isolation, a process of reaction? What do you do when you realize fundamentally or deeply that the thought cannot end itself? What happens? Watch yourselves, sirs, and tell me. When you are fully aware of this fact, what happens? You then understand that any reaction is conditioned, and that, through conditioning, there can be no freedom either at the beginning or at the end. Freedom is always at the beginning, and not at the end.

When you realize that any reaction is a form of conditioning and therefore giving continuity to the self in different ways, what actually takes place? You must be very clear in this matter. Belief, knowledge, discipline, experience, the whole process of achieving the result or the end, ambition, becoming something in this life or the next one, future life—all these are a process of isolation, a process which brings destruction, misery, wars from which there is no escape through collective action, however much you might be threatened with concentration camps and all the rest of it. Are you aware of that fact? What is the state of the mind? What is the state of the mind which says, "It is so," "That is my problem," "That is exactly where I am," "I have rejected," "I see what knowledge and discipline can do, what ambition does"? Surely, there is a different process at work.

We see the ways of the intellect. We do not see the way of love; the way of love is not to be found through the intellect. The intellect with all its ramifications, with all its desires, ambitions, pursuits, must come to an end for real love to come into existence. Don't you know that when you love, you cooperate, you are not thinking of yourself? That is the highest form of intelligence—not when you are loved as a superior entity or when you are in good position, which is nothing but fear. When your vested interests are there, there can be no love; there is only the process of exploitation culminating in fear. So, love can come into being only when the mind is not there. Therefore, you must understand the whole process of the mind, the function of the mind. Only then can you find out when deep revolution will take place.

This process of the mind is not understood in a couple of minutes or by listening to one or two talks. It can only be understood when there is a big revolution in you, a deep interest to find out this discontent, this despair. But you are not in despair. You are well-fed intellectually and physically. You prevent yourself from coming to that state in which you are in despair. You have always something to lean on. You can always escape, go to the temple, read books, listen to a talk, run away, and a man who escapes cannot be in despair. If you are in despair, you are trying to find a way to be hopeful, to go away from despair. It is only a man who is really unconscious, who has discarded completely all these things, stands naked, who will find what love is; and without that, there is no transformation, there is no revolution, there is no renewal. There is nothing but imitation and ashes, and that is what our culture is at present. It is only when we know how to love each other that there can be cooperation, there can be intelligent functioning, coming together over any question. It is only then possible to find out what God is, what truth is. Now, we are trying to find truth through intellect, through imitation—which is idolatry, whether it is made by hand or by mind. Only when you discard completely, through understanding, the whole structure of the self, that which is eternal, timeless, immeasurable, comes; you cannot go to it; it comes to you.

Question: Can the root of a problem like greed be completely eradicated by awareness? Are there various levels of awareness?

KRISHNAMURTI: That is a problem to the questioner. Is it to each one of us a problem? Greed cannot be chipped away little by little. That which you chip away, set aside, grows into greed in another form, and you know what greed does in society, between two individuals' relationship; you know the whole process of greed, economic or spiritual, of greed to be. The questioner asks how greed can fundamentally be eradicated because he feels there must be a way, a process which will go to the root of the thing. If you say, "I wish to get rid of it slowly, gradually, until I become perfect," it is just a way of avoiding the issue. Is there a way of fundamentally eradicating it? Let us find out.

First of all, why do you want to get rid of greed? Is it not in order to get something else, in order to be something, because books say so or because you see results in society? What is the urge that makes you say, "I must do away with it"? That is very important to find out. You may be the root when you say, "I do not want to be this, but I want to be that." The want to be, positive or negative, may be the root. You are only saying, "I will do this and that"; by chipping that, by becoming that, you have not understood the motive, have you? Can greed be destroyed by will, by denial, by repression, by control, or by identifying with something which is not greed? Can you destroy it? If you have tried it, the very process of identifying with something, is that not also greed? Certainly, it is also greed because you want to avoid the pains, conflicts, and sufferings of greed without really solving it. You are trying to be something else. The motive, the desire, is still to be something. Is not desire to be something the very nature of greed? To be something is greed. Can you live in this world without being something? Can you live without being anything, without titles, degrees, positions, capacities? Until you are prepared to be nothing, you must be greedy in different forms.

Have you true awareness of this function of greed and its destructive pursuits? Can the mind—after all, mind is greed—can the mind be nothing, not seeking, not desiring to be, to become? Obviously it can. It is only then that you are full; only then, you do not ask, you do not demand to be fulfilled. But you do not want to be nothing. All your struggle is to be something, is it not? If you are a clerk, you want to be something higher, to have better pay, more position, higher prestige, more ambitions, to be near the Master, far away from the Master, promise of reward in the future. You don't throw away all that, be simple, be nothing, be really naked. Surely, until you come to that state, there must be greed in different forms. And you cannot come to that state without being nothing. Your experiencing of nothing is a projection of the self and therefore a strengthening of the self. So, you cannot experience the state of nothingness any more than you can experience the state of love. When you experience anything, love is not because, as I explained yesterday, that which you call experience is only a projection of your own desire and therefore a strengthening of the self. So if you see all this, if you are aware of all this—not only at the superficial level, which is to have little, to possess only one or two suits—if you are aware of the whole significance of the desire to transform yourself from this to that, when you are fully cognizant of the whole process of greed, then greed will drop away.

Obviously, there are many layers of awareness. The spirit or marvel of what all is taking place, of the trees, the moonlight, the poor unfed child, the half-starved, the bloated tummies—they are all superficial awareness, observations. But if you can go a little deeper, there is awareness of how we are conditioned, not only at the conscious level but at a deeper level, awareness which comes through dreams, or movement when there is a little space between two thoughts, a certain unthought of, unmeditated observation. When you can go still deeper, that is, when the mind is absolutely without any reflection, recognition, when the mind is still, not experiencing, when the mind is not seeing what is stillness, there is intelligence.

Mind is always verbalizing experience and therefore giving strength to the memory and therefore to the self. Surely, the more we are conscious of all the ways of the self, the more we are aware of all our feelings; we understand every sorrow, every movement of thought; we not only observe it but live with it without brushing it aside. That gives maturity—not age, not knowledge, not belief. That brings about integrated intelligence, which is not separative.

Question: We are all Theosophists interested fundamentally in truth and love, as you are. Could you not have remained in our Society and helped us rather than separate yourself from us and denounce us? What have you achieved by this?

KRISHNAMURTI: First of all, many of you are amused; others are a little bit agitated; there is apprehension. Don't you feel all this? Let us find out.

Fundamentally, are we, you and I, seeking the same thing? Can you seek truth in any organization? Can you give yourself a label and seek truth? Can you be a Hindu and say, "I am seeking truth"? Then, when you are seeking, is not truth but fulfillment of belief. Can you belong to any organization, spiritual group, and seek truth? Is truth to be found collectively? Do you know love when you believe? Don't you know that when you believe in something very strongly and I believe in something contrary, there is no love between us. When you believe in certain hierarchical principles and authorities and I do not, do you think there is communion between us? When the whole structure of your thinking is the future, the becoming through virtue, when you are going to be somebody in the future, when the whole process of your thinking is based on authority and hierarchical principles, do you think there is love between us? You may use me for convenience, and I may use you for convenience. But that is not love. Let us be clear. Do not get agitated about these matters. You will not understand if you get excited about it.

To find out whether you are really seeking truth and love, you must investigate, must you not? If you investigate, if you find out inwardly and therefore act outwardly, what would happen? You would be outside, wouldn't you? If you question your own beliefs, won't you find yourself outside? As long as there are societies and organizations—so-called spiritual organizations that have vested interests in property, in belief, in knowledge—obviously, the people there are not seeking truth. They may say so. So, you must find out if we are fundamentally seeking the same thing. Can you seek truth through a Master, through a guru? Sirs, think it out. It is your problem. Can you find truth through the process of time, in becoming something? Can you find truth through the Master, through pupils, through gurus; what can they tell you fundamentally? They can only tell you to dissolve the 'me'. Are you doing that? If you are not, obviously you are not seeking truth, It is not that I am saying that you are not seeking truth, but the fact is that, if you are saying, "I am going to be somebody," if you occupy a position of spiritual authority, you cannot be seeking truth. I am very clear about these matters, and I am not trying to persuade you to accept or to denounce, which will be stupid. I cannot denounce you, as the questioner says.

Even though you have heard me for twenty years, you go on with your beliefs because it is very comforting to believe that you are being looked after, that you have special messengers for the future, that you are going to be something beautiful, now or eventually. You will go on because your vested interests are there, in property, in job, in belief, in knowledge. You do not question them. It is the same all the world over. It is not only this or that particular group of people but all groups—Catholics, Protestants, communists, capitalists—are in the same position; they have all vested interests. The man who is really revolutionary, who is inwardly seeing the truth of all these things, will find truth. He will know what love is, not in some future date which is of no value. When a man is hungry, he wants to be fed now, not tomorrow. But you have convenient theories of time, of eventuality, in which you are caught. Therefore, where is the connection, where is the relationship between you and me, or between yourself and that which you are attempting to find out? And yet, you all talk about love, brotherhood, and everything you do is contrary to that. It is obvious, sirs, that the moment you have organization, there must be intrigues for position, for authority; you know the whole game of it.

So, what we need is not whether I denounce you or whether you denounce or throw me out. That is not the problem. Obviously you must reject a man who says that what you believe or do is wrong; you have done so, or inwardly you should do so, because I say I am opposed to that which you want. If you would really seek, if you would find truth and love, there must be singleness of purpose, complete abandonment of all vested interests, which means you must be inwardly empty, poor, not seeking, not acquiring positions of authority as displayers or bringers of messages from the Masters. You must be completely naked. Since you do not wish that, naturally, you acquire labels, beliefs, and various forms of security. Sirs, do not reject; find out whether you are really, as you say, fundamentally seeking truth. I really question you, I really doubt you when you say, "I am seeking truth." You cannot seek truth because your search is a projection of your own desires; your experiencing of that projection is an experience which you want. But when you do not seek, when the mind is quiet and tranquil without any want, without any motive, without any compulsion, then you will find that ecstasy comes. For that ecstasy to come, you must be completely naked, empty, alone. Most people join these societies because they are gregarious, because they are clubs, and joining clubs is very convenient socially. Do you think you are going to find truth when you are seeking comfort, satisfaction, social security? No, sirs; you must stand alone without any support, without friends, without guru, without hope, completely and inwardly naked and empty. Then only, as the cup which is empty can be filled up, so the emptiness within can be filled up with that which is everlasting.

January 20, 1952

Seventh Talk in Madras

Perhaps this evening we can discuss the problem and the full implication of what is suffering and what is sorrow. I think that before we enter into that subject, we should consider what we mean by the word *understanding,* because if we can understand the profound significance, the depth and the meaning of sorrow, perhaps then we shall be able to free the mind entirely from those reactions which we term, or to which we give the name *sorrow,* which is a feeling. So, it is important to find out what we mean by understanding.

Is understanding reason or deduction? Is understanding merely the outcome of an intellectual or verbal process, or is it something entirely different from deduction, from comprehension? By careful analysis, do we solve a deep psychological problem? Is not understanding the comprehension, recognition, seeing the whole of the problem in its entirety? The mind can only reason, put several things together, deduce, analyze, compare, have knowledge about; but can the mind, which is a process of thinking in which time is involved, which is memory, and which is the accumulation of beliefs, knowledge, can such a mind understand the full significance of a problem? In other words, can the time process which is essentially a process of the mind, a process of thinking, solve a problem? That is particularly important to find out for most of us. For most of us, the instrument which we have cultivated so diligently is the mind, the intellect, with which we approach a problem hoping thereby to resolve it.

We are asking ourselves, "Can the mind which is a process of time, which is the result of yesterday, today, and tomorrow, be the instrument of understanding?" Can the mind see the whole problem in its entirety? Does understanding come into being through time? Or is it irrespective of time? If we dissociate the process of understanding from reasoning, from deduction, from analysis, which is a process of time, then we can probably comprehend fully a problem at one glance. That is very important, is it not? If we are to understand the full significance of sorrow, we must eliminate the time process altogether. Time will not resolve the process of building up sorrow nor will it help in the resolution of sorrow. It can only help you to forget it, to evade it, to postpone it, but still the sense of sorrow is there.

So, please come forward this evening as two individuals, not as groups of people trying collectively to think about it; come forward as two individuals and look at this problem of sorrow without introducing the process of time as a means to understanding, to resolving. In other words, can we see this problem of sorrow in its entirety? It is only when we see something completely, wholly, integrally, there is a possibility of its dissolution, and not otherwise. The possibility of this dissolution does not lie through the process of what we call the mind, the reason, the thought. That is why I said we must understand that word ***understanding;*** we must grasp the significance of that word. I think if we can do that, perhaps we shall get to the root of the problem of sorrow.

If I would understand something, first I must love it, must I not? I must have communion with it. I must have no barrier. There must be no resistance. There must be no apprehension, no fear, which translate themselves into condemnation, justification, or a process of identification. I hope you are following all this. Forget the words for the moment; the words I am using need not have any value for you; keep in contact, in communion with what I am saying, the spirit of it, which is not mere verbalization. To understand something, there must be love. If I would understand you, I must love you, I must have no prejudice. We know all these things. You say, "I have no prejudice." But all of us are a bundle of prejudices, antagonisms, and we put on verbal screens. Let us remove this screen and see what the significance of sorrow is. I feel that only through that way shall we resolve this enormously complex problem of sorrow.

So, understanding requires communion; understanding requires a mind that is capable of perceiving the unknown, the unnameable, because a mind that wishes to understand something must itself be quite still, which is not a state of recognition. If there is to be understanding, there must be communion, which means love, not only at one particular level but at all levels. When we love somebody, it is a process of timeless quality. You can't name it. There is no barrier of fear, of reward, of condemnation; nor is there identification with somebody else—which is a mental process. If we can really see the significance of that word, then we can go into the problems of suffering. If there is that feeling of communion, of really loving that problem which we call sorrow, then we shall be able to understand it fully; otherwise, we shall merely run away from it, find various escapes. So, let us, if we can, put ourselves in that position. Only then can we understand what is called sorrow. There should be no mental barrier, no prejudice, no condemnation, no justification through tradition. Then we can approach, you and I as individuals, this thing that is consuming most of us—sorrow.

Energy in movement, in action, is desire, is it not? That desire when thwarted is pain, and that desire in fulfillment is pleasure. For most of us, action is a process of fulfillment of desire. "I want" and "I don't want" govern our attitude. That energy which is canalized, identified as the 'me' through desire, is ever seeking a fulfillment. Desire in its movement, in its action, is a process of fulfillment or denial. There are various forms of fulfillment and various forms of denial likewise—each binding, each bringing about different kinds of sorrow. When there is sorrow, there are various forms of resolution of it, various forms of escapes from it.

We know sorrow at different levels, don't we? Physical sorrow, physical pain, sorrow of death, sorrow that comes when there is no fulfillment, sorrow resulting from a state of emptiness, sorrow that comes when ambition is not fulfilled, sorrow in not coming up to the standard or the good example, sorrow of the ideal, and finally sorrow of identification. We know various forms of sorrow at different psychological and physiological levels; and also we know the various forms of escapes: drink, rituals, repetition of words, the turning to tradition, looking to the future, looking for better times, better hopes, better circumstances; we know all these forms of escapes—religious, psychological, physical, and material. The more we escape, the greater and more complex the problems become. When we look at the problem, our whole structure is a series of escapes. You explain away sorrow; to you then, explanation has more significance than the depth, the meaning, the vitality of sorrow. After all, the explanations are merely words, however subtle, however justified, and we are satisfied with words. This is another escape.

We have our whole mental process in approaching a problem like that of sorrow. We have our basis of a series of escapes, justifications, and condemnation. So, there is not direct and vital communion with the problem of sorrow. Then you are a different entity looking at sorrow. You are trying to dissolve, inquire into, analyze the problem of sorrow. You are different, and something else is suffering in this process of analysis, condemnation, and justification.

There is no question of you as an entity that is in sorrow or that is sorrowful. Sorrow is not different from the thinker. The thinker, the feeler, the entity that desires, is itself sorrow. It is not as if he is different from sorrow, and he is going to dissolve sorrow. The very process of desire, which is energy in action, is a process of frustration, of suffering, of fulfillment, of pain. You are not different from sorrow. That is the whole picture, is it not? We can enlarge it more verbally, paint it more in detail, but that is the problem, is it not? You are not different from sorrow, and therefore you cannot resolve sorrow. You can't analyze yourself as a separate entity looking at sorrow, nor can you go to the analyzer to get it resolved, nor can you escape, put away direct sorrow by energy spent in social activities.

Most of our efforts, most of our intentions, and our search are for saying, "I am different from that which I feel, and how am I to resolve that?" This is really an important issue not to be easily brushed aside and cunningly replied. You have to look at it though your whole being revolts because we have been brought up to think that you can operate on it. You are not at all a different entity from your thought, or from your desire or your ambition, from your ladder you are climbing, spiritually or sociologically. To understand this problem there must be communion with the whole, and you cannot commune with the whole if you are looking at it partially as you and the object. That is a partial comprehension, partial understanding—which is not at all understanding—if you think you are a different entity looking at the thing which you call sorrow.

So, you are the creator of sorrow, you are the entity that suffers, and you are not separate from sorrow, from pain. As long as there is a division between you and suffering, there is only a partial understanding, partial comprehension, partial view of the thing, which means really that you must put aside all previous explanations, which means you are face to face, not as two separate processes but as a unitary process, with the thing that you call sorrow. When you really love, there is no barrier; then there is communion. It is not an identification with another; identification does not exist in love. It is only a state of being.

Can you look at this problem of sorrow, sorrow not only of the reaction of sympathy, a hope or failure, but also the sorrow that is so enveloping, so deep, so profound that no verbal description can cover it? Can you and I be in full communion with it? We must not make virtue of sorrow, as a means of understanding, a means of progress.

Actually what is this sorrow? When you suffer, when your son dies, there is one kind of sorrow; when you see the poor unfed children, that is another kind of sorrow; when you are struggling to reach the top of the ladder and you don't succeed, that is a third kind of sorrow; when you are not fulfilling the ideal, you have sorrow. Surely, sorrow is a process of desire ever increasing, ever multiplying, self-enclosing. Can I understand that whole process of energy in movement as desire and put an end to desire, not to energy? What we know is that energy in action is desire—desire being the 'me', the 'me' advancing, the 'me' fulfilling, the 'me' postponing.

Can I understand this whole problem of sorrow and desire and thereby put an end to desire as a movement of the 'me', and not come back but be in that state of energy which is pure intelligence? It is not a question to be answered yes and no. It is not a schoolboy's affair. This needs a great deal of meditation, meditation not in the sense of pitching up your thought to a certain level and holding it—that would be absurdity. We are not discussing meditation here. As I said, this requires a great deal of insight, and you can't have insight if there is any sort of distortion of desire.

Energy is pure intelligence, and when once we comprehend that, or let it come into being, then you will see that desire has very little significance. That is our whole problem, is it not?—how to shape the desire, how to mold it sociologically or spiritually. How is the 'me' or desire to be shaped for collective use, to be shaped for individual use? How is all this done?

As long as desire is not fully comprehended, fully understood, there must be sorrow because we cannot have the pure reason that will resolve it, the pure intelligence that is necessary for it. Reason can't dissolve sorrow; it can't dissolve desire. Therefore it is necessary to understand the whole problem not by deduction, not by reasoning but by seeing the whole thing, which means to really love the problem, to really love sorrow. You understand? There are people who love sorrow, but their hearts are empty; instead of loving a man, they love sorrow, which is an ideal. Haven't you seen people who love virtue? They love sorrow because they feel good in loving; they feel a certain enthusiastic response, a certain well-being. I do not mean that kind of love at all. When you love, there is no identification, but there is communion; there is open receptivity between that and you. That is essential to understand this whole problem.

As I said, understanding is not a process of time; it is not of time. Don't say, "I will understand tomorrow," "I will go," "I will come," "I will be aware more and more." Understanding has nothing to do with time or process of time, which is thinking. So mind cannot solve the problem of sorrow. So, what can solve it? If you try to understand the problem with your mind, you justify, you condemn, or you identify yourself with it. The mind that can understand the problem fully is the mind that is not in a state of agitation; the mind that would understand the problem is not seeking a result; it does not want to find an answer; it does not say, "I must be free from sorrow in order to experience, in order to have more." There is no "more." "More" is the sorrow, which means, the less. So if you can look at it completely, not as 'I' or 'me' looking, observing, shaping, destroying, but with a mind to which the observer and the observed are the same, then you will find there comes love that is not sensation, intelligence that is not of time or of thought process—and it is only that that can resolve this immense and complex problem of sorrow.

Question: I have spent ten of the best years of my life in prison for my political activities which promised great things. Now there is disillusionment, and I feel completely burned out. What am I to do?

KRISHNAMURTI: You may not spend ten years in prison, but you may spend a year or two in pursuit of false hope, in pursuit of false activity, in doing something to which you have given your whole being, your whole devotion or thought, and then find it empty. We have done that, have we not? You follow a certain path and action hoping it will bring great things, hoping it will help people, will free people, hoping there will be at the end of it compassion, love; and you have given your life to it. And then one day you find it is utterly empty, that is, the thing you have lived for has no meaning any more; you are emotionally burned out. Don't you know such cases? Are you not one of the cases? Are you not in that position? Have you not had such experience; have you not known that you have followed the path of the Master, the initiator—political or religious, promising an ideal state through revolution—and you have given out your zeal and energy and your life to it, and at the end you are disillusioned, burned out emotionally? You work for it and then leave it. But there is another fellow, stupid and ignorant, who comes and fills your place. He carries on; he adds fuel to the useless fire. And if he is burned out, he walks away and goes out of it. But there is another fellow to take up. And the movement of stupidity goes on in the name of religion, politics, God, peace—call it what you will. Another problem arises: how to prevent the stupid from falling into the useless fray that has no meaning.

Societies, organizations, are such empty things, especially the religious; so, what are you to do when you are burned out? Your elasticity is gone. You are getting old. All the things you are striving for have no meaning. And either you turn cynical, bitter, or you remain like a log of dead wood, secluded, in isolation. That is an obvious fact, is it not? All that, we know; there are hundreds of examples; perhaps you are yourself one of them. What is one to do when one is in that state? Can that which is dead be revived? Can that which is hollow, false, give its life to the false? Can that suddenly come to life and see what it has done, pursue the real, and renew? That is the problem, is it not? Can I who have given the greater part of my life to something which has no meaning—no meaning in the sense that it has no deep, everlasting significance—can I who have lost that state, been burned out, can I find life again, can I find the zeal again? I think I can.

When I am burned out, when I realize I have wasted, instead of becoming bitter, if I can see the whole significance of what I have done, how I have pursued the ideal and how ideal always destroys—because ideal has no meaning, ideal is only self-projection, ideal is only postponement, ideal prevents me from understanding that which is, ideal prevents me from comprehending the whole; if I can sit quietly, not pulled off in another direction; if I recognize the whole process of what I have done and see what had led me to false hopes, what awakened all kinds of ambitions in me; if I can see all that, without any movement in the other direction, either of justification or condemnation; if I can remain with it, live with it, then there is the possibility of reviving, is there not? Because, the mind has pursued something which, it hoped, would produce results, utopias, marvels, etc. If the mind realizes what it has done, there is renewal, is there not? If I know I have done a grievous thing, false thing, if I am aware of it, understand it, then surely that very understanding is light, is the new.

But most of us have no patience or wisdom or silent acceptance of that which we have done, without bitterness. All I know is I have wasted my life, and I want a new life. I am eager to grasp the new thing. When I am eager to grasp, then I am again lost. Then there is the guru, the political leader, the promise of utopia carrying me away. So, I am back again at the same process as before. But recognizing this process is to be patient, to be aware, to know what I have done, not to attempt anything more. That requires great wisdom. That requires great affection, to know I am not going to participate in any of those things. It does not matter where it will lead me, but I am not going to do that. When we do that, when we are in that state, I assure you there is renewal, new beginning. But I must see that my mind does not create new illusion, new hope.

Question: What is meant by ''accepting what is''? *How does it differ from resignation?*

KRISHNAMURTI: What is acceptance? What is the process of acceptance? I accept sorrow. What does it mean? I suffer through loss of a friend, brother, or son, and there is suffering. The acceptance of that suffering through explanation is resignation, is it not? I say it is inevitable, and the suffering dies; I rationalize, or I turn to karma or reincarnation, and I accept. Acceptance is the process of recognition, is it not? Don't define the word but see the meaning. That is, I accept in order to be peaceful. I resign myself to an event, to the circumstance, to the incident. I accept them because they pacify me, they put me out of the state of conflict. There is an ulterior motive in resignation, of which I may not be conscious. Deep down, unconsciously, I want to have peace, I want to have satisfaction, I do not want to be disturbed. But loss causes disturbance which we call suffering. And in order to escape from suffering, I explain, I justify and then say, "I am resigned to the inevitable, to karma." That is the most stupid way, is it not, of living. But that will not bring about understanding, will it?

If I am capable of looking at *what is*—that is, what has taken place, the death of someone, an incident—without any mental process, if I can observe it, be aware of it, follow it, be in communion with it, love it, there is no resignation, no acceptance. I shall have to accept the fact. Fact is fact. But, if you can prevent yourself from translating it, interpreting it, giving it justification, putting it in a place that will be suitable for you, if you are aware of that and therefore put it aside naturally, without any effort, then you will see that which is quite different, which is significant. Then it begins to narrowly unfold, begins superficially, but as it begins to unfold, it is more and more; it is like reading a book. But if you have already concluded what the book is about, know the end, you are not reading.

Understanding of *what is* cannot come about through any justification, condemnation, or identifying yourself with *what is.* We have lost the way of love. That is why all this superficial process exists. Don't ask what love is. You talk all the time of love. What do you mean by it? You can only find out what love is by negation. As the life we lead is negation, there can be no love. As our life is mostly destructive, the way of our life, the way of our communion is self-enclosing. That which is all embracing can be understood only when the negation has ceased to be. The understanding of *what is* can come when there is complete communion with that which is.

Question: For truth to come, you advocate action without idea. Is it possible to act at all times without idea, that is, without a purpose in view?

KRISHNAMURTI: I am not advocating anything. I am not a propagandist, political or religious. I am not inviting you to any new experience. All that we are doing is trying to find out what action is. You are not following me to find out. If you do, then you will never find out. You are only following me verbally. But if you want to find out, if you as an individual want to find out what idea and action are, you have to inquire into it, and not accept my definition or my experience, which may be utterly false. As you have to find out, you have to put aside the whole idea of following, pursuing, advocating, propagandist, leader, or example.

Let us therefore find out together what we mean by action without idea. Please give your thought to it. Don't say, "I do not understand what you are talking about." Let us find out together. It may be difficult, but let us go into it.

What is our action at present? What do you mean by action? Doing something, to be, to do; our action is based on idea, is it not? That is all we know; you have idea, ideal, promise, various formulas about what you are and what you are not. That is the basis of our action—reward in future or fear of punishment or seeking self-enclosing ideas upon which we can base our action. We know that, don't we? Such activity is isolating. Watch yourselves in action. Don't go to sleep over my words. You have an idea of virtue, and according to that idea you live—that is, you act in relationship. That is, to you, relationship is action which is towards ideal, towards virtue, towards self-achievement, so on and so on, collective or individual.

When my action is based on an ideal, which is an idea, that idea shapes my action, guides my action—such as, I must be brave, I must follow the example, I must be charitable, I must be socially conscious, and so on. So I say, you say, we all say, "There is an example of virtue, I must follow''; which means again, ''I must live according to that.'' So action is based on that idea. So between action and idea, there is a gulf, there is a time process, there is division of time. That is so, is it not? That is, ''I am not charitable, I am not loving, there is no forgiveness in my heart—but I must be charitable.'' There is time between what I am and what I should be, and we are all the time trying to bridge between what I am and what I should be. That is our activity, is it not?

Now what would happen if the idea did not exist? At one stroke, you would have removed the gap, would you not? You would be what you are. Have I frightened you all? You say, ''I am ugly, I must become beautiful; what am I to do?'' which is action based on idea. You say, ''I am not compassionate, I must become compassionate.'' So you introduce idea separate from action. Therefore there is never action, but always ideal of what you will be, never of what you are. The stupid man always says he is going to become clever. He sits working, struggling to become; he never stops, he never says, ''I am stupid.'' So his action, which is based on idea, is not action at all.

Action means doing, moving. But when you have idea, it is merely ideation going on, thought-process going on, in relation to action. And if there is no idea, what would happen? Please follow it through. You are that *which is*. You are uncharitable, you are unforgiving, you are cruel, stupid, thoughtless. Can you remain with that? If you do, see then what happens. Please follow this. Don't be impatient, don't push it away—now, not tomorrow, actually now when you are facing it—then what happens? When I recognize I am uncharitable, stupid, what happens when I am aware it is so? Is there not charity, is there not intelligence, when I recognize uncharitableness completely, not verbally, not artificially, when I realize I am uncharitable and am unloving? In that very seeing of *what is*, is there not love? Don't I immediately become charitable? Please let us not have your acceptance. Look at it. Go into it. If I see the necessity of being clean, it is very simple; I go and wash. But if it is an ideal that I should be clean, then what happens? Don't you know the answer? Cleanliness is then very superficial.

So action based on idea is very superficial, which is not action at all, which is merely ideation, which is a different kind of action; but we are not discussing that kind of action which is merely thought-process going on.

But the action which transforms human beings, which brings regeneration, redemption, transformation—call it what you will—such action is not based on idea. It is action irrespective of sequence, reward, or punishment. Then you will see such action is timeless because mind does not enter into it, and mind is time process, calculating process, dividing process, isolating process.

This question is not so easily solved. Most of you put questions and expect an answer—yes or no. It is easy to ask questions like ''What do you mean?'' and then sit back and let me explain, but it is much more arduous to find out the answer for yourselves, go into the problem so profoundly, so clearly and without any corruption, that the problem ceases to be. And that can only happen when the mind is really silent in the face of the problem. The problem is as beautiful as sunset, if you love the problem. If you are antagonistic to the problem, you will never understand. And most of us are antagonistic because we are frightened of the result, of what may happen if we proceed, so we lose the significance and purview of the problem.

January 26, 1952

Eighth Talk in Madras

It must have occurred to many of us how quickly everything deteriorates. Great revolutions slaughtering millions with good promise soon deteriorate. They fall into the hands of bad people. Great movements, political and religious, soon wither away. It must have occurred to many of us why it is that this constant process of renewal and decay takes place. Why is it that something that has been started by a few people with good intentions, with right motives, is soon usurped by bad people and destroyed?

What is this process of withering, this decay? I think if we can answer this question and find out the truth of the matter, then perhaps we as individuals can set about an action which will not utterly wither away. I think we should look to the cause of it, not merely at the superficial level, but at the deeper level as well. I think there is a deeper and more fundamental reason why this deterioration takes place so rapidly, and I hope that is one of your problems too. Don't think I am trying to introduce a new problem or I am taking up something to talk about. This must have occurred to you, as it has occurred to me. If you are at all alert, aware of the process of history, in everyday life, you must have observed that something is behind this process of deterioration; having observed it, probably you have brushed it aside; or having sacrificed yourself to a cause which soon withers away, you do not know what to do.

You must find out what exactly is that which is behind this process of deterioration, this renewal which soon withers away. It seems to me that we should inquire into this whole question, and perhaps there lies the true answer to our problem.

In our everyday life, we make effort to become, don't we? All our effort is to be something, to become, positively or negatively. We see that there is sociological conflict in "becoming," in the individual becoming more and more, and the force behind that "becoming" is ever directed that way. To control individual effort, which is self-enclosing, there are social laws, and in order to control the individual religiously, there are religious sanctions; but in spite of these laws and sanctions, deteriorations exist in our effort to be good, to be noble, to be beautiful, to seek truth. Until we really discover for ourselves—not imitatively, not through tradition, not through mere verbal rationalization—that which is behind this process of decay and deterioration, which is apart from our being, there will be no end to the world's turmoils.

The state of creativeness is very important. I am afraid we shall not be in that state which is so essential to bring about or to maintain a constant state in which there is no deterioration of any kind.

Now to go into this matter fully, you must inquire into this process of the experiencer and the experience because whatever we do contains this dual process. The effort or the will to experience, to acquire, to be or not to be, is always there. The will is the factor of our deterioration; the will to become—individually, collectively, nationally, or in different levels of our societies—the will to be is the important factor. If we observe, we shall find that, in this will, there are the actor and the thing he acts upon. That is, I exert my will to transform or change something; I am greedy, and I exert my will not to be greedy; I am provincial, nationalistic, and I exert my will not to be so. I act; that is, I use my will to transform that which I consider evil, or I try to become or keep that which is good. So, there is this dualistic action in will, which is the experiencer and the experience. I think that, therein, is the root of our deterioration.

As long as I am experiencing, as long as I am becoming, there must be this dualistic action; there must be the thinker and the thought, two separate processes at work; there is no integration; there is always a center which is operating through the will, of action to be or not to be—collectively, individually, nationally, and so on. Universally, this is the process. As long as effort is divided into the experiencer and the experience, there must be deterioration. Integration is only possible when the thinker is no longer the observer. That is, we know at present there are the thinker and the thought, the observer and the observed, the experiencer and the experienced; there are two different states. Our effort is to bridge the two.

The will or action is always dualistic. Is it possible to go beyond this will which is separative and discover a state in which this dualistic action is not? That can only be found when we directly experience the state in which the thinker is the thought. We now think the thought is separate from the thinker, but is that so? We would like to think it is, sirs, because then, a thinker can explain matters through his thought. The effort of the thinker is to become more or become less, and therefore, in that struggle, in that action of the will, in "becoming," there is always the deteriorating factor; we are pursuing a false process, and not a true process.

Is there a division between the thinker and the thought? As long as they are separate, divided, our effort is wasted; we are pursuing a false process which is destructive and which is the deteriorating factor. We think the thinker is separate from the thought. When I find that I am greedy, possessive, brutal, I think I should not be all this. The thinker then tries to alter his thoughts, and therefore effort is made to "become"; and in that process of effort, he pursues the false illusions that there are two separate processes whereas there is only one process. I think therein lies the fundamental factor of deterioration.

Is it possible to experience that state when there is only one entity, and not two separate processes, the experiencer and the experience? Then perhaps we shall find out what it is to be creative, and what the state is in which there is no deterioration at any time, in whatever relationship man may be.

In all our experiences, there is the experiencer, the observer, and the experiences; or the observer is gathering to himself more and more or denying himself. Is that not a wrong process, and is that not a pursuit which does not bring about the creative state? If it is a wrong process, can we wipe it out completely and put it aside? That can come about only when I experience, not as a thinker experiences, but when I am aware of the false process and see that there is only a state in which the thinker is the thought.

I am greedy. I and greed are not two different states; there is only one thing, and that is greed. If I am aware that I am greedy, what happens? Then, I make an effort not to be greedy, either for sociological reasons or for religious reasons; that effort will always be in a small, limited circle; I may extend the circle, but it is always limited. Therefore the deteriorating factor is there. But when I look a little more deeply and closely, I see that the maker of effort is the cause of greed, and he is greed itself; and I also see that there is no 'me' and greed, separately existing, but that there is only greed. If I realize that I am greedy, that there is not the observer who is greedy but I am myself greed, then our whole question is entirely different; our response to it is entirely different; then our effort is not destructive.

What will you do when your whole being is greed, when whatever action you do is greed? But unfortunately, we don't think along those lines. There is the 'me', the superior entity, the soldier who is controlling, dominating. To me that process is destructive. It is an illusion, and we know why we do that. I divide myself into the high and the low in order to continue the desire to be secure. If there is only greed, completely, not 'I' operating greed, but I am entirely greed, then what happens? Surely then, there is a different process at work altogether, a different problem comes into being. It is that problem which is creative, in which there is no sense of 'I' dominating, 'I' becoming positively or negatively. We must come to that state if we would be creative. In that state, there is no maker of effort. I think it is not an action of verbalizing or of trying to find out what that state is; if you set about that way, you will lose and you will never find. What is important is to see that the maker of effort and the object towards which he is making effort are the same. That requires enormously great understanding, watchfulness, to see how the mind divides itself into the high and the low—the high being the security, the permanent entity—but still remains a process of thought and therefore of time. If we can understand this as directly experiencing, then you will see that quite a different factor comes into being.

The unknown can't be understood by the maker of effort, the will of action. To understand, mind must be completely silent, which ultimately means complete self-abnegation; the self, which is the maker of effort to "become" positive or negatively, is not there.

Question: What makes something I say to another gossip? Is speaking the truth or speaking good or bad about another gossip? Can it be gossip so long as what is said is true?

KRISHNAMURTI: Behind this question, there lie many things. First of all, why do you want to speak about another? What is the motive, what is the urge? That is more important to find out. You must know if what you say about another is true. Why do you want to talk about another? If you are antagonistic, your motives are based on violence, hatred, and then, it is bound to be evil; your intention is to give pain to another through your words or through your expression. Why do you talk about another, good or bad, and what is the necessity that urges you to talk about somebody else? First of all, does it not indicate a very shallow and petty mind? If you are really concerned, interested in anything, you should know the time for it, the time to talk about another, however good, noble that another may be, or however stupid or irresponsible he may be. A stupid or shallow mind always wants to have something to talk about, chat or be agitated about. It must either read, acquire, or believe. You know the whole process of being occupied with something. Then the problem arises, how am I to stop gossiping.

Both the gossiper and the subject of the gossip, good or bad about another, have a kind of relationship to one another, and both he and the man to whom he gossips have a kind of mutual pleasure, the one to tell and the other to listen. I think it is very important to find out the motives, and not how to stop gossiping. If you can discover the motive and rather keep looking at it directly without any condemnation or justification, then perhaps your mind will begin to discover a deeper level, which consequently makes you put away this gossip, this talking about another. But to discover that motive, that urge, is quite an arduous task, is it not?

First of all, the man or woman who is occupied with gossiping is so interested in telling about somebody, good or bad, that he or she has no time to think. After all, gossip is one of the ways of self-knowledge, is it not? If you talk about another cruelly, it indicates antagonism, hatred. As you do not want to face your own antagonisms and hatreds, you escape through talk, and if you talk and gossip about another, it is another form of escape from yourself.

The man who would really understand this whole process of life must have profound self-knowledge—not the knowledge which you acquire from a book or a psychologist, but direct knowledge which comes through relationship, the relationship which comes as a mirror in which you see yourself constantly, both the pleasant and unpleasant. But that requires earnestness. Very few are earnest, and many are petty and stupid.

Question: How can individual regeneration alone possibly bring about, in the immediate, the collective well-being of the greatest number, which is the need everywhere?

KRISHNAMURTI: We think that individual regeneration is opposed to collective regeneration. We are not thinking in terms of regeneration, but only of individual regeneration. Regeneration is anonymous. It is not "I have redeemed myself." As long as you think of individual regeneration as being opposed to the collective, then there is no relationship between the two. But if you are concerned with regeneration, not of the individual, but *regeneration,* then you will see there is quite a different force—intelligence—at work; because after all, what are we concerned with? What is the question with which we are concerned, profoundly and deeply? One might see the necessity for united action of man to save man. He sees that collective action is necessary in order to produce food, clothing, and shelter. That requires intelligence, and intelligence is not individual, is not of this party or that party, this country or that country. If the individual seeks intelligence, it will be collective. But unfortunately, we are not seeking intelligence, we are not seeking the solution of this problem. We have theories of our problems, ways of how to solve them, and the ways become individual and collective. If you and I seek an intelligent way to the problem, then we are not collective or individual; then we are concerned with intelligence that will solve the problem.

What is collective, what is mass? You in relationship with another, is it not? This is not oversimplification because in my relationship with you, I form a society; you and I together create a society in our relationship. Without that relationship, there is no intelligence, there is no cooperation on your side or on my side that is wholly individual. If I seek my regeneration and you seek your regeneration, what happens? We, both of us, are pursuing opposite directions.

If both of us are concerned with the intelligent solution of the whole problem because that problem is our main concern, then our concern is not how I look at it or you look at it, not my path or your path; we are not concerned with frontiers or economic bias, with vested interests and stupidities which come into being with those vested interests. Then you and I are not collective, are not individual; this brings about collective integration which is anonymous.

But the questioner wants to know how to act immediately, what to do the next moment, so that man's needs can be solved. I am afraid there is no such answer. There is no immediate moral remedy, whatever politicians may promise. The immediate solution is the regeneration of the individual, not for himself, but regeneration which is the awakening of intelligence. Intelligence is not yours or mine; it is intelligence. I think it is important to see this deeply. Then our political and individual action, collective or otherwise, will be quite different. We shall lose our identity; we shall not identify ourselves with something—our country, our race, our group, our collective traditions, our prejudices. We shall lose all those things because the problem demands that we shall lose our identity in order to solve it. But that requires great, comprehensive understanding of the whole problem.

Our problem is not the bread and butter problem alone. Our problem is not feeding, clothing, and shelter alone, but it is more profound than that. It is a psychological problem, why man identifies himself. And it is this identification with a party, with a religion, with knowledge, that is dividing us. And that identity can be resolved only when, psychologically, the whole process of identifying, the desire, the motive, is clearly understood.

So the problem of the collective or of the individual is nonexistent when you are pursuing the solution of a particular problem. If you and I are both interested in something, vitally interested in the solution of the problem, we shall not identify ourselves with something else. But unfortunately, as we are not vitally interested, we have identified ourselves, and it is that identity that is preventing us from resolving this complex and vast problem.

Question: Although you have used the word truth *often, I do not recall that you have ever defined it. What do you mean by it?*

KRISHNAMURTI: You and I as two individuals are going to find this out, not tomorrow, but perhaps this evening. If you are very quiet, let us discover it. Definitions are not valuable. Definitions have no meaning to a man who is seeking truth. The word is not the thing; the word *tree* is not the tree; but we are satisfied with words. Please follow this closely. To us, definitions, explanations are very satisfactory because we can live with them. We can pursue words, and words have certain effects on us physically and psychologically. The word *God* awakens all kinds of neurological and psychological reactions, and we are satisfied.

So to us, definition is very important. Is that not so? Definition we call knowledge, and knowledge we think is truth. The more we read about it, the nearer we think we are to it. But the explanation of the word is not the thing. So we have to realize, to understand—we must not be caught by definitions, by words. Therefore, we must put aside the word. And how difficult it is, is it not, because the word is the process of thought! There is no thinking without verbalizing, without using words, images, concepts, formulas. Please follow all this, meditate with me now, to find this out.

When the mind perceives that it is caught in words, that the very process of its thinking is word which is memory, how can such a mind—which is memory, which is time, which is caught in definitions and conclusions—understand what is truth, what is unknowable. If I would know the unknowable, the mind must be completely silent, must it not? That is, all verbalization, all imagination, all projection must cease. You all know how difficult it is for the mind to be still, not compelled, not disciplined to be still; which means, the mind is no longer verbalizing, no longer recognizing, no longer the center of recognition of any experience.

When the mind recognizes the experience, that experience is projected. When I experience the Master, truth, God, that experience is self-projected because I recognize. There is the center of me which recognizes that experience; that recognition is the process of memory. Then I say, "I have seen the Master, I know he exists, I know there is God." That is, the mind is the center of recognition, and recognition is the process of memory. When I experience something as God, as truth, it is my projection, it is recognition; it is not truth, it is not God.

The mind is quite still only when it is incapable of experiencing, that is, when there is no center of recognition. But that does not come about through any form of action of will. That does not come about through discipline. That comes about when the mind observes its own activities, which I hope you are doing now. And when you observe, you will see how every minute there is the process of recognition going on, and how when you recognize, there is nothing new.

Truth is something that is timeless, that is not measurable by words. Since truth is measureless, timeless, mind cannot recognize it. Therefore, for truth to be, it is imperative that the mind should be in a state of nonexperiencing. Truth must come to you, the mind; you cannot go to it. If you go to it, you will experience it. You cannot invite truth. When you invite, when you experience, you are in the position of recognizing it; when you recognize it, it is not truth; it is only your own process of memory, of thought that says, "It is so, I have read, I have experienced." Therefore, knowledge is not the way to truth. Knowledge must be understood and put away for truth to be. If your mind is quiet, not asleep, not drugged by words, but actually pursuing, observing the process of the mind, then you will see that quietness comes into being, darkly, mysteriously; and in that state of stillness, you will see that which is eternal, immeasurable.

Question: There is an urge in every one of us to see God, reality, truth. Is not the search for beauty the same as the search for reality? Is ugliness evil?

KRISHNAMURTI: Sirs, do realize you cannot seek God. You cannot seek truth. Because, if you seek, what you will find is not truth. Your search is the desire to find that which you want. How can you seek something of which you do not know? You seek something of which you have read, which you call truth, or you are seeking something which inwardly you have a feeling for. Therefore, you must understand the motive of your search, which is far more important than the search for truth.

Why are you seeking, and what are you seeking? You would not seek if you were happy, if there were joy in your heart. Because we are empty we are seeking. We are frustrated, miserable, violent, full of antagonism; that is why we want to go away from that and seek something which would be more. Do watch yourselves and realize what I am saying to you; don't merely listen to words. In order to escape from your present psychological conflicts, miseries, antagonisms, you say, "I am seeking truth." You will not find truth because truth does not come when you are escaping from reality, from that which is. You have to understand that. To understand that, you must not go to seek the answer outside. So you cannot seek truth. It must come to you. You cannot beckon God, you cannot go to Him. Your worship, devotion, is utterly valueless because you want something; you put up the begging bowl for Him to fill. So, you are seeking someone to fill your emptiness. And you are interested more in the word than in the thing. But if you are content with that extraordinary state of loneliness without any deviation or distraction, then only that which is eternal comes into being.

Most of us are so conditioned, so trained, that we want to escape, and the thing to which we escape, we call beauty. We are seeking beauty though something—through dance, through rituals, through prayer, through discipline, through various forms of formulations, through painting, through sensation, are we not? So as long as we are seeking beauty through something, through man, woman, or child, through some sensation, we shall never have beauty because the thing through which we seek becomes all-important. Not beauty, but the object through which we seek it becomes all-important, and then we cling to that. Beauty is not found through something; that would be merely a sensation which is exploited by the cunning. Beauty comes into being through inward regeneration, when there is complete, radical transformation of the mind. For that, you require an extraordinary state of sensitivity.

Ugliness is an evil only when there is no sensitivity. If you are sensitive to the beautiful, denying the ugly, then you are not sensitive to the beautiful. What is important is not ugliness or beauty, but that there should be sensitivity which sees, which reacts to the so-called ugly as well as to the beautiful. But if you are only aware of the beautiful and deny the ugly, then it is like cutting off one arm; then your whole existence is unbalanced. Don't you shut out the evil, deny it, call it ugly, fight it, be violent about it? You are only concerned with the beautiful—you want it. In that process, you lose the sensitivity.

The man that is sensitive to both the ugly and the beautiful goes beyond, far away from the things through which he seeks truth. But, we are not sensitive to either beauty or ugliness; we are so enclosed by our own thoughts, by our own prejudices, by our own ambitions, greeds, envies. How can a mind that is ambitious spiritually or in any other direction be sensitive? There can be sensitivity only when the whole process of desire is completely understood, for desire is a self-enclosing process, and through enclosing, you cannot see the horizon. The mind then is stifled by its own "becoming." Such a mind can only appreciate beauty through something. Such a mind is not a beautiful mind. Such a mind is not a good mind; it is an ugly mind which is enclosed and is seeking its own perpetuation. Such a mind can never find beauty. Only when the mind ceases to enclose itself by its own ideals and pursuits and ambitions—such a mind is beautiful.

January 27, 1952

Ninth Talk in Madras

As I was saying last Saturday, the problem of deterioration of the mind is a grave one. It not only affects the older generation but also the young people. This deterioration is a common factor throughout the world.

This deterioration is bound to come when there is the exercise of the will in action, the will being the choice between two opposites, the essential and the non-essential, the desire to be or to become. Obviously, the will is a deteriorating factor in our life and most of us would not admit it because we have been brought up through our educational and psychological systems, through our religion and so on, to use the will as a means of achieving, of acquiring, of gaining an end in which is involved the whole process of choosing. Is it not one of the major factors in our life which brings about deterioration, repetition, imitation, conformity of idea?

What I would like this evening, if we can experiment, is to go into this whole problem of the mind, mind as a repetitive machine, as a storehouse of memory, guiding, shaping, controlling, and therefore producing no creative action, mind as a process of consciousness which when thwarted becomes the 'I', the 'me'. The self-conscious individual seeks fulfillment, and therefore, in the very desire for fulfillment, there is frustration from which arises sorrow.

One of the major factors of deterioration is the process of thought which is repetitive, imitative, conforming, because we know what happens when we are repetitive, conforming, and imitative; the mind becomes merely a machine automatically responding, functioning, reacting according to circumstances, according to memory, like a physical machine put together. All that, we know. We do not know any other process. Our thinking is purely repetitive; though we think it is a new idea, a new reaction, it is a process of the past in conjunction with the present. You can only meet the present with the screen, the limitation of the past. So, if you watch your mind, you will see it is conforming, it is repetitive, it is imitating.

Here arises the problem of how you listen. Are you listening to me at the verbal level, or are you watching what I am saying with what is actually happening in your mental process? Are you merely responding to the verbal vibration, or are you watching—which is a stimulation—what I am saying? It is a very important thing that you should go slowly into this matter, and as you have got a full hour before you, you can go into it very carefully. If you are watching your own mind using me, using what I am saying as a mirror and therefore observing, then what I am saying will be of extraordinary significance. But if you are merely listening, then you are imitating; you are merely responding to the words; words create an image, and the pursuit of that image is referred to as thinking, which is 'I', the 'me' stimulating you to observe. Therefore that stimulation becomes weary, dull, but if you observe your own thinking in relation to what I am saying, then you will discover whether your mind is merely repetitive or it is something beyond the mechanical quality of a machine. I hope you have understood the point. Have I made myself clear?

The question we are discussing is the deteriorating factor of the mind, whether in the old or in the young. This deteriorating factor is observed as we grow older; old age is to most of us a problem because we see the mind obviously deteriorating. You may not be conscious of it, but others may be conscious of the deterioration in you.

The application of the ideal as a means of action is an imitative, repetitive, conforming process like tradition. You may throw off the outward tradition, being forced by the modern economic pressure, but inwardly, you are still following tradition, which is repetitive, conforming. So, the problem is: is the mind merely a machine, incapable of going beyond this mechanical quality, or can the mind be made to be nonmechanical? That is, we have so far used the mind as a machine to achieve a result, to be something, to gain something, in which process, conformity, or repetition is essential. If I want to be successful, I must conform, I must repeat, I must imitate. So, we have used the machinery of the mind, which is a thought process, as a way of bringing about the desired end. That is, we want to produce a certain end, and we use the thought process as the machine, like the one we find in a factory. The machine is the mind, and when we want a result, we use it. In this process, the mind becomes merely repetitive.

Is not repetition, imitation, a sign of disintegration, which is observable as we grow older? You can see how old people talk—the same thing over and over again, the same beliefs, the continuity, crystallized, stabilized, and held firmly. All these are signs of deterioration, are they not? Don't ask what would happen to society or what would happen to our relationship if there were no repetition or conformity. We will find that out. A mind that thinks about what will happen if one is not mechanical is obviously a mind already in the process of deterioration.

It is very important for us to go into this matter very carefully and with intelligence because we see more and more how the old people govern the young—not that the young are very much more intelligent, but we are observing the fact. All the government places, all the religious positions, and all other high offices are filled by people who are in their sixties and seventies. The perfect bureaucratic machine, which the average citizen worships, is made up of these old people. Don't apply this to any particular person, please. I see several of you smiling at the idea of your old leaders or some other particular person being referred to as repetitive. Well, aren't you yourself repetitive? We are discussing not any individual but this whole process of repetition and deterioration.

Is the mind, which is the only instrument we have, merely to be used as a machine, routine-ridden, repeating and conforming? How is the mind to be made nonmechanical—that is, how to remove the factor or factors that bring about deterioration? Surely, this is an important question, is it not? This seems to me to be one of the gravest issues in the present crisis of our culture—the world culture, and not the Madras culture, the whole cultural process—because every sensation, every experience, every problem becomes repetitive.

Is it possible for the mind to free itself from this mechanical process? What do we mean by the mechanical process? Is not thought itself, please follow this, a factor of deterioration? We mean by thought a verbalizing reaction to experience. I am not defining, so don't learn the definitions. Is not thought the verbalizing process of memory, the memory being the past in conjunction with the present? Please watch your own mind. Don't listen to me verbally, but watch the process of your thinking. That is what we are discussing. It is not my problem; it is a problem which you and I must solve. Unless we are creative in a wholly different sense, all our education, religious system, political system, civilization, ideas are utterly useless because they contain deteriorating factors. So, it is a problem which you and I must solve; to solve it, we must consider this question of thought. That is the only instrument we have, or that is the only instrument which we are using. If that instrument is not valid in the process of bringing about integrated society, integrated beings, there must be some other means. That is what we are out to discover.

As I was saying, is not thought a process which is the continuation of the past modified by the present response? What is our thinking? It is memory in action. Please do not ask what we would do if we had no memory. That is not the problem. If you have no memory, you will be locked up for suffering from amnesia. Our problem is this: Thought is repetitive; the thought process is the result of continued response according to a certain background, which can only produce mechanical results, and therefore it is merely a process of repetition. Can thought be any other factor than deterioration? We think thought will produce a new sensation, a new way of living, a new culture, and so on. That is, we think intellect, which is thought, is the way of creation. If that is not, then what have we?

The mind which is so accustomed to the thought process, the mind which is thought itself, which is accumulated memory, responding to every experience, observable and nonobservable, conscious and unconscious, is certainly repetitive. The whole content of consciousness, as we function now, is thus repetitive. I think that is fairly clear, is it not? When you seek to go beyond the repetitive, you will find that the projection of that thought, that image, is all the outcome of the past, and that which you pursue as the ideal is the outcome of the past. Therefore, the whole content of consciousness, whether we are conscious of it or not, is a mechanical process. I mean by mechanical process a response of the past conditioned by the present, which is nothing but repetitive.

Please do not learn the definition because definitions are not going to solve the problem. What we have to do is to find out how the mind, how the whole machinery of the mind, can be changed so that it is not repetitive. After all, creation at any level, truth, is nonrepetitive. So the mind, to recognize the truth, must be nonrepetitive.

Take a very simple example. You have an experience of the beauty of a flower or of the sunset or of the shade of a tree. At the moment of experiencing, there is no recognition; there is only a state of being. As that moment slips away, you begin to give it a name; you say, "How beautiful that was!" That is, a process of recognition comes into being, and there is the desire for repetition of that sensation. This is simple and not complicated; just follow it and you will see. I see the tree lit by the evening sun; at that moment there is perception, experience, and there is nothing more; it is a state of being which is not describable. Then, as the state of being moves forward, I give it a name and thereby recognize it; and that creates a sensation in me. Then I say, "How beautiful, how marvelous that feeling was." I want to repeat that sensation. So, I begin next evening to look at the tree in the evening light, and there is a certain vague sensation that I want it. So, I have set the repetitive machinery going.

You watch your own process of mind, and you will see the truth of this. You have a beautiful statue in your room, or a picture. The first moment, it gives a great delight; you see something extraordinary, and the mind captures it. You then say, "I want more of it." So you sit down in front of the picture or image and repeat; you hope to repeat that sensation. You have therefore set the mechanical process of the mind going; it is not only at the conscious level but more profound; it brings about conflict, struggle.

Our mind is used to routine, repetition, imitation, conformity, and it knows nothing else. If it perceives something, it immediately wants to make it a daily affair. That is clear, is it not? Nobody denies this. This is a psychological, observable fact of our daily existence.

Now, how can the mind, which is the only instrument we have, not be mechanical? First of all, how few of us have asked this question? Or, how few of us are aware of this whole problem? Now that I put it in front of you and that you are aware of it, what is your response? I observe this whole process, and do I know anything else? I do not, obviously. That is, if I said there was something else, it would still be a process of thought, which is a projection of the past into the present. This is a very complex problem because in this is involved the whole process of naming, the giving of symbols and the importance of words, not only neurologically but psychologically, not only at the conscious level but at the deeper level. That is the deteriorating factor.

Can the mind, which is so much used to functioning mechanically, stop? This machinery has to be stopped before you can find an answer. If you project the answer either according to Marx or Bhagavad-Gita, then you are repetitive and destructive. Can the mind, which has been going on for centuries, stop? The 'me' is the result of the whole human being, rather, of the whole humankind, and the mind involves the 'me'. Can that process of the mind, can that machinery which is so cunning, so devouring, so urgently demanding, so mighty, stop? That is, can it come to an end? If it cannot, you cannot find out the answer.

If you use the mind, then you are only continuing thought as a means of achieving something. Please watch it. If you are tired, do not listen. If you are not tired, just watch it. Can the machinery which has been functioning for generations, centuries, can that come voluntarily to an end—not forced, cornered, or compelled? If you are compelled, then your response will be one of continuance and therefore of thought.

How will the mind come to an end? That is an important question, but you do not know how to solve it. The mind must be stopped so that it can jump to the other state. You cannot let it function mechanically and jump. In speculation, it is the past responding, and there is nothing new. A mind that is mechanical can never find anything new. It must come to an end. Now how is this to be done? Is that the right question? The "how" is important. You are following all this?

We know the mind is mechanical. Then the next response is: How am I to stop it? In putting this question, the mind has become mechanical. Do you follow? That is, I want a result, the means is there, and I follow it. What has happened? The "how" is the response of a mechanical mind, the response of the old, and the following or the practicing of the "how" is the continuation of the machine. See how false our thinking has become. We are always concerned with the past, the how, the way, the practice, and so on. You see all this process. The "how" is empty, and an inquiring mind really becomes the old repetitive mind through the practice of this "how."

There are two different states of the mind, one pursuing the "how" and the other inquiring and not seeking a result. The mind which inquires, which pursues in research, will only help us. Inquiry and seeking a result are two entirely different states. Now which is the state of your mind—the one that seeks a result or the one that is inquiring? If you seek a result, you are merely pursuing mechanically; then, there is no end; that leads to deterioration and destruction. That is obvious.

Is your mind really inquiring to find out the answer whether the mind can come to an end, not how to make it come to an end? The "how" is entirely different from the "can." Can it? Have you put that question yourselves? If you have, with what motive, with what intention, with what purpose have you put it? That is very important. If you have put the question "Can it?" with the motive that you want a result of which you are conscious, then you are back again in the mechanical process. So, you have to be extraordinarily alert and extremely subtle to answer that question—not to me but to yourself. If you really put the question without the intention to find out what happens, if you inquire, you will find that your mind is not seeking a result, it is waiting for an answer; it is not speculating about an answer; it is not desiring for an answer; it is not hoping for an answer; it is waiting.

Look at this. I ask you a question; what is your response? Your immediate response is to think, to reason, to look, to find out a clever argument to reply. Question and response is a daily observable psychological action, verbally and psychologically. That is, you are not answering, you are responding, you are giving what are the reasons; in other words, you are seeking an answer. If you want to find out the answer to a question, the response is mechanical, other than waiting. That is, the mind that waits for an answer to come is nonmechanical, because the answer must be something which you don't know; the answer which you know is mechanical. But if you are faced with the question, and you wait for the answer, then you will see your mind is entirely in a different state. Waiting is more important than answer. You understand? Then, mind is no longer mechanical but quite a different process; it is quite a different thing that comes into being without being invited.

Question: You said that it is our idea of fear that stands in the way of facing it. How is one to overcome fear?

KRISHNAMURTI: First of all, one must be conscious of it, one must be aware of it. Are you? May we try together and experiment? Let us see, in our explaining this thing, whether fear will not completely go away from us. I am going to take you on the journey. If you willingly come, so much the better. If you are willing to come, let us go to the end of it, not stop in the middle of it.

We know various forms of fear—fear of public opinion, fear of death of someone, fear of what people will say, fear of losing an object; there are innumerable forms of fear. You ask, "How am I to overcome fear?" Can you overcome anything? You know what is meant by overcoming, conquering, being on top of it, suppressing it, going beyond it. When you overcome something, you have still again to conquer it, haven't you? So the very process of overcoming is a continuation of constant conquering. You cannot overcome your enemy because, in the very overcoming, you strengthen the enemy. That is one factor.

We are concerned with understanding fear and seeking the implications of it. We are going to take the journey together. How does fear come into being? Is it the word *fear* or the fact of fear? You understand? Is it the word that is causing me fear, or the fact of something in relationship to something else? Which is causing fear? It is not complex; it is very simple if you watch.

Am I afraid of the word *fear?* We are going to find out. Now what happens when one is afraid? The obvious reaction is to run away from it in many ways—drink, women, temple, Master, beliefs; they are all at the same level, they are no better, no worse. A man who runs away from fear through drink is as righteous as one who runs away from fear through virtue. Sociologically, it may have different values, but they are all the same, mentally, psychologically.

What is the reaction to fear? To escape from it. That is, our reaction to fear is condemnation, is it not, or justification. Am I really afraid? Do I think of the term *I am afraid of* when I am running away from it? Obviously not. I cannot understand fear if I run away from it, if I justify or condemn it, or even if I identify myself, or say, "I am afraid," and reason. So if I am to understand fear, there must be no escape. And our mind is made up of escapes. So mind is unwilling to face that thing, understand, respond to, discover what is causing fear, and so I run away from it.

What is then important, fear or running away from it? What is the most important thing in our life when there is fear? Running away from it, is it not? Not how to dissolve fear, but how to escape from it. I am more concerned with escapes rather than understanding. And can I understand it when I am looking in the other direction? I can look at it when I am completely concentrating about it. Is there any possibility of complete awareness, full concentration of it, when I am all the time dreading it? Obviously not.

To understand fear, you don't run away by suppression, domination, by belief, virtue, and so on. Then, you are nearer to the fact which is causing you fear. What is your relationship to it? Is it verbal?—verbal in the sense that the mind speculates about it and is afraid of the speculation. The mind foresees and says, "If that happens, this will happen, and therefore I am afraid." So what is your relationship to it? Follow this closely because on that relationship depends your solution. Are you related to what is causing fear, merely verbally—that is, speculatively—or are you confronting it without speculation, which is nonverbalization? If you are related to it verbally, you have no direct communication with it, you have escaped from it. If you confront it, you have ceased to run away; there is no escape whatsoever.

Let us next consider the relationship of words and their meaning. Is fear caused by the word or by the fact? Do you understand? The word being the mind, the mind is creating a screen through verbalization and not facing it. So, is fear created by the word—that is, the mind by thinking about it, thought being the process of verbalization? If so, your thought about it is to escape from it. Otherwise, you are facing the fact without verbalization, without thought process, without escape; then you are directly in relationship with it, directly in communion with it.

When you are directly in communion with something, what happens? Have you been directly in communion with anything without thought process, have you? Obviously not. When you are, the thing which you have named as fear has ceased to be. It is these screens, these escapes, this verbalization, this mental process, that create fear, not the fact itself. So these screens between you and the fact are productive of fear, not the fact; there is no overcoming of the fact. If you see the whole process and have followed this step by step, you will see you have no fear. Then, you are observing the fact, and the fact is going to alter; the fact is going to take action, and not you in movement towards an escape.

Question: How can the thinker and the thought be united?

KRISHNAMURTI: The "how" is a school boy's question. But we are going to find out if it is possible to bring together the two separating processes of things at work. First, we know the thinker and the thought are separate. Are we aware of it? To you, the thinker and the thought are two separate entities, and you want to find out if they can be brought together. If the thinker is separate and always dominating thought, thought is always crippled and the thinker is always conquering. There will be no alleviation; there will be constant battle between the thinker and the thought. I want to find out if it is possible for the two to be together so that there is no division, no battle, because I see that it is only when there is no struggle, there is something new.

Violence does not produce peace; it is only when violence is not, peace is. Similarly, I have to find out if the thinker and the thought are two separate entities, eternally dividing, never brought together.

You and I are going to take the journey of discovering and really experiencing the fact. We know that the thinker and the thought are separate. Most of us have never even thought about it; we take it for granted. It is only when somebody outside of you asks the question, then you are inquiring. I am asking, and therefore you are inquiring, you are taking the journey of inquiry.

Taking the journey is understanding *what is,* what is actually taking place, not what you would like, but what actually happens.

Why are the thought and the thinker separate? Not that they should not be or must not be, but why are they separate? They are separate because of habit. We have not doubted it; we have accepted it, taken it for granted; therefore, it has become a habit for us. The thinker is separate from his thought, and the struggle between the two, the domination of the thinker over the thought, is our daily habit—habit being routine, repetitive. That is a fact, is it not?

What would happen if the thinker and the thought were not separate? My mind is used to this habit. What would happen to my mind if this habit stops? The mind would feel lost, would it not? It would be puzzled, bewildered by something unexpected, something new; so the mind prefers to live in habit; so it says, "I keep my habit going. I don't know what would happen if these two come together and I shall prefer the old things to continue." So you are more interested in the continuation of habit rather than in inquiring what would happen if they come together.

Why do we want the old to continue? For the obvious reason that we want security, certainty, something to hold on to; because it is the only thing we know. We are sure of the thinker and the thought. We have not thought of what would happen if they come together. Certainty makes us hold on to the old. That is a psychological fact, an observable fact. Our problem then is not how to bring the thinker and the thought together, but why the mind is seeking security, certainty. Can the mind exist without certainty, without seeking something to which it can hold on—knowledge, belief, what you will? The mind cannot be without the process of security. The mind that we know is secure; it is not interested in finding out; it is interested in being completely safe, completely secure.

Why does the mind seek security? Because you realize that thought suddenly changes any moment; there is no actuality in thought. So thought creates the thinker as a permanent entity which will go on indefinitely; so, in the thinker, it has vested interests. And so the mind has found security in the thinker, certainty, which is the old habit.

Our problem then is whether the mind can ever have security, or is it only an illusion of security to which it clings. The mind has the power to create the illusion of security and clings to it; therefore, so long as it is seeking security, it cannot understand the other. So long as the mind is not interested in discovering what will happen if the thinker and the thought come together, it will hold on to something it is already sure of.

So our problem is whether there is security, certainty. Is there? Obviously not—neither in God, nor in wife, nor in property which you would want to have. There is no security. Of that you are not convinced; of that, you have had no experience. There is complete loneness without any dependability, without anything on which the mind can rest, hold, and cling to. Because the mind is afraid to be alone, it invents the thinker as a permanent entity that will continue. Or if the thinker is not, it would invent God, or property, or wife, anything—a tree would do, a stone would do, a carved image.

The mind, in its desire for security, has created the thinker as separate from the thought and has accustomed itself to this division by habit. Where there is habit there is permanence, and mind becomes mechanical. When you realize, not merely verbally but in actual experience, that the thinker is the result of thought, that it seeks permanency, that it seeks continuity, then you will see there is no effort by the mind to bring the two together. Then there is only a state of understanding, without any words, without the thought process of the thinker and the thought. For that, you must have an extraordinary insight into the whole process of consciousness which we have been considering this evening, which is the process of meditation. That meditation is only possible when the mind understands the whole content of consciousness, which is yourself.

February 2, 1952

Tenth Talk in Madras

As I was saying yesterday, one of the fundamental causes of deterioration is the will in action. I also said that imitation, repetition, the mechanical response of the mind, of memory, is another factor of deterioration of the mind. Is not self-perpetuation one of the major factors that brings about destruction, deterioration of the mind?

We see that every religion, every philosophy, even the totalitarian state, desires to destroy the separative process of the mind. No revolution, no outward economic change or the so-called inward discipline, has in any way destroyed or brought about the ending of the self. I think most of us perceive or are aware that the self must come to an end, not theoretically but actually. One can philosophize over it and speculate about it; most people do it only surreptitiously or with an aggressive purpose like most politicians by whom we are ruled, or like the rich men who control most of our outward economy, or like those who pursue the spiritual path. All of them in different forms, more subtly or more aggressively, pursue self-expansion. Is not that one of the vital factors that destroy the mind?

The only instrument we have is the mind. We have used it hitherto, wrongly. Is it possible now to bring to an end this whole process of the self with all its deteriorating factors, with all its destructive elements? I think most of us realize that the self is separative, destructive, anti-social; outwardly and inwardly, it is an isolating process in which no relationship is possible, in which love cannot exist. We more or less feel this actually or superficially, but most of us are not aware of it. Is it possible to really bring that process to an end, not substitute something else for it, or postpone, or explain it away?

As we have seen, mere discipline, mere conformity, does not end the self; it only gives it a vital strength in another direction. Most intelligent people, thoughtful people, must have inquired into this. Apart from religious sanctions, totalitarian compulsions, injunctions, and concentration camps, most of us must have asked if the self can really come to an end. When we do put that question to ourselves, the automatic, the natural response is the "how." How is it to come to an end? So to us, the "how" becomes very important. Only the "how," the practical way, the manner, matters to us. If we can examine a little more closely the whole question of the "how" and its technique, perhaps we shall understand that the "how," the practical way of achieving a result, will not end the self.

When we want to know the method of ending the self, the way to bring it about, what is the process of the mind? Is there the "how," the way of doing, the method, the system? If we do follow the system, does it end the self? Or, does it give strength in another direction? Most of us are anxious, particularly those who are somewhat earnest and religiously inclined, desire to know or find out the method of ending, the way of becoming, the way of achieving a result. If we look deeply into our hearts and mind, it is obvious that we would pursue the method of ending the self, should there be one.

Now, why does the mind ask the way, the technique, the method? Is not that an important question? What happens is this. You have a system, a method, the "how," the technique; and the mind shapes after the technique, the pattern. Does that end the self? You may have a very rigorous and disciplining method, or a method that will gradually ease you out of the conflict of self, a method that will give you solace, but essentially, the desire for a method only indicates really the strengthening of the self, does it not? Please follow this closely, and you will see whether or not the "how" indicates a thought process, an imitative process, through which the mind, the self, can gather strength and have greater capacity and not end at all.

Take the question of envy. Most of us are envious at different levels, which causes untold misery to others and to ourselves; you have envy of the rich, envy of the learned, envy of the guru, envy of the man who achieves. Envy is the social motive, a drive in our existence. It is clothed sometimes in a religious form but essentially it is the same; it is the desire to be something, spiritually, economically. That is one of our major drives. Is there a method, a means, by which you can get rid of it? Our instinctive response, if we are at all thoughtful, is to find a way to make it come to an end or to bring it to an end. What happens? Can envy be brought to an end by a method, by a technique? Envy implies the desire to be something here or hereafter. You have not tackled the desire which makes you envious, but you have learned a way to cover up that desire by expressing it in another way; but essentially, it is still envy.

So, if you can understand this process of how we want a method to achieve a result, and if we also understand the mind that cultivates the technique, we can then see that essentially it is the strengthening of thought. Thought is one of the major factors that brings about deterioration because thought is a process of memory, which is verbalization of memory and is a conditioning influence. The mind that is seeking a way out of this confusion is only strengthening that thought process. So, what is important is not to find a way or a method—because we have seen what the implications in it are—but to be aware of the whole process of the mind.

Thought can never be independent; there is no independent thinking because all thought is a process of conformity to the past. There is no independence or freedom through thinking. How can a mind which is essentially the result of the past, which is conditioned by various memories, climatically, socially, and environmentally and so on, how can such a mind be independent? So, if you seek independence of thought, you are only perpetuating the self. What is the process of this independence? Most of us are lonely, and there is a constant craving for fulfillment. Being aware of this emptiness in ourselves, we seek various forms of escapes from it—religious, social—you know the whole business of escapes. As long as we do not solve that problem, the independence that we are seeking in thinking will only be the perpetuation of the self.

For most of us, creation is nonexistent; we do not know what it means to create. Without that creativeness which is not of time, which is not of thought, we cannot bring about a vitally different culture, a different state of human relationship. Is it possible for the mind to be in that receptive state in which creativeness can take place? Thought is not creative. The man who pursues the idea can never be creative. The pursuit of an ideal is thought process and is conditioned after the mind. So, how can the mind which is thought process, which is the result of time, which is the result of education, of influence, of pressure, of fear, of the search for reward, of the avoidance of punishment, how can such a mind be ever free so that creativeness can take place? When we put that question to ourselves, we want to know the method, the "how," the practical way to achieve that mental freedom. Trying to know the "how," the method, is the most absurd thing and is a school boy's affair. The "how" implies always the method which is the pursuit of thought, the conformity to a particular technique. We see also that only when the mind with its thought process comes to an end is there creation.

Surely, in the present crisis of the world and with the politicians and their cunning exploitations, creation is the most difficult thing to achieve. We do not want more theories, more ideals, more leaders, more and newer techniques, the means of supporting a pattern. The only minds that are creative are those of human beings that are integrated.

Is it possible for the mind, which is the result of centuries of thought process, ever to be in that creative state? That is, can the thought ever receive, or ever cultivate, that creative urge? It seems to me that that is one of the most important things we should ask ourselves because the mere following of a pattern has not led us anywhere, socially or religiously. No leader can give us the real creative urge; no example can do that. Every example is the expansion of the self; the hero is the expansion of the 'me' glorified. So is the pursuit of the ideal an expansion of myself, fulfilling of myself in an idea; it is continuation of thought as time, and therefore there is no creative state. I think it is very important to find this out, to be aware how essential it is for each of us to discover for ourselves that creative spirit. The mind can never discover that, do what it will; thought can never understand or bring about that creative state.

What is that creative state? Surely it cannot be stated positively. To describe it is to limit it. The description will be a process of measuring, and to measure it is to use a thought process. Obviously it is so. Therefore thought can never capture it. It is of no value to describe it. But what we can do is to find out what are the barriers, by negatively approaching it, obliquely coming upon it. Most of us will object to it because most of us are accustomed to being direct. "Do this thing and you will get that" is the attitude that governs your approach. What we are discussing is not to describe that state, but to find out what you should do to discover for yourself the impediments that prevent that creative state, that extraordinary state in which the mind, the observer is nonexistent.

What is the first thing that stands in the way? Surely, the whole desire to be powerful, to dominate, stands in the way. The desire for power is a process which is separative; though it may be identified with the whole, with a country, or with a group, it is an isolating process. The impediment is the mind which is ambitious at any level—the so-called spiritual ambition, the mind of the politician, of the rich and of the poor man. All these persons desire to have more. The urge for more is the most destructive element that stands in the way. That is very difficult to grasp because the mind is so subtle. You may not seek power in the crude form, but you may seek it as a politician with his excuse of doing things in the interests of the state, or you may be an electioneer. There are different forms of pursuit of power which are all essentially the will to be, the will to become something, which expresses itself through virtue, through respectability, through the action of the mind, the sense of domination, the pride of having power.

So, one of the major factors, major barriers, is this desire for power, this desire for domination. Do watch in your own lives and you will see the separative, the destructive desire in action. That will obviously defeat love. It is only love that is our redemption. But you cannot have love if there is any sense of domination, any sense of the desire for power, position, authority, the will in action, the desire to achieve a result. We know all this. Vaguely we are aware of it also. We are caught in the stream of becoming, in the stream of desire for power, and we are incapable of stopping it and stepping out. To step out, there is no "how." You see the full implications of power, and when you realize it fully, you step out; there is no "how."

One of the hindrances that prevents creativeness is authority, authority of the example, the authority of the past, authority of experience, authority of knowledge, authority of belief. All these are impediments for a creative state. You do not have to accept what I am saying. You can observe it in your own life, and you will see how belief, knowledge, and authority strengthen the separative process of the mind.

Obviously, another factor that prevents the creative state is repetition, imitation, perpetuation of an idea. Repetition is not only of sensation but of rituals, vain repetition of the pursuit of knowledge, repetition of experience, which have no significance at all. All these are hindrances. There is no new experience. All experience is a process of recognition. When there is no recognition, there is no experience, and the process of recognition is a process of the mind, which is verbalization.

Another factor that divides us from that creative state is this desire for a method, the "how," the way, practicing something so that our mind can achieve a result. This is a process of continuity, repetition, and the mind which is caught in repetition can never be creative.

So, if you can see all that, then you will find that it is the mind actually that is preventing the creative state from coming into being.

So when the mind is aware of its own movement, mind comes to an end. It is only then that the creative state can be; it is the only salvation because that creative state is love. Love has nothing to do with sentiment. It has nothing to do with sensation. It is not a product of thought, nor can the mind manufacture it. Mind can only create images, images of sensation, of experience; and images are not love. We do not know what it means though we use that word very freely. But we know sensation, and it is the very nature of the mind to feel sensation, and pursue sensation through images, through words, through every form of conceit. But the mind can never know love, and yet we have cultivated the mind for centuries.

It is extremely arduous for the mind to see all this process so that the experiencer is never apart from the experienced. It is this division between the observer and the observed that is the process of thought. In love, there is no experiencer or the experienced. And as we do not know it and as that is the only redemption, surely an earnest man must watch the whole process of the mind, the hidden and the open. That is very arduous. Most of us are wasting our energies through climate, through diet, through idle gossip—I am sorry, there is no idle gossip, there is only gossip—through our envy. We have not the time for inquiry. It is only through meditative search that we can have awareness of the mind and its content; then the mind comes to an end and love can be.

Question: How is man to fulfill himself if he has no ideals?

KRISHNAMURTI: Is there such a thing as fulfillment, though most of us seek fulfillment? We know we try to fulfill ourselves through family, through son, through brother, through wife, through property, through identification with a country or a group, or through pursuit of an ideal, or through the desire for continuity of the 'me'. There are various, different forms of fulfillment at different levels of consciousness.

Is there such a thing as fulfillment? What is the thing that is fulfilling? What is the entity that is seeking to be, in or through certain identification? When do you think of fulfillment? When are you seeking fulfillment?

As I said, this is not a talk at the verbal level. If you treat it at the verbal level, then go away; it is a waste of time. But if you want to go deeply, then pursue, then be alert and follow it because we need intelligence, not dead repetition, not repetition of phrases, words, and examples with which we are fed up.

What we need is creation, intelligent integrated creation; which means, you have to search it out directly through your own understanding of the mind process.

So in listening to what I am saying, relate it to yourself directly, experience what I am talking about. And you cannot experience it through my words. You can experience it only when you are capable, when you are earnest, when you observe your own thinking, your own feeling.

When is desire to be fulfilled? When are you conscious of this urge to be, to become, to fulfill? Please watch yourself. When are you conscious of it? Are you not conscious of it when you thwart it? Are you not aware of it when you feel extraordinary loneliness, a sense of inexhaustible nothingness, of yourself not being something. You are aware of this urge for fulfillment only when you feel an emptiness, loneliness. And then, you pursue fulfillment through innumerable forms, through sect, through relationship with property, with trees, with everything at different layers of consciousness. The desire to be, to identify, to fulfill, exists only when there is consciousness of the 'me' being empty, lonely. The desire to fulfill is an escape from that which we call loneliness. So our problem is not how to fulfill, or what is fulfillment because there is no such thing as fulfillment. The 'me' can never fulfill; it is always empty. You may have a few sensations when you are achieving a result; but the moment the sensations have gone, you are back again in that empty state. So you begin to pursue the same process as before.

So the 'me' is the creator of that emptiness. The 'me' is the empty; the 'me' is a self-enclosing process in which we are aware of that extraordinary loneliness. So being aware of that, we are trying to run away through various forms of identification. These identifications we call fulfillments. Actually, there is no fulfillment because mind, the 'me', can never fulfill; it is the very nature of the 'me' to be self-enclosing.

So what is the mind which is aware of that emptiness to do? That is your problem, is it not? For most of us, this ache of emptiness is extraordinarily strong. We do anything to escape from it. Any illusion is sufficient, and that is the source of illusion. Mind has the power to create illusion. And as long as we do not understand that aloneness, that state of self-enclosing emptiness—do what you will, seek whatever fulfillment you will—there is always that barrier which divides, which knows no completeness.

So our difficulty is to be conscious of this emptiness, of this loneliness. We are never face to face with it. We do not know what it looks like, what its qualities are, because we are always running away from it, withdrawing, isolating, identifying. We are never face to face, directly, in communion with it. We then are the observer and the observed. That is, the mind, the 'I', observes that emptiness, and the 'I', the thinker, then proceeds to free itself from that emptiness or to run away.

So, is that emptiness, loneliness, different from the observer? Is not the observer himself empty, and not that he observes emptiness? Because, if the observer was not capable of recognizing that state which he calls loneliness, there would be no experience. He is empty; he cannot act upon it, he can do nothing about it. Because, if he does anything whatever, he becomes the observer acting upon the observed, which is a false relationship.

So when the mind recognizes, realizes, is aware that it is empty and that it cannot act upon it, then that emptiness of which we are aware from outside has a different meaning. So far, we have approached it as the observer. Now the observer himself is empty, alone, is lonely. Can he do anything about it? Obviously, he cannot. Then his relationship to it is entirely different from that of the relationship of the observer. He has that aloneness. He is in that state in which there is no verbalization that "I am empty." The moment he verbalizes it or externalizes it, he is different from that. So when verbalization ceases, when the experiencer ceases as experiencing loneliness, when he ceases to run away, then he is entirely lonely. His relationship is in itself loneliness; he is himself that, and when he realizes that fully, surely, that emptiness, loneliness, ceases to be.

But loneliness is entirely different from aloneness. That loneliness must be passed to be alone. Loneliness is not comparable with aloneness. The man who knows loneliness can never know that which is alone. Are you in that state of aloneness? Our minds are not integrated to be alone. The very process of the mind is separative. And that which separates knows loneliness.

But aloneness is not separative. It is something which is not the many, which is not influenced by the many, which is not the result of the many, which is not put together as the mind is; the mind is of the many. Mind is not an entity that is alone, being put together, brought together, manufactured through centuries. Mind can never be alone. Mind can never know aloneness. But being aware of the loneliness when going through it, there comes into being that aloneness. Then only can there be that which is immeasurable. Unfortunately most of us seek dependence. We want companions; we want friends; we want to live in a state of separation, in a state which brings about conflict. That which is alone can never be in a state of conflict. But mind can never perceive that, can never understand that; it can only know loneliness.

Question: You said that truth can come only when one can be alone and can love sorrow. This is not clear. Kindly explain what you mean by being alone and loving sorrow.

KRISHNAMURTI: Most of us are not in communion with anything. We are not directly in communion with our friends, with our wives, with our children. We are not in communion with anything directly. There are always barriers—mental, imaginary, and actual. And this separativeness is the cause, obviously, of sorrow. Don't say, "Yes, that we have read, that we know verbally." But if you are capable of experiencing it directly, you will see that sorrow cannot come to an end by any mental process. You can explain sorrow away, which is a mental process, but sorrow is still there, though you may cover it up.

So to understand sorrow, surely you must love it, must you not? That is, you must be in direct communion with it. If you would understand something—your neighbor, your wife, or any relationship—if you would understand something completely, you must be near it. You must come to it without any objection, prejudice, condemnation, or repulsion; you must look at it, must you not? If I would understand you, I must have no prejudices about you. I must be capable of looking at you, not through barriers, screens of my prejudices and conditionings. I must be in communion with you, which means I must love you. Similarly, if I would understand sorrow, I must love it, I must be in communion with it. I cannot do so because I am running away from it through explanations, through theories, through hopes, through postponements, which are all the process of verbalization. So words prevent me from being in communion with sorrow. Words prevent me—words of explanations, rationalizations, which are still words, which are the mental process—from being directly in communion with sorrow. It is only when I am in communion with sorrow, I understand it.

The next step is: Am I who is the observer of sorrow different from sorrow? Am I, the thinker, the experiencer, different from sorrow? I have externalized it in order to do something about it, in order to avoid, in order to conquer, in order to run away. Am I different from that which I call sorrow? Obviously not. So I am sorrow, not that there is sorrow and I am different—I am sorrow. Then only is there possibility of ending sorrow.

As long as I am the observer of sorrow, there is no ending of sorrow. But when there is the realization that sorrow is the 'me', the observer himself is the sorrow, which is an extraordinarily difficult thing to experience, to be aware of, because for centuries we have divided this thing; when the mind realizes it is itself sorrow—not when it is observing sorrow, not when it is feeling sorrow—it is itself the creator of sorrow, it is itself the feeler of sorrow, it is itself sorrow, then there is the ending of sorrow. This requires not tradition or thinking but very alert, watchful, intelligent awareness. That intelligent, integrated state is aloneness. When the observer is the observed, then it is the integrated state. And in that aloneness, in that state of being completely alone, full, when the mind is not seeking anything, neither seeking reward nor avoiding punishment, when the mind is truly still, not seeking, not groping, only then, that which is not measured by the mind comes into being.

February 3, 1952

Eleventh Talk in Madras

During the past several weeks that we have met, we have been considering the problems that affect our whole being, not at any one particular level but the whole process of consciousness, the way of thinking and the effects that produce the false process of thought. We see that the process of thinking is a deteriorating factor. Perhaps this may be, for those who are here for the first time, rather startling or surprising, or they may think that it is rather an idiotic statement, but those who have been earnestly pursuing these talks need no further explanations. For, explanations are really detrimental to understanding. We are so easily fed by words; we are so easily satisfied by explanations, by a sound sensation; the oft repeated explanation or the word is sufficient to make the mind dull.

So, those who have carefully and somewhat seriously followed these talks will, I think, have observed or be aware that thinking, as we now practice it, indulge in it, is one of the major factors that divide man from man. It is one of the factors that bring about no action, that postpone action, because ideas are the result of thought and they can never produce action. There is a gap between idea and thought, and our difficulty is to bridge the gap into which we have fallen.

I would like to discuss or consider this evening this question of self-deception, the delusions that the mind indulges in and imposes upon itself and upon others. That is a very serious matter, especially in a crisis of this kind which the world is facing. But in order to understand this whole problem of self-deception, we must follow it, not merely verbally, not at the verbal level, but intrinsically, fundamentally, and deeply. As I was saying, we are too easily satisfied with words and counter-words; we are word-wise, and being word-wise, all that we can do is to hope that something will happen. We see that the explanation of war does not stop war; there are innumerable historians, theologians, and religious people explaining war and how it comes into being, but wars still go on, perhaps more destructive than ever. Those of us who are really earnest, must go beyond the word, must seek this fundamental revolution within oneself; that is the only remedy which can bring about a lasting, fundamental redemption of mankind.

Similarly, when we are discussing this kind of self-deception, I think we should guard ourselves against any superficial explanations and rejoinders. We should, if I may suggest, not merely listen to a speaker, but follow the problem as we know it in our daily life; that is, we should watch ourselves in thinking and in action, watch ourselves how we affect others and how we proceed to act from ourselves.

What is the reason, the basis, for self-deception? How many of us are aware actually that we are deceiving ourselves? Before we can answer the question "What is self-deception and how does it arise?" must we not be aware that we are deceiving ourselves? Do we know that we are deceiving ourselves? What do we mean by this deception? I think it is very important because the more we are deceived, the more we deceive ourselves, the greater is the strength in the deception which gives us a certain vitality, a certain energy, a certain capacity which entails the imposing of my deception on others. So, gradually, I am not only imposing deception on myself but on others. It is an interacting process of self-deception. Are we aware of this process because we think we are very capable of thinking clearly, purposefully, and directly? Are we aware that, in this process of thinking, there is self-deception?

Is not thought itself a process of search, a seeking of justification, seeking security, self-protection, a desire to be well thought of, a desire to have position, prestige, and power? Is not this desire to be, politically or religio-sociologically, the very cause of self-deception? The moment I want something other than the purely materialistic, do I not produce, do I not bring about, a state which easily accepts? Take for example this: I want to know what happens after death, which many of us are interested in—the older we are, the more interested we are. We want to know the truth of it. How will we find it? Certainly not by reading, nor through the different explanations.

Then, how will you find it out? First, you must purge your mind completely of every factor that is in the way—every hope, every desire to continue, every desire to find out what is on that side. Because, the mind is constantly seeking security, it has the desire to continue and hopes for a means of fulfillment, for a future existence. Such a mind, though it is seeking the truth of life after death, reincarnation or whatever it is, is incapable of discovering that truth, is it not? What is important is not whether reincarnation is true or not but how the mind seeks justification, through self-deception, of a fact which may or may not be. So, what is important is the approach to the problem—with what motivation, with what urge, with what desire you come to it.

The seeker is always imposing upon himself this deception; no one can impose it upon him; he himself does it. We create deception, and then we become slaves to it. So, the fundamental factor of self-deception is this constant desire to be something in this world and in the world hereafter. We know the result of wanting to be something in this world; it is utter confusion where each is competing with the other, each is destroying the other in the name of peace. You know the whole game we play with each other, which is an extraordinary form of self-deception. Similarly, we want security in the other world, a position.

So, we begin to deceive ourselves the moment there is this urge to be, to become, or to achieve. That is very difficult for the mind to be free from. That is one of the basic problems of our life. Is it possible to live in this world and be nothing? Because, then only there is freedom from all deception, because then only the mind is not seeking a result, the mind is not seeking a satisfactory answer, the mind is not seeking any form of justification, the mind is not seeking security in any form, in any relationship. That takes place only when the mind realizes the possibilities and subtleties of deception, and therefore understands. The mind abandons every form of justification, security—which means the mind is capable then of being completely nothing. Is that possible?

Surely as long as we deceive ourselves in any form, there can be no love. As long as the mind is capable of creating and imposing upon itself a delusion, it obviously separates itself from collective or integrated understanding. That is one of our difficulties; we do not know how to cooperate; all that we know is to work together towards an end which both of us bring into being. Surely, there can be cooperation only when you and I have no common aim created by thought. Go slowly with me because I see several people are not following me. What is important to realize is that cooperation is only possible when you and I do not desire to be anything. When you and I desire to be something, then belief and all the rest of it become necessary, a self-projected utopia is necessary. But if you and I are anonymously creating without any self-deception, without any barriers of belief and knowledge, without a desire to be secure, then there is true cooperation.

Is it possible for us to cooperate, for us to be together without an end, without a result, which you and I are not seeking? Can you and I work together without seeking a result? Surely that is true cooperation, is it not? If you and I think out, work out, plan out a result, and we are working together towards that result, then what is the process involved in it? Our minds are meeting; our thoughts, our intellectual minds are of course meeting. Emotionally, the whole being may be resisting it, which brings about deception, which brings about conflict between you and me. It is an obvious and observable fact in our everyday life. You and I agree to do a certain piece of work intellectually, but unconsciously, deeply, you and I are at battle with each other. I want a result to my satisfaction; I want to dominate; I want my name to be ahead of yours though I am said to be working with you. So, we both, who are creators of that plan, are really opposing each other even though outwardly you and I agree as to the plan; inwardly, we are at battle with each other though consciously we may agree.

So, is it not important to find out whether you and I can cooperate, commune, live together in a world where you and I are nothing, whether we are able really and truly to cooperate not at the superficial level but fundamentally? That is one of our greatest problems, perhaps the greatest. I identify myself with an object and you identify yourself with the same object; both of us are interested in it; both of us are intending to bring it about. Surely, this process of thinking is very superficial because, through identification, we bring about separation—which is so obvious in our everyday life. You are a Hindu and I, a Catholic; we both preach brotherhood, and we are at each other's throats. Why? That is one of our problems, is it not? Unconsciously and deeply, you have your beliefs and I have mine. By talking about brotherhood, we have not solved the whole problem of beliefs, but we have only theoretically and intellectually agreed that this should be so; inwardly and deeply, we are against each other.

Until we dissolve those barriers which are a self-deception, which give us a certain vitality, there can be no cooperation between you and me. Through identification with a group, with a particular idea, with a particular country, we can never bring about cooperation.

Belief does not bring about cooperation; on the contrary, it divides. We see how one political party is against another, each believing in a certain way of dealing with the economic problems, and so they are all at war with one another. They are not resolved in solving the problem of starvation, for instance. They are concerned with the theories which are going to solve that problem. They are not actually concerned with the problem itself but the method by which the problem will be solved. So, there must be contention between the two because they are concerned with the idea and not with the problem. Similarly, religious people are against each other though they verbally say they have all one life, one God; you know all that. But inwardly, their beliefs, their opinions, their experiences are destroying them and are keeping them separate.

So, experience becomes a dividing factor in our human relationship; experience is a way of deception. If I have experienced something, I cling to it; I do not go into the whole problem of the process of experiencing; but because I have experienced, that is sufficient, and I cling to it, and thereby I impose, through that experience, self-deception.

So, our difficulty is that each of us is so identified with a particular belief, with a particular form or method in bringing about happiness, economic adjustment, that our mind is captured by that and we are incapable of going deeper into the problem; therefore, we desire to remain aloof individually in our particular ways, beliefs, and experiences. Until we dissolve and understand them, not only at the superficial level but at the deeper level, there can be no peace in the world. That is why it is important for those who are really serious to understand this whole problem—the desire to become, to achieve, to gain—not only at the superficial level but fundamentally and deeply; otherwise, there can be no peace in the world.

Truth is not something to be gained. Love cannot come to those who have a desire to hold on to it or who like to become identified with it. Surely such things come when the mind does not seek, when the mind is completely quiet, when the mind is no longer creating movements and beliefs upon which it can depend or from which it derives a certain strength, which is an indication of self-deception. It is only when the mind understands this whole process of desire, can the mind be still. Only then, the mind is not in movement to be or not to be; then only is there the possibility of a state in which no deception of any kind is possible.

Question: One starts with good will and the desire to help, but unfortunately, to help constructively, one joins various organizations, political or religio-sociological. Presently, one finds oneself cut off from all goodness and charity. How does this happen?

KRISHNAMURTI: Can we think out the problem now together? That is, don't merely listen to me explaining the question, but observe yourself in action in daily life. Most of us, especially if we are young and still sensitive and impressionable, want to do something about this world with its misery and starvation. As we grow older, unfortunately, that sensitivity gets dull.

Being sensitive, desiring to do good, being compassionate, you see all this misery, the village next door, hunger, squalor, every form of desire, corruption, and you want to do something. So, you look around. Then what happens? You go to various meetings of the extreme left, middle, or of the right, or pick up a religious book and try to solve the problem. If you are religiously inclined, you explain it away—karma, reincarnation, growth, evolution, "It is so" or "It is not so," and so on. But if you are politically mindful of it, then you attend various meetings; the more left promise immediate results; they show what can be done immediately; they are completely adhering to a particular idea, particular concept, particular formula; they keep photographs of what they have done or what they will do, and they have all their literature. All that convinces you more than what others say, and so you are caught in it. You start out wanting to do good with a certain compassionate desire to bring about a result, and you end up in a political organization which promises a future reward, a future utopia.

You who are so eager to bring about a result join the organization; your eagerness has gone into political activity, into an idea and not immediate action but a future through certain ideological methods, practices, and discipline and so on. You are concerned then more with the method, with the party, with the group, with the particular dialectical ideas, and so on, rather than with how you should act now to produce a change. Have we not introduced deception, a postponement, a forgetfulness, a deception not of the problem, of the evil that creates the problem, but the deception of the opposing parties which prevents us from doing anything? The result is that we have lost goodness, we have lost charity, we are cut off from all that, from the source of compassion and love. We call this immediate action. That is the case with most of us, is it not?

We join groups, we join societies hoping something good will come out of it, and soon we are lost in beliefs, in contention, in ambitions, in appalling stupidities. The difficulty with most of us is that we are cut off; we are in the midst of the society, the group, the political party. We are all prisoners, and it is so difficult to break away because the parties, the groups, the religious organizations have the power to excommunicate you. They threaten you because they have the power, economic and psychological power, and you are at their mercy; you have committed yourself, and your interests are with them, both psychologically and economically. It requires a great deal of understanding to break away from all this. No one will help us because everybody believes something and has committed himself to something or other. Being caught in all this, one grows old; then there is despair and tragedy, and one accepts it as the inevitable.

Is it possible to see this whole, total process of how goodness, charity, love are destroyed by our stupidity because we are all so eager to do something? The very desire to want to do something brings about self-deception. We have not the patience to wait, to look, to observe, to know more deeply. The very desire to be active in doing good is a deception because the clever man is waiting there to use your goodness, your desire to help; we give ourselves over to him to be exploited, to be used.

Is it not possible to look at all this, be aware of the whole content of this problem, and to break away, not theoretically but actually, face the problem so as to revive again that pristine goodness, that sense of being intimate with people, which is really being in a state of love? That is the only way to act. When there is love, that will bring about an extraordinary state, an extraordinary result, which you and I cannot plan to produce, cannot think out. All the clever people have planned, thought out; look at what is happening; they are at each others' throats, each destroying the other.

Seeing this whole problem, those who are serious have obviously to break away. In the very breaking is the renewal; in the very seeing is the action which is not idea first and action afterwards.

Question: Why do you say that knowledge and belief must be suppressed for truth to be?

KRISHNAMURTI: What is your knowledge and what is your belief? Actually when you examine your knowledge or your belief, what is it? Memories, are they not? What have you knowledge of? Of your past memories, knowledge of other people's experiences written down in a book! Actually when you think about your knowledge, what is it? It is past memory; you are acquiring certain explanations from others, and you have your own experiences based upon your memories. You meet an incident, and you translate that incident according to your memory, which you call experience. Your knowledge is a process of recognition. We know what beliefs are. They are created by the mind in its desire to be certain, to be safe, to be secure.

So, how can such a mind, crippled with knowledge, which is the accumulation of the past translating the present in terms of its own convenience, how can such a mind burdened with such knowledge understand what truth is? Truth must be something beyond time. It cannot be projected by my mind; it cannot be carved out of my experience; it must be something unknowable from my past experience. If I know it is from the past, I recognize it. Therefore, it is not true. If it is merely a belief, then it is a projection of my own desires.

Why are we so proud of our knowledge? We are enclosed in our beliefs, in the state of knowledge—in the sense it is understood commonly. You are afraid to be nothing. That is why you put so many titles; you give yourselves names, ideas, reputation, a vulgar show. With all this burden on your mind, you say, "I am seeking truth, I want to understand the truth." When you closely examine the whole process of acquisition of knowledge and the erection of belief, what happens? Surely, you see that they are the tricks of the mind, to believe, to know, because they give you a certain prestige, certain powers; people respect you as an extraordinary man who has read so much and who knows so much. As you grow older, you demand more respect because you have grown in wisdom—at least you think so; all that you have done is to be ripened in your own experience. Belief destroys human beings, separates human beings. A man who believes can never love because to him belief is greater than being kind, gentle, thoughtful; belief gives a certain strength, a certain vitality, a false sense of security.

So, when you examine this whole thing, what have you? Nothing but words, nothing but memory. Truth is something that must be beyond the imagination, beyond the process of the mind. It must be eternally new, a thing that cannot be recognized, that cannot be described. When you quote what Shankara, Buddha, XYZ has said, you have already begun to compare—which shows that through comparison you have stopped thinking, feeling, experiencing. That is one of the tricks of the mind. Your knowledge is destroying the immediate perception of what is truth.

That is why it is important to understand this whole process of knowledge and belief and to put them away. Be simple; see these things simply, not with a cunning mind. Then you will see the mind which has acquired so much experience, so many explanations, which is bound by so many beliefs, itself becoming new. Then the mind is no longer seeking the new, it is no longer recognizing, it has ceased to recognize, and therefore, it is in a state of constant experiencing, not in relation to the past. There is a new movement which is not repeatable.

That is why it is important that all knowledge, all belief, should be understood. You can't suppress knowledge; you have to understand it; you can't lock the door on knowledge. Now what is your reaction? You will go away from here and proceed in the same old manner because you are afraid to move from the old pattern.

To find the truth, there is no guru, there is no example, there is no path. Virtue will not lead to truth; practice of virtue is self-perpetuation. Knowledge obviously leads only to respectability. That man who is respectable and enclosed by his own importance will never find truth. The mind must be completely empty, not seeking, not projecting. It is only when the mind is utterly still that there is a possibility of that which is immeasurable.

Question: What is the relationship between what the psychologists call intuition and what you call understanding?

KRISHNAMURTI: Don't let us bother about what the psychologists say. What do you mean by intuition? We use that word, don't we? I have used the word *understanding* very often. Let us find out what it means.

What do we mean by intuition? Don't introduce what other people say. You use that word *intuition.* What is an intuitive feeling? Whether it is right or wrong, you have a feeling that it must be so or it must not be so. By intuitive feeling, we mean a feeling that is not rationalized, that is not very logically thought out, a feeling which you ascribe to beyond the mind, which you call a flash from higher consciousness. We are not seeing if there is intuition or not, but we want to find out the truth of it.

First of all, it is very easy to deceive oneself, is it not? I have an intuitive feeling that reincarnation is true. Don't you have it? Not because you have read about it, but you have a feeling about it; your intuition says so, and you grant it. I am only taking that as an example; we are not considering the truth of the matter whether there is or there is not continuity. Now, what is involved in the intuitive feeling? Your hope, your desire, continuity, fear, despair, feeling of emptiness, loneliness, all these are driving you; all these urge you to hold on to the idea of reincarnation. So, your own desire unconsciously projects that intuitive feeling.

Without understanding this whole process of desire, you cannot depend on intuition which may be extraordinarily deceptive. In some cases, intuition is deceptive. Don't talk about scientists having intuitive perception of a problem; you are not scientists. We are just ordinary people with our everyday problems. The scientists work impersonally about a mathematical problem; they work at it, work at it, can't see an answer and then let it go. As they work, they suddenly see the answer, and that is their intuition. But we don't tackle our problems that way. We are too intimate with our problems; we are confined, limited by our own desires, and our own desires dictate, consciously or unconsciously, the attitude, the response, the reaction. We use the word *intuition* in this connection.

Understanding is the whole perception of the problem—which is understanding the desire and the ways it acts. When you understand, you will see there is no entity as the examiner who is looking at the examined problem. This understanding is not intuition. This understanding is the seeing of the process of how the desire works, entirely, not just at the superficial level; it is going completely into the thing, in which every possibility of deception is revealed.

Understanding is an integrated process whereas intuition, as we use it, is departmental. The latter operates occasionally; the rest of the time, we are all stupid. What is the good of having such intuition? One moment, you see things clearly, and for the rest of the time, you are just the old, stupid entity that you were. Understanding is an integrated process, functioning all the time, and that comes into being when we are aware of the total process of desire.

Question: You say that life, as we live, is negation, and so there cannot be love. Will you please explain.

KRISHNAMURTI: Why do you want my explanation? Don't you know this? Are our lives very creative, very positive? At least we think we are positive. But the result is negation. We are very positive in our greed, in our hatreds, in our envy, in our ambition. We know that, don't we? Class division, communal division, natural divisions, every form of destruction, separation, isolation—all these are there.

Our life, though it appears positive, is actually a negation because it leads to death, destruction, misery. You will not accept that because you will say, "We are doing everything positive in this world; we can't live in a state of negation." But what you are doing is a negative act. Whatever you are doing is an act of death. How can such an activity be anything but negation? If you are ambitious, you are destructive, corrupting, corroding in your relationships. Every act of yours is a negative act.

How can a mind whose whole existence is a series of negation know love? Then you ask me what love is. Imitation is death, yet we have examples which we want to follow—we have power, we have gurus, we follow the process of repetition, imitation, routine—which is what? Death, abnegation! Is it not? How can such a thing comprehend anything? Such an entity can't know love.

The only thing that is positive is love. That comes into being only when the negative state is not, when you are not ambitious, when you are not corrupt, when you are not envious. First you must recognize that which is, and in understanding that which is, the other comes into being.

February 9, 1952

Twelfth Talk in Madras

This is the last talk of the series. There won't be any more talks after this meeting is over, at least for the time being.

Most of us, I think, are aware that every form of persuasion, every kind of inducement, has been offered us to resist self-centered activities. Religions, through fear, through promises, through fear of hell, through every form of condemnation, have tried in different ways to dissuade man from this constant activity that is born from the center of the 'me'. These having failed, political organizations have taken over. There again, persuasion; there again the ultimate utopian hope. Against any form of resistance, concentration camps and every form of legislation—from the extreme to the very limited—have been used and enforced; and yet we go on in our self-centered activity. That is all we know. If we at all think about it, we try to modify. If we are aware of it, we try to change the course of it, and fundamentally, deeply, there is no transformation, there is no radical cessation of that activity. We know this. At least, the thoughtful are aware of this; they are also aware that when that activity from the center ceases, only then can there be happiness. Most of us are not aware of this. We take it for granted that it is natural and that the consequential action is inevitable, only to be modified, controlled, and shaped. Now, those who are a little more serious, more earnest, not sincere—because sincerity is the way of self-deception and therefore is out of the question—must find out how one, being aware of this extraordinary total process of self-centered activity, can go beyond.

To understand what this self-centered activity is, one must obviously examine it, look at it, be aware of this entire process. If one can be aware of it then there is the possibility of its dissolution; but to be aware of it requires a certain understanding, a certain intention to face the thing as it is, to look at the thing as it is, and not to interpret it, not to modify it, not to condemn it. We have to be aware of that activity which we are doing from that self-centered state; we must be conscious of it. That is one of our primary difficulties because the moment we are conscious of that activity, we want to shape it, we want to control it, we want to condemn it, or we want to modify it; but we are never in a position to look at it directly, and when we do, very few of us are capable of knowing what to do.

We realize that self-centered activities are detrimental, are destructive, and that every form of self-centered activity—such as that of identification with the country, with a particular group, with a particular desire, with desires that produce action, the search for a result here or hereafter, the glorification of an idea, the pursuit of example, worship of virtue and the pursuit of virtue, and so on—is essentially the activity of a self-centered person. All his relationships with nature, with people, with ideas are the outcome of that activity. Knowing all this, what is one to do? All such activity must voluntarily come to an end, not self-imposed, not influenced, not guided. I hope you see the difficulty in this.

Most of us are aware that this self-centered activity creates mischief and chaos, but we are only aware of it in certain directions. Either we observe it in others and are ignorant of our own activities, or being aware, in relationship with others, of our own self-centered activity, we want to transform, we want to find a substitute, we want to go beyond. Before we can deal with it, we must know how this process comes into being, must we not? In order to understand something, we must be capable of looking at it; and to look at it, we must know its various activities at different levels, conscious as well as unconscious, and also the conscious directives, the self-centered movements of the unconscious motives and intentions. Surely, this is a self-centered process, the result of time, is it not?

What is it to be self-centered? When are you conscious of being the 'me'? As I have suggested often during these talks, don't merely listen to me verbally but use the words as a mirror in which you see your own mind in operation. If you merely listen to my words, then you are very superficial and your reactions will be very superficial. But if you can listen, not to understand me or what I am saying, but to see yourself in the mirror of my words, if you use me as a mirror in which you discover your own activity, then it will have a tremendous and profound effect. But if you merely listen as in political or any other talks, then I am afraid you will miss the whole implication of the discovery for yourself of that truth which dissolves the center of the 'me'.

I am only conscious of this activity of the 'me' when I am opposing, when consciousness is thwarted, when the 'me' is desirous of achieving a result. The 'me' is active, or I am conscious of that center, when pleasure comes to an end and I want to have more of that pleasure; then there is resistance and there is a purposive shaping of the mind to a particular end which will give me a delight, a satisfaction. I am aware of myself and my activities when I am pursuing virtue consciously. That is all we know. A man who pursues virtue consciously is unvirtuous. Humility cannot be pursued, and that is the beauty of humility.

So, as long as this center of activity in any direction, conscious and unconscious, exists, there is this movement of time, and I am conscious of the past and the present in conjunction with the future. The center of this activity, the self-centered activity of the 'me', is a time process. That is what you mean by time; you mean the psychological process of time; it is memory that gives continuity to the activity of the center which is the 'me'. Please watch yourselves in operation; don't listen to my words or be mesmerized by my words. If you watch yourself and are aware of this center of activity, you will see that it is only the process of time, of memory, of experiencing and translating every experience according to memory. You also see that self-activity is recognition, which is the process of the mind.

Now can the mind be free from it? That may be possible at rare moments; that may happen to most of us when we do an unconscious, unintentional, unpurposive act. Is it possible for the mind ever to be free from self-centered activity? That is a very important question first to put to ourselves, because in the very putting of it, you will find the answer. That is, if you are aware of the total process of this self-centered activity, fully cognizant of its activities at different levels of your consciousness, then surely you have to ask yourselves if it is possible for that activity to come to an end—that is, not to think in terms of time, not to think in terms of what I will be, what I have been, what I am. From such thought, the whole process of self-centered activity begins; there also begin the determination to become, the determination to choose and to avoid, which are all a process of time. We see, in that process, infinite mischief, misery, confusion, distortion, deterioration taking place. Be aware of it as I am talking, in your relationship, in your mind.

Surely the process of time is not revolutionary. In the process of time, there is no transformation; there is only a continuity and no ending. In the process of time, there is nothing but recognition. It is only when you have complete cessation of the time process, of the activity of the self, is there the new, is there revolution, is there transformation.

Being aware of this whole, total process of the 'me' in its activity, what is the mind to do? It is only with the renewal, it is only with the revolution—not through evolution, not through the 'me' becoming, but through the 'me' completely coming to an end—that there is the new. The time process can't bring the new; time is not a way of creation.

I do not know if any of you have had a moment of creativity, not action—I am not talking of putting something into action—I mean that moment of creation when there is no recognition. At that moment, there is that extraordinary state in which the 'me', as an activity through recognition, has ceased. I think some of us have had it; perhaps most of us have had it. If we are aware, we will see in that state that there is no experiencer who remembers, translates, recognizes, and then identifies; there is no thought process which is of time. In that state of creation, creativity, or in that state of the new which is timeless, there is no action of the 'me' at all.

Now, our question surely is: Is it possible for the mind to experience, to have that state, not momentarily, not at rare moments, but—I would not use the word *everlasting* or *for ever* because that would imply time—to have the state, to be in that state without regard to time? Surely, that is an important discovery to be made by each one of us because that is the door to love; all other doors are activities of the self. Where there is action of the self, there is no love. Love is not of time. You can't practice love. If you do, then it is a self-conscious activity of the 'me' which hopes through loving to gain a result.

So, love is not of time; you can't come upon it through any conscious effort, through any discipline, through identification, which are all a process of time. The mind, knowing only the process of time, cannot recognize love. Love is the only thing that is new, eternally new. Since most of us have cultivated the mind, which is a process of time, which is the result of time, we do not know what love is. We talk about love; we say we love people, love our children, our wives, our neighbor; we say we love nature; but the moment I am conscious that I love, self-activity has come into being; therefore, it ceases to be love.

This total process of the mind is to be understood only through relationship—relationship with nature, with people, with our own projection, with everything. In fact, life is nothing but relationship. Though we may attempt to isolate ourselves from relationship, we cannot exist without relationship; though relationship is pain from which we try to run away through isolation by becoming a hermit and so on, we cannot do that. All these methods are an indication of the activity of the self. Seeing this whole picture, being aware of this whole process of time as consciousness, without any choice, without any determined, purposive intention, without the desire for any result, you will see that this process of time comes to an end voluntarily, not induced, not as a result of desire. It is only when that process comes to an end, that love is, which is eternally new.

We do not have to seek truth. Truth is not something far away. It is the truth of the mind, truth of its activities from moment to moment. If we are aware of this moment to moment truth, of this whole process of time, this awareness releases consciousness or that energy to be. As long as the mind uses consciousness as the self-activity, time comes into being with all its miseries, with all its conflicts, with all its mischiefs, its purposive deceptions; and it is only when the mind, understanding this total process, ceases, that love will be. You may call it love or give it some other names; what name you give is of no consequence.

Question: How can one know if one is deceiving oneself?

KRISHNAMURTI: How do you know anything? What is the process of knowing? Please follow this and you will soon find out whether you are deceiving yourself or not. That is, if you are earnest in your question, you can find out.

You want to know when you are deceiving yourself. Now, what do we mean by deceiving? When do you know? When you are interpreting, is it not? You only know when you recognize, when there is the interpretation process going on, when you are experiencing and translating that experience; then you say, "I know." As long as there is the process of recognition, there is knowing.

What do we mean by self-deception? When do we deceive ourselves, consciously or unconsciously? Most of us, though we deceive ourselves, are totally unaware that this process is going on. We may be superficially aware, aware at the superficial levels of consciousness of the word; we may be aware of the self-deception in a vague way. But that will not do. We must know that at all levels, fundamentally. That is rather difficult. We must inquire, we must find out, we must search and understand what we mean by deception. When do we deceive ourselves, delude ourselves? Only when there is an imposition on ourselves or on others. That word *delusion* surely implies that, does it not? Imposing a certain experience on others or being attached to that experience, which is the imposing of that experience on ourselves. What I am saying is not difficult to follow. If you go step by step, it is quite simple. Self-deception exists as long as I am trying to impose an experience on others or on myself, as long as I am translating an experience through attachment or through identification or through the desire to convince another.

So self-deception is a process of time. It is an accumulated process: "I have had an experience as a boy, and I want that experience to continue. I am convinced that experience as a lad is true, and I want to convince you of it because I have experienced it and I hold on to it''; that is how we know. So, the knowing, which is the interpretation of experience, brings about self-deception, which is a process of time.

Don't you know when you are deceiving yourselves? Don't you know it? There is a fact, and you translate that to suit your own vested interests, your own likes and dislikes; and immediately, there has begun self-deception. When you are incapable of facing a fact and are translating that fact in terms of your memory, immediately self-deception has begun. I have a vision which I translate and to which I hold on; there is the experience which I translate according to my like or dislike, and I proceed to deceive myself through my past experience—there self-deception begins, starting with interpretation.

When I am capable of looking at the fact without any kind of comparison or judgment, without translating, then only there is the possibility of not being deceived. When I do not want anything out of it, when I do not want a result, when I do not want to convince you of it or convince myself about it, this possibility of not being deceived exists. I must look directly, be in contact with the fact, without any interpretation between me and that fact. Between me and that fact, the time process which is deception should not be there.

I have an experience as a boy, as a lad, of a guru, a Master, or what you will; then what happens? I interpret it according to my likes, my conditioning. Then I say, ''I know.'' There begins self-deception. I cling to an experience which is translatable. An experience that is translatable is the beginning of self-deception. From there I proceed; I build up this whole process of knowing. If I have capacities, I convince you of my experience; and you, uncritical, superstitious, follow me because you also want to be deceived, you also want to be in the same net. The net has to be thrown away. You can plow the ground every day, do nothing but plow, plow, and plow, but until you sow a seed, you won't get anything. That is how we are deceiving ourselves constantly and deceiving others.

So, to discover for oneself if there is self-deception is very simple, very clear. As long as there is the interpreter translating the experience, there must be deception. Don't say there is infinite time to get free from the experiencer, from the translator. That is another of your ways of self-deception; that is your desire to evade the fact.

If we want to know whether we are deceiving ourselves, it is very clear and it is very simple. It is only when you do not ask, when you do not put out the begging bowl for another to fill, then only you will know the state in which no deception is possible.

Question: You say that through identification we bring about separation, division. Your way of life appears to some of us to be separative and isolating and to have caused division among those who were formerly together. With what have you identified yourself?

KRISHNAMURTI: Now, let us first see the truth of the statement that identification divides, separates. I have stated that several times. Is it a fact or not?

What do we mean by identification? Don't just merely and verbally indulge in it, but look at it directly. You identify yourself with your country, don't you? When you do that, what happens? You immediately enclose yourself through that identification with a particular group. That is a fact, is it not? When you call yourself a Hindu, you have identified yourself with particular beliefs, traditions, hopes, ideas, and that very identification isolates you. That is a fact, is it not? If you see the truth of that, then you cease to identify; therefore, you are no longer a Hindu or a Buddhist or a Christian, politically or religiously. So, identification is separative, is a deteriorating factor in life. That is a fact; that is the truth of it whether you like it or not.

The questioner goes on to ask if I have, through my action, brought about division among those who were formerly together. Quite right. If you see something true, must you not state it? Though it brings trouble, though it brings about disunity, should you not state it? How can there be unity on falsity? You identify yourself with an idea, with a belief, and when another questions that belief, the idea, you throw that other fellow out; you don't bring him in, you push him out. You have isolated him; the man who says what you are doing is wrong has not isolated you. So, your action is isolating, and not his action, not the action of the person who points to the truth. You don't want to face the fact that identification is separative.

Identification with a family, with an idea, with a belief, with any particular organization is all separative. When that is directly put an end to, or when you are made to look at it and are given a challenge, then you who want to identify, who want to be separative, who want to push the other fellow out, say that that man is isolating.

Your way of existence, your way of life, is separative, and so you are responsible for separation. I am not. You have thrown me out; I have not gone out. Naturally, you begin to feel that I am isolating, that I am bringing division, that my ideas and my expressions are destroying, are destructive. They should be destructive; they should be revolutionary. Otherwise, what is the value of anything new?

Surely, sirs, there must be revolution, not according to any particular ideology or pattern. If it is according to an ideology or pattern, then it is not revolution; it is merely the continuation of the past; it is identification with a new idea, and therefore it gives continuity to a particular form, and that is certainly not revolution. Revolution comes into being when there is an inward cessation of all identification, and you can only do that when you are capable of looking straight at the fact without deceiving yourself and without giving the interpreter a chance to tell you what he thinks of it.

Seeing the truth of identification, obviously I am not identified with anything. Sir, when I see a truth that something hurts, there is no problem; I leave it alone. I cease to identify there or elsewhere. You realize that the whole process of identification is destructive, separative; whether this process takes place in religious beliefs or in the political dialectical outlook, it is all separative. When you recognize that, when you see that and are fully aware of it, then obviously you are freed; therefore, there is no identification with anything. Not to be identified means to stand alone, but not as a noble entity facing the world. This has nothing to do with being together. But, you are afraid of disunity.

The questioner says I have brought disunity. Have I? I doubt it! You have discovered for yourself the truth of it. If you are persuaded by me and therefore identify yourself with me, then you have not done a new thing; you have only exchanged one evil for another. Sirs, we must break to find out. The real revolution is the inward revolution; it is a revolution that sees things clearly and that is of love. In that state, you have no identification with anything.

Question: You say there can be cooperation only when you and I are as nothing. How can this be true? Is not cooperation positive action whereas being as nothing is almost unconscious negativity? How can two nothingnesses be related, and what is there for them to cooperate about?

KRISHNAMURTI: The state of nothingness must obviously be an unconscious state. It is not a conscious state. You can't say, "I am as nothing." When you are conscious as being nothing, you are then something. This is not a mere amusing statement, but this is a fact. When you are conscious that you are virtuous, you become respectable; a person who is respectable can never find what is real. When I am conscious that I am as nothing then that very nothingness is something. Simply because I have made that statement, don't accept it.

There can be cooperation only when you and I are as nothing. Find out what it means, think out and meditate about it. Don't just ask questions. What does that state of nothingness mean? What do you mean by it? We only know the state of activity of the self, the self-centered activity. Whether you are following some guru, Master, that is all irrelevant. We only know the state which is self-action. That obviously creates and engenders mischief, misery, turmoil, confusion, and noncooperation. And then the problem arises: How is one to cooperate?

We know now that any cooperation based on an idea leads to destruction, as has already been shown. Action, cooperation, based on an idea is separative. Just as belief is separative, so is action based on an idea. Even if you are convinced, or millions are convinced, still there are many to be convinced, and therefore there is contention going on all the time. So, we know that there cannot be fundamental cooperation though there may be superficial persuasion through fear, through reward, through punishment, and so on—which is not cooperation obviously.

So, where there is activity of the self as the end in view, as the utopia in view—that is nothing but destruction, separation, and there is no cooperation. What is one to do if one is really desirous, or one wants really to find out, not superficially but really, and bring about cooperation? If you want cooperation from your wife, your child, or your neighbor, how do you set about it? You set about by loving the person. Obviously!

Love is not a thing of the mind; love is not an idea. Love can be only when the activity of the self has ceased to be. But you call the activity of the self positive; that positive act leads to destruction, separativeness, misery, confusion, all of which you know so well and so thoroughly. And yet, we all talk of cooperation, brotherhood. Basically, we want to cling to our activities of the self.

So, a man who really wants to pursue and find out the truth of cooperation must inevitably bring to an end the self-centered activity. When you and I are not self-centered, we love each other; then you and I are interested in action, and not in the result, not in the idea but in doing the action; you and I have love for each other. When my self-centered activity clashes with your self-centered activity, then we project an idea towards which we both quarrel; superficially we are cooperating, but we are at each other's throats all the time.

So, to be nothing is not the conscious state, and when you and I love each other, we cooperate, not to do something about which we have an idea, but in whatever there is to be done.

If you and I loved each other, do you think the dirty, filthy villages would exist? We would act; we would not theorize and would not talk about brotherhood. Obviously, there is no warmth or sustenance in our hearts, and we talk about everything; we have methods, systems, parties, governments, and legislations. We do not know that words cannot capture that state of love.

The word *love* is not love. The word *love* is only the symbol, and it can never be the real. So, don't be mesmerized by that word *love*. It is not something new. That state can only come into being when the activity of the 'me' has ceased, and in that cessation of the 'me', you are cooperating with what is to be done and not with any idea. Don't you know all this, sirs? Don't you know that when you and I love each other, we do things so easily and so smoothly; we do not talk about cooperation; we do not talk about a system of how to do a thing and then battle over the system and forget the action. You smile and you all pass it by. We have grown old in our cleverness and not in wisdom.

Question: What system of meditation should I follow?

KRISHNAMURTI: We are going to find out. You are not going to listen to my truth and make it yours. You can only imitate the words, but that won't be truth. The symbol is not the real. When you worship the symbol you become idolatrous, and the man who is idolatrous can never find what is truth.

Now, you are going to find out what is the truth, not the ultimate, absolute, and final truth but the truth of the system which will help you to meditate. That is, we are going to find out the truth if systems, methods, help you to meditate. You understand?

The questioner probably asks whether systems, methods, and definite steps will help you to meditate. We are going to find that out. Truth is not something far away, miles away, for which we have to go. It is there right under your very nose, to be discovered every minute; it is there for you to discover with a fresh mind which is creative. We shall discover in this way the truth, the whole implication of meditation.

What is the implication of a system? Practice, doing the thing over and over again, repetition, copying, and imitation, is it not? All systems imply only this, do they not? Through practice, through repetition, are you going to find happiness? That happiness, bliss, something which is not measurable, cannot come that way.

At the beginning of your practice, you have both the beginning and the ending of that practice; that is, what you begin with is also what you end up with; the beginning is the end. If I practice, if I copy, I will end up as an imitator, as a machine repeating. If my mind is only capable of repeating, practicing day after day a certain method, following a certain system, at the end my mind is still copying, imitating, repeating. Surely this is obvious, is this not? Therefore at the beginning, I have set the course which the mind shall follow; if I do not understand at the beginning, I shall not understand at the end. That is the obvious truth.

So, I have discovered that the end is at the beginning. Systems through promises, through pleasure, rewards, punishments, make the mind mechanical, stupid, drunk. And at the beginning there is no freedom, and therefore there is no freedom at the end. The beginning matters enormously.

To you, meditation is quite a different process. You want to learn concentration; you want to learn the method of achieving a result; you want to worship God, female or male, some stupid image; you want to pursue virtue. All this is meditation for you. When you pursue virtue, cultivate virtue, what happens? You have the action of the 'me'. The 'me' desires to be kind, to be generous, to have no greed, and you practice, day after day, month after month. Thereby, are you not strengthening greed in a different way? Because, you are becoming conscious that you are not greedy, and the moment you are conscious that you are not greedy, you are certainly greedy.

Your pursuit of virtue is a form of self-centered activity. That is not meditation. When you want to concentrate, your mind goes wandering, and you try to pull it up; and therefore, you set up a battle. The mind is wandering off, and you attempt to concentrate. What does that indicate? When you are here, for the duration you are here, are not your minds really concentrated? That is, is there not instinctive, natural concentration which is not a process of exclusion?

If your mind is petty, narrow, clever, cunning, ambitious, what is the good of your meditation, what is the good of your learning concentration? If you learn it, then it is another action of the self which will help you to deceive others or to deceive yourself. So, you have seen the truth that concentration is not meditation; it is only a narrowing, exclusive process designed to force the mind to a particular pattern.

Imagine you have abolished all systems; the whole idea of systems has fallen away. What then? The idea of concentrating your mind on a particular object—Master, some image—which is only exclusion, which is a process of identification and therefore of separation, has also dropped away. Then what happens? Your mind becomes more cognizant, more aware. Do you not then see that any pursuit of the mind, any form of achievement, is a burden?

Please follow all this; meditate as I am talking, and you will see that any form of achievement of success, any sense of becoming, is still the action of the self, and therefore of time. When you see that clearly, fully recognize it, then there is no longer the pursuit of virtue. Then all sense of achievement, of being somebody, drops away; therefore, the mind becomes quieter, more serene, not looking for a reward or punishments; it becomes completely indifferent to flattery and insult alike. What has happened to your mind? Don't go home and think about it there; think now. The things that were agitating you before, the things that acted in a separative way, being unconscious and fearful, seeking a reward, avoiding punishment—all these have gone away. The mind has become more quiet, more alert. There is gripping silence, not induced, not disciplined, not forced. Then what happens? Then, in that quiet state, ideas come up, feelings come up, and you understand them and put them away. Then, if you proceed a little further, you will see that in that state there are certain activities which are not self-projected, which come darkly and mysteriously without invitation, like the breeze, the sunset, like beauty. The moment they come, the mind, seeing the beauty, may like to hold on to it; it may then say, "I have experienced that state"; and then it clings to it and thereby creates the process of time, which is memory. That possibility also must go away.

You know how the mind is operating and how it wants a series of sensations, which are called marvelous, and how it is naming them. When you see the truth of all that, these things also go away. Now, what is the state of the mind that is not seeking, that is not pursuing, that is not desiring, that is not searching out a result, that is not naming, that is not recognizing? Such a mind is quiet; such a mind is silent; the silence has come very naturally without any form of enforcement, without any compulsion, without any discipline. It is the truth that has liberated the mind. In that state, the mind is extraordinarily quiet. Then that which is new, which is not recognizable, which is creation, which is love, call it what you will, which is not different from the beginning, comes. And such a mind is a blessed mind, is a holy mind. Such a mind alone can help. Such a mind can cooperate. Such a mind can be without any identification, be alone, without any self-deception.

What is beyond is not measurable by words. That which is not measurable comes, but if you seek like the foolish, then you will never have it. It comes when you are least expecting it; it comes when you are watching the sky; it comes when you are sitting under the shade of a tree; it comes when you are observing the smile of a child or the tears of a woman. But we are not observant; we are not meditating. We meditate only about a mysterious, ugly thing to be pursued, to be practiced, and to be lived up to. A man who practices meditation shall never know, but the man who understands the true meditation, which is from moment to moment, only shall know. There is no experience of the individual. Where truth is concerned, the individuality disappears—the 'me' has ceased to be.

February 10, 1952

London, England, 1952

First Talk in London

It seems to me that having so many problems, each so complex, few of us find a happy solution for them. Intellectually, we have many theories, many ways of solving our human complex problems. Politically, the left offers a certain type, either through compulsion, conformity, or by accepting a certain set of ideas; and religions throughout the world offer a hope, either in the future or through living according to a certain pattern laid down by teachers. And yet, most of us find that our problems are growing more and more complex, our relationship to society more and more intricate, and our individual relationships with one another extremely difficult, conflicting, and painful. Few of us are really inwardly content and happy. We do not seem to find a way out—and when we do, it is an escape, which brings about further complications, further problems, greater intricacies and illusions.

Thought has not solved our problem, and I don't think it ever will. We have relied on the intellect to show us the way out of our complexity. The more cunning, the more hideous, the more subtle the intellect is, the greater the variety of systems, of theories, of ideas. And ideas do not solve any of our human problems; they never have and they never will. The mind is not the solution; the way of thought is obviously not the way out of our difficulty. And it seems to me that we should first understand this process of thinking and perhaps be able to go beyond—for when thought ceases, perhaps we shall be able to find a way which will help us to solve our problems, not only the individual, but also the collective.

And may I suggest here that in listening, we should not reject anything that we may hear for the first time; for most of us have so many ideas, so many prejudices, so many biases through which we cannot listen, which hamper our understanding of anything that is put forward, anything that may be new. So may I suggest that we should listen, not in order to condemn or justify or oppose what is said by our own ideas, but listen so that both of us can understand this problem of living. You and I are talking as two individuals, and if we can think individually—that is, think over our problems as two friends, going deeply into them—then perhaps we shall come upon that intelligence which is neither collective nor individual. It is that intelligence alone that can solve our intricate, ever-increasing problems. To listen properly is not to oppose one idea by another idea. Probably you know already what you think, the way of your thought; you are familiar with your own reactions. And I presume that you have come here to find out what I have to say. To find out what I have to say, you have to listen, surely, with a mind that is free from prejudices, that is watching to find out what the other fellow is saying—which means, with a mind that is willing to examine the problem, a mind that is capable of discovering freely, and not merely a mind that is comparative, that judges, weighs, balances. So, if I may suggest it, as you would listen to a friend to whom you go with a problem, let us with that same attitude, with that same feeling of two individuals trying together, solve this complex problem of living.

As I said, thinking has not solved our problems. The clever ones, the philosophers, the scholars, the political leaders, have not really solved any of our human problems—which are, the relationship between you and another, between you and myself. So far we have used the mind, the intellect, to help us investigate the problem and thereby are hoping to find a solution. Can thought ever dissolve our problems? Is not thought, unless it is in the laboratory or on the drawing-board, always self-protecting, self-perpetuating, conditioned? Is not its activity self-centered? And can such thought ever resolve any of the problems which thought itself has created? Can the mind, which has created the problems, resolve those things that it has itself brought forth?

Before we can say yes or no, surely we must find out what this process of thinking is, this thing which we worship, this intellect to which we look up. What is this thought which has created our problems and which then tries to resolve them? Surely, until we understand that, we cannot find another way of living, another way of existence. Seeing that thought has not freed man, you and me, from our own conflicts, surely we must understand the whole process of thinking and perhaps, thereby, let it come to an end. We may find out, then, if we have love—which is not the way of thought.

What is thinking? When we say, "I think," what do we mean by that? When are we conscious of this process of thinking? Surely, we are aware of it when there is a problem, when we are challenged, when we are asked a question, when there is friction. We are aware of it as a self-conscious process. Please do not listen to me as a lecturer holding forth, but you and I are examining our own ways of thought, which we use as an instrument in our daily life. So I hope you are observing your own thinking, not merely listening to me—that is no good. We shall arrive nowhere if you are only listening to me and not observing your own process of thinking, if you are not aware of your own thought and observing the way it arises, how it comes into being. That is what we are trying to do, you and I—to see what this process of thinking is.

Surely, thinking is a reaction. If I ask you a question, to that you respond—you respond according to your memory, to your prejudices, to your upbringing, to the climate, to the whole background of your conditioning; and according to that you reply, according to that you think. If you are a Christian, a communist, a Hindu, or what you will—that background responds, and it is this conditioning that obviously creates the problem. The center of this background is the 'me' in the process of action. So long as that background is not understood, so long as that thought process, that self which creates the problem, is not understood and put an end to, we are bound to have conflict, within and without, in thought, in emotion, in action. No solution of any kind, however clever, however well thought out, can ever put an end to the conflict between man and man, between you and me. And realizing this, being aware of how thought springs up and from what source, then we ask: Can thought ever come to an end?

That is one of the problems, is it not? Can thought resolve our problems? By thinking over the problem, have you resolved it? Any kind of problem—economic, social, religious—has it ever been really solved by thinking? In your daily life, the more you think about a problem, the more complex, the more irresolute, the more uncertain it becomes. Is not that so—in our actual, daily life? You may, in thinking out certain facets of the problem, see more clearly another person's point of view, but thought cannot see the completeness and fullness of the problem; it can only see partially, and a partial answer is not a complete answer; therefore, it is not a solution.

The more we think over a problem, the more we investigate, analyze, and discuss it, the more complex it becomes. So is it possible to look at the problem comprehensively, wholly? And how is this possible? Because that, it seems to me, is our major difficulty. For our problems are being multiplied—there is imminent danger of war, there is every kind of disturbance in our relationships—and how can we understand all that comprehensively, as a whole? Obviously it can be solved only when we can look at it as a whole—not in compartments, not divided. And when is that possible? Surely, it is only possible when the process of thinking—which has its source in the 'me', the self, in the background of tradition, of conditioning, of prejudice, of hope, of despair—has come to an end. So can we understand this self, not by analyzing, but by seeing the thing as it is, being aware of it as a fact and not as a theory?—not seeking to dissolve the self in order to achieve a result, but seeing the activity of the self, the 'me', constantly in action. Can we look at it without any movement to destroy or to encourage? That is the problem, is it not? If in each one of us the center of the 'me' is nonexistent, with its desire for power, position, authority, continuance, self-preservation, surely our problems will come to an end!

The self is a problem that thought cannot resolve. There must be an awareness which is not of thought. To be aware, without condemnation or justification, of the activities of the self—just to be aware—is sufficient. Because if you are aware in order to find out how to resolve the problem, in order to transform it, in order to produce a result, then it is still within the field of the self, of the 'me'. So long as we are seeking a result—whether through analysis, through awareness, through constant examination of every thought—we are still within the field of thought, which is within the field of the 'me', of the 'I', of the ego, or what you will.

As long as the activity of the mind exists, surely there can be no love. When there is love, we shall have no social problems. But love is not something to be acquired. The mind can seek to acquire it, like a new thought, a new gadget, a new way of thinking, but the mind cannot be in a state of love as long as thought is acquiring love. So long as the mind is seeking to be in a state of nongreed, surely it is still greedy, is it not? Similarly, so long as the mind wishes, desires, and practices in order to be in a state in which there is love, surely it denies that state, does it not?

So, seeing this problem, this complex problem of living, and being aware of the process of our own thinking, and realizing that it actually leads nowhere—when we deeply realize that, then surely there is a state of intelligence which is not individual or collective. So, the problem of the relationship of the individual to society, of the individual to the community, of the individual to reality, ceases because then there is only intelligence, which is neither personal nor impersonal. It is this intelligence alone, I feel, that can solve our immense problems. And that cannot be a result; it comes into being only when we understand this whole, total process of thinking, not only at the conscious level, but also at the deeper, hidden levels of consciousness.

Perhaps, as we are going to meet during the whole of this month, we shall be able to talk over this problem more fully, exchange ideas, discuss them. But what I feel is that to understand any of these problems, we have to have a very quiet mind, a very still mind, so that the mind can look at the problem without interposing ideas, theories—without any distraction. And that is one of our difficulties because thought has become a distraction. When I want to understand, look at something, I don't have to think about it—I look at it. The moment I begin to think, to have ideas, opinions about it, I am already in a state of distraction, looking away from the thing which I must understand. So thought, when you have a problem, becomes a distraction—thought being an idea, opinion, judgment, comparison—which prevents us from looking and thereby understanding and resolving the problem. But unfortunately, for most of us thought has become so important. You say, "How can I exist, be, without thinking? How can I have a blank mind?" To have a blank mind is to be in a state of stupor, idiocy, or what you will, and your instinctive reaction is to reject it. But surely, a mind that is very quiet, a mind that is not distracted by its own thought, a mind that is open, can look at the problem very directly and very simply. And it is this capacity to look without any distraction at our problems that is the only solution. For that, there must be a quiet, tranquil mind.

Such a mind is not a result, is not an end-product of a practice, of meditation, of control. It comes into being through no form of discipline or compulsion or sublimation, without any effort of the 'me', of thought; it comes into being when I understand the whole process of thinking—when I can see a fact without any distraction. In that state of tranquillity of a mind that is really still, there is love. And it is love alone that can solve all our human problems.

I have several questions here, and I will try to answer them. May I suggest that in listening to the answers you do not merely listen to me—that you are not caught by my words, but that actually we go through the problem together and try to resolve it together. That is, do not, if I may suggest, follow verbally the description of the problem or intellectually try to resolve it. Any of these questions is a problem for most of us, and it will be beneficial, I think, if you can follow them as they are happening in yourselves. If you can listen to each problem, not as of another, but as of yourself, then we can deal with it directly and tackle it immediately.

Question: I have been to several psychoanalysts to free myself from the fear which dominates me. I have not been able to get rid of it. Would you kindly suggest how I am to set about freeing myself from this constant oppression.

KRISHNAMURTI: Surely most of us have fears, conscious or unconscious, of various kinds. We are not discussing the kind of fear but fear as a whole. When I can understand fear as a whole, then after having understood it I can deal with the particular.

So, let us find out how to resolve this fear—not theoretically, not as something to be thought over the day after tomorrow, when you have leisure, but actually do it now as we go along. Let us see if we can experiment with this.

How do we look at fear? When we are aware of it, how do we regard it? What is our attitude, our state of mind, when we are aware that there is fear? Please, follow this step by step, and if it is not fear, substitute for it your own particular nightmare, your own particular burden. And let us go into it step by step, completely, if we can, and see if we cannot resolve it. What is the state of the mind when it discovers that there is fear? What happens to the mind? What do you do? You have opinions about it, have you not? You have ideas about it, have you not? You look at it from a distance, do you not? You do not look at it directly; you are not in immediate contact with it. You are far away from it and regard it as something to be avoided, something to be got rid of, something about which you can have theories. You look at it either with condemnation or with a desire to run away from it, so that you are never directly in contact with it; you never look at it immediately, directly, simply. You have all these barriers of distraction.

So, we are going to look at it directly. And to do that, you must approach it, you must come nearer to it. And you cannot come nearer to it if you have opinions about it or about the cause of it. You cannot see it directly if your mind is occupied with analysis—the why and the wherefore, going backwards indefinitely. The discovery of the cause of fear will not dissolve fear. It can be dissolved only when you can directly look at it, when you can have direct relationship with it. Merely analyzing, groping in the past to discover its cause, will not dissolve it because your mind is distracted, because you are not facing the fact of fear.

So, having an opinion about it or analyzing it will not bring you close to it, direct to it. So, that must go away. And it will disappear, this opinion with regard to it, when you feel the urgent necessity of looking at that fear. Then what happens? You have come a little nearer to it, have you not?—to the thing that you call fear. Then what happens? What is the reaction then? You still have ideas about it, have you not?—the idea that you must get rid of it, the idea that you cannot bear to look at it, the idea that even if you do look you will not know how to resolve it. So, the idea about fear creates fear, does it not? That is, I am afraid, there is fear in me; I am trying to understand what that fear is—that is, to look at it. I cannot look at it if I have ideas about it—the idea being the word, the image. As long as I have an idea about fear, surely idea creates fear. If I recognize, if I am aware of that, what is my relationship to the thing that I have called fear? I hope you are following this. How do I look at the thing that I call fear now? I've come closer; the barrier of opinion, judgment, analysis, has gone; I am no longer in a position where idea dominates. So, what is my relationship to the thing that I call fear? Is that thing called fear separate from me, the observer, the onlooker? Surely it is not. The observer is fear. The observer is not watching fear; the observer himself is the fear. So, that is a fact.

Now, let us go a little closer, still further. Is that thing which I call fear the result of a word? Is it the product of a word—the word being thought? If it is, then the word is very important, isn't it? And for most of us the word is very important. Verbalizing is the process of thinking. So for us the word *fear* is fear. The word is fear, not the thing which we call fear. So, when I can look at myself in a state which I have called fear—which is merely the word—surely then the word disappears, and I realize that as long as the mind is active, verbalizing, in any direction—which is to have symbols—there must be fear.

So, I am not different from fear; the thinker is the thought. And for thought to come to an end, the thinker cannot discipline thought—because it is himself. All that he can do is to be in a state without any movement in any direction. Only then, surely, fear ceases.

Question: We all recognize that inward peace and tranquillity of the mind are essential. What is the method or the "how" which you suggest?

KRISHNAMURTI: Now again, let us try to see the truth of this "how," of this method. You say, "Tranquillity of the mind and a peaceful heart are essential." Is that so? Or, is that merely a theory, merely a desire? Because we are so disturbed, distracted, we want that quietness, that tranquillity—which then is merely an escape. It is not a necessity; it is an escape. When we see the necessity of it, when we are convinced it is the only thing that matters, the only thing that is essential—then do we ask the method for it? Is a method necessary when you see something is essential?

Method involves time, does it not? If not now, then eventually—tomorrow, in a couple of years—I shall be tranquil. Which means you do not see the necessity of being tranquil. And so the "how" becomes a distraction; the method becomes a way of postponing the essentiality of tranquillity. And that is why you have all these meditations, these phoney, false controls to get eventual tranquillity of the mind, and the various methods of how to discipline in order to acquire that tranquillity. Which means you do not see the necessity, the immediate necessity, of having a still mind. When you see the necessity of it, then there is no inquiry into the method at all. Then you see the importance of having a quiet mind, and you have a quiet mind.

Unfortunately, we do not see the necessity of having a still mind, a tranquil mind. We are too fond of our distractions, and we want to be weaned away from our distractions through the process of time. And therefore we ask the method, the "how," the practice. I think that is a very false approach. A tranquil mind is not a result; it is not the end of a practice. A tranquil mind is not a static mind, and that which is result is static. When you have a quiet mind as a result, through discipline, it is no longer a still mind. It is a state which is a product, and that which has been put together can be dismembered again.

So, what is important in this question is not the method—because there are innumerable methods to produce a result, and a man who is seeking a result has no tranquil mind. But what is important in this is to see directly, simply, that only a tranquil mind can understand; that a still mind is essential, not in some future, but immediately. When you see such a necessity, then the mind is still.

Such a still mind will know what it is to be creative. Because in that state, which is not a result, which is not the product of years of practice, in that still mind, you will find that all movement of thought is nonexistent. Thought does not create; thought can never create. It can project its own desires, its own sensations, its own imagery, symbols, but that which it has projected is not true; it is of itself. Let thought be of Christ, of a Master, or what you will—it is its own projection. And the worship of that projection is self-worship. Such a mind is not a tranquil mind. But you will see, if it is truly tranquil, quiet, that there is no movement in it. Therefore all experiencing, as we know it, has ceased. Because that which we experience is recognizable, and as long as there is the center of recognition, the mind is not tranquil. For reality, or God, is not to be recognized, is not to be experienced by the mind. When experiencing ceases—which is, when recognizing comes to an end—then there is that which is not to be experienced, that which is not to be recognized. And only when we see the necessity of such tranquillity, such stillness—only then it comes into being.

April 7, 1952

Second Talk in London

As we were saying yesterday, we look to ideas for the solution of our problems, and we base our action on ideas—at least we approximate our action to a certain set of ideas. And is it ever possible to be free from the conflict of idea and action? Because, between action and idea there is a wide gap, and we are everlastingly trying to bridge this gap, and so we are in constant conflict. And when the mind is in conflict, obviously there is confusion. And when we are in a state of confusion, any choice of idea, any choice of action, is bound to be equally confused. And so we are caught in a series of conflicts, never ending, but always getting more and more complex. And we can see that only when the mind is very still and quiet, not choosing, is there a possibility of tranquillity.

When the mind is merely accumulating knowledge—either of the past or of the future, accumulating ideas, and thereby trying to find an action which will bring about the cessation of conflict, not only within ourselves, but with society and all about us—does not the mind merely become then the instrument of conflict, the source of conflict? That is, does knowledge—the accumulating process of ideas, of information, of that which is of the past or the hope of the future—does knowledge help in bringing about the cessation of conflict? And must conflict go on indefinitely—conflict within and without, in our relationships and in ourselves?

If that conflict is to continue—and that seems the lot of all of us, everlastingly and without end—then we must find escapes—political, religious, every kind of escape—so that we can at least drown ourselves in some kind of darkness, illusion, in some theory, in some complicated action, which never produces freedom.

If we would really go more deeply into this question of conflict—whether it will ever produce greater progress, a greater understanding, a greater freedom in our relationships, more love—then we must find out the source of conflict. For if conflict is ultimately to produce a sense of freedom of the mind, and therefore love, then conflict is necessary. We have taken it for granted that it is essential in one form or another, and without conflict we think we shall become stagnant. We have built our life, our philosophy, our religious thinking, on this series of conflicts, hoping that it will eventually bring about freedom—be ennobling, and so on. So should we not, before we accept the inevitability of conflict, find out whether conflict ever brings understanding?

When you and I are in conflict—emotionally, verbally, deeply—is there understanding? And does conflict cease with knowledge? Is not knowledge the very center of the 'me', of the self, which is everlastingly acquiring, trying to become something? And does not this conflict lie in this desire to become, to be? This process of accumulating knowledge—which is really information, words put together—will that bring about the cessation of conflict, put an end to the 'me', which is the center of accumulation, which is the center of conflict? Is it ever possible to suppress knowledge and this process of accumulation? We may possess very little—a few clothes, a little property; we may be unknown, living in a small place, but we are always accumulating knowledge; we are always trying to gather to ourselves virtue. And that is the process of the mind.

I do not know if you have ever thought of this problem of acquiring knowledge—whether knowledge does ultimately help us to love, to be free from those qualities that produce conflict in ourselves and with our neighbors; whether knowledge ever frees the mind of ambition. Because ambition is, after all, one of the qualities that destroys relationship, that puts man against man. And if we would live at peace with each other, surely ambition must completely come to an end—not only political, economic, social ambition, but also the more subtle and pernicious ambition, the spiritual ambition—to be something. Is it ever possible for the mind to be free from this accumulating process of knowledge, this desire to know?

What is it we want to know? We want to know about ourselves, what we have been and what we shall be. We may want to know about scientific information, but that is merely a side issue. Fundamentally, we all want to know—what?—to know if we are loved, and if we ourselves love; to know if we are free, if we are happy, if we are creative, if we are somebody, something. We want to know either what we have been or what we shall be, so that knowledge becomes a means of personal security, a psychological necessity for one's continuance. And so we gather information—religious, political, social, and so on—and with that we are satisfied, for we use that knowledge to exploit others or cover ourselves.

So surely, one of our problems is, is it not, whether it is possible to live in this world without the psychological process of accumulation, without this constant battle to know what one will become, psychologically. So long as we are trying to become something—accepting certain principles, ideals, beliefs, and then approximating ourselves to them—surely knowledge becomes a means of self-satisfied security, certainty. And the moment you have acquired, you want more, and so there is the battle, the struggle of this constant desire to be something more, to become something. And for that we must have knowledge. And this accumulating process of the 'me', the 'I', the ego, is the center of this recognition, is the knower, is the knowledge. And this center is always translating every experience according to its knowledge, according to its prejudices. And so, this center of knowledge, this entity that is everlastingly inquiring in order to know, can only experience that which it has known; it cannot experience anything new. The mind that is burdened with knowledge can never be creative; it cannot know what it is to be in that state wherein creation can take place. Every experience has already been tasted, and whatever it experiences is its own projection.

A mind that would be in a state in which the new can take place—whether it be the truth, whether it be God, or what you will—must surely cease to acquire, to gather; it must put aside all knowledge. Because that which is capable of recognizing is still within the field of time. And a mind which is the result of time, which is the result of accumulation, a mind burdened with knowledge, cannot possibly understand, surely, that which is real, which is not measurable. But most of us are afraid to be in that state, to be entirely free from this center which is everlastingly accumulating.

All this is not a matter of conviction. You are not being persuaded by me to accept any set of ideas—that would be a horror. Then our relationship would be one of propagandists. But surely, what we are concerned with is to find out the truth of this thing which we call the 'me', the center that is the cause of conflict, and whether that center can ever be resolved. And one of its qualities, part of its nature, is the accumulating process of knowledge, the gathering in of memories, of the past and of the future, so that it can be secure. I am not trying to convince you of it, and we need not argue about it. It is not a matter of logic—logic is always rather cheap. But we can surely try to find out if the mind can be free, can be in that state of not-knowing, when it is not gathering or projecting from its own knowledge. Surely that requires investigation, not conviction, not belief. For that you do not have to read any books. All that one has to do is to watch oneself, go into the intricacies of the mind, watch the ways of the self, gathering and rejecting. And then one can see that conflict is not necessary; conflict is not the way to an integrated existence, to a complete life. But so long as the mind is trying to become—acquiring, reaching for more experience, for a greater wealth of information and knowledge—the more there must be conflict.

Reality or God or what you will is not to be reached through conflict. On the contrary, there must be the cessation of the 'me' as the center of accumulation—either of information or of virtue or experience, or of any of those qualities that the mind seeks in order to enlarge itself. Only then, surely, is it possible for that state of reality to come into being.

Question: I have tried out many of the things you have suggested in your various talks, but I don't seem to get very far. What is wrong with you or with me?

KRISHNAMURTI: You see, the difficulty is that we want to get "very far," we want to reach a result, we want the 'more'. So we experiment in order to arrive; we study, we listen, in order to compare, in order to become something. What I say may be utterly wrong; you have to find out, not accept it. What is important in this question is, is it not, the desire to become more, to reach far, to arrive somewhere. And so, with that motive in the background, you study, you experiment, you observe yourself, you are aware of your actions. With that hidden motive—to progress, to achieve, to become a saint, to know more, to reach the Master—with that hidden, subtle motive driving you, you do all: you read, you study, you inquire. And naturally, you do not get very far. So what is important is to understand that motive, that drive. Why should you get very far? Far in what?—in your knowledge, in your ambitions, in your so-called virtues, which are really not virtues at all but the becoming greater in yourself?

You see, the difficulty is that we are so deeply ambitious. As the clerk strives to become the manager, so we want to become the Masters, the saints. We want to arrive ultimately at a state of peace. So ambition is the motive; ambition is driving us. And instead of understanding that ambition and putting an end to it completely, we turn our face towards becoming more and more, to reaching deeper, going very far. So we deceive ourselves, we create illusions. Obviously, the man who is ambitious is not only antisocial, destructive, but he will never understand what truth is, what God is, or whatever name you like to give to it.

So, if I may suggest, do not try to get "very far," but inquire into the motive, into the activities of the mind that desires to go far. Why do we want this? Either we want to escape from ourselves, or we want to have influence, prestige, position, authority. If we want to escape from ourselves, any illusion is good enough.

And it is not a matter of time. The mind is the instrument of achievement, and with the mind, which is the result of time, one cannot understand that which is beyond measure, which is not vague, not mysticism as opposed to occultism—a very convenient division of the thoughtless. To understand this motive, this drive to become something, is what is important, and that we can observe in our daily actions, in our everyday thought—this urge to be something, to dominate, to assert. It is there that the truth lies, not away from it. It is there that we must find it.

Question: Is it possible for the ordinary individual to lead a spiritual life without having a set of beliefs or taking part in ceremonies and ritual?

KRISHNAMURTI: I wonder what we mean by a spiritual life? Do you become spiritual by performing ceremonies and rituals, having innumerable beliefs, or by having principles according to which you are trying to live? Does that make you spiritual? Ceremonies and rituals sometimes, perhaps at the beginning, give a certain sensation, so-called uplift. But they are repetitious, and every sensation that is repeated soon wearies of itself. The mind likes to establish itself in a routine, in a habit; and rituals, ceremonies, provide this and give to the mind an opportunity to separate itself, to feel itself superior, to feel that it knows more, and to enjoy the sensations of repetitious pleasures. Surely there is nothing spiritual about rituals and ceremonies; they only divide man against man. Since they are repetitious, they do not free the mind from its own self-projected sensations. On the contrary, for a spiritual life—a free life, a free mind, a mind that is not burdened by the ego, the 'me'—it is essential to see the falsity of ceremonies. To find reality or God or what you will, there must be no ceremonies, no rituals round which the mind can wrap itself and feel itself different, enjoying the sensations of oft-repeated action.

And a mind burdened with belief—is such a mind capable of perception, of understanding? Surely, a mind burdened with belief is an enclosed mind—no matter what belief it is, whether it is in nationalism, or any particular principle, or the belief in its own knowledge. A mind that is burdened with beliefs, either of the past or of the future, is surely not a free mind. A mind crippled with belief is incapable of investigation, of discovery, of looking within itself. But the mind likes beliefs because belief gives to it a certain security, makes it feel strong, energetic, aloof, separative.

We know all this as an everyday fact. And yet we continue in our beliefs—that you are a Christian and I am a Hindu—I with my set of idiosyncrasies, traditions, and experience handed down from the past, and you with yours. Obviously, belief does not bring us together. Only when there is no belief, only when we have understood the whole process of belief—then perhaps we can come together. The mind desires constantly to be secure, to be in a state of knowledge, to know; and belief offers a very convenient security. Belief in something, belief in a certain economic system for which one is willing to sacrifice oneself and others—in that the mind takes shelter; it is certain there. Or, belief in God, in a certain spiritual system; there again the mind feels secure, certain.

Belief, after all, is a word. The mind lives on words; it has its being in words, and there it takes shelter and finds certainty. And a mind that is sheltered, secure, certain, is surely incapable of understanding anything new, or receiving that which is not measurable. So belief acts as a barrier, not only between man and man, but also, surely, as a block, as a hindrance, to something that is creative, that is new. But to be in a state of uncertainty, of not knowing, of not acquiring, is extremely difficult, is it not—perhaps not difficult, but it requires a certain earnestness, without any distraction, inward or outward. But unfortunately most of us inwardly want to be distracted, and beliefs, ceremonies, rituals offer good, respectable distractions.

So, what is important in this question is, is it not, to free the mind from its own self-created habits, from its own self-projected experiences, from its own knowledge—which is, from the entity which is gathering, accumulating. That is the real problem—to be free inwardly, to be in that state when the mind is no longer inviting or accumulating experience. That is extremely arduous. And it is for everyone, not for the few, to free themselves from the process of time, which is the process of accumulation, gathering in, the desire for the 'more'. This is only possible when we understand the ways of the mind, how it is constantly seeking security, permanency, either in beliefs, in rituals, in ceremonies, or in knowledge. All these are distractions, and a mind that is distracted is incapable of quietness. To go into this problem very deeply, one has to be aware inwardly, both at the conscious and at the unconscious level, of those attractions and distractions that the mind has cultivated—to observe them, and not try to transform them into something else but merely observe. Then begins the freedom in which the mind is no longer acquiring, accumulating.

Question: I feel that much of my unhappiness is due to my strong urge to help and advise those I love—and even those I do not love. How can I really see this as domination and interference? Or, how can I know if my help is genuine?

KRISHNAMURTI: You mean to say that you are unhappy because you cannot help another! I should have thought you would help others because you are happy. Because you love, you help, and if you do not help, you are not unhappy. I think that is where the key of this problem is; you are unhappy because you cannot help. That is, helping gives you happiness. So, you are deriving your happiness from helping others. You are using others to get your own satisfaction. Please, this is not a clever, smart remark. But most of us are in that state: we want to be active; we want to do things, interfere, help, love, be generous; we want to be active doing something. And when that is thwarted, we are unhappy. And as long as we have the freedom to act, to fulfill, and that activity is not thwarted, we call it happiness.

Surely, the action of help is not of the mind. The generosity of the mind is not the generosity of the heart. But because we have lost the generosity of the heart, we are generous with our mind, which when thwarted, rebels—and there is the ache. And so we join groups, parties, create societies to help. When we have lost generosity, we turn to social service; when we have lost love, we turn to systems. So surely, in this problem the underlying difficulty is that we are seeking satisfaction, and that is a very difficult thing to be free of because it is so subtle. We want to be satisfied in everything that we do, or we go to the other extreme and become martyrs, put up with anything. Until we understand this desire to be satisfied, then help becomes interference and domination. The desire to help another becomes interference and domination until we understand the urge, the craving, to find satisfaction.

The mind is always seeking satisfaction, is it not?—which is, seeking a result, to be sure that one is helping. And when you are certain that you are giving help, you feel satisfied, from which comes so-called happiness. So, is it possible for the mind to be free from this urge to be satisfied? Why do we seek satisfaction? Why do we seek gratification in everything? Why are we not merely content to be what we are? For, if we can see what we are, then perhaps we can transform it. But always seeking satisfaction away from what we are brings about the whole problem of interference and domination—whether your help is genuine or not, and so on.

So, the problem of satisfaction is very difficult to resolve because it is so extraordinarily subtle and varied. And it can only come to an end by constant watching, being aware of how the mind is seeking to be certain in its own satisfaction. Again, this is not a matter for disputation, for argument, to be convinced of it—but it is to be inquired into, to be found. To really see that your mind is seeking satisfaction—not merely to repeat what has been said, which leads nowhere, but to see the truth of it—brings about an extraordinary discovery. Then it is something new which you have found. To find out for yourself the ways in which the mind is subtly seeking satisfaction, to discover it, to see it, to be aware of it, brings freedom from it.

Question: How do you "see" a fact without any reaction—without condemnation or justification, without prejudice or the desire for a conclusion, without wanting to do something about it, without the sense of thine and mine? What is the point of such "seeing" or awareness? Have you actually done this, and could you exemplify from your own experience?

KRISHNAMURTI: First of all, do we see a fact?—not how do we see a fact, but do we see a fact? Do we see the fact, for example, of greed, of contradiction, in ourselves? What exactly do we mean by "seeing"? Am I aware that I am greedy? And how do I regard it? Am I capable of seeing that I am greedy, without explanations, without condemnation, without trying to do something about it, without justifying it, without the desire to transform it into nongreed? Let us take the example of envy or greed, or feeling inferior or superior, or jealousy, and so on. Take one thing like that, and see what happens.

First of all, most of us are unaware that we are envious; we brush it casually aside as a bourgeois thing, as being superficial. But deeply, inwardly, profoundly, we are envious. We are envious beings. We want to be something, we want to achieve, we want to arrive—which is the very indication of envy. Our social, economic, spiritual systems are based on that envy. First of all, be aware of it. Most of us are not. We justify it; we say, "If we hadn't envy, what would happen to civilization? If we did not make progress and had no ambition, and so on, what would we do?—everything would collapse, would stagnate." So, that very statement, that very justification, surely prevents us from looking at the fact that we are, you and I, envious.

Then, if we are at all conscious, aware, seeing all this—then what happens? If we do not justify, we condemn, don't we?—because we think that state of envy, or whatever state it is you feel, is wrong, not spiritual, not moral. So we condemn, which prevents us seeing *what is,* does it not? When I justify or condemn or have a desire to do something about it, that prevents me from looking at it, doesn't it? Let us examine this glass in front of me on the table. I can look at it without thinking who made it, observing the pattern, and so on; I can just look at it. Similarly, is it not possible to look at my envy, not to condemn it, not to have the desire to alter it, to do something about it, to justify it? Then, if I do not do all that, what happens? I hope you are following this, substituting for envy your own particular burden. I hope you are not merely listening to me telling you something about it but are observing your own relation to a certain fact which is causing you disturbance or pain or confusion. Please watch yourself, and apply what we are saying to yourself—watch your own mind in the process of thinking. We are partaking together, sharing together in this experiment to find out what "seeing" is, going more and more deeply into it.

So, if I would see that I am envious, be aware of it, see the content of it, then the desire to do something, to condemn, to justify, obviously comes to an end because I am more interested to see what it is, what is behind it, what is its inward nature. If I am not interested to know more deeply, more intimately, the content of this whole problem of envy, then I am satisfied by merely condemning.

So, if I am not condemning, not desiring to do something about it, I am a little nearer, intimate, more close to the problem. Then how do I look at it? How do I know I am greedy? Is it the word that is creating the feeling of wanting more? Is the reaction the outcome of memory, which is symbolized by a word? And is the feeling different from the word, the name, the term? And by recognizing it, giving it a name, a label, have I resolved it, have I understood it?

All this is a process of seeing the fact, isn't it? And then, to go still further, is the 'me', the observer, experiencing greed? Is greed something apart from me? Is envy, that extraordinarily exciting and pleasurable reaction, something apart from me, the observer? When I do not condemn, when I do not justify, when I am not desirous of doing something about it, have I not removed the censor, the observer? And when the observer is not, then is there the word *greed*—the very word being a condemnation? When the observer is not, then only is there a possibility of that feeling coming to an end.

But in looking at the fact, I do not start with the desire to bring it to an end; that is not my motive. I want to see the whole structure, the whole process; I want to understand it. And in this process I discover the ways of my own thinking. And it is through this self-knowledge—not to be gathered from books, from printed words and lectures, but by actually sharing together as in this talk—that we find out the ways of the self. It is seeing the truth of the fact—which I can only do when I have been through this process—which frees the mind from that reaction called envy. Without seeing the truth of that, then do what you will, envy will remain. You may find a substitute for it; you may do everything to cover it up, to run away from it, but it is always there. Only when we can understand how to approach it, to see the truth of it, is there freedom from it.

April 8, 1952

Third Talk in London

It seems to me that our problems are not so much concerned with the illusions that the mind creates, but rather in the fact that we avoid coming face to face with our own inadequacy. We do not see that we are really escaping from ourselves constantly. It is these escapes, these illusions, that create the conflict, and not the discovery of ourselves as we are, and I think that is the real crux of our problem. We have got so many illusions, so many beliefs, so many certainties and prejudices, and these create the problem. We are trying constantly, are we not, to adjust our inward urges, our inward experiences, our inward difficulties—to adjust them to the beliefs, to the knowledge, to the superficial conditions of our lives. And so we are forever avoiding facing the real issue, which is ourselves. We are extremely bored with ourselves, with what we are—and so we seek superficial knowledge or acquire beliefs that will act as security, as permanency—and constantly we are running away from what we are. And perhaps this evening we can see what these escapes are and actually cut ourselves off from them—not theoretically, not verbally or intellectually, but actually face them, realize their full significance, and thereby let them drop away—so that without the suggestions or persuasions of others we can directly experience for ourselves, directly face, that which we are.

I think it is important not to discuss what our beliefs are and how to get rid of them; what our superstitions are; whether rituals, ceremonies, Masters are necessary or not—those are all childish things. Because, our central problem is not those illusions but what is actual—and from that we are running away. And if we can experience, come into contact with what actually is—not from a distance, but come very close and examine it, look at it, observe it, go into it deeply—then we shall see that though we are in despair, though there is war, though there is anxiety, a sense of eternal loneliness from which we are continually running away, we can deal with it, we can deal with the direct issue. That is where our difficulty lies because we have surrounded ourselves, have we not, with so many fancies, so many illusions, so many myths, and all these are utterly valueless if we would discover what we actually are, and go beyond. As religious people, so-called religious—which presumably most of us here are—we have created many systems of philosophy, disciplines, beliefs, and we have formed many societies, organizations, which actually take us away from the central issue—which is, what we actually are.

So, until we face that—not intellectually, not verbally—we cannot proceed to bring about an integration between what verbally we understand and action. Intellectually we see that we are actually running away, taking flight from ourselves. We are conscious of it intellectually; verbally we accept it. Which again creates another problem, does it not? For the problem then arises: How am I to act in order to come near, to understand, what actually I am? So, we make the "how" into another problem. And so, we increase one problem by another—what to believe and what not to believe, what kind of meditations, disciplines we shall follow, how to still the mind, how to reject, what to acquire and what not to acquire, and so on and on—which only brings further confusion, further problems, ever multiplying and increasing.

Can we not see all this as illusion?—not theoretically, but really see that the mind is projecting these things and escaping through them in order to avoid the central issue of what we actually are? We can never find out what is actually the present state of the mind and what lies beyond unless we put aside or understand these illusions—like beliefs in reincarnation, in Masters, dozens of beliefs—with which we have crippled the mind and which have made it so enclosed that it can never be free. It is only when we have relinquished these, actually set them aside—then only, when the mind is free, can we approach our central difficulty, which is ourselves.

Surely that is the problem, is it not? You may have wonderful philosophies, theories, of economic relationship—how to bring about brotherhood, unity, and so on. But they will all be worthless, will they not, unless we have solved the problem of the center, of the motive, of the drive which makes us what we are. Surely that is the problem, is it not? And what is the difficulty that makes us incapable of meeting our problem fully? Why is it that we cannot, by understanding the escapes, come to the central point?—which is, our own anxiety, our own fear, that sense of utter loneliness, despair, which we are everlastingly trying to fill, to cover up. Is not our difficulty primarily the fear of uncertainty? The mind obviously dislikes a state in which it is uncertain, in which it cannot rely on something—on a belief, on a person, on an idea. So, is not our difficulty the fact that most of us are seeking a permanency?—a permanent explanation, a permanent answer, a permanent relationship, an idea that cannot be shattered under any circumstances, the idea of God, or what you will—to which the mind clings. And so, the mind projects the permanent and holds on to it.

Now, can we not, seeing all this—how the mind acts, its process—can we not put aside those escapes? Not as a separate entity putting these things aside—and thereby again dividing the mind in itself and producing another problem of how to bring about integration of the mind. But can we not see the full significance of these escapes and be in direct relationship, then, with that central issue instead of going round in circles about things that really do not matter?—what nationality you belong to, what belief you have, what gods you worship—which are all really the result of immature thinking. Can we not put those aside? Can the mind not see their actual value, their significance, and thereby be free from them and so come to the central point?

Can we not experiment with this problem as I am talking, so that you actually experience the freedom from these self-created illusions of the mind? And being free of them, then you can look directly at that thing which we call fear, anxiety, loneliness. It is only when the mind is free from anxiety, from fear, from loneliness, that it can then understand that which is not measurable by the mind; only then is it possible for that to take place—not by seeking an explanation for that infinite anxiety, not by trying to reason it out, not by trying to escape from it, but by going through it. And it can only be gone through when the mind is not agitated with finding an answer, when it is not trying to look at what lies beyond it, when it is not measuring its own experiences in relation to the future, to the thing that it hopes to discover. Only then, surely, can we find out what is reality, what God is, or whatever name you may give to it. But merely to speculate from this side, to have theories, to have dogmas, is surely immature and only creates further confusion and misery.

Surely the earnest, the thoughtful, must have gone through all this. But perhaps we have not gone further—that is, to know the process of our own minds. And when we understand the full significance of our own minds, then the division between the thinker and the thought, the observer who is looking at that anxiety or fear and trying to overcome it, surely disappears. There is only then that state of being which is fear or anxiety or loneliness—not the observer of fear.

That integration between the thinker and the thought takes place only when the mind has completely put aside all escapes and is not trying to find an answer. Because, whatever movement the mind makes in trying to understand the central issue must be based on time, on the past. And time comes into being only when there is fear and desire.

So, realizing all that, is it not possible for the mind, being free from those escapes, to look at itself, not as the thinker looking at his thoughts, as the experiencer experiencing, but merely observing the state of the mind, being aware without this division? That integrated state comes only when there is no desire to experience something more, the greater than *what is*.

And, if we can understand *what is* and go beyond it, then we shall find out what love is. And love is the only remedy and the only revolution that can bring about order. But unfortunately, most of us are not very serious or earnest. Earnestness, surely, means discovering the process of one's own thinking—not multiplying beliefs or rituals or all that nonsense, but understanding the ways of our own thinking: the motives, the pursuits, the activities, the chatterings of the mind, from which all mischief arises. Having understood them, they will naturally come to an end; and thereby the mind, being free from its own pettiness, can penetrate without effort, without that constant battle, and discover what is beyond itself.

Question: I have tried writing down my thoughts with a view to bringing thought to an end, as you once suggested. Do you still suggest this? I have not found it very helpful myself, as it seems to become a sort of diary.

KRISHNAMURTI: Without understanding the process of thought, how thought comes into being, the ways of your own individual thinking, how your thought is driven by motives, by desires, by anxieties—without knowing the whole content of thought, you cannot possibly bring about tranquillity. I suggested once that by writing down, being acquainted with your own thinking, with your own thought, perhaps self-knowledge would come out of it. For without self-knowledge there is no understanding. Without knowing the intricacies of your own thought, at both the conscious and the unconscious levels, without knowing the depths of it, then, do what you will, all superficial activities of control, of domination, of adjustment, of what to believe and what not to believe, are utterly useless. So, perhaps you can get to know yourself more deeply, not only by observing superficially your daily thoughts, but also by writing them down; and perhaps thereby you will release the unconscious motives, the unconscious pursuits, desires, and fears.

But, if you have a motive—that by writing down your thoughts you will put an end to thinking—then obviously the thing becomes a diary. Because, you want a result, and it's very easy to produce a result. You can have an end and achieve a goal, but that does not mean you understand the whole process of yourself, the total process of yourself. The intention is, surely, not how to achieve a result, but to understand yourself, and also to understand why the mind craves for a result. In achieving a result the mind feels secure; there is a satisfaction, a sense of permanency, a vanity, a conceit.

So, after all, what is important is, is it not, to understand yourself. Not what your values are—your nationality, belief, religion, church, and all the rest of it; those are all immature activities of the mind. But what is important is, is it not, to understand the ways of your thinking, to know yourself. And you can only do that by observing your own thinking, your own reactions, being aware of your dreams, of your words, of your gestures, of your whole being. And that you can observe in the bus, in relationship, all the time if you wish. But for most of us that becomes very strenuous, and so, without actually experiencing, we repeat phrases and thereby prevent the actual discovery of the process of our own thinking.

After all, as long as the mind is active, or merely concentrated on a particular idea or a particular desire, it is not free. Thought can project and worship that which it has projected. With us, that is almost always the case. So, one has to be aware of the activities of the mind, its reactions. And only then can thought come to an end. Not as a result, as a thing to be willed, towards which the mind disciplines itself, suppressing, rejecting, sublimating itself, and so on. But the ending of the thought is an indication that the mind is actually tranquil, still. But if it is merely a result, then the mind is in a state of stagnation. Because, the mind again wants to go further; so every result, everything that has been conquered, has to be reconquered, broken again.

So the mind, through understanding itself at all its different levels, comes to a state when it is still. And this is not a long, tedious, tiresome, boring process. You know very well what you think and what you feel if you are at all aware, sensitive to yourself. You do not have to be analyzed, dissected—that is a lazy man's game. But we know, actually, inwardly, our own conflicts and the cause of those conflicts—their significance, what lies behind them. But we don't want to look at it, we don't want to face it. And so we play around in circles, never coming to the center.

So, the ending of thought is essential because the mind must be utterly tranquil, without any movement backwards or forwards, for movement indicates time, in which there is fear and desire. So, when the mind is utterly tranquil, then only is it possible for that which is not nameable to come into being.

Question: My wife and I quarrel. We seem to like each other, but yet this wrangling goes on. We have tried several ways of putting an end to this ugliness, but we seem unable to be psychologically free of each other. What do you suggest?

KRISHNAMURTI: As long as there is dependency, there must be tension. If I depend on you as an audience in order to fulfill myself, in order to feel that I am somebody talking to a vast number of people, then I depend on you, I exploit you, you are necessary to me psychologically. This dependence is called love, and all our relationship is based on it. Psychologically I need you, and psychologically you need me. Psychologically you become important in my relationship with you because you fill my needs—not only physically, but also inwardly. Without you, I am lost, I am uncertain. I depend upon you; I love you. Whenever that dependence is questioned, there is uncertainty—and then I am afraid. And to cover up that fear, I resort to all kinds of subterfuges which will help me to get away from that fear. We know all this—we use property, knowledge, gods, illusions, relationship, as a means to cover our own emptiness, our own loneliness, and so these things become very important. The things which have become our escapes become extraordinarily valuable.

So, as long as there is dependence, there must be fear. It is not love. You may call it love; you may cover it up with any pleasant-sounding word. But actually, beneath it there is a void; there is the wound which cannot be healed by any method, which can only come to an end when you are conscious of it, aware of it, understand it. And there can be understanding only when you are not seeking an explanation. You see, the questioner demands an explanation; he wants words from me. And we are satisfied by words. The new explanation—if it is new—you will repeat. But the problem is still there; there will still be wrangling.

But when once we understand this process of dependence—the outward as well as the inward, the hidden dependencies, the psychological urgencies, the demand for the 'more'—when we understand those things, only then, surely, is there a possibility of love. Love is neither personal nor impersonal; it is a state of being. It is not of the mind; the mind cannot acquire it. You cannot practice love, or through meditation acquire it. It comes into being only when there is no fear, when this sense of anxiety, loneliness, has ceased, when there is no dependence or acquisition. And that comes only when we understand ourselves, when we are fully cognizant of our hidden motives, when the mind can delve into the depths of itself without seeking an answer, an explanation, when it is no longer naming.

Surely one of our difficulties is, is it not, that most of us are satisfied with the superficialities of life—with explanations, chiefly. And we think we have solved all things by explaining them—which is the activity of the mind. As long as we can name, recognize, we think we have achieved something, and the moment there is the idea of no recognition, no naming, no explanation, then the mind gets confused. But only when there are no explanations, when the mind is not caught in words, is it possible for love to come into being.

Question: Does not what you are talking about require time and leisure?—whereas most of us are occupied with earning a livelihood, which takes most of our time. Are you speaking for those who are old and retired, or for the ordinary man who has to work?

KRISHNAMURTI: What do you think? You have leisure, you have time, even though you have to earn a livelihood. It may take most of your time, but you have at least an hour to yourself during the day, have you not? There is sometime when you have leisure. We use that leisure for various activities, to relax from the things which we have been doing all day, which are boring, routine. But even after you have relaxed, surely you still have more leisure, have you not? And even while you are working, you can be aware of your own thoughts. Even while working at things that do not please you, a routine, a job which is not your vocation but which modern civilization forces you into—even while you are turning over a machine, surely you have time, you can observe your own thinking! Most of your work is automatic because you are highly trained. But there is a part of you that is observing, that is looking out of the window, that is seeking an answer to this confusion, that goes and joins societies, that goes in for meditation, rituals, churches.

So, you have enough leisure which, if rightly employed, will break your routine, will bring about action, a revolution, in your life—which the respectable do not want, of which those well-established with name, with property, with position, have a dread. We want to alter the outward things without inward revolution. But there must be the inward revolution first, which will bring about outward order. This is not just a phrase. But that inward revolution is not possible, either collectively or individually, if each one of us does not go into this whole problem of ourselves. You see, it is you and I who are tackling the problem; the problem is not outside you and me. The problems of war, peace, competition, ruthlessness, cruelty—we are creating these, you and I. And without understanding the total process of ourselves, mere change of occupation, or having leisure, will have little significance. This is not, surely, for the old or for the young. For anyone who thinks at all, who wants to find out, surely age is not of importance. But we put wrong values on these things and thereby create more problems.

Question: I have read a great deal and have studied the religions of both East and West, and my knowledge of these things is fairly extensive. I have listened to you now for several years, but what eludes me is this thing which you call the creative being or state. Could you go a little further into the matter.

KRISHNAMURTI: Perhaps you and I can experiment for the next ten minutes and see if we cannot go further, more deeply—not theoretically but actually—into what it means to be creative. The difficulty with most of us is that we know too much about these matters. We have read a great deal about Eastern philosophy, or Western theories—which actually becomes a barrier to discovery, does it not? So our knowledge becomes an impediment. Because, our knowledge has already tasted what the creative state is, what God is; because, we have read the descriptions of the experiences of others. So, when we are full of that, we can only compare, and comparison is not experiencing; comparison is not discovery.

So, the thing which we have acquired through centuries as knowledge, that which is measurable by memory—that has to come to an end, has it not? Which means that our mind, with all its experience, its knowledge of what we have experienced yesterday, or what we have read of the descriptions by others of that state—all that must be set aside, must it not? Because this thing must be completely original. God must be something never experienced before. It must be something unrecognizable by the mind. If it is recognized, it is not the new; it is not the timeless.

So, seeing the truth of that—not theoretically but actually—cannot the mind be free of the old? Not free through suggestion, but through seeing the truth of it—that as long as the mind, which is the result of time, is capable of measuring, recognizing, projecting, desiring, then it cannot possibly be in a state which is creative. The new cannot be in the old. The old can recognize nothing but its own projections. So, the activity of the mind must completely cease. And it ceases when we understand all these things, when we see the truth of them.

So, let us just listen—not exercise our minds, but listen—to find out, to discover, how the mind by its own activities, which are based on time—of the past, of memories of what we have learned, and of the things we have forgotten—is preventing the creative state. When that is seen, understood, then there is a freedom from it. So, knowledge must be completely set aside for the mind to be still. And then only is it possible for that state which cannot be described to come into being. That state is not a permanent state, a thing of time, continuous. It is not a state to be cultivated, to be acquired and held. It exists from moment to moment, without any invitation from the mind. And no amount of reading about it, no amount of your practice, discipline, theories, will ever actually bring that state into being. Only when the mind is completely free from its own activities, from its own demands, is it possible for that creative state to come into being.

April 15, 1952

Fourth Talk in London

It seems to me that one of our most difficult problems is to coordinate or integrate idea with action. Most of us are aware that there is a gap between action and idea, and we are everlastingly trying to bridge this gap. And I think it is important to understand that there will always be a division between idea and action so long as we do not understand and go fully into the question of consciousness, and experience direct relationship between the idea and action itself. For most of us, idea is very important—idea being symbol, image, words. And we try to approximate action to that idea. And the problem then arises of how to bridge the gap, how to put idea into action. And I would like to go into that problem this evening.

Most of us are aware that envy is the basis of most of our action. Envy or acquisitiveness—our social structure is based on that. And the thoughtful, the earnest, obviously see that there must be freedom from envy. And being aware that there must be freedom, how does one set about it? There is the idea first, and then we inquire how to relate it to action. Obviously, there must be freedom from envy because it is a deteriorating factor, antisocial, and so on. For innumerable reasons we are well aware that envy is a quality, an impulse, a reaction, which must be eradicated.

Now how is one to do it? Can one do it through the process of time, through constant denial, through suppression? Or is there a different approach, a different way of looking at it altogether? How can the mind be free from that reaction called envy, upon which most of our existence is based? Because obviously, if we take time, practice a gradual diminution of it, we are not entirely free of it. The process of time will not give to the mind a freedom from envy. Virtue, after all, is freedom—not a cultivation of any particular quality. The more you cultivate a quality, the more you strengthen the self, the 'me'. So it must have struck most of us that we are faced with this problem of how to be free from a particular quality, how to set about it. If we merely cultivate its opposite, we are still held in the opposite, and there is no freedom. Virtue is, after all, a state of being free, and not being held in a particular quality—which limits the mind.

So, the problem is, is it not, how can one deal with a particular quality—let us say, for example, envy—and be free of it, immediately? Not take time, gradually eradicate it, but be immediately free. Is it possible to be free completely? To answer that question deeply, and not merely superficially, we must examine, must we not, the process of consciousness. That is, we must know, or be aware of, our approach to the problem—how we think, how we regard the problem, in what way we approach it, with what attitude—not only at the superficial level of the mind, but in the hidden layers. All that is surely the process of consciousness. So, if we are to be completely rid of this thing called envy, we must know how we are looking at it—with what attitude, with what motive, with what intention we approach it. Which means—how does our mind, both the conscious as well as the unconscious, react to it? That is, are we in direct relationship with it, or are we merely dealing with words and ideas without being in direct contact with the quality?

I do not know if I am making myself clear on this point—perhaps not. So, let me elaborate a little more. What is our consciousness?—consciousness being our mind, both the hidden and the superficial. It is obviously the result of time—time being memory, images, words—all of which, accumulated, respond to any particular problem, to any challenge, to any question. And our thinking, based on that memory, is verbal. That is, there is no thinking without words, without symbols, without images. So with that background, with that consciousness, we approach the problem of envy, which we are taking as an example. We are never directly in relation with the reaction called envy, but only with the word. Am I directly experiencing envy; am I in relation with it—or with the word called *envy?* Am I in contact with that reaction, immediately and fully aware of it, without giving it a name, without giving it a term? Or, do I recognize envy through the word? If I can experience envy directly—without giving it a term, a name—then there is quite a different experience. But if I am only in relation with that reaction verbally, through a word, through an image, then it is not a true experience.

So, if we would be completely free from a particular quality such as envy, surely we must find out whether we are experiencing it directly, without the medium of words, or whether the word is giving us the so-called experience. If we are concerned with the word, with the idea, and are in relation only with the idea, then the problem arises—how to relate the idea to action. That is, we are aware that we are envious, but are we aware merely verbally, or are we experiencing envy directly, without giving to that reaction a name? I do not know if you have ever tried it. Take, for example, your sudden awareness that you are jealous. How are you aware of it? Are you aware of it because you recognize it through the word, or are you aware of it as an actual experience, without giving it a word, a name, a term? I think it is important to find this out. Because if you can have direct relationship with it, then you will see that there is complete freedom from the thing which we have named. But if you are aware of the feeling through the word, through the symbol, through memory, then the problem arises of how to relate the idea to action.

Perhaps we can make this a little more simple. I am envious; I am jealous. How am I to get rid of it? I see its complications, its conflicts, the uselessness of it. And how am I to proceed to be free from it? Am I to suppress it, analyze it, discipline myself to resist it?—which all takes time, and which brings about conflict between idea and action, does it not? I want to be free from it, but actually I am not. So, there is the idea of wanting to be free, and the actuality of not being free. What is important is the actuality, the reality, not "I want to be free." So, how am I to set about being free from this quality which I have termed envy? Obviously, discipline does not get rid of it. If I create a resistance against it, that resistance does not bring understanding—nor does the cultivation of its opposite, which only creates further conflict. So, how am I to be free from it?

We know the usual, habitual, traditional approach—which is, by gradually attacking, resisting, disciplining ourselves against it—and one sees that still one is not actually free from it. I wonder if you have ever thought about it in a different way? There must be a different approach, and that is what we are trying to find out. There is a different approach if I can experience the reaction of envy directly, without naming it. And that is why we have to examine, understand, how our consciousness works, which is really quite a complicated process. We think we understand something when we give it a name; when we can put a label on something, we think we have grasped the full significance of it. So to us, words, symbols, ideas are very important. And our consciousness is made up of these—of words, of symbols, of ideas—which represent our memories. So our memories recognize the reaction called envy, and therefore there is no direct experience of that feeling but only the recollection of it.

But if you can look at that reaction without verbalizing it, without giving it a name, then you will see you are experiencing it directly for the first time. And I think that is most important—to experience the feeling, the reaction, for the first time, as it were, afresh, without giving it a name. It is the name that creates the barrier. Perhaps you will experiment with this, and you will see how difficult it is to experience something new. Because memory is always intervening, recognizing, and saying, "Yes, that is jealousy, that is envy, the thing which I must get rid of." So, memory creates the idea, and that idea creates its own feeling, its own reactions, and therefore you are only in relationship with the idea, and not in direct relationship with the problem.

So when we have a problem from which we feel there must be complete freedom—such as envy—it is important, is it not, to find out how our minds approach it, what our reactions are, how we are experiencing that quality, whether the experience is direct or merely through a word. And it is surely only when we can experience something anew, afresh, that there is a possibility of understanding it fully, completely. If we bring to it all our recollections, all our memories, the names, the conditioning influences, then we are not experiencing it directly at all; and so the problem ever increases, multiplies, and keeps going. Most of us know that although we have struggled against envy we are not free from it. It is virtue which brings freedom—not being caught in words, which bring only a limitation, a respectability, a habit, to the mind.

Question: I have lived through two catastrophic world wars. I fought in one and became a displaced person in the other. I realize that the individual who has no control over these events has very little purpose in life. What is the point of this existence?

KRISHNAMURTI: I wonder how you and I as two individuals regard this problem? There is the historical process, and what is the relationship of the individual to that process? As an individual, what can you do about the wars? Probably very little. Because wars come into being for various reasons—economic, psychological, and so on—and how can you stop all that? You cannot, surely, stop the process of war, which multitudes have set going. But you as an individual can step out of it, can you not, whatever the consequences to yourself. Can you as an individual eradicate from your own heart and mind those qualities that create antagonism, hatred, enmity? If you cannot, you are obviously contributing to the cause of war.

Take, as an example, nationalism—the feeling of being a separate group of people—in which the individual fulfills himself, finds satisfaction. Inwardly we are poor, insufficient, lonely; and when we identify ourselves with a particular group of people as Hindu, Russian, or English, obviously we feel secure. And that security we must protect. In pursuing the security we long for, we exploit and are exploited. Now, can you as an individual be free from that nationalistic feeling? And when you are free, is it not possible to look upon this historical process with an entirely different attitude? The questioner wants to know if he is not responsible for these wars, if he has no control over them, what is the purpose of living? But is it not important to find out first if you as an individual cannot be free from all the forces, influences, that create war? Can you not actually bring about an inward revolution—not theoretically but actually—so that you are a free human being who experiences love, and who, because he is free from antagonism, from hatred, will find the right answer to the question?

You see, our problem is, is it not, that we have no love. If the mother really loved her child, if the parents loved, they would jolly well see that there was no war! But to the parents, the prestige and well-being of the country, of a certain group, is more important than love of the child. If one really loved, if there were that feeling of love, then surely you would prevent war. But, not having that inward reality, we resort to all kinds of systems, governments; we look to politicians, various methods, to prevent war. And we will never succeed. Because, we have not as individuals solved the problem in ourselves. We would rather remain segregated, enclosed within nationalistic ideologies, in a world of beliefs, and so be separated, be one against the other. And until we solve that problem—how the individual is seeking security and thereby causing antagonism, hatred, enmity—wars of one kind or another will always go on.

When we know for ourselves that we are free, then the purpose of existence comes into being without our asking. Freedom does not come into being through the mere cultivation of virtue but only when there is that quality of love which is not of the mind.

Question: When trying to empty the mind in order to still it, I obtain a kind of blank mind. How do I know that this state is not simply dozing?

KRISHNAMURTI: Why do we want a still mind? Why do we want tranquillity? Is it because we are so tired, exhausted, by an agitated mind—a mind that is constantly chattering, a mind that is so occupied—and to escape from that we desire a still mind? Is that it? Or do we see the necessity of a still mind, of a quiet mind, because a quiet mind understands, can see things directly, can experience immediately? Do we see that if the mind is agitated, there is no possibility of discovering anything new, of understanding, of being free? And is this a necessity, or merely a reaction from its opposite? Surely that is important to find out, is it not? Do you want tranquillity of the mind because you are fed up with the mind which is so active, so agitated? Surely, that you have to find out, have you not? If it is merely a reaction, then obviously the mind goes into sleep.

Then the mind is not tranquil; it merely puts itself to sleep through various forms of discipline, controls, and so on.

So, our problem is not how to bring about a quiet, still mind, but to look at those things that agitate the mind, to understand those things that bring about disturbance. And when we understand those, then there will be tranquillity; when we are free from the problem, then there is a stillness. But to induce a stillness when the mind is crippled with problems, obviously brings about a dullness of the mind. So, our problem is not how to make the mind tranquil, still, peaceful, but to understand, to be free from those problems which agitate the mind. The mind obviously creates the problems. If there is a problem, how do we approach it, with what attitude? How do we experience it? It is that which it is important to understand, and not how to escape from the problem into tranquillity.

How can the mind which is producing problems be quiet? It is impossible. All that it can do is to understand each problem as it arises and be free from it. And through freedom comes tranquillity. As I was saying previously, without virtue there is no freedom. And virtue is not a thing to be cultivated. If I am jealous, envious, I must be free from it immediately. The immediacy is important, is essential. And if I realize that the immediacy of freedom from that particular quality is essential, then there is freedom. But we do not realize the urgency of it. And that is where our difficulty lies. We like the feeling, the sensation, of being envious—the pleasure of it; we want to indulge in it. And so gradually we build the idea that we must eventually be free from it. And so, there is never a complete freedom from a particular reaction. And only when the mind is free is there the possibility of tranquillity.

Question: Unless the mind is occupied, it soon goes to sleep or deteriorates. Should it not be occupied with the more serious things of life?

KRISHNAMURTI: Is not a mind that is occupied—with the great or with the trivial—incapable of being free? Is not mere occupation a distraction, however noble it is? What concerns us is that the mind is so vagrant, wandering all over the place, distracted, and we want it to be occupied with something, for then it feels at rest. Most of our minds are occupied with trivial things, with the daily chatterings. And rejecting those, we begin to occupy ourselves with more serious things—the serious things being ideas, images, speculations. And as long as the mind is occupied with these so-called serious things, we feel it is more quiet, more concentrated, not wandering. But such an occupied mind is never a free mind. It is only in freedom that you can begin to understand anything—not with a mind that is crippled by its own concentrations.

You see, we are so afraid to discover the process of our own thinking, of our own state; we are so apprehensive of knowing ourselves as we are. And so, we begin to invent cages, ideas, in which the mind can be held, which offer a convenient escape from ourselves. So, what is important is the understanding of ourselves—not with what we should occupy our minds. There is no good occupation or bad occupation. As long as the mind is occupied, it is not free. And it is only through freedom that we can understand, that we can know, what truth is. So, instead of asking whether our minds should be occupied, we should find out how our minds work, what our motives are—the whole process of our existence.

After all, we live through sensation—contact, perception, sensation—from which arises desire. And when desire is not fulfilled there is conflict, and there is fear. So, fear and desire create time, the sense of tomorrow, the acquiring more, being secure, the importance of the 'me', the 'I', the ego. And instead of understanding, going into, that whole problem of consciousness, we want superficial results; we want to be occupied; we want to know how to meditate, how to be this or that—which are all escapes, distractions.

So, what is important in all these questions is to go into the process of our thinking—which is self-knowledge. Without self-knowledge, do what you will, there can be no peace in the world. Without self-knowledge, there can be no love. The thing which the mind calls love is not love; it is only an idea. And you can only begin to know yourself deeply, widely, in relationship—with your wife, with your husband, with your society. Be aware of it; be aware of your reactions, and do not condemn them; because any form of judgment, any form of justification, surely puts an end to a feeling, a reaction—brushes it aside and does not let it flow out so that you can follow it. After all, if I would understand a child, I must study him in all his moods—when he plays, when he talks. Merely to condemn prevents understanding. Similarly, if I would understand the process of my thinking, there must obviously be not condemnation but observation. But all our training, socially, morally, and religiously, is to condemn, to resist—which prevents a direct experience, a direct understanding of the problem.

So, the more you go into the problem of your reactions, without condemnation, without justification, then you will see that you are beginning to understand the whole process of your consciousness, of the 'me', with all its hidden motives. Then you will see whether you are merely reacting to the word or are directly experiencing a certain feeling—whether you are meeting any challenge through the screen of memory or idea, or whether you are meeting it directly. The more you begin to know yourself, to be aware of every subtle reaction, every process, every intention, then you will see that quite a different state comes into being—a state which is not induced by the mind. Because, the mind can induce any kind of state; it can believe in anything, experience anything. But that which the mind experiences, believes in, is not the real. Reality can come into being only through self-knowledge, when the mind, through understanding its own processes, the hidden as well as the superficial, becomes quiet—not is made quiet, but becomes quiet. Then only is there a possibility for that reality to come into being.

But all this does not imply a series of stages which the mind must go through. What is essential is to see the necessity of being quiet. And it is the urgency, the necessity, that brings this about, and not the cultivation of a particular quality or method.

April 16, 1952

Fifth Talk in London

Perhaps this evening we could go into the problem of effort. It seems to me that it is very important to understand the approach we make to any conflict, to any problem with which we are faced. We are concerned, are we not, most of us, with the action of will. And to us, effort is most essential in every form; to us, to live without effort seems incredible, leading to stagnation and to deterioration. And if we can go into that problem of effort, I think perhaps it will be profitable because we may then be able to understand what is truth—without exercising will, without making an effort—by being capable of perceiving directly *what is*. But to do that, we must understand this question of effort, and I hope we can go into it without any opposition, any resistance.

For most of us, our whole life is based on effort, some kind of volition. And we cannot conceive of an action without volition, without effort; our life is based on it. Our social, economic, and so-called spiritual life is a series of efforts, always culminating in a certain result. And we think effort is essential, necessary. So we are now going to find out if it is possible to live differently, without this constant battle.

Why do we make effort? Is it not, put simply, in order to achieve a result, to become something, to reach a goal? And if we do not make an effort, we think we shall stagnate. We have an idea about the goal towards which we are constantly striving, and this striving has become part of our life. If we want to alter ourselves, if we want to bring about a radical change in ourselves, we make a tremendous effort to eliminate the old habits, to resist the habitual environmental influences, and so on. So we are used to this series of efforts in order to find or achieve something, in order to live at all.

And is not all such effort the activity of the self? Is not effort self-centered activity? And, if we make an effort from the center of the self, it must inevitably produce more conflict, more confusion, more misery. Yet we keep on making effort after effort. And very few of us realize that the self-centered activity of effort does not clear up any of our problems. On the contrary, it increases our confusion and our misery and our sorrow. We know this. And yet we continue, hoping somehow to break through this self-centered activity of effort, the action of the will.

That is our problem—is it possible to understand anything without effort? Is it possible to see what is real, what is true, without introducing the action of will?—which is essentially based on the self, the 'me'. And if we do not make an effort, is there not a danger of deterioration, of going to sleep, of stagnation? Perhaps this evening, as I am talking, we can experiment with this individually and see how far we can go through this question. For I feel the thing that brings happiness, quietness, tranquillity of the mind, does not come through any effort. A truth is not perceived through any volition, through any action of will. And if we can go into it very carefully and diligently, perhaps we shall find the answer.

How do we react when a truth is presented? Take, for example, what we were discussing the other day—the problem of fear. We realize that our activity and our being and our whole existence would be fundamentally altered if there were no fear of any kind in us. We may see that; we may see the truth of it, and thereby there is a freedom from fear. But for most of us, when a fact, a truth, is put before us, what is our immediate response? Please, experiment with what I am saying; please do not merely listen. Watch your own reactions, and find out what happens when a truth, a fact, is put before you—such as, "Any dependency in relationship destroys relationship." Now, when a statement of that kind is made, what is your response? Do you see, are you aware of the truth of it, and thereby dependency ceases? Or have you an idea about the fact? Here is a statement of truth. Do we experience the truth of it, or do we create an idea about it?

If we can understand the process of this creation of idea, then we shall perhaps understand the whole process of effort. Because, when once we have created the idea, then effort comes into being. Then the problem arises, what to do, how to act? That is, we see that psychological dependency on another is a form of self-fulfillment; it is not love—in it there is conflict, in it there is fear, in it there is dependency, which corrodes; in it there is the desire to fulfill oneself through another, jealousy, and so on. We see that psychological dependency on another embraces all these facts. Then we proceed to create the idea, do we not? We do not directly experience the fact, the truth of it, but we look at it and then create an idea of how to be free from dependency. We see the implications of psychological dependence, and then we create the idea of how to be free from it. We do not directly experience the truth, which is the liberating factor. But, out of the experience of looking at that fact, we create an idea. We are incapable of looking at it directly, without ideation. Then, having created the idea, we proceed to put that idea into action. Then we try to bridge the gap between the idea and action—in which effort is involved.

So, can we not look at the truth without creating ideas? It is almost instinctive with most of us when something true is put before us to create immediately an idea about it. And I think if we can understand why we do this so instinctively, almost unconsciously, then perhaps we shall understand if it is possible to be free from effort.

So, why do we create ideas about truth? Surely that is important to find out, is it not? Either we see the truth nakedly, as it is, or we do not. But why do we have a picture about it, a symbol, a word, an image?—which necessitates a postponement, the hope of an eventual result. So, can we hesitantly and guardedly go into this process of why the mind creates the image, the idea?—that I must be this or that, I must be free from dependence, and so on. We know very well that when we see something very clearly, experience it directly, there is a freedom from it. It is that immediacy that is vital, not the picture or the symbol of the truth—on which all systems and philosophies and deteriorating organizations are built. So, is it not important to find out why the mind, instead of seeing the thing directly, simply, and experiencing the truth of it immediately, creates the idea about it?

I do not know if you have thought about this. It may perhaps be something new. And to find the truth of it, please do not merely resist. Do not say, "What would happen if the mind did not create the idea? It is its function to create ideas, to verbalize, to recall memories, to recognize, to calculate." We know that. But the mind is not free, and it is only when the mind is capable of looking at the truth fully, totally, completely, without any barrier, that there is a freedom.

So, our problem is, is it not, why does the mind, instead of seeing the thing immediately and experiencing it directly, indulge in all these ideas? Is this not one of the habits of the mind? Something is presented to us, and immediately there is the old habit of creating an idea, a theory, about it. And the mind likes to live in habit. Because, without habit the mind is lost. If there is not a routine, a habitual response to which it has become accustomed, it feels confused, uncertain.

That is one aspect. Also, does not the mind seek a result? Because, in the result is permanency. And the mind hates to be uncertain. It is always seeking security in different forms—through beliefs, through knowledge, through experience. And when that is questioned, there is a disturbance, there is anxiety. And so the mind, avoiding uncertainty, seeks security for itself by making efforts to achieve a result.

I hope you are following all this—not merely listening to me, but actually observing your own minds in operation. If you are only listening to me and not really following what I am talking about, then you will not experience, then it will remain on the verbal level. But if you can, if I may suggest it, observe your own mind in operation and watch how it thinks, how it reacts, when a truth is put before it, then you will experience step by step what I am talking about. Then there will be an extraordinary experience. And it is this direct approach, direct experience of what truth is, that is so essential in bringing about a creative life.

So, why does the mind create these ideas instead of directly experiencing? That is what we are trying to find out. Why does the mind intervene? We said, it is habit. Also, the mind wants to achieve a result. We all want to achieve a result. In listening to me, are you looking for a result? You are, are you not? So, the mind is seeking a result; it sees that dependency is destructive, and therefore it wants to be free of it. But the very desire to be free creates the idea. The mind is not free, but the desire to be free creates the idea of freedom as the goal towards which it must work. And thereby effort comes into being. And that effort is self-centered; it does not bring freedom. Instead of depending on a person, you depend on an idea or on an image. So, your effort is only self-enclosing; it is not liberating.

So, can the mind, realizing that it is caught in habit, be free from habit?—not have an idea that it should achieve freedom as an eventual goal, but see the truth that the mind is caught in habit, directly experience it. And similarly, can the mind see that it is pursuing incessantly a permanency for itself, a goal which it must achieve, a god, a truth, a virtue, a being, a state—what you will—and is thereby bringing about this action of will, with all its complications? And when we see that, is it not possible to directly experience the truth of something without all the paraphernalia of verbalization? You may objectively see the fact; in that there is no ideation, no creation of idea, symbol, desire. But subjectively, inwardly, it is entirely different. Because there we want a result; there is the craving to be something, to achieve, to become—in which all effort is born.

And I feel that to see what is true, from moment to moment, without any effort, but directly to experience it, is the only creative existence. Because it is only in moments of complete tranquillity that you discover something—not when you are making an effort, whether it is under the microscope or inwardly. It is only when the mind is not agitated, caught in habit, trying to achieve a result, trying to become something—it is only when it is not doing that, when it is really tranquil, when there is no effort, no movement, that there is a possibility of discovering something new.

Surely, that is freedom from the self; that is the abnegation of the 'me'—and not the outward symbols, whether you possess this or that virtue or not. But freedom only comes into being when you understand your own processes, conscious as well as unconscious. And it is possible only when we go fully into the different processes of the mind. And as most of us live in a state of tension, in constant effort, it is essential to understand the complexity of effort, to see the truth that effort does not bring virtue, that effort is not love, that effort does not bring about the freedom which truth alone can give—which is a direct experiencing. For that, one has to understand the mind, one's own mind—not somebody else's mind, not what somebody else says about it. Though you may read all the volumes, they will be utterly useless. For you must observe your own mind, and penetrate into it deeper and deeper, and experience the thing directly as you go along. Because there is the living quality, and not in the things of the mind. Therefore the mind, to find its own processes, must not be enclosed by its own habits, must occasionally be free to look. Therefore it is important to understand this whole process of effort. For effort does not bring about freedom. Effort is only more and more self-enclosing, more and more destructive—outwardly as well as inwardly—in relationship with one or with many.

Question: I find a regular group that meets to discuss your teachings tends to become confusing and boring. Is it better to think over these things alone, or with others?

KRISHNAMURTI: What is important? To find out, is it not, to discover for yourself the things about yourself. If that is your urgent, immediate, instinctive necessity, then you can do it with one or with many, by yourself or with two or three. But when that is lacking, then groups become boring things. Then people who come to the groups are dominated by one or two in the group who know everything, who are in immediate contact with the person who has already said these things. So, the one becomes the authority and gradually exploits the many. We know this too familiar game. But people submit to it because they like being together. They like to talk, to have the latest gossip or the latest news. And so, the thing soon deteriorates. You start with a serious intention, and it becomes something ugly.

But if we are really, insistently needing to discover for ourselves what is true, then all relationship becomes important; but such people are rare. Because, we are not really serious, and so we eventually make of groups and organizations something to be avoided. So it surely depends, does it not, on whether you are really earnest to discover these things for yourself. And this discovery can come at any moment—not only in a group, or only when you are by yourself, but at any moment when you are aware, sensitive to the intimations of your own being. To watch yourself—the way you talk at table, the way you talk to your neighbor, your servant, your boss—surely all these, if one is aware, indicate the state of your own being. And it is that discovery which is important. Because it is that discovery which liberates.

Question: What would you say is the most creative way of meeting great grief and loss?

KRISHNAMURTI: What do we mean by "meeting"? You mean, how to approach it, what we should do about it, how to conquer it, how to be free of it, how to derive benefit from it, how to learn from it so as to avoid more suffering? Surely that is what we mean, do we not, by how to "meet" grief?

Now, what do we mean by "grief"? Is it something apart from you? Is it something outside of you, inwardly or outwardly, which you are observing, which you are experiencing? Are you merely the observer experiencing? Or, is it something different? Surely that is an important point, is it not? When I say, "I suffer," what do I mean by it? Am I different from the suffering? Surely that is the question, is it not? Let us find out.

There is sorrow—I am not loved, my son dies, what you will. There is one part of me that is demanding why, demanding the explanation, the reasons, the causes. The other part of me is in agony for various reasons. And there is also another part of me which wants to be free from the sorrow, which wants to go beyond it. We are all these things, are we not? So, if one part of me is rejecting, resisting sorrow, another part of me is seeking an explanation, is caught up in theories, and another part of me is escaping from the fact—how then can I understand it totally? It is only when I am capable of integrated understanding that there is a possibility of freedom from sorrow. But if I am torn in different directions, then I do not see the truth of it.

So, it is very important to find out, is it not, whether I am merely the observer experiencing sorrow. Please follow this question slowly and carefully. If I am merely the observer experiencing sorrow, then there are two states in my being—the one who observes, who thinks, who experiences, and the other who is observed—which is, the experience, the thought. So as long as there is a division, there is no immediate freedom from sorrow.

Now, please listen carefully, and you will see that when there is a fact, a truth, there is understanding of it only when I can experience the whole thing without division—and not when there is the separation of the 'me' observing suffering. That is the truth. Now, what is your immediate reaction to that? Is not your immediate reaction, response, "How am I to bridge the gap between the two?" I recognize that there are different entities in me—the thinker and the thought, the experiencer and the experience, the one who suffers and the one who observes the suffering. And, as long as there is a division, a separation, there is conflict. And it is only when there is integration that there is freedom from sorrow. That is the truth; that is the fact. Now, how do you respond to it? Do you see the thing immediately and experience it directly, or do you ask the question, "How am I to bridge the division between the two entities? How am I to bring about integration?" Is that not your instinctive response? If that is so, then you are not seeing the truth. Then your question of how to bring about integration has no value. For it is only when I can see the thing completely, wholly, without this division in myself, that there is a possibility of freedom from the thing which I call sorrow.

So, one has to find out how one looks at sorrow. Not what the books or what anybody else says, not according to any teacher or authority, but how you regard it, how you instinctively approach it. Then you will surely find out, will you not, if there really is this division in your mind. So long as there is that division, there must be sorrow. So long as there is the desire to be free from sorrow, to resist sorrow, to seek explanations, to avoid, then sorrow becomes the shadow, everlastingly pursuing.

So, what is very important in this question is, is it not, how each one of us responds to psychological pain—when we are bereaved, when we are hurt, and so on. We need not go into the causes of sorrow. But we know them very well—the ache of loneliness, the fear of losing, not being loved, being frustrated, the loss of someone. We know all this very well; we are only too familiar with this thing called sorrow. And we have many explanations, very convenient and satisfying. But there is no freedom from sorrow. Explanations do not give freedom. They may cover up, but the thing continues. And we are trying to find out how to be free from sorrow, not which explanations are more satisfactory. There can be freedom from sorrow only if there is an integration. And we cannot understand what integration is unless we are first aware of how we look at sorrow.

Question: For one who is caught in habit, it seems impossible to see the truth of a thing instantaneously. Surely time is needed—time to break away from one's immediate activity and really seek to go into what has been happening.

KRISHNAMURTI: Now what do we mean by "time"? Please—again let us experiment. What do we mean by "time"? Obviously not time by the clock. When you say, "I need time," what does it mean? That you need leisure—an hour to yourself, or a few minutes to yourself? Surely, you do not mean that. You mean, "I need time to achieve a result." That is, "I need time to break away from the habits which I have created."

Now, time is obviously the product of the mind; mind is the result of time. What we think, feel, our memories, are basically the result of time. And you say that time is necessary to break away from certain habits.

That is, this inward psychological habit is the outcome of desire and fear, is it not? I see the mind is caught in it, and I say, "I need time to break it down. I realize it is this habit that is preventing me from seeing things immediately, experiencing them directly, and so I must have time to break down this habit."

First, how does habit come into being? Through education, through environmental influences, through our own memories. And also, it is comfortable to have a mechanism that functions habitually so that it is never uncertain, quivering, inquiring, doubtful, anxious. So, the mind creates the pattern which you call the habit, the routine. And in that it functions. And the questioner wants to know how to break down that habit so that experience can be direct. You see what has happened? The moment he says, "How?" he has already introduced the idea of time.

But if we can see that the mind creates habits and functions in habit, and that a mind which is enclosed by its own self-created memories, desires, fears, cannot see or experience anything directly—when we can see the truth of that, then there is a possibility of experiencing directly. The perception of the truth is not a matter of time, obviously. That is one of the conveniences of the mind—eventually, next life, I shall reach perfection, whatever I want. So, being caught, then it proceeds to say, "How am I to be free?" It can never be free. It can only be free when it sees the truth of how it creates habit—that is, by tradition, by cultivating virtues in order to be something, by seeking to have permanency, to have security. All these things are barriers. In that state, how can the mind see or experience anything directly? If we see that it cannot, then there is a freedom, immediate freedom. But the difficulty is, is it not, that most of us like to continue in our habits of thought and feeling, in our traditions, in our beliefs, in our hopes. Surely, all those compose our mind. The mind is made up of all those things. How can such a mind experience something which is not its own projection? Obviously it cannot. So, it can only understand its own mechanism and see the truth of its own activities. And when there is freedom from that, then there is a direct experience.

Question: You have said that neither meditation nor discipline will create a still mind, but only the annihilation of the 'I' consciousness. How can the 'I' annihilate the 'I'?

KRISHNAMURTI: Surely any movement of the 'I', however lofty, however noble, is still within the field of self-consciousness, is it not? You may divide the 'I' into the higher self and the lower self—the higher dominating, controlling, directing the lower; but it is still within the field of thought, is it not?

The question is, How can the 'I', the 'me', destroy itself? I am saying that the 'I' is a series of movements, a series of activities, responses, a series of thoughts. And thought may divide itself into the higher and lower, but it is still the process of thinking; it is still within its own field. And, can one part of thought destroy another part? That is, can one part of me put aside, resist, conceal, drive away, the other part which it does not like? Obviously it does; it covers it up. But it is still there in the unconscious. So, any movement of thought, any movement of the 'me', is still within the field of its own consciousness. It cannot destroy itself. All that it can do is to make no movement in any direction. Because, any movement in any direction is to perpetuate itself—under a different name, under a different cloak.

Please, experiment with what I am talking about. One part of me can say, "I will subjugate anger, jealousy, control my irritability, envy, and so on." One part that controls is desirous of dominating some other part. But it is caught, is it not, within the field of time, and whatever it does is of its own projection. That is fairly clear, surely? If it says, "I must through belief understand God or attain God," it is caught in its own projection, is it not? And so long as the mind, the 'me', is active in projecting, in demanding, in craving, the 'I' cannot destroy itself. It only perpetuates itself.

If you see the truth of that, then the mind is still. Because, it cannot do anything. Any movement, negatively or positively, is its own projection; therefore, there is no freedom from it. Seeing the truth of that brings about a quietness of the mind which obviously cannot come through any form of self-discipline, through any form of spiritual exercise, because they are all indications of self-perpetuation, ideation.

Tranquillity of the mind is not a result; it is not something put together which can be undone again. It is not the result of the mind seeking an escape from ideation. It comes into being only when the mind is no longer manufacturing or projecting. And that can only happen when you understand the process of thinking, your own reactions and responses to everything—not only the conscious, but the unconscious as well—the hidden responses, the motives, the urges that are concealed. And this does not demand time. Time exists only when you want to achieve a result, when you say, "I must have tranquillity within a couple of years, or tomorrow." Then come all the spiritual exercises in order to achieve a result. Such a mind is a stagnant mind; it can have no experience of what is real; it is only seeking a result, a reward. And how can such a mind experience something which is immeasurable, which cannot be grasped by any word? The mind is only still when it sees the truth of that—immediately. And the urgency is what is necessary.

April 23, 1952

Sixth Talk in London

Instead of the usual talk, this evening I will try to answer some of the many questions that have been put.

It seems to me it is very important to understand the deteriorating factors that destroy us, not only inwardly but outwardly. I have tried during these talks to indicate that there are definite factors that cripple the mind, that pervert and destroy the capacity to discover what is true. The discovery of what is true is not for the few—though only the few are serious. And those who are earnest can obviously find that which cannot be destroyed. But most of us are caught in things that create constant conflict between what we are and what we should be, and we think this endless struggle is necessary, will bring about a revolution, happiness. We consider this conflict between thesis and antithesis is progress, and we hope it will create a synthesis. But when we go very deeply into it we find this conflict exists only when there is no comprehension of the inward, deeper things of life.

In answering these questions, I hope you will not merely listen to what is being said but actually experience. What is important, I feel, is not merely the experience of a projection but to experience something which is not of the mind. It is very important, I feel, to understand this thing which we call experience. This so-called experience comes to us when there is recognition of it. When we say, "I have had an experience," surely we mean something that we have recognized, that we have named, that memory can respond to. But what is recognizable is not true. And it is the truth that is the liberating factor, and not the thing that we recognize. Because, recognition is of the mind, of memory, of time, of desire, and fear. And so long as we indulge in these things, which we call experience, the other is not. So I hope this evening, if we can, we shall really experience something—not sentimentally, not something which is the response of memory, of what you have read, that you have accumulated and stored up, which reacts or projects—all of which we call experience. But perhaps, if we go into this problem very deeply, we shall really experience something which is not nameable, which is not a thing of the mind, of memory.

Surely, so long as we are functioning within the field of memory, there is no possibility of freedom. And that is why it is important, I feel, to understand the whole process of thought and, if possible, to go beyond the projections of thought. The difficulty is that in listening we are apt to merely follow the words, which evoke certain responses; and through those responses we have further reactions of sentiment, sensation. But surely, sensation, which is of the mind, cannot possibly uncover that which is timeless. So, in answering these questions, perhaps we can both go together beyond the verbal level and experience directly that which is not merely of the mind.

Question: I feel deeply moved when you talk. Is this just sentimentality?

KRISHNAMURTI: Probably it is. But if you can go beyond the mere suggestions, mere reactions, which the words evoke, then you put aside the speaker, then the speaker is not important at all. But what is important, surely, is to find out for yourself what is true; not some distant truth—unattainable, imaginary, mythical—not something that you have read or heard of, but something which you have discovered directly. And that discovery is not possible if we are merely depending on sensations.

Most of us want to find something which is really indestructible, which is not of time. Everything around us is transitory; all our relationships soon weary and end. Though we are comfortable or not comfortable, have much to do or little, the thoughtful obviously recognize the transiency of everything. And the incessant battle—not only within but outwardly, between groups of people, between nations—further increases war and misery. Knowing all this, we must find out something which is not of the mind, which is not merely knowledge. And perhaps if we can discover that, not through the suggestions of the speaker, but by watching our own daily activities, thoughts, impressions, reactions, then we shall go beyond the mere veil of sentiment; and that is what is important. What the individual is, the society is. What you are matters infinitely. That is not a mere slogan, but if you go into it really deeply, you will discover how significant your actions are, how what you are affects the world in which you live—which is the world of your relationships, however small, however limited. And if we can fundamentally alter, bring about a radical revolution in ourselves, inwardly, then there is a possibility of creating a different world, a different set of values.

But so long as we only treat these talks as a new sensation, something with which to be entertained—instead of going to the cinema come here—then obviously it has very little value and very little significance. But those who are really serious, ardent to discover what is true, do not depend on others. They do not follow, they have no authority. And it is their own discovery, from moment to moment, that is essential, for the discovery of that which is true is the only liberating factor.

Question: What is the function of the mind if thought is to come to an end?

KRISHNAMURTI: What is the present function of the mind? It is used as an instrument of survival, is it not—to exist, to survive.

And in the process of survival we have created various forms of society, various values—moral, ethical, spiritual, and so on. But the whole activity of our present mind is, in some form or other, the continuance of the self, of the 'me'. That is our present activity—cunning, subtle—at any cost to survive; to survive in this world, and in the hereafter; to identify with a group, or with a nation, or with a country; or to identify with anything larger, with a word, with knowledge, with projection; ever seeking permanency, always demanding security, physically or psychologically. That is the present state of our mind—a self-centered activity, except at rare moments; and we are not discussing the rare moments.

Those things are all that we know. And, that has not led us very far. We destroy each other, we exploit each other, our relationships are constant conflicts—with that we are all familiar. Though the mind seeks security, it is destroying itself and destroying others. Physically, we are insecure; there is always the threat of war. So, in its very search to be secure, the mind is inviting destruction.

That is the state of our mind, its present state. And we say, "What is the function of the mind if there is no thought?" Obviously, we can see what thought, self-centered activity, has produced. And is it not possible to go beyond that self-centered activity? Every form of inducement has been offered—religiously, psychologically, and outwardly; every form of compulsion, threat, we have endured; and yet, the self-centered activity has never stopped; it is always the 'me' in subtle form. And surely, to find out what is beyond thought—which is the result of time—thought has to come to an end.

I do not know if you have ever found that creative state which comes when the mind is not active, agitated, but is very quiet—naturally, spontaneously, not induced. That state of mind, that state of being, cannot be understood by the thought process. And because we are unhappy, because everything we touch deteriorates, every relationship soon withers away, we want something beyond time. I think it is the function of the mind to discover that, to experience that. But it cannot experience that as long as there is the self-centered activity. And that discovery is not something to be pursued relentlessly. It comes, but you cannot invite it. If you do invite it, then it is your own projection—it is but another form of self-centered activity.

So, recognizing what the mind is, as it is now, is it possible to go beyond and discover? I say it is. But you cannot discover if it is merely a hobby, something you occasionally turn to. But it becomes a reality when the process of the mind and its activities are understood.

Question: The memory of an incident recurs over and over again. How is one to be free from the memory of that incident and from the incident itself?

KRISHNAMURTI: What do we mean by "memory"? How does memory come into being? Perhaps if we can go a little deeply into the matter, we may be able to answer this question fully. Is not the whole process of memory, the recollection, the recognizing process—is not that of consciousness? Please, I am not trying to complicate the question. The question itself sounds simple, but if you would really understand it, you will find it is very complex. So, we must go into the problem of what we mean by consciousness. Please, have patience, and you will answer the question for yourself.

When are we conscious of anything? Only when there is friction, when there is a blockage, when there is a hindrance. Otherwise, the movement of thought or consciousness is not self-conscious. It is only when we are frustrated, when there is fear, when there is the desire to achieve a result that there is self-consciousness—that is, the 'me' being conscious of itself in action. I want to fulfill; I want to achieve a result—and as long as I am progressing towards what I want there is no hindrance, but the moment I am blocked, there is a conflict. And the process of consciousness is one of recognizing, which means naming. That which I recognize I can only recognize when I name, when I give it a symbol, a term. So, the 'me' is a bundle of memories; the 'me' is the product of time; it is always in the process of accumulating, gathering.

And an incident is an experience, is it not? And that experience comes only when we are capable of recognizing it. If I am not capable of recognizing an experience, it is not an experience. So memory, which is the storehouse of words, of experiences—not only one's own, but the collective—is always functioning, whether you are conscious or unconscious of it. So, it retains an incident. Having recognized it, verbalized it, it stores it away. Take a simple thing like being hurt by another. You are hurt; someone says something cruel—or something pleasant. It is retained, and the incident is stored away. If you are hurt, the feeling of antagonism, of pain, is retained. And then you begin to forgive the person—if you are morally inclined. So, you first retain, keep the hurt; and then, being trained morally, you begin to forgive. So, the incident is held.

For, if we collected no incidents, if we were not constantly active, either receiving hurts or forgiving, being greedy or not being greedy—if the mind were not in this constant activity, it would feel lost, would it not? For it, this activity is necessary to know it is alive.

So, as long as you are accumulating and rejecting, you cannot forget the incident, or the memory of it; the memory remains with you. And the problem is, what are you to do with it?—because it keeps on repeating. How is one to be free from it? To really be free from it, not superficially, you have to go into the problem of habit, have you not? Because the mind lives in habit, and the memory of the incident has become a habit. And so the mind keeps constantly going back to it. So you discover how the mind lives in the past, and you discover how habits are created. The mind is the past; there is no present mind; there is no future to the mind; the mind exists because of the past; the mind is the past. And you say, "How am I to be free from the past?" You can only be free when you understand the process of accumulation, which is essentially based on the desire to protect oneself, to be secure, to be certain. So long as that urge, compulsion, exists, there must be the memory of incidents and the struggle with those memories. So, this question can only be resolved when we understand the whole process of accumulation, which is the process of time, which is the 'me', from which all activities take place.

So, to be really free from memory is to meet incidents, experiences, fully—which is, to be aware of them without condemning, without justifying, without identifying, without naming. By being aware of every movement of thought, whether good or bad, without justifying—merely observing, without any sense of prejudice—then you will see that every incident, every experience, indicates its own truth. And what is true is the liberating factor.

Question: How is one to expose the hidden depths of the unconscious?

KRISHNAMURTI: Before we ask how to discover the hidden depths of the unconscious, I wonder if we are aware of the conscious? Are we aware consciously of what we are doing? Are you conscious of what you are saying, what you are thinking? Most of us are not. Not being consciously aware of the superficial level, we ask how to uncover the deeper levels. You cannot—which is an obvious fact. If I am not aware of what I am actually doing, thinking, at the surface level, how can I go deeper? But if we want to go deeper, to expose the hidden motives, intentions, purposes, obviously the conscious mind must be somewhat tranquil. If I want to find out what my deeper motives are, which are not obvious—if I want to bring them to the surface, the conscious mind must be alert, must it not, must be somewhat quiet, inquiring, hesitant, tentative, patient. But if the surface mind is incessantly agitated, active—as most of our minds are—then what happens? Then there is a conflict between the conscious and the unconscious. And this conflict becomes more and more accentuated, strong, acute, until there are all kinds of psychological and physiological diseases.

So, if I would discover the deeper levels of consciousness, I have to be extraordinarily awake on the surface, superficially, outwardly. The unconscious is not only the recently acquired but also it is the storehouse, is it not, of the past—of tradition, of the race, of all hopes. Your unconscious is not only limited to the 'you' but is of the whole past. You are the result, surely, of all the past; you are the summation of all mankind. And to understand that, to go into it really profoundly, mere study of psychology will not help, nor being analyzed. Analysis of the unconscious by the conscious mind cannot reveal the truth. If I want to discover the deeper levels of the unconscious, I may analyze myself, or go to somebody who will help me to analyze, but what happens? In that process of analysis, of digging down deeply, can I investigate every movement, every nuance, every subtle response? Not only would it take time, but it is almost impossible, is it not? Because I may miss one memory, one layer, one prejudice—which, if missed, will obviously thwart or pervert my judgment. Also there is the projection of the unconscious through dreams, which need interpreting, and what if I do not interpret them rightly? Even if the analyst does interpret them rightly, the conflict goes on, does it not?

So, the question is, How is it possible to open the unconscious, to let all the hidden pursuits come to the surface, not to have any one blank spot? How does one set about it? We see that analysis, introspection, will not do it; it may uncover a few spots, but the totality of it cannot be understood or revealed by a part of the mind, a division which merely observes. Surely, to understand something, there must be total perception of it. I do not know if you are following all this! If I would understand a picture, a painting, I must see the whole of it, not take a part and investigate that part. Similarly, I must be able to look at this whole process of consciousness as a total thing, as a whole, not as the conscious and the unconscious; I must be able to have an integrated understanding of the whole. If I merely look at it partially, it will be a partial understanding, and a partial understanding is no understanding at all.

So, can I, the observer, the investigator, look at the total process, and not at the part? Please follow this carefully, and you will see. Is not the investigator always the part, and not the whole? When you analyze, when you look, when you say, "How am I to expose all the layers, intimations, accumulations of the unconscious, the residue of the past?"—are you not looking at it, investigating it, as an entity apart from the whole, total process? Obviously you are. The analyzer is something apart, looking, investigating, trying to understand, trying to interpret, translate. So the analyzer is always a separate entity, looking into the unconscious, trying to fathom it, trying to expose it, trying to do something about it. Therefore, the entity who keeps himself apart cannot understand the whole, total process. Please follow this.

So, as long as there is the interpreter, the analyzer, the total process cannot be understood. And to eliminate the analyzer is to eliminate the unconscious—that is, to bring the whole thing out and understand the total process, because it is the separate entity, the analyzer, that is looking. And the analyzer, the separate being, is itself the result of the past, of the total accumulation, of the race, of the individual, of the group. Surely the 'me', the investigator, is the result of tradition, of memory. And when the investigator, who is the result of memory, tries to understand part of himself, he is incapable of understanding it. You can only understand it when there is complete identity, the cessation of the analyzer. It is only then, when the mind is really quiet, that the intimation of the totality is projected, is seen. But as long as the superficial mind, through partial awareness, separates itself and analyzes, it cannot understand the totality.

You can experiment with this yourself very simply. Occasionally, when you are not concerned about yourself and your activities, about what you think and do not think, when you are quietly walking in the country, you suddenly perceive some hidden motive, hidden totality. In that moment there is no conscious investigator; you see the whole thing completely. But then the conscious mind comes in, intervenes, wants to pursue the thing further—because at that moment it was an extraordinary experience. And the moment the conscious mind intervenes, it becomes a memory, and you pursue that memory. Memory is of the part, and not the whole.

So, if you can be in that state of unselfconscious perception, without pursuing the memory, then you will see from moment to moment how the unconscious totality comes up in different forms, different ways of expression. Then you will find that as the truth of each expression is seen, there is a freedom—freedom from the accumulated prejudices, the racial antagonisms, the incessant desires which have been thwarted, the blind spots. These are all seen in moments when the mind is quiet, when the mind is not a separate entity investigating, censoring, judging. Then only is it possible to find that which is indivisible.

Question: I have done a great many spiritual exercises to control the mind, and the image-creating process has become less powerful. But still I have not experienced the deeper implications of meditation. Would you please go into this.

KRISHNAMURTI: Right meditation is important. But to discover what is the right kind of meditation is very difficult. Because we are so eager to still the mind, to find out something new, to experience something which the teachers, the books, the religious persons have experienced. But perhaps this evening we can go into it and discover what is true meditation. And perhaps if we can experience it as we go along, step by step, we shall know how to meditate.

We think a petty mind, a small mind, a narrow mind, a greedy mind, by disciplining itself will become nonpetty, something great. And is that not an illusion? A petty mind will always remain petty, however much it disciplines itself. That is so, is it not? If I am narrow, limited, and my mind is stupid, however much I may discipline, I will still remain stupid; and my gods, my meditations, my exercises will still be limited, stupid, narrow. So, first I have to realize that I have a petty mind, that my mind is prejudiced, that it is seeking something as a reward, that it is escaping—which are all indications of its narrowness. And how can such a mind, though it practices spiritual exercises, controls, disciplines—how can such a mind be free? Surely, it is only in freedom that you discover, not when your mind is bound, trained, controlled, shaped. So that is the first thing to realize—that a mind seeking a reward, a result, however much it may train itself, will experience only its own projection. Its Masters, its gods, its virtues are its own projections. That is the first thing to see the truth of, to realize.

Then we can proceed to the next thing—which is, that a mind which has learned concentration is incapable of understanding the total, the whole. For concentration is a process of exclusiveness, is a process of discarding, putting aside, in search of a result. A mind that is merely narrowed down through effort, through the desire to achieve a result, a reward—surely, such a mind can only be exclusive; it is not aware of its total process. But most of us are trained to concentrate in our daily work. And those who are seeking so-called spiritual heights are equally as ambitious as the worldly people; they want to arrive, they want to experience. And it is this drive to experience that forces them to narrow down their consciousness, their thought, excluding all but the one thing they desire to attain—be it a phrase, an image, a picture, or an idea. Again, such a mind is incapable of comprehending the whole.

This does not mean the mind must wander all over the place. On the contrary, the moment there is awareness of the wandering, there is no resistance, there is the understanding of each wandering. Then each thought has its significance and is understood, not excluded, not put down, suppressed. Then the mind, instead of being petty, narrow, greedy, is no longer fettered by its own compulsions. It is then beginning to be open, to inquire, to discover. Which means, really, that we must discard the whole process of what we have learned as meditation. Then meditation is not for a few minutes or an hour during the day, but is a constant process, all the time seeking, discovering, what is true.

Then, as you go deeper into the problem, you will see that the mind becomes extraordinarily quiet—not disciplined, not the quietness of stagnation, of enclosure, but a quietness, a tranquillity, in which all movement of thought has ceased. And in that silence the entity who experiences has completely ceased. But what most of us want is to experience, to gather more. It is the desire for the 'more' that makes us meditate, that makes us do spiritual exercises, and so on. But when all that is understood, when all that has dropped away, then there is a silence, then there is a tranquillity of the mind in which the experiencer, the interpreter, is absent. Then only is there a possibility for that which is not nameable to come into being. It is not a reward for good deeds. Do what you will, be as selfless as you like, force yourself to do the good things, the noble things, to be virtuous—all those are self-centered activities, and such a mind is only a stagnant mind. It can meditate, but it will not know that state of silence, quietness, in which the real can be.

And that reality is not the word; the word *love* is not love. One knows in that silence that which is love without the word. And that love without the word is neither yours nor mine, neither personal nor impersonal. It is a state of being. There are no words to describe it. It is an experience which is not recognizable because the recognizer is absent. You can call it what you like—love, God, truth, what you will. It is that experience which puts an end to all conflict, to all misery.

Question: I have listened to all your talks, and I have read all your books. Most earnestly I ask you, what can be the purpose of my life if, as you say, all thought has to cease, all knowledge be suppressed, all memory lost? How do you relate that state of being, whatever it may be according to you, to the world in which we live? What relation has such a being to our sad and painful existence?

KRISHNAMURTI: Since the questioner is earnest, let us go into it seriously. We want to know what this state is which can only be when all knowledge, when the recognizer, is not; we want to know what relationship this state has to our world of daily activity, daily pursuits. We know what our life is now—sad, painful, constantly fearful, nothing permanent; we know that very well. And we want to know what relationship this other state has to that, and if we put aside knowledge—become free from our memories, and so on—what is the purpose of existence?

What is the purpose of existence as we know it now—not theoretically but actually? What is the purpose of our everyday existence? Just to survive, isn't it?—with all its misery, with all its sorrow and confusion, wars, destruction, and so on. We can invent theories, we can say, "This should not be, but something else should be." But those are all theories; they are not facts. What we know is confusion, pain, suffering, endless antagonisms. And we know also, if we are at all aware, how these come about. Because, the purpose of life, from moment to moment, every day, is to destroy each other, to exploit each other, either as individuals or as collective human beings. In our loneliness, in our misery, we try to use others, we try to escape from ourselves—through amusement, through gods, through knowledge, through every form of belief, through identification. That is our purpose, conscious or unconscious, as we now live. And, is there a deeper, wider purpose beyond, a purpose that is not of confusion, of acquisition? And has that effortless state any relation to our daily life?

Certainly, that has no relation at all to our life. How can it have? If my mind is confused, agonized, lonely, how can that be related to something which is not of itself? How can truth be related to falsehood, to illusion? But we do not want to admit that. Because our hope, our confusion, makes us believe in something greater, nobler, which we say is related to us. In our despair we seek truth, hoping that in the discovery of it, our despair will disappear.

So, we can see that a confused mind, a mind ridden with sorrow, a mind that is aware of its own emptiness, loneliness, can never find that which is beyond itself. That which is beyond the mind can only come into being when the causes of confusion, misery, are dispelled or understood. All that I have been saying, talking about, is how to understand ourselves. For without self-knowledge, the other is not; the other is only an illusion. But if we understand the total process of ourselves, from moment to moment, then we shall see that in clearing up our own confusion, the other comes into being. Then, experiencing that will have a relation to this. But this will never have a relation to that. Being this side of the curtain, being in darkness, how can one have experience of light, of freedom? But when once there is the experience of truth, then you can relate it to this world in which we live.

That is, if we have never known what love is, but only constant wrangles, misery, conflicts, how can we experience that love which is not of all this? But when once we have experienced that, then we do not have to bother to find out the relationship. Then love, intelligence, functions. But to experience that state, all knowledge, accumulated memories, self-identified activities must cease, so that the mind is incapable of any projected sensations. Then, experiencing that, there is action in this world.

Surely that is the purpose of existence—to go beyond the self-centered activity of the mind. And having experienced that state, which is not measurable by the mind, then the very experiencing of that brings about an inward revolution, which is the only true revolution. Then, if there is love, there is no social problem. There is no problem of any kind when there is love. Because we do not know how to love, we have social problems and systems of philosophy on how to deal with our problems. And I say, these problems can never be solved by any system, either of the left or of the right or of the middle. These can be solved—our confusion, our misery, our self-destruction—only when we can experience that state which is not self-projected.

April 24, 1952

Questions

Rajamundry, 1949

Madras, 1949–50

Colombo, 1949–50

Bombay, 1950

Paris, 1950

New York, 1950

Seattle, 1950

Madras, 1952

London, 1952

Index

For further information about Krishnamurti Libraries, Retreats, Study Centers, Schools and events world-wide, as well as other publications, please contact the following:

Krishnamurti Foundation of America
P.O. Box 1560
Ojai, California 93024 U.S.A.
E-mail: kfa@kfa.org
www.kfa.org

Krishnamurti Foundation Trust, Ltd.
Brockwood Park
Bramdean, Hampshire
England SO24 0LQ
E-mail: info@brockwood.org.uk
www.brockwood.org.uk

Krishnamurti Foundation India
64-65 Greenways Road
Vasanta Vihar
Chennai
India 600 028
E-mail: kfihq@vsnl.com
www.kfionline.org